MESSIAEN PERSPECTIVES 2:
TECHNIQUES, INFLUENCE AND RECEPTION

For Claude Samuel

Messiaen Perspectives 2: Techniques, Influence and Reception

Edited by

CHRISTOPHER DINGLE
Birmingham Conservatoire, UK

ROBERT FALLON
Carnegie Mellon University, USA

ASHGATE

© Christopher Dingle, Robert Fallon and the contributors 2013

All rights reserved. No part of this publication may be reproduced, stored in a retrieval system or transmitted in any form or by any means, electronic, mechanical, photocopying, recording or otherwise without the prior permission of the publisher.

Christopher Dingle and Robert Fallon have asserted their right under the Copyright, Designs and Patents Act, 1988, to be identified as the editors of this work.

Published by
Ashgate Publishing Limited
Wey Court East
Union Road
Farnham
Surrey, GU9 7PT
England

Ashgate Publishing Company
110 Cherry Street
Suite 3-1
Burlington, VT 05401-3818
USA

www.ashgate.com

British Library Cataloguing in Publication Data
A catalogue record for this book is available from the British Library

The Library of Congress has cataloged the printed edition as follows:
Messiaen perspectives / edited by Christopher Dingle and Robert Fallon.
   volumes cm
   Includes bibliographical references and index.
   ISBN 978-1-4094-2696-7 (hardcover : alk. paper) — ISBN 978-1-4724-1517-2 (ebook) — ISBN 978-1-4724-1518-9 (epub) 1. Messiaen, Olivier, 1908–1992—Criticism and interpretation. I. Dingle, Christopher Philip, editor. II. Fallon, Robert, editor.
   ML410.M595M494 2013
   780.92—dc23
                                                                    2013007758

ISBN 9781409426967 (hbk)
ISBN 9781472415172 (ebk – PDF)
ISBN 9781472415189 (ebk – ePUB)

Bach musicological font developed by © Yo Tomita

Printed and bound in Great Britain by
TJ International Ltd, Padstow, Cornwall.

Contents

List of Illustrations	*ix*
List of Figures and Tables	*xi*
List of Music Examples	*xiii*
Acknowledgements	*xvii*
Editors' Note	*xix*

Introduction	1
Christopher Dingle and Robert Fallon	

PART I   TECHNIQUES

Perspectives on Techniques	9
Christopher Dingle and Robert Fallon	

1	Sacred Machines: Fear, Mystery and Transfiguration in Messiaen's Mechanical Procedures	13
	Christopher Dingle	

2	*La Fauvette des jardins* and the 'Spectral Attitude'	33
	Roderick Chadwick	

3	Aspects of Compositional Organization and Stylistic Innovation in *Petites Esquisses d'oiseaux*	51
	David Kopp	

4	Messiaen's Counterpoint	77
	Christoph Neidhöfer	

Intermède 1

5	A Catalogue of Messiaen's Birds	113
	Robert Fallon	

PART II INFLUENCE

Perspectives on Influence   149
Christopher Dingle and Robert Fallon

6   Messiaen and Ohana: Parallel Preoccupations or Anxiety
of Influence?   153
Caroline Rae

7   The Messiaen–Xenakis Conjunction   175
Anne-Sylvie Barthel-Calvet

8   From France to Quebec: Messiaen's Transatlantic Legacy   201
Heather White Luckow

9   Messiaen and the Spectralists   227
Marilyn Nonken

Intermède 2

10   The Tombeaux of Messiaen: At the Intersection of Influence
and Reception   243
Robert Fallon

PART III RECEPTION

Perspectives on Reception   277
Christopher Dingle and Robert Fallon

11   The Reception of Olivier Messiaen in Italy: A Historical
Interpretation   281
Raffaele Pozzi

12   Three Decades of Messiaen's Music in Spain: A Brief Survey,
1945–1978   301
Germán Gan-Quesada

13   Placing Mount Messiaen   323
Robert Fallon

14	Genesis and Reception of Olivier Messiaen's *Traité de rythme, de couleur, et d'ornithologie*, 1949–1992: Toward a New Reading of the Composer's Writings	341
	Jean Boivin	

Appendix: A Critical Catalogue of Messiaen's Musical Works	363
1. Complete List of Messiaen's Works	369
i. Acknowledged Works	369
ii. Other Pieces	373
2. Messiaen's Works, Listed by Year of Première	379
3. Messiaen's Acknowledged Works, Listed by Instrumentation	385
4. Annotations	391
Christopher Dingle and Robert Fallon	

Select Bibliography	*407*
Discography	*427*
Notes on Contributors	*429*
Index	*435*
Contents of Messiaen Perspectives 1: Sources and Influences	*443*

List of Illustrations

6.1   Leaflet for Le Groupe Musical Le Zodiaque concert at the Salle
Gaveau, 29 April 1949   158

7.1   Olivier Messiaen decorating Iannis Xenakis with the Légion
d'Honneur in Xenakis's apartment on the Rue Chaptal   176

12.1   Dedication by Olivier Messiaen and Yvonne Loriod to Maurice
Legendre, director of the 'Casa de Velázquez' in Madrid
(28 March 1949)   306

12.2   Concert programme of the Pianist Pilar Bayona (Zaragoza,
10 January 1951), featuring 'Regard des prophètes, des bergers
et des Mages' by Olivier Messiaeu (sic). Archivo Pilar Bayona,
Madrid   310
    a) Front and back cover   310
    b) Inside pages   311

12.3   Luis de Pablo, 'Clave y ejemplo', *La Estafeta literaria*, 188
(1 March 1960): 20   317

List of Figures and Tables

Figures

10.1	The number of works composed each year for the same instrumentation as the *Quartet for the end of Time*, from 1953 to 2012	252
10.2	The number of tombeaux composed each year from 1952 to 2011	253

Tables

1.1	Select list of musical machines from Messiaen's output	16
2.1	Cadential chords in the Garden Warbler solos	40
2.2	The flight of the Black Kite	44
3.1	Alternative parsings of overall form in *Petites Esquisses d'oiseaux*	53
3.2	Occurrence of invented chords in the three Robin pieces	69
5.1	A Catalogue of Messiaen's Birds	116
10.1	Music composed in recognition of Messiaen in jazz, rock and electronica traditions	262
10.2	Music composed in recognition of Messiaen in classical traditions	263

List of Music Examples

1.1	'La Rousserolle effarvatte', opening	18
1.2	'Les sept Anges aux sept trompettes', rhythmic cells	19
2.1	Concluding chords of the Garden Warbler's 'preliminary trials'	39
2.2	The 'couleurs de couchant' chords	41
2.3	Climactic chords of the Black Kite's spiral flight	43
2.4	Messiaen's augmented sixth chord	45
2.5	*La Fauvette des jardins* – opening	45
2.6	*La Fauvette des jardins* – contrapuntal voice-leading in the lowest register	46
2.7	'la nuit vient'	47
2.8	*La Fauvette des jardins* end of penultimate line	47
3.1a	The six transpositions of mode 7, identified by their absent tritone complements	57
3.1b	Generation of mode 7^2 by transpositional combination of tritone related pentatonic sets	57
3.2	Important pitch collections in *Petites Esquisses* and their prime-form pitch-class set equivalents	59
3.3	Two appearances of the Robin in *Catalogue d'oiseaux* (1956–58)	60
	a) From II, 'Le Loriot' (The Golden Oriole)	60
	b) From IX, 'La Bouscarle' (The Cetti's Warbler)	60
3.4	'Le Rouge-gorge' (The Robin) I, mm. 1–5: invented chords, inexact doubling and pentatonic content	62
3.5	Pitch-map showing the transformation of the opening motto in the first two strophes of the Robin pieces	63
3.6	Pitch-map showing the indirect doubling patterns in the first two strophes of the three Robin pieces (octava indications in this and succeeding reductions affect the upper line only)	65
3.7	Pitch-map for 'Le Rouge-gorge' I, mm. 62–67: shifting registral placement of black-key and white-key material	66
3.8	'Le Rouge-gorge' III: three upward spiraling gestures	68
3.9	'Le Rouge-gorge' II, mm. 50–55: transfer of completion function from Total Chromatic chord to other chord types	70
3.10	Pitch-map for 'Le Rouge-gorge' III, mm. 55–62: dissolution of scales	71
3.11	'Le Merle noir', mm. 1–4	72
3.12	'La Grive musicienne', mm. 7–10	73

3.13	'L'Alouette des champs': triplet figurations and B ceiling	74
4.1	*Chants de terre et de ciel*, 'Résurrection', bars 30–32, motivic imitation and modes marked	80
4.2	*Chants de terre et de ciel*, 'Minuit pile et face', bars 14–19, piano part only, first three fugal entries	81
4.3	*Vingt Regards sur l'Enfant-Jésus*, 'Par Lui tout a été fait', opening of fugue, bars 1–9	82
4.4a	*Préludes*, 'Instants défunts', bars 23–24	83
4.4b	*Préludes*, 'Les sons impalpables du rêve', bars 22–24	83
4.5	Analytic reduction of *Messe de la Pentecôte*, 'Offertoire', bars 25–34, with chords in the right hand numbered, durations labelled and modes identified	85
4.6a	Rhythmic interversions in bars 25–32	85
4.6b	Voice-leading patterns in chords 1–20 of the right hand (in mode 3^1)	86
4.7	Marcel Dupré, *Traité d'improvisation à l'orgue*, 'Modulations by Symmetrical Chords' (excerpt, p. 24 of English edition)	87
4.8	*Vingt Regards sur l'Enfant-Jésus*, 'Le baiser de l'Enfant-Jésus', bars 1–6 with modes and harmonies marked	89
4.9a	Voice leading in 'Le baiser de l'Enfant-Jésus' bar 1 illustrated (in mode 2^1)	90
4.9b	Voice leading in 'Le baiser de l'Enfant-Jésus' bar 2 illustrated (in mode 2^2)	90
4.9c	Voice leading in 'Le baiser de l'Enfant-Jésus' bar 4 illustrated (in mode 2^2)	91
4.10	*La Nativité du Seigneur*, 'Dieu parmi nous', bars 60–63	91
4.11a	Voice-leading patterns in 'Dieu parmi nous' bar 60 illustrated (in mode 2^2)	92
4.11b	Voice-leading patterns in 'Dieu parmi nous' bar 63 illustrated (in mode 2^2)	92
4.12	*Chants de terre et de ciel*, 'Arc-en-ciel d'innocence', bars 15–16, modes and sequence marked	93
4.13	Sequential parallel voice-leading patterns in the piano part (analysed in numbers of scale degrees)	93
4.14	*Poèmes pour Mi*, 'Le collier', bars 1–5, piano part only	95
4.15	Voice-leading patterns in 'Le collier' bars 1 and 5	95
4.16a	*Poèmes pour Mi*, 'Paysage', vertical-shifting counterpoint in the piano part of bars 8 and 13	96
4.16b	'Boris' motive in the right hand and its intervallic diminution in the left, before and after the vertical shift	96
4.17	*La Transfiguration de Notre-Seigneur Jésus-Christ*, 'Terribilis est locus iste', p. 339, excerpt, annotated	97

4.18	'Terribilis est locus iste', p. 339, Verticals I–IV from the array, with pitches that do not belong to mode 2^2 indicated by filled-in note heads	99
4.19	'Terribilis est locus iste', p. 339, Rotational array schematized	99
4.20a	'Terribilis est locus iste', p. 339, Pitch-class cycle for verticals I, III, V, VII, IX	100
4.20b	'Terribilis est locus iste', p. 339, Pitch-class cycle for verticals II, IV, VI, VIII, X	101
4.21	Analytical sketch for 'Thème A' from *Concert à quatre*, I, 'Entrée'	106
6.1	Ohana, *Cinq sequences*, 'Polyphonie' (bars 1–5)	165
6.2	Ohana, *Messe*, 'Gloria' (figure 35)	167
6.3	Ohana, *Lys de madrigaux*, 'Star Mad Blues' (renotated harmonic reduction, figure 22)	171
6.4	Ohana, *24 Préludes* for piano, no. 13 (closing section)	172
7.1	Xenakis, *Zyia*, bars 354–363	194
7.2	Xenakis, *Le Sacrifice*, series with note-lengths assigned to pitches	195
8.1	Chords of Contracted Resonance in context, melodic 'recitation tones' and linear movement primarily by ic 1 in Serge Garant's *Concerts sur terre* (1952), movement 1	205
8.2	Comparison of Messiaen's CCR to similar chords in Garant's *Concerts sur terre*, movement 1	206
8.3	Melodic line saturated with ics 1 and 6 in the first phrase of *Concerts sur terre*, movementt 2 (1952)	207
8.4	Theme comprising a *Candrakalâ tâla* Hindu rhythm and two *monnayages* in Garant's incomplete 'Variations pour deux pianos'	209
8.5	The compositional realization, left, of the four inversionally symmetrical readings on the right, 'Variations pour deux pianos', m. 86	210
8.6	Reduction of mode 2^2 thematic fragments and cascading woodwind scales in *Guernica*, movement 1, mm. 279–93	214
8.7	Mode 2^2 woodwind descending scales in the 'Introduction' of Messiaen's *Turangalîla-Symphonie*, figure 6, mm. 37–9	214
8.8	The I_7 row with interjecting mode 3 scales in Variation VII of Pépin's *Variations*, mm. 14–29	216
8.9	An illustration of the four- and eight-interversion palindromes with the eight reordered rows A–H of the *partie médiane* of Sonate pour violon et piano, movement 2	221
8.10	A direct comparison between similar permutations used by Messiaen and Prévost, applied to the same original chromatic collection	223

9.1	Murail, *Comme un oeil suspendu et poli par le songe…*, page 2, systems 3–4	234
9.2	Murail, *Comme un oeil suspendu et poli par le songe…*, chords, set-class and interval-class content, page 2, system 3 to page 4, system 2	235
12.1	Luis de Pablo, Sonata para piano, op. 3 (1958), bars 1–4	316

Acknowledgements

Two large, complex and international collections of this nature are clearly the product of a great many hands and eyes and we should like to thank all those involved in making these volumes possible. Our thanks first of all to the staff at Ashgate, which has published an impressive library of Messiaen scholarship for which all music scholars should be grateful. In particular, Heidi Bishop and Emma Gallon have shown immense patience, support and understanding of various surprises. We should also like to thank the proofreader, Sarah Price, and desk-editor, the indefatigable Barbara Pretty.

Many of the chapters within the two volumes have their seeds in the Messiaen 2008 International Centenary Conference at Birmingham Conservatoire and we should like to thank all of the delegates at this event for creating such a fertile atmosphere of intellectual exchange and for innumerable conversations that provided some of the hinterland to this collection. The Messiaen 2008 conference was generously supported by The British Academy. We are also grateful for support from colleagues at our respective institutions, notably Liz Reeve and Ronald Woodley from Birmingham Conservatoire and research assistants Matthew Brahm, Michael Ceurvorst and Devon Maloney as well as music librarian Kristin Heath at Carnegie Mellon University. In addition, colleagues at the University of Pittsburgh Department of Music, especially Anna Nisnevich, provided much inspiration.

Among the many ways in which Peter Hill has helped, we are especially grateful for his providing two pictures of Messiaen that appear as part of the cover illustration. We are also extremely pleased that Eric Prenshaw agreed to the inclusion of his photographs in the cover illustration, and would like to thank Yian Ling Cheong for the overall composition of the cover. Thanks should also go to Ruth Milsom for advice and support with many of the music examples. For Peter Hill's chapter, Madame Yvonne Loriod-Messiaen granted unrestricted access to the cahiers and to Messiaen's diaries and correspondence.

The greatest thanks, of course, should go to our marvellous contributors. Their scholarship is inspiring, while their understanding of sometimes infuriating requests is immensely appreciated. We hope we have done them justice. Finally, for their unstinting love and support, our families, especially William and Catherine Fallon, and Marie, Liz, Wilfred and Nathaniel Dingle.

Christopher Dingle and Robert Fallon

Alongside two pictures of Messiaen, the cover includes two photographs by Eric Prenshaw. These photos come from the 'Illuminating Messiaen' photography competition, sponsored by Duke Divinity School Initiatives in Theology and the Arts. Entrants were invited to listen to Messiaen's *Visions de l'Amen*, and submit responses to the seven movements in the form of photography. The winners were displayed at King's College, Cambridge, UK and Duke Divinity School, USA, in conjunction with a concert performance of the work by Jeremy Begbie and Cordelia Williams.

The first photograph (the mountain) tries to capture the third movement, 'Amen de l'Agonie de Jésus'. In the garden, sweating with blood, we hear Jesus' agonized 'Let it be' to his Father: 'My Father, if this cup may not pass away from me, except I drink of it, thy will be done'. Christ bears the intensity of God's verdict on the world's wrongdoing. He cries out, laments, sighs, sweats blood. Only in this way can humanity be re-made.

The second photograph (the leaves) responds to the fifth movement, 'Amen des Anges, des Saints, du Chant des Oiseaux'. Transparent and effortless, the angels and saints offer their 'Amen' of praise to God in pure song. Nightingales, blackbirds, finches and warblers, join the ecstatic vocal chorus of unselfconscious adoration.

Eric Prenshaw is a photographer who lives in Raleigh, NC, USA. He is a 2011 MDiv. Graduate from Duke Divinity School, where he studied with Dr Jeremy Begbie on issues regarding Theology and the Arts. Among other awards, he won four honourable mentions in the 'Illuminating Messiaen' photography exhibition. Eric currently serves as Minister of Children and Youth at Sunrise United Methodist Church. Inquiries can be directed to eprenshaw@gmail.com.

Editors' Note

Language

Where an English translation readily exists for a source, references are to that version. Similarly, the original French for quotations has generally been omitted where the source is readily available. The exception in both cases is where specific linguistic points are being made.

Technique de mon langage musical

Originally published in two volumes, text and musical examples respectively, Leduc has recently published single-volume French (1999) and English (2001) editions of *Technique de mon langage musical*. In the text, it is given simply as *Technique*, with specific references being to the music examples, which are numbered identically in every edition.

Traité de rythme, de couleur, et d'ornithologie

References to this are given as '*Traité*', followed by the volume number in Roman numerals, followed by the page reference as usual (e.g. *Traité VI*, p. 143).

Messiaen's Conversations with Claude Samuel

Page references are to Glasow's 1994 translation of Messiaen's 1986 conversations with Claude Samuel, given simply as *Music and Color*, as this is the most widely available English version. The exception is where the 1967 conversations (translated into English in 1976 by Felix Aprahamian) contain different material. Messiaen did not wish to appear as author of the conversations and, as a consequence, the author is given in the bibliography as Samuel.

Hill and Simeone

References to Peter Hill and Nigel Simeone's seminal work, called simply *Messiaen*, are given as 'PHNS', followed by the page number. References are to the English edition unless specified.

Yvonne Loriod

Messiaen's widow is referred to in the main text as Yvonne Loriod. Bibliographical references follow the source document. The variants are Yvonne Loriod-Messiaen, Yvonne Messiaen-Loriod and Yvonne Messiaen.

Capitalization and Orthography

Where possible, the capitalization of titles of works and movements follows that used by Messiaen where evidence exists for his clear preference. The editors have considered published scores, work lists, materials written in Messiaen's hand and the norms of French capitalization. There is no consistent norm we have followed, but rather have sought in each case to adopt the spelling that we think Messiaen would have preferred. This does not always follow any usual publishing convention, but it is our view that Messiaen's capitalization, despite the vagaries in orthography of his titles, is often revealing for the way in which it emphasizes (or de-emphasizes) key words. We point out especially that an ellipsis should always end the titles *Des Canyons aux étoiles…* and *Éclairs sur l'Au-Delà…* and the word 'Temps' is capitalized in the *Quatuor*.

Birds

When referring to the species itself, all words are capitalized. When referring to a title named after a bird, Messiaen's capitalization is followed.

Introduction

Christopher Dingle and Robert Fallon

> It's always dangerous to think you've got a great composer buttoned up. In Messiaen's case, there is much real thinking still to be done ... above all, not taking all Messiaen's own remarks about his music at face value.[1]

More than 20 years have now passed since Olivier Messiaen's death in 1992. So much has been discovered and so much has changed in our understanding of the man and his music that it is easy to forget how sparse the resources were at that time. All the readily available music, books, articles and recordings could fit comfortably onto a single shelf. In the field of scholarship since then, the imperative identified by Roger Nichols for 'much real thinking', the need to get beyond the composer himself, has increasingly borne rich fruit, including now the chapters included in the two volumes of *Messiaen Perspectives*.

Since his death, Messiaen's output has become increasingly prominent in musical life. Part of the growth in acceptance and recognition undoubtedly stems from the 2008 centennial celebrations, but the worldwide exposure these prompted seems only to have increased programming and recording of his music. That Renée Fleming sang the orchestral version of *Poèmes pour Mi* in the broadcast opening gala of the New York Philharmonic season in 2009 (and later recorded it) indicates the extent to which Messiaen's music has entered the repertoire. Looking at some of the numerous performances of his music around the world in 2012 and the first half of 2013, it is little surprise that works such as *Quatuor pour la fin du Temps*, *Turangalîla-Symphonie*, *Oiseaux exotiques* and *Et exspecto resurrectionem mortuorum* crop up with regularity. *Turangalîla* alone is on concert programmes in Tampere (Finland), Miami, Essen (Germany), Berlin, Erlangen (Germany), Heidelberg, Hamburg, Frankfurt, Ludwigsburg, Castilla y Leon (Spain), Taipai, Medellin (Columbia), Birmingham, Aldeburgh (UK), London, Hiroshima, Madrid, Munich, Paris, Seattle, Estonia, Weimar, London (again) and Frankfurt (again).[2] Even more noteworthy than that global litany, perhaps, is that more challenging or difficult to mount works are also featured. To take just two examples, *Chronochromie* is being given several times by the Chicago Symphony Orchestra under Pierre Boulez and by the National

---

[1] Roger Nichols, 'Messiaen: *Éclairs sur l'Au-Delà...*', *Musical Times*, 135/1812 (February 1994): p. 117.

[2] These are merely the performances listed on Malcolm Ball's Messiaen website (www.oliviermessiaen.org) from the beginning of January 2012 until the summer of 2013. It is entirely possible that there are others.

Orchestra of Belgium with Lothar Zagrosek, while *Des Canyons aux étoiles...* can be heard in performances by different ensembles in New York, Ann Arbor, Aspen and (back in New York) at Carnegie Hall. Meanwhile, Messiaen's music appears regularly in the recital programmes of students in conservatoires. That Durand have published an album entitled *Olivier Messiaen en treize morceaux pour piano* [Olivier Messiaen in thirteen pieces for piano] and Deutsche Grammophon a CD compilation called *Messiaen: Garden of Love's Sleep* underlines the extent to which the composer has moved beyond the specialist niche towards the mainstream of the classical music world. Even in jazz and pop, Messiaen has made a mark with Björk, Radiohead, and numerous other artists quoting his music, a remarkable achievement for any composer soon after death.

Unsurprisingly, there has been a similar growth in scholarship about Messiaen. The publication of the final volume of Messiaen's *Traité de rythme, de couleur, et d'ornithologie* in 2002, then of Hill and Simeone's *Messiaen* in 2005, which drew upon access to the composer's personal archive, each marked a seminal moment in providing general access to his life and thought hitherto available to a select few.[3] In his call, quoted above, for much-needed thinking, Roger Nichols notes that this would follow 'in the footsteps most notably of Robert Sherlaw Johnson and Paul Griffiths'.[4] In other words, just two significant books on Messiaen in English were available in 1994, to which anyone else would have added Roger Nichols's own study. The German literature was no more extensive and even in France there was hardly an abundance of riches. Now those published in English alone since the appearance of Hill and Simeone's seminal book in 2005 would fill a bookshelf (see the Bibliography for full details):

- Siglind Bruhn, *Messiaen's Contemplations of Covenant and Incarnation: Musical Symbols of Faith in the Two Great Piano Cycles of the 1940s* (2007)
- Christopher Dingle, *The Life of Messiaen* (2007)
- Christopher Dingle and Nigel Simeone (eds), *Olivier Messiaen: Music, Art and Literature* (2007)
- Peter Hill and Nigel Simeone, *Olivier Messiaen:* Oiseaux exotiques (2007)
- Robert Sholl (ed.), *Messiaen Studies* (2007)
- Vincent Benitez, *Olivier Messiaen: A Research and Information Guide* (2008)
- Siglind Bruhn, *Messiaen's Explorations of Love and Death: Musico-Poetic Signification in the "Tristan Trilogy" and Three Related Song Cycles* (2008)
- Siglind Bruhn, *Messiaen's Interpretations of Holiness and Trinity: Echoes of Medieval Theology in the Oratorio, Organ Meditations, and Opera* (2008)
- Andrew Shenton, *Olivier Messiaen's System of Signs* (2008)
- Jon Gillock, *Performing Messiaen's Organ Music: 66 Masterclasses* (2009)
- Sander van Maas, *The Reinvention of Religious Music: Olivier Messiaen's Breakthrough Toward the Beyond* (2009)

---

[3] Subsequent references to Hill and Simeone's *Messiaen* are given as 'PHNS'.

[4] Roger Nichols, 'Messiaen: *Éclairs sur l'Au-Delà*': p. 117.

- Judith Crispin (ed.), *Olivier Messiaen: The Centenary Papers* (2010)
- Andrew Shenton (ed.) *Messiaen the Theologian* (2010)
- Stephen Broad, *Olivier Messiaen: Journalism, 1935–39* (2012)
- Christopher Dingle, *Messiaen's Final Works* (2013)
- Gareth Healey *Messiaen's Musical Techniques: The Composer's View and Beyond* (2013)

Furthermore, in 2008 Caroline Rae updated Robert Sherlaw Johnson's classic book on the composer and feature articles on Messiaen have recently appeared in the world's top musicology journals.

To this abundance of recent scholarship, these two volumes stand out for presenting a wealth of new material and thinking that extends beyond the face value of Messiaen's remarks. Equally notable, though, is that, far from being the last word on the matter, the enclosed chapters tend to be the first detailed examinations of their respective avenues of enquiry. In some cases this is because material has not been generally available until now, in others because time was needed for a sense of historical perspective, and in others because the ideas are fresh. One charge that was levelled at Messiaen scholars in the past, with some justification, is of an insularity of thought. If this was symptomatic of both the viewpoint (from without and within) that Messiaen stood apart and a concurrent over-reliance on the composer's own explanations, the outward-facing nature of many of the contributions along with the broader frame of reference suggests that such a claim is becoming ever harder to substantiate.

The two volumes collect 29 chapters from an international and multilingual group of leading and emerging scholars of Messiaen. The chapters draw heavily, but not exclusively, from research presented at the Messiaen 2008 International Centenary Conference, organized by Christopher Dingle at Birmingham Conservatoire. However, these volumes are more than a simple set of conference proceedings; they also move beyond the theoretical divisions – rhythm, colour, ornithology and faith – that Messiaen himself espoused and much scholarship has adopted. Focusing on Messiaen's relationship with history – both his own and the history he engendered – the Messiaen Perspectives volumes convey the growing understanding of his deep and varied interconnections with his cultural milieux. Read from beginning to end, the five ways of examining Messiaen, which we have called *perspectives*, provide a chronological sequence of historiographical lenses in order of the creative lifecycle, from provenance to audience, or, in terms he would prefer, from genesis to revelation. *Messiaen Perspectives 1: Sources and Influences* explores the origins and cultural pressures that shaped Messiaen's music. By contrast, *Messiaen Perspectives 2: Techniques, Influence and Reception* analyses select compositions and the repercussions of his music. While each book offers a coherent collection in itself, together these complementary volumes elucidate how powerfully Messiaen was embedded in his time and place and how his relevance has not diminished today.

Many of the chapters range broadly across Messiaen's life and output while others look outward from him to the work of others. Some works or episodes of Messiaen's life are explored in detail, filling significant gaps, but several major works receive comment within *Messiaen Perspectives* as part of a broader context rather than as standalone case studies for they have already been explored elsewhere. So, while there is no specific chapter, for instance, on the opera *Saint François d'Assise*, anglophone readers can already find extensive information on this work in books, chapters or articles by Benitez, Bruhn, Dingle, Fallon, Griffiths and Camille Crunelle Hill, not to mention Hill and Simeone.[5] Similar lists can be produced for other major works, such as the *Quatuor*, *Turangalîla*, *La Transfiguration* or *Éclairs sur l'Au-Delà...*, and it is to be hoped that the literature specifically on each will continue to expand. Each perspective presented here shines a light on a particular facet of the composer. If we were French, it would have been sorely tempting to call these chapters 'regards', not that we could have culled nine of them to make the analogy complete. That said, prompted by the lightest movement of the *Quatuor pour la fin du Temps*, both books contain 'Intermède' (Interlude) chapters, placed between the principal parts, but related to them and the whole.

The perspectives contained within these two volumes both deepen and broaden our knowledge and understanding of Messiaen. An important feature is that several of the contributors write from the perspective of having performed the music at the highest level, with their professional practice informing their research, while Julian Anderson brings a composer's insights to Messiaen's creative imperatives in his chapter in the first volume. As with any scholarship, each discovery made, each issue addressed and each insight expounded suggests additional questions and lines of enquiry. In other words, it is fervently hoped that these chapters will act as a catalyst for further reflection, study and performance of Messiaen's music.

---

[5]   Vincent Benitez, 'Simultaneous Contrast and Additive Designs in Olivier Messiaen's Opera *Saint François d'Assise*', *Music Theory Online*, 8/2 (August 2002); Siglind Bruhn, *Messiaen's Interpretations of Holiness and Trinity: Echoes of Medieval Theology in the Oratorio, Organ Meditations, and Opera* (Hillsdale, NY: Pendragon, 2008); Christopher Dingle, 'Frescoes and Legends: the sources and background of *Saint François d'Assise*', in Christopher Dingle and Nigel Simeone (eds), *Olivier Messiaen: Music, Art and Literature* (Aldershot: Ashgate, 2007); Christopher Dingle, *The Life of Messiaen* (Cambridge: Cambridge University Press); Paul Griffiths, '*Saint François d'Assise*', in Peter Hill (ed.), *The Messiaen Companion* (London: Faber and Faber, 1995); Camille Crunelle Hill, 'Saint Thomas Aquinas and the Theme of Truth in Messiaen's *Saint François d'Assise*', in Siglind Bruhn (ed.), *Messiaen's Language of Mystical Love* (New York: Garland, 1998); PHNS; Nils Holger Petersen, 'Messiaen's *Saint François d'Assise* and Franciscan Spirituality', in Siglind Bruhn (ed.), *Messiaen's Language of Mystical Love* (New York: Garland Publishing, 1998).

Messiaen Perspectives 2: Techniques, Influence and Reception

This second volume of perspectives falls into three parts, each containing four chapters and exploring different ways in which Messiaen left an imprint on musical life. The first part scrutinizes aspects of his own compositional technique in terms of counterpoint, spectralism and later piano music, while the second charts ways in which Messiaen's influence is manifest in the music and careers of Ohana, Xenakis, Murail and Quebecois composers. The third part provides case studies of Messiaen's reception: general reception in Italy and Spain, a geological and personal odyssey about Mount Messiaen in the USA, and the view thus far of his posthumous *Traité de rythme, de couleur, et d'ornithologie*. Between the three parts come two 'Intermèdes'. The first is an ornithological catalogue of Messiaen's birds and the second collates information on the numerous 'tombeaux' and other pieces written with a direct element of tribute to Messiaen. The volume concludes with a substantial appendix that we call 'A Critical Catalogue of Messiaen's Musical Works'. This catalogue seeks to clarify his output in the light of recent discoveries, supported by annotations discussing pieces that pose problems regarding their status as works.

Composers need champions at every stage of their careers. It is hard to think of a better advocate not just for Messiaen, but for new music in general than Claude Samuel. The books and recordings of conversations between Messiaen and Samuel are just one aspect of this exceptional contribution, a lasting legacy that will remain of vital importance. All of us who study Messiaen's music return time and again to these conversations and owe Samuel a debt of gratitude. In recognition of his service to Messiaen and to music generally, this volume is dedicated to him.

PART I
Techniques

Perspectives on Techniques

Christopher Dingle and Robert Fallon

Solid technique is an essential, yet oft-maligned ingredient for a creative artist. It is often played down, as it can smack of the unglamorous, workaday aspect of what an artist does. Yet it is the product of many hours, days, months and years of formation, in being bound by the methods and rules of others, of repetition and habit, of disciplined time spent alone in self-imposed splendid isolation and self-abnegation. It is understandable, then, that artists may especially value the rare moments of inspiration, of new ideas and novel ways of doing things, of the message, purpose or function of what they do, of how they have broken the shackles of technical convention.

It is true, of course, that technique alone is of little or no value. One of the most damning charges that can be made is that an artist is an excellent technician, but no more, the implication being that all those years of learning the craft have not resulted in anything of value artistically. In performance, this is bound up with suspicions of the virtuoso dating back at least to the nineteenth century, so that, even now, there are those who dismiss much of Liszt's output as being little more than a vehicle for bravura display with little artistic integrity. For some, to concentrate on matters of technique is to reduce the artist to the status of artisan, while others have suggested that it is misguided to have pretensions to do more than provide art as a utility. Nonetheless, while technique is generally regarded as requiring a purpose, what can easily be overlooked is that it is also what makes realizing the moment of inspiration possible. Christopher Dingle's chapter on Yvonne Loriod was placed at the heart of *Messiaen Perspectives 1* for her position as an influence upon, and source of information and insight about the composer. Nonetheless, she is a relevant figure here as well for, as is made clear, it was her extraordinary technical facility that revolutionized and galvanized Messiaen's compositional thinking about the piano. Her technique did not just enable inspiration to be realized, but was itself a catalyst for inspiration.

Messiaen was immensely proud of his compositional technique, as is obvious from the amount of time and effort he expended in explaining his compositional language. While his interviews and prefaces to scores contain numerous technical expositions, by far the most important writings on his compositional methodology are the *Traité* and *Technique*. These have understandably spawned extensive discussion of specific aspects of his compositional arsenal, such as the modes of limited transposition or Transposed Inversion chords. Nonetheless, despite the impression sometimes given by Messiaen himself, such isolated technical resources were not simply bolted together in his music like compositional Lego®. He certainly did not feel bound by his own rules and, like Bach or Beethoven, Messiaen made full use of the intersections and ambiguities between elements of his music. He believed in the strength of his all-around musical education, and his music is a product of that deeper technique and, yes, his artistic inspiration. That Messiaen's craftsmanship was of the highest order was readily apparent to his students, as Alexander Goehr has recalled: 'None of us, including Stockhausen, were technically up to that standard. ... It would be like trying to draw like Picasso. ... He was very, very good! ... as a craftsman, the *écriture*, he was simply sensational'.[1]

Messiaen's *Vingt Leçons d'Harmonie*, originally published in 1939, reflects one aspect of the solid foundations of his craft, a thorough grounding in the style of others through pastiche, but other aspects tend to be overlooked. For all sorts of reasons, it is easy to forget that Messiaen had rigorous training in counterpoint, especially fugue. Christoph Neidhöfer's essay is thus especially welcome for shining a light on how counterpoint resonates throughout the composer's career. Some of Messiaen's techniques, such as the modes, or use of additive rhythm, are constant features of his music from the moment they are developed, readily malleable for any situation. However, others appeared only intermittently, accruing a set of associations through their relative rarity. One such group is explored in Dingle's essay, 'Messiaen's Sacred Machines', which, like Neidhöfer's, draws upon passages from across the composer's output.

The automated procedures discussed by Dingle are often rhythmic in nature, and, for many, this was the field where Messiaen's contribution was greatest. A new approach to, and emphasis on, rhythm lay at the heart of his compositional thinking from at least *La Nativité* in 1935, though the fluidity of plainchant and Stravinsky's developments were absorbed earlier and the different approach to time was there from the outset. Rhythm also drove the experiments of 1949–52, the period when exploration of technique came to the forefront of Messiaen's music. The emphasis he placed on it is reflected by the fact that both *Technique* and the *Traité* begin with, and dwell for some time upon, rhythm.

Remarkable as it may seem, Messiaen's harmony was long given relatively scant attention. However, as is clear from a review of recent literature, it has finally begun to receive serious scrutiny.[2] Like a number of other composers working

---

[1] Alexander Goehr, unpublished interview with Christopher Dingle, Cambridge, 4 July 1996.

[2] Some notable examinations of Messiaen's technique include: Amy Bauer, 'The Impossible Charm of Messiaen's *Chronochromie*', in Robert Sholl (ed.), *Messiaen Studies* (Cambridge: Cambridge University Press, 2007); Vincent P. Benitez, 'Aspects of Harmony in Messiaen's Later Music: An Examination of the Chords of Transposed Inversions on the Same Bass Note', *Journal of Musicological Research*, 23/2 (April–June, 2004): pp. 187–226; Wai-Ling Cheong, 'Rediscovering Messiaen's Invented Chords', *Acta Musicologica*, 75/1 (2003): pp. 85–105; Christopher Dingle, *Messiaen's Final Works* (Farnham: Ashgate, 2013); Allen Forte, 'Olivier Messiaen as Serialist', *Music Analysis*, 21/1 (2002): pp. 3–34; Robert Sherlaw Johnson, *Messiaen*, 2nd paperback edition, updated and additional text by

in the latter part of the twentieth century, Messiaen's harmony explored a free-ranging, post-tonal landscape, in which major triads nestle alongside much more intricate sonorities. The music is neither tonal nor atonal, but it includes inferences, echoes and resonances of tonal writing within both simple and complex chords, and for that matter of atonal writing. The difficulty for the analyst is in finding an appropriate label for it. In *Messiaen's Final Works*, Dingle suggests the term 'omnitonal' as possibly appropriate for music by the composer of *Éclairs sur l'Au-Delà...*, while acknowledging that it may not suit the music of others.[3]

One area that Messiaen did not expound upon at any length, and which remains little discussed in the literature, is his use of texture and orchestration, especially from the mid-1960s onwards. The way that he highlights aspects of the harmony or rhythm in his orchestral works is one aspect of this, placing his instrumental expertise at the service of other aspects of his technical armoury. A study of his chord spacing, for example, would be invaluable, but it would be important, also, not to overlook Messiaen's orchestration in its own right. Any composition student trying to develop the art of orchestration could do a lot worse than to study the score of *Des Canyons aux étoiles...*. The compositional scope of the music is on the same level as *La Transfiguration*, and the impression is of a massive work, and yet the ensemble is relatively modest. In particular, Messiaen manages to balance just 13 strings with full wind and percussion sections.

What is soon clear from examining Messiaen's music is that, while any analytical approach is likely to reveal insights, to follow a single systematic approach to the exclusion of others is crudely myopic for a composer with such a rich range of resources. Messiaen does not squeeze into neat boxes. His own terminology has limitations, and can obscure, but it provides labels that are useful so long as the analyst is not restricted by them. The essays by Roderick Chadwick and David Kopp provide examples of how to negotiate the information from Messiaen intelligently. They are much needed examinations of Messiaen's final two piano works, *La Fauvette des jardins* and *Petites Esquisses d'oiseaux* respectively. In both cases they demonstrate an ease with Messiaen's own viewpoint and terminology, but are far from bound by it in terms of analytical (and performance) insight. Chadwick focuses on form and situates *La Fauvette des jardins* within the context of Messiaen's students' development of spectralism. Among many other things, Kopp, too, focuses on Messiaen's form and the interplay between supposedly distinct types of material. Even Robert Fallon's first complete

---

Caroline Rae (London: Omnibus Press, 2008); Stefan Keym, '"The Art of the Most Intensive Contrast": Olivier Messiaen's Mosaic Form up to Its Apotheosis in *Saint François d'Assise*', in Robert Sholl (ed.), *Messiaen Studies* (Cambridge: Cambridge University Press, 2007); Andrew Shenton, *Olivier Messiaen's System of Signs: Notes towards Understanding His Music* (Aldershot: Ashgate, 2008); Mirjana Simundza, 'Messiaen's Rhythmical Organisation and Classical Indian Theory of Rhythm I–II', *International Review of the Aesthetics and Sociology of Music*, 18/1–2 (June 1987): pp. 117–44 and 19/1 (June 1988): pp. 53–73.

[3] Dingle, *Messiaen's Final Works*, p. 315.

published listing of Messiaen's birds reveals a kind of negotiated methodology in its melding of Messiaen's avian nomenclature with that of contemporary ornithology, his catalogue showing at a glance the enormous role that birdsong played in his toolkit of techniques. What emerges from each of these chapters is that there is much more going on in Messiaen's music than meets the ear and eye, or than he was willing or able to reveal.

Chapter 1
Sacred Machines: Fear, Mystery and Transfiguration in Messiaen's Mechanical Procedures[1]

Christopher Dingle

> As the conditions of life become more and more hard, mechanical and impersonal, music must ceaselessly bring to those who love it its spiritual violence and its courageous reactions. (Manifesto of La Jeune France)[2]

It is well known that Messiaen regarded himself as a man of nature. He loved the birds, he loved sunsets and he loved the mountains. His annual routine was built around spending the summer composing at his house in Petichet, surrounded by his perennial muse, the Dauphiné countryside, while, from his earliest to his latest works, his music is replete with depictions of natural phenomena. The corollary of this, a dislike of urbanization, is equally apparent. Messiaen lamented to Claude Samuel that 'Paris has become unbearable'[3] and that he had 'an absolute horror of cities, a horror of the one I live in [Paris], despite all its beauties'.[4] He went on to say that:

> In France, I'd like to get away from the automobiles, the factories, the big cities. Living in Paris is tolerable thanks only to the Saint-Chapelle's stained glass, the Louvre, the Opéra and a few beautiful churches like Notre Dame. … What can I tell you – I love nature, and it's really in spite of myself that I live in a city! But how would I find my beautiful Parisian organ in the Causses [region]?[5]

He even stated that living in Paris was responsible for his mother's death.[6] This all fits neatly with the manifesto of La Jeune France, of which Messiaen was a

---

[1] I am grateful to Robert Fallon for some typically perspicacious comments on this chapter.

[2] Serge Gut, *Le Groupe Jeune France* (Paris: Honoré Champion, 1977), p. 16.

[3] *Music and Color*, p. 155.

[4] Ibid., p. 33.

[5] Ibid., p. 171.

[6] Brigitte Massin, *Olivier Messiaen: Une poétique du merveilleux* (Aix-en-Provence: Éditions Alinéa, 1989), p. 52.

Messiaen Perspectives 2: Techniques, Influence and Reception

signatory, as does his statement that 'mechanized civilization is overwhelming'.[7] Admittedly, the manifesto of La Jeune France was as much a statement about what its members were against as the artistic path that they espoused. In particular, they were against neoclassicism and the aesthetic espoused by Jean Cocteau in *Le coq et l'arlequin*, with its flippant remarks decrying nature as an inspiration for art and exalting machinery in its place.[8] Moreover, the Jeune France manifesto goes on to say that the group wished to be 'as far removed from revolutionary formulas as from academic formulas' and that 'their aim is to create and to promote a living music'.[9] None of this is at odds with a man whose music was increasingly suffused with the sounds of nature, and whose *magnum opus* would be an opera about St Francis of Assisi.

Given Messiaen's devotion to the vitality of music and nature, it is remarkable that within five years of putting his name to the manifesto of La Jeune France, his compositions began to include on a regular basis what can only be described as mechanical music. In one sense, it is easy to see what attracted Messiaen to explore systematic methods of composing by creating passages that write themselves once the parameters are set, for they held both an intellectual fascination and the prospect of new sound worlds. Moreover, as is well-documented, the robust intellectual curiosity of the postwar generation of younger composers and its move towards serialism was difficult to resist. What is fascinating, though, is not merely that Messiaen used compositional machines, but that he continued to employ them long after the experiments of the early 1950s had lost their lustre.

What follows is an exploration of the occurrence and impetus behind Messiaen's use of passages of mechanized composition. For the purposes of this chapter, mechanical music refers to any section of music in which, once the parameters have been set, no further compositional input is required for that feature. Although a certain amount of explanation of these devices is inevitable, the principal aim of this chapter is not to examine the specific techniques being used in themselves. Instead, this is an attempt to step back, surveying the broad span of Messiaen's output and life. Two distinct types of mechanization are identified, manifest and mysterious, the latter subdividing into serial modes and coloured time. What emerges is that the persistent attraction of compositional machines appears to have been prompted, at least in part, by the emotion that mechanization induced in Messiaen: fear. In part this is engendered by the impersonality and lifelessness of the machine. The intention here is to explore some relationships between these passages as musical entities and to consider how and why Messiaen harnessed the fear and disquiet provoked by the mechanical. Crucially, while direct evocations of the fearful occur, Messiaen transfigured his emotive response to the fear and

---

[7] *Music and Color*, p. 155.

[8] For an excellent discussion of Messiaen's reaction to Cocteau, see Stephen Broad, 'Messiaen and Cocteau', in Christopher Dingle and Nigel Simeone (eds), *Olivier Messiaen: Music, Art & Literature* (Aldershot: Ashgate, 2007).

[9] Gut, *Le Groupe Jeune France*, p. 16.

impersonality of machines so that they became symbols of transcendent mystery.[10] Before considering the machines themselves, though, a brief consideration of manifestations of fear in Messiaen's music is in order.

Fear, in its various guises, occurs more often in Messiaen's music than might initially be expected for a composer associated with conveying hope and joy. It was a lifelong fascination for him, with fearful elements being found in just about all of his major cycles. To name but a few instances, fear and disquiet is present in the central 'sin' panel of *Les Offrandes oubliées*, is a regular factor in *Turangalîla-Symphonie* in the three movements which share their title with the symphony, is a feature of the various 'abyss' movements such as 'Abîme des oiseaux' (*Quatuor pour la fin du Temps*) or 'Les Mains de l'abîme' (*Livre d'orgue*), is the overriding emotion of 'Terribilis est locus iste' (*La Transfiguration*) and underpins the opening of 'Les stigmates' (*Saint François*).[11] Indeed, one of Messiaen's mother's letters relates the eight-year-old Messiaen saying: 'I think I really prefer things which make me afraid.'[12] In this context, the presence of mechanization in all its horror would be unsurprising were it not for the fact that Messiaen's most common subjects are the divine and nature.

Table 1.1 provides a selective list of mechanized passages in Messiaen's works. It is not exhaustive in terms of either techniques or passages containing them, but includes some prominent examples of Messiaen's musical machines. Several of the passages in question defy a succinct label, while others can be categorized in two or more ways even when using Messiaen's terminology. Nor should it come as any surprise that there is plenty of overlap between the various techniques categorized by Messiaen, such as 'personnages rythmiques' and 'agrandissement asymétrique'. The passages listed in Table 1.1 fall into the two broad categories of, respectively, manifest and mysterious processes. For the latter, it is clear that some organizational force is at work, but, to the innocent ear at least, its governing features remain inscrutable. Conversely, with manifest procedures the process is clearly and explicitly audible.

Manifest Mechanical Processes

Unsurprisingly for a man who resided firmly on the transcendent wing of the Roman Catholic Church, Messiaen utilized manifest processes only rarely. Just three pieces from Table 1.1 can be said to fall into this category: 'L'Échange', the opening (and closing) music from 'La Rousserolle effarvatte' and the percussion writing in 'Les sept Anges aux sept trompettes'. What 'L'Échange', 'La Rousserolle effarvatte' and

---

[10]   This sense of the fearful is not unrelated to the 'spiritual violence' discussed by Philip Weller in his chapter 'Messiaen, the *Cinq Rechants* and "Spiritual Violence"' in *Messiaen Perspectives 1*.

[11]   Please see the editors' note explaining the capitalization of the titles of Messiaen's works. For a full listing of Messiaen's musical works, please see the appendix to this volume.

[12]   Cécile Sauvage, *Œuvres complètes* (Paris: La Table Ronde, 2002), p. 244.

Table 1.1   Select list of musical machines from Messiaen's output

Title of work	Movement	Technique	Concurrent material	Surrounding material
Quatuor pour la fin du Temps	1. 'Liturgie de cristal'	pno and vc isorhythms	Birdsong	N/A
Vingt Regards sur l'Enfant-Jésus	3. 'L'Échange'	Agrandissement asymétrique	None	N/A
Turangalîla-Symphonie	9. 'Turangalîla III'	'Mode rhythmique', percussion, with string chords added later	Joined by variant of opening melody	
Quatre Études de rythme	*Mode de valeurs et d'intensités*	Mode of pitches, durations and intensities	None	N/A
	Île le de feu 2	Permutations	None	Variants of theme, etc.
Livre d'orgue	3. 'Les Mains de l'abîme'	Agrandissement asymétrique	None	Tutti chords
	5. 'Pièce en Trio 2'	Personnages rythmiques	None	N/A
	7. '64 durées'	Chromatic durations, grouped and given in retrograde canon	birdsong	N/A
Catalogue d'oiseaux	5. 'La Chouette hulotte'	Mode of pitches, durations and intensities	None	Birdsong
	7. 'La Rousserolle effarvatte'	Personnages	None	Birdsong
Chronochromie	'Strophes I & II'	Permutations symétriques	Birdsong	N/A

La Transfiguration de Notre-Seigneur Jésus-Christ	6. 'Candor est lucis aeternae'	Personnages rythmiques	Chorus and birdsong	N/A
	10. 'Adoptionem filiorum perfectam'	Permutations symétriques	None	Chorus and birdsong
	12. 'Terribilis locus iste'	Chromatic modal canon and rhythmic augmentation/ diminution	String clusters	Fully chromatic cluster, choral declamation
Saint François d'Assise	7. 'Les stigmates'	Mode of durations, timbres and intensities	None	Fully chromatic cluster and Chouette Hulotte
Livre du Saint Sacrement	12. 'La Transsubstantiation'	Mode of pitches, timbres and durations	None	Birdsong and plainchant
Éclairs sur l'Au-Delà...	4. 'Les élus marqués du sceau'	Permutations symétriques	Birdsong	N/A
	6. 'Les sept Anges aux sept trompettes'	Personnages rythmiques	Wind monody	N/A

'Les sept Anges' have in common is an ineluctability. Their purpose, and a large part of their impact, comes from inculcating a sense of inevitability about what is happening.

In the case of 'L'Échange', the entire movement works through a process of asymmetrical enlargement ('agrandissement asymétrique'). Some elements, such as the descending thirds that open each pair of bars, remain static. Other elements are gradually and systematically stretched. For instance, the second left-hand octave descends by a semitone on each appearance, while the third rises by the same interval. This automatic process continues resolutely until the intervals between these three left-hand semiquavers have stretched to an octave. It is only at this point that Messiaen reasserts his compositional authority by rounding the piece off with a brief coda.

While not quite as transparent, the opening music of 'La Rousserolle effarvatte' is also governed by a clear process (see Example 1.1). The right hand alternates a pair of major ninth dyads, heard in ticking semiquavers. The first (G♭–A♭) initially has one semiquaver, the second (A♭–B♭) has 13, but the first dyad steals a semiquaver on each successive cycle, giving 2 and 12, 3 and 11, and so on. This aspect of the machine can be easily perceived. The left hand is a little more abstruse, having a set of nine chords (which freely select from the nine pitches not used by the right hand) and seven durations (♪♪♪♪♩ ♪♪). Moreover, a semiquaver

Example 1.1   'La Rousserolle effarvatte', opening

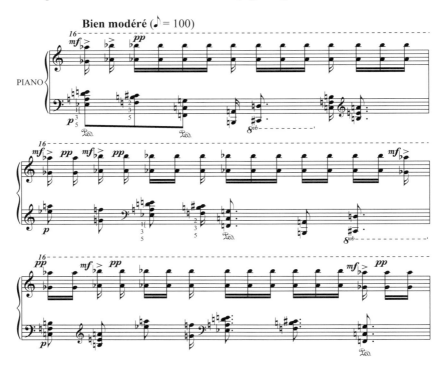

is added to the penultimate duration on each occasion, so that, by the end of the second page, the rhythm reads (♪♪♪♪. ♩ ♪[♪]).[13] As with 'L'Échange', it is readily apparent that a process has been set in motion that requires no further intervention. The process is reversed, though heard in fragmentary form, at the close of the movement.

In 'Les sept Anges', the systematic enlargement and contraction in the percussion is a readily audible example of what Messiaen calls *personnages rythmiques*, a device that is the equivalent in pure rhythm of *agrandissement asymétrique*. After the initial trinity of bass drum whacks, three descending notes are played on cymbals, gongs and tam-tams. These are followed by an emphatic semiquaver whip crack. Throughout the movement, the semiquaver of the whip and the three bass drum quavers provide an unchanging cell, lasting seven semiquavers. Each of the three descending notes that form the first cell of cymbals, gongs and tam-tams lasts three semiquavers. On the next appearance of this cell, a semiquaver has been added to each note so that each of the three elements of the rhythm lasts for four semiquavers. By adding (or subtracting) semiquavers to the descending notes of the cymbal, gong and tam-tam cells on each occasion, the durations fluctuate between three and seven semiquavers (Example 1.2).

It can be seen, then, that the percussion section consists of two elements, or *personnages*: the telescopic machinations of the metallic instruments and the

Example 1.2   'Les sept Anges aux sept trompettes', rhythmic cells

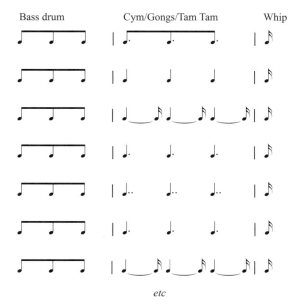

---

[13]   The rhythm is cut off before the final value.

immutable whip and bass drum. Numerology is clearly at play here, with the durations fluctuating between a Trinitarian three and a perfect seven, which has added resonance in terms of the seven angels of the title and is also the duration of the unchanging whip and bass drum cell. In addition, it is worth noting that the process is halted arbitrarily at the beginning of the 21st (3 × 7) cycle.

The ineluctability of these three movements is essentially objective. In 'La Rousserolle effarvatte', for example, the 'music of the ponds' simply encapsulates the broader, relentless daily cycle of observed nature. The irony in this instance is that the mechanical represents the absence of human input within the workings of the natural cycle. In a work in which Messiaen frequently and necessarily abandons any pretence of the emotional or artistic objectivity of *Réveil des oiseaux*, this is a crucial reminder at the heart of the *Catalogue* that he is a bystander to the action he portrays. Nature may provoke wonder, joy, fear and myriad other responses in Messiaen, but it remains impervious to his observation.

There is something of the same spirit in the depictions of immutable divine workings, whether the mysterious machines to be discussed later, or the manifest machines of 'L'Échange' and 'Les sept Anges'. Rather than impervious nature, they convey aspects of implacable divine workings. In 'Les sept Anges' this is not merely the unleashing of apocalyptic forces in themselves, but also a sense of this being a pre-ordained event, part of the divine plan since the dawn of time. Indeed, once the trumpets of the title have had their say, as also depicted in the *Quatuor pour la fin du Temps*, the machine measuring durations in the percussion is cut off – the workings of Time cease.

The sense of relentless unfolding of the divine will is strongest in 'L'Échange', the only instance of Messiaen allowing an automated process to be the sole provider (aside from the brief coda) of musical material in a movement. *Agrandissement asymétrique* is used within several later movements of *Vingt Regards*, perceptibly so for those minded to listen out for such techniques. However, in 'L'Échange' the machine is the movement so that the process is writ large, readily audible to all. It is perhaps no accident that, while some find it overwhelming, this movement has also drawn criticism from those otherwise well disposed towards Messiaen's music. For instance, in reviewing Peter Hill's recording of *Vingt Regards*, David Fanning described 'L'Échange' as being 'aridly composed'.[14] In its proper context of a cycle lasting more than two hours, 'L'Échange' forms an essential ingredient in the build-up of vast potential energy during the first five movements of *Vingt Regards*, which finds an outlet only in the kinetic frenzy of 'Par Lui tout a été fait'. Moreover, 'L'Échange' is only one of a number of occasions where Messiaen is prepared to let the theological symbolism of the work override purely musical considerations.[15] In this case, the inscription to the score makes clear that the

---

[14] David Fanning, 'Messiaen. Vingt Regards sur l'Enfant-Jésus. Peter Hill', *Gramophone* (September 1992): p. 137.

[15] Another instance of musical concerns being subservient to symbolism is found in the final two movements of the oratorio *La Transfiguration de Notre-Seigneur Jésus-Christ*, in

movement depicts 'the terrible trade between humans and God. God becomes man to make us Gods…'. It is theologically essential that the process is asymmetrical in order to reflect the balance of the relationship being portrayed, even while simultaneously conveying a fundamental rebalancing in that relationship. What is being made explicit here is not merely the exchange itself, but the sense that, from the outset, the consequence of humanizing the divine is a sacralizing of humanity.

In this sense, 'L'Échange' looks forward more than 20 years to the second septenary of *La Transfiguration*, in which notions of affiliation are explored more fully. The importance of the Transfiguration for the Church is that, in the revelation of Christ's true nature, the divine potential of all humanity is also made apparent. This underpins the ninth movement of the oratorio, 'Configuratum corpori claritatis suae', the principal text being an extract from Paul's letter to the Philippians (3:20–21): 'We are expecting the Saviour, our Lord, Jesus Christ, who will transform our humble bodies that they may be conformed to His glorious body'. It is reinforced with a quotation from St Thomas Aquinas in 'Terribilis est locus iste' (How awesome is this place), the 12th movement: 'The splendour which was in His garments signified the future splendour of the saints, which will be surpassed by that of Christ, just as the brightness of the snow is surpassed by that of the sun'.[16] Finally, the sense of the divine potential for humanity through the fact of Christ being both God and human is at the heart of the 'Collect' for the Feast of the Transfiguration, which provides the text for 'Adoptionem filiorum perfectam', the 10th movement of *La Transfiguration*:[17]

Deus, qui fidei, sacramenta in Unigeniti tui gloriosa Transfiguratione, patrum testimonio roborasti, et adaptionem filiorum perfectam voce delapsa in nube lucida mirabiliter praesignasti: concede propitius, ut ipsius Regis gloriae nos coheredes efficias, et ejusdem gloriae tribuas esse consortes. Alleluia, Allelluia.	O God, who confirmed the sacraments of faith by the testimony of the fathers [i.e. Moses and Elijah] at the Transfiguration of your only begotten Son and in marvellous fashion signified ahead of time our perfect adoption as sons by the voice that came down with a cloud of light, grant most graciously that you may make us fellow heirs of the King of Glory and allow us to have a share in that Glory. Alleluia, Alleluia.[18]

which Messiaen essentially repeats the end of the work in order to make a theological point; see Christopher Dingle, '"La statue reste sur son piédestal": Messiaen's *La Transfiguration* and Vatican II', *Tempo*, 212 (April, 2000): pp. 8–11.

[16]   St Thomas Aquinas, *Summa Theologiæ*, Part 3, Question 45, Article 2, Answer 3.

[17]   The Collect is sometimes referred to as the 'Opening Prayer' or just as the 'Prayer' (as in the score to *La Transfiguration*). It is said at the end of the Introductory Rites of the Mass, bringing together the prayers of the congregation and setting the theological tone for that particular day's celebration.

[18]   Translation by Paul Parvis. The text of the prayer was slightly altered in the Third Latin Typical Edition of 2002 and, hence, in the 2010 English translation now used in Catholic churches.

What links these three texts is the perspective of being between Christ's time on earth and the time of humanity achieving its divine potential, as if between two key moments. In 'L'Échange', by contrast, there is a continuous transfiguration of aspects of the material, the sense being of a process that is ongoing until completion. Moreover, the endpoint is inevitable from the moment the movement commences – it is viewed from the perspective of God rather than humanity. Nonetheless, in musical terms, Messiaen takes the feeling of inevitability to the limit of what can be sustained within his output. 'L'Échange' is the closest that he comes to producing a process piece in the manner of early Reich and, if Fanning's comments find any resonance, it is because this open approach sits uneasily within the transcendence that is Messiaen's usual practice.

The preface to *Un Vitrail et des oiseaux*, with its closing statement that 'More important than all the rest is the invisible aspect', is a simple example of this more usual penchant for the mysterious, and further examples will be discussed below. It is one of the fascinating contradictions of Messiaen that a cultivation of the mysterious should run through his output, given his apparent compulsion to provide some form of elucidation for his music. That said, his explanations are often striking as much for what is not said as for the insights provided. Moreover, a distinction should be drawn between description of the tools used to evoke a mystery and explaining the mystery itself. It is a simple matter to state what is done during the consecration in a Mass, but a bald statement that the gifts are blessed and (according to Catholic doctrine) transubstantiation occurs does not even begin to address the nature of the mystery involved for its adherents. Messiaen states what musical procedures are involved, and even what they represent, but he rarely touches upon the resulting emotive effect. In the case of the musical machines, this is especially pertinent, above all in what this chapter has defined as the mysterious processes, for there is often a deliberate abnegation of the compositional self in the face of the deepest mysteries.

Mysterious Mechanical Processes 1: Serial Modes

The unstoppable forces embodied in the manifest processes, whether representing the divine plan or the emotionless cycles of nature, are unnerving in their implacability, not merely in the aural experience, but also in the awareness of what is to come. It is one way in which Messiaen adapts the fear engendered by machines, the apprehension of the known. In the first category of mysterious processes, by contrast, Messiaen draws upon fear of the unknown, the perplexing, the unknowable. The machines in question here are the various passages where Messiaen employs a mode in which pitch, duration, attack and/or timbre are systematized, with each note becoming a distinct atom of sound with a unique combination of features that remains the same whenever it is heard. The most famous instance of this approach is in *Mode de valeurs et d'intensités*. Writing in 1958, Messiaen was proud of being 'the first' to develop the idea of a 'super-series applied to all the elements of music', first in passages of *Cantéyodjayâ*, then in *Mode de valeurs et d'intensités*.[19] He soon became dismissive, though, describing the 'three pages' of *Mode de valeurs* as 'perhaps, prophetic and historically important, but, musically, it's three times nothing'.[20] Not that this prevented him from putting adapted versions of the technique to good use in works as late as 'La Transsubstantiation', the 12th movement of the organ cycle *Livre du Saint Sacrement*, written in 1984, just two years before the comments to Samuel, and first performed on 1 July 1986, days before the Samuel conversations.

Two of the most prominent uses of this kind of serial mode are in 'La Chouette hulotte' (the Tawny Owl) from *Catalogue d'oiseaux* and the opening of 'Les stigmates', the seventh tableau of *Saint François d'Assise*. Blood-curdling imagery permeates 'La Chouette hulotte', with the composer describing the cry of the bird as being 'vociferous in terror like the cry of a murdered child' (preface to the score). The mode sets the scene to this nightmare, and a similar one, this time incorporating timbre, is used for the foreboding nocturnal scene of 'les stigmates'. In conversation with Samuel, Messiaen was explicit about his choice of technique: 'This super-serial passage gives you some sense of my feelings about serial music: I find it capable of expressing only fear, terror, and night … it is black! I see it without colour. Always black, grey, black, grey … only darkness remains'.[21] This is a damning indictment of serialism coming from a composer who not only viewed colour as an integral factor in his compositional processes, but who also spent so much of his time writing about 'the light'. As in 'La Chouette hulotte', the series in 'les stigmates' is juxtaposed with the cry of a Tawny Owl.

In the context of this clear correlation between serial modes and uneasy night-time settings, the use of the technique in 'La Transsubstantiation' might seem to be puzzling. However, the darkness here is that of a veil of inscrutability, and it is not so much fear itself that the movement evokes, but rather one of its key components: the unknown or, to be more precise, matters beyond human apprehension. The doctrine of transubstantiation is one of the most profound mysteries of Messiaen's faith. It should be remembered, too, that the theology surrounding transubstantiation is inextricably linked with the events of the Passion, to which 'les stigmates' also alludes. Messiaen's meditation upon transubstantiation draws upon three types of music: the quasi-serial mode, birdsong and plainchant. The mode is mechanical, while the birdsong and plainchant are found materials; the common factor to this trinity of materials is that each involves a minimum of compositional input from Messiaen. Just as he felt unworthy to compose a true Passion setting,[22] the transubstantiation is one of the areas of faith that were so precious to Messiaen that they were almost taboo as compositional subjects. In this context it is worth observing that among the 18 meditations of *Livre du Saint Sacrement*, an entire

---

[19] Notes for Adès CD 12.233-2, originally released as Vega C30A139 with same text.

[20] *Music and Color*, p. 47. Translation emended.

[21] Ibid., pp. 241–2. Translation emended.

[22] See ibid., p. 209.

cycle dedicated to the Eucharist, there is a 'Prière avant la Communion' (XIV) and a 'Prière après la Communion' (XVI), but there is no direct representation of the sacrament itself. The intervening movement is a birdsong extravaganza, 'La Joie de la grace', the title of which refers to the spiritual benefits of receiving Communion.[23] Rather than 'compose' a movement, Messiaen allows God's musicians to convey what cannot be conveyed. As far as the serial aspect of 'La Transsubstantiation' is concerned, the inscription at the head of the first 'Pièce en trio' from *Livre d'orgue*, which has some similarity of spirit, comes to mind: 'For now we see through a glass darkly' (1Corinithians 13:12).

Another factor that may be relevant to Messiaen's use of a process associated elsewhere with fear is the notion of awe. Speaking about 'Cedar Breaks et le don de crainte' (Cedar Breaks and the gift of awe), the fifth movement of *Des Canyons aux étoiles...*, Messiaen explained that:

> Cedar Breaks was a frightening place, and to evoke it, I thought of the different stages of fear: first the fear of the policeman or, if you prefer, the fear of punishment, then the fear that the Bible calls awe, which is the beginning of wisdom. Awe here signifies the sense of the sacred. When Moses approaches the burning bush and a voice says to him, 'I am the One who is,' he is afraid. It's not the fear felt before death, but a feeling caused by an extraordinary event that is beyond you. It's a reverence for the sacred .... I wanted to translate this feeling of awe, which is not fear but a feeling of reverence before something higher. ... The gift of awe is ... the impossibility of understanding.[24]

This notion of awe, a sense of 'reverence before something higher', is certainly pertinent for 'La Transsubstantiation', not merely for the mystery itself, but also for the consequent interaction of believers with the consecrated hosts. Transubstantiation is the foundation of the notion of the 'real presence' of Christ in the Eucharist, resulting not only in its consumption in Communion, but also prompting Exposition, where the host is displayed for prayerful adoration.

Messiaen may make a distinction between awe and fear, but it is significant that his thoughts on awe started with fear, and with a place that he found frightening. For Messiaen, fear and awe had a close kinship, as is clear in movements such as 'Terribilis locus iste' from *La Transfiguration*. Indeed, it is surely no accident in this context that the momentous vocalization just before the end of this movement is another aurally mysterious machine, though in this case it is modal in origin.[25] The use of a serial process in 'La Transsubstantiation' similar to those found in 'La Chouette hulotte' and 'les stigmates' reflects Messiaen's catholic approach

---

[23]   Even this was only included at the very last moment of the work's composition (see PHNS, p. 350).

[24]   *Music and Color*, p. 164.

[25]   This is discussed at some length in Christoph Neidhöfer's chapter, 'Messiaen's Counterpoint', later in this volume.

to expressing his Catholicism, his creative reach extending to a mechanistic compositional approach that he found contrary to his nature.

Mysterious Mechanical Processes 2: Coloured Time

The second category of transcendent mechanical processes covers the various movements or passages where harmony and duration combine to create a gradually evolving kaleidoscope of sound:

- 'Liturgie de cristal' (*Quatuor*)
- 'Turangalîla III' (*Turangalîla*)
- 'Soixante-quatre durées' (*Livre d'orgue*)
- 'Strophe I' and 'Strophe II' (*Chronochromie*)
- 'Candor est lucis aeternae' (*La Transfiguration*)
- 'Adoptionem filiorum perfectam' (*La Transfiguration*)
- 'Les élus marqués du sceau' (*Éclairs*)

With just two exceptions, 'Turangalîla III' and 'Adoptionem filiorum perfectam', the coloured time of these movements provides the backdrop to a web of birdsong. From 'Liturgie de cristal' to 'Les élus marqués du sceau', Messiaen returned repeatedly to this idea of a movement with two distinct strata, creating, on the one hand, a tightly organized, mechanized, mysterious, dazzling band of coloured rhythm and, on the other, the freedom of birdsong. These movements might be regarded as combining two sides of the divine, or, perhaps, the rigorous logic of Saint Thomas Aquinas with the nature loving spirit of Saint Francis of Assisi.

There are a variety of techniques employed. 'Liturgie de cristal' is undoubtedly the most famous example of a compositional machine in Messiaen's music. As has been discussed at length elsewhere,[26] the piano part has a cycle of 29 chords combined with a set of 17 durations. Both being prime numbers, it would take 17 times 29 cycles to return to the same starting point. To this should be added the cello, which plays a cycle of 5 pitches and a sequence of 15 durations. For this machine to return to its starting point would take 4 hours 40 minutes,[27] but Messiaen simply presents a short fragment. The effect is of a door being opened to reveal the ongoing workings, and then being closed again.

The machinations of 'Turangalîla III', the ninth movement of the *Turangalîla-Symphonie*, are discussed at some length by Messiaen in the *Traité*.[28] Much of the movement is underpinned by a 'rhythmic mode' based upon a distribution

---

[26] See, for instance, Anthony Pople, *Messiaen: Quatuour pour la fin du Temps* (Cambridge: Cambridge University Press, 1998) for an extensive discussion of this movement.

[27] Ibid., p. 26.

[28] *Traité II*, pp. 333–68.

of values from 1 to 17 semiquavers between five percussion instruments. There is then a systematic exchange and inversion of values between high and low instruments. For instance, whereas in the first rendition the woodblock plays the series (♩♩♪♪♪♪♪♪♩.♩.) and the tam-tam has the values (♩♩♪♪♪♩♩♩♪), on the second the woodblock plays the tam-tam's original (♩♩♪♪♪♩♩♩♪) while the tam-tam takes the woodblock's opening (♩♩♪♪♪♪♪♩.♩.) as its own. As the movement progresses, additions are made before each value, gradually increasing from one to five semiquavers, with these new series also being exchanged and inverted. What links this to the other processes discussed here is that, from about figure 5 of the score, five groups of solo strings appear. These provide what Messiaen calls 'the resonance of the five percussion instruments',[29] thus making this a passage of coloured rhythm.

A similar colouring occurs in 'Soixante-quatre durées', in which the 64 durations of the title are heard simultaneously in what Messiaen calls an open and a closed fan, that is, working from the middle outwards, or from the edges inwards. As Robert Sherlaw Johnson observes, this machine is coloured in three ways, 'by timbre, by sustained chords (harmony) and by the birdsong'.[30] Coming at the end of the *Livre d'orgue*, this movement might seem to be the culmination of the experimental period, during which Messiaen's fascination with compositional methodology in general, and machines in particular, was most apparent. However, the boundaries are not so clear cut, and it is notable in this context that Peter Hill has described Messiaen's approach to the central tutti of *Réveil des oiseaux* as possessing '"automatic" characteristics in the composing that reflect his reluctance to alter his birdsong data'.[31] Indeed, this moment of conjunction between the automatic and the natural also confirms the importance for Messiaen of the near removal of his compositional personality, as is explicit in his instructions for the première at Donaueschingen: 'Don't include my biography, or any personal or musical information with my analytical note: I'm anxious to disappear behind the birds.'[32] While far from being the case for all of his birdsong writing, this appears to be the intent behind the birdsong strata of all of the coloured time passages. At the risk of creating a circular argument, viewed the opposite way, the similarity of intent between Messiaen's disappearance behind the birds in *Réveil* and the impersonality of his musical machines provides more specific understanding of

---

[29]   Ibid., p. 360. Two first violins join the woodblock with an ostinato of 13 chords in mode 3^2, four second violins join the suspended cymbal with an ostinato of 10 chords in mode 2^1, three violas join the maracas with an ostinato of 9 chords in mode 6^1, two cellos join the *tambourin provençal* (a type of drum) with an ostinato of 14 chords in mode 4^5 and two double basses join the tam-tam with an ostinato of 8 chords in mode 1^1.

[30]   Robert Sherlaw Johnson, *Messiaen*, 2nd paperback edn, updated and additional text by Caroline Rae (London: Omnibus Press, 2008; first published 1975), p. 115.

[31]   See Peter Hill's chapter, 'From *Réveil des oiseaux* to *Catalogue d'oiseaux*: Messiaen's *Cahiers de notations des chants d'oiseaux*, 1952–59', in *Messiaen Perspectives 1*.

[32]   PHNS, p. 208.

the manner in which this work fulfils Messiaen's claim that 'every subject can be a religious one on condition that it is viewed through the eye of one who believes'.[33]

Messiaen expanded the principles of 'Soixante-quatre durées' for an orchestral canvass with the development of a technique he called *permutations symétriques*. He had employed permutational devices since the *Quatre Études de rythme*, notably in *Île de feu 2*, but it was only with the two 'Strophe' movements of *Chronochromie* that the device became fully formalized and related to a specific group of rhythms. Messiaen's starting point was a chromatic series of durations from 1 to 32 demisemiquavers. He then permutated these durations, not as a whole, but in five groups so that, rather than an astronomical number of permutations, he ended up with a manageable 36. Six out of the seven movements of *Chronochromie* draw upon these 36 permutations,[34] but it is the 'Strophe' movements that utilize them to most spectacular effect. A group of three consecutive permutations is superposed from the group of 36, with each permutation having a palette of string chords, one harmony per duration.[35] As Messiaen explains, a complete rendition of a permutation takes 33 bars of $\frac{4}{4}$.[36] This is the length of each 'Strophe' movement.

After *Chronochromie* these 'symmetrical permutations' appear in numerous movements, up to and including 'Les élus marqués du sceau'. However, while the durations in 'Les élus' follow the 'Strophe' movements in being 'coloured' both by harmony and by birdsong, there are also passages where the birds are absent. These tend to be partial unfoldings, such as in 'Adoptionem filiorum perfectam', the tenth movement of *La Transfiguration*. The first section features the first seven durations of permutation 7 (♪ ♩ ♪ ♪♪ ♪. ♩ ♪[♩ ♩ ♪.])[37] while the third section of the movement contains an equally fleeting glimpse of permutation 8, starting with the seventh duration (♩ ♪ ♪♪ ♪ ♩ ♪ ... ♪[♩ ♩ ♪]).[38] The way in which these kaleidoscopic rhythm machines are cut off is no different in essence from the way in which only a fragment of the full isorhythm of 'Liturgie de cristal' is heard. These passages in 'Adoptionem filiorum perfectam' offer just the briefest moments of mysterious colour, a few seconds each in a substantial movement, yet the composer felt compelled to draw attention to them in an otherwise relatively brief programme note. This means nothing to the majority of those reading it, and provides no sense of their purpose or how they sound. Messiaen's reference to permutations may reflect his pride in the technique, or even a brandishing of intellectual armour

---

[33] Messiaen, 'Autour d'une parution', *Le Monde musical* (April 1939), cited in PHNS, p. 80.

[34] The exception is the 'Épôde', which is constructed exclusively from birdsong.

[35] For a fuller discussion of the *permutations symétriques*, see *Traité III*, pp. 5–76 and Johnson, *Messiaen*, pp. 159–69 and 176–7. Note that there is an error on p. 28 of Messiaen's chapter in *Traité III*, as the sixth value of *permutation 18* should be a dotted quaver, not a quaver.

[36] *Traité III*, p. 39.

[37] The final duration is interrupted.

[38] The final duration is interrupted.

in discussing a work that marked the decisive reintroduction of tonally derived harmony as a key structural element. Nonetheless, it also raises the suspicion that, behind the genial façade of elucidation, there lurked a mischievous need periodically to perplex in order to satisfy his ubiquitous predilection for mystery.

The aural complexity of passages using symmetrical permutations is matched in *La Transfiguration* by different means in 'Candor est lucis aeternae', despite the machine in question being more straightforward. Rhythmically, it is the same as that used in 'Les sept Anges', being a systematic process of asymmetrical augmentation and diminution. The augmentation takes place in the form of adding semiquavers to each constituent value of the Çârngadeva rhythm *Candrakalâ*,[39] except for the final semiquaver, which remains unchanged throughout the movement (♪♪♪♪ ♪ ♪ ♪). Augmentation continues until three semiquavers have been added to the original values, at which point diminution commences by removing semiquavers until we return to the original rhythm. The entire process of augmentation and diminution then recommences and the telescopic rhythmic process threatens to continue *ad infinitum*. This purely rhythmic process is coloured by a set of ten chords played by tubular bells and eight second violins. Above this, the choir sings the movement's text in a rare occurrence of mode 1 (the whole-tone scale). If this were the extent of 'Candor est lucis aeternae' it would be placed firmly in the manifest category of automatic processes, the only difference from 'Les sept Anges' being that the telescopic rhythm is coloured by harmony. However, the perception of the process in 'Candor est lucis aeternae' is markedly different on account of the greater complexity of texture in the movement. The rhythmic machinations of the tubular bells and eight second violins are barely comprehensible beneath a confusion of additional material, notably birdsong, which is pervaded by irrational rhythms. As the composer himself notes, this is a more complex movement than anything in *Chronochromie* and looks forward to 'Le Prêche aux oiseaux' in *Saint François*. Birdsong is the focus and distracts the ear from the more mechanical processes so that the compositional tree on which the birds sit is barely registered.

Regardless of the technique, from the isorhythms of 'Liturgie de cristal', via the marginal durational distinctions of 'Soixante-quatre durées', to the *permutations symétriques* of the 'Strophe' movements in *Chronochromie*, there is a clear similarity of intent. This concurrence is underlined by the tendency to combine the coloured time element with birdsong. Three of these birdsong movements – 'Candor est lucis aeternae', 'Les élus marqués du sceau' and 'Liturgie de cristal' – have an explicit symbolism attached to them. 'Candor est lucis aeternae' is an evocation of the transfigured (that is, 'true') figure of Christ. Rather than attempting a direct musical depiction, Messiaen constructs a complex movement containing admittedly personal, allegorical musical elements in order to convey a text that itself does not refer to Christ directly:[40]

---

[39]   No. 105 in Çârngadeva's table of 120 deçî-tâlas.

[40]   Using Wisdom as synonym for Christ is a common feature of Christian theology, particularly in the Patristic tradition. For further discussion of how this applies to *La*

Candor est lucis aeternae, speculum sine macula, et imago bonitatis illius.	[Wisdom] is the brightness of the eternal light, a mirror without fault, and the image of His goodness.

(Wisdom 7:26)

As with 'La Transsubstantiation', Messiaen draws upon what might be regarded as impersonal elements, namely birdsong, the uncharacteristic mode 1 and a rhythmic machine. The resultant impression is of a swirling, controlled chaos, in which a sense of order is apparent, though its nature is beyond apprehension.

'Les élus marqués du sceau' marks a significant moment in the Book of Revelation and, again, there is a sense of forces at work that are beyond human understanding:

> Next I saw four angels standing at the four corners of the earth, holding back the four winds of the world to keep them from blowing over the land or the sea or any tree. Then I saw another angel rising where the sun rises, carrying the seal of the living God; he called in a powerful voice to the four angels whose duty was to devastate land and sea, 'Wait before you do any damage on land or at sea or to the trees, until we have put the seal on the foreheads of the servants of our God'. (Revelation 7:1–3)

The *Quatuor pour la fin du Temps* is also inspired by *Revelation*, specifically Chapter 10. Crucially, in his preface to the score, Messiaen explains the symbolism of his dual-level creation in 'Liturgie de cristal': 'Between three and four in the morning, the awakening of birds: a solo blackbird or nightingale improvises, surrounded by a shimmer of sound, by a halo of trills lost very high in the trees. Transpose this onto a religious plane and you have the harmonious silence of heaven.' Although this phrase is a general allegory rather than tied to a specific piece of scripture,[41] it is worth noting that, at the beginning of Chapter 8, immediately after the passage that inspired 'Les élus', the narrative of Revelation denotes a pause, explaining that: 'there was silence in heaven for about half an hour' (Revelation 8:1). It is hardly surprising that there is a concurrence of celestial symbolism in these pieces with, on the one hand, the 'harmonious silence of heaven' and, on the other, the divine nature of Christ, for these are far from uncommon subjects for Messiaen. The inspiration in these coloured-time movements is markedly different from that found underpinning some of the other compositional machines. The passages in Revelation are moments of respite amidst cataclysmic events, while the Wisdom text in 'Candor est lucis

---

Transfiguration, see Christopher Dingle, *Olivier Messiaen:* La Transfiguration de Notre-Seigneur, Jésus-Christ – *A Provisional Study*, MPhil thesis (University of Sheffield, 1994).

[41]   Messiaen uses the same expression with regard to the end of 'Amen du désir', the fourth movement of *Visions de l'Amen*.

Messiaen Perspectives 2: Techniques, Influence and Reception

aeternae' portrays Christ as the image of light and goodness. As has already been suggested, Messiaen's other machines are more imposing.

Transfiguring Fear

Messiaen's remark to Claude Samuel in 1986 that he found mechanization 'overwhelming' merely reiterates a sentiment inherent in the manifesto for La Jeune France. Typically, though, for a composer who declared 'I abandon nothing',[42] Messiaen found a use for the mechanical in his music. Rather than reflecting the machines and life of the cities that he abhorred, Messiaen translated the bafflement and fear that city life and automation aroused in him into an allegory for something higher, namely the divine plan. Whether the machines are manifest or mysterious, abstruse quasi-serial passages or clangourous mélanges of coloured time, depictions of natural phenomena or theological concepts, they convey glimpses of the all-seeing, all-knowing aspects of God. This is the music of the spheres, or the Newtonian view of God as geometer, updated for the century of Einstein. Moreover, while some of these machines are deliberately abstruse, as the 'creator' of his music, Messiaen wished to possess an intimate knowledge of the components of the devices he set in motion. An exchange during the thesis defence of Iannis Xenakis, for which Messiaen was on the panel of examiners, is illuminating:

> *Olivier Messiaen*: You know as well as I do that a certain number of objects gives a certain number of permutations, and the more the number of objects increases, the more the number of permutations increases and with a speed and in quantities which can seem disproportioned. So, three objects give six permutations, six objects give seven hundred and twenty, and twelve objects give (if I'm not mistaken) four hundred and ninety-seven million, one thousand six hundred permutations. Suppose these objects correspond to durations: I would have to write out these durations in order to know what gesture or what movement they could create in time. There has been a lot of talk about retrograde movements these days: this is but one movement, one single movement among thousands of others, and its permutation follows the original trajectory. And all the other permutations? I can't write out the millions and millions of permutations ... and yet I must write them out in order to know them and to love them (I insist on the verb *to love*!). In your case, a machine will give you the millions of permutations within a few minutes: it's a cold and unexplicit list. How can and do you choose directly from within this immense world of possibilities without intimate knowledge or love?

---

[42] Almut Rößler, *Contributions to the Spiritual World of Olivier Messiaen*, trans. Barbara Dagg and Nancy Poland (Duisberg: Gilles and Francke, 1986), p. 75.

Iannis Xenakis: … The question … of having to love something in order to use it naturally implies an initial taming. To tame or 'win over' means live with, and live with means to love and also to not love; for loving leads to its corollary.

Olivier Messiaen: I've expressed myself poorly. What I wanted to say was 'to know!' To know with a real and emotional knowledge, out of love or hate.[43]

Messiaen evidently felt the need to have creative omniscience when it came to representing the workings of the divine, even while using them to remove a sense of his compositional self.[44]

Machines are used in Messiaen's music as metaphors for the mysterious, the fearful, the awe-inspiring, things visible and invisible, the impenetrable and abstruse. The use of mechanization as an allegory for such things is easy to comprehend. More remarkable, though, is the spectacular way that Messiaen adapted his most complex compositional machines, painting them in myriad colours as vibrant expressions of nature and inspiring divine moments. Messiaen harnessed the mechanical to the natural, the controlled to the free, not so much to neutralize them as to transform and sacralize them to create the harmonious silence of heaven.

---

[43] Iannis Xenakis, *Arts/Sciences: Alloys – The Thesis Defense of Iannis Xenakis*, trans. Sharon Kanach (New York: Pendragon Press, 1985), pp. 31–2.

[44] Incidentally, Messiaen also stated that, as he was a composer, he could not write and discuss rhythms in terms of sequences of numbers, but had to use musical durations (crotchets, quavers, etc.). See Olivier Mille, *Olivier Messiaen: La Liturgie de Cristal*, film made in 2002, Idéale Audience International DVD (2007), DVD9DS44.

Chapter 2
La Fauvette des jardins and the 'Spectral Attitude'

Roderick Chadwick

If location is one aspect of music's world, the life-history of the composer is another.[1]

Messiaen used the metaphor of night for compositional and spiritual struggles when both writing music and discussing it. The nocturnal 'Stigmata' scene in *Saint François d'Assise* is an example of his most disorientating material, and his earlier, apprehensive view of musical progress in the mid-1950s was famously recounted by Alexander Goehr: 'Gentlemen, we are all in a profound night; I'm as lost as you.'[2] (The echo of Debussy's Golaud here is striking.)[3] Given the countless early mornings the composer spent notating the song of Fauvettes des Jardins (Garden Warblers) outside his summer home at Petichet in the 1960s, it is tempting to imagine him reliving the emergence from his 'experimental' period into his 1950s bird style as the sun rose.[4] His preoccupation with passing time and the hours of the day was translated into music in the post-experimental solo piano works:

> But it's in my *Catalogue d'oiseaux* and in *La Fauvette des jardins* that you'll find my great formal innovation. There, instead of referring to an antique or classical

---

[1] Arnold Whittall, *Exploring Twentieth-century Music: Tradition and Innovation* (Cambridge: Cambridge University Press, 2003), p. 9.

[2] Goehr's recollection of Messiaen's words to his class in 1956, quoted in Peter Hill and Nigel Simeone, *Olivier Messiaen: Oiseaux Exotiques* (Aldershot: Ashgate, 2007), p. 214.

[3] 'Je suis perdu aussi', from Debussy, Claude *Pelléas et Mélisande*, Act I, scene 1, concluding line. Messiaen later identified Golaud's voice (and Boris Godunov's) with that of St Francis.

[4] On 21 July 1960 he wrote 'réveil des oiseaux' when two Garden Warblers sang together at 5 am. *Réveil des oiseaux* (1953) is widely seen as a turning-point in Messiaen's output, though nuanced versions of this view can be found in, amongst others, Hill and Simeone, *Messiaen: Oiseaux exotiques'*, p. 27 and Wai-Ling Cheong, 'Neumes and Greek Rhythms: The Breakthrough in Messiaen's Birdsong', *Acta Musicologica*, 80/1 (2008): pp. 1–32. I am grateful to Peter Hill for allowing me to view reproductions of several unpublished *cahier* pages from the 1960s, where Garden Warblers are featured extensively.

mold, or even to some mold I might have invented, I sought to reproduce in condensed form the vivid course of the hours of day and night.[5]

Attending Messiaen's class the year *La Fauvette des jardins* was composed (1970) were a number of composers, including Tristan Murail and Gérard Grisey, who were on the verge of creating new ways of working with sound by stretching time, seeing it as part of a continuum along with timbre, harmony and rhythm. Could their achievements illuminate Messiaen's 'great formal innovation'? The fluid approach to continuity and form of these pioneering 'spectral' composers is seemingly the polar opposite of Messiaen's in *La Fauvette*, where 'limpid, virtuosic'[6] Garden Warbler solos alternate with a succession of episodic blocks (other birdcalls and souvenirs of the Dauphiné). My aim in this chapter is to challenge this apparent opposition by referring in particular to Grisey and his seminal article '*Tempus ex Machina*: A Composer's Reflection on Musical Time',[7] with the intention of moving beyond the notion of *La Fauvette*'s hard-edged form and identifying more organic, 'respirational' processes (Grisey's term) behind the splices. This approach will enable conclusions to be drawn about the nature of the Garden Warbler's song, how Messiaen simulates the passage of time, and ultimately his integration of 'sinusoidal forms'[8] with a tonal substructure – the principal technical reason for granting the work the exalted status he afforded it.[9]

La Fauvette des jardins is a rich and inspired portrait of a landscape Messiaen knew probably better than any other.[10] If the life-history of a composer is as much an aspect of music's world as location, it should prove instructive to look back through the lens of a movement with which the composer had a discernible affinity, particularly given the extent to which technique was – for him – wrapped up in all other aspects of life. I will steer clear, however, of overstating any kinship or influence between teacher and students, and instead observe how a state of mind (which is

---

[5]   *Music and Color*, p. 117.

[6]   Messiaen's description in the preface to the score, *La Fauvette des jardins* (Paris: Leduc, 1972).

[7]   Gérard Grisey, '*Tempus ex Machina*: A Composer's Reflection on Musical Time', *Contemporary Music Review*, 2/1 (1987): pp. 239–75.

[8]   This is Murail's description of the waves of sound in *Territoires de l'oubli* ('Realms of oblivion'), the other great 30-minute French piano work of the 1970s alongside *La Fauvette*.

[9]   He does so purely in the context of birdsong composition: 'To them [the birds of the ponds] I've dedicated 'La Rousserolle effarvatte' in my *Catalogue d'oiseaux*, a piece I've long considered my greatest success in bird songs, but which I now think has twice been surpassed, by my *Fauvette des jardins* for piano and 'The Sermon to the Birds' from *Saint François d'Assise*', *Music and Color*, p. 92.

[10]   The landscape is an idealized one; frogs are completely absent, despite their ubiquity in the Petichet *cahier* pages, tipping the balance of the work towards the more harmonious upper register in contrast to 'La Rousserolle effarvatte'.

after all what the practitioners of spectralism professed it to be) can influence an investigation and help to demonstrate Messiaen's command of his resources.

The 'Spectral Attitude'

What are the origins of the expression 'spectral attitude'? No single definition has primacy. Joshua Fineberg identifies Hugues Dufourt as the first to use the 'spectral' epithet (memorably described by Grisey as a 'sticker' in 1996[11] – one that he hoped would eventually peel off?); Tristan Murail first issued the qualification in the early 1980s, coining a phrase that has become common currency.[12] Needless to say, this was in part a rebuttal of the emerging notion of a 'school' of composition.

An established modern-day definition of spectralism is 'any music that foregrounds timbre as an important element of structure or musical language'.[13] Merging musical parameters (most commonly timbre and harmony, but also rhythm) by 'putting a microscope on the sound'[14] is a process that has led to the most celebrated passages in spectral music, such as the 'instrumental synthesis' at the opening of Grisey's *Partiels*, or the modulated bell sounds of Murail's *Gondwana*. More abstract considerations tend to determine how the 'attitude' is struck; the running theme is an 'obsession with organic continuity ... well outside the twentieth-century French tradition of discontinuously juxtaposing *objets sonores*, a characteristic of both Boulez and Murail's teacher Messiaen'.[15] Further observations from the key players range from the pithy to the mildly satirical – and are not always entirely in accordance with each other:

---

[11] Gérard Grisey and David Bündler, 'Gérard Grisey', interview with David Bündler, 18 January 1996, available at www.angelfire.com/music2/davidbundler/grisey.html (March 1996).

[12] It is outlined most extensively, in print, in Tristan Murail's 'Target Practice': 'I do not believe, therefore, that one can speak of a "spectral system" as such, if by that we understand a body of rules that will produce a product of a certain hue. I do believe, however, that one can speak of a "spectral attitude"'. Trans. Joshua Cody, in Joshua Fineberg and Pierre Michel (eds), 'Models and Artifice: The Collected Writings of Tristan Murail', *Contemporary Music Review*, 24/2–3 (April/June 2005): p. 152.

[13] Istanbul Spectral Music Conference 2003. See, Robert Reigle and Paul Whitehead (eds), *In Spectral World Musics: Proceedings of the Istanbul Spectral Music Conference* (Istanbul: Pan Yayıncılık, 2008).

[14] Thereby observing the partials that constitute the sound and using them as the basis for a wide variety of musical procedures. The microscope notion is attributed to Grisey in Joshua Fineberg, *Classical Music, Why Bother? Hearing the World of Contemporary Culture through a Composer's Ears* (New York: Routledge, 2006), p. 115.

[15] Julian Anderson, 'In Harmony – Julian Anderson Introduces the Music and Ideas of Tristan Murail', *The Musical Times*, 134/1804 (June 1993): pp. 321–3. Anderson could be having fun at Boulez's expense, given the latter's infamous put-down of Messiaen as a 'juxtaposer'.

- 'Music is ultimately sound evolving in time' (Joshua Fineberg).[16]
- 'We are musicians and our model is sound not literature, sound not mathematics, sound not theatre, visual arts, quantum physics, geology, astrology or acupuncture' (Gérard Grisey).[17]
- 'Thinking in terms of continuous, rather than discrete, categories' (Tristan Murail).[18]
- '[The] potential for interplay between fusion and continuity, on one side, and diffraction and discontinuity, on the other' (Grisey again).[19]

Grisey acknowledged Messiaen's importance in opening up spectral realms:

> There is music that has been important for me at certain periods. Like the music of Conlon Nancarrow because he deals with music in compressed time – the sort of music written for and by insects or for small animals. Extremely compressed in time. I'm fascinated by that. … I think there are three composers that have had a strong impression upon me as a young composer. Messiaen, who was my teacher for four years, for the sense of colour and harmony and translucence. Second, I would name Stockhausen for the sense of dramaturgy, the sense of form and time. And Ligeti, as third, for his use of extended time and continuity.[20]

It is notable that, of the three, Messiaen is not the one credited with being an adept handler of time. Is this anxiety of influence? Perhaps, though unlikely: Grisey was critical of Messiaen's approach to rhythm in *Tempus ex Machina*.[21] Though they were pursuing similar rhythmic goals (asymmetry on the one hand and malleable periodicity on the other), differences undoubtedly existed. Nevertheless, as shown below, Grisey's understanding of musical time illuminates the effects Messiaen was aspiring to create on a large-scale rhythmic basis.

Many composers of the pre-1970 generation could be credited with aspects of a spectral attitude, not least the three cited above (amongst others there are Per

---

[16] Fineberg, *Classical Music, Why Bother?*, p. 112.

[17] Quoted in ibid., p. 105.

[18] Murail, 'Target Practice', p. 152.

[19] The last two quotations are brought together by Sean Ferguson in 'De-composing Tristan Murail: The Collected Writings, 1980–2000 (Review of 'Models and Artifice: The Collected Writings of Tristan Murail', *Contemporary Music Review*, 24/2–3 (April/ June 2005)', *Circuit: Musiques contemporaines*, 17/1 (2007): p. 118. The second of these originates from Grisey's article, 'Did you say spectral?', trans. Joshua Fineberg, *Contemporary Music Review* 19/3 (2000): pp. 1–3.

[20] Grisey and Bündler, 'Gérard Grisey'.

[21] He describes Messiaen's non-retrogradable rhythms as an 'avatar': 'It shows the level of contempt for or misunderstanding of perception our elders had attained', Grisey, *Tempus ex Machina*, p. 242.

Nørgård, Giacinto Scelsi and even Paul Hindemith).[22] Right from the final bars of the first *Prélude*, 'La colombe', Messiaen demonstrates sensitivity towards resonance as an integral part of his language. The penultimate page of 'Première Communion de la Vierge', the depiction of Christ's heart beating in the Virgin's womb, shares many characteristics with one of the archetypal moments in spectral music, the opening of Grisey's *Partiels*. Grisey often mentioned heartbeats in connection with the 'fuzzy periodicity' of his own rhythms, and the similarities between the two passages are both rhythmic (the manner in which the number of bass notes accumulates: two steps forward, one back, more precisely so in the *Regard*) and harmonic (varying harmonicity above a static bass; this time the process is more systematic in *Partiels*).[23]

The fact that these memorable sonorities illustrate one of Messiaen's most moving, poetic images enhances their importance and relevance to this discussion.

'Chronotropy'

Returning to *La Fauvette des jardins* and simulation of the hours of the day, Grisey transports the issue to the wider cosmos in his *Le Noir de l'étoile* for six percussionists, tape and pulsar-transmitting radio signal:

> When music succeeds in conjuring up time, it finds itself vested with a veritable shamanic power, that of connecting us to the forces that surround us. In bygone civilisations, the lunar or solar rites had a conjuring function. Thanks to them, the seasons could return and the sun rise every day.[24]

It is hard to imagine Messiaen claiming to possess the powers of a shaman,[25] but in *La Fauvette* he invests his avian subject with the opposite power during its immense solos, observing in the preface that 'Its rapid *vocalises*, its tireless virtuosity, the regular flow of its discourse seem to arrest time'; it emulates the Angel of the Apocalypse, no less. So through large parts of the work the passage of time is simulated by the illusory suspension thereof. Grisey describes this kind of texture in more analytical terms in '*Tempus ex Machina*':

> If this continuity is maintained throughout the duration of a work it is virtually impossible to memorize anything ... all that emerges is a hazy memory of the

---

[22] Julian Anderson's 'A Provisional History of Spectral Music' (*Contemporary Music Review*, 19/2: pp. 7–22) contains a definitive survey of the prehistory of spectralism.

[23] Julian Anderson remarks on the similarity of the opening of *Partiels* to the trombone and clarinets' 'abyss' in *Couleurs de la Cité céleste*; see Anderson, ibid., p. 11.

[24] Liner notes to Gérard Grisey, *Le Noir de l'Etoile*, trans. John Tyler Tuttle, CD Accord 476 1052.

[25] Messiaen's student François-Bernard Mâche nonetheless refused to laugh off this idea when it was suggested by the author.

contours of the sound's evolution. Time past is no longer measurable. I would call this process psychotropic or better still chronotropic.[26]

This aptly describes the effect of the Garden Warbler solos, which are unquestionably long enough for memory of them to start eroding. Messiaen's apparent paradox does not need to be seen as such, however. Time 'stops' on a regular basis (during each solo); all the more opportunity to be aware of it when it begins again, at the key moments in an accumulating musical architecture.

La Fin des Périodes

When it comes to spectralist preoccupation with the merging of parameters, Messiaen's students would surely have been intrigued by his comment to pianists at the foot of p. 7 of *La Fauvette des jardins*, had they reason to notice it: 'Pour les Solos de Fauvette des jardins: bien observer les durées des accords de fin de périodes, pour que les couleurs en soient perceptible.'[27] This is perhaps more practical than his direction for the conductor to 'transmit' the colours of *Couleurs de la Cité céleste* to the players, implying that if, but only if, you do what the score says, alchemy will occur. It could be seen as the flip side of works such as *Timbres-durées* and *Chronochromie*, where timbres 'colour' the durations.

What happens if one focuses on these chords in order to see what makes the Garden Warbler tick? As Peter Hill observes, many of them are chords of transposed inversion[28] and, in line with Messiaen's common practice, they reflect the world around them: the refrain-like harmonies that elsewhere in *La Fauvette* describe the reflection of the sun in the Lac du Laffrey are complete *renversement transposées* progressions.

Added notes at the top of the chords that end the 'two preliminary trials'[29] of the warbler enhance a feature already present in the basic harmony: polarization of black and white notes. There are three black notes above six white in both sonorities; they are the same chord of transposed inversion, the second transposed five semitones lower, though the bass is only three semitones lower (it still doubles the lowest note in the right hand due to the recommended employment of a double-thumb in the first chord, but not the second). Transposition by a perfect interval facilitates the retention of *blanc/noir* duality (though it would still theoretically be

---

[26]   Grisey, '*Tempus ex Machina*', p. 273.

[27]   'For Garden Warbler solos: stay true to the durations of chords at the ends of phrases, in order for the colours to be perceptible.' *La Fauvette des jardins*, plate no. A.L. 24 588 (p. 7).

[28]   Peter Hill, 'Piano Music II' in Peter Hill (ed.) *The Messiaen Companion* (London: Faber and Faber, 1995), pp. 345–6. Other types, such as chords of contracted resonance, also occur.

[29]   Messiaen's description in the preface to the score, *La Fauvette des jardins*.

Example 2.1   Concluding chords of the Garden Warbler's 'preliminary trials'

a) Chord of transposed inversion 2A with added D♯

b) Chord of transposed inversion 9A with added A♯

achievable in any other transposition). Literal transposition is avoided (the most inventive birds usually refrain from such activity!). In short, great care – including pianistic care – has been taken in fashioning these sonorities (Example 2.1a and b).

Is there any significance in the notes being distributed this way? It makes for greater pianistic convenience: if one can approach the black keys at an angle with the third, fourth or fifth fingers of either hand, as these chords allow, the chances of landing in the right place are increased, and the resulting confidence can in turn affect both the timbre and the fluency of the song. As David Kopp attests elsewhere in this book, such chords are a prominent feature of *Petites Esquisses d'oiseaux* (1985). Furthermore, Pierre-Laurent Aimard has sagely commented that non-synaesthetic pianists can utilize Messiaen's chord-shapes as a proxy for colours, linking 'feel' and timbre. His extraordinary playing testifies to the effectiveness of this approach.[30]

How many 'fin des périodes' chords exhibit this black/white polarization throughout the course of the day? Though it is occasionally difficult to tell where phrases begin and end, I have taken my cue from Messiaen's analyses in *Traité V* and extracted all chords with resonance slurs (unless clearly in the middle of a phrase), and/or followed by a rest (Table 2.1, below).

There is nothing deliberate about this pattern, but clearly there is a trend: as morning advances, and exchanges between the Garden Warbler and other birds (particularly the Great Reed Warbler) grow more animated and insistent, there is a much lower proportion of polarized chords.[31] The percentage then grows again as the day progresses further. The central solos feature some of the most inventive and virtuosic singing of the warbler, in particular the spectacular closing salvo of 121 uninterrupted demisemiquavers that concludes solo 9, the longest solo with no polarized cadential chords. The marathon solo 11 is the most varied cadentially; here the polarized chords are often emphatic and *fortissimo*, and occasionally repeated.

---

[30] An example of a similarly-polarized sonority elsewhere in Messiaen's music is the opening right hand arabesque of 'Première Communion de la Vierge'.

[31] Solo 4, a relatively short solo, is the only anomaly.

40   Messiaen Perspectives 2: Techniques, Influence and Reception

Table 2.1   Cadential chords in the Garden Warbler solos[32]

Time of day	Fauvette des jardins solos (with characteristics)	Sequence of 'fin des périodes' [1 = polarized, 0 = not polarized]	%
Dawn	Solo 1 'preliminary trial 1'	1 1	100
	Solo 2 'preliminary trial 2'	1 1	100
	Solo 3	0 1 1 0	50
	Solo 4	0 0	0
5am	Solo 5	1 1 1 0 0	60
	Solo 6 crescendi to high ends of phrases	1 0 0 0 0 0 1 0 0 0 0 1 0	21
Morning advances	Solo 7	1 0 0	33
	Solo 8 closes with imitation of Golden Oriole	0 0 0	0
	Solo 9 extended closing volley (121 notes)	0 0 0 0 0 0 0 0	0
	Solo 10 gradual ascent, last note highest	1 1 0 0 0 0	33
… the most beautiful hours of the afternoon …	Solo 11 longest (6 pages)	1 0 1 0 1 1 0 1 0 1 0 1 1 1 0 0 0 1 0 1 0 0 1 0 0	48
Towards nightfall	Solo 12 discursive	1 1 0 0 1	60

How should this all be interpreted? In spite of the prevailing impression of undifferentiated 'chronotropic' time, evolution (of a periodic nature) is slowly taking place. Grisey always places utmost emphasis on the listeners' perception, and at 268 semiquavers per minute there is admittedly little time for an ear to analyse the sounds. Nevertheless, there is a clear sense that the character of the solos changes throughout the day, and all factors must be permitted to account for this, not least harmonic ones. Overall, the warbler's calls seem to reflect the thousand-coloured light of the sun as it changes through the day (just as the lake reflects its hues); the bird sings about what is around it, as happens so often in the *Catalogue*.[33] Its song has a 'respirational' profile: 'sound evolving in time' as the spectralists would

---

[32]   In his analysis in the *Traité V:1* (p. 377) Messiaen also counts 12 warbler solos. (I counted 12 before reading his account; we both seem to have counted the 'preliminary trials' as solos in themselves.)

[33]   Wai-Ling Cheong made this valuable observation during her paper 'Birdsong, Revelation and Messiaen's *Visions de l'Amen*' at the 2008 Messiaen Centenary Conference, illustrating the point with a delightful quotation from *Traité V:1* (p. 18): 'Les oiseaux sont émus par le beauté des couleurs' [the birds are moved by the beauty of the colours]. Solo 8

Example 2.2   The 'couleurs de couchant' chords

Lent ($\flat$=40)   *(contemplation extatique)*

later have it. The calls are more virtuosic towards the height of the day, rising to a peak at the end of solo 10. The relationship between the polarized chords and their surroundings is revealed in the set of four chords Messiaen employs to mark the last moments of sunset (the 'couleurs de couchant') (Example 2.2).

This bar settles on an 11-note polarized chord as the sun disappears; the rotational teleology of the hours of the day is summed up in this progression and elaborated in the warbler solos. There is no colour-correspondence suggested in the seventh volume of the *Traité* for a chord as dense as this. It is notable that while Messiaen is a keen advocate of the double-thumb throughout the warbler solos, sometimes to the point of inconvenience, here he is sparing in its advocacy, recommending it only when strictly necessary in order to keep open all options for varying the balance and timbre. The surrounding page (p. 53) is self-contained harmonically: the 'couleurs de couchant' bar is immediately preceded by the nightingale's 12-note *accord à total chromatique*; and the note F♯ that begins the 'couleurs de couchant' melody is the pitch class missing from the 11-note chord. F♯ goes on to function as the Blackcap's recitation tone (and the added note in the A major harmony that underpins its song) in the *following* bar. There is goal-orientation even in the slowest *extatique* music.

In other words, the issues of chromatic saturation and integration of tonality into the surrounding harmonic tapestry are well out in the open on this page. I will now deal with each of these in turn to demonstrate Messiaen's command of his language, and argue that the long-awaited task of portraying his home surroundings inspired him to write particularly extraordinary music.

Chromatic Saturation

There is a feature, unmentioned as yet, that is of great significance to spectral composers: continuous progression to and from white noise, or at least extremely

in Table 2.1 gives an example of the warbler also responding to the bird most redolent of sunlight, the Golden Oriole.

complex noises. This is a key part of the landscape in Grisey's *Prologue* and *Partiels* in particular. In Messiaen's case white noise is commensurable with the densest instances of chromatic saturation, sounds that are more homogenous than the registrally separated *accord à total chromatique* (and they do occur).[34] In *La Fauvette de jardins* he lets such a sonority impact upon the dynamism of the music at a structural crux.

For the spectralists, when sounds move between harmonicity and inharmonicity, rhythm is an integral factor. In his article '*Tempus ex Machina*' Grisey describes five types of rhythmic continuity. He lists them as smooth ('rhythmic silence'), statistical ('punpredictability' [sic] of durations, maximum discontinuity), discontinuous-dynamic ('acceleration or deceleration by stages or elision; statistical acceleration or deceleration'), continuous-dynamic ('continuous acceleration or deceleration') and periodic (including the category of 'fuzzy periodicity').[35] In his music relatively harmonious sounds often coincide with periodic rhythms, especially in *Les Espaces acoustiques*.

La Fauvette des jardins evades these classifications much of the time, but there is one notable exception. Peter Hill and Harry Halbreich enthuse, with much justification, about p. 49 of *La Fauvette des jardins*,[36] a grand plagal manoeuvre that depicts 'the most beautiful hours of the afternoon' (Messiaen's words in the preface). I will discuss this juncture shortly but the passage that immediately precedes it, the 'grandes spirales' of the Black Kite, is also remarkable. Here chromatic saturation gradually reaches its highest pitch and in doing so sets off by far the most extended example of 'continuous-dynamic' transition in the work (in the shape of a drawn-out *molto rallentando* from $\flat$ = 132 to $\flat$ = 50: 'The orbs of its flight contract'). The circular flight of the kite, borne on air currents, precedes a definite temporal arrival point (late afternoon), and is unique in that Messiaen uses its motion to turn the wheel of time in front of our eyes, rather than moving sequentially from one episode to the next.[37]

After claiming that *accelerandi* cause progressive loss of memory (in the local rather than pathological sense), Grisey goes on to say:

> With deceleration, *the listener is pulled backwards* since the arrow of musical time had somehow turned in the opposite direction. But because our listener also perceives that the arrow of his own biological time had not changed course, he

---

[34]   It is, nonetheless, still possible to hear the constituent colours, even in the case of a sonority such as the foghorn blast in 'Le Courlis Cendré'. See also Grisey, '*Tempus ex Machina*', p. 249.

[35]   Ibid., p. 244.

[36]   Hill, 'Piano Music II', p. 347; Harry Halbreich, *Olivier Messiaen* (Paris: Fayard, 1980), pp. 261–2.

[37]   This episode is a very substantial development of earlier music of the alders and, more obliquely but also more recently, the undulations of the lake.

will oscillate indefinitely between these two senses of time going in opposite but concomitant directions, in a sort of state of *temporal suspension*.[38]

He nonetheless later concedes that there are as many realities as there are listeners. What one is unquestionably aware of during the *molto rallentando* is the sensation of being parachuted from the uppermost realms of resonance (the Garden Warbler, though it sings consistently high, is never quite *that* high) as the kite descends, back to the *terra firma* of melody and harmony and a re-established sense of temporal orientation.

The passage proceeds from an average of 11 different pitch classes in each bar to an average of 12,[39] as shown in Table 2.2. Complete chromatic saturation occurs at the apparent zenith of the flight at the top of p. 47, the *fortississimo* start of the long *rallentando*. The accumulation is systematic and reminiscent of the *personnages rythmiques* technique: the bars that feature all 12 notes appear in 'groups' of one, then two, then one, three, one, three, one and four. The climactic chords take a similar form to the polarized chords of the Garden Warbler solos (Example 2.3).

Example 2.3   Climactic chords of the Black Kite's spiral flight

The sustaining pedal is required to be depressed, without release, throughout the 'long' bar and the succeeding four climactic bars, building up an immense sonority from the bottom note of the piano (the accumulated pitches are shown in Example 2.6). It is the closest Messiaen gets to the effects of Murail's *Territoires de l'oubli*, where the pedal is held down for the entire 30 minutes of the work.

The concept of entropy is worth mentioning here, as both Murail and Grisey see entropy as an important aspect of spectral awareness. Murail defines it as 'the passage from order to disorder' and relates it to the progression towards white

---

[38]   Grisey, '*Tempus ex Machina*', p. 249; emphases in original. I do not take this to mean that time *itself* is suspended.

[39]   There is a maximum of 20 notes in a bar, apart from the one long bar that occupies the last line and a half of p. 46. Sustaining pedal changes are marked at every barline. 'I happen to use the 12 notes in bundles and they sound absolutely unlike a series or a partial series; they sound like colours' (*Music and Color*, p. 49).

Table 2.2 The flight of the Black Kite

'Grandes Spirales' of the Black Kite (bar numbers)	Total number of pitch classes in each bar
p. 44 b. 17 – p. 45 b. 6	11 12 11 11 11 11 11 12 12
p. 45 b. 7 – b. 13	11 12 10 11 12 12 12
p. 45 b. 14 – p. 46 b. 5	10 12 10 11 12 12 12
p. 46 b. 6 – b. 10	11 11 11 11 11
p. 46 b. 11 – p. 47 b. 4	12 LONG BAR 12 12 12 12
p. 47 b. 5 – b. 13	11 11 11 6 7 7 7 6 6

noise. Grisey also associates entropy with the gradual erosion of memory in a 'chronotropic' process.[40] Both of these are at play, as we have now seen, in *La Fauvette des jardins*, and Messiaen's skilful control of them proves essential given the abundance of material.

The polarized structure of the climactic chords is important.[41] It is not uncommon in Messiaen to find passages of birdsong (or music describing birds) that have great structural force, but remarkable that he should find a way to link colour, time and movement in such a complex work, and create a *rapprochement* between the episodic formal texture of much of *La Fauvette* and its most extended passage of continuously evolving music. Overall, a counterpoint of respirational forms is now beginning to emerge: a full-blown arch form for the Garden Warbler, contrasted with various peaks of chromatic saturation or near-saturation, of which the Black Kite transition is by far the most intense. Smaller peaks include the undulating water of the Lac du Laffrey, the Nightingale, and the 'couleurs du couchant' as seen above; the encroaching night on the penultimate page, p. 54, is an atonal, *secco*, strung-out example (see Example 2.7).

Whilst these organic processes are doubtless worth observing, it is also necessary to step outside the spectral mindset to see how Messiaen ingeniously links them up with the tonal backdrop of the work.

Tonality and Large-scale Bass Motion

Pianists with *La Fauvette* in their fingers may have had the experience of playing, and enjoying, the final pages many times over before learning the warbler solos. To do so is to become quickly familiar with the poignant variant of the augmented sixth chord on the final page – an 'Alpine' augmented sixth (more French than

---

[40]   Grisey, '*Tempus ex Machina*', p. 273.

[41]   Both between and within each hand there is beauty in the way Messiaen breaks this down gently once the '*rall. e dim.*' takes hold.

Italian or German), perhaps? (Example 2.4). Its root is at the beginning of the work, where acoustic space is opened up for the first time (Example 2.5). The richest bar is bar 4, where the lowest B♭ is first sounded; note the appearance of the first white-on-black music above it.

The two long bass notes (C♯ and B♭) are prolonged for much of the day and resolve semitonally, from C♯ to D in the late afternoon and B♭ to A (the lowest note on the instrument) in the final line of the piece. The result is the large-scale

Example 2.4   Messiaen's augmented sixth chord

Example 2.5   *La Fauvette des jardins* – opening

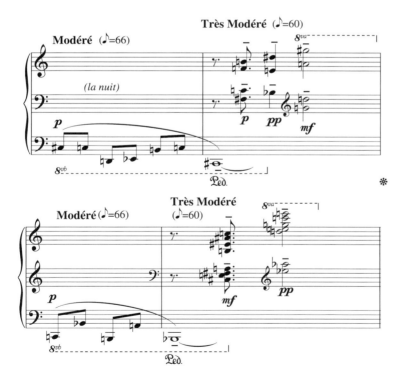

IV–I described earlier; both p. 49 and the final page, p. 55 (where the resolutions occur), are moments of great beauty, colour and intensity. The two black 'leading' notes are prolonged in contrasting ways. The C♯ is replayed several times, though not heard for much of the work's central section. The B♭ is more covert, largely absent in fact – it can be, because large-scale voice-leading is more explicit when it occurs between the two lowest notes of the instrument.

When all the bass notes in this register are shown (they are irregular enough that each sounding is an event), with their dynamics included, a multi-dimensional view of the work's voice-leading emerges (Example 2.6).

Example 2.6   *La Fauvette des jardins* – contrapuntal voice-leading in the lowest register

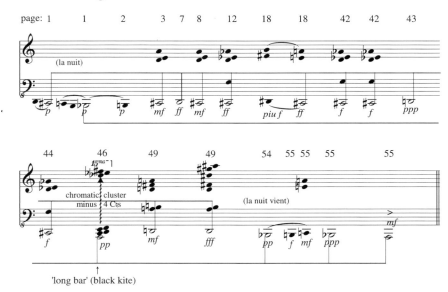

There is clear teleology here. The contrapuntal voicing shows a 'tonal' strand (C♯ to D) and a strand that supports altogether more diverse harmonies. The most complex sonority is the 'long bar' of the Black Kite's flight, which, when verticalized, displays its own polarization. There is a splash of brilliant colour at its peak (see also Example 2.3), arguably anticipated by the *fortissimo* polarized chords of the warbler's preceding solo number 11. The dynamics indicate why the final, nocturnal A, though a clear goal, does not need to be played more forcefully than accented *mezzo-forte* (compare with the devastating shards of 'solemnité de la nuit' in 'La Rousserolle effarvatte', as angular as the hidden skull in Holbein's *The Ambassadors*, and always landing on the same bottom A, fortississimo). The plagal motion on pp. 46, 49 and 55 is deliberately shown as the coincidence of two strands. There is no great sense of leverage between the final D and final A, but this does not adversely affect the architectural sweep of the piece. The warmth and power of the second D on p. 49 is highlighted on Yvonne Loriod's 1973 Erato recording, where she seems to play an additional A (a twelfth above the bass), although the third harmonic could be ringing out with exceptional clarity.[42] Either way, it is a glorious sonority.

Returning to the 'Alpine' augmented sixth chord on the final page,[43] the black-and-white topic has a final part to play here, too. The outer notes, B♭ and G♯, are set up by the inexorable motion of night drawing in (Example 2.7).

Example 2.7 'la nuit vient'

Their final sounding as darkness closes in is a dyad that will feel familiar to any pianist who plays 'Scarbo'. The pitches are low and quiet enough to be on the limits of audibility, this being the point that the structural threads draw together, when returning to dusk in the lowest register (Example 2.8).

Example 2.8 *La Fauvette des jardins* end of penultimate line

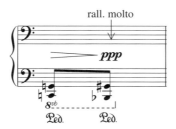

On the final two pages of the score the augmented sixth interval has therefore been heard in three ways: in a bare contrary motion texture at registral extremes; as part of a lush tonal harmony (receptive to much emotional emphasis); and, finally, as a compact summation of polarized warbler harmonies, the motion of the

---

[42] Warner Classics 2564 62162-2.
[43] This chord is, intriguingly, an augmented sixth in D rather than A.

water and the Black Kite, the oppressiveness of night, and the waxing and waning musical argument of the whole work.

Conclusions

An attitude, whether compositional or analytical, is only a means to an end; the world of the work itself is usually something bigger. Nevertheless, I would argue that spectral awareness in its many guises can and should increase our understanding of music from the decades, or even centuries, before spectralism's apparent inception.

Viewing *La Fauvette des jardins* in this way reveals much about how Messiaen reacted to his environment in musical terms and the breadth of musical language he used to convey it. He was clearly in possession of a keen spectral sensibility,[44] and able to integrate this expertly with large-scale tonal processes on a sizable canvas. He simulates the hours of the day in both a single 'breath' (the Garden Warbler's evolving song) and a series of musical events of varying intensity, some organic, some less so. The work's naturalism resides in these contrapuntal impressions: nature's inexorable daily cycle, coupled with the smaller-scale events at which we marvel. These simultaneous threads have their own harmonic/timbral characteristics, a crucial condition for Messiaen in ensuring polyphonic intelligibility. Alexander Goehr again comes to mind, here in his admiration for Messiaen's 'masterly' instrumental counterpoint in *Oiseaux exotiques*.[45]

Of all Grisey's reflections in '*Tempus ex Machina*', it is one not immediately related to music that particularly resonates: a hectic day, experienced quickly, can seem lengthy on reflection; an interminable day free of events, the opposite.[46] The arrow of time does not fly uniformly, particularly when travelling back and forth through musical forms. In his 1980 monograph Harry Halbreich celebrates the richness of the harmonies in *La Fauvette des jardins*.[47] One can be equally enraptured by richness of temporal experience, without knowing precisely where one stops and the other begins. In no other work of Messiaen is there more, in Grisey's words, 'interplay between fusion and continuity, on one side, and diffraction and discontinuity, on the other'.[48] There is little doubt that by the time

---

[44] His realization of the timbre of the Garden Warbler's song as a constant stream of harmonies is ample evidence of this.

[45] Quoted in Hill and Simeone, *Olivier Messiaen: Oiseaux Exotiques*, p. 113.

[46] Messiaen also makes this observation twice in his reflections on time at the beginning of *Traité I*, on pages 10 and 23. He ascribes the theory to the philosopher Armand Cuvillier.

[47] Halbreich, *Olivier Messiaen*, p. 262.

[48] See Ferguson, 'De-composing Tristan Murail', p. 118 and the list of spectral quotations from Fineberg, Grisey and Murail early in this chapter.

he composed *La Fauvette* the anxieties of the 1950s were well behind him, and he was secure in what he sensed was his position, poised between unresonant serialism and an emerging sonic organicism. And given what was to come, he was hardly even in the late afternoon of his career.

Chapter 3

Aspects of Compositional Organization and Stylistic Innovation in *Petites Esquisses d'oiseaux*

David Kopp

Olivier Messiaen's *Petites Esquisses d'oiseaux*, written in 1985, comprise what appears to be a very modest element of his compositional output. Their very petiteness is a contributing factor: six pieces, each between two and three minutes in length, collectively no more than a brief moment in the vast temporal extent of Messiaen's œuvre. The circumstances of their composition must also be considered, as they represent the first tentative steps toward writing music after a period of profound creative exhaustion at a late point in the composer's career. The title further contributes to a perception of modest ambition, 'sketches' implying an unfinished, unpolished quality. And the composer's own initial opinion of the work reinforces it all: it is documented that on presenting it as a surprise gift to Yvonne Loriod, Messiaen, unsure of himself, declared that the pieces were not very good.

Yet it is equally documented that Loriod, for her part, countered that, on the contrary, the pieces were wonderful.[1] They saw publication, are now regularly heard in performance, and have been recorded a number of times. Messiaen himself evidently took enough pride in the work eventually to write about it, citing two of the pieces in volume V, part 1 of the *Traité*, where he documents his rendering of the many individual species of birdsong populating his work. One citation treats the last piece, on the Skylark, focusing on his technique of composing against a treble pedal, plus brief commentary on select passages.[2] The other citation is more significant. Rounding off the *Traité*'s discussion devoted to the European Robin's music, Messiaen provides a complete, measure-by-measure resumé of the second of three Robin episodes in the group, affirming the piece's central role within the set, to demonstrate the multiple ways in which the Robin's complex call is instantiated in the music.[3] It is doubtful that such a lengthy and detailed exposition would have

---

[1] The coming-to-be of the *Petites Esquisses* is recounted in PHNS, pp. 352–3, and by Christopher Dingle in *The Life of Messiaen* (Cambridge: Cambridge University Press, 2007), pp. 225–6. For a detailed exploration of the post-*Saint François* works, see Dingle's *Messiaen's Final Works* (Farnham: Ashgate, 2013).

[2] *Traité V:1*, pp. 265–73.

[3] Ibid., pp. 171–81.

been included in the *Traité* were Messiaen not confident of the quality of the work. Thus whatever the prominence of the *Petites Esquisses* in the Messiaen canon, we may trust that they are good music and deserving of attention. Their chronological status as the first work of Messiaen's last creative period suggests their importance for understanding that period's stylistic trends. Peter Hill and Nigel Simeone relate that Loriod found 'in their spareness a completely new style, with a new kind of pianism, "poetic and sublime"'. They state further, 'in the *Petites Esquisses d'oiseaux* ... Messiaen's birdsong style was refined to an exquisite transparency'.[4] Similarly, Christopher Dingle observes that 'the *Petites Esquisses* represent a new economy of means in Messiaen's music'.[5] Moreover, the small scale of the individual sketches gives the rare advantage, for Messiaen, of allowing for close analysis of entire pieces. This chapter will attempt to shed some light on the inner workings of several aspects of this music: overall and individual form; texture and continuity; pitch organization, both harmonic and intervallic; and motive and gesture. All of these factors in combination contribute to the impression of stylistic development and concentrated expression in the music.

Distinctive Features of Birdsong in the Robin Pieces

The dynamic structure of the set as a whole is intriguing. From one vantage point, the work consists of two parallel, discrete streams, as depicted in Table 3.1a. The first contains pieces 1, 3 and 5, the three Robin episodes; the second, pieces 2, 4 and 6, dedicated to the Blackbird, Song Thrush and Skylark. Each stream has its own internal logic. From another view, shown in Table 3.1b, the work groups into three successive pairs, each beginning with a Robin episode and terminating with the song of a different bird, creating three different relationships with the Robin's music, the movements of which themselves stand in developmental relation to each other. Naturally, both perspectives are analytically relevant. Here we will privilege the dual-stream approach, focusing on the odd-numbered Robin trace, because it is arguably the fundamental music of the set. We know that a significant inspiration for the *Petites Esquisses* was Yvonne Loriod's expressed desire for music devoted to the Robin, which comprises fully half of the work.[6] Moreover, we have it from Messiaen himself, in the *Traité*, that the second of the three Robin episodes is the heart of the set. Messiaen also tells us that the three Robin episodes actually represent a single work divided into three.[7] Though separated in time, all bear the identical name: 'Le Rouge-gorge'. For discussion's sake, we will refer to the first, second and third Robin pieces as 'Rouge-gorge' I, II and III. If we are truly to view

---

[4] PHNS, pp. 353, 363.

[5] Dingle, *Life of Messiaen*, p. 226.

[6] Peter Hill, 'Piano Music II' in Peter Hill (ed.), *The Messiaen Companion* (London: Faber and Faber, 1995), p. 347; Dingle, *Life of Messiaen*, p. 225.

[7] *Traité V:1*, p. 171.

them in some way as a single discontinuous piece, this amplifies the interest for analysis, since the three episodes do not stand in any typical relation for a three-part piece. There is no ABA structure, no departure and return, no dramatic arc. Nor is any clear variation or developmental process from piece to piece apparent, despite their similar internal structures. The composer states that 'all three pieces were written in the same harmonic style, with the same pianistic writing, and the same melodic and rhythmic aesthetic which is proper to the Robin'.[8] There are indeed many similarities between the three pieces at several levels, from large-scale structure to details of harmony and figuration, and I will begin by describing some of these. But there are also notable differences, aspects special to one or another piece, and subtle developmental or transformational processes between them that we will investigate following some general comments on the music and a word on Messiaen's seemingly detailed précis of 'Rouge-gorge' II.

Table 3.1   Alternative parsings of overall form in *Petites Esquisses d'oiseaux*

a) Parallel streams

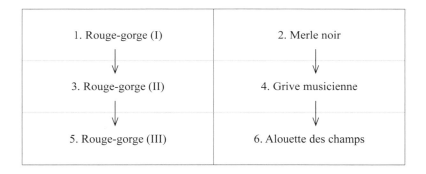

b) Successive pairs

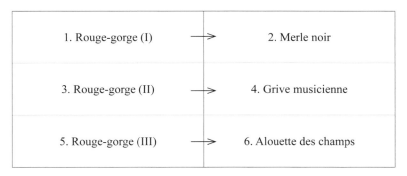

---

[8] Messiaen, preface to the published edition of *Petites Esquisses d'oiseaux* (Paris: A. Leduc, 1988).

54 *Messiaen Perspectives 2: Techniques, Influence and Reception*

In the *Traité*, Messiaen states that the Robin is a bird full of contrasts.[9] This is amply reflected in the *Petites Esquisses*, where tempo, texture, expression and dynamics change for nearly every measure of the Robin pieces, often independently of each other. The three pieces contain 69, 69 and 73 measures, respectively, and in each piece the tempo changes at the beginning of all but about ten of the measures, as do texture and dynamics. Throughout these pieces, Messiaen employs seven different tempi arranged in no particular pattern or succession, about a half dozen different textures, and a dynamic range from *pianissimo* to *forte*, in a kaleidoscope of unpredictable combinations, although the two extreme tempi become associated with very particular material, whereas three others in the moderate range emerge as primary.[10]

Textures generally remain consistent within individual gestures of a measure or two. They vary from sonorous background chords to fleeting, delicately pearled single-line scales, along with intermediate two- and three-part textures in which Messiaen extensively employs his technique of inexact doubling.[11] This technique, used to mimic the timbre of birdsong, manifests in a variety of dyadic and trichordal configurations and combinations, and a variety of shapes and contours, for a palette of continual change.[12] The parallel chord successions so distinctive to Messiaen's music (and the subject of important recent theorizing) are completely absent in the Robin pieces, contributing to the stylistic paring-down mentioned above.[13]

---

[9] *Traité V:1*, p. 146.

[10] These primary tempi are *Un peu lent* ♪ = 63, *Modéré* ♪ = 88, and *Un peu vif* ♪ = 120. Andrew Shenton has observed that Messiaen did not always follow his own tempo indications scrupulously in performance. Moreover, Shenton cites Loriod's observation, quoted in an interview with Peter Hill (*The Messiaen Companion*, p. 288), that the indications may not always be exact. The tempo changes in the Robin pieces are so constant and diverse that a meticulously accurate performance would likely necessitate a click track, if only for preparation. Perhaps, though, the notated tempi may serve as much to indicate character and timbre as speed per se, requiring the performer to be – in Robert Fink's terminology, appropriated by Shenton – both an executor and an interpreter. Shenton, 'Composer as Performer, Recording as Text: Notes towards a "Manner of Realization" for Messiaen's music', in Robert Sholl (ed.), *Messiaen Studies* (Cambridge: Cambridge University Press, 2007), pp. 179–82.

[11] *Traité V:1*, pp. 178–81. He describes the music resulting from this technique in two ways: (1) doubled inexactly, in a literal sense; (2) doubled poorly, evidently referring to the ear's perception rather than the composer's skill: 'Le mouvement mélodique est mal doublé, pour rendre le timbre.'

[12] While the two earlier appearances of the Robin in the solo piano music, in the *Catalogue d'oiseaux* (no. 2, 'Le Loriot' and no. 9, 'La Bouscarle'), have similar pitch and gestural content, their multiple gestures generally occur within a single tempo. The rapid tempo changes for this bird are new to the *Petites Esquisses*.

[13] Significant studies include Wai-Ling Cheong, 'Messiaen's Triadic Colouration: Modes as Introversion', *Music Analysis*, 21/1 (2002): pp. 53–84, and Christoph Neidhöfer, 'A Theory of Harmony and Voice Leading for the Music of Olivier Messiaen', *Music Theory Spectrum*, 27/1 (Spring 2005): pp. 1–34.

The chord progressions that do occur intermingle various invented and modally derived chord types having unequal numbers of elements.

Rhythm, on the other hand, shows little variety within gestures. Durations either remain uniform or else articulate in relatively unremarkable combinations of two values in 2:1 proportion, although accentual patterns do differ. Durational values between gestures, however, vary significantly, magnified by the wide gradations in tempo, from slow quavers at $\flat$ = 40 to rapid demisemiquavers at $\flat$ = 184. Very generally, the denser chords last the longest, particularly Messiaen's invented chords, some types occurring in abundance in the Robin pieces, while the scalar gestures contain the shortest values, with the intermediate textures occupying the intermediate states. There are, however, many instances of speedy successions of chords, and the two-part textures in particular run the gamut of all but the slowest and swiftest durations.

As for register, the *Petites Esquisses* as a whole virtually ignore the bass regions, which are completely absent in the Robin episodes.[14] Elsewhere in the work these depths are only accessed sporadically: in the Blackbird and Skylark (nos 2 and 6) mostly as phrase punctuation, and in the Song Thrush (no. 4) to initiate certain quickly rising gestures.

While we have just considered each dimension separately in a typical analytical manner, this is hardly how they are meant to function in the music. One need only read Messiaen's précis of 'Rouge-gorge' II to understand this. Characteristically, the presentations of his birdsong music in volume V of the *Traité* involve a measure-by-measure recounting of content, in a manner often frowned upon as mere description. But what is Messiaen actually relating to us? Here is a brief excerpt:

> Measure 9: repeated notes in high register, in chords of four tones. Measure 10: an anacrustic group with grace note carries an accent and a mute. ... In measure 11: tempo *un peu vif* – a torculus resupinus – then stronger emphasis on the superposed seconds – and a Bacchian rhythm (short–long–long), which ends on a Transposed Inversion chord no. 2D, from top to bottom: very clear violet above clear green. In measure 12: the tempo 'un peu lent' and the character 'amical' contrast with the preceding vivacity and brilliance.[15]

Messiaen's focus shifts constantly, mercurially, among the various dimensions, from measure to measure, veering from pitch organization to shape and direction to accentual profile to texture to colour. Different aspects are associated idiosyncratically. Each individual dimension is repeatedly lost and regained during the course of the full narrative of the piece. The discussion on the whole lacks the emphasis on relatedness, musical logic, and structural connections that many of us

---

[14] Dingle (*Life of Messiaen*, pp. 226, 237) notes that, beginning with the *Esquisses*, the absence of music in lower registers becomes a hallmark of Messiaen's later style.

[15] *Traité V:1*, p. 178.

have come to expect from analysis. Instead, it projects a sense of discontinuity and even fickleness of attention.

But this is not a shortcoming. Messiaen is, among other things, showing us that the continuity in this music lies in the integration of the shifts of compositional and perceptual focus among dimensions into the temporal flow. This is suggested by his descriptions of one of the very few things in 'Rouge-gorge' II that recurs without changing, a certain invented-chord progression. At the first appearance, he describes the colour qualities of the chords in typically eloquent detail and depth. Several measures later, at the second appearance, we get exactly the same description. Were Messiaen simply providing information, this would be unnecessary; he might simply say 'as before'. Rather, he is communicating to us the experience of the birdsong through music, something that for him must necessarily be just as vivid and precise the second time as the first, within the larger interdimensional continuity. In addition, Messiaen's descriptive language neatly and characteristically blurs the distinction between art and nature, at points assuming the composer's active voice ('the pitches are inexactly doubled to produce the timbre'), while at others following the will of the subject ('the bird ends its strophe with a podatus and climacus resupinus'), as if in collaboration.

Formal, Harmonic and Motivic Features of the Individual Robin Pieces

We turn now to analysis. Some common elements between the three Robin pieces have already been discussed. Along with their similar lengths, there are similar formal structures. Each piece consists of a series of strophes, from six to eight, further organized by common large-scale structural identifiers. Every Robin episode begins with a similar series of three or four chords, which in their original and varied forms become a recognizable motto throughout the Robin pieces and to a lesser extent in the entire set of six. Each first strophe lasts six measures, followed by a second appearance of a varied and extended version of the motto. From there, the strophic structures of the individual pieces diverge, but in each one the motto makes a third, varied appearance about two-fifths of the way through. All of the Robin pieces make significant use of several types of invented chords: Transposed Inversion chords, Total Chromatic chords, chords derived from mode 3, and the two varieties of chord pairs of Contracted Resonance. These are distributed differently in each piece, with one curious concurrence: measure 48 in all three pieces contains a pair of second chords of Contracted Resonance.[16]

---

[16] The genesis and development of Messiaen's invented chord types over several decades has been carefully charted by Wai-Ling Cheong. Given the late date of composition of the *Petites Esquisses*, Messiaen's *Traité* descriptions are appropriate for identification here. See Cheong, 'Rediscovering Messiaen's Invented Chords', *Acta Musicologica*, 75/1 (2003): 85–105.

Equally prominent in the three Robin pieces is the musical rendering of what Messiaen repeatedly extols in the *Traité* as the most distinctive aspect of the Robin's call: the descending pearled scale, very delicate and quick. The scale serves as a paradigmatic occurrence of important harmonic materials. Its basic form is defined at the outset, in measure 4 of the first Robin: alternating patterns of black-key and white-key pentatonic on G♭ and C, in other words the pentatonic collections having major triads on these roots. These tritone-related pentatonic sets unite through transpositional combination to form a ten-note collection that is identical to Messiaen's mode 7^2, the complete chromatic scale save the tritone F–B, shown in Example 3.1. This combination of black-key and white-key pentatonic collections inhabits the Robin pieces well beyond the scales – in all of the tempi and textures, sometimes with an added diatonic note or two, and occasionally using the white-key pentatonic on F or on G, although the mode 7 version is paramount. Moreover, a significant amount of all of the Robin music, taken measure by measure, no matter what the means of pitch organization, can be understood as being in one of the six transpositions of mode 7, containing at least eight or more pitch classes (pcs) that taken together fit into mode 7 and no other mode of limited transposition, and often containing a chromatic pentachord. About two-thirds of the first Robin piece, for example, can be read this way, invoking five of the six possible transpositions, with mode 7^2 most prominent throughout.

Example 3.1a   The six transpositions of mode 7, identified by their absent tritone complements

7^1: [E, B=] 7^3: [C, G=] 7^5: [D, A=]

7^2: [F, B] 7^4: [D=, G] 7^6: [E=, A]

Example 3.1b   Generation of mode 7^2 by transpositional combination of tritone related pentatonic sets

white notes = white-key pentatonic with major triad on C
black notes = black-key pentatonic with major triad on G♭

Messiaen conspicuously omitted discussion of mode 7 as a compositional tool among the modes of limited transposition in the *Traité*, having included it with the others in the earlier *Technique de mon langage musical*.[17] The later presentation of modes, framed solely in the context of colour, is limited to those (modes 2, 3, 4 and 6) serving as a source of harmonies, and thus colours, for Messiaen. There is no explicit repudiation of the other modes in this discussion.[18] Now, in Messiaen's précis of the second Robin piece in *Traité V:1*, only the invented chords and mode 3 chords are specifically described in terms of colour. All other chords and textures are described in terms of other more prominent dimensions. While I am far from arguing that Messiaen deliberately used mode 7 as a compositional device in the Robin pieces, evidence suggests its utility as an analytic construct against which to measure the pitch content of the music, particularly when not associated directly with colour.[19] Also, note that mode 3 is the only mode of limited transposition that is not a subset of mode 7; thus the two modes most evident in the Robin pieces contrast qualitatively.[20] The pentatonic set, in addition to defining the mode-7 pearled scales, permeates a considerable amount of the rest of the music. It appears frequently in both linear and chordal contexts and is imbedded in many of the invented chords used in the piece, as indicated in Example 3.2. It is also imbedded in the diatonic collection, with which Messiaen associates it in this music, as discussed below.[21]

---

[17] *Traité VII*, p. 107, footnote by Loriod; *Technique*, example 355, also cited in Cheong, 'Messiaen's Triadic Colouration': p. 55. In line with the *Technique* presentation, Cheong broadly incorporates mode 7 into her investigation of modal properties, while acknowledging its rarity in the music along with certain attributes that set it apart from the other colour modes.

[18] Jonathan Bernard has speculated that the colour aspect of mode 7, just two elements short of chromatic saturation and a superset of most of all of Messiaen's other colour modes, might either approach the grey-black that Messiaen, ironically, associated with the total chromatic, or else invoke the simultaneous presence of all colours. But there is no word on this from the composer. See Bernard, 'Messiaen's Synesthesia: The Correspondence between Colour and Sound Structure in His Music', *Music Perception*, 4/1 (Fall 1986): p. 46.

[19] Vincent Benitez states that 'one can find various instances of modes 1, 5, and 7 in [Messiaen's] music'. In his opinion, this can reflect compositional intent, although these modes remain much less significant than the others, since they are not sources of harmonic colour. Benitez, 'Aspects of Harmony in Messiaen's Later Music: An Examination of the Chords of Transposed Inversions on the Same Bass Note', *Journal of Musicological Research*, 23/2 (April–June 2004): pp. 195–6.

[20] For an illustration of how Messiaen's modes relate to one another, see Example 1.2 on p. 21 of Anthony Pople, 'Messiaen's Musical Language: An Introduction', in Hill (ed.), *The Messiaen Companion*, pp. 15–50.

[21] The technique of pentatonic embedding in diatonic contexts has, of course, a long legacy. A particularly sophisticated case in Debussy is described in David Kopp, 'Pentatonic Organization in Two Piano Pieces of Debussy', *Journal of Music Theory*, 41/2 (Fall 1997): pp. 261–87.

Organization and Stylistic Innovation in Petites Esquisses d'oiseaux   59

Example 3.2   Important pitch collections in *Petites Esquisses* and their prime-form pitch-class set equivalents

Mode 7:	(0 1 2 3 4 6 7 8 9 10)*
Chord of total chromatic:	(0 1 2 3 5 7 8 9)*
Chord of transposed inversion:	(0 1 2 5 6 7 9)*
1st chord(s) of contracted resonance:	(0 1 2 3 5 6 8) appog., resolves to
	(0 1 2 3 4 7 9)*
2nd chord(s) of contracted resonance:	(0 1 3 4 7 8) appog., resolves to
	(0 1 2 5 6 8)
Mode 3 chord	(0 1 2 4 5 8)
Pentatonic mode:	(0 2 4 7 9)(*)

* contains the pentatonic collection as a subset

A short digression will help to contextualize the later style. The only other appearances of the Robin in Messiaen's solo piano music are relatively minor ones in two pieces from the *Catalogue d'oiseaux* dedicated to other birds.[22] Both instances include pearled pentatonic scales and resonant doubling, and contain shapes and textures similar to those in the *Petites Esquisses*.[23] Style characteristics, however, are somewhat different. In the excerpt from 'Le Loriot' (The Golden Oriole) shown in Example 3.3a, right hand and left hand play black keys and white keys, respectively, as pentatonic and diatonic scales run in parallel without gaps, save one at the beginning of the diatonic. The black/white distinction continues through a progression of trichords built from fourths: vertical in the right hand, horizontal in the left. The following measure contains a succession of richly tonal sonorities, all ninth chords or greater, by descending whole tone in the bass, leading to a cadential triad a semitone below the expected pitch level. In the excerpt from 'La Bouscarle' (The Cetti's Warbler), shown in Example 3.3b, the same black/white distinction persists until the final interval.[24] Tritone-related pentatonic scales, tonally based on G♭ and C, run similarly in parallel without gaps, at the closest possible intervals to the unison, yielding an unbroken succession of diminished

---

[22]   The other appearances of the European Robin in all of Messiaen's music are in *Livre d'orgue, Réveil des oiseaux, Chronochromie, La Transfiguration, Saint François d'Assise* and *Un Vitrail et des oiseaux*. Most of the examples of Robin settings in the *Traité* come from *Saint François*.

[23]   'Le Loriot' contains two two-measure Robin calls (mm. 13–14, cited, and 30–31). 'La Bouscarle' contains three extended one-measure calls (mm. 62, cited, 101 and 213).

[24]   The terminal left-hand B♭ was likely introduced to conserve the cadential effect of parallel minor sixths at the gesture's end.

Example 3.3 Two appearances of the Robin in *Catalogue d'oiseaux* (1956–58)

a) From II, 'Le Loriot' (The Golden Oriole)

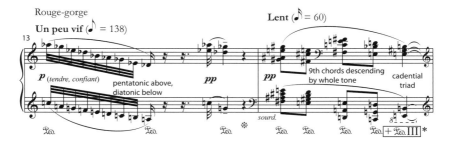

b) From IX, 'La Bouscarle' (The Cetti's Warbler)

octaves save one minor seventh, a semitone smaller. The gestures framing the scale also contain parallel doubling, all minor sixths save one diminished seventh, a semitone larger. Note that in this and succeeding examples, vertical intervals are indicated in two ways: the exact size as Messiaen would indicate, and the interval class. The interval class, too, signifies two things: first, the acoustic quality of the interval and its degree of consonance or dissonance, and, second, the degree of deviation in semitones from the unison or octave, with 1, the semitone, being the least, and 6, the tritone, the greatest.

Here in the 'Bouscarle' example we see that all of the vertical intervals of the scale are dissonant, while all of the vertical intervals of the framing gestures are consonant.[25] The two later appearances of the Robin in 'La Bouscarle', about twice as long, are not as strictly composed. Nonetheless, they alternate gestures of successive minor sixths and/or diminished octaves with freer gestures that still favour these intervals overall, while incorporating others, notably the terminal tritone. The black/white key distinction in either orientation is present about half

---

[25] Although the third interval of the first gesture is notated as a diminished seventh, as interval class 3 it is acoustically equivalent to a consonant major sixth.

the time. All in all, though, these Robin's scales and their surroundings from the *Catalogue d'oiseaux* exhibit a greater degree of regularity and tonal grounding than those of the *Petites Esquisses*, as we will discover. The parallel scales in the earlier music are also less complex than the hand-over-hand ones of the *Esquisses*, which change in every octave and in every appearance.[26]

Returning to our subject, we find further significant differences between the three Robin pieces. Note the three-chord motto that begins the first piece (Examples 3.4 and 3.5a). On the surface this comprises a progression of two Transposed Inversion chords linked by a chord derived from mode 3, all of which are quite similar. Vincent Benitez has argued that we should consider the lower parts of these chord types, usually versions of tonal seventh chords taken by the left hand, as foundational, whatever the formal derivation.[27] Accordingly, if we take off the tops of these three chords, retaining the F♯ in the mode 3 chord, we get a very different-sounding progression: an unmistakable $^V/_V$–V–I progression to G, a hidden relic of more explicit tonal references present in the earlier style.[28] At the motto's restatement and expansion in measure 7 (Example 3.5b), Messiaen appends an additional mode 3 chord at a different transposition level, followed by a more dissonant Total Chromatic chord. This final chord has an A major 63 chord at its base, while the preceding chord contains a D major triad in the right hand along with a B♭-rooted sonority in the left. Assigning some contextual priority to the D major given its previous appearance, we find a palindromic fifth-progression from A to D to G and back again – not an untypical construct for Messiaen.[29] In the second Robin piece, the original motto reappears verbatim

---

[26] The Robin's scales from *Saint François* that Messiaen cites in the *Traité* are altogether different again, with an octave-to-octave inconsistency that prefigures the *Esquisses*, close semi-exact doubling, and a mix of scalar elements including short stretches of pentatonic, whole-tone and chromatic scales. See *Traité V:1*, pp. 152–70.

[27] Benitez, 'Aspects of Harmony': 205–8.

[28] The identities of the three chords in this progression are (1) Transposed Inversion chord no. 1B; (2) chord derived from mode 3^3; (3) Transposed Inversion chord 11B. Messiaen singles out an occurrence of Transposed Inversion 11B in *Saint François* for its colour aspect of lemon yellow with red spots, analogous to the Robin's orange breast (*Traité V:1*, p. 156). Given its prominence, we could assume similar significance for the chord here in the *Esquisses*. The first two chords, however, have general colour aspects of blue and violet, and blue and green, respectively (*Traité VII*, pp. 142, 122), while Messiaen describes the bird's other colour attributes as an olive-brown body and whitish belly (*Traité V:1*, p. 146). Since he considers the three-chord motto to be a decorative or background theme (*thème de décor*; *Traité V:1*, p. 178), we might imagine the blend of harmonic and colour properties of the progression to be a cadential focus on the Robin within its environment. I am not arguing, though, that Messiaen deliberately either coordinated these two dimensions or structured the colour progressions.

[29] On another level, Total Chromatic chord 2 unites colour aspects of the preceding chords, with its attribute of deep gentian blue surrounded by a circle streaked with violet, red and orange (*Traité VII*, p. 188).

Example 3.4 'Le Rouge-gorge' (The Robin) I, mm. 1–5: invented chords, inexact doubling and pentatonic content

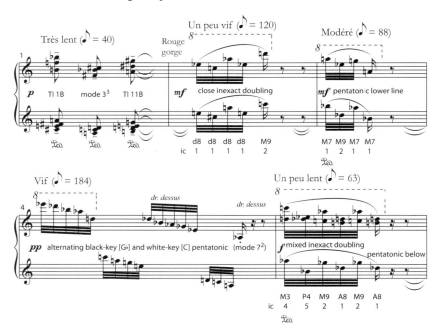

In this and the following examples, the following abbreviations and conventions are used:

TI = Transposed Inverstion chord
TC = Total Chromatic chord
CR1, CR2 = first and second chords of Contracted Resonance
Interval sizes follow Messiaen's convention of expressing intervals larger than a ninth within the octave.
ic = interval class

at the beginning but returns varied in a different way (Example 3.5c). After the fourth chord in the succession, an extra mode 3 chord at a new transposition level leads to a Transposed Inversion chord with root C. The change of root of the goal chord, plus the dominant-seventh foundation of the Transposed Inversion chord, in place of the triadic 6/4 underlying the Total Chromatic chord at the parallel moment in the first Robin, lends this new progression a much more open effect than before.[30] A more dramatic change occurs at the beginning of the third Robin piece, where the opening three-chord progression returns once

---

[30] Concurrently, TI7B introduces several new colours with its aspects of red, white, rose and black (*Traité VII*, p. 145).

Example 3.5   Pitch-map showing the transformation of the opening motto in the first two strophes of the Robin pieces

a) Robins I and II, m. 1   b) Robin I, m. 7   c) Robin II, m. 7
              d) Robin III, m. 1   e) Robin III, m. 7

more, but transposed down a semitone, leading to G♭ (Example 3.5d). Heard in relation to the beginnings of the first two Robins, this progression gives a very different impression of colour, whether or not as specific as the composer himself would perceive. It continues with a Total Chromatic chord on D, creating a new intervallic relation that amplifies the impression of harmonic change from previous iterations of the opening motto. At its varied return in m. 7, however, the motto reverts to its original transposition level, appending one of the chords from the new level at the end (Example 3.5e).

Following the initial statements of the motto in all three Robin pieces, we find two or more measures of two-part texture, inexactly doubled. When recounting examples of this doubling technique in the *Traité*, Messiaen often names each vertical interval in succession, in order to communicate precisely the effect of twittering birdsong. Such focus on his part led me to examine these interval progressions in detail, revealing many different types of inexact doubling in the Robin pieces, distinct enough to suggest that they are employed strategically. Note, for example, the close doubling in measures 2 and 3 of the first Robin (Example 3.6a); all of the intervals are either a semitone or a whole tone, giving a sense of tight coordination and consistent dissonance. The doubling in measure 5, on the other hand, moves from wide intervals to narrow and from consonance to dissonance, while the doublings in measures 8 and 10 are mixed, giving a jangly effect; the unusual tritones framing the measure 10 gesture are striking against the pentatonic underlay. Overall, narrower intervals closer to the octave (ics 1–3) are more prevalent than wider, more open ones (ics 4–6), with the vertical tritone surprisingly rare given the composer's fondness for the interval. By contrast, consider the beginning of the second Robin piece in Example 3.6b, which contains the longest stretch of music in the same tempo and texture in all of the Robin pieces: three entire measures' worth, enough to resemble a conventional segmented phrase. Note the absence of semitones at the beginning, the gradual increase in displacement from the octave, and motion from dissonance to consonance, with a slight contraction at the end of measure 3 followed by a clear convergence into dissonance and semitones at the end of the gesture in measure 4. This intervallic play lends a very clear acoustic shape to the semantics of the birdcall. In the second strophe, at the bottom of the page, note the wide, consonant intervals of the call in measure 8, followed by the contrast of narrow, dissonant intervals in measure 10. A similar wide/narrow contrast occurs quite audibly in successive measures at the beginning of the third Robin (Example 3.6c, measures 2–3), reinforcing the change in dynamics and tempo between the two. The descending figure at measure 10 represents another instance of intervallic convergence, here in the absence of semitones. Throughout the Robin pieces, these sorts of relationships and intervallic patterns, ranging from organized and directed to loose and chaotic, contribute meaning and distinctiveness to the many passages of inexact doubling.

One further aspect of doubling deserves mention. In measures 3, 5 and 10 of Example 3.6a, and in many other places in the Robin excerpts shown here, the lower part is completely pentatonic while the upper part has mixed black and white keys. With the pedal depressed, this creates the distinctive sound of a layer of pentatonic sonority below and a chromatic or diatonic layer above. This technique is frequent in the Robin pieces in both linear and chordal textures. Occasionally at a moment of emphasis, Messiaen inverts the texture, placing the pentatonic sonority on top, to marked effect (e.g. the end of the first Robin, shown in Example 3.7, with several black-key/white-key registral shifts). When describing these sonorities in the *Traité*, Messiaen never refers directly to the pentatonic mode, but rather to tonal, sensory cues, for example 'an atmosphere of G♭ major' or 'a light scent of

Example 3.6 Pitch-map showing the indirect doubling patterns in the first two strophes of the three Robin pieces (octava indications in this and succeeding reductions affect the upper line only)

a) Robin I

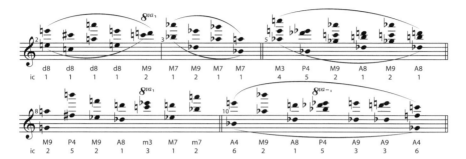

b) Robin II

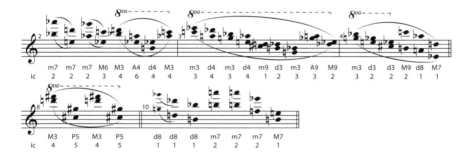

c) Robin III

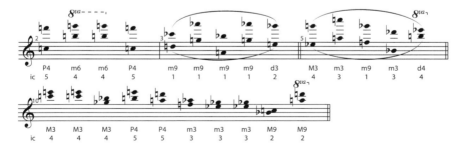

Example 3.7 Pitch-map for 'Le Rouge-gorge' I, mm. 62–67: shifting registral placement of black-key and white-key material

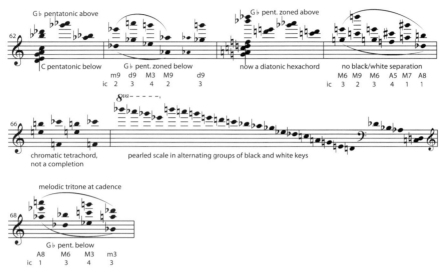

flat keys'. He does not mention pentatonicism even when discussing the pearled scales, simply citing the alternation of black and white piano keys.[31]

Satisfying as it would be to identify some common syntax of textural and gestural succession in this music, it appears that the elements combine every which way. However, three basic types of cadence or strophe ending can be discerned. At the end of the first strophe of the first Robin (Example 3.4, m. 5) is a melodic descent of a tritone atop a trichordal texture. The cadential tritone is, of course, a Messiaen signature. This first cadence type also occurs at the end of the first Robin (Example 3.7, m. 68), both times conveying a somewhat open quality. The second type of cadence is even more distinctive and most decisive: a descending melodic whole tone, which is usually, though not always, associated here with a pair of Contracted Resonance chords. These whole-tone cadences occasionally end the interior strophes of the first Robin, but do so more prominently in the second Robin's first and last strophes, among others, giving the music a grounding and gravity that may contribute to this particular episode's central role. The third type of cadence is the most open, a wide leap. These occur occasionally in the first two Robins but are most prominent in the third, particularly at the end, for reasons to be outlined shortly.

---

[31] *Traité, V:1*, pp. 178, 181. Earlier in the same discussion of Robin calls, however, he does identify the 'mode pentaphone' as the source for a brief four-note 'black-key' measure from *Saint François d'Assise* (*Traité, V:1*, p. 150).

There are a few other important differences between the Robin pieces in addition to the ones already mentioned. One concerns the length and shape of the two-part twittering gestures. In the first Robin they often change direction frequently and are of moderate length, around seven to twelve notes. In the second Robin, past the extended call of the opening, they tend to be much shorter, around five to seven notes, and simpler in shape; Messiaen often describes them as a single neume. In the last Robin, by contrast, the twitterings reach their greatest length and complexity of shape; they tend upward more often than in the previous episodes. Several of these gestures acquire an upward-spiralling contour, traced mostly by successive groups of three descending dyads. Given similar contour and tempo, expression in this music may nonetheless vary considerably according to doubling and context. Example 3.8a shows a spiral gesture occurring in the middle of the piece, directly following a statement of the three-chord motto at the beginning of a strophe. The soft dynamic, gradual rise, and very consistent doubling, with a prefix of consonant ic4 followed by a spiral favouring almost-octave ic1, transmit a controlled, introductory quality. Example 3.8b occurs in the middle of a very long and complex strophe. Here a louder dynamic, constantly shifting doublings, and a climactic passage coupling unusually wide linear intervals with atypically narrow vertical intervals that initiate a final succession of all six pcs produce a clear effect of intensification. Example 3.8c takes place just before the end, on the heels of a similar, shorter downward gesture. Its soft dynamic, relatively quick spiral rise and semitone-free intervallic content favouring consonance and wider intervals, followed by a relatively long pause, give an open, ethereal quality that sets up, and sets off, the piece's final cadential gesture.

A different element, the shorter four-note-calls that often complete the total chromatic, describes an even simpler but related overall progression. In the first Robin, the calls' direction is invariably down (e.g. Example 3.7, m. 66). In the second, they are less frequent and often oscillate back and forth, until near the end, when they reverse direction (see Example 3.9, mm. 51 and 53). In the third Robin, they occur most frequently and invariably go up, culminating prominently at the end of the piece (Example 3.8c, m. 72). This upward trending in the third Robin, along with the spiral gestures, may serve to foreshadow the ebullient, joyful outburst of the Skylark in the final piece of the set.

A further important difference between the Robin pieces involves Messiaen's use of invented chords. While all of the chords mentioned above appear in all of the pieces, they do so with varying frequency, as shown in Table 3.2.[32] The Transposed

---

[32] Values in the table do not include instances of the same set class in non-chordal textures, often as only one of what is theoretically a pair. But their placement sometimes suggests compositional relevance. For example, a progression of first chords of Contracted Resonance (CR1A and CR1B) at measure 20 in the first Robin is directly preceded in measure 19 by a short passage of unequal doubling whose pitch content also amounts to CR1B at a different transposition level. Toward the end of the first Robin, two disjunct but parallel measures of similar unequal doubling (mm. 63 and 65) have content equivalent to

Example 3.8 'Le Rouge-gorge' III: three upward spiraling gestures

a) m. 32, near the beginning of a strophe

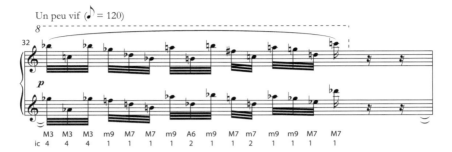

b) m. 54, in the middle of a long strophe

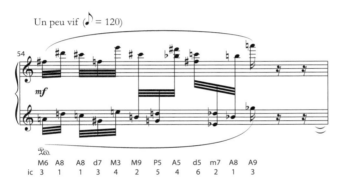

Inversion chords that begin the first Robin occur nowhere else in the piece save the three appearances of the slow motto, all at the same transposition level. In the second and third Robins, there are twice as many of these chords, appearing at a number of transposition levels in different contexts and different inversions. The same is true with the mode 3 chords, which only appear in the mottos in the first Robin, then proliferate in the second and third Robins while remaining at only four transposition levels throughout. Contracted Resonance chords occur with slightly increased frequency as the Robins parade by. The Total Chromatic chord, on the other hand, is twice as common in the first Robin as in the others.

CR1B and CR1A (the latter plus a note), respectively, while the final measure (m. 68), in three-part unequal doubling, also defines CR1A.

Example 3.8 *concluded*

c) m. 70, just before the end

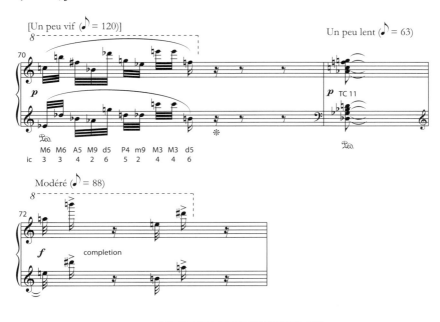

Table 3.2   Occurrence of invented chords in the three Robin pieces

	TI	TC	CR1	CR2	Mode 3
Rouge-gorge I	4 (2)	6	3	2	4 (3)
Rouge-gorge II	9 (6)	3	5	4	9 (6)
Rouge-gorge III	8 (4)	3	4	1	10 (7)

Where more than one chord of the same type appears in the same gesture, the number in parentheses indicates the number of separate gestures in the piece in which the chords occur.

Wai-Ling Cheong has remarked on Messiaen's 'deep-seated concern for twelve-tone completion'.[33] This is true to an extent in the Robin pieces, although not always strictly speaking. A great number of measures or measure pairs contain 10 or sometimes 11 distinct pcs, for example at the beginning of the third Robin, which is distinguished by an abundance of 10-pc measures. Full chromatic

---

[33] Cheong, 'Messiaen's Invented Chords': p. 101.

Example 3.9 'Le Rouge-gorge' II, mm. 50–55: transfer of completion function from Total Chromatic chord to other chord types

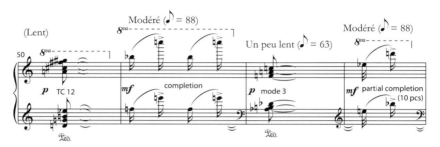

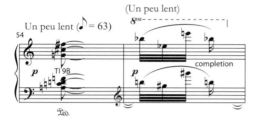

completion in the *Esquisses* is initially associated with the Total Chromatic chord followed by its four complementary pcs, a frequent occurrence in the first Robin and the beginning of the second. Toward the end of the second Robin, though, this function is deliberately and audibly transferred to some of the other invented chords, as shown in Example 3.9. At this point a Total Chromatic chord and its completion are directly followed by a mode 3 chord and a similar gesture of completion, though amounting to only 10 pcs in all, immediately followed by a Transposed Inversion chord and a gesture containing all five complementary pcs.[34] This transfer of the completion function to chords other than Total Chromatic ones is a significant factor in the decreased presence of that chord type and the increased presence of the others as the pieces progress, enhancing the prominence of the Total Chromatic chord's return in the third Robin's final cadence (Example 3.8c).

A final, and perhaps most important, analysis traces the transformation of the Robin's descending scale through the pieces. In the first Robin the scale appears near the end of each of the six strophes, as a culminating pre-cadential figure (see Example 3.4, m. 4, and Example 3.7, m. 67). Additionally, Messiaen varies the appearances so that five of the scales begin on a different note of the G♭ pentatonic collection, with the first note of the other being notated as a sharp (D♯). In the second Robin the scales become a bit longer and less orderly in appearance. There are only five of them in seven strophes; they occur in interior parts of the strophe

---

[34] Cheong (ibid: p. 101) discusses the completion aspects of measures 50–51 and 54–5 in the more general context of Messiaen's style.

Organization and Stylistic Innovation in Petites Esquisses d'oiseaux 71

Example 3.10   Pitch-map for 'Le Rouge-gorge' III, mm. 55–62: dissolution of scales

and begin on only three different notes. In the third Robin they are dramatically transformed, becoming more frequent and irregular in appearance, gradually shorter, and increasingly less scalar and pentatonic, eventually dissolving into brief, truncated arpeggios, while the twitterings and upward leaps become more prominent. Example 3.10 shows the end of this process, where the dissolution of the scales is interwoven with the gradual expansion of a shaped gesture (a torculus) to produce, in measure 62, one of the distinctive elongated rising gestures characterizing this last Robin piece. The perception of gestural expansion as a process over time is strengthened by the inexact doubling, which is relatively consistent both within and between gestures. Within each gesture, difference of interval size never exceeds two semitones, interval classes often repeat in pairs, and interval size tends to expand a bit toward the end. Between gestures, an overall range of ics 1–3 in measures 55 and 57 expands slightly to ics 2–4 in measures 60 and 62, shifting toward increased consonance. This process effectively counterbalances the scalar disintegration. The gesture in measure 62 also relates

72   *Messiaen Perspectives 2: Techniques, Influence and Reception*

to the end of the piece through its marked similarity of pitch and contour to the culminating gesture in measure 70, described above (Example 3.8c).

Contrasts of Content in the Blackbird, Song Thrush and Skylark

The pieces of the even-numbered stream are as dissimilar as the Robin pieces are similar, progressing from simplicity and tranquility to complexity and agitation. The second piece of the set, on the Blackbird, looks back strongly to Messiaen's earlier style and his much earlier piece on the same subject, *Le Merle noir* for flute and piano. Quasi-parallel chord successions infuse the texture. As in the Robin pieces, the Blackbird's strophes begin with a chordal motto. But whereas the tonal implications of the Robin mottos are largely subdued and localized, here in the Blackbird they are fully exploited. The music proceeds slowly through four strophes of similar construction, beginning with an extended series of chords culminating in a perceptible cadence, followed by a short birdcall, and topped off with soft chromatic clusters in the extreme registers of the instrument. This patterned content is associated with a very conventional if slightly askew harmonic scheme. The first strophe features an arrival on a clearly cadential C chord (see Example 3.11); the second on G, its dominant; the third, with some developmental additions, on D; the fourth back conclusively to C. Striking in this piece is the strong similarity of the Transposed Inversion chords, which permeate

Example 3.11   'Le Merle noir', mm. 1–4

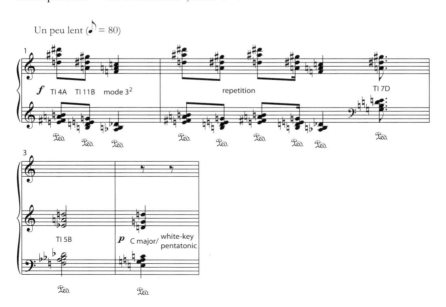

Example 3.12 'La Grive musicienne', mm. 7–10

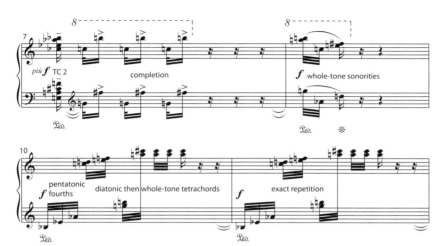

the initial chord progressions, to the more consonant, fully tonal goal chords of the progressions. The difference between the two chord types amounts to only a couple of semitones in the upper parts, e.g. in measures 3–4 of Example 3.11.

The fourth piece, on the Song Thrush, most resembles the Robin pieces in strophic structure, texture and character. It also features appearances of a three-chord motto and occasional tempo shifts against a steadier, moderate tempo. The predominant effect is nonetheless one of immediate contrast with the Robin, as the Song Thrush's calls introduce a strong and pervasive element of exact repetition, both immediate and disjunct in time, that is almost completely absent in the Robin pieces. One of the most distinctive calls, for example, is a bold upward gesture beginning in pentatonic black-key fourths, continuing through a diatonic tetrachord and terminating in a whole-tone tetrachord.[35] It appears first, repeated, in measures 9–10 (Example 3.12), returns exactly as before in measures 27–28 and surfaces again verbatim near the end of the piece at measures 75–76. Gestures occasionally emerging from the bass register also contrast with the Robin's music. The Song Thrush's pitch materials, however, generally recall the Robin's: a potpourri of chromatic, pentatonic, diatonic and whole-tone elements intermingled with invented chords and elements deriving from modes 3, 4 and 7.

The sixth and final piece of the *Petites Esquisses*, portraying the Skylark, confirms the second stream's progression toward increased activity with an

---

[35] While bits of music like this appear to be whole tone, Messiaen denied ever deliberately using his first mode of limited transposition: 'Je ne me suis jamais servi de la gamme par tones.' See *Traité, VII*, p. 51. Yet we have already seen that four successive notes are enough for him to identify a traditional mode. An equally convincing alternative explanation for this straightforward example is hard to come by.

exuberant toccata, a relentless outpouring of chatter and shrieks. Unlike all of the preceding music, there is not a single rest in the entire piece. One brisk tempo prevails, disturbed only infrequently by brief, slight adjustments. The texture is also more uniform, consisting mostly of passages of inexact doubling punctuated regularly by chords. Pitch material is somewhat similar to that of the Robin and Song Thrush, intermingling elements from modes 3, 4 and 7 along with invented chords. However, the previously prominent pentatonic and diatonic material is largely absent here, perhaps in line with the more restricted range of tempo and texture. Up close, Messiaen's favoured intervals of fourths, sevenths and ninths are pervasive in the Skylark's music. Their frequent incorporation into prominent triplet or three-note figures in inexact doubling produces an abundance of hexachordal sonorities, differing slightly from one to the next, whose semitonal content often associates them with mode 4. This concentration on hexachords, apparent in Example 3.13a, is unique to the Skylark within the *Petites Esquisses*.

Messiaen's approach to repetition in this final piece also combines techniques from previous pieces. Some of the Skylark's calls involve exact repetition of local motives or entire gestures, like that of the Song Thrush (Example 3.13a). Others vary content with every motivic repetition or gestural recurrence, recalling the Robin (Example 3.13b). There are even some cases of systematic transposition, for instance Example 3.13c, in which the upper four notes of each triplet figure move up a semitone with each iteration, while the lower two notes move down a semitone, with a divergence at the final dyad. The very end of the piece also features

Example 3.13   'L'Alouette des champs': triplet figurations and B ceiling

a) mm. 4–10 (excerpts): literal repetition and dense, shifting hexachordal content, all mode 4 except mode 3 in m. 8

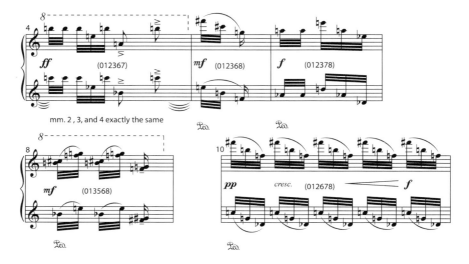

b) m. 43: changing iterations

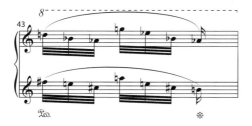

c) m. 51: systematic transposition

a gradual, terraced descent of oscillating figures in systematically ever-increasing repetitions (2×, 3×, 4×, 6×, 12×) as the music dies away. A final distinctive and unifying repetitive element in the piece is Messiaen's use throughout of an upper limit or 'ceiling' in the treble register, the pitch B6.[36] The ceiling can function as a kind of pedal, as in Example 3.13a, or as a directional goal, as in Example 3.13c. While these varying approaches to recurrence could be attributed to the inherent nature of the birdcalls Messiaen transcribes, they can also be seen as an element serving to unify aspects of the two concurrent streams at the end of the set. What is more, the piece concludes with a loud, sustained cacophony and graded decrescendo, whose expansive scope serves as a culmination not only for the piece but, even more so, for the entire work.

Conclusion

We return now to the issue of overall form. Alongside the odd-even and successive-pair groupings, another alternative might come to mind: a straight succession of

---

[36] Messiaen refers to this element both as 'sons tenues', although the notes are not literally held, and as a 'si plafond'. *Traité V:1*, pp. 265–9.

six pieces. However, the way in which they are organized, particularly the Robins, works against this perception. Moreover, for the three Robin episodes to give a strong impression of a single piece in a conventional sense, they would project a beginning, middle and end, binding the whole into a temporal progression whose structure could incorporate the other pieces in alternation. But the parallel beginnings and similar scope of the three Robin pieces project something else, akin to what Peter Hill has termed an 'elegant continuity'.[37] In their similarity, they naturally represent formal articulations, suggesting internal relationships to be further defined in context: either three parallel beginnings with different outcomes (successive-pair) or a separate content stream (odd-even). Furthermore, there is no cause for these two perceptions of dynamic structure to be opposed or mutually exclusive. Both are implicit in the organization of the *Petites Esquisses* and their coexistence lends the set a unique depth and complexity. A performance managing to convey this multiplicity within the formal dimension would add coherence to the music and serve it well.

The foregoing analysis is neither exhaustive nor authoritative. Nonetheless, it suggests that the apparently slight pieces of Messiaen's *Petites Esquisses d'oiseaux* show evidence of abundant compositional skill and musical substance. They convey the impression not of a composer in a diminished state, but much the opposite: a master in considerable technical and creative command, still capable of significant innovation.

---

[37] Hill, 'Piano Music II', p. 347.

Chapter 4
Messiaen's Counterpoint[1]

Christoph Neidhöfer

Lazy: those artisans of sub-Fauré and sub-Ravel. Lazy: the fake Couperin maniacs, writers of rigadoons and pavans. Lazy: the odious contrapuntalists of the 'return to Bach' who offer us, without remorse, dry and doleful lines poisoned by a semblance of atonality.[2]

Olivier Messiaen's music has been noted for its apparent dearth of contrapuntal writing. In his 1945 review of *Trois Petites Liturgies de la Présence Divine*, Roland-Manuel concluded that 'despite appearances, Olivier Messiaen is much more the master of harmony than the slave of counterpoint'.[3] His student George Benjamin maintained that 'background harmonic motion, tension and, above all, polyphony – were foreign to his thought'.[4] This view seems to be supported by Messiaen's own commentaries on his music – in interviews, prefaces to his scores and the theoretical treatises – which address counterpoint far less frequently than the hallmark features of his compositional technique such as the modes of limited transpositions, their synaesthetic colour associations, his typical harmonies, birdsong and rhythm. This chapter takes a fresh look at Messiaen's voice-leading practices and demonstrates that judging his commitment to counterpoint solely through the lens of his writings and only with a view toward overtly recognizable polyphonic features in his music considerably undervalues Messiaen's engagement with counterpoint in his compositional practice.

---

[1] Earlier versions of this chapter were read in 2008 at the Messiaen International Centenary Conference at Birmingham Conservatoire, the Annual Meeting of the American Musicological Society in Nashville and the Journées d'Étude Messiaen hosted by l'Observatoire International de la Création et des Cultures Musicales, Université de Montréal. I would like to acknowledge the support from the Social Sciences and Humanities Research Council of Canada for this research.

[2] Olivier Messiaen, 'Contre la paresse', *La Page musicale* (17 March 1939): p. 1, quoted and translated in Stephen Broad, 'Messiaen and Cocteau', in Christopher Dingle and Nigel Simeone (eds), *Olivier Messiaen: Music, Art and Literature* (Aldershot: Ashgate, 2007), p. 7.

[3] Roland-Manuel, 'Georges Auric, Olivier Messiaen', *Les Lettres françaises*, 28 April 1945, as quoted in English translation in PHNS, p. 149.

[4] George Benjamin, 'The Master of Harmony', in Peter Hill (ed.), *The Messiaen Companion* (London: Faber and Faber, 1995), p. 271.

As the analyses to follow will show, Messiaen, both as a composer and improviser thoroughly trained and brilliantly conversant in the polyphonic practices of the past, recast contrapuntal techniques in novel and often covert ways in his music. In so doing, he steered traditional contrapuntal concepts in new directions and applied them in new dimensions. As will be evident, the novelty of Messiaen's particular approaches – veiling and transforming familiar procedures to create something new – has led to the misperception of Messiaen's limited involvement with counterpoint.

In the following examples I first address more traditional forms of imitative counterpoint in Messiaen's music from the 1930s and 1940s, contrasting them with the neoclassical contrapuntal practices to which he was so strongly opposed. Following a brief overview of how Messiaen used the term 'counterpoint' in his own writings, I go on to show how he engaged contrapuntal devices in a variety of circumstances, including in contexts that are no longer necessarily openly polyphonic. With analytical examples that span Messiaen's entire career, I demonstrate how he generated harmonic progressions from intricate voice-leading patterns and how he varied harmonic combinations via contrapuntal transformations. In addition, my examples show how Messiaen expanded contrapuntal concepts beyond their historical models, such as in the canons of a rotational array or in the augmentation/diminution of melodic intervals inspired by similar procedures in the rhythmic domain of proportion canons. By and large, the analyses presented here demonstrate how tightly Messiaen's counterpoint is integrated with his harmonic language.

Preliminary Considerations

In setting themselves apart from the neoclassical movement, Messiaen and the other members of La Jeune France strongly opposed the mechanical polyphonies (as they perceived them) found in the music of the neoclassicists. Messiaen repeatedly singled out neoclassical counterpoint as a point of contention. In his 1939 article 'Contre la paresse' ('Against Laziness'), from which an excerpt is cited at the beginning of this chapter, he lamented in particular the 'return to Bach' of the neoclassical 'odious contrapuntalists'.[5] Almost 30 years later, in his 1967 interviews with Claude Samuel and in their later editions, he kept reiterating his rejection of the neoclassicists' 'return to Bach' that took inspiration from Cocteau's 1918 manifesto *Le coq et l'arlequin*.[6] Instead of a 'retour à Bach', Messiaen and La Jeune France advocated the return to a different aesthetic, one

---

[5] Messiaen, 'Contre la paresse'.

[6] See, for instance, Samuel, *Music and Color*, pp. 112–13. For an excellent analysis of the sources that document Messiaen's position vis-à-vis the neoclassical movement and Les Six, as well as his role in La Jeune France, see Stephen Broad, 'Messiaen and Cocteau', pp. 1–12.

that valued emotion and the spiritual.[7] Evidently, extended passages too closely modelled on baroque counterpoint were unsuited to this endeavour, because to Messiaen their lines were 'dry', 'dull' and lacking in rhythmic resourcefulness. In his 1939 article on Stravinsky, Messiaen deplores the absence of 'rhythmic gear' – the sophisticated rhythms of *Le sacre* and *Les noces* – in the 'retour à Bach' of *Symphony of Psalms*, whose second movement notably is a fully grown neo-baroque double fugue.[8]

Beyond occasional echoing effects such as those shown in Example 4.1, Messiaen seems largely to have avoided extended passages of imitative counterpoint of a more traditional kind, canons excepted. In the example, the motives marked in the voice are imitated in the piano, sometimes reinforced by one or two additional lines that move parallel within the respective modes.[9]

We do, however, find a number of longer fugal passages in Messiaen's music. Yet with the exception of an exposition like the one whose beginning is shown in Example 4.2 (piano part only), Messiaen's fugues are a far cry from the models of a 'school fugue'. While in Example 4.2 subject and answer still enter on the 'tonic' and 'dominant', with the usual steady increase in the number of voices, other fugal passages in Messiaen's compositions clearly steer away from those traditional features.[10] This is true as much for the fugue in the third movement of *L'Ascension* (orchestral version) as it is for the sixth movement from *Vingt Regards sur l'Enfant-Jésus*, a grand fugue that stands worlds apart from a neoclassical recasting of the genre.

Christopher Dingle observes that in the third movement from the original orchestral version of *L'Ascension*, 'Messiaen lacks the necessary tools to whip up a genuine head of steam towards the end of the movement, instead creating pseudo-Stravinsky with added fugue but without the impetus'.[11] Messiaen's idiosyncratic fugue at the end of this movement, starting at rehearsal 17, is built from a long

---

[7] 'Quant aux "tout jeunes", ils suivent des voies très différentes de leurs aînés; ils retournent au sensible, au spirituel.' Olivier Messiaen, 'Le rythme chez Igor Strawinsky' [sic], *La Revue musicale*, 191 (June 1939): p. 91. The opening of the 1936 manifesto by the group La Jeune France (which aside from Messiaen included Yves Baudrier, André Jolivet and Daniel-Lesur) contrasts their quest for the spiritual in music with the harsh and mechanical conditions of contemporary life: 'Les conditions de la vie devenant de plus en plus dures, mécaniques et impersonnelles, la Musique se doit d'apporter sans répit à ceux qui l'aiment sa violence spirituelle et ses réactions généreuses.' Manifesto of La Jeune France quoted in Serge Gut, *Le Groupe Jeune France* (Paris: Honoré Champion, 1977), pp. 16–17.

[8] Messiaen, 'Contre la paresse', and 'Le rythme chez Igor Strawinsky', p. 92.

[9] Motive c is part of Messiaen's 'Boris' contour shown in Example 4.16b below.

[10] The fugue in Example 4.2 – a dance of sins – is also noteworthy for its asymmetrical metric structure in light of Messiaen's disparaging remarks on the 'lamentable bars in 3s and 4s' in neoclassical music. See Messiaen, 'Le rythme chez Igor Strawinsky', p. 91.

[11] Christopher Dingle, *The Life of Messiaen* (Cambridge: Cambridge University Press, 2007), p. 40.

Example 4.1 *Chants de terre et de ciel*, 'Résurrection', bars 30–32, motivic imitation and modes marked

subject (lasting 25 bars in quick $\frac{2}{4}$ meter) that is replete with syncopations. It first enters in the low string register and is subsequently imitated exclusively at the octave, moving into the next higher register with each imitation. Messiaen does not develop a repeating countersubject, but instead provides a fresh multi-voiced accompaniment below each new statement of the subject. The texture gradually extends into the highest register, progressively dropping the lower range before reclaiming it in the final gesture. Except for a chromatic passing tone in the latter, the entire fugue is built on mode 2^1.

The exposition of the fugue in the sixth movement from *Vingt Regards*, whose beginning is reproduced in Example 4.3, goes against convention by immediately restating the subject in altered form: the unprepared listener will find it difficult to recognize that the subject in the left hand of bars 1–2 reappears in the right hand of bars 3–5 in different rhythm and contour (and with an occasional added

Example 4.2   *Chants de terre et de ciel*, 'Minuit pile et face', bars 14–19, piano part only, first three fugal entries

inner voice), accompanied by other successively altered statements of the same subject in the left hand. In these, Messiaen continuously distorts the pitch(-class) succession by transposing certain pitches while keeping the rest fixed as marked on the example.[12] The very opening in bars 1–2 pairs the subject in the left hand with a countersubject in the right hand.[13] The answer in bars 7–8 presents this two-part combination in modified mirror-inversion with the inverted countersubject doubled in octaves. The mirror-inversion is modified in that the vertical intervals between subject and countersubject in bars 1–2 differ from those between the inverted subject and countersubject in bars 7–8. In straightforward mirror-inversion, in which two simultaneous lines are each inverted around the *same* pitch axis, the vertical intervals between the lines are preserved after the inversion. By contrast, Messiaen's subject and countersubject are mirrored around two different pitch axes: the subject

---

[12]   The gradual transformation of the pitch succession in the left hand of bars 3–6, which continues in bar 9 and beyond, is what Messiaen calls an *agrandissement asymétrique*: certain intervals are enlarged (or reduced) while others remain unaltered. Messiaen discusses the method in his analysis of the movement in *Traité II*, p. 445. The procedure is also examined in Siglind Bruhn's detailed analysis of the entire movement. See Siglind Bruhn, *Messiaen's Contemplations of Covenant and Incarnation: Musical Symbols of Faith in the Two Great Piano Cycles of the 1940s* (Hillsdale, NY: Pendragon Press, 2007), p. 258. The continuous transposition up and down by semitone creates a larger composed-out chromatic wedge. Messiaen would call this a 'passing group' (the enlargement of a chromatic passing note progression). See *Technique*, example 305. The gradual enlargement and reduction of targeted intervals that arises from *agrandissements asymétriques* parallels the asymmetrical augmentations and diminutions of durations in the rhythmic domain elsewhere in Messiaen's music, thus transferring a particular strategy from one parameter to another. Messiaen mentions this in *Traité II*, p. 34.

[13]   Some analysts would thus call this a double fugue.

Example 4.3   *Vingt Regards sur l'Enfant-Jésus*, 'Par Lui tout a été fait', opening of fugue, bars 1–9

in bars 1–2 maps onto the inverted subject in bars 7–8 around pitch F♯3, while the countersubject maps onto its inversion via pitch axis F3 (to get the upper notes of the inverted countersubject). I conjecture that Messiaen must have chosen those pitch axes so that *both* the subject and countersubject would be answered at the tritone (subject begins on D♯ and is answered in bar 7 starting on A, countersubject begins on D and is answered in bar 8 on G♯). Messiaen mentions that the inverted subject in bar 7 starts on the 'dominante à la quarte augmentée de la tonique'.[14]

In bar 9 the left hand continues the transformations begun in bars 3–6 while the right hand restates the inverted subject (the 'answer') in a new rhythm and contour, continuing beyond the example. All in all, this movement presents us with a compilation of some of Messiaen's most characteristic compositional devices to

---

[14]   *Traité II*, p. 445.

date, including rhythmic and pitch canons (stretto), non-retrogradable rhythms, colour chords and the gradual expansion and truncation of material. By means of these densely presented complex features, and by calling upon the prototype of musical learned style – the fugue – the movement portrays the world's Creation-through-the-Word ('Par "Lui" [le Verbe] tout a été fait ').[15]

Examples 4.4a and 4.4b show two contrapuntal passages typical of the early *Préludes* for piano. In both cases, the right and left hands present canons in inversion. In Example 4.4a, the contour outlined by the chords in the right hand (first in mode 6^4, then 6^1) is imitated in inversion by the chords in the left hand (first in mode 3^4, then 3^1) one quaver later. In Example 4.4b, the outer voices forming a canon in inversion, also at the time interval of a quaver, are accompanied by two inner voices that, with one exception, move parallel with each other within the mode (6^5). Messiaen's proficiency in counterpoint and the frequent display of contrapuntal devices in his earlier works are not surprising in light of his studies in counterpoint and fugue at the Conservatoire, the influence of Paul Dukas and Charles Tournemire, and especially his training in fugal improvisation under Marcel Dupré.

In his organ improvisation treatise first published in 1926 – much of which focuses on improvised counterpoint, including canon at the octave and fifth, chorale prelude, fugue and double fugue – Dupré not only emphasizes that a 'good improviser' must know counterpoint and fugue alongside harmony, plainsong, and

Example 4.4a   *Préludes*, 'Instants défunts', bars 23–24

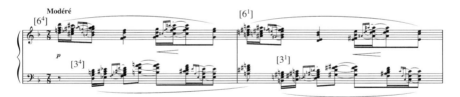

Example 4.4b   *Préludes*, 'Les sons impalpables du rêve', bars 22–24

---

[15] For a very detailed interpretation of the many facets of this movement in the context of the entire piano cycle, see Bruhn, *Messiaen's Contemplations of Covenant and Incarnation*, pp. 255–67.

84   *Messiaen Perspectives 2: Techniques, Influence and Reception*

so on, but moreover that improvised harmonization 'must be only the consequence of the contrapuntal movement of voices'.[16] As Robert Sholl observed, Dupré's affection for counterpoint is 'evident not only in Dupré's own compositions but in his preference for contrapuntal forms in his recorded improvisations'.[17] In the preface to *Technique*, Messiaen acknowledges Dupré, 'who oriented me toward counterpoint and form'. Tournemire, whose improvisations likewise had a strong impact on Messiaen, also stresses in his organ performance treatise the importance of counterpoint skills in improvisation.[18] Incidentally, some of the lists of chords found in Dupré's treatise, such as the one that shows ninth chords built on each scale degree as we move up the major and harmonic minor scales, bear clear resemblance with Messiaen's own published lists of chords moving in parallel voice-leading up and down the scales of the modes of limited transpositions.[19] Given Messiaen's improvisatory skills, we can easily imagine him developing modal harmonic progressions and contrapuntal passages such as the ones in Examples 4.4a and 4.4b through improvisation.

The same holds for the excerpt analysed in Example 4.5. According to Messiaen, *Messe de la Pentecôte* for organ was developed through improvisation over a number of years.[20] The passage shown superimposes three individual strands of material in the dark lower to middle register. While it would probably require enormous skill to improvise the rhythmic complexities involved – each strand contains a different chain of rhythmic interversions – those with Messiaen's modes under their fingers (and feet) could well extemporise the layering of the pitch materials.

With one exception, Messiaen produces the rhythmic interversions by applying the same ordered permutations to all three layers, as Example 4.6a illustrates. Each layer starts with a different ordering of durations between 1 and 5 semiquavers, but permutes them in the same way (the second permutation differs in the right hand from that used in the left hand and pedal). This process continues beyond Example 4.5 for another six

---

[16]   Marcel Dupré, *Cours complet d'improvisation à l'orgue*, Vol. 2, *Traité d'improvisation à l'orgue*, English trans. John Fenstermaker (Paris: Alphonse Leduc, 1974), Introduction (no page number) and p. 16.

[17]   Robert Sholl, 'Making the Invisible Visible: The Culture, Theology and Practice of Olivier Messiaen's Improvisations', paper given at the annual meeting of the American Musicological Society, Washington, D.C., October 2005.

[18]   See Charles Tournemire, *Précis d'éxécution, de registration et d'improvisation à l'orgue* (Paris: Eschig, 1936), p. 102. The influence of Dupré and Tournemire on Messiaen is discussed in Vincent Benitez, 'Messiaen as Improviser', *Dutch Journal of Music Theory*, 13/2 (2008): pp. 129–44.

[19]   Dupré's list of ninth chords appears in *Traité d'improvisation à l'orgue*, p. 21. The purpose of this list is to show all the possible ninth chords available in the two modes. Dupré does not suggest playing them in ascending or descending parallel motion in actual improvisation, but we can imagine an improviser practising the chords in this order. From here it is only a small step to Messiaen's parallel modal chord progressions.

[20]   *Traité IV*, p. 83.

Example 4.5 Analytic reduction of *Messe de la Pentecôte*, 'Offertoire', bars 25–34, with chords in the right hand numbered, durations labelled and modes identified

Example 4.6a Rhythmic interversions in bars 25–32

interversions in each layer. The order permutations applied in each layer (not shown here) are, with three exceptions: (1)(2354), (1)(2)(3)(45), (1)(2)(4)(35), (1)(2)(3)(45), (1)(2)(4)(35), (1)(2)(3)(45). In *Traité IV*, p. 95, Messiaen writes out the interversions in rhythmic reduction – albeit without specifying the order permutations – and in a gesture of self-criticism observes (on p. 96) that too many simultaneous attacks occur among the three layers because all durations are multiples of a semiquaver.

Example 4.6b   Voice-leading patterns in chords 1–20 of the right hand (in mode 3[1])

Chords:	1-2	2-3	3-4	4-5	5-6	6-7	7-8	8-9	9-10	10-11	11-12	12-13	13-14	14-15	15-16	16-17	17-18	18-19	19-20
Line 1:	+1	+2	-1	-1	+5	-2	+3	+2	+1	-1	-1	-1	-1	-2	-3	+3	-4	-1	-1
Line 2:	-1	+2	+1	+1	+1	+1	+1	+3	+1	-1	-1	-1	-3	-1	-3	+3	-5	+1	+1
Line 3:	-1	+2	+1	+1	+1	+1	+1	+2	+3	-1	-1	-1	-4	+1	-3	+3	-7	+1	+1

The pedal repeats a pitch ostinato (in mode 2^1, 4^5, 6^5 or 7^2) while the left hand presents two lines moving up and down in parallel motion in mode 4^1.[21] The upper line hovers two scale degrees above the lower, in a progression that would have been familiar to an improviser from preparatory exercises in the mode.[22] The chords in the right hand follow less regular voice-leading patterns. These are illustrated in Example 4.6b, which tabulates the voice-leading intervals in each of the three lines in the right hand. Intervals are measured in numbers of scale degrees within the mode (3^1), rather than with respect to chromatic distance. Hence the top line is shown as moving up first by one scale degree, from D to E♭, then by two scale degrees, from E♭ to F♯ (which corresponds to a chromatic distance of three semitones), then moving down by one scale degree from F♯ to E (a distance of two semitones), and so forth. As this voice-leading analysis shows, unlike in the patterns in the pedal and left hand, the right hand sustains neither a pitch ostinato nor parallel motion in all of its lines throughout. Instances of parallel voice-leading in all three lines, shaded in the example, account for about one third of the progressions. Successions that have parallel voice-leading in two of the three lines, with the third line moving in some other way, are more common; they account for a little over half of the progressions. We can imagine in these instances the improviser's fingers still largely following parallel voice-leading patterns in at least two lines (a skill honed by preparatory exercises) while exploring other patterns in the third line.[23] One is also reminded here of exercises like the one from Dupré's treatise partially reproduced in Example 4.7, where the improviser learns how to move from the symmetrical and tonally ambiguous augmented triad to tonal chords in various keys via smooth voice-leading by semi- and/or whole-tone exclusively. Messiaen's progressions in the left and right hands of Example 4.5 are not about modulation, but they show a similar focus on smooth voice leading (motion by one scale degree predominates).

---

[21]   Messiaen identifies the mode in the pedal only as mode 2^1. Ibid., p. 96.

[22]   In the section on Hindu modes in *Traité VII*, Messiaen recommends practising modes in two and more voices in ascending and descending parallel motion 'in order to make them [the modes] thoroughly one's own and to be able to handle them almost automatically'. The exercise is also meant to prevent the improviser from 'always falling back into tonal sonorities' (*Traité VII*, p. 31).

[23]   With one exception, parallel voice-leading always involves adjacent voices in the example, further strengthening the hypothesis that the passage largely elaborates on patterns acquired through parallel chord progression exercises.

Example 4.7   Marcel Dupré, *Traité d'improvisation à l'orgue*, 'Modulations by Symmetrical Chords' (excerpt, p. 24 of English edition)

1. Two notes stationary, one note descending a half-step.

2. Two notes stationary, one note rising a half-step.

3. One note stationary, two notes rising a half-step.

4. One note stationary, two notes descending a half-step.

5. One note stationary, one note rising a half-step, one note descending a half-step.

6. One note rising a half-step, two notes descending a half-step.

7. One note descending a half-step, two notes rising a half-step.

8. One note descending a whole-step, two notes descending a half-step.

In his own analysis of *Messe de la Pentecôte*, Messiaen does not discuss any of the voice-leading features in Example 4.6b.[24] In fact, his writings in general hardly ever address the nitty-gritty details of this type of counterpoint. Perhaps Messiaen found it unnecessary to point out such features because he thought interested analysts would

---

[24]   *Traité IV*, pp. 93–6.

recognize them without his help. As he states in the preface to *Technique*, Messiaen expects his readers to have a thorough grasp of 'counterpoint and fugue', alongside the other subjects of the conservatoire curriculum. This knowledge presumably is not only required because Messiaen uses basic contrapuntal terminology without defining it, but also so that the reader would be able to appreciate the more subtle instances of counterpoint in his music, whether they are explicitly discussed or not. The term 'counterpoint' itself is used straightforwardly in Messiaen's writings, in line with traditional uses of the term, either identifying an independent voice ('contrepoint de flûte', 'the light formulas of the violin create a secondary counterpoint', 'contrepoint contrastant'), an independent layer of material ('contrepoint d'accords'), the combination of different layers ('contrepoint de rythmes'), or a specific contrapuntal device ('canon', 'stretto', 'augmentation').[25] Such devices occur repeatedly in Messiaen's music, but are often resourcefully concealed, as we shall see.

In the examples to follow I pass over Messiaen's polyphonic textures that superimpose different layers of materials that have little in common with each other in terms of rhythm and pitch, but instead focus on the more intricate voice-leading patterns in situations where different lines or layers nonetheless relate to each other in some tangible way. As we shall see, such counterpoints are often embedded in what appear to be predominantly harmonic contexts, in the form of note-against-note counterpoint where the intimate link between Messiaen's harmonic and contrapuntal thinking is particularly evident. I first discuss various voice-leading patterns and then turn to techniques of contrapuntal transformation, including double counterpoint, intervallic augmentation/diminution and order rotation. Lastly, I briefly address counterpoint in Messiaen's orchestration.

Voice-leading Patterns in Note-against-note Counterpoint

As the following analyses of two excerpts from *Vingt Regards* and *La Nativité du Seigneur* demonstrate, Messiaen frequently built successions of harmonies from carefully constructed contrapuntal patterns. Example 4.8 shows the 'Theme of God' that opens the 15th movement from *Vingt Regards*. Starting with a calm and soothing harmonic progression that moves back and forth between tonic and dominant harmonies, this lullaby is rich in contrapuntal activity. As analysed in Example 4.9a, the anacrusis in bar 1 can be heard as a combination of five lines, the outer of which are stationary and the inner three move stepwise within mode 2^1 (which is associated with the tonic harmony). The anacrusis at the end of bar 2, analysed in Example 4.9b, works similarly in mode 2^2 (itself associated with the dominant harmony, over the tonic pedal F♯ foreign to this mode). The voice leading of the expanding gesture in bar 4 – moving through the main accent of the entire phrase – is analysed in Example 4.9c, omitting the F♯ pedal. As marked by the boxes,

---

[25]   The expressions in the first through third parentheses are from *Traité VII*, p. 65; *Technique*, example 60; *Traité IV*, p. 96; and *Traité II*, pp. 175 and 156–7.

Example 4.8 *Vingt Regards sur l'Enfant-Jésus*, 'Le baiser de l'Enfant-Jésus', bars 1–6 with modes and harmonies marked

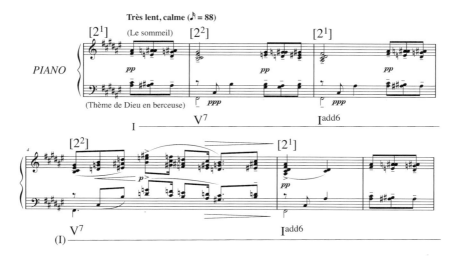

Messiaen superimposes two strands, each of which projects a distinct melodic interval succession in parallel motion within the mode. In other words, Messiaen combines here two distinct melodies, in the manner of melody and countermelody, reinforcing each with one or two additional lines that, seen from a modal perspective, move in parallel motion (i.e. in each box the lines always move or skip by the same number of scale degrees). As a consequence, the chords in the right hand (lines 1–3) are all built from the same vertical intervals if considered from a modal perspective, but not if viewed from a chromatic perspective: the uppermost and middle pitch, as well as the middle and lowest pitch of each chord, are always three scale degrees apart, which translates into a vertical major third or perfect fourth depending on the location within the mode. As a result, these chords form major *or* minor triads. Similarly, the vertical intervals between lines 4 and 5 alternate between perfect and diminished fourths, with the two lines again moving at a vertical distance of three scale degrees from each other. Altogether, these changing interval sizes (from a chromatic perspective) projected by parallel motion (from a modal perspective) produce the 'shimmering, stained-glass' quality so characteristic of Messiaen's music.[26]

---

[26] *Music and Color*, p. 115. I have discussed elsewhere how Messiaen's modal harmonic progressions owe their 'stained-glass quality', in part, to the multidimensional listening perspective they entail. I suggest that his modal harmonies are heard simultaneously from three perspectives, namely: (1) from within the mode (by way of the scale degrees they occupy in the mode); (2) with reference to diatonic tonality and tonal functions; and (3) from a more abstract, set-class perspective (with respect to chromatic interval sizes, measured in semitones). Christoph Neidhöfer, 'A Theory of Harmony and Voice Leading for the Music of Olivier Messiaen', *Music Theory Spectrum*, 27/1 (2005): pp. 1–34.

Example 4.9a Voice leading in 'Le baiser de l'Enfant-Jésus' bar 1 illustrated (in mode 2^1)

Example 4.9b Voice leading in 'Le baiser de l'Enfant-Jésus' bar 2 illustrated (in mode 2^2)

Another instance of how Messiaen builds harmonies from carefully crafted voice-leading patterns is shown in Example 4.10. The left hand of bar 60, analysed in Example 4.11a, contains three descending lines, with the stepwise descent of line 2 getting underway one chord later than in lines 3 and 4. I have marked this as canon α. The right hand in Example 4.10 plays this progression an octave higher, substituting the pitches shown in parentheses in Example 4.11a. Following two repeats of this material in bars 61 and 62 over the entrance of the pedal, Messiaen

Example 4.9c Voice leading in 'Le baiser de l'Enfant-Jésus' bar 4 illustrated (in mode 2^2)

Example 4.10 *La Nativité du Seigneur*, 'Dieu parmi nous', bars 60–63

moves to a higher chord at the beginning of bar 63. This chord is also a harmony on E, substituting a minor-minor seventh chord for the major triad on the earlier downbeats. Example 4.11b illuminates the voice-leading patterns in bar 63 where we again find instances of imitation, marked b and g.

Example 4.11a Voice-leading patterns in 'Dieu parmi nous' bar 60 illustrated (in mode 2^2)

Example 4.11b Voice-leading patterns in 'Dieu parmi nous' bar 63 illustrated (in mode 2^2)

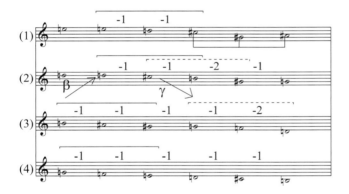

While one would normally classify the progressions in the two excerpts from *Vingt Regards* and *La Nativité* in Examples 4.8 and 4.10 as harmonic rather than contrapuntal, my analysis shows how Messiaen assembled these harmonies from carefully crafted individual lines. There is nothing arbitrary about the number of pitches per chord nor about the way one chord moves to the next, because of the linear voice-leading forces at play. The same also holds for the three excerpts to be discussed next, where contrapuntally conceived harmonic progressions are subjected to further transformation.

Vertical-shifting Counterpoint

In the following examples Messiaen transforms harmonic progressions by altering the vertical distance between superimposed blocks of chords when they are repeated and transposed. In the polymodal passage of Example 4.12, the harmonies in the right hand of the piano belong to mode 3^1, those in the left hand to mode 2^2. The four lines in each hand move parallel to one another within the mode while each hand follows a different melodic contour. This is examined in Example 4.13, which illuminates the sequential nature of the progressions: each hand repeats – in four parallel lines – the succession of intervals that I have underlined (the intervals are again measured in numbers of scale degrees within the respective mode). The corresponding segments are also marked by the brackets in Example 4.12. The sequence preserves the types of chords in each hand: the chords under the second bracket in each hand are an exact transposition of the corresponding chords under the first bracket. However, the left-hand and right-hand chords form a different vertical relationship with one another the second time around. This is so because under the second bracket the chords in the right hand are transposed down a major third and the ones in the left hand a minor third, reflecting the transpositional symmetry of each mode. (Mode 3 maps onto itself under transposition by a major third or a multiple thereof, and mode 2 maps onto itself under transposition by

Example 4.12 *Chants de terre et de ciel*, 'Arc-en-ciel d'innocence', bars 15–16, modes and sequence marked

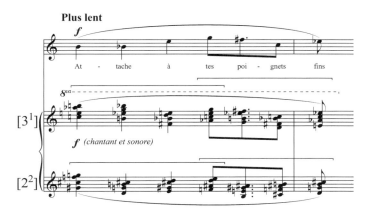

Example 4.13 Sequential parallel voice-leading patterns in the piano part (analysed in numbers of scale degrees)

In the right hand, all four lines move (in mode 3^1):   -1   -4   +2   -1   -4   +2

In the left hand, all four lines move (in mode 2^2):   -4   +1   +1   -4   +1   +1

94   *Messiaen Perspectives 2: Techniques, Influence and Reception*

a minor third or a multiple thereof.) In other words, the chords in the two hands have moved one semitone closer to each other the second time.[27] The harmonic combination has been transformed by way of 'vertical-shifting counterpoint', to borrow the terminology of Sergei Taneiev.[28] The shift is a contrapuntal device insofar as it takes the combination of right-hand and left-hand chords under the first bracket and alters that combination by transposing each hand by a different interval under the second bracket. In counterpoint instruction such shifts, applied to a combination of two or more melodies, are commonly classified as invertible or double counterpoint. In invertible counterpoint two melodies switch relative position (the upper melody becomes the lower and vice versa); in double counterpoint – as I will use the term here – they remain in the same relative position but with the vertical distance between them altered.[29] Example 4.12 represents an instance of double counterpoint involving two melodies (left and right hand), each of which moves in four parallel lines.

In another way, the first and fifth bar of Example 4.14 are also related via double counterpoint. The chords in the right hand of bar 5 are lower than but not an exact transposition of the chords in bar 1. As Example 4.15 reveals, these chords are generated by the same melodic intervals read in different modes for which reason different chord qualities arise. Meanwhile, on the downbeat of both bars we hear a second inversion E major triad in the left hand. Bar 5 thus presents a vertically shifted combination of the chords from bar 1, with the chords in the right hand in addition subjected to modular transformation (they switch from minor to major).[30] The two hands swap mode between bars 1–4 and 5: the right hand moves from mode 3^1 to mode 2^2 while the left hand uses them in reverse order.[31] The technique of modular transformation – reading the same intervals (in terms of the number of scale degrees they span) in two different modes – reminds us of similar

---

[27]   The alteration of the vertical distance between the chords in the right and left hands can easily be recognized by examining the intervals between the lowest note in the right hand and the highest note in the left hand in the corresponding places. For instance, on the very first beat that interval is a perfect fourth (G5–C6), reduced to a diminished fourth (E5–A♭5) three chords later where the transposed repetitions begin.

[28]   Sergei Ivanovitch Taneiev, *Convertible Counterpoint in the Strict Style*, trans. G. Ackley Brower (Boston: Bruce Humphries Publishers, 1962). Taneiev's treatise, originally published in 1909, explores vertical-shifting, horizontal-shifting and double-shifting counterpoint in the context of tonal and (Renaissance) modal music.

[29]   My terminological distinction between 'invertible' and 'double' counterpoint follows Peter Schubert, 'A Lesson from Lassus: Form in the Duos of 1577', *Music Theory Spectrum*, 17/1 (1995): pp. 1–26.

[30]   On the third quaver of bar 5, Messiaen assigns to the left hand a new harmony, one that nevertheless follows the E major $^6_4$ chord via some of the same voice-leading intervals as those in bar 1 as boxed in Example 4.15.

[31]   Messiaen calls this situation a 'modulation by inversion of the superposed modes' (*Technique*, example 380). In *Traité VII*, p. 262, the exchange of modes is called 'modulation polymodale par interversion [sic] des modes superposés'.

Example 4.14 *Poèmes pour Mi*, 'Le collier', bars 1–5, piano part only

Example 4.15 Voice-leading patterns in 'Le collier' bars 1 and 5

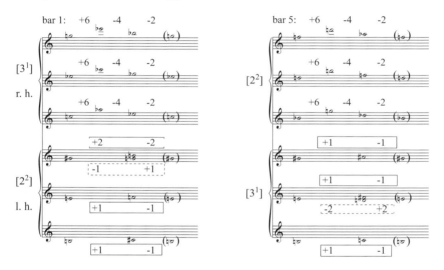

approaches in the music of Debussy, Bartók, Stravinsky and others, whereby a melody is mapped from one mode onto another.[32] Such transformations preserve the melodic contours while changing the 'flavour' of the sound. For Messiaen, such transformations lead to a change in colour.

A third instance of double counterpoint is shown in Example 4.16. The two passages in Example 4.16a (bars 8 and 13) use the same melodies and chords. But, as illustrated, in the second instance the left hand is transposed down a whole-tone while the right hand stays in place. Again, the counterpoint between the right and left hand is vertically shifted to produce new harmonic combinations the second

---

[32] Well-known examples include the chromatic opening theme from Bartók's *Music for Strings, Percussion, and Celesta* – composed the same year as *Poèmes pour Mi* – which is mapped in the last movement onto the acoustic scale, or the theme from Debussy's 'Feux d'artifice' (*Préludes* II), which is mapped from the pentatonic (diatonic) onto the whole-tone collection and vice versa. For a discussion of these and other examples, see Matthew Santa, 'Defining Modular Transformations', *Music Theory Spectrum*, 21/2 (1999): pp. 200–29.

Example 4.16a *Poèmes pour Mi*, 'Paysage', vertical-shifting counterpoint in the piano part of bars 8 and 13

Example 4.16b 'Boris' motive in the right hand and its intervallic diminution in the left, before and after the vertical shift

time around. Melodically, bars 8 and 13 are led by the 'Boris' motive shown in Example 4.16b, which occurs in intervallically diminuted form in the left hand (in counterpoint above ascending parallel fourths).[33]

Rotational Array

The following examples examine a passage from a highly complex texture generated via an elaborate procedure of horizontal- and vertical-shifting counterpoint that carries powerful extra-musical significance. Evoking the terrifying moment of the Transfiguration through images of mountain heights and the splendour of the sun and eternal light, the 12th movement from the monumental *La Transfiguration de Notre-Seigneur Jésus-Christ* concludes with what Messiaen describes as 'a collective vocalise written in twenty real parts [that] brings about the final word: "Terribilis"'.[34] Example 4.17 extracts the beginning of this counterpoint from the full score. The remaining string and percussion parts that do not participate in this particular polyphony are not shown. The 20 vocal lines, each of which is doubled by strings, form a rotational array: each line states the same series in a different rotation and/or transposition. I have bracketed the series in the top line (after the

---

[33] The 'Boris' motive is identified, with examples from *La Nativité du Seigneur* and *Les Corps glorieux*, in *Technique*, examples 75–9. It occurs frequently in Messiaen's music.

[34] *Traité VII*, p. 295.

Example 4.17   *La Transfiguration de Notre-Seigneur Jésus-Christ*, 'Terribilis est locus iste', p. 339, excerpt, annotated

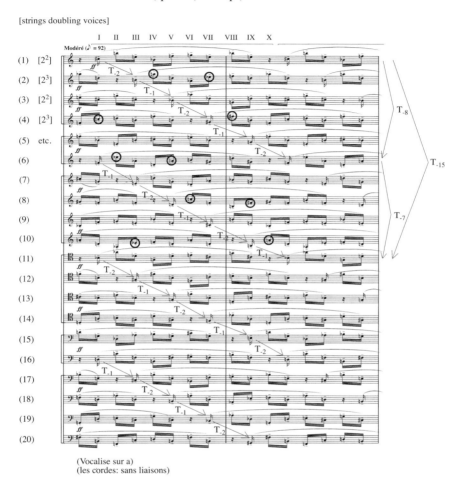

(Vocalise sur a)
(les cordes: sans liaisons)

first statement it is repeated three times beyond the excerpt shown). It is in mode 2^2 and consists of a succession of nine semiquaver notes – some of which repeat the same pitch classes – followed by a semiquaver rest. Line 2 presents this succession in transposed canon, in mode 2^3: the series is shifted down a whole-tone and rotated two positions (semiquavers) to the right. The third line rotates the result another two positions to the right and transposes it down by a semitone (thus returning to mode 2^2). This is followed by further rotations, alternating transpositions down by one and two semitones, that is, by alternating modes 2^2 and 2^3.

As can be gleaned from the transpositional paths marked by arrows on the score, the combination of the first ten lines as a whole is replicated from the 11th

98   *Messiaen Perspectives 2: Techniques, Influence and Reception*

line down a minor tenth lower, that is, 15 semitones lower, marked T_{-15}. From this we can conclude that each of the verticals (harmonies) numbered I–X consists of an upper half that is an exact transposition of the vertical's lower half, since in each vertical the pitches from lines 1–10 map onto the pitches from lines 11–20 via T_{-15}.

Although the counterpoint of the array moves at a moderately quick tempo and is somewhat blurred by the additional sliding and chromatically ascending/descending string harmonics and the percussion parts not shown, it projects an overall consistent flavour of mode 2^2. The following examples demonstrate why this is the case.

Christopher Dingle has explained the passage as 'an advanced mode 2^2 canon', with each entry of the 'theme' starting one step down the mode (C♯, B, B♭, etc.). Since the transposition is exact rather than modal, the lines alternate transpositions 2 and 3 of the mode. Dingle concludes, concerning the expressive meaning of the passage:

> Messiaen covers his compositional tracks by starting all the parts together in relation to the first part, with the consequence that sixteen of the twenty parts begin mid-cycle. … The complex vocalisation in *La Transfiguration* is another example of Messiaen not being content with merely creating a remarkable effect but rather feeling it necessary to imbue it with mysterious elements. In this case he has used the second transposition of mode two, the mode which lies at the heart of *La Transfiguration*, as a basis for creating a structure which, by virtue of its inevitable processes, obscures any trace of the original mode from the listener. The music is again under the control of 'unseen' forces.[35]

Let us now take a closer look at the ten verticals of the array, which consist predominantly of pitch classes from mode 2^2. The first four verticals excerpted in Example 4.18, for instance, each contain only two pitches (shown as filled-in note heads) that are not a member of this mode. As we shall see, this also holds for the remaining verticals. This may at first seem surprising, since only every other line of the array is in this mode, with the rest being in mode 2^3. The following tables explore this and other properties of the verticals in more detail, demonstrating how Messiaen's harmonies (verticals) resulted from his particular contrapuntal decisions or, conversely, in what might have been a more likely scenario, how his harmonic preferences must have motivated his contrapuntal choices.

In order to understand Messiaen's array we need to consider it in two ways: general and specific. As concerns the array's general properties, Example 4.19 schematizes its first seven lines. Letters a through i stand for the nine pitches of the series in line 1 that are followed by a rest. On line 2, these pitches are transposed down by two semitones, shown as 'a-2', 'b-2', etc., and rotated two positions to the right. On line 3 these pitches are transposed down another semitone, that is, a

---

[35]   Christopher Dingle, *Olivier Messiaen:* La Transfiguration de Notre-Seigneur Jésus-Christ – *A Provisional Study*, MPhil thesis (University of Sheffield, 1994), Vol. 1, pp. 76–7.

Example 4.18   'Terribilis est locus iste', p. 339, Verticals I–IV from the array, with pitches that do not belong to mode 2^2 indicated by filled-in note heads

Example 4.19   'Terribilis est locus iste', p. 339, Rotational array schematized

vertical:	I	II	III	IV	V	VI	VII	VIII	IX	X
line 1 (series):	a	b	c	d	e	f	g	h	i	(rest)
line 2:	i-2	(rest)	a-2	b-2	c-2	d-2	e-2	f-2	g-2	h-2
line 3:	g-3	h-3	i-3	(rest)	a-3	b-3	c-3	d-3	e-3	f-3
line 4:	e-5	f-5	g-5	h-5	i-5	(rest)	a-5	b-5	c-5	d-5
line 5:	c-6	d-6	e-6	f-6	g-6	h-6	i-6	(rest)	a-6	b-6
line 6:	a-8	b-8	c-8	d-8	e-8	f-8	g-8	h-8	i-8	(rest)
line 7:	i-9	(rest)	a-9	b-9	c-9	d-9	e-9	f-9	g-9	h-9
etc.	etc.									

for a = C♯, b = B, c = E, d = B♭, e = F, f = G, g = E, h = B♭, i = E

total of three semitones down from line 1 ('a-3', 'b-3', etc.) and rotated another two positions to the right, and so forth. As a result of the specific rotation and the length of the series – rotation by two positions of a series with an even number of elements – the pitches in the first vertical (marked by the open box) are derived from every second element of the series, namely from a, c, e, g and i exclusively. The same holds for verticals III, V, VII and IX. On the other hand, the pitches of the remaining verticals are all obtained exclusively from b, d, f, h and the semiquaver rest of the original series.

The leftmost column in Example 4.20a shows the first vertical in generalized form (first 20 entries bracketed α and β) and extends it further down, according to what would have happened had Messiaen continued the array beyond the 20 lines until the entire permutation/transposition procedure would have run its course. As the example demonstrates, this would have been the case after a total of 40 lines, after which the 'super-array' would have started over. In other words, the first column in the example – which represents the first vertical of the 'super-array' – wraps around to the top after 40 entries ('a', 'i-2', 'g-3' and so on below the double line correspond to these same entries at the top). As demarcated by the four curly brackets to the left, the cycle of 40 entries divides into four groups, labelled α–δ,

Example 4.20a 'Terribilis est locus iste', p. 339, Pitch-class cycle for verticals I, III, V, VII, IX

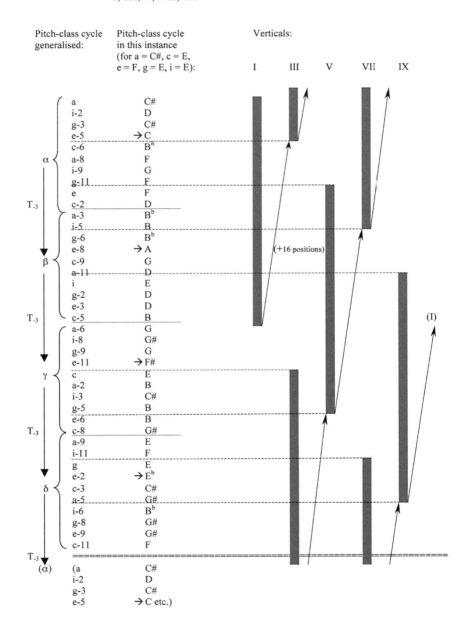

Example 4.20b 'Terribilis est locus iste', p. 339, Pitch-class cycle for verticals II, IV, VI, VIII, X

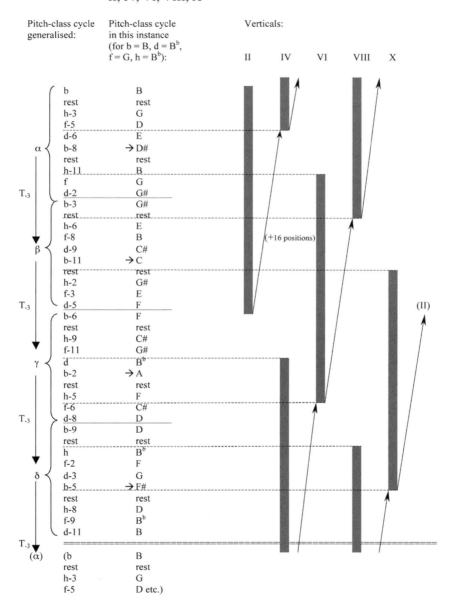

that are exact transpositions of each other: β transposes the entries from α down three semitones, that is, {a, i-2, g-3, e-5 etc.} of α map onto {a-3, i-5, g-6, e-8 etc.} of β via subtraction of three semitones from each entry. The same applies between β and γ, γ and δ, and δ and α (modulo 12). We had already observed this property for α and β, whereby the lower half β of vertical I in Example 4.18 replicated the upper half α 15 semitones lower. Since in the generalization of Example 4.20a intervals are calculated modulo 12, i.e. irrespective of register, T_{-15} (Example 4.18) now appears reduced to T_{-3}.

The transpositional relationships among α, β, γ and δ hold no matter what pitches were originally chosen for the series of the array. Considering Messiaen's specific pitch choices, the second column in Example 4.20a lists the pitch classes that are obtained once we feed Messiaen's particular series into the array.[36] The top 20 entries comprise vertical I. This is indicated by the shaded bar to the right, under I, which demarcates the segment covered by this vertical. As shown by the further shaded bars under III, V, VII and IX, the remaining odd-numbered verticals from Messiaen's array correspond to other segments from the same larger pitch-class cycle. These segments are distributed evenly, at a distance of 16 positions from one to the next, as shown by the diagonal upward-pointing arrows in the example.

In the second column, I have marked with → those pitch classes that are not part of mode 2^2. They occur in only four locations of the larger pitch-class cycle, and each of verticals I, III, V, VII and IX includes exactly two of them. These verticals are thus all predominantly in mode 2^2. As Example 4.20b demonstrates, the same also holds for all the even-numbered verticals from the array. They are based on a different pitch-class cycle, shown in the second column. Again, pitch classes that are foreign to mode 2^2 are marked with → . As they did in Example 4.20a, they occur in only four locations, and each of the verticals again contains exactly only two of them. The even-numbered verticals are thus also predominantly in mode 2^2, as in the previous example, a property that arises from Messiaen's specific choice of the series: if we were to substitute other pitch classes for variables a through i in Examples 4.20a and 4.20b, different verticals would arise that may or may not be predominantly in one particular mode. Hence Messiaen must have chosen his series with certain modal properties of the verticals in mind, the intricate counterpoint of the array thus serving a larger harmonic objective.

The reason why Messiaen's particular series generates verticals that are predominantly in mode 2^2, each containing two and only two pitches (pitch classes) foreign to that mode, can be explained in the two following ways:

1. Messiaen's series (C♯–B–E–B♭–F–G–E–B♭–E–rest) is entirely in mode 2^2 (Example 4.17, line 1). This means that each pitch(-class) of the series is a member of either the diminished seventh chord C♯/E/G/B♭ (henceforth 'dim1') or the diminished seventh chord B/D/F/A♭ (henceforth 'dim2'). When the entire series is transposed down a whole tone on line 2 of the

---

[36] That is, for values a = C♯, b = B, c = E, d = B♭, e = F, f = G, g = E, h = B♭ and i = E.

array, pitch classes that were members of dim1 on the first line are mapped onto members of dim2 on the second line (because dim2 is a transposition down by a whole tone of dim1). Pitch classes that were members of dim2 on the first line are mapped on the second line onto members of the diminished seventh chord A/C/E♭/F♯ (henceforth 'dim3'). These are the ones that lie outside mode 2^2 as dim3 is foreign to it. Via the same principle, pitch classes outside mode 2^2 occur exclusively in the following even-numbered lines of the array (lines 4, 6, 8, etc.) while the odd-numbered lines, as observed earlier, stay entirely in mode 2^2. In order to identify the places in the array where pitch classes foreign to mode 2^2 occur, we thus simply need to track what happens to the members of dim2 from the original series on line 1 (pitch classes B and F in second and fifth position). Via transposed rotation, they project pitch classes foreign to the mode as circled in Example 4.17, namely in positions 4 and 7 of the second line (A and E♭), positions 8 and 1 of the fourth line (F♯, C), 2 and 5 of the sixth line (E♭, A), 6 and 9 of the eighth line (C, F♯) and 10 and 3 of the tenth line (A, E♭). In other words, in the first ten lines we find a pitch class foreign to the mode exactly once in each of positions 1 to 10. The same holds for lines 11–20 of the array because they are an exact transposition by T_{-15} of lines 1–10, as we have seen. Since that transposition is not by octave or any compound thereof, each of verticals I–X of the 20-part counterpoint contains exactly *two* different pitch classes (pitches) that are foreign to mode 2^2.

2. Another way of predicting the number of pitches foreign to mode 2^2 in each vertical goes as follows: In the pitch-class cycle for the odd-numbered verticals in Example 4.20a, four of the five variables are members of dim1 (a = C♯, c = E, g = E, i = E). Under the transposition operations listed in the first column, these pitch classes map onto pitch classes of either dim1 itself (via transposition by -3, -6 and -9) or dim2 (via transposition by -2, -5, -8 and -11). The resulting pitch classes thus are all still members of mode 2^2 (which consists of dim1 + dim2). One of the five variables (e = F) will map onto a pitch class foreign to this mode half of the time, namely under transposition by -2, -5, -8 and -11. (Under transposition by -3, -6 and -9 the result stays within the mode. No other transpositions are used anywhere in the pitch-class cycle). Since the five variables (a, c, e, g, i) are evenly distributed over the entire cycle (see the first column), with each occurring eight times overall, the eight occurrences of e will produce exactly four results outside mode 2^2 (i.e. half of the time), evenly spaced in the cycle as marked by → . Since each of verticals I, III, V, VII and IX uses exactly half of the pitch-class cycle (a segment of size 20), it contains exactly two pitches (pitch classes) foreign to mode 2^2. The same can be shown for the even-numbered verticals in Example 4.20b, where again only one out of the five variables (now b = B) leads to pitch classes outside the mode, half the time.

Counterpoint and Contrapuntal Transformation

Many of the contrapuntal techniques we have seen in the foregoing examples appear to be inspired by music of the past that is commonly studied in counterpoint classes. A perusal of counterpoint treatises with which Messiaen would have been familiar corroborates this observation. Such treatises usually proceed from an introduction of voice-leading rules to various techniques of imitation and contrapuntal transformation, including – to quote from one of the leading texts – 'simple and invertible counterpoint, ... imitation in direct, contrary, retrograde motion; augmentation, diminution, canons, etc.'[37] These contrapuntal devices can all be found in Messiaen's music and yet they are at times easily overlooked because the musical surface may sound more 'harmonic' than 'contrapuntal'. The harmonic quality of a given passage may distract attention from its inner contrapuntal life; we may not notice that a harmonic progression is built from individually crafted distinct lines or that a harmonic progression may have been transformed via vertical-shifting counterpoint where the result, although generated via contrapuntal transformation, still sounds 'harmonic' rather than polyphonic. All in all, Messiaen's contrapuntal devices are often hidden.[38]

---

[37] '*Contrepoint simple et renversable*, ... *imitations* par *mouvements* DIRECT, CONTRAIRE, RÉTROGRADE; AUGMENTATION, DIMINUTION, CANONS, etc.' (italics and capital letters in the original). André Gedalge, *Traité de la fugue 1re partie: De la fugue d'école* (Paris: Enoch & Cie, 1901), p. 7. The four parts of *Traité de contrepoint et de Fugue* by Théodore Dubois (Paris: Heugel & Cie., 1901) follow the same overall outline ('Contrepoint simple' to 'Contrepoint fleuri', 'Imitations', 'Contrepoint Double, Triple et Quadruple' and 'Fugue').

[38] The close association of, and hence often blurred distinction between, counterpoint and harmony is stressed by many encyclopedia and textbook authors, while others insist on a clearer differentiation. To quote from three sources that were likely familiar to Messiaen: In his entry on 'contrepoint' in the *Encyclopédie de la Musique* (Paris: Fasquelle, 1958, p. 585) Messiaen's former student Pierre Boulez states that 'Il est évident qu'aucune musique ne peut être dite strictement contrapuntique ou strictement harmonique' and that 'Au fur et à mesure que la musique évolua, ces deux tendances se sont interpénétrées de plus en plus pour donner naissance à une espèce de style libre, avec de nombreux degrés de variation entre l'homophonie pure et la polyphonie pure'. In the section on counterpoint at the end of Henri Reber's *Traité d'Harmonie* (Paris: Colombier, n.d., p. 265) – a textbook originally published in 1862 and widely used at the Conservatoire – the author observes that 'il [le mot CONTREPOINT] a donc, sous beaucoup de rapports, la même signification que le mot *harmonie*, et dans beaucoup de cas, la distinction entre ces deux termes devient illusoire et inutile'. On the other hand, in the descriptive index of *Histoire de la Langue Musicale* (Paris: H. Laurens, 1951, Vol. 2, p. 644), Maurice Emmanuel (with whom Messiaen studied) stresses that 'Il faut distinguer formellement le Contrepoint, de l'Harmonie simultanée. Celle-ci codifie les ressources sonores offertes par la Résonance plus ou moins largement interprétée, et rectifiée. Le Contrepoint ne se gêne pas pour contrevenir aux formules harmoniques et il tolère, il favorise même certaines âpretés de langage qui sont, en harmonie

The following final example examines traces of contrapuntal thinking in an excerpt from Messiaen's last and unfinished work, *Concert à quatre*. Admittedly, the 23 bars of 'Thème A' that open the first movement do not sound particularly contrapuntal (nor does the rest of the movement) because individual lines move mostly note-against-note with each other. The upper part of Example 4.21 summarizes the pitch materials of 'Thème A' (bars 1–23, octave doublings mostly omitted). The lower part shows how this material is transformed when it recurs in the second half of the movement (bars 83–107).[39] I have identified modes and chord types, marked melodic intervals in bars 1–4 and 9–13, highlighted motivic associations in bars 14–18 and analysed the motivic contours inside the turning chords of bars 21–23.[40] In addition, I have indicated at the bottom how Messiaen transposes individual segments of 'Thème A' when it reappears in the second half of the movement.

Each of the three lines that open the movement follows the same melodic contour, itself inspired by the opening melody of Susanna's aria from *Le nozze di Figaro*.[41] The three lines do not move exactly parallel within the mode throughout, perhaps because Messiaen wanted the progression to alternate between minor and major harmonic triads. In parallel motion this would only be possible if all lines were to move by odd-numbered intervals (as is the case from the third to the fourth chord). In bars 12–13 the three upper lines also share the same contour, again without moving parallel throughout probably in order to obtain the desired chord types (quartal harmony at the lowest points of the motive and triads for the rest) and to avoid too many common tones between successive triads.[42]

Interesting contrapuntal details also characterize the remainder of 'Thème A'. As beamed in the section of bars 14–18, the solo line (oboe) embellishes a contour that is also found in the top two lines of the accompaniment (a motive that moves by +1, -1, -2 scale degrees – perhaps in a hidden reference to *Silent Night*?). The

---

pure, de véritables accidents.' In other words, for Emmanuel non-chordal dissonances no doubt belong exclusively in the realm of counterpoint, not harmony.

[39] The binary form of the movement is mentioned in Messiaen's own notes to the work as reported by Yvonne Loriod in the Preface to the score published by Alphonse Leduc in 2003 (p. vii).

[40] The distinction between the two kinds of chords of contracted resonance (1st CCR, 2nd CCR) follows Wai-Ling Cheong, 'Rediscovering Messiaen's Invented Chords', *Acta Musicologica*, 75/1 (2003): pp. 85–105.

[41] The source of this melodic contour is identified in Messiaen's notes, as reported in the preface to the score, though ambiguously so – see Christopher Dingle, 'Messiaen and Mozart: A Love without Influence?' in *Messiaen Perspectives 1*, and the discussion of the *Concert à quatre* in chapter 24 of Christopher Dingle, *Messiaen's Final Works* (Farnham: Ashgate, 2013).

[42] This contour – which unlike the one from *Figaro* is not identified in the preface to the score – is based on Grieg ('Solveig's Song' from *Peer Gynt*) and also has a long history in Messiaen's music. In *Technique*, examples 80–84, he gives several examples of its use in his early works.

Example 4.21 Analytical sketch for 'Thème A' from *Concert à quatre*, I, 'Entrée'

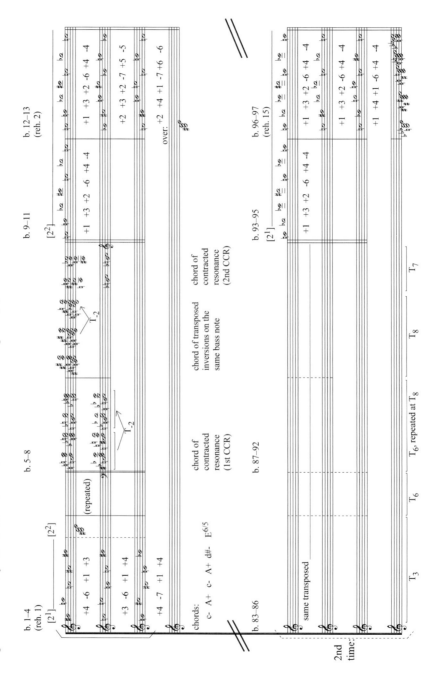

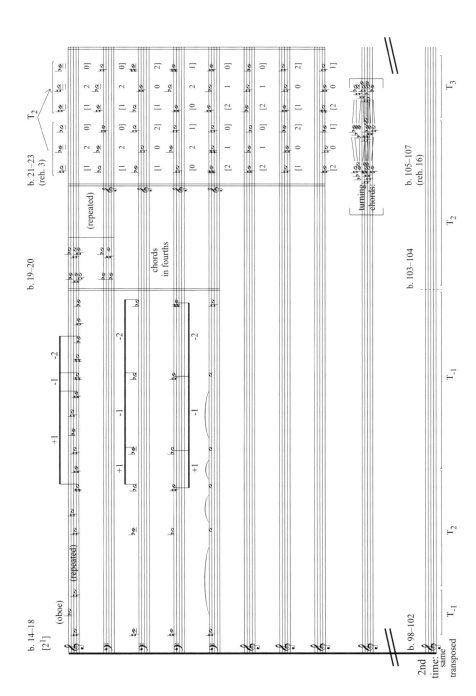

motive progresses at a slightly different pace in the accompaniment, creating a kind of transposed heterophony. In bars 21–23 'Thème A' comes to a close with two statements of the turning chord progression in which the eight individual lines move as shown, in contradistinction to a more straightforward voice-leading realization indicated in parenthesis below these bars on the example, in which the top line would follow the succession of highest notes, the second line the string of second-to-highest notes, and so on. In the latter voice-leading, some of the lines would have to repeat pitches (lines 2, 3, 5, 6).[43] Messiaen evidently avoids this by having his lines crisscross more actively, as the analysis of the contours in square brackets further illustrates. In each turning chord progression each line sounds three different pitches, abbreviated in the analysis as 0, 1, 2 according to their relative position from lowest to highest. Six of the lines zigzag (contours [120], [102], [021], [201]) and hence are related via contour inversion, retrogradation and retrograde-inversion. Two of the lines descend ([210]).[44] The overall result is a carefully orchestrated contrapuntal texture with intricate internal motivic relationships. The zigzagging in most of the lines reinforces the 'turning' aspect of the chord progression.[45]

Transformations inspired by contrapuntal thinking play out on the larger formal scale of this movement as well. When the entire 'Thème A' (bars 1–23) is repeated later in the second half (bars 83–107), individual segments are transposed by different intervals as noted at the bottom of the example. This strategy recalls the *agrandissements asymétriques* shown earlier in the sense that here too a passage is parsed into shorter units that are then transposed by different intervals. However, unlike in the continuously reapplied transpositions of *agrandissements asymétriques* (Example 4.3, left hand of bars 3–6 and 9), 'Thème A' as a whole is subjected to transpositional transformation only once. The modification of 'Thème

---

[43] This is in part due to the fact that the first and second chords share six pitch classes, as do the second and third chords.

[44] In other words, only one of the six possible contours with three different pitches is not used, the ascending [012].

[45] Latry and Mallié attribute the name 'accords tournants' to the *tournoiement inégal* in the eight lines of the more straightforward realization of the progression (the one indicated in parenthesis). See Olivier Latry and Loïc Mallié, *L'œuvre d'orgue d'Olivier Messiaen: Œuvres d'avant-guerre* (Stuttgart: Carus, 2008), pp. 30–31. In essence, Messiaen's orchestration of the progression further amplifies this contrapuntal feature. According to the foreword to the score of *Concert à quatre*, the first part of the first movement was orchestrated at the time of Messiaen's death. Without access to the manuscript sources I have not, however, been able to verify this. I assume that the contours just examined are as Messiaen intended them. Similarly orchestrated crossing contours inside turning chords can already be found much earlier in Messiaen's music, as for instance in the fourth movement of *Et exspecto resurrectionem mortuorum* (at rehearsal 6) or the eighth movement from *La Transfiguration* (at rehearsal 6). Messiaen specifically points out the need for crossing instrumental lines in the orchestration of the latter passage, in order to avoid repeating notes. See *Traité VII*, p. 277. Messiaen also permutes the order of the chords.

A' also bears resemblance to Messiaen's vertical-shifting counterpoints, but with the notable distinction that various transpositions are applied here to *juxtaposed* and not to *superimposed* materials.[46] Proper vertical-shifting counterpoint does occur in bars 96–97, on the other hand: the three upper lines move mostly in parallel motion within the mode, almost entirely a perfect fourth above the corresponding passage in bars 12–13. However, in bars 96–97 the three upper lines are accompanied not by a stationary harmony as was the case earlier (bars 12–13) but by different transpositions of that harmony (dominant seventh chords in first inversion). These create new relationships with the triads in the upper three lines and thus new overall harmonies result, generated via double counterpoint.

Concert à quatre was posthumously published with the four movements partially completed by Yvonne Loriod 'in consultation with Heinz Holliger and George Benjamin'.[47] As we learn from the preface to the score, Messiaen had planned a fifth movement that would have been a 'fugue with four subjects'.[48] There could be no clearer sign of Messiaen's continuing interest in counterpoint, and while it seems pointless to speculate what this final fugue would have looked like, the biographical circumstances would certainly have rendered it a most personal reference to the great baroque master whose appropriation by the neoclassicists decades earlier had so irritated Messiaen.

The examples we have seen demonstrate how Messiaen engaged and modified contrapuntal strategies throughout his career. Beyond more direct allusions to traditional counterpoint such as in motivic imitation, we can discern in particular five characteristic ways in which his music employs and transforms contrapuntal principles. First, Messiaen may take a contrapuntal combination, such as a melody and countermelody, and attach a string of (parallel) chords to one or both. Second, he may superimpose layers of more or less independent material where each layer presents a different type of texture, mode and so on. Third, he may construct chord progressions from intricate voice-leading patterns, with or without internal motivic correspondences. Fourth, he may subject a given passage to invertible or double counterpoint or various other transformational procedures. And fifth, he may expand a typical contrapuntal pattern, such as a passing tone motion, into a larger group, a 'passing group' (the large-scale chromatic wedges

---

[46] I have been unable to discern a particular principle behind the transpositions to which Messiaen subjects 'Thème A' the second time. The transpositions by 3, 6 and 8 semitones in bars 83–92 (T_3, T_6, T_8) relate, via retrogradation, to the end of motive (D♭)–E♭–D♭–B♭ in bars 16–18 (E♭ corresponding to 8, D♭ to 6 and B♭ to 3 semitones over pedal G). Likewise, the transpositions by –1, 2 and 3 semitones in bars 98–107 (T_{-1}, T_2, T_3) relate to the end of motive (A)–B♭–A–F♯ in bars 16–18 (B♭ corresponding to 3, A to 2 and F♯ to –1 semitones over pedal G). Using T_3 followed by T_6 in bars 83–86 allows Messiaen to stay within the same modes as in the beginning of the movement. Transposition by T_{-1} and T_2 in bars 98–102 keeps this entire passage in one and the same mode (2^3).

[47] PHNS, p. 377.

[48] Preface, p. vii.

underlying *agrandissements asymétriques* exemplify this).[49] Further, Messiaen may carry transformational procedures from one dimension into another, as when a rhythm's systematic augmentation and diminution inspires the augmentation and diminution of the intervals in a motive. Most of these techniques go back to traditional contrapuntal concepts. But rejecting a more literal, neoclassical use of historical contrapuntal models, Messiaen takes their principles and applies them in new ways, transforming counterpoint into something distinctively his own.

---

[49] Passing groups and other enlargement techniques are discussed in Chapter XV of *Technique* (examples 302–11).

Intermède 1

Chapter 5
A Catalogue of Messiaen's Birds

Robert Fallon

Wisdom begins with calling a thing by its proper name. (Chinese proverb)

The names of Messiaen's birds have proved vexatious from the start. In the preface to the score of *Quatuor pour la fin du Temps*, Messiaen writes ambiguously that 'a Blackbird or a Nightingale soloist improvises', as if he himself did not know which bird was singing in his music. And in the second 'Note de l'auteur' of *Oiseaux exotiques,* which lists all the work's species, there is no mention of the White-throated Sparrow [Pinson à Gorge Blanche], whose song appears in the flute on page 41. Neither Messiaen's prefaces nor his scores are wholly reliable inventories of his birds. Performers wishing to follow Messiaen's recommendation in *Réveil des oiseaux* to 'walk in the forest, in spring, especially early in the morning, in order to study his models' may therefore have difficulties when the species are misnamed or not named at all. Such problems are found throughout his works. The purpose of this catalogue (Table 5.1) is to free Messiaen's birds from their current ragged state of nomenclature by providing a proper name for when one is needed.

From the ornithological perspective, the one proper name in the lists of birds that front Messiaen's scores is the Latin scientific binomial (e.g. *Homo sapiens*), whose principles of nomenclature Linnaeus laid out in 1753. While this system remains in use, Latin names are increasingly sharing space with vernacular names. In January 2012, for example, botanical taxonomists adopted a new International Code of Nomenclature for algae, fungi and plants that permits the description of new taxa to be submitted in English or Latin, instead of Latin alone. In a similar move from the mid-1980s, the International Ornithological Congress – now the International Ornithologists' Union (IOU) – initiated a project to standardize the vernacular names of the world's birds, which frequently suffer from the confusion of contending or outdated names, as when the Bullock's Oriole and Baltimore Oriole were once thought to be the same species called the Northern Oriole. The new, standardized French names were published in 1993 and the English names followed in 2006; both are endorsed by the IOU.[1] The present catalogue matches

---

[1] The French names first appeared in P. Devillers and H. Ouellet, *Noms français des oiseaux du monde avec les equivalent latins et anglais: Commission internationale des noms français des oiseaux* (Sainte-Foy, Québec and Chabaud, Bayonne, France: Multimondes, 1993). The first edition of these names is published in Frank Gill and Minturn Wright, *Birds of the World: Recommended English Names* (Princeton: Princeton University Press, 2006).

114   *Messiaen Perspectives 2: Techniques, Influence and Reception*

the IOU's recommended English names with Messiaen's French names in order to avoid the confusion created by the use of nonstandard names.

This catalogue also aims to redress some of the problems found in the two previously published lists of Messiaen's birds, beginning with drawing its data not from the prefaces, but from every page of every relevant score. The earliest published list is the third appendix in Robert Sherlaw Johnson's *Messiaen*, which appeared while Messiaen was still composing and thus went quickly out of date. The publisher of the 2008 edition of Johnson's book did not permit the updating of this list, which consequently omits species heard in such final works as *La Ville d'En-Haut, Éclairs sur l'Au-Delà...* and *Concert à quatre*. Johnson includes 342 species, this catalogue lists 357. Like Johnson's list, the one prepared by Yvonne Loriod in Chapter 8 of *Traité V:2* is incomplete and lacks 40 of the species listed here, as she acknowledges: 'It's a list frequently requested by musicians, musicologists, and ornithologists. It can only be incomplete because this is a treatise and not a catalogue.'[2] These lists are organized according to different principles. Johnson groups birds by their continent of origin and subdivides some continents by country, leading him to list some birds, such as the Moqueur des Tropiques, twice. Loriod organizes her list by composition and orders the compositions by their instrumentation, from solo piano to opera. Some of Messiaen's multi-movement works list the birds within each movement, but others do not.

In contrast to previously published lists, this catalogue:

- includes all of the bird species in Messiaen's compositions
- names all species in each movement, listed chronologically by work
- uses the recommended English names on the IOU's World Bird List (www. worldbirdnames.org)

The advantage of offering a complete (rather than incomplete) listing of Messiaen's named birds is self-evident. This catalogue begins with *Quatuor pour la fin du Temps*, which initiated both a significant increase in the *style oiseau* and in Messiaen's practice of attributing species to his birdsong; the songs in many of his early works – and even in later ones such as *Harawi* and *Île de feu 1* – cannot be identified with a particular species and are often marked 'comme un oiseau'.[3] The birds are not listed in taxonomic, zoogeographical or alphabetical order, however, but by the order they appear movement by movement and within each movement.

An updated list with names in 20 languages may be found online at www.worldbirdnames. org. Another useful online resource is the Cornell Lab of Ornithology's website, www. allaboutbirds.org, which provides a French name for many species (listed in the Other Names section under the tab for a species's life history).

    [2]   *Traité V:2*, p. 628.

    [3]   For an account of these 'early' birds and their significance, see Robert Fallon, *Messiaen's Mimesis: The Language and Culture of the Bird Styles*, PhD diss. (University of California at Berkeley, 2005).

This mode of presentation enables the reader to distinguish the movements with many, few or no birds, and to track the appearance of birds, including individual species, as they occur throughout Messiaen's works. This presentation may prove particularly useful in discerning any symbolic meaning in his birds, as the movement titles often provide them with a theological context. The correlation of the French name with the standard ornithological name in English is designed to solve several problems faced by performers and scholars of Messiaen. First, the use of ornithological nomenclature raises awareness of basic differences such as those between the European Robin and the American Robin. Second, it provides an authoritative and frequently reviewed standard for the shifting and contentious naming of birds. Third, this catalogue facilitates the proper identification of several of Messiaen's birds, whose species have been made uncertain by Messiaen's own dubiety and use of invented or anachronistic names. Fourth, it may enable anglophone readers to remember the names of birds more easily than if they are presented in Messiaen's original French.

The use of IOU names will prove particularly useful for studies that involve the comparison of Messiaen's birds with those of other composers or with actual birdsong as well as for studies referring to ornithological literature. These names may have little relevance for studies whose purview remains principally within that of a single score.

Both Johnson and Loriod acknowledge the difficulties that arise from creating such a list.[4] The reasoning behind each problematic species's identification is beyond the scope of this introduction, but takes into account evidence from the prefaces to Messiaen's scores, his other writings, and other sources that help to confirm the identity of the species.[5] Two caveats may interest some readers. First, Messiaen portrays the flight, rather than the song, of two species: the Aigle Royal [Golden Eagle] in 'Le Chocard des Alpes' and the Hirondelle de Cheminée [Barn Swallow] in *La Fauvette des jardins*. Second, the indicated zoogeographical regions (indicating their mating locations) do not always correspond to Messiaen's, though they may provide a kind of initial geographical setting for his birds as well as his music.

This catalogue reveals several unusual facts about how Messiaen used birds in his music. He transcribed 357 different species in his compositions. Counting species once per movement, he composed a total of 757 birdsongs, not including the unlabelled ones that enliven his music composed before *Réveil des oiseaux*, his first ornithologically informed piece. Most of the species in Messiaen's bird style appear only once or twice in all of his compositions. In fact, 91 per cent of

---

[4]   See Robert Sherlaw Johnson, *Messiaen* (London: Omnibus Press, 2008), p. 211, and *Traité V:2*, pp. 636–7.

[5]   For example, see the justification for including the unnamed Manus Friarbird in movement 9 of *Éclairs*, listed here in brackets, in Christopher Dingle, *Messiaen's Final Works* (Farnham: Ashgate, 2013), p. 343, note e. Dingle's identification of the bird as the Manus Friarbird is highly plausible.

his 357 species appear in no more than three of the 186 movements he composed after the *Quatuor pour la fin du Temps*. Despite his overriding concern for variety, Messiaen did have a few favourite species. The Common Blackbird sings in 28 movements, the Garden Warbler in 22, and the Common Nightingale in 20. One surprising source of variety is the large number of non-songbirds that he set to music. Although Messiaen claimed to have been interested in the best avian singers, fully 16 per cent of his birds are drawn from the weak songsters of the nonpasserines.[6] This sizeable percentage of birds that squawk rather than sing underscores Messiaen's commitment to representing a wide variety of bird species. In all, his transcriptions represent 3.6 per cent of the world's species, 38 per cent of its families, and 47 per cent of its orders.

The catalogue's four columns provide the composition title and date in bold (with the movement titles below it), the French name as it appears in the score (or sometimes, for works composed before 1952, in his programme notes), the IOU name, and the IOU listing of the species's zoogeographical region.

Table 5.1   A Catalogue of Messiaen's Birds

Title	French Name	IOU English Name	Region
Quatuor pour la fin du Temps (1940–41)			
1. Liturgie de cristal	Merle Noir	Common Blackbird	EU, OR
	Rossignol	Common Nightingale	EU
3. Abîme des oiseaux	Merle Noir	Common Blackbird	EU, OR
4. Intermède	Merle Noir	Common Blackbird	EU, OR
Visions de l'Amen (1942–43)			
5. Amen des Anges, des Saints, du chant des Oiseaux	Merle Noir	Common Blackbird	EU, OR
	Pinson	Common Chaffinch	EU
	Rossignol	Common Nightingale	EU
	Fauvette des Jardins	Garden Warbler	EU

---

[6]   Ornithologists divide the world's nearly 10,000 bird species into three large categories. The true songbirds are called the oscine passerines; the suboscine passerines are related to these because they, too, perch on branches, though they generally do not sing as mellifously as the oscine passerines. The remaining birds constitute the nonpasserines, which include seagulls, ostriches and eagles.

A Catalogue of Messiaen's Birds

Title	French Name	IOU English Name	Region
Trois Petites Liturgies (1943–44)			
1. Antienne de la Conversation intérieure	Merle Noir	Common Blackbird	EU, OR
	Pinson	Common Chaffinch	EU
	Rossignol	Common Nightingale	EU
	Alouette des Champs	Eurasian Skylark	EU
	Fauvette des Jardins	Garden Warbler	EU
Vingt Regards sur l'Enfant-Jésus (1944)			
8. Regard des hauteurs	Rossignol	Common Nightingale	EU
	Merle Noir	Common Blackbird	EU, OR
	Alouette des Champs	Eurasian Skylark	EU
Turangalîla-Symphonie (1946–48)			
6. Jardin du sommeil d'amour	Merle Noir	Common Blackbird	EU, OR
	Rossignol	Common Nightingale	EU
	Fauvette des Jardins	Garden Warbler	EU
Messe de la Pentecôte (1950–51)			
3. Offertoire	Merle Noir	Common Blackbird	EU, OR
4. Communion	Merle Noir	Common Blackbird	EU, OR
	Rossignol	Common Nightingale	EU
5. Sortie	Alouette des Champs	Eurasian Skylark	EU
Livre d'orgue (1951–52)			
4. Chants d'oiseaux	Merle Noir	Common Blackbird	EU, OR
	Rossignol	Common Nightingale	EU
	Grive Musicienne	Song Thrush	EU
	Rougegorge	European Robin	EU
7. Soixante-quatre durées	Mésange Charbonnière	Great Tit	EU, OR
	Merle Noir	Common Blackbird	EU, OR
	Pic Vert	European Green Woodpecker	EU
	Grive Musicienne	Song Thrush	EU

Title	French Name	IOU English Name	Region
	Fauvette à Tête Noir	European Blackcap	EU
	Rossignol	Common Nightingale	EU
Le Merle noir (1952)	Merle Noir	Common Blackbird	EU, OR
Réveil des oiseaux (1953)	Rossignol	Common Nightingale	EU
	Chouette Chevèche	Little Owl	EU, AF
	Torcol	Eurasian Wryneck	EU
	Bouscarle	Cetti's Warbler	EU
	Alouette Lulu	Woodlark	EU
	Merle Noir	Common Blackbird	EU, OR
	Engoulevent	European Nightjar	EU
	Pouillot Véloce	Common Chiffchaff	EU
	Rougegorge	European Robin	EU
	Grive Musicienne	Song Thrush	EU
	Pinson	Common Chaffinch	EU
	Grive Draine	Mistle Thrush	EU
	Fauvette Grisette	Common Whitethroat	EU
	Coucou	Common Cuckoo	EU
	Pic Épeiche	Great Spotted Woodpecker	EU
	Hypolaïs Polyglotte	Melodious Warbler	EU
	Huppe	Eurasian Hoopoe	EU, OR
	Pic Vert	European Green Woodpecker	EU
	Accenteur Mouchet	Dunnock	EU
	Moineau	House Sparrow	EU, OR, AF
	Rouge-queue à Front Blanc	Common Redstart	EU
	Loriot	Eurasian Golden Oriole	EU
	Corneille Noire	Carrion Crow	EU
	Pie	Eurasian Magpie	EU
	Fauvette à Tête Noire	Eurasian Blackcap	EU
	Tourterelle	European Turtle Dove	EU
	Mésange Bleue	Blue Tit	EU

Title	French Name	IOU English Name	Region
	Linotte	Common Linnet	EU
	Troglodyte	Winter Wren	NA, EU
	Fauvette des Jardins	Garden Warbler	EU
	Pouillot Fitis	Willow Warbler	EU
	Verdier	European Greenfinch	EU
	Serin des Canaries	Atlantic Canary	AF
	Sittelle	Eurasian Nuthatch	EU
	Chardonneret	European Goldfinch	EU
	Étourneau Sansonnet	Common Starling	EU
	Pouillot Bonelli	Western Bonelli's Warbler	EU
	Pigeon Ramier	Common Wood Pigeon	EU
Oiseaux exotiques (1955–56)			
	Mainate Hindou	Hindou Gracula	OR
	Garrulaxe de l'Himalaya	White-crested Laughingthrush	OR
	Leiothrix de Chine	Red-billed Leiothrix	OR
	Grive des Bois	Wood Thrush	NA
	Verdin de Malaisie	Lesser Green Leafbird	OR
	Troupiale de Baltimore	Baltimore Oriole	NA
	Grive de Californie	California Thrasher	NA
	Cardinal Rouge de Virginie	Northern Cardinal	NA, MA
	Tétras Cupidon des Prairies	Greater Prairie Chicken	NA
	Troupiale des Vergers	Orchard Oriole	NA, MA
	Carouge à Épaulettes Jaunes	Yellow-shouldered Blackbird	NA
	Bulbul Orphée	Red-whiskered Bulbul	OR
	Merle Migrateur	American Robin	NA, MA
	Chouette de la Louisiane	Barred Owl	NA, MA

Title	French Name	IOU English Name	Region
	Pape Indigo ou Ministre	Indigo Bunting	NA
	Merle de Swainson	Swainson's Thrush	NA
	Guiraca à Poitrine Rose	Rose-breasted Grosbeak	NA
	Grive Ermite	Hermit Thrush	NA
	Shama des Indes	White-rumped Shama	OR
	Pinson à Couronne Blanche	White-crowned Sparrow	NA
	Amazone	Orange-winged Amazon	SA
	Bruant Renard	Fox Sparrow	NA
	Gros-bec à Tête Noire	Black-headed Grosbeak	NA
	Engoulevent Criard	Whip-poor-will	NA
	Tangara Rouge	Summer Tanager	NA
	Pinson Chanteur d'Amérique	Song Sparrow	NA
	Tangara Écarlate	Scarlet Tanager	NA
	Colin de Gambel	Gambel's Quail	NA, MA
	Moqueur Polyglotte	Northern Mockingbird	NA, MA
	Serin des Canaries	Atlantic Canary	AF
	Pinson à Ailes Baies	Vesper Sparrow	NA
	Colin de Californie	California Quail	NA, MA
	Pinson à Gorge Blanche	White-throated Sparrow	NA
	Dindon Sauvage	Wild Turkey	NA, MA
	Sturnelle à Collier	Eastern Meadowlark	NA, LA
	Oiseau-chat	Grey Catbird	NA
	Bobolink	Bobolink	NA
	Tangara de la Louisiane	Western Tanager	NA, MA
	Troglodyte de Caroline	Carolina Wren	NA, MA
	Grive Rousse	Brown Thrasher	NA

Title	French Name	IOU English Name	Region
	Viréo aux Yeux Rouges	Red-eyed Vireo	NA, LA
	Alouette Oreillard	Horned Lark	NA, MA, EU
	Roselin Pourpré	Purple Finch	NA
	Viréo Gris-olive	Warbling Vireo	NA, MA
	Viréo à Front Jaune	Yellow-throated Vireo	NA
	Pape Lazuli	Lazuli Bunting	NA
	Viréo à Tête Bleue	Blue-headed Vireo	NA
Catalogue d'oiseaux (1956–58)			
1. Le Chocard des Alpes	Chocard des Alpes	Alpine Chough	EU
	Aigle Royal	Golden Eagle	NA, MA, EU
	Grand Corbeau	Northern Raven	NA, MA, EU
2. Le Loriot	Loriot	Eurasian Golden Oriole	EU
	Rouge Queue à Front Blanc	Common Redstart	EU
	Troglodyte	Winter Wren	NA, EU
	Rougegorge	European Robin	EU
	Merle Noir	Common Blackbird	EU, OR
	Grive Musicienne	Song Thrush	EU
	Fauvette des Jardins	Garden Warbler	EU
	Pouillot Véloce	Common Chiffchaff	EU
3. Le Merle bleu	Martinet Noir	Common Swift	EU
	Merle Bleu	Blue Rock Thrush	EU, OR
	Cochevis de Thékla	Thekla Lark	AF
	Goéland Argenté	Herring Gull	NA, MA, EU
4. Le Traquet stapazin	Traquet Stapazin	Black-eared Wheatear	EU
	Bruant Ortolan	Ortolan Bunting	EU
	Fauvette à Lunettes	Spectacled Warbler	EU

Title	French Name	IOU English Name	Region
	Goéland Argenté	Herring Gull	NA, MA, EU
	Grand Corbeau	Northern Raven	NA, MA, EU
	Chardonneret	European Goldfinch	EU
	Fauvette Orphée	Orphean Warbler	EU
	Bruant Fou	Rock Bunting	EU
	Bruant Proyer	Corn Bunting	EU
	Hypolaïs Polyglotte	Melodious Warbler	EU
	Cochevis de Thékla	Thekla Lark	AF
5. La Chouette hulotte	Hibou Moyen-duc	Long-Eared Owl	NA, MA, EU
	Chouette Chevèche	Little Owl	EU, AF
	Chouette Hulotte	Tawny Owl	EU
6. L'Alouette lulu	Alouette Lulu	Woodlark	EU
	Rossignol	Common Nightingale	EU
7. La Rousserolle effarvatte	Rousserolle Effarvatte	Eurasian Reed Warbler	EU
	Merle Noir	Common Blackbird	EU, OR
	Pie-grièche	Red-backed Shrike	EU
	Rougequeue Noir	Black Redstart	EU, OR
	Faisan	Common Pheasant	EU
	Bruant des Roseaux	Common Reed Bunting	EU
	Pic Vert	European Green Woodpecker	EU
	Étourneau Sansonnet	Common Starling	EU
	Mésange Charbonnière	Great Tit	EU, OR
	Bergeronnette Grise	White Wagtail	EU
	Locustelle Tachetée	Common Grasshopper Warbler	EU
	Phragmite des Jones	Sedge Warbler	EU
	Rousserolle Turdoïde	Great Reed Warbler	EU
	Mouette Rieuse	Common Black-headed Gull	EU

A Catalogue of Messiaen's Birds

Title	French Name	IOU English Name	Region
	Foulque	Eurasian Coot	EU, OR, AU
	Alouette des Champs	Eurasian Skylark	EU
	Râle d'Eau	Water Rail	EU
	Héron Butor	Eurasian Bittern	Eu
	Rossignol	Common Nightingale	EU
8. L'Alouette calandrelle	Alouette Calandrelle	Greater Short-toed Lark	EU
	Faucon Crécerelle	Common Kestrel	EU, AF
	Caille	Common Quail	AF, EU
	Cochevis Huppé	Crested Lark	EU, AF
	Alouette des Champs	Eurasian Skylark	EU
9. La Bouscarle	Bouscarle	Cetti's Warbler	EU
	Poule d'Eau	Common Moorhen	Worldwide
	Martin-pêcheur	Common Kingfisher	EU, OR
	Merle Noir	Common Blackbird	EU, OR
	Rougegorge	European Robin	EU
	Râle des Genêts	Corn Crake	EU
	Grive Musicienne	Song Thrush	EU
	Troglodyte	Winter Wren	NA, EU
	Pinson	Common Chaffinch	EU
	Fauvette à Tête Noire	Eurasian Blackcap	EU
	Huppé	Eurasian Hoopoe	EU, OR
	Rossignol	Common Nightingale	EU
	Hirondelle de Rivage	Sand Martin	Worldwide
	Bergeronnette Printanière	Western Yellow Wagtail	EU
10. Le Merle de roche	Grand Duc	Eurasian Eagle-Owl	EU
	Choucas	Western Jackdaw	EU
	Rougequeue Noir	Black Redstart	EU, OR
	Merle de Roche	Rufous-tailed Rock Thrush	EU
11. La Buse variable	Buse Variable	Common Buzzard	EU
	Pinson	Common Chaffinch	EU

Title	French Name	IOU English Name	Region
	Bruant Jaune	Yellowhammer	EU
	Grive Draine	Mistle Thrush	EU
	Chardonneret	European Goldfinch	EU
	Hirondelle de Cheminée	Barn Swallow	Worldwide
	Pie-grièche	Red-backed Shrike	EU
	Corneille Noire	Carrion Crow	EU
	Fauvette Grisette	Common Whitethroat	EU
12. Le Traquet rieur	Traquet Rieur	Black Wheatear	EU
	Goéland Argenté	Herring Gull	NA, MA EU
	Merle Bleu	Blue Rock Thrush	EU, OR
	Traquet Stapazin	Black-eared Wheatear	EU
	Martinet Noir	Common Swift	EU
	Fauvette à Lunettes	Spectacled Warbler	EU
13. Le Courlis cendré	Courlis Cendré	Eurasian Curlew	EU
	Sterne Caugek	Sandwich Tern	NA, LA, AF, EU
	Mouette Rieuse	Common Black-headed Gull	EU
	Petit Gravelot	Little Ringed Plover	EU, OR
	Chevalier Gambette	Common Redshank	EU
	Goéland Argenté	Herring Gull	NA, MA, EU
	Goéland Cendré	Mew Gull	NA, EU
	Guillemot de Troïl	Common Murre	NA, EU
	Huîtrier Pie	Eurasian Oystercatcher	EU
	Tournepierre à Collier	Ruddy Turnstone	NA, EU
	Sterne Naine	Little Tern	AF, EU, OR, AU
Chronochromie (1959–60)			
1. Introduction	Balbuzard	Osprey	Worldwide
	Merle Japonais	Japanese Thrush	EU

Title	French Name	IOU English Name	Region
	San Kô Chô Globe-mouches de Paradis du Japon	Japanese Paradise Flycatcher	EU
	Gobemouche Narcisse	Narcissus Flycatcher	EU
	Bouscarle du Japon	Japanese Bush Warbler	EU
	Pygargue	White-tailed Eagle	EU
2. Strophe I	Rouseserolle Verderolle	Marsh Warbler	EU
	Troglodyte	Winter Wren	NA, EU
	Mésange Charbonnière	Great Tit	EU, OR
	Hypolaïs Ictérine	Icterine Warbler	EU
	Fauvette à Tête Noire	Eurasian Blackcap	EU
	Sittelle	Eurasian Nuthatch	EU
3. Antistrophe I	Grive Musicienne	Song Thrush	EU
	Alouette des Champs	Eurasian Skylark	EU
	Attila	Bright-rumped Attila	LA
	Solitaire Ardoise	Slate-coloured Solitaire	MA
	Oropendola de Montezuma	Montezuma Oropendola	MA
	Moqueur des Tropiques	Tropical Mockingbird	LA
	Saltator Grisâtre	Greyish Saltator	LA
	Moqueur Bleu	Blue Mockingbird	MA
	Grive de Gray	Grayson's Thrush	MA
4. Strophe II	Merle Noir	Common Blackbird	EU, OR
	Fauvette des Jardins	Garden Warbler	EU
	Rossignol	Common Nightingale	EU
	Rougegorge	European Robin	EU
	Gorge Bleue	Bluethroat	EU
	Fauvette à Tête Noire	Eurasian Blackcap	EU
	Chardonneret	European Goldfinch	EU
	Hypolaïs Ictérine	Icterine Warbler	EU

Title	French Name	IOU English Name	Region
5. Antistrophe II	Grive Musicienne	Song Thrush	EU
	Alouette des Champs	Eurasian Skylark	EU
	Ani	Groove-billed Ani	LA
	Attila	Bright-rumped Attila	LA
	Solitaire Ardoise	Slate-coloured Solitaire	MA
	Oropendola de Montezuma	Montezuma Oropendola	MA
	Moqueur des Tropiques	Tropical Mockingbird	LA
	Saltator Grisâtre	Greyish Saltator	LA
	Moqueur Bleu	Blue Mockingbird	MA
	Grive de Gray	Grayson's Thrush	MA
6. Épôde	Merle Noir	Common Blackbird	EU, OR
	Bruant Jaune	Yellowhammer	EU
	Chardonneret	European Goldfinch	EU
	Pouillot Véloce	Common Chiffchaff	EU
	Fauvette Grisette	Common Whitethroat	EU
	Fauvette Babillarde	Lesser Whitethroat	EU
	Pinson	Common Chaffinch	EU
	Verdier	European Greenfinch	EU
	Rossignol	Common Nightingale	EU
	Loriot	Eurasian Golden Oriole	EU
	Linotte	Common Linnet	EU
	Fauvette des Jardins	Garden Warbler	EU
7. Coda	Gobemouche Narcisse	Narcissus Flycatcher	EU
	Bouscarle du Japon	Japanese Bush Warbler	EU
	Balbuzard	Osprey	Worldwide
	Zosterope à Lunettes	Japanese White-eye	EU
	Merle Japonais	Japanese Thrush	EU
	Petit Coucou	Lesser Cuckoo	EU
	Cyornis Japonais	Blue Flycatcher	EU
	Pygargue	White-tailed Eagle	EU

Title	French Name	IOU English Name	Region
Verset (*pour la fête de la Dédicace*) (1960)			
	Grive Musicienne	Song Thrush	EU
Sept Haïkaï (1962)			
3. Yamanaka–cadenza	Aoji = Bruant Masqué du Japon	Black-faced Bunting	EU
	Nojiko = Bruant Soufré	Yellow Bunting	EU
	Kuro Tsugumi = Merle Japonais	Japanese Thrush	EU
	Mejiro = Zosterope à Lunettes	Japanese White-eye	EU
	Iwahibari = Accenteur Alpin	Alpine Accentor	EU
	Binzui = Pipit des Arbres	Tree Pipit	EU
	Kibitaki = Gobemouche Narcisse	Narcissus Flycatcher	EU
	San Kô Chô = Gobe-mouches de Paradis du Japon	Japanese Paradise Flycatcher	EU
	Ôruri Cyornis Japonais	Blue Flycatcher	EU
	Aka Hara = Grive à Flancs Roux	Brown-headed Thrush	EU
	Uguisu = Bouscarle du Japon	Japanese Bush Warbler	EU
	Hôaka = Bruant à Tête Grise	Grey-headed Bunting	EU
	Hibari = Alouette des Champs	Japanese Skylark	EU
	Ruribitaki = Rossignol à Flancs Roux	Red-flanked Bluetail	EU, OR
	Sendai Mushikui = Pouillot Couronné	Crowned Willow-warbler	EU
	Juichi = Coucou Épervier du Japon	Large Hawk-Cuckoo	OR

Title	French Name	IOU English Name	Region
	Misosozai = Troglodyte Japonais	Eurasian Wren	EU
	Komadori = Rougegorge du Japon	Japanese Robin	EU
	Nobitaki = Tarier Pâtre	European Stonechat	EU, AF
	Ikaru = Gros-bec Masqué	Japanese Grosbeak	EU
6. Les Oiseaux de Karuizawa	Uguisu = Bouscarle du Japon	Japanese Bush Warbler	EU
	San Kô Chô = Gobe-mouches de Paradis du Japon	Japanese Paradise Flycatcher	EU
	Hototoguisu = Petit Coucou	Lesser Cuckoo	EU
	Komadori = Rougegorge du Japon	Japanese Robin	EU
	Kuro Tsugumi = Merle Japonais	Japanese Thrush	EU
	Kibitaki = Gobemouche Narcisse	Narcissus Flycatcher	EU
	Binzui = Pipit des Arbres	Tree Pipit	EU
	Mejiro = Zosterpoe à Lunettes	Japanese White-eye	EU
	Nojiko = Bruant Soufré	Yellow Bunting	EU
	Aka Hara = Grive à Flancs Roux	Brown-headed Thrush	EU
	Iwahibari = Accenteur Alpin	Alpine Accentor	EU
	Nobitaki = Tarier Pâtre	European Stonechat	EU, AF
	Sendai mushikui = Pouillot Couronné	Crowned Willow-warbler	EU
	Ikaru = Gros-bec Masqué	Japanese Grosbeak	EU
	Hôjiro = Bruant des Prés	Meadow Bunting	EU
	Fukuro = Chouette de l'Oural	Ural Owl	EU

Title	French Name	IOU English Name	Region
	Ruribitaki = Rossignol à Flancs Roux	Red-flanked Bluetail	EU, OR
	Hôaka = Bruant à Tête Grise	Grey-headed Bunting	EU
	Oruri = Ôruri Cyornis Japonais	Blue Flycatcher	EU
	Aoji = Bruant Masqué du Japon	Black-faced Bunting	EU
	Hibari = Alouette des Champs	Japanese Skylark	EU
	Ko-mukudori = Martin aux Joues Rouges	Chestnut-cheeked Starling	EU
	Juichi = Coucou Épervier du Japon	Large Hawk-Cuckoo	OR
	Ô-yoshikiri = Rousserolle Turdoïde	Great Reed Warbler	EU
Couleurs de la Cité céleste (1963)			
	Oiseau Tui	Tui	AU
	Benteveo	Great Kiskadee	NA, LA
	Troglodyte barré	Stripe-backed Wren	SA
	Mohoua à Tête Jaune	Yellowhead	AU
	Oiseau-cloche	New Zealand Bellbird	AU
	Stournelle	Western Meadowlark	NA, MA
	Araponga	Bare-throated Bellbird	SA
	Toucan	Green-billed Toucan	SA
	Engoulevent à Collier Blanc	Pauraque	LA
	Saltator Cendré	Greyish Saltator	LA
	Nestor de Nouvelle-Zélande	New Zealand Kaka	AU
	Cassique Cela	Yellow-rumped Cacique	LA

Title	French Name	IOU English Name	Region
	Grive à ventre Roux	Rufous-bellied Thrush	SA
	Troglodyte à Long Bec	Long-Billed Wren	SA
	Râle Takahé	Takahe	AU
	Hornero	Rufous Hornero	SA
	Moqueur du Venezuela	Venezuelan Mockingbird	SA
Et exspecto resurrectionem mortuorum (1964)			
3. L'heure vient où les morts entendront la voix du Fils de Dieu…	Uirapuru-verdadeiro	Musician Wren	SA
4. Ils ressusciteront, glorieux, avec un nom nouveau	Alouette Calandre	Calandra Lark	EU
La Transfiguration de Notre-Seigneur Jésus-Christ (1965–69)			
2. Configuratum corpori claritatis suae	Grand Indicateur	Greater Honeyguide	AF
	Bulbul	Dark-capped Bulbul	AF
	Grive Grise	Grey Butcherbird	AU
3. Christus Jesus, splendor Patris	Engoulevent de la Caroline	Chuck-will's widow	NA
	Chouette de la Louisiane	Barred Owl	NA, MA
	Chocard des Alpes	Alpine Chough	EU
	Accenteur Alpin	Alpine Accentor	EU
	Chouette des Terriers	Burrowing Owl	NA, LA
	Barbu à Tête Rouge	Red-and-yellow Barbet	AF
	Ani à Bec Lisse	Smooth-billed Ani	NA, LA
	Tangara Rouge	Summer Tanager	NA, MA
	Spréo Superbe	Superb Starling	AF
	Sabía-poliglota	Lawrence's Thrush	SA
	Sabía-verdadeiro	Cocoa Thrush	SA

Title	French Name	IOU English Name	Region
	Fauvette à Tête Noire	Eurasian Blackcap	EU
	Troupiale de Baltimore	Baltimore Oriole	NA
	Perdrix Bartavelle	Rock Partridge	EU
	Grive de Swainson	Swainson's Thrush	NA
5. Quam dilecta tabernacula tua	Rougegorge Bleu d'Amérique	Eastern Bluebird	NA, MA
	Rhipidure de Willie	Willie Wagtail	AU
	Rossignol	Common Nightingale	EU
	Melliphage à Joues Blanches	White-cheeked Honeyeater	AU
	Merle de Roche	Rufous-tailed Rock Thrush	EU
	Accenteur Alpin	Alpine Accentor	EU
	Carouge Noir	Brown-headed Cowbird	NA, MA
6. Candor est lucis aeternae	Fauvette à Tête Grise	Grey-capped Warbler	AF
	Cisticole du Natal	Croaking Cisticola	AF
	Merle Noir	Common Blackbird	EU, OR
	Accenteur Alpin	Alpine Accentor	EU
	Oiseau-chat	Grey Catbird	NA
	Fauvette des Jardins	Garden Warbler	EU
	Hibou Oreillard	Long-eared Owl	NA, MA, EU
	Gelinotte	Hazel Grouse	EU
	Merle de Roche	Rufous-tailed Rock Thrush	EU
	Grive Musicienne	Song Thrush	EU
	Rougegorge	European Robin	EU
	Fauvette à Tête Noire	Eurasian Blackcap	EU
	Merle Gris du Brésil	Andean Slaty Thrush	SA
	Évêque Bleu	Blue-black Grosbeak	LA
	Colombe Talpacoti	Ruddy Ground Dove	LA
	Engoulevent Roux	Rufous Nightjar	LA
	Troglodyte	Winter Wren	NA, EU

Title	French Name	IOU English Name	Region
	Tarin de Magellan	Hooded Siskin	SA
	Chardonneret	European Goldfinch	EU
9. Perfecte conscius illius perfectae generationis	Stournelle de Prés de l'Ouest	Western Meadowlark	NA, MA
	Tichodrome Échelette	Wallcreeper	EU
	Loriot	Eurasian Golden Oriole	EU
	Accenteur Alpin	Alpine Accentor	EU
	Long Bec à Collier Châtain	Long-billed Thrasher	NA, MA
	Viréo Gris Olive	Grey Vireo	NA, MA
	Merle Noir	Common Blackbird	EU, OR
	Fauvette des Jardins	Garden Warbler	EU
	Chocard des Alpes	Alpine Chough	EU
	Pic Noir	Black Woodpecker	EU
	Troglodyte Strié	Band-backed Wren	LA
	Fauvette Orphée	Orphean Warbler	EU
	Hypolaïs des Oliviers	Olive-tree Warbler	EU
	Oropendola de Montezuma	Montezuma Oropendola	MA
	Melocichla Mentalis	Croaking Cisticola	AF
	Moqueur Bleu	Blue Mockingbird	MA
	Merle de Roche	Rufous-tailed Rock Thrush	EU
	Cassique du Mexique	Mexican Cacique	SA
	Bruant Mélanocéphale	Black-headed Bunting	EU
	Solitaire Ardoise	Slate-coloured Solitaire	MA
	Troglodyte à Poitrine Tachetée	Spot-breasted Wren	MA
	Saltator Grisâtre	Greyish Saltator	LA
	Moqueur des Tropiques	Tropical Mockingbird	LA
	Fauvette à Tête Noire	Eurasian Blackcap	EU
	Bobolink	Bobolink	NA

Title	French Name	IOU English Name	Region
10. Adoptionem filiorum perfectam	Bouvreuil à Ailes Roses	Crimson-winged Finch	EU
	Téléphone Tschagra	Black-crowned Tchagra	
	Tangara Écarlate	Summer Tanager	NA, MA
	Spréo Superbe	Superb Starling	AF
	Pape Indigo	Indigo Bunting	NA
	Fauvette à Tête Noire	Eurasian Blackcap	EU
	Merle Noir	Common Blackbird	EU, OR
	Guiraca à Poitrine Rose	Rose-breasted Grosbeak	NA
	Cardinal Rouge de Virginie	Northern Cardinal	NA, MA
	Fauvette Passerinette	Subalpine Warbler	EU
	Alouette Hausse-col	Horned Lark	NA, MA, EU
	Shama des Indes	White-rumped Shama	OR
	Dromoïque du Sahara	Scrub Warbler	EU
	Rubiette de Moussier	Moussier's Redstart	AF
	Bruant Striolé	House Bunting	AF
12. Terribilis est locus iste	Aigle de Bonelli	Bonelli's Eagle	EU, OR
	Faucon Pélerin	Peregrine Falcon	Worldwide
	Pie Grièche à Tête Rousse	Woodchat Shrike	EU
	Autour	Northern Goshawk	Worldwide
	Circaète	Short-toed Snake Eagle	EU, OR
13. Tota Trinitas apparuit	Calao Concolor	African Grey Hornbill	AF
	Siffleur Doré	Australian Golden Whistler	AU
	Moqueur à Tête Noire	Black-capped Donacobius	LA
	Koel	Asian Koel	OR
	Loriot Vert	Olive-backed Oriole	AU

Title	French Name	IOU English Name	Region
	Rouxinol do Rio Negro	Coraya Wren	SA
	Cisticole à Moustaches	Croaking Cisticola	AF
	Siffleur à Ventre Roux	Rufous Whistler	AU
	Grive d'Alice	Grey-cheeked Thrush	NA
	Bobolink	Bobolink	NA
Méditations sur le mystère de la Sainte Trinité (1969)			
2.	Troglodyte	Winter Wren	NA, EU
	Merle Noir	Common Blackbird	EU, OR
	Pinson	Common Chaffinch	EU
	Fauvette des Jardins	Garden Warbler	EU
	Fauvette à Tête Noire	Eurasian Blackcap	EU
	Bruant Jaune	Yellowhammer	EU
4.	Pic Noir	Black Woodpecker	EU
	Merle à Plastron	Ring Ouzel	EU
	Chouette de Tengmalm	Boreal Owl	NA, EU
	Grive Musicienne	Song Thrush	EU
5.	Bruant Jaune	Yellowhammer	EU
7.	'Oiseau de Persepolis', which Messiaen later identified as a Bulbul des Jardins	Common Bulbul	AF
8.	Bruant Jaune	Yellowhammer	EU
9.	Fauvette des Jardins	Garden Warbler	EU
	Fauvette à Tête Noire	Eurasian Blackcap	EU
	Bruant Jaune	Yellowhammer	EU
La Fauvette des jardins (1970)			
	Rossignol	Common Nightingale	EU
	Caille	Common Quail	AF, EU
	Fauvette des Jardins	Garden Warbler	EU
	Troglodyte	Winter Wren	NA, EU

Title	French Name	IOU English Name	Region
	Pic Vert	European Green Woodpecker	EU
	Alouette des Champs	Eurasian Skylark	EU
	Pinson	Common Chaffinch	EU
	Rousserolle Turdoïde	Great Reed Warbler	EU
	Loriot	Eurasian Golden Oriole	EU
	Hirondelle de Cheminée	Barn Swallow	
	Corneille	Carrion Crow	EU
	Pie-grièche	Red-backed Shrike	EU
	Milan Noir	Black Kite	EU, AF, OR, AU
	Merle Noir	Common Blackbird	EU, OR
	Bruant Jaune	Yellowhammer	EU
	Chardonneret	European Goldfinch	EU
	Fauvette à Tête Noire	Eurasian Blackcap	EU
	Chouette Hulotte	Tawny Owl	EU
Des Canyons aux étoiles… (1971–74)			
1. Le désert	Pie Grièche à Plastron Noir	Bokmakierie	AF
	Moqueur Polyglotte	Northern Mockingbird	NA, MA
	Gobemouche Narcisse	Narcissus Flycatcher	EU
	Sirli du Désert	Greater Hoopoe-Lark	AF, EU
2. Les Orioles	Troupiale des Vergers	Orchard Oriole	NA, MA
	Troupiale de Scott	Scott's Oriole	NA, MA
	Boubou	Tropical Boubou	AF
	Troupiale de Lichtenstein	Altamira Oriole	NA, MA
	Merle de Swainson	Swainson's Thrush	NA
	Troupiale de Baltimore	Baltimore Oriole	NA
	Troupiale de Bullock	Bullock's Oriole	NA
	Troupiale à Capuchon Orange	Hooded Oriole	NA, MA

Title	French Name	IOU English Name	Region
3. Ce qui est écrit sur les étoiles…	Solitaire de Townsend	Townsend's Solitaire	NA, MA
	Merle Bleu des Montagnes	Mountain Bluebird	NA
	Viréo de Bell	Bell's Vireo	NA, MA
	Viréo Mélodieux	Warbling Vireo	NA, MA
	Viréo Gris	Grey Vireo	NA, MA
	Ko-mukudori = Martin aux Joues Rouges	Chestnut-cheeked Starling	EU
	Nogoma = Calliope à Gorge Rubis	Siberian Rubythroat	EU
	Tétras Centrocerque	Sage Grouse	NA
	Geai de Californie	Scrub Jay	NA
	Pic Maculé	Ladder-backed Woodpecker	NA, MA
	Troglodyte de Bewick	Bewick's Wren	NA
	Viréo à Tête Noire	Black-capped Vireo	NA, MA
	Troglodyte des Cactus	Cactus Wren	NA, MA
	Troglodyte des Canyons	Canyon Wren	NA, MA
4. Le Cossyphe d'Heuglin	Cossyphe d'Heuglin	White-browed Robin	AU
5. Cedar Breaks et le Don de Crainte	Pic Flèche Rouge	Northern Flicker	NA, MA
	Tétras Obscur	Blue Grouse	NA
	Viréo Gris	Grey Vireo	NA, MA
	Martinet à Gorge Blanche	White-throated Swift	NA, MA
	Casse-noix de Clark	Clark's Nutcracker	NA
	Merle Migrateur	American Robin	NA, MA
	Buse à Queue Rousse	Red-tailed Hawk	NA, MA
	Bruant Renard	Fox Sparrow	NA
	Tohi d'Abert	Abert's Towhee	NA, MA

Title	French Name	IOU English Name	Region
6. Appel interstellaire	Grive Geai de Pékin	Chinese Thrush	EU
	Troglodyte des Canyons	Canyon Wren	NA, MA
7. Bryce Canyon et les rochers rouge-orange	Merle Noir à Tête Jaune	Yellow-headed Blackbird	NA, MA
	Geai Bleu de Steller	Steller's Jay	NA, MA
	Tangara de l'Ouest	Western Tanager	NA
	Troupiale de Scott	Scott's Oriole	NA, MA
	Carouge Bronzé	Bronzed Cowbird	NA, MA
	Mainate Rouillé	Rusty Blackbird	NA
	Tourterelle à Ailes Blanches	White-winged Dove	NA, MA
	Moqueur Polyglotte	Northern Mockingbird	NA, MA
8. Les ressucités et le chant de l'étoile Aldébaran	Grive Ermite	Hermit Thrush	NA
	Grive de Wilson	Veery	NA
	Grive Rousse	Brown Thrasher	NA
	Merle de Swainson	Swainson's Thrush	NA
9. Le Moqueur Polyglotte	Moqueur Polyglotte	Northern Mockingbird	NA, MA
	Siffleur Doré	Australian Golden Whistler	AU
	Oiseau-lyre Superbe	Superb Lyrebird	AU
	Gymnorhine Flûteur à dos Blanc	Australian Magpie	AU
	Oiseau lyre du Prince Albert	Albert's Lyrebird	AU
	Grive Grise	Grey Butcherbird	AU
10. La Grive des bois	Grive des Bois	Wood Thrush	NA
	Grive de Wilson	Veery	NA
	Grive Ermite	Hermit Thrush	NA
	Troglodyte de Caroline	Carolina Wren	NA, MA
11. Omao, Leiothrix, Elapaio, Shama	Shama	White-rumped Shama	OR
	Leiothrix	Red-billed Mesia	OR

Title	French Name	IOU English Name	Region
	Moqueur Polyglotte	Northern Mockingbird	NA, MA
	Kibitaki (Gobemouche Narcisse)	Narcissus Flycatcher	EU
	Fauvette Naine	Grey-capped Warbler	AF
	Bulbul verdâtre	Little Greenbul	AF
	Merle à Poitrine Tachetée	Spotted Palm Thrush	AF
	Tisserin Bicolore	Dark-backed Weaver	AF
	Geai Bleu	Blue Jay	NA
	Bruant Masqué du Japon	Black-faced Bunting	EU
	Dyal Malgache	Madagascar Magpie-Robin	AF
	Gonolek à Ventre Blanc	Swamp Boubou	AF
	Téléphone Tschagra	Black-crowned Tchagra	
	Elepaio	Elepaio	PO
	Alala	Hawaiian Crow	PO
	Omao	Hawaiian Thrush	PO
	Grive Geai de Pékin	Chinese Thrush	EU
	Boubou Shrike	Tropical Boubou	AF
	Moqueur des Armoises	Sage Thrasher	NA
	Apapane	Apapane	PO
	Gorge Blanche	White-throated Sparrow	NA
	Chouette des Terriers	Burrowing Owl	NA, LA
	Pie grièche à Plastron Noir	Bokmakierie	AF
	Grand-duc de Virginie	Great Horned Owl	NA, LA
12. Zion Park et la Cité céleste	Pinson à Ailes Baies	Vesper Sparrow	NA
	Stournelle des Prés de l'Ouest	Western Meadowlark	NA, MA
	Bruant à Nuque Grise	McCow's Longspar	NA
	Pape Pazuli	Lazuli Bunting	NA

A Catalogue of Messiaen's Birds

Title	French Name	IOU English Name	Region
	Roselin de Cassin	Cassin's Finch	NA
	Tétras Centrocerque	Sage Grouse	NA
	Viréo Gris	Grey Vireo	NA, MA
	Carouge Noir	Brown-headed Cowbird	NA, MA
	Junco à Tête Grise	Dark-eyed Junco	NA
	Tohi à Queue Verte	Green-tailed Towhee	NA
	Troglodyte des Canyons	Canyon Wren	NA, MA
	Guiraca Bleu	Blue Grosbeak	NA, MA
	Pyrrhuloxia	Pyrrhuloxia	NA, MA
	Moqueur des Armoises	Sage Thrasher	NA
Saint François d'Assise (1975–83)			
1. La Croix	Alouette des Champs	Eurasian Skylark	EU
	Chouette Chevèche	Little Owl	EU, AF
	Chouette Hulotte	Tawny Owl	EU
2. Les Laudes	Merle Noir	Common Blackbird	EU, OR
	Fauvette des Jardins	Garden Warbler	EU
	Fauvette à Tête Noire	Eurasian Blackcap	EU
	Fauvette des Seychelles	Seychelles Warbler	IO
	Pie chanteuse des Seychelles	Seychelles Magpie-Robin	IO
3. Le baiser au lépreux	Chouette de l'Oural	Ural Owl	EU
	Gérygone	Fan-tailed Gerygone	PO
	Merle Bleu	Blue Rock Thrush	EU, OR
	Merle Noir	Common Blackbird	EU, OR
4. L'Ange voyageur	Oiseau-moine	New Caledonian Friarbird	AU
	Notou	New Caledonian Imperial Pigeon	AU
	Rousserolle Effarvatte	Eurasian Reed Warbler	EU
	Gérygone	Fan-tailed Gerygone	PO
5. L'Ange musicien	Merle Noir	Common Blackbird	EU, OR

Title	French Name	IOU English Name	Region
	Pie Chanteuse des Seychelles	Seychelles Magpie-Robin	IO
	Fauvette des Seychelles	Seychelles Warbler	IO
	Grive Musicienne	Song Thrush	EU
	Gérygone	Fan-tailed Gerygone	PO
	Faucon Crécerelle	Common Kestrel	EU, AF
	Zostérops	Green-backed White-eye	AU
	Fauvette des Jardins	Garden Warbler	EU
	Fauvette à Tête Noire	Eurasian Blackcap	EU
	Bruant à Tête Grise	Chestnut-eared Bunting	EU
	Rougegorge	European Robin	EU
	Rossignol	Common Nightingale	EU
6. Le Prêche aux oiseaux	Alouette des Champs	Eurasian Skylark	EU
	Grive Draine	Mistle Thrush	EU
	Fauvette à Tête Noire	Eurasian Blackcap	EU
	Grive Musicienne	Song Thrush	EU
	Merle Noir	Common Blackbird	EU, OR
	Uguisu = Bouscarle du Japon	Japanese Bush Warbler	EU
	Tourterelle	European Turtle Dove	EU
	Troglodyte	Winter Wren	NA, EU
	Rougegorge	European Robin	EU
	Fauvette Passerinette	Subalpine Warbler	EU
	Coucou	Common Cuckoo	EU
	Pinson	Common Chaffinch	EU
	Hototoguisu = Petit Coucou	Lesser Cuckoo	EU
	Eopsaltria = Rossignol à Ventre Jaune	Yellow-bellied Flyrobin	AU
	Zostérops	Green-backed White-eye	AU

A Catalogue of Messiaen's Birds

Title	French Name	IOU English Name	Region
	Lichmera = Meliphage à Oreillons Gris	Grey-eared Honeyeater	PO
	Pachycephala Rufiventris = Siffleur à Ventre Roux	Rufous Whistler	AU
	Bruant à Tête Grise	Chestnut-eared Bunting	EU
	Gérygone	Fan-tailed Gerygone	PO
	Coucou à Éventail	Fan-tailed Cuckoo	AU
	Fauvette des Jardins	Garden Warbler	EU
	Oiseau-moine	New Caledonian Friarbird	AU
	Roselin Cramoisi	Common Rosefinch	EU
	Traquet à Tête Grise	Red-rumped Wheatear	EU, AF
	Téléphone Tschagra	Black-crowned Tchagra	
	Gorge Bleue	Bluethroat	EU
	Bouvreuil à Ailes Roses	Crimson-winged Finch	EU
	Pigeon Ramier	Common Wood Pigeon	EU
	Oiseau-lyre Superbe	Superb Lyrebird	AU
	Loriot	Eurasian Golden Oriole	EU
	Linotte	Common Linnet	EU
7. Les stigmates	Chouette Hulotte	Tawny Owl	EU
8. La mort et la nouvelle vie	Faucon Crécerelle	Common Kestrel	EU, AF
	Fauvette à Tête Noire	Eurasian Blackcap	EU
	Rossignol	Common Nightingale	EU
	Fauvette des Jardins	Garden Warbler	EU
	Gérygone	Fan-tailed Gerygone	PO
	Alouette des Champs	Eurasian Skylark	EU
Livre du Saint Sacrement (1984)			
3. Le Dieu caché	Etourneau de Tristram	Tristram's Starling	EU

Title	French Name	IOU English Name	Region
	Hypolaïs Pale	Eastern Olivaceous Warbler	EU
5. Puer natus est nobis	Hypolaïs des Oliviers	Olive-tree Warbler	EU
6. La manne et le Pain de Vie	Traquet Deuil	Mourning Wheatear	EU, AF
	Ammomane du Désert	Desert Lark	AF, EU
8. Institution de l'Eucharistie	Rossignol	Common Nightingale	EU
11. L'Apparition du Christ resuscité à Marie-Madeleine	Iranie à Gorge Blanche	White-throated Robin	EU
12. La Transsubstantiation	Bulbul des Jardins	Common Bulbul	AF
	Tourterelle Maillée	Laughing Dove	AF, EU, OR, AU
13. Les deux murailles d'eau	Hypolaïs Polyglotte	Melodious Warbler	EU
	Rousserolle Turdoïde d'Egypte	Great Reed Warbler	EU
15. La Joie de la grâce	Bulbul des Jardins	Common Bulbul	AF
	Etourneau de Tristram	Tristram's Starling	EU
	Iranie à Gorge Blanche	White-throated Robin	EU
Petites Esquisses d'oiseaux (1985)			
1. Le Rouge-gorge	Rougegorge	European Robin	EU
2. Le Merle noir	Merle Noir	Common Blackbird	EU, OR
3. Le Rouge-gorge	Rougegorge	European Robin	EU
4. La Grive musicienne	Grive Musicienne	Song Thrush	EU
5. Le Rouge-gorge	Rougegorge	European Robin	EU
6. L'Alouette des champs	Alouette des Champs	Eurasian Skylark	EU
Un Vitrail et des oiseaux (1987)			
	Rossignol	Common Nightingale	EU
	Pinson	Common Chaffinch	EU
	Fauvette à Tête Noire	Eurasian Blackcap	EU
	Fauvette des Jardins	Garden Warbler	EU
	Merle Noir	Common Blackbird	EU, OR

Title	French Name	IOU English Name	Region
	Rougegorge	European Robin	EU
	Fauvette Passerinette	Subalpine Warbler	EU
La Ville d'En-Haut (1987)	Hypolaïs Polyglotte	Melodious Warbler	EU
	Fauvette à Tête Noire	Eurasian Blackcap	EU
	Fauvette des Jardins	Garden Warbler	EU
Un Sourire (1989)	Cossyphe d'Heuglin	White-browed Robin	AF
Pièce (1991)	Fauvette des Jardins	Garden Warbler	EU
Éclairs sur l'Au-Delà… (1987–91)			
2. La constellation du Sagittaire	Accenteur Alpin	Alpine Accentor	EU
	Fauvette Orphée orientale	Orphean Warbler	EU
	Merle à Poitrine Tachetée	Spotted Palm Thrush	AF
	Cossyphe de Ruppell	Rüppell's Robin-Chat	AF
	Cossyphe Choriste	Chorister Robin-Chat	AF
	Cossyphe du Natal	Red-capped Robin-Chat	AF
	Troglodyte Musicien	Musician Wren	SA
3. L'Oiseau-Lyre et la Ville-Fiancée	Oiseau-lyre Superbe	Superb Lyrebird	AU
4. Les élus marqués du sceau	Kuangkuit Rimau = Timalie Cimeterre	Large Scimitar Babbler	OR
	Cossyphe Choriste	Chorister Robin-Chat	AF
	Merle de Roche	Rufous-tailed Rock Thrush	EU
	Sourd Papou	Brownish Whistler	AU
	Merele à Poitrine Tachetée	Spotted Palm Thrush	AF
	Lève Queue à Gorge Blanche	White-throated Fantail	OR
	Oiseau-moine Papou	Papuan Friarbird	AU
	Corbeau Flûteur Pie	Pied Butcherbird	AU
	Gérygone à Gorge Blanche	White-throated Gerygone	AU

Title	French Name	IOU English Name	Region
	Sucrier à Poitrine Fauve	Tawny-breasted Honeyeater	AU
7. Et Dieu essuiera toute larme de leurs yeux…	Alouette Calandrelle	Greater Short-toed Lark	EU
	Merle Noir	Common Blackbird	EU, OR
8. Les étoiles et la Gloire	Oiseau-lyre d'Albert	Albert's Lyrebird	AU
	Fauvette des Jardins	Garden Warbler	EU
	Perruche à Collier Jaune	Mallee Ringneck	AU
	Fauvette à Tête Noire	Eurasian Blackcap	EU
	Oiseau-fouet	Eastern Whipbird	AU
	Cassican à Tête Noire	Hooded Butcherbird	AU
	Shama	White-rumped Shama	OR
	Corbeau Flûteur Pie	Pied Butcherbird	AU
	Grive Grise	Grey Butcherbird	AU
	Oiseau-moine Papou	Papuan Friarbird	AU
	Pie Grièche Rousse	Brown Shrikethrush	AU
	Loriot Brun	Brown Oriole	AU
	Sucrier de Lewin	Lewin's Honeyeater	AU
	Martin Chasseur Géant	Laughing Kookaburra	AU
	Brève Criarde	Noisy Pitta	AU
9. Plusieurs oiseaux des arbres de Vie	Bulbul à Huppe Noire	Black-Crested Bulbul	OR
	Bulbul Brès	Grey-cheeked Bulbul	OR
	Merle de Roche	Rufous-tailed Rock Thrush	EU
	Burung Gembala Palanduk = Grand Rimeur	Large Wren-Babbler	OR
	Murai Mata Putih = Garrulaxe à Tête Rousse	Chestnut-capped Laughingthrush	OR
	Merbah Berjanggut = Bulbul Ochré	Ochraceous Bulbul	OR
	Shama	White-rumped Shama	OR

A Catalogue of Messiaen's Birds

Title	French Name	IOU English Name	Region
	[Polochion à Nuque Blanche]	[Manus Friarbird]	AU
	Mohoua à Tête Jaune	Yellowhead	AU
	Loriot à Gorge Noire	Dark-throated Oriole	OR
	Murai Bukit = Fulvette Montagnarde	Mountain Fulvetta	OR
	Monarque Noir et Jaune	Golden Monarch	AU
	Brève Criarde	Noisy Pitta	AU
	Murai Rimba Bukit = Garrulaxe à Tête Rousse	Chestnut-crowned Laughingthrush	OR
	Burung Takar Kapala Kuning = Barbut à Sourcils Jaunes	Yellow-crowned Barbet	OR
	Mésia à Joues Argentées	Silver-eared Mesia	OR
	Riroriro	Grey Warbler	AU
	Mésange Sultane	Sultan Tit	OR
	Malure Pie	White-winged Wren	AU
	Pie Grièche Rousse	Brown Shrikethrush	AU
	Sourd Papou	Brownish Whistler	AU
	Timalie Cimeterre	Large Scimitar Babbler	OR
	Rhipidure à Gorge Blanche	White-throated Fantail	OR
	Échenilleur Choucari	White-bellied Cuckooshrike	AU
	Burung Takat Bukit = Barbut Malais	Black-browed Barbet	OR
10. Le chemin de l'Invisible	Corbeau Flûteur Pie	Pied Butcherbird	AU
Concert à quatre (1990–92)			
1. Entrée	Fauvette des Jardins	Garden Warbler	EU
	Kokako	Blue Wattled Crow	AU
	Mohoua à Tête Jaune	Yellowhead	AU
	Kakapo	Kakapo	AU

Title	French Name	IOU English Name	Region
2. Vocalise	Merle de Roche	Rufous-tailed Rock Thrush	EU
3. Cadenza	Oiseau-lyre Superbe	Superb Lyrebird	AU
	Troglodyte Musicien	Musician Wren	SA
	Fauvette des Jardins	Garden Warbler	EU
	Cossyphe du Natal	Red-capped Robin-Chat	AF
4. Rondeau	Oiseau-cloche	New Zealand Bellbird	AU
	Loriot	Eurasian Golden Oriole	EU
	Fauvette des Jardins	Garden Warbler	EU
	Riroriro	Grey Warbler	AU
	Cossyphe Choriste	Chorister Robin-Chat	AF
	Râle Takahé	Takahe	AU
	Hypolaïs Ictérine	Icterine Warbler	EU
	Grive Musicienne	Song Thrush	EU
	Grand Tétras	Western Capercaillie	EU
	Plongeon Arctique	Black-throated Loon	EU
	Bruant Ortolan	Ortolan Bunting	EU
	Linotte Mélodieuse	Common Linnet	EU
	Fauvette Orphée Orientale	Orphean Warbler	EU
	Hypolaïs Polyglotte	Melodious Warbler	EU
	Merle de Roche	Rufous-tailed Rock Thrush	EU
	Oiseau-Tui	Tui	AU

PART II
Influence

Perspectives on Influence

Christopher Dingle and Robert Fallon

As both a word and an idea, influence has accrued a bad reputation in artistic and scholarly circles. Sensitivity to an artist's integrity may suggest that the artwork be allowed to stand on its own without the implication of its being strong-armed by the past. It has become fashionably polite, therefore, to speak of *inspiration* rather than *influence*, a distinction that places artistic decisions in the hands of the artist, rather than an external, fateful force. As a theory of artistic creation, influence has become encumbered by the fusillade of attacks (formerly) or devastating silence (recently) in response to Harold Bloom's famous theory of poetic influence. Bloom's idea, to which he has returned repeatedly for the last 40 years, holds that art emerges from a imaginative misreading of other art, not from the pressures of history, and that the creative process is agonistic rather than benign. Most recently he has defined influence as 'literary love, tempered by defence'.[1] His critics have chided his adherence to an outdated ideology of aestheticism when nearly everyone now professes that the boundaries between art and non-art are thoroughly porous and often meaningless. One poem may 'answer' another, but it also answers to social, political, religious and economic pressures. Art no longer reflects life, it is life – and, in reverse, 'All the world's a stage', as Jaques says in Shakespeare's *As You Like It*, his playwright ventriloquist himself cribbing from a predecessor.

Despite the word's heavy baggage, influence seems to be an inevitable and even useful category of historical inquiry. In a world supersaturated by media and microniche markets, by -isms, -wasms and postmodern all-of-the-abovisms, the idea of influence can fruitfully provide genealogies in which to contextualize, read from and impart meaning to art. For the artisan described above in 'Perspective on Techniques', earlier art is an important context, and in our culture that increasingly lacks shared experience, such artistic context is not only invaluable but necessary for art to reach its fullest communicative potential. Seen in this way, influence is less an exertion of power on art and more an empowerment of its audience, which is now better equipped to listen to composers such as Maurice Ohana, Serge Garant, Iannis Xenakis and Tristan Murail in the context of their relationship to Olivier Messiaen, as the chapters in this section show.

Readers are asked here both to associate and differentiate *influences* and *influence*. The plural form refers to the multiplicity of cultural pressures that shapes an artist. The second part of *Messiaen Perspectives 1* involves the *influences*

---

[1] Harold Bloom, *The Anatomy of Influence: Literature as a Way of Life* (New Haven: Yale University Press, 2011), p. 8.

Messiaen received from engaging with, for example, Mozart, Chopin and the *art sacré* movement. In the chapters here, the singular *influence* refers to Messiaen as a collective agency, his influence on the cultural production of other composers to be regarded as a productive field in which to situate later music, not as a limiting force that asserts both chronological and aesthetic priority.

The 'Perspective on Sources' from *Messiaen Perspectives 1* asserts that sources are said to shape music as influences are said to shape a composer. In a similar way, the final two parts of *Messiaen Perspectives 2* are two sides of the same coin: influence can be seen as a prospective view and reception as a retrospective view. Robert Fallon discusses this idea in his chapter on music written in memory of Messiaen, where his concern is artistic influence. But when 'all the world's a stage', influence may easily be discerned in non-artistic spheres, as Fallon does with Mount Messiaen and Jean Boivin does with Messiaen's *Traité*.

Messiaen's influence on later generations is gradually being documented, most often in monographs on younger composers, such as Boulez, Dutilleux and Saariaho. A book devoted entirely to Messiaen's influence, however, has yet to appear in print.[2] It could, of course, investigate his brief roles as a leader of hyperserialism and *musique concrète*. Good candidates for studies of his influence on individuals must include George Crumb, Jonathan Harvey, Toru Takemitsu, and Gilles Tremblay. His influence on spectralist and post-spectralist composers is also ripe for a detailed look. Not only did he teach the founding fathers of spectralism, above all Grisey and Murail, but the 'natural resonance' guiding his music plainly foreshadows the overtone-rich harmonies and virtuosic orchestration of spectralist music. Furthermore, Grisey's own rhetoric baldly borrows from Messiaen when he writes about *personnages rythmiques* or the differing times of whales, humans and birds. Yet a more challenging type of influence demands to be written one day, where Messiaen's role among still larger trends is defined. How did his spirituality inspire late twentieth-century composers, his love of nature the subjects of environmentally conscious composers, his synaesthesia the collaborations between musicians and artists?

The chapters in Part II describe a variety of relationships between Messiaen and younger (or contemporary) composers. Caroline Rae shows that the music of Maurice Ohana shares numerous surprising correlations of topic and technique with Messiaen. She resists the temptation to ascribe the 'close parallels' to

---

[2] Existing studies on Messiaen's influence include: Jean Boivin, 'Messiaen's Teaching at the Paris Conservatoire: A Humanist's Legacy', in Siglind Bruhn (ed.), *Messiaen's Language of Mystical Love* (New York: Garland, 1998); Jean Boivin, 'Convictions religieuses et modernité musicale au Québec avant la Révolution tranquille: L'example de Nadia Boulanger et d'Olivier Messiaen, Pédagogues et Transmetteurs du Renouveau Musical', in Sylvain Caron and Michel Duchesneau (eds), *Musique, Art et Religion dans l'Entre-deux-guerres* (Lyon: Symétrie, 2009); and Mark Delaere, 'Olivier Messiaen's Analysis Seminar and the Development of Post-War Serial Music', *Music Analysis*, 21/1 (2002): pp. 35–51.

causation, saying there are no 'direct lines of influence' between the composers. Rather, she argues that in spite of the French musical politics that separated them into different camps, they shared a common background in Debussy and even a common friend in Jolivet. Rae does suggest, however, that Ohana's reluctance to discuss Messiaen could be caused by a Bloomian anxiety of influence. Fallon mentions this possibility, too, when in his chapter on tombeaux he queries whether such anxiety could account for the absence of memorial compositions for Messiaen by composers such as Claude Vivier, François-Bernard Mâche, Elliott Carter and Witold Lutosławski.

Uncovering Xenakis's student notebooks from his studies with Messiaen, Anne-Sylvie Barthel-Calvet describes Messiaen's influence on Xenakis as 'intellectual contact', relating less to sounds than to abstractions and concepts concerning rhythmic permutations and music history. Heather White Luckow demonstrates how three Québecois students of Messiaen, Serge Garant, Clermont Pépin and André Prévost, 'adopted and developed techniques of Messiaen'. She shows the substantial but often hidden influence on his students, whose music exhibits a variety of his harmonic, rhythmic and permutational ideas. Where all three composers had spoken of Messiaen's aesthetic influence, White demonstrates how this aesthetic is manifest in specific musical techniques and suggests how their later developments as composers are productively seen in relation to their early studies with Messiaen. Marilyn Nonken, who has worked with Tristan Murail in recording his complete piano works, addresses Messiaen's influence not on any one individual but on an artistic movement. Positioning spectralism in relation to the competing camps of post-serialism and aleatory music and finding it 'influenced' by the Parisian upheavals of May 1968, Nonken identifies the relation as one of sharing a common objective. This objective does not separate rhythm, pitch, attack and dynamic from one another but rather embraces them as interdependently creating harmonic-timbral colour.

Geometrical metaphors appear regularly in these pages on influence. Where Rae refers to 'close parallels', Anne-Sylvie Barthel-Calvet refers to 'points of convergence' and Marilyn Nonken mentions both a 'point of intersection' and 'parallels' between 'political and aesthetic arenas'. Such spatial language demonstrates how studies of influence locate the Bloomian 'revisionary ratio' on coordinates as varied as biography, technique, aesthetic, intellect and politics, thereby inviting audiences to hear the music from a rich variety of perspectives.

Chapter 6
Messiaen and Ohana: Parallel Preoccupations or Anxiety of Influence?

Caroline Rae

Olivier Messiaen and Maurice Ohana belonged to the same distinguished generation of French composers born before the First World War. They carved-out their careers and lived most of their lives in Paris, both also departing this world in that same city within a few months during the same year.[1] Major figures of the French musical avant-garde of the last century, they each made significant contributions to the repertoires of the piano as well as orchestra, acknowledged the importance of Debussy's influence on their respective compositional developments, composed works for Rostropovich, and as crowning achievements of their late years, had operas commissioned by the Opéra de Paris that were first performed at the Palais Garnier during the 1980s: Messiaen's *Saint François d'Assise* on 28 November 1983, Ohana's *La Célestine* on 13 June 1988, both works being premièred around the time of the composers' 75th birthdays.[2] *La Célestine* received the additional distinction of being the last new opera to be premièred at this historic location before the inauguration of the Opéra de la Bastille in 1989.[3]

Despite even these superficial parallels, the work of Messiaen and Ohana has rarely been a subject for comparative discussion. The self-proclaimed aesthetic standpoints of each composer served to emphasize their differences, commentators discreetly and diplomatically accepting that such individual figures should remain separate even in a critical environment. Yet, the music of Messiaen and Ohana demonstrates similarities that merit scrutiny not only because they are indicative of broader compositional trends in French music since 1945, but also as they suggest closer parallels than the composers themselves may have wished to admit. Many features in the music of Messiaen and Ohana reveal their respective contributions

---

[1]   Both Messiaen and Ohana died in 1992, Messiaen on 27 April at Beaujon Hospital in Clichy, Ohana on 13 November at his home in the 16th arrondissement, 31 rue du Général Delestraint.

[2]   Messiaen's 75th birthday was on 10 December 1983 (during the period of his opera's run of 11 performances), Ohana's was on 12 June 1988 (the day before his opera's première).

[3]   The Opéra Bastille was officially opened with a gala concert on 14 July 1989, the bicentenary of the storming of the Bastille. The inaugural operatic production (of Berlioz's *Les Troyens*) took place on 17 March 1990.

to be branches of a compositional tree rooted in Debussy and nourished by kindred influences from the exotic to the esoteric, the religious to the mystic. This chapter will explore these parallel preoccupations, such as their love of nature and awe at the non-human reality of the cosmos, and investigate points of stylistic and technical convergence while acknowledging the crucial differences that defined their respective musical personalities.

Ohana avoided making public statements about the music of his illustrious contemporary Messiaen, his regrettable silence reflecting certain tensions among the sometimes less than fraternal society of Parisian composers of the last century. Even by the 1980s, when Ohana had long achieved international recognition and was among the esteemed of his generation, two distinct compositional factions could still be identified; one comprising those who had been students of Messiaen or whose music had been promoted through the Concerts du Domaine Musical and Ensemble InterContemporain, and the other comprising those who had not. Ohana, like Dutilleux and many others, belonged to the latter category, and for many years composers from one group could not comfortably be mentioned in the company of those from the other.[4] Although such tensions have since waned, Ohana did not live long enough to experience the gradual mellowing that has characterized the period since his death, and Messiaen's, in 1992.[5]

Another reason for Ohana's regrettable silence about Messiaen is what might be called anxiety of influence. While Ohana agreed privately that his music shared certain features with aspects of Messiaen's work,[6] his reluctance to draw public attention to points of convergence stemmed not only from a fear of being overshadowed by his eminent contemporary but also, and more importantly, from a deep-seated desire to emphasize his independence from any perceived compositional school or aesthetic trend, a characteristic he shared with his friend Dutilleux that owed much to the influence of Debussy's thinking. While Dutilleux has questioned the logic of being labelled an 'independent' composer,[7] Ohana sought to make a virtue of such positioning. To assert his independence Ohana consciously distanced himself from Messiaen and his circle, with the result that his many works for solo piano remained notably unperformed by Yvonne Loriod who was otherwise an enthusiastic supporter of new music by her French contemporaries. Dutilleux's wife Geneviève Joy, on the other hand, was among

---

[4]   For a more detailed exploration of these issues, see Caroline Rae, 'Henri Dutilleux and Maurice Ohana: Victims of an Exclusion Zone', *Tempo,* 212 (April 2000): pp. 22–30.

[5]   Any frustration Dutilleux may have felt in being overlooked by Boulez was tempered by the recognition he achieved in the United States early in his career. Ohana was not so fortunate.

[6]   My first meeting with Maurice Ohana was in October 1982. I visited him frequently in Paris throughout his last decade, undertaking many long discussions with him about his own music and that of others.

[7]   See Claude Glayman, *Henri Dutilleux: Music – Mystery and Memory; Conversations with Claude Glayman*, trans. Roger Nichols (Ashgate: Aldershot, 2003), p. 90.

the early champions of Ohana's piano music. Due to the many tensions resulting from Ohana having been overlooked by Boulez,[8] it would have been surprising for Ohana to align himself in any way with Messiaen, whose music featured prominently at the Concerts du Domaine Musical, a forum at which Ohana's music was notably absent. Boulez conducted Ohana's music only once; while musical director of the Renaud-Barrault theatre company, he gave the first performance of Ohana's *La soirée des proverbes* (incidental music for Georges Schéhadé's play of the same title) at the Petit Théâtre Marigny in Paris on 30 January 1954.

While admitting certain similarities with Messiaen in private conversation, Ohana was at pains to underline important differences, not least concerning the theological associations of Messiaen's music, which he found overpowering, even alienating. Although of Jewish origin (Ohana's father originated from Gibraltar), Ohana was raised within the Catholic faith through his mother, but as an adult distanced himself from the practice of any formalized religion.[9] Yet, the deeply spiritual aspects of Ohana's musical persona, combined with his lifelong admiration for the sacred vocal repertories of the medieval and renaissance periods, led him in 1977 to compose a Mass, a form that Messiaen conspicuously avoided throughout his mature years despite his long and intimate involvement with the Church.[10] Resulting from a commission from the Avignon Festival, Ohana's *Messe* (for soprano, mezzo-soprano, two mixed choirs and an ensemble comprising oboe, clarinet, bassoon, trumpet, trombone, organ and percussion) is designed for liturgical as well as concert performance. It incorporates settings of the Ordinary (excepting the Credo)[11] with additional music designed to accompany, precede or follow important stages within the Mass (Entrance, Alleluia, Psalm, Epistle,

---

[8] The wounds from Messiaen's short-lived rift with Boulez of many years earlier healed comparatively quickly.

[9] Ohana's cultural background is full of contradictions that conspire to make him difficult to place for those who desire convenient labelling by bureaucratic nationality. He was born in Casablanca, French colonial Morocco, to parents of Andalusian-Spanish origin, yet was technically British because of the family's connection with Gibraltar, but later adopted French nationality. After completing his secondary musical and general education in the French Basque region, at Bayonne and Biarritz, he settled permanently in Paris in 1932. For more detailed discussion of these issues, see Caroline Rae, *The Music of Maurice Ohana* (Aldershot: Ashgate, 2000), pp. 1–3.

[10] Messiaen's *Messe* (1933), a setting of the Ordinary for eight sopranos and four violins, was composed while working on *L'Ascension* but remains unpublished. Reputedly, Messiaen attached little importance to this work during his lifetime. His later *Messe de la Pentecôte*, for organ, is not a setting of the Ordinary but comprises five sections designed to accompany the main actions of the Mass: Entrance, Offertory, Consecration, Communion and Exit.

[11] Ohana's score indicates the liturgical version of his *Messe* to be 35–40 minutes' duration; together with the Kyrie, Gloria, Sanctus and Agnus Dei, an additional setting of the Credo, with its extensive text, would have increased the overall duration of the work to unmanageable proportions.

156   *Messiaen Perspectives 2: Techniques, Influence and Reception*

Communion).[12] Ohana's *Messe* was performed at his memorial service at the Église Saint-Séverin de Paris on 18 December 1992, the officiating priest being Ohana's close friend and former student, the composer Félix Ibarrondo.[13]

Le Groupe Musical Le Zodiaque and La Jeune France

Ohana was Messiaen's junior by only five years but his compositional chronology places him with the generation that emerged after 1945.[14] While his first career had been as a concert pianist (he performed throughout much of Europe as well as in prestigious Paris and London venues during the 1930s and 1940s),[15] his real beginnings as a composer were delayed by his service with the British Army during the Second World War.[16] Thus, when other composers in France were continuing to make their mark during the difficult years of the Occupation, Ohana was absent from Parisian musical life due to active service in Madagascar, Kenya, North Africa, Greece and Italy.[17] When he returned to Paris after demobilization in 1946 (following a period of study at the Accademia di Santa Cecilia in Rome with Alfredo Casella) Ohana was keen to assert his compositional presence, and in 1947 reunited with former colleagues from his Schola Cantorum days to form Le Groupe Musical Le Zodiaque. The group initially comprised three composers, Ohana, Alain Bermat (b. 1926) and Pierre de la Forest Divonne (b. 1926), all of whom had studied at the Schola Cantorum with Daniel-Lesur, an erstwhile

---

[12]   A short 'Prélude' is interpolated between the 'Entrée' and 'Kyrie', while a 'Trope' follows the Communion. The text of the relevant psalm is to be read over an instrumental accompaniment.

[13]   I had the privilege of attending Ohana's memorial service. Ohana's *Messe* (liturgical version) was first performed at the Église Saint-Agricol, Avignon on 31 July 1977 as part of the Avignon Festival, with Isabel Garcisanz (soprano), Nicole Oxombre (mezzo) and the Ensemble Vocal et Instrumental de Provence conducted by Daniel Chabrun. The concert version has been recorded by the Coeur Contemporain d'Aix-en-Provence and Musicatreize under Roland Hayrabedian (Opus 111 OPS30-246).

[14]   Ohana was born on 12 June 1913. By his own admission, he was profoundly superstitious, especially so in matters involving the number 13, and throughout his lifetime suppressed knowledge of his true date of birth; most studies and recordings published before 1992 state 1914 as Ohana's year of birth, respecting the composer's unusual eccentricity. His superstition may have had just cause: Ohana died at 13.00 hours on Friday 13 November 1992.

[15]   See Caroline Rae, *The Music of Maurice Ohana*, pp. 8–9.

[16]   Despite volunteering for the British Army in September 1939, Ohana was required to clarify his national status with the British authorities and was not able to join-up until November 1940 following his escape from France to England (via Portugal) in June that year.

[17]   Ohana took commando training, served with the Intelligence Corps and was periodically seconded to the Royal Marines, Royal Scots Fusiliers and Argyll and Southerland Highlanders. He ended the war in Rome after a period as liaison officer with the French Maquis.

member of La Jeune france. Forest Divonne had also been a student of Messiaen at the Paris Conservatoire. They were joined in 1948 by a further two members: the Polish composer and conductor Stanisław Skrowaczewski (b. 1923), who was then studying with Nadia Boulanger, and the Argentinean Sergio de Castro (b. 1922), who had been a composition pupil of Falla but later became known as a painter and poet. (Sergio de Castro was also a friend of Dutilleux.[18])

Initially a compositional protest group, Le Zodiaque, with Ohana at their helm, vigorously rejected post-war serialism, considering the new freedoms of the Liberation culturally at risk. While the political structure of the Third Reich had been defeated militarily, they feared Austro-German musical thinking was in danger of conquering aesthetically (not for the first time in France), and that Mediterranean and Latinate traditions were under threat of annihilation through the pervasive influence of the Schoenberg- and Webern-inspired serial techniques that predominated at the time.[19] United as much by their stylistic and cultural diversity as their opposition to serialism, Le Zodiaque mounted concerts of their music at the Salle Gaveau and on French Radio, the latter through the enthusiastic support of Daniel-Lesur and Dutilleux, both of whom were sympathetic to the group's aims and provided broadcast opportunities through their influential positions at the Radiodiffusion Française (RDF). The Zodiaque concerts contributed to the explosion of musical pluralism that characterized French music broadcasting during the immediate post-war years.[20]

Gradually developing more positive aims as their presence became established, Le Zodiaque promoted music based on ancient Mediterranean and Latinate traditions, including folksong, emphasized their independence from aesthetic dogma and avoided pre-compositional systems. Ohana particularly advocated a musical language based on plainchant that could acknowledge the techniques of the medieval and renaissance periods, this being among the sympathies he shared with Messiaen. Le Groupe Zodiaque promoted freedom of musical expression and independence from academic convention with a spirit of sincerity and generosity that echoed La Jeune France, which had opposed contemporary trends during the inter-war years and, like Le Zodiaque, comprised a group of composers similarly unified by stylistic diversity.

---

[18]   See also Henri Dutilleux and Martine Cadieu, 'Rencontre: chez le peintre Sergio de Castro', in *Constellations – entretiens* (Paris: Michel de Maul, 2007): pp. 47–54.

[19]   The vigorous opposition to contemporary trends by the Zodiaque composers may have been in part associated with the cultural origins of the group, their aversion to serialism being one of geography as well as of musical taste. While Skrowaczewski is Polish and thus has a tradition of kinship with France, Poland having long considered itself independent of Germanic culture (a feeling that was particularly strong after the war), the remaining four members were of Latinate origin. For further discussion of the Groupe Zodiaque see Caroline Rae *The Music of Maurice Ohana*, pp. 16–21.

[20]   Dutilleux later commissioned Ohana to compose a number of works for his radio series of 'illustrations musicales'.

Illustration 6.1 Leaflet for Le Groupe Musical Le Zodiaque concert at the Salle Gaveau, 29 April 1949

In another parallel with La Jeune France, Le Zodiaque's resistance to the intellectualism of serialism can also be considered in terms of spiritual dissatisfaction, their aim to promote freedom of musical expression being a means of restoring human and very personal values to a world in turmoil at the end of the Second World War and seemingly devoid of real meaning or purpose.

Many concerts of Le Zodiaque, like those of La Jeune France, also included works by non-group members. Featuring Rameau and Roussel among their programmes, the Zodiaque composers sought to reconstruct continuity with a particularly French past (Illustration 6.1). While the inclusion of Roussel suggests the influence of the Schola Cantorum, the programming of Rameau had even greater resonance; his music featured in many concert programmes during the Paris Occupation, serving as a clarion call for the revival of French national pride. Through programming Rameau, the Zodiaque composers linked themselves both with an established cultural resistance to Germanic influence and with the quest to re-establish a line of tradition that connected with acknowledged greats of French musical culture. Berlioz had served a similar purpose for La Jeune France.

Unlike La Jeune France, whose concert activities extended over a period of more than twenty years,[21] those of Le Zodiaque were comparatively short-lived; the group lacked any secure financial support or a figurehead who already enjoyed widespread

---

[21] The concerts of La Jeune France ran from June 1936 to May 1945 with two additional concerts taking place in May 1954 and in November 1966, the latter celebrating the thirtieth anniversary of the group. See Nigel Simeone, 'La Spirale and La Jeune France: Group Identities', *The Musical Times*, 143/1880 (Autumn 2002): pp. 10–36.

recognition, and by 1950 their activities were disintegrating.[22] Nonetheless, their concerts served to announce the presence of composers who were independent of the serialism of the post-war years and to establish a sense of stylistic pluralism that was later rekindled by Marius Constant in 1963 when he founded the Ensemble Ars Nova specifically to counter the aesthetic trends of the Domaine Musical. Constant and his Ensemble Ars Nova performed and recorded many works of both Ohana and Messiaen during the 1960s and 1970s. They gave the first performance of Ohana's instrumental chamber work *Signes* (1965) as well as his chamber opera *Syllabaire pour Phèdre* (1966–67) of which Constant is the dedicatee, and the first Paris performance of Messiaen's *Des Canyons aux étoiles....*[23]

Although the Zodiaque composers did not publish their ideas as a manifesto, Ohana served as the group representative and spokesman to explain their aims and purpose. The esoteric title of the group was also chosen by Ohana as an allusion to ancient pagan beliefs concerning the enduring power of nature's primary forces – earth, fire, water and air – the four cyclic elements to which the signs of the zodiac belong and to which he related the creative personalities of the group members. There was also a deeper symbolism. In the ancient Mediterranean world, the Zodiac Dodecahedron was not only associated with the sacred host of the Greek *Dodecatheoi*, but also an idealized form for representing divine thought or idea, 12 being symbolic of cosmic order through the 12 points of the zodiac. Immersed in Greek mythologies, Ohana was fascinated by the geometric construction of the dodecahedron, a polyhedron built from a sphere of 12 regular pentagons;[24] five (the number of group members) thus represented the structural element that produced the sphere of symbolic wholeness, the dodecahedron expanding the pentagon into three-dimensional space. In drawing on this symbolism, Ohana aimed to diffuse the idea that the number 12 was connected only with serial composition, wishing to emphasize instead its older, metaphysical associations. He sought to revitalize continuity with the ancient past as a means of opposing what were for him the ephemeral trends of the then predominantly serial present. The group's esoteric

---

[22] Of the five members of Le Groupe Zodiaque, only Ohana secured an international reputation as a composer. Skrowaczewski established an international career as a conductor after winning the Santa Cecilia Conducting Competition and being appointed musical director of the Minneapolis Symphony Orchestra in 1960; Sergio de Castro devoted himself to painting from 1951 onwards, also establishing international recognition (several of his paintings are reproduced as covers on CD recordings of Ohana's music); Alain Bermat continued composing in private, dividing his time between composition and dealing in antiques; and Pierre de la Forest Divonne abandoned his career in music.

[23] The first performance of *Signes* on 23 May 1965 was part of the festival 'Mai musical', Bordeaux, while that of *Syllabaire pour Phèdre* took place at the Théâtre de la Musique, Paris on 5 February 1968. The first Paris performance of *Des Canyons aux étoiles...* was on 29 October 1975 at the Théâtre de la Ville.

[24] At the insistence of his father, Ohana studied architecture at the École des Beaux Arts and École Nationale Supérieure des Arts Décoratifs in Paris from 1932 to 1936.

name was thus a cipher for a mysterious, even magical, symbolism that could resonate with the initiated, a concept not unknown in Messiaen.[25]

The programming of the inaugural Jeune France concert on 3 June 1936 also asserted connections with the past; Daniel-Lesur's *Suite française* alluded to baroque forms in very French guise, Messiaen's *Hymne au Saint-Sacrement* and *Les Offrandes oubliées* created symbolic links with more than a millennium of Christian symbolism, while Jolivet's *Danse incantatoire* evoked imagined ritual from a pre-Christian world. The many references to pagan and pre-Christian beliefs that abound in Ohana's music parallel those found in Jolivet, although Ohana refuted any idea that Jolivet had influenced his own compositional thinking despite their mutual fascination for the incantatory, a feature that links many aspects of their music also with Messiaen.[26]

Nature

Ohana's allusion to the zodiac was also a cipher for his fascination with nature and the cosmos which, in his later music, spawned a complex web of symbolic and mythological references that provided the stimulus for many of his mature works. For example, his two large orchestral works of the 1970s, *T'Harân-Ngô* (1973–74) and *Livre des Prodiges* (1978–79), both relate to cosmogonic creation myths. The title of *T'Harân-Ngô* is derived from the name of Taranis the Celtic God of thunder, the work being as climactic, austere and intentionally terrifying as Messiaen's 'Amen des étoiles, de la planète à l'anneau' in *Visions de l'Amen* as well as sections of *Éclairs sur l'Au-Delà...*, not least through its violent rhythmicism. While the orchestral forces are not as large as those of *Éclairs*, Ohana's percussion section is equivalent to Messiaen's, and both scores juxtapose contrasting blocks of sound-texture to create a sense of the monumental. Ohana's objective of portraying the immense power of nature is underlined by the work's subtitle: 'Conjuration, Contemplation, Glorification of the Primary Forces of Nature'. His short preface also refers to stars, light, night, fire, earth, air and water.[27] While the influence of Stravinsky's *The Rite of Spring* looms large in *T'Harân-Ngô* (the work also contains a number of near quotations, as do other works by Ohana of the 1970s and 1980s), *Livres des Prodiges* was designed as a musical commentary on *The Rite* and follows much of its internal structure as well as the bi-partite form. *The Rite of Spring* served as an important mine of technical vocabulary for Ohana,

---

[25]   *Music and Color*, p. 78.

[26]   In my many conversations with Ohana, it was clear that he had been on good terms with Jolivet for many years (and taught for Jolivet's class from time to time at the Paris Conservatoire) but asserted that any aesthetic parallels in their music did not result from a direct line of influence.

[27]   'Conjuration, Contemplation, Glorification des forces premières de la Nature'. Preface to the score of *T'Harân-Ngô*.

as well as for Messiaen, and was a cornerstone of Messiaen's analytical teaching at the Paris Conservatoire.

The celebration of nature and awesome power of the cosmos appear as recurrent themes in Ohana's music from the mid-1960s, thus paralleling Messiaen's enthrallment with the transcendental power of planets and stars, which can be traced in many works from the 1940s, up to and including *Éclairs*. Ohana also contemplates the cosmos in terms of its vast spaces of silence that can be both peaceful as well as terrifying. 'La Chevelure de Bérénice', the fifth movement of *Si le jour paraît...* (1963–64), for 10-string guitar, concerns the serenity of constellations in the night sky, as does part of 'Étoiles', the third movement of the harpsichord concerto *Chiffres de clavecin* (1967–68). The more awesome *Silenciaire* (1969), for strings and percussion, was intended by the composer as a 'breviary' on silence, the externalized emptiness of the macrocosm reflecting an internalized microcosm in a spiritual contemplation of life, nature and all creation.[28] The concept of this work has much in common with *Déserts* (1950–54) of Varèse, whose music Ohana, like Messiaen, greatly admired. (Ohana almost certainly attended the notorious Paris première of the work in December 1954.) *Silenciaire* also anticipates spiritual concepts in Messiaen's 'astronomical' work *Des Canyons aux étoiles...*, which not only celebrates nature but is similarly concerned with ideas of contemplation and praise, exploring experiences of the divine through silence in its first movement 'Le désert'. While there is a spiritual element in much of Varèse, not least in *Déserts*, the respective awe for the cosmos found in both Messiaen and Ohana is also deeply spiritual; where Messiaen's connections are ultimately related to his faith, God being the creator of all, Ohana's references suggest an archetypal symbolism.[29]

Other allusions to nature in Ohana's music, such as in his *24 Préludes* (1972–73) for piano, which abound in evocations of wind, rain, mists, barren landscapes and even the raw burning of the sun, owe much to the influence of Debussy, as did Messiaen's early piano *Préludes*, notably 'Un reflet dans le vent'. As is often the case in Debussy, as in Messiaen, Ohana's nature exists in a world free from human intervention overlooked dispassionately by the sun, moon and stars. Ohana often signed his manuscripts enigmatically with a cipher depicting a sunburst in which the letters of his name (excluding the non-aspirate 'h') appear within four rays of light extending to each point of the compass.[30] Sometimes he also drew in the moon and stars, as well as the Latin inscription 'nox et dies sum', the implication being that Ohana, as author of his music, is the creator of all within his musical

---

[28]   See Ohana's programme note for the work reproduced in Christine Prost, 'Catalogue raisonnée', *La Revue musicale*, 351–2 (1982): pp. 52–3.

[29]   See Caroline Rae, 'Symbolism and Allegory: Images of the Archetype', in *The Music of Maurice Ohana*, pp. 31–67.

[30]   Ohana's 'sunburst' signatures are also reproduced in a number of his published scores including *T'Harân-Ngô* and the Piano Concerto. See also Rae, *The Music of Maurice Ohana*, pp. 41–3.

162   *Messiaen Perspectives 2: Techniques, Influence and Reception*

universe. Paraphrasing Debussy's remark to listen to no one's advice except that of the wind and the trees, Ohana asserted the importance of nature as among the primary elements of his music:

> The great lessons of music were not given to me by musicians. I received them solidly from the sea, the wind, the rain on the trees and from light, even more from the contemplation of certain landscapes that I seek out because they seem to belong more to the origin of the world than to any civilized place.[31]

Messiaen also contemplated landscapes and cited nature as a great teacher:

> Nature is primarily a great force in which to lose oneself, a sort of nirvana, but above all it's a marvellous teacher. ... I've listened passionately to the waves of the sea, to mountain streams and waterfalls, and to all the sounds made by water and wind. ... All this always represents music.[32]

The importance of Debussy for both Ohana and Messiaen (as well as Dutilleux) was recognized in a commission from French Radio and the Ministry of Culture for all three composers to write a large-scale orchestral piece to commemorate the Debussy centenary in 1962. While Dutilleux did not manage to fulfil the commission, and Messiaen's planned concerto for piano, xylophone and flute eventually emerged as *Sept Haïkaï*, Ohana provided his *Tombeau de Claude Debussy* (1961–62) for soprano, piano, concert zither (tuned to third-tone microintervals) and orchestra, which received its broadcast première on 27 December 1962.[33] Dedicated to Henri Dutilleux, the work received its concert première on 4 January 1966 at the Théâtre des Champs-Elysées with the same soloists and the Orchestre Philharmonique de l'ORTF under Charles Bruck. Avoiding any use of text, the vocal part comprises a succession of wordless vocalizations recalling 'Sirènes' in Debussy's *Nocturnes*, while the orchestral and piano parts incorporate borrowings from Debussy's *Préludes*, *Études* and *En blanc et noir*. Ohana's distinctive third-tone micro-intervals occur both harmonically and as a colouristic means of enhancing the expressiveness of melodic lines, particularly in the voice, and are derived from dividing each step of the whole-tone scale equally. Precisely

---

[31]   'Les grandes leçons de musique ce ne sont pas des musiciens qui me les ont données. Je les ai reçues concrètement de la mer, du vent, de la pluie sur les arbres et de la lumière, ou encore de la contemplation de certains paysages que je recherche parce qu'ils ont l'air d'appartenir plus à la création du monde qu'à des contrées civilisées.' Alain Grunenwald, '*T'Harân-Ngô*: Conversation avec Maurice Ohana', *Arfuyen*, no. 2 (1975): p. 58.

[32]   *Music and Color*, p. 35.

[33]   The first performance of *Tombeau de Claude Debussy* was given by Geneviève Roblot (soprano), Monique Rollin (zithers), Christian Ivaldi (piano) and the Orchestre Philharmonique de l'ORTF under André Girard (who also conducted many of the Groupe Zodique concerts).

pitched and notated, Ohana's third-tone microintervals were intended as a means of extending Debussy's harmonies, the whole-tone scale also representing the first of Messiaen's modes of limited transposition.[34]

Debussy's influence is also significant in Ohana's chamber work *Signes* (1965), for flute/piccolo, two concert zithers (one tuned in semitones, the other in third-tone microintervals), piano and percussion. Drawing its inspiration from nature, *Signes* presents a series of enigmatic 'portraits' of a tree, the work's title emanating from graphic symbols placed at the head of each of the six movements instead of textual titles. According to Ohana, his drawings represent different, albeit esoteric, images of the imagined tree: 'at night', 'alive with birds', drowned with rain', 'imprisoned by spiders' webs', 'beaten by the wind', and 'burnt by the sun'.[35] The fifth movement featuring the piano is intended as a commentary on Debussy's *Prélude* 'Ce qu'a vu le vent d'ouest'. Identifying *Signes* as the work demonstrating the crystallization of his mature musical language, Ohana chose the potent image of a tree to represent his psychological and musical maturity; like the tree, his composition has taken root, is growing and will proliferate. This work has an intriguing and unexpected parallel with Messiaen. Although clearly imaginary, the tree depicted in *Signes* was identified by Ohana to be located in a Japanese landscape. As in Messiaen's *Sept Haïkaï* of three years earlier, the instrumental writing in *Signes* paraphrases the style and character of specific Japanese (and some Chinese) instruments, including the bamboo flute, shamisen, koto and sho, while the percussion (notably woodblocks and bells) evokes the ritual ceremonial associated with Japanese theatre music. Ohana's use of microintervals dilutes the effect of Western equal temperament, and as in *Sept Haïkaï*, the work is static and ritualistic. While Ohana did not visit Japan (unlike Messiaen), he immersed himself in the study of Japanese theatrical and musical traditions, including Gagaku and Noh, being drawn to the repertoire both for its ritualistic qualities and evocations of nature. His chamber opera *Syllabaire pour Phèdre* (1966–67) is another work with Japanese associations; in addition to certain Japanese musical borrowings, the staging is based on Noh theatre, which he felt ideally suited to the stylized ritualism of the ancient Greek subject matter. Ohana was also amused to discover (from a Japanese composition pupil) that his name in Japanese means 'Honourable Flower', a feature exploited in his later Bunraku-inspired *Trois contes de l'Honorable Fleur* (1978), which adapts original fairy tales by the composer for a music-theatre setting.

---

[34] For a more detailed discussion of Debussian references in Ohana, see Caroline Rae, 'Debussy et Ohana: Allusions et références', *Cahiers Debussy*, no. 17–18 (1993–94): pp. 103–20.

[35] The author in conversation with the composer in Paris.

Plainchant and 'Combinatoire' Counterpoint

Messiaen described himself as 'a composer of the Middle Ages',[36] a statement indicative of the importance of his personal faith yet also suggestive of his use of plainchant, plainchant parodies, adaptation of early polyphonic techniques and his recourse to numerous texts and religious paintings of the period. For Ohana, too, plainchant and music of the medieval and renaissance periods were among his most enduring sources of inspiration, as is evidenced most obviously in his vocal works: his adaptation of the thirteenth-century mystic texts and melodies of King Alfonso X in the choral work *Cantigas* (1953–54); his *Messe* (1977); and his golden summer of late vocal works of the 1980s and 1990s, *Lux noctis – Dies solis* (1981–88), *Swan Song* (1987–88), *Tombeau de Louize Labé* (1990) and *Nuit de Pouchkine* (1990). Ohana regularly cited Guillaume de Machaut and Josquin Desprès as decisive influences on his approach to vocal writing and treatment of polyphony;[37] the score of Machaut's *Messe de Notre Dame* was one of few works Ohana kept beside his piano and composing table at his Paris flat. Claude Le Jeune's *Printemps* played a similar role for Messiaen.

While Messiaen once said that 'people of the Middle Ages were linked to the past through melody',[38] Ohana remarked that his music stemmed from vocal origins: 'The most fundamental aspect of my music is that it should be able to be sung. It must be accessible to the human being in the simplest form in which he can apprehend music.'[39] He applied these principles to his instrumental music as well, often describing plainchant as one of the building blocks of his musical language. Attracted to the sound, melodic shape and rhythmic flexibility of plainchant, Ohana immersed himself in its study while at the Schola Cantorum with Daniel-Lesur and analysed not only Gregorian repertory but also Mozarabic chant which he heard at Toledo Cathedral (Ohana travelled frequently to Spain during his formative years). Unlike Messiaen, Ohana avoided using actual plainchant melodies, but their shape and contour influenced his melodic style from the 1950s onwards, as is first revealed in the vocal writing of *Cantigas*, which incorporates features from various chant traditions associated with the Iberian peninsula, including Gregorian, Mozarabic, Sephardic and Muezzin. He immediately began extending these principles to his instrumental music. For example, the second movement of the *Trois caprices* (1954) for piano, 'Hommage à Luis Milán' (which commemorates the innovative harmonic sonorities of the sixteenth-century vihuela composer) presents a non-metrical, chant-like melody

---

[36] Cited in Peter Hill (ed.), *The Messiaen Companion* (London: Faber and Faber, 1995), p. 303.

[37] See, for example, Richard Langham Smith, 'Ohana on Ohana: An English Interview', *Contemporary Music Review,* 8/1 (1993): p. 126.

[38] *Music and Color*, p. 192.

[39] Ohana in interview [in English] with Michael Oliver, *Music Weekly*, BBC Radio 3 (10 June 1984).

Example 6.1   Ohana, *Cinq sequences*, 'Polyphonie' (bars 1–5)

that is clearly articulated in vocal phrase lengths and texturally thickened through harmonic parallelism.

Ohana's first extensive instrumental adaptation of plainchant parodies and techniques associated with early polyphony, including organum, trope and discant, occurs in his first string quartet, *Cinq séquences* (1962–63). The first movement, 'Polyphonie', presents one of his most characteristic fragments of plainchant parody (see Example 6.1), which, after its initial statement, is subject to extension, intervallic expansion, heterophony and dense contrapuntal imitation. Sections of the movement also make use of Ohana's distinctive third-tone microintervals to extend the melodic expressivity inherent in the chant melody.[40] The second movement, 'Monodie', presents a succession of elaborated chants, expanded with microintervals and sequentially developed through virtuosic commentaries in the different instruments, descending from the first violin to the cello. The fourth movement, 'Déchant', superimposes slowed-down chant melodies in which the component intervals are transformed into third-tones to create a harmonically disorienting effect that is further emphasized through the requirement for the strings to play senza vibrato. The homophonic final movement, 'Hymne', explores organum-like textures in which the melodic line is harmonically thickened through parallelism to make the focus of the movement monodic, rather than polyphonic, in accordance with Ohana's self-declared maxim: 'My music is monodic and that which is added to it is just a trail or shadow. The soul of it is fundamentally monodic

---

[40]   Although Ohana experimented periodically with isolated quarter- and third-tone microintervals during the 1950s, the consistent use of precisely notated third-tone microintervals (which he derived from subdividing the whole-tone scale, and thus precludes semitones) became a characteristic feature of his musical language from the early 1960s.

166   *Messiaen Perspectives 2: Techniques, Influence and Reception*

and whether it is a sequence of chords or masses of sound, it is fundamentally monodic.'[41]

Other notable examples of Ohana's plainchant parodies occur in his concerto for two pianos, percussion and orchestra, *Synaxis* (1965–66), and the harpsichord concerto, *Chiffres de clavecin*, the latter incorporating extended sections based on cantus firmus technique to coordinate freely juxtaposed blocks of aleatory counterpoint. Explicitly notated cantus firmi also occur in *Office des oracles* (1974) for three choruses and orchestra, as well as in *Sacral d'Ilx* (1975) for oboe, horn and harpsichord (a work based on the instrumentation of one of Debussy's projected *Sonates pour divers instruments*). Plainchant parodies abound, not surprisingly, in Ohana's *Messe*, which exploits diverse antiphonal effects, incorporates organum at the interval of a fifth and adapts techniques of conductus and trope. The overall effect is more incantatory than other works, emphasizing the repetitive and stylized nature of the liturgical ritual as if written from the perspective of someone looking in from the outside. Many of Ohana's plainchant melodies are notated as note-heads without stems to underline the importance of rhythmic flexibility and to create the effect of improvisation, albeit within a precisely notated score. Such an example occurs in the opening solo of the Piano Concerto (1980–81). The final section of the 'Gloria' from Ohana's *Messe* combines this feature in layers of aleatory counterpoint in which subdivided choral parts form a sound-mass of melodic chant fragments that are freely combined (and freely repeated) without vertical coordination. This textural use of plainchant parody is juxtaposed against the metrical instrumental parts that support the solo vocal lines subdividing the text 'Cum Sancto Spiritu in Gloria Dei Patris' (see Example 6.2). This type of melodic sound-mass occurs frequently throughout Ohana's mature music.

While the sound-mass in the 'Gloria' is subdued, contemplative and primarily melodic, Ohana's horizontally conceived aleatory counterpoint, in which there is no vertical coordination between parts, also extends to rhythm. By the mid-1960s, sections of independently superimposed rhythmic patterns in free or multiple tempi had become a feature of his musical language; these create more energetic sound-masses that are designed to contrast with those of the melodic type in terms of both texture and mood. While these techniques owe much to his study of isorhythm at the Schola Cantorum, they also derive from his knowledge and experience of African drumming, both in sub-Saharan Africa during the war as well as during his youth in North Africa (specific African and Afro-Cuban, rhythms are features of Ohana's rhythmic vocabulary).

His ballet for solo percussion *Études chorégraphiques* (1955) illustrates the beginnings of his experimentations with these layering principles, or what might be called 'combinatoire' counterpoint.[42] Although Ohana avoided Messiaen's more rigorous adaptations of 'colour' and 'talea', his technique of superimposing

---

[41]   Ohana in interview [in English] with Michael Oliver, *Music Weekly*, BBC Radio 3 (10 June 1984).

[42]   See Rae, *The Music of Maurice Ohana*, pp. 125–6.

Example 6.2 Ohana, *Messe*, 'Gloria' (figure 35)

independently repeated (sometimes *ad libitum* and usually unmetered) rhythmic patterns to create sound-masses not only provided blocks of textural contrast within a work or movement, but also impetus and drive to counteract the stasis of more sustained melodic sections. Ohana's approach to structure, like that of Messiaen, is thus primarily sectional and non-developmental. His layering principles anticipate the partially aleatory counterpoint in free tempo first used by Messiaen in the sixth tableau of *Saint François d'Assise* ('Le Prêche aux oiseaux') and subsequently explored in *Un Vitrail et des oiseaux* as well as in the second and ninth movements of *Éclairs*, these sections comprise collages of different superimposed birdsongs. Messiaen also stipulated a cadenza section of birdsong in free tempo and bells in the final movement, 'Rondeau', of his *Concert à quatre*. Although unfinished at the time of his death, Yvonne Loriod completed the work (in consultation with Heinz Holliger and George Benjamin) following Messiaen's detailed instructions. As in Ohana's aleatory counterpoint (both rhythmic and melodic), the individual parts are precisely notated, with only the vertical coordination being undefined. In each case, the composer maintains control over pitch and thus overall harmonic colour.

Other Stylistic and Technical Parallels

Ohana's music is not without the occasional twitter of birds, as in the second movement of *Signes*, which presents a stylized, incantatory evocation of birdsong on flute and piccolo to depict the tree that is 'alive with birds'. Ohana neither attempted to be ornithologically accurate (no species of bird is specified), nor did he study the structure of individual birdsongs, his evocation being a suggestion of birdsong analogous to that of Dutilleux some years later in 'Appels', the first movement of *Mystère de l'instant* (1985–89). Another example of birdsong occurs in Ohana's *Office des oracles* (1974), although here the association is more ironic, providing a tongue-in-cheek reference almost certainly to Messiaen. A large-scale music theatre work for vocal soloists, three choral groups, three ensembles and three conductors, *Office des oracles* presents a witty commentary on the state of contemporary music and questions the future of musical composition through consulting a succession of different 'oracles', ranging from tarot cards, dreams and weather forecasts to horoscopes, automatic writing and those from ancient Greece.

In the eighth of the work's 12 movements, 'Interrogation des oiseaux', Ohana questions the birds to see whether they can tell him how music should be composed. He combines the three choral and instrumental groups in a gigantic sound-mass of 37 individual unmetered parts, each of which freely evokes birdsong in a massive block of aleatory counterpoint. Comprising independently superimposed repeated rhythmic and percussive fragments (the vocal parts are enunciated with percussive onomatopoeic phonemes), the effect is more that of multitudinous chirping than actual song; the section is startlingly prophetic of Messiaen's approach in the sixth tableau of *Saint François d'Assise*. The context of the work tells us that the 'oracle' of birds did not help this particular composer resolve his creative quest.

Ohana turns finally to the Oracle of Delphi who gives what he proposes as the true source of all music: the human voice. In the penultimate movement 'Pythié', the high priestess of Delphi, in the guise of a contralto soloist, presents an ecstatic and intensely expressive monodic vocalization in which the phonetic enunciations articulating the melodic line more than suggest the composer's name 'O-HA-[N]-A'. This proceeds seamlessly into the work's intimate and contemplative final section, 'Omega', which reintroduces the full vocal ensemble in layers of melodic counterpoint that gradually evaporate into silence. Dutilleux considered these final two sections to be among Ohana's most eloquent writing.[43]

Another point of stylistic convergence with Messiaen lies in Ohana's work for unaccompanied voices, *Cris* (1968–69), which parallels *Cinq Rechants* not only in terms of its unaccompanied vocal forces, which are periodically treated as a group of soloists, but also in its use of invented language and experimentation with different rhythmic and percussive textures; textual articulation in both works becomes a discrete colour and sound-object. The disintegration of text into onomatopoeic phonemes and morphemes characterizes much of Ohana's vocal writing, but first came to prominence in a set of experimental vocal works composed within a three-year period: the chamber opera *Syllabaire pour Phèdre* (1966–67), *Sibylle* (1968) for soprano, percussion and tape and *Cris*. Like *Sibylle*, *Syllabaire* makes use of a pre-recorded tape and develops new solo and choral vocal techniques within a dramatic context, its title referring to the breaking-up of text into syllables that are chosen for their sonoric quality. *Sibylle* explores textural interactions between the solo voice and percussion, while *Cris* extends the principles further, its objective being to investigate different types of vocal utterance, or cries, in a catalogue of techniques ranging from percussive exclamation to expressive and lyrical lamentation. Recognizable text is not entirely absent in *Cris*, but its sparing use highlights its effect. The inspirational sources of *Cris* and *Cinq Rechants* are, however, quite different. Ohana's work has a political slant, commemorating the student demonstrations of 1968 in its final movement, 'Slogans', and the Jewish Holocaust in its powerfully expressive fourth movement, 'Mémorial 44', which recites the names of the concentration camps and uses a range of vocal effects to evoke the sound of falling shells, explosives and distant gunfire.

The parallel with *Cinq Rechants* indicates another connection that links, albeit indirectly, with *Harawi* and the *Turangalîla-Symphonie*, namely Latin American references. While Messiaen borrowed much of *Harawi*, both musically and mythologically from Peruvian folklore via Raoul and Marguerite Béclard d'Harcourt's study of Inca music,[44] and incorporated Quechua words (including the title) in both this work and in *Cinq Rechants*, he also suggested that the 'Statue' theme in *Turangalîla* evoked the terrifying brutality of old Mexican monuments.

---

[43]   Henri Dutilleux,'Regards croisés', in Jean Roy and Frédéric Duval (eds), 'Maurice Ohana le musicien du soleil*', Le monde de la musique*, no. 2 [special edition] (1994): 18.

[44]   Marguerite and Raoul Béclard d'Harcourt, *La musique des Incas et ses survivances* (Paris: Paul Geuthner, 1925).

Latin America was a potent source of inspiration for Ohana, representing the ideal fusion of the music of Spain and black Africa, the two musical sources that stimulated much of his early compositional development. While these traditions may appear disconnected from a northern European perspective, they are closely related in an Iberian context; Spanish and African cultures cross-fertilized through the myriad transatlantic migrations resulting from conquest of the New World and the slave trade, then mixed with indigenous populations of South and Central America. Through his acquaintance with the Cuban writer Alejo Carpentier (who was a friend of Varèse, an associate of Jolivet, and who published an article on Ohana's music in 1956),[45] Ohana learned much about Cuban music and its fertile blend of Spanish and African traditions.[46] The incorporation of actual Afro-Cuban rhythms became an important feature of Ohana's musical vocabulary from the 1960s onwards, the recourse to non-European sources representing another parallel with Messiaen.

Ohana's fascination for the blending of Spanish and African musical traditions in the New World of Latin America is illustrated in his operas *Autodafé* (1971–72) and *La Célestine* (1982–87), but culminated in his last major work, *Avoaha* (1990–91) for mixed chorus, two pianos and percussion, where he synthesizes these musical traditions with their respective mythological and religious beliefs. A quotation from the anthropologist J. Mauss heads the preface to the score of *Avoaha*: 'European music, however great, is only one music. It is not all music.'[47]

Both Messiaen and Ohana also incorporated Greek rhythms, Ohana particularly favouring the 'epitrite' pattern because of its association with Spanish music, although his use of Greek rhythm overall is neither as systematic nor as extensive as that of Messiaen. In Ohana, this interest was intimately bound together with his fascination for Greek mythology, which imbues a large body of his music and is extended to his adaptation of forms associated with Greek theatre and poetry such as appear in his dramatic works *Syllabaire pour Phèdre* and *Autodafé*. Similar adaptations occur in, for instance, the 'Strophe' and 'Antistrophe' movements of Messiaen's *Chronochromie*.

Other features in Ohana's musical language parallel specific procedures in Messiaen. Although Ohana's harmonic palette is primarily atonal, based on the juxtaposition of different harmonic 'colours' through processes of intervallic differentiation, he occasionally makes use of referential tonality as a special effect to underline highly expressive personal statements. These special moments of

---

[45]   Alejo Carpentier, 'Revelación de un compositor', *El Nacional* (Caracas, 29 April 1956), reproduced in 'Ese músico que llevo dentro', *Obras completas de Alejo Carpentier*, Vol. 10 (Mexico City: Siglo veintiuno, 1987): pp. 214–17.

[46]   Alejo Carpentier (1904–80) undertook a detailed study of Afro-Cuban musical traditions for his novel *¡Ecué Yamba-O!* (Madrid, 1933), and published a history of Cuban music, *La música en Cuba* (Mexico City, 1946).

[47]   'La musique européenne, si grande soit-elle, n'est qu'une musique. Elle n'est pas toute la musique.' Preface to Ohana's score of *Avoaha*.

Example 6.3   Ohana, *Lys de madrigaux*, 'Star Mad Blues' (renotated harmonic reduction, figure 22)

tonal clarity and stillness are always connected with major keys. The ninth of his *24 Préludes* for piano, an affectionate tribute to the memory of Fats Waller and Count Basie, is oriented within a jazzy E♭ major with added notes, although the notation is designed to obscure the harmonic reference through the use of numerous enharmonic equivalents. The expressive heart of his vocal work *Lys de madrigaux* (1975–76), for female chorus, concert zithers, piano, organ and percussion, occurs in its third movement, 'Star Mad Blues', which comprises another jazz-based reference incorporating a setting of a Negro spiritual melody centred in F♯ major, replete with added sixths (see Example 6.3). Again, the reference is visually obscured through enharmonic notation in the original score. This F♯ major tonality is of great expressive significance in Messiaen, not least in *O sacrum convivium!* and 'Le baiser de l'Enfant-Jésus' from *Vingt Regards sur l'Enfant-Jésus*. In 'Star Mad Blues' Ohana provides his own poetic English text (the only text in the work) to underline the magic of his intimate *mezza-voce* setting. Another more fleeting tonal reference, this time in F major, occurs in 'Miroir de Sapho' [sic], the sixth and final movement of the same work. Here, nine layers of independently moving melodic cells repeated *ad libitum* in aleatory counterpoint are quietly underpinned by the organ part, which provides the tonal environment. Ohana incorporates other referential tonalities in his *Douze études d'interprétation* for piano (Book 1: 1981–82, Book 2: 1983–85), notably B♭ major for an Andalusian folk melody in 'Cadences libres' (Book 1) and C major for a paraphrase of a Bartókian folk melody in 'Septièmes' (Book 2), a piece dedicated to the memory of Bartók. B♭ major is similarly is found in Messiaen, notably in the 'Première communion de la Vièrge' from *Vingt regards* and in 'L'Alouette lulu' from *Catalogue d'oiseaux*. As in the Andalusian folk melody in Ohana's 'Cadences libres', both the Messiaen examples are contemplative in mood.

With *Catalogue d'oiseaux* in mind, it is worth pointing out that the closing section of the thirteenth of Ohana's *24 Préludes* bears a striking resemblance to the final haunting moments of Messiaen's 'Le Courlis cendré' composed almost 15 years earlier, although Ohana never revealed whether the similarity was intentional (see Example 6.4).

The piano works of both Messiaen and Ohana may be considered among the most significant contributions to the French repertoire for the instrument since

Example 6.4　Ohana, *24 Préludes* for piano, no. 13 (closing section)

Debussy and Ravel, this being among the similarities with Messiaen that Ohana was, understandably, entirely willing to acknowledge publicly. When the first recording of Ohana's *24 Préludes* won the Grand Prix de l'Académie Charles Cros in 1975, he was pleased to discover a short article in the journal *La musique* discussing his own piano music with that of Messiaen, but observed that no one hitherto had drawn comparisons between the two composers (although his piano music has since been subject for study).[48] Like Messiaen, Ohana wrote piano preludes, a substantial work for two-pianos, *Sorôn-Ngô* (1969–71) and two large-scale cycles that if performed in their entirety would comprise complete programmes: the *24 Préludes* and *Douze études d'interprétation*. Ohana's *Trois caprices* (1944–54) compare with Messiaen's *Petites esquisses d'oiseaux* in that they comprise sets of short yet technically demanding pieces. While both Ohana's and Messiaen's piano works as a whole are highly virtuosic, those of Ohana particularly exploit the use of cluster chords that acknowledge his exceptionally large hands and long thumbs. He frequently requires the pianist to play with the side and palms of the hands as well as forearms (felt-covered rulers can be used as an alternative), while dense chordal structures often necessitate two notes to be played with the thumb or middle finger.

Although, of the two composers, only Ohana composed a work bearing the title Piano Concerto, the instrument features prominently in Messiaen's many concertante works, including his last and unfinished work, the *Concert à quatre*. Similarly, Ohana incorporated many important piano parts in his ensemble and orchestral music and featured the instrument as soloist in several concertante works.[49] Like Messiaen, Ohana's pianism is both innovative yet rooted in tradition, both composers sharing common pianistic ancestors from Chopin and Albéniz to Debussy and Ravel. Both composers also admired the keyboard writing of Domenico Scarlatti. While elements of Lisztian pianism can be traced in Messiaen's and Ohana's piano works, Liszt was not among those Ohana claimed as having directly influenced his approach to the piano. (Liszt's music was conspicuously absent from Ohana's recital programmes of his concertizing years.) Ohana's piano writing makes frequent use of resonant effects at extremes of the instrument that equate with Messiaen's concept of 'added-resonance', while both composers often feature gently pulsating, usually descending parallel chords that conclude with a tritonal cadence, often coloured with an added sixth. While this characteristic gesture may ultimately be derived from their common musical ancestor Debussy,

---

[48] R. A. Lacassagne, 'Ohana et Messiaen, un regard neuf sur le piano', *La musique* (15 April 1975); For more on Ohana's piano music, see Brigitte Massin, 'Écrire aujourd'hui pour le piano', *Panorama de la musique* (March–April, 1980): pp. 12–13; Paul Roberts, 'La musique de piano de Maurice Ohana', *La Revue musicale*, nos 391–3 (1986): pp. 27–50; and Caroline Rae 'The Piano Music of Maurice Ohana', *Revista Musica*, 6/1–2 (Saõ Paulo, May–November, 1995): pp. 44–74.

[49] Ohana's concertante works featuring the piano as soloist comprise: *Tombeau de Claude Debussy* (1961–62), *Synaxis* (1965–66), the Piano Concerto (1980–81) and *Avoaha* (1990–91). Other works with important piano parts include: *Cantigas* (1953–56), *Prométhée* (1956), *Récit de l'an Zéro* (1958–59), *Signes* (1965), *Syllabaire pour Phèdre* (1966–67), *Autodafé* (1971–72), *T'Harân-Ngô* (1973–74), *Office des oracles* (1974)*, Lys de madrigaux* (1975–76), *Trois contes de l'Honorable Fleur* (1978), *Livre des Prodiges* (1978–79), *Kypris* (1983–84) and *La Célestine* (1982–87).

Ohana's music as a whole, like that of Messiaen, abounds with strident, cascading homophonic chordal structures that recall the vibrant colourings of *Turangalîla*.

Conclusion

While it would be misleading to suggest direct lines of influence between Messiaen and Ohana, there are nevertheless striking parallels in the works of the two composers that suggest a closer aesthetic bond than the tensions of their Parisian musical milieu allowed them to admit. Their respective contributions reveal them to be branches of a compositional tree rooted in Debussy that was nourished by kindred influences; in keeping with well-established French tradition, both were instinctive eclectics. While Ohana felt distanced by the intense theological associations in so much of Messiaen's music, spirituality and religiosity (albeit of a pre-Christian kind) were an important part of his compositional *raison d'être*, as they were for their mutual friend, André Jolivet. Although Ohana sought to make a virtue of his independent, some might say isolated, position, the presence of an underlying unity within the stylistic diversity of both Ohana and Messiaen reveals that the inspirational ideals of both composers were central to the mainstream of twentieth-century French music.

Chapter 7
The Messiaen–Xenakis Conjunction[1]

Anne-Sylvie Barthel-Calvet

It is well known that the 40-year relationship between Olivier Messiaen, the fervent Catholic, and Iannis Xenakis, the self-declared atheist, was one of mutual esteem, artistic admiration and even friendship.[2] The strength of their ties was publicly demonstrated on a number of occasions: Xenakis's oral examination for his doctoral thesis on 18 May 1976; Messiaen decorating Xenakis with the Légion d'Honneur in 1982 (see Illustration 7.1); Xenakis's induction into the French Académie des Beaux-Arts on 2 May 1984 (marked by a friendly introduction from his *maître*, Messiaen);[3] and Xenakis's tribute to Messiaen published in commemoration of the world première of *Saint François d'Assise*.[4] This long relationship developed thanks to Messiaen's remarkable confidence in Xenakis and his musical capacities from their very first encounter.[5]

Beyond simple friendship, much can be learned from considering the intellectual connections that formed between these creative personalities during two periods in particular: Xenakis's time as an auditor in Messiaen's class at the

---

[1] I would like to thank Christopher Brent Murray for his patient re-reading and correction of this text.

[2] Françoise Xenakis spoke of this relationship in the following terms: 'I'm afraid to say that I believe that Messiaen was the first person in Paris to show him kindness, kindness that Xenakis dared show in return' [Je crois, je crains, que Messiaen ait été le premier, à Paris, à lui montrer une tendresse que Xenakis a osé lui render.], Françoise Xenakis, 'Ce que je sais de lui', in François-Bernard Mâche (ed.), *Portrait(s) de Iannis Xenakis* (Paris: Bibliothèque Nationale de France, 2001), p. 14. Françoise Xenakis also recalled that Messiaen loved coming to the Xenakis family home to eat the cookies and sweets he was forbidden by Yvonne Loriod!

[3] Olivier Messiaen, 'Discours de réception à l'Institut de France-Mercredi 2 mai 1984', in Mâche (ed.), *Portrait(s) de Iannis Xenakis*, pp. 83–6.

[4] Iannis Xenakis, 'Olivier Messiaen', *Opéra de Paris,* 12 (November 1983): pp. 6–7.

[5] The only passing gloom on this otherwise warm relationship can be found in a short note, jotted in Greek in Xenakis's notebook 1 on 20 October 1953 (notebook 1, p. 52). Xenakis notes 'Messiaen's pettiness' ('Μικροπρέπεια τοῦ Messiaen'), when Messiaen claimed to have urged the younger generation to write series of rhythms and dynamics in the 1940s, an error according to Xenakis's note. However, Xenakis repeated Messiaen's words two years later in his famous manifesto 'La crise de la musique sérielle' (*Gravesaner Blätter* 1 (1955): pp. 2–4, new edition in *Keleütha: Écrits* (Paris: L'Arche, 1994), pp. 39–43). Perhaps Xenakis's remark was just a passing outburst?

Illustration 7.1   Olivier Messiaen decorating Iannis Xenakis with the Légion d'Honneur in Xenakis's apartment on the Rue Chaptal

Conservatoire from 1951 to 1954 (a period that coincided with a drastic evolution in Xenakis's musical style that calls for a re-evaluation of the impact of Messiaen's teachings on his music), and later, during the 1960s, when Xenakis embarked upon an ambitious theoretical project to study what he called 'outside-time structures'[6] (in which he considered Messiaen's work and thought as a critical historical turning point).

As a composer and teacher, Messiaen showed great interest in Xenakis's music from the 1960s onward.[7] According to the programme of Messiaen's classes established by Jean Boivin,[8] Messiaen analysed *Metastasis* in 1965–66 and added *Pithoprakta*, *Eonta*, *Herma* and stochastic music the following year. There are also references to Xenakis's music in Messiaen's sketches for the seventh scene of *Saint François d'Assise*, where Messiaen wrote: 'Ensemble of cluster glissandos which move at different speeds – see Bali, gagaku, [Boulez's] *Pli selon pli*, Xenakis, Ligeti.'[9]

[6]   See Iannis Xenakis, *Musique Formelles: Nouveaux principes formels de composition musicale* (Paris: Richard-Masse, 1963), pp. 183–208; English edn: *Formalized Music: Thought and Mathematics in Composition* (New York: Pendragon, 1991), pp. 155–77.

[7]   Sadly, no traces of Messiaen's personal notes could be found in the Xenakis scores of Messiaen's former collection now conserved at the Médiathèque Hector-Berlioz of the Paris Conservatoire.

[8]   Jean Boivin, *La classe de Messiaen* (Paris: Bourgois, 1995), pp. 336–7 and pp. 443–4.

[9]   PHNS, p. 325.

The Messiaen–Xenakis Conjunction

Although scholars have commented on the similarities that appeared between these two creative personalities as early as the 1950s,[10] newly accessible documents in the Xenakis archives at the French National Library have shed new light on the convergence of their musical practices.[11] In the pages that follow I will first outline examples of Messiaen's support of Xenakis and describe Xenakis's studies and notes as an auditor in Messiaen's class at the Conservatoire. In the second part of this chapter I will examine several points of convergence between the two composers' musical poetics, including their use of additive rhythm, serial techniques and permutations.

Messiaen's Support of Xenakis

Messiaen was the first composer of influence to take Xenakis's efforts at writing music seriously. The first example of this can be found in his acceptance of the young Greek composer-to-be as an auditor in his class in 1951 in spite of the fact that Xenakis had not completed any formal harmony or counterpoint studies.[12] In November of the following year, Xenakis showed Messiaen his *Zyia* for flute, piano, soprano and chorus of male voices. Messiaen was taken by the piece, recognized that it showed real talent, and offered to show it to Marcel Couraud, the respected choir director who premièred Messiaen's own *Cinq Rechants*, for

---

[10]   See Boivin, *La classe de Messiaen*; André Baltensperger, *Iannis Xenakis und die stochastische Musik* (Berne: Paul Haupt, 1996), pp. 183–5 and 219–36; François-Bernard Mâche, 'L'Hellénisme de Xenakis', in *Un demi-siècle de musique… et toujours contemporaine* (Paris: L'Harmattan, 2000), pp. 302–22; Makis Solomos and Peter Hoffmann, 'Xenakis et Messiaen', in Christine Wassemann Beirão, Thomas Daniel Schlee, Elmar Budde (eds), *La cité céleste: Olivier Messiaen zum Gedächtnis* (Berlin: Weidler, 2006), pp. 289–306.

[11]   Xenakis's archives were deposited at the French National Library by Françoise and Mâkhi Xenakis in 2001.

[12]   For more details, see Nouritza Matossian, *Iannis Xenakis* (London: Kahn & Averill, 1986), pp. 47–8 and Jean Boivin, *La classe de Messiaen*, pp. 112–15. Xenakis had tried to fill the gaps in his musical education by attending Honegger's classes at the École Normale de Musique – but he ultimately gave up, discouraged by Honegger's remarks. He later took private lessons with Nadia Boulanger and Annette Dieudonné. As Messiaen recalled in his speech for Xenakis's induction into the French Academy in 1984: 'Having learned he was Greek, that he had studied mathematics and he was working with Le Corbusier as an architect, I told him: "Keep doing all that! Be Greek, be a mathematician, be an architect, and make your music from all that!" Without knowing it, I had just given a quite precise definition of his future work …'. [Ayant appris qu'il était grec, qu'il avait fait des mathématiques, et qu'il travaillait avec Le Corbusier comme architecte, je lui dis: "Continuez comme cela! Soyez grec, soyez mathématicien, soyez architecte, et du tout faites de la musique!" Sans le savoir, je venais de donner une définition presque exacte de son œuvre future …] (Olivier Messiaen, 'Discours de réception à l'Institut de France', p. 83).

a potential public performance. This was a tremendously important gesture that helped Xenakis find a certain degree of self-confidence. He related the event in his first notebook on 15 November 1951:[13]

> Messiaen a vu la Ζυγιά. Il l'a lue attentivement en trouvant des fautes de copie. Il m'a dit: 'Mais c'est formidable le progrès que vous avez fait depuis les harmonisations. Vous avez maintenant une langue, un style. C'est très très bien. Comment avez-vous fait? Vous vous rendez compte?'
> J'ai dit que c'était grâce à lui, à son encouragement, à ses leçons, ensuite à la rythmique hindoue, à Le Corbusier et à la musique populaire grecque.
> Il m'a répété son étonnement à plusieurs reprises.
> Il m'a dit qu'il voudrait bien entendre la partie centrale soprano, flûte et piano qu'il trouve exceptionnelle à cause de la combinaison des timbres, mélodies et rythmes.
> Il a eu un doute quant au raccord de la strette avec les doubles croches de Bartók, mais, a-t-il dit, ce sera très bien quand même.
> Il a trouvé la partie du piano solo avec la variante du refrain, très bien et pas du tout longue et statique, à cause des accidents rythmiques (changement des mesures).
> Il m'a proposé de montrer la Ζυγιά de sa part à Marcel Couraud pour qu'il la mette dans ses programmes.
> Je commence à me sentir à nouveau un homme parce que les paroles de Messiaen sont très encourageantes et parce que je suis d'accord avec lui.
> C'est le début de la fin du Moyen-Âge?

> [Messiaen saw Ζυγια. He read it carefully and found some copy mistakes. He said: 'But it's incredible, the progress you've made since the harmonizations. Now you have a language, a style. It's very, very good. How did you do that? Did you realize?'
> I said I owed it to him, to his encouragement, his lessons, then to the Hindu rhythms, to Le Corbusier and to Greek folk music.
> He retold me several times he was amazed.
> He said to me he would like to hear the central part for soprano, flute and piano that he finds outstanding for the combination of timbres, melodic lines and rhythms.
> He had a doubt about the link of the stretto with the Bartók sixteenth notes, but he said, it will be very good even so.
> He found the piano solo part with the variation of the refrain very good and not long and static at all, because of the rhythmic disruptions (changing of metres).
> He offered to show Ζυγια to Marcel Couraud so that he can include it on one of his programmes.

---

[13] Iannis Xenakis, notebook 1, pp. 40–42, Xenakis Archives, BnF, Music Department.

I'm starting to feel human again because Messiaen's words are very encouraging and because I agree with him. Is this the beginning of the end of the Middle Ages?]

Unfortunately, the story did not end as happily as it had begun. Xenakis's letters and diaries from 1953 and 1954 record his tireless efforts and communication with Marcel Couraud and Pierre Capdevielle, director of the chamber music programmes at the French Radio, in the hopes of having *Zyia* premièred. His efforts were backed by the support of Irène Colassi, the Greek soprano who was supposed to sing the solo soprano part. Capdevielle initially seemed quite open to the idea and tried to convince Couraud to perform the piece,[14] but Xenakis's diary entries from April 1954 show that he failed to get a clear response from either.[15] By the end of the year, after a promising meeting with Hermann Scherchen on 5 December, Xenakis turned his attention to the project of getting *Metastasis* performed and left *Zyia* by the wayside. It would ultimately receive its première some 40 years later on 5 April 1994.

Messiaen used his influence on Xenakis's behalf on at least one other occasion, writing a letter of recommendation to Pierre Schaeffer that Xenakis himself called *formidable*. It has since become well known:[16]

> 6 juillet 1954
> À Pierre Schaeffer
> > de la part de Messiaen
>
> > Cher Ami,
>
> Je viens vous recommander tout spécialement mon élève et ami
>
> > Yannis Xénakis
>
> qui est Grec et très extraordinairement doué pour la musique et le rythme. Il m'a montré tout dernièrement une partition assez volumineuse intitulée 'Le Sacrifice', utilisant un petit orchestre (bois, cuivres, cordes, percussion), dont l'esprit de recherche rythmique m'a séduit dès l'abord et qui est de nature à vous intéresser, j'en mets ma main au feu!… Xénakis serait très heureux de

---

[14] Pierre Capdevielle, letter to Marcel Couraud, 18 January 1954, Xenakis Archives, file O.M. 17/5: 'je vous demande de vouloir bien étudier sans trop attendre l'éventuelle réalisation de ce projet' [I ask you to be kind enough to examine the possibility of realizing this project without too much delay].

[15] As Xenakis summed up the situation in a letter to Louis Saguer: 'ZYIA, rewritten and accepted by Colassi is stuck because of Couraud who does not give a damn about me. He has not given a damn for a year. Capedevielle too, although more polite.' [La ZYIA refaite et acceptée par Colassi est restée en panne à cause de Couraud qui se fout de ma gueule. Il s'est foutu [de ma gueule] depuis un an. Capdevielle aussi quoique plus poli] (Lettre de Yannis Xenakis à Louis Saguer, 9 janvier 1952–1959, BnF, Music Department).

[16] File OM 17/5, Xenakis Archives, reprinted in Mâche, *Portrait(s) de Iannis Xenakis*, p. 14; quoted in Matossian, *Iannis Xenakis*, p. 76, and Boivin, *La classe de Messiaen*, p. 115.

s'entendre: si vous pouvez faire jouer cette oeuvre, ce serait pour lui une grande joie et une occasion de progrès. D'autre part, il est désireux de faire de la 'musique concrète' – c'est un esprit jeune, aventureux, neuf, aigu, il pourrait devenir un de vos précieux collaborateurs.

Espérant que vous serez favorable à toutes mes requêtes, je vous adresse l'hommage de mon admiration toujours sincère – et j'y joins de bonnes amitiés pour Pierre Henry et vous-même.

Olivier Messiaen[17]

[6 July 1954
To Pierre Schaeffer
    From Messiaen

    Dear Friend,

I have come to recommend to you, very specially, my pupil and friend

    Yannis Xénakis

who is Greek and very extraordinarily gifted in music and rhythm. Very recently, he showed me a rather voluminous score entitled 'The Sacrifice', for small orchestra (woodwind, brass, percussion), whose spirit of rhythmic research appealed to me at once and which is likely to interest you, I swear to it!... Xénakis would be very happy to hear his work: if you could have it played, it would be a great joy for him and an opportunity for progress. Besides, he would like to make 'musique concrète' – he is a young, adventurous, new, and sharp spirit, and could become one of your valued collaborators.

In the hopes that you will look favourably upon all of my requests, I send the homage of my ever sincere admiration – and I add to it my best wishes to Pierre Henry and yourself.

Olivier Messiaen]

This letter was originally requested by Schaeffer.[18] Xenakis sent it on 10 July and on 17 September he got a positive response from Schaeffer inviting him to come and work at the Studio de Musique concrète.[19] *Le Sacrifice*, like *Zyia*, would only be premièred much later, in Munich on 15 December 2000.

---

[17]   Olivier Messiaen, Lettre à Pierre Schaeffer, 6 July 1954, file O.M. 17/5, Xenakis Archives.

[18]   Xenakis noted in his 1954 diary, on 2 July: 'Telephoner Scheffer [sic] / Vu Schaeffer à 3h de l'après-midi. / Jamais vu le Sacrifice. / Gardé pour interroger Pierre Henry. / Demandé une lettre de recom. de Messiaen pour travailler concrète.' [Phone Scheffer [sic] / Met Schaeffer at three o'clock p.m. / Has never seen le Sacrifice. / Kept to question Pierre Henry. / asked for a letter of introduction from Messiaen to study concrete] (Xenakis Archives).

[19]   Diary, 17 September 1954: 'Telephoné Schaeffer. / m'a dit qu'il accepte que je travaille à Concrète' [Phoned Schaeffer / said to me he agreed for me to study Concrete

When Xenakis sent the score of *Metastasis* to Heinrich Strobel, hoping to get a first performance at the Donaueschinger Musiktage, Xenakis mentioned the support he had received from Messiaen and Fred Goldbeck:

Paris le 4–5–55

Dr. H. STROBEL   YANNIS XÉNAKIS

SWFunk Baden-Baden   35, rue de Sèvres

Paris 6e

Cher Monsieur,

J'ai été encouragé à vous écrire et à vous soumettre ma partition pour orchestre 'Les MÉTASTASSIS', par Olivier Messiaen dont j'ai été l'élève et par F. Goldbeck dont je vous envoie une lettre de recommandation.[20]

[Dear Sir,

I was encouraged to write and to submit to you my orchestra score 'Les MÉTASTASSIS' by Olivier Messiaen, of whom I was a student, and by F. Goldbeck, from whom I send you a letter of introduction.]

While a warm letter of recommendation from Goldbeck is found in the Donauschingen archives, there is none from Messiaen. However, Strobel was on very good terms with Messiaen and could have easily verified Xenakis's claims.[21]

From the première of *Metastasis* on 16 October 1955 onwards, Xenakis's early career benefitted most from his relationship with Hermann Scherchen, who, as conductor and editor of the Ars Viva Verlag, was in a better position than Messiaen to get Xenakis's works played. Scherchen gave the first performances of *Pithoprakta* in Munich in 1957, *Achorripsis* in Buenos Aires in 1957 and Paris in 1959, *Polla ta Dhina* in 1962, and *Terretektorh* in 1966, two months before he died. From time to time, Xenakis continued to ask Messiaen to lend a word of support on his concert programmes – for the French première of *Achorripsis* on 22 November 1959 and the Festival Xenakis held on 20 May 1965 at the Salle Gaveau.[22]

[music]]. Also, 23 September: 'J'ai vu Schaeffer 37 rue de l'Université. / Pierre Henri [sic] m'a dit qu'il allait me faire signe d'ici 15 jours. Accepte travailler même comme manipulateur.' [I met Schaeffer 37 rue de l'Université./ Pierre Henri [sic] said to me he will get in touch with me within two weeks. I agree to work even as operator.]

[20]   Iannis Xenakis, Letter to Heinrich Strobel, 4–5–55, Donaueschinger Musiktage 1955, finder PO 66260, Historic Archives of the SWF.

[21]   As Director of the Music Programmes of the Südwestfunk, Strobel had already invited Messiaen, not only to the Donaueschingen Festival (*Harawi* in 1951) but also for the SWF concert season, which included the first German performance of the *Turangalîla-Symphonie* in April of the same year.

[22]   See letter to Olivier Messiaen, 26 October 1959, file O.M.3/ 4 and file Writings 4/10, Xenakis Archives.

Xenakis's Time in Messiaen's Class

In order to understand their relationship better, I will now turn my focus to the three academic years during which Xenakis was in regular contact with Messiaen's manner of 'thinking music' (to borrow a turn of phrase from Boulez), an intellectual contact that is clearly recorded in Xenakis's notes from Messiaen's class. Citing Nouritza Matossian, Jean Boivin has written that Xenakis went to introduce himself to Messiaen at the end of one of his classes in 1951. Although the exact date of this first meeting is not known, we may assume it took place either in July, at the end of the 1950–51 academic year, or the following October.[23] In any case, according to Boivin's lists of pupils,[24] Xenakis was registered as an auditor during three consecutive academic years, from 1951–52 to 1953–54. In her biography of Xenakis, Matossian suggests that Le Corbusier advised Xenakis to meet Messiaen,[25] and in Marc Kidel's film *Something Rich and Strange*, she seems certain of it, although there is no documentation to support these claims. It is certain that Xenakis had in his possession a short, undated note of introduction from Annette Dieudonné, solfège professor at the Conservatoire and long time friend of Nadia Boulanger (one of the first musicians in Paris to show Xenakis a certain degree of kindness). It seems probable that Xenakis used this note as his letter of introduction to Messiaen:

> Mon cher Maître (Messiaen),[26]
> Puis-je vous demander de faire bon accueil à Monsieur Xenakis, qui est un jeune compositeur plein de talent, très désireux d'assister à quelques-unes de vos classes.
> Je vous remercie d'avance de ce que vous voudrez bien faire et vous prie de croire à mes sentiments de haute estime artistique.[27]

> [My dear Maître (Messiaen),
> May I ask you to welcome Mister Xenakis, who is a young composer full of talent, very eager to attend some of your classes.
> Thank you in advance for what you are willing to do, and please believe in my sentiments of high artistic esteem.]

---

[23] In Solomos and Hoffmann, 'Xenakis et Messiaen', p. 290, it is said that Xenakis met Messiaen in 1950, without giving the precise source of this information.

[24] See Boivin, *La classe de Messiaen*, pp. 415–17.

[25] See Matossian, *Iannis Xenakis*, p. 47. Le Corbusier and Messiaen seem to have got in contact later, through Xenakis, in preparation for the inauguration of Ronchamp in 1955. See Le Corbusier, letter to Messiaen, 21 May 1955 in Le Corbusier, *Choix de lettres*, ed. Jean Jenger (Basel: Birkhäuser, 2002), p. 215.

[26] 'Messiaen' added in Xenakis's hand.

[27] Visiting card, entitled 'Annette Dieudonné/Professeur au Conservatoire', file O.M. 17/5, Xenakis Archives.

Xenakis's Notebooks

There are some forty notebooks conserved in Xenakis's archives, the most recent of which date to the mid-1970s. The first 13 notebooks date from the period of Xenakis's studies with Messiaen, and only two of these contain actual notes from Messiaen's class: notebook 7, which is a music book for the examples given by Messiaen, and notebook 9,[28] for actual class notes. Xenakis often used four or five notebooks during the same period of time without devoting a special theme to each one. These notebooks constitute a genuine record of a creative personality in active formation. Their content varies, and often shifts from reading notes to sketches, unpublished texts or drafts of later developed publications, and so on. The sudden, eruptive character of Xenakis's ideas can be seen in the very nature of his handwriting – often ideas are quickly jotted down. The urgent need to write ideas down on whatever was at hand can be seen in the elements connected to the same work or idea that are often scattered across a variety of different notebooks. Only the notes from Messiaen's classes seem to have been carefully and regularly kept in the same place, although notes concerning other topics are also found at the end of notebooks 7 and 9. The notebooks provide insight into Xenakis's compositional thought process for the works he was composing at the time of his studies with Messiaen, but also reveal embryonic ideas that would only be developed much later.

Xenakis's Notes from Messiaen's Class

Xenakis's notes reveal not only what Xenakis heard in Messiaen's class, but how he reacted to Messiaen's lectures, helping us deduce what part of Messiaen's teaching most interested him.

The archive inventory titles for notebooks 7 and 9 are Xenakis's own: 'Xenakis//1952//Messiaen' and 'Carnet 1952' respectively.[29] Surprisingly, notebook 9 only contains information from the second and third years that Xenakis audited Messiaen's class, beginning in October 1952 and ending with notes on the *Livre d'orgue* from 6 July 1954.[30] One might even question whether Xenakis attended Messiaen's class during the 1951–52 school year, if notebook 7 (containing the musical examples) did not appear to have been used during that period. Although the first three pages of notebook 7 are dedicated to plainchant[31] and are undated, the fifth page is marked '3–4–52', suggesting that class notes corresponding to the musical examples from 1952 may have existed, but did not survive. As notebook 7 seems to have been filled chronologically from beginning to end, these first four pages

---

[28]   This numbering system was established by the Bibliothèque Nationale de France, not by Xenakis. The description of the notebooks can be found below.

[29]   For convenience, these will henceforth referred to as 'notebook 7' and 'notebook 9'. Notebook 7 is composed of manuscript paper in Italian format (16.4 cm × 11.5 cm) and notebook 9 is composed of graph paper (13.3 cm × 21 cm).

[30]   Xenakis, notebook 9, pp. 72–7.

[31]   Xenakis wrote: 'Formes du plein chant [sic]'.

184   *Messiaen Perspectives 2: Techniques, Influence and Reception*

were probably written earlier in 1952.[32] After this, notebook 7 was only used in Messiaen's class in October and November 1953 (pp. 8–11, 32). In notebook 9, only the first 77 pages are used for class notes. A music notebook devoted to examples for notes taken between November 1953 and July 1954 may have also disappeared.

Notebook 9 opens with notes on Byzantine neumes (October 1952) whose precision suggests that they might be reading notes rather than class notes. On 22 November, Xenakis wrote out the programme of the courses until the end of December. The following undated pages relating to Hindu rhythms, are written very meticulously, and seem to have been taken at the same session or at the following one. The entry dated 9 December 1952 features vague notes on medieval neumes, followed by the description of the five *ordres rythmiques* dear to Messiaen, set forth in the same manner as in the *Traité* (ordres quantitif, dynamique, des hauteurs, phonétiques, cinématique).[33] Then 16 December features terse notes on Debussy and notes on rhythm whose relative precision shows Xenakis's interest in rhythmic issues.[34] On 17 January 1953, Xenakis noted an analysis of Mozart's *Don Giovanni* as well as the class programme for January, alternating between *Don Giovanni* and Debussy's *Préludes*.[35] The next entry is dated 15 October 1953, meaning that, after the *Don Giovanni* analysis in January either Xenakis stopped taking notes, or he did not return to any of Messiaen's courses for the remainder of the academic year. Another improbable hypothesis, considering Xenakis's orderly note-taking in class, would be that he used another notebook that has since been lost.

On 15 October 1953, Xenakis noted some very general reflections about Chinese and Hindu modes and tonal music followed by a carefully copied analysis of Beethoven's Fifth Symphony with the corresponding musical examples in notebook 7. At the same session or in the following one, he took down the general principles of serial composition. This theme continues on 20 October with notes on Webern's opp. 18[36] and 27. On 23 October 1953, Xenakis started to take fairly developed notes about Messiaen's modes of limited transposition (with corresponding musical examples in notebook 7) as well as the theories of Ivan

---

[32]   According to Jean Boivin, 'music of the Middle Ages' was studied on 5 January 1952, which confirms our assumptions (Boivin, *La classe de Messiaen,* pp. 437–8).

[33]   *Traité I*, p. 44.

[34]   'La syncope est à la base de la musique à temps égaux. Guill. De Machaux [sic] syncopes à profusion. Pas dans le plein chant [sic] / Augmentation et diminution côte à côte (l'une après l'autre).' [Syncopation lies at the basis of music with equal beats. Guill. De Machaux [sic] syncopations in profusion. Not in full chant [sic]/ Augmentation and diminution side by side (one after the other).] (Xenakis, notebook 9, p. 11).

[35]   In fact, Xenakis wrote only 'Prélude Debussy' but Jean Boivin (*La classe de Messiaen,* p. 439) indicates that the subject was the *Préludes* for piano and not the *Prélude à l'après-midi d'un faune.*

[36]   Completed on notebook 7, pp. 8–9, with an overview of the four forms of the series for Webern's op. 19 on p. 8.

Wyschnegradsky, John Cage and Nicolas Slonimsky.[37] On 29 October, he took a few short notes on birdsongs, and on 23 November 1953 there are carefully recorded notes from a class about the *Prélude à l'après-midi d'un faune*, where Xenakis sometimes voices his personal opinions alongside those of Messiaen. The next page (undated) shows an analysis for the opening of *Pelléas*, but notebook 7 (which contains the Golaud and forest themes) dates the *Pelléas* class to 26 November 1953. The highly detailed character of these notes contrasts with the idle doodling of 5 December – the only trace of Messiaen's analysis of the 'Scène de la fontaine' from *Pelléas*.[38] Messiaen returned to birdsong on 10 December 1953 and this time, Xenakis took more detailed notes. Conversely, on 19 December, he filled only a half page with very vague notes about the symphony and the rondo sonata form, jotting down Mozart's name without specifying which symphony was studied. The following pages record extremely detailed notes on *Turangalîla-Symphonie*, which seems to have been analysed exhaustively. In particular, Xenakis precisely transcribed the rhythmic modes used in the seventh movement ('Turangalîla II') designating them as 'la plus originale' – undoubtedly Messiaen's own opinon. This analysis is undated, but the final page of this analysis bears a note of a concert at the École Normale de Musique on 9 March, which may suggest the analysis was taught during the weeks preceding this date, between January and March 1954. After this, Xenakis took down some superimposed permutations from the *Messe de la Pentecôte* in numerical values. A new analysis dedicated to Stravinsky's *Sacre du printemps* starts on page 66; the first four pages of which are undated, but 3 July 1954 is inscribed on page 70, where an analysis of the 'Danse sacrale' is developed in relative detail over two pages. It may be assumed that the first notes on the *Sacre* were written in sessions just a few days earlier, meaning that Xenakis may have again missed classes for several weeks or even months, either between the class on the *Messe de la Pentecôte* and the class on the *Sacre* or between the classes on *Turangalîla-Symphonie* and the *Messe de la Pentecôte*. The notes on the *Sacre* are fairly detailed, dedicated primarily to harmony and orchestration, with Messiaen's celebrated 'personnages rythmiques' relegated to a brief passage on the 'Danse sacrale'. Xenakis also recorded the rhythms from rehearsal 46 (the end of the 'Ritual of Abduction') in numerical form.

Xenakis's final class with Messiaen, dedicated to the *Livre d'orgue*, seems to have been on 6 July 1954. Xenakis took meticulous notes on the rhythmic interversions of the Hindu rhythm 'niçcanka' and the '64 durées', writing down the disposition of the 64 note-lengths, divided into groups of four and expressed forwards and backwards. It is worth noting that Messiaen used the word 'sériel' to describe his piece, detailing the emergence of series in the score for his students.

---

[37] 'Vischnegradsky / gamme ¾ tons ≈ gamme par tons / Slonimsky / Thesaurus of scales / ajout 1 ou plusieurs tons dans la gamme / interpolation / ultra[polation] / infra[polation]', notebook 9, p. 25.

[38] *Pelléas*, Act II, scene 1.

186   Messiaen Perspectives 2: Techniques, Influence and Reception

I have already observed that Xenakis's notebooks contain no entries from the first part of the 1951–52 academic year, with breaks also occurring from January 1953 to the end of the 1952–53 school year, and from February or March 1954 until July of the same year. Given his tendency to take notes at even classes that seem to have little interested him, it seems unlikely that Xenakis went to class without taking notes during such a long stretch of time. One very plausible reason for these absences may have been his professional duties at Le Corbusier's studio. Though we know that Le Corbusier held Messiaen in great esteem and may have occasionally overlooked Xenakis missing work for class,[39] it seems Xenakis was often unable to regularly attend all three weekly sessions of Messiaen's classes which then took place on Tuesdays, Thursdays and Saturdays. It should also be pointed out that in 1953, Le Corbusier had granted Xenakis's request to work on the project for the Dominican convent of La Tourette.[40] This new role in Le Corbusier's studio as an architect and not just an engineer surely reduced free time for attending Messiaen's classes during a period when Xenakis was also claiming to need more time for composing. In this sense, the mid-1950s might be seen as a period marking the emergence of Xenakis's independent creative spirit in both architecture and music. In any case, Xenakis seems to have regretted missing so many of Messiaen's classes, writing to Louis Saguer[41] in May 1953, 'Ça fait longtemps que je n'ai pas vu Messiaen'.[42] This also supports the theory that the gap in Xenakis's notes from January to July 1953 corresponds to a period during which he did not attend Messiaen's class.

Another explanation for these absences might be that certain topics were often repeated. For instance, in November–December 1952, Xenakis took meticulous notes on Hindu rhythms; a year later in November 1953, among his notes on *Pelléas*, he recorded the current programme: 'tous les mardis rythmes hindous /

---

[39]   See Matossian, *Iannis Xenakis*, p. 47.

[40]   For Xenakis's request to participate in the Notre Dame de la Tourette project, see Iannis Xenakis, *Musique de l'Architecture*, Sharon Kanach (ed.) (Marseille: Parenthèses, 2006), p. 105. For Xenakis's role in the project, see Sergio Feero, Chérif Kebbal, Philippe Potié et Cyrille Simonnet, *Le Corbusier: Le Couvent de la Tourette* (Marseille: Éd. Parenthèses, 1988) and Anne-Sylvie Barthel-Calvet, 'De l'ubiquité poïétique dans l'œuvre de Iannis Xenakis: Espace, Temps, Musique, Architecture', *Intersections*, 29/2 (2009): p. 10.

[41]   Louis Saguer (1907–91) whose real name was Wolfgang Simoni, was a French composer of German birth who was naturalized in 1947. After studies in Berlin (with Hindemith among others), he settled in Paris in 1933. After the war, he was very involved in performing contemporary music, particularly in Darmstadt. His own style is based on the fusion of modal and atonal languages. Xenakis wrote to him on 9 January 1952 – while he was at the same time attending Messiaen's class – introducing himself as a 'Greek musician' and asking if Saguer would agree to give him 'music lessons (fugue, composition, etc.)' (letter dated 9 January 1952, *Lettres de Yannis Xenakis à Louis Saguer*, BnF, Music Department).

[42]   'I have not seen Messiaen for a long time', letter dated 4 May 1954, *Lettres de Yannis Xenakis à Louis Saguer*, BnF, Music Department.

jeudi et samedi Debussy'[43] after which no further notes on Hindu rhythms can be found. It might be that Xenakis thought it pointless to attend a class for which he had already taken exhaustive notes.

There are no notes at all on other topics taught at least twice during those three years, including Debussy's *Préludes* for piano and Messiaen's own *Vingt Regards sur l'Enfant-Jésus*. Was Xenakis really not able to make the time for these classes, or was he simply uninterested in these subjects? A similar question might be posed concerning the variable density of his notes: why are they sometimes very detailed and at other times distracted and vague? The greatest contrast appears in his notes on *Pelléas*. On pp. 35–9 of notebook 9 he took precise notes, mainly on questions of harmony and orchestration on the third scene of Act I, but on page 40 he merely doodled, idly noting 'gamme par tons dans les deux transpositions pour harmoniser une mélodie'.[44] Generally speaking, these different levels of intensity may reflect either a lack of interest or fatigue. Xenakis had a hectic schedule, working days at Le Corbusier's studio and spending his nights composing. The content of these more densely written passages demands more careful analysis insofar as they relate the tenor of Messiaen's teaching, and more particularly, the individual subjects that captured Xenakis's attention.

Xenakis's notebooks seem to show that Messiaen did not always analyse using the same standards and techniques. In a classical work, such as Beethoven's Fifth Symphony, he tended to emphasize thematic organization, whereas in early twentieth-century works, such as Debussy's *Pelléas* or Stravinsky's *Sacre du printemps*, he was more likely to make observations about the orchestration. Xenakis's abundant notes on orchestration show his interest in the subject and also seem to indicate that Messiaen intended his teaching, involving both principles of abstract construction and orchestration tricks, for future composers. His most detailed notes on orchestration were taken at the end of 1953 when he had just finished *Le Sacrifice*, in which he developed very particular treatments of timbre involving the play of sonic interferences. Xenakis also seems to have been very interested in Messiaen's classes on rhythm, as is evidenced by the carefully transcribed successions of rhythmic motives in numerical form. This is most apparent in his reproduction of tables of Hindu rhythms and in the analyses of *Le sacre du printemps, Turangalîla-Symphonie, Messe de la Pentecôte* and the *Livre d'orgue*. The fact that Xenakis was most interested in Messiaen's own compositions, those closest to his own, historically speaking, will provide terrain for further reflection below.

In three different examples, Xenakis's personal reactions to Messiaen's ideas or statements can be gleaned from his notes. In his 17 January 1953 notes on *Don Giovanni*, Xenakis writes: 'changement de couleur total à l'apparition de la statue. / élément de contraste', commenting, 'Le manque de changement de couleur est à la base de la crise actuelle. Les moyens sont trop riches aujourd'hui. / Époque analogue à celle entre le plain-chant et l'harmonie. Guillaume de Machaut qui

---

[43] 'Tuesdays Hindu rhythms / Thursdays and Saturdays Debussy.'

[44] 'whole-tones scale in both transpositions to harmonize a melody.'

188   *Messiaen Perspectives 2: Techniques, Influence and Reception*

a pressenti l'avenir' and, in a vertical line alongside this paragraph, the words 'crise moderne' [modern crisis].[45] Some elements appear to come from Messiaen, especially the reference to music history; on the other hand, the terms 'crise moderne' and 'crise actuelle' belong more to Xenakis's vocabulary.[46] In this case, it is difficult to ascribe the entire remark to one or the other.

In the middle of his notes about the modes of limited transposition (23 October 1953), Xenakis writes: 'Considération harmonique seulement / ni série ni mode grec ou hindou / ni mélodie ni tonique / pas d'initiale pas de finale / "pas de lien" par des series / seulement couleur. / "synopsie"'.[47] The generally critical tone that opens this commentary would seem to preclude its sole attribution to Messiaen, particularly for the diminishing words 'considération harmonique seulement' and 'seulement couleur'. This note is rather equivocal: it could reveal the fact that, at that time, in the early 1950s, Messiaen was critical towards his own compositional techniques – expressing his doubts even in his own teaching; it could also indicate that Messiaen's modes did not correspond to the sorts of musical organization Xenakis sought during this period, although his position would later change when he returned to Messiaen's modes in formalizing his ideas on sieve theory. At this time, Xenakis was already working on *Le Sacrifice* in which he links the organization of pitches and note-values.

A remark on Messiaen's harmonic analysis of Debussy indicates Xenakis's intellectual maturity and independence. On 23 November 1953, for the analysis of *Prélude à l'après-midi d'un faune*, he noted:

> Théorie Messiaen / Une seule harmonie vraie pour une mélodie
> Chez Debussy / 1) sans harmonie / 2) harmonie 1 ton plus bas / 3) est la vraie/
> 'chaude naturelle' / (pour moi platte) [sic] / les critiques l'appellent sensuelle /
> assez compliquée [with an arrow from 'chaude naturelle'].[48]

The words 'pour moi platte' clearly reflect an assertion of Xenakis's own harmonic taste.

---

[45]   'complete change of colour with the statue's appearance/element of contrast'. 'The lack of changing colour is at the base of the current crisis. The means are now too rich. / Analogous time with the one between plainsong and harmony. Guillaume de Machaut had the path to the future' (notebook 9, p. 13).

[46]   See Xenakis's 1955 essay 'La crise de la musique sérielle'.

[47]   'Harmonic consideration only / neither series nor Greek or Hindu mode/ neither melody nor tonic / no initial no final note / no "link" with series / only colour/ "synopsia"' (notebook 9, p. 25).

[48]   'Messiaen Theory: Only one true harmony for a melody. For Debussy / 1) without any harmony / 2) Harmony 1 tone below / 3) is the true one / "natural warm" / (for me flat) / critics call it sensual / quite complicated' (notebook 9, pp. 28–9). For Xenakis's ideas about Debussy, see Anne-Sylvie Barthel-Calvet, 'Le regard de Xenakis sur Debussy', in Myriam Chimènes and Alexandra Laederich (eds), *Regards sur Debussy* (Paris: Fayard, 2013): pp. 517–31.

Comparing Xenakis's Class Notes with his Other Notebooks

It is also necessary to study Xenakis's other notebooks from this period in order to appraise interactions between the two composers' ideas and the impact of Messiaen's teaching on his pupil's artistic evolution. Making the use of these sources is a painstaking affair, but the rewards include the possibility of understanding the impact of ideas taught in Messiaen's class. Sometimes the examples of Messiaen's teachings coincide chronologically with their evocation in Xenakis's notes, sketches and writings; sometimes they do not.

Serial Techniques
A first important case of chronological coincidence between Messiaen's class and Xenakis's personal notes may be observed between notebook 9 and notebook 1. On 20 October 1953,[49] Xenakis took notes from Messiaen's class on Webern's op. 18, indicating the process of dividing series into short, superposable segments.[50] A brief and rapidly written text in Greek ('Μικροπρέπεια τοῦ Messiaen' [Messiaen's pettiness]), bears the same date and can be found in notebook 1. Here, Xenakis criticizes Messiaen's claim to have played a leading role in the evolution of serialism.[51] Ten days later, on 30 October 1953, Xenakis hastily scribbled an outline for a text, 'Musique sérielle', in which he emphasized the musical significance of segmenting the 12-tone row 'for more richness and complexity'. He experimented with this technique in *Metastasis*, begun in early 1954:[52] different segmentations are used in each of the four serial sections of the work, the segmentations are derived from different organizational processes set out in the text 'MÉTASTASSIS-Analyse'.[53] Understood from this point of view, 'Musique sérielle' almost reads like a programme for the techniques used in Metastasis. Such close alignment between Xenakis's class notes and personal notes is rare and suggests that Messiaen's class on Webern corresponded with Xenakis's compositional concerns.

---

[49]   Notebook 9, p. 21. As noted above, Messiaen had already started his theme of serial music at an undated earlier session.

[50]   'en superposition de fragments/tronçons de la série' [in superposition of fragments/ sections of the series].

[51]   See n. 5 above.

[52]   Although the dates usually given for this work, as indicated in Xenakis's hand on the score, are 1953–54, a study of the sketches proves that he actually started composition at the end of January 1954 (notebook 13, p. 10 ff. and file O.M. 1/4, Xenakis Archives, BnF). See also Barthel-Calvet, 'Xenakis et le sérialisme: L'apport d'une analyse génétique de Metastasis', *Intersections: Revue Canadienne de Musique*, 31/2 (2011): pp. 3–22. The score of *Metastasis* from Messiaen's personal collection now held at the Médiathèque of the Paris Conservatoire (a facsimile version of one of Xenakis's manuscripts) bears the date 1954–55.

[53]   Anne-Sylvie Barthel-Calvet, '*MÉTASTASSIS-Analyse*: Un texte inédit de Iannis Xenakis sur *Metastasis*', *Revue de Musicologie*, 89/1 (2003): pp. 129–87.

Permutation as a Compositional Tool

Another meaningful convergence occurs with the use of permutations. Notes on permutations appear very early in Xenakis's notebooks: on the first page of notebook 8, in January 1952,[54] he wrote out permutations of three elements without indicating what they corresponded to:

$$A = 123 \qquad B = 312 \qquad C = 231$$

and the reverse forms:

$$\bar{A} = 321 \qquad \bar{B} = 213 \qquad \bar{C} = 132$$

It may be assumed that these numbers refer to note length since a larger set of numerical values displayed on the following pages turns out to correspond to the succession of note-lengths in the central piano part of *Tripli Zyia* (bars 116–164). Beyond its meaning as a sketch of a particular work, this document falls within a larger genetic perspective as it represents the oldest identifiable example of Xenakis's use of permutations, a compositional process that he would extensively develop later in his career.

Almost two years later, in December 1953,[55] Xenakis made an attempt at composing with permutations of four sounds labelled 'a, b, c, d', without taking his sketches to their logical conclusion. However, this process would be used for the first four sounds of the basic series of the central part of *Metastasis*, finalized between January and April 1954, in which the possible permutations were indeed exhausted in a mathematical organization.[56] This was also the case in Xenakis's June 1954 plans for the interior glass panels at the La Tourette Convent, although Le Corbusier did not ultimately retain this project.[57] This principle would later see highly elaborate developments in Xenakis's music from the mid-1960s onward, with the composition of permutation groups set out in 'Towards a Philosophy of Music', published in the *Gravesaner Blätter* in 1966 and used in both *Akrata* (1964–65) and *Nomos Alpha* (1966).[58]

---

[54] Page 3 bears the indication '7/γν.52', which, in Greek, means 7 January 1952.

[55] Notebook 11, p. 90.

[56] This is according to the principles of group composition, comparable to Messiaen's techniques of interversions and symmetrical permutations. For further details on this point, see Barthel-Calvet, '*MÉTASTASSIS-Analyse*': pp. 137–41 and 'De l'ubiquité poïétique dans l'œuvre de Iannis Xenakis': pp. 11–14.

[57] See Xenakis, *Musique de l'architecture*, pp. 105–19 and Barthel-Calvet, 'De l'ubiquité poïétique dans l'œuvre de Iannis Xenakis': pp. 14–16.

[58] Iannis Xenakis, 'Zu einer Philosophie der Musik' /'Towards a Philosophy of Music': this text is given either in German or English in the *Gravesaner Blätter*, 29 (1966): pp. 23–38, 39–52; revised and enlarged edition: 'Vers une philosophie de la musique', *Revue*

According to his class notebooks and the meticulous notes he took during Messiaen's class on the topic of permutations (particularly in the analysis of the *Livre d'orgue* on 6 July 1954), it is clear that Xenakis was very aware of this element of his teacher's musical poetics. As we shall see, some 30 years later, he emphasized Messiaen's crucial role in the development of permutations as a compositional tool, mainly in the field of rhythm.

The Concept of Additive Rhythm

Although he developed different rhythmic systems (polymetrics, note-lengths, sieves, etc.) across his entire career,[59] Xenakis always worked within the framework of an additive organization of rhythm, based on the succession of note-values built in reference to a common elementary unit, for instance a quaver or semiquaver. It is therefore worthwhile to study how this type of rhythmic writing emerged in his early intellectual development as well as possible connections with Messiaen's thinking on rhythm.

Starting his first notebook in September 1951 with thoughts on rhythm, Xenakis turns on page 3 to a four-page text dated October 1951 titled 'Hindu music' that is nearly exclusively devoted to rhythm.[60] It is not certain he had already heard about Hindu (Indian) music from Messiaen, as the first course on this topic during the academic year 1951–52 seems to have been held two months later on 18 December.[61] According to François-Bernard Mâche, this interest for 'Hindu music' might have been stimulated at concerts Xenakis attended at the Musée Guimet and from recordings in the collection of André Schaeffner at the Musée de l'Homme.[62] At any rate, the first notes about Hindu music that may be found in his class notebook date from 4 and 6 December 1952, a full year later. The care with which these notes were taken seems to indicate his interest for the topic.

Describing Hindu music as the 'most civilized and perfect organization of rhythm' [organisation la plus civilisée du rythme et la plus parfaite], Xenakis pointed out its additive organization: 'Le temps de base, le continuum, forme la trame saisissable. Le reste est un jeu d'antithèses p.ex. 3+2, 3+2+2'.[63] Although Xenakis was also interested in more complicated alternations of values of two and three with longer values of five and seven,[64] the main source of his interest in

---

d'esthétique, 21/2–3–4 (1968): pp. 173–210; *Musique. Architecture* (Tournai: Casterman, 1971), pp. 71–119; 'W strone filozofii Muzyki', *Res Facta,* 2 (1968).

[59]   See Anne-Sylvie Barthel-Calvet, *Le rythme dans l'œuvre et la pensée de Iannis Xenakis*, PhD thesis, 4 Vols (École des Hautes Études en Sciences Sociales, Paris, 2000).

[60]   Notebook 1, pp. 4–8, this text is published in François-Bernard Mâche, 'Xenakis et la musique indienne', *Filigrane*, 10 (2009).

[61]   See Boivin, *La classe de Messiaen*, p. 437.

[62]   Mâche, 'Xenakis et la musique indienne': *Filigrane*, 10 (2009): p. 21.

[63]   'The basic time, the continuum, forms the perceptible frame. The rest is a play of antithesis, for instance, 3+2, 3+2+2' (notebook 1, pp. 3–4).

[64]   Ibid., p. 4.

Hindu rhythms lay in the possibility of expressing their structures mathematically, noting 'Ceci relève de l'esprit, de l'ordre mathématique des nombres simples.'[65] He continues:

> On devrait pouvoir étudier le rythme à l'aide des formules mathématiques. Des mathématiques très primitives, des théories des nombres entiers …
> Organiser le temps mathématiquement veut dire rythme hindou.[66]

> [It should be possible to study rhythm with mathematic formulas. Very primitive mathematics, whole number theories …
> Organizing time mathematically means Hindu rhythm.]

It is worth pointing out that Xenakis showed great interest in the possibility of organizing note-values through arithmetic principles also observable in Messiaen's rhythmic thinking, particularly in the works of the late 1940s and early 1950s.

In Xenakis's notes from October 1951, these concepts were still in embryonic form, but a few months later, in April–May 1952, Xenakis used them in composing *Tripli Zyia*. The sketches for this work make it possible to understand the development of his thoughts. On 11 April 1952, Xenakis extended his previous reflections in a fairly long text entitled 'Conclusion sur la Section d'Or dans le temps' in which he uses the example of a sequence of note-values built up from a hemidemisemiquaver whose presentation suggests an affinity with the division of values in *Mode de valeurs et d'intensités*.[67]

While both Messiaen's and Xenakis's rhythmic sequences share an additive organization and reflect the will to create an intrinsic link between musical parameters, Xenakis's series distinguishes itself in that the proportions between the different values are not just arithmetic, but geometric, following the Fibonacci sequence whose progression ratio is 1.618, the Golden Number. According to Boivin's recreation of the schedule of classes, Messiaen analysed his *Quatre Études de rythme* in April–May 1952.[68] For now, it is impossible to know whether Xenakis attended Messiaen's class on this topic, as he had not begun his classbook 9 at that date. There is no trace of this class on the *Quatre Études* course in notebook 7. It is also worth noting that, as Le Corbusier's assistant, Xenakis frequently dealt with modulor scales based on Fibonacci Series. He may have been tempted to apply this principle to build his sequence of note-values.

Xenakis soon noted that a row built on such proportions brought about difficulties in execution:

---

[65] 'This is the spirit, the order of simple numbers' (ibid., p. 4).
[66] Ibid., pp. 6–8.
[67] 'Conclusion on Golden Section in time' (ibid., pp. 27–35).
[68] Boivin, *La classe de Messiaen*, p. 438.

Mathématiquement déterminé puis réalisé, ce rythme est injouable. ... La grande difficulté réside dans le fait que plus on veut augmenter l'approximation c'est-à-dire employer des décimales très petites, plus l'unité commune (comme mesure) devient petite donc, dans le spectre de très courtes durées, avant même d'atteindre la limite de la perceptibilité, l'exécution est pour ainsi dire impossible.[69]

[Mathematically determined and realized, this rhythm is unplayable. ... The great difficulty lies in the fact that the more you want to increase the approximation, that is to use very small decimals, the more the common unit (as measure) becomes small, therefore, in the spectrum of very short note-values, even before reaching the limits of perceptibility, the performance becomes impossible.]

Xenakis would get around this practical difficulty by using the medium of tape: he cut pieces of tape whose lengths fit the Golden Number ratio[70] and corresponded to note-values that were long enough to be played with reasonable ease. With an acceptable approximation of the Golden Number ratio and tempo adaptations, Xenakis managed to express these values in coherent musical notation using an arithmetic expression, building a satisfying set of note-values based on 5, 8, 13 and 21 units that he used in *Zyia* (Example 7.1 below).

Later, in *Metastasis*, Xenakis set up a similar ratio for what he called 'differential duration' corresponding to the time between two notes in a polyphonic context – another concept made possible thanks to additive rhythmic thinking.[71]

I have already noted that Xenakis took particularly careful notes on rhythm on Hindu rhythmic modes in November 1952, on the modes of the seventh movement of *Turangalîla* and on '64 Durées' from the *Livre d'orgue* in July 1954. Xenakis also showed a special interest for the statement of note-length successions expressed arithmetically. Conversely, and somewhat surprisingly, his notes about the 'personnages rythmiques' in Messiaen's analysis of *Le sacre du printemps* are not very detailed: Messiaen may have been more allusive that day, but his talk also may have simply failed to capture Xenakis's interest.

At the beginning of the 1950s, Messiaen composed the most abstract music of his career. It is clear that his presentation of rhythmical matters was most likely not only to catch Xenakis's interest, but also to provide him with tools and concepts that, given his scientific background, he would be in position to easily use. Both composers shared the practice of a rhythmic writing based on a succession of note-lengths as well as a taste for mathematical games and the abstract organization of rhythmic values using interversions or the Golden Number.

---

[69]   Notebook 1, p. 27.

[70]   Ibid., pp. 30–31.

[71]   See Barthel-Calvet, 'MÉTASTASSIS-*Analyse*': pp. 131–6; 'De l'ubiquité poïétique dans l'œuvre de Iannis Xenakis': pp. 22–5. For Xenakis's notes, see notebook 13, pp. 22–9.

Example 7.1   Xenakis, *Zyia*, bars 354–363

Le Sacrifice as a Tribute to Messiaen

All of the works composed during Xenakis's time in Messiaen class bear, in varying degrees, the mark of Messiaen's teachings, but *Le Sacrifice* (*I Thysia*, in Greek, part of the *Anastenaria* cycle), turned out to be a true tribute to Messiaen's compositional models insofar as it willingly integrates compositional models typical of Messiaen. This work, dedicated to 'mon maître et ami Olivier Messiaen' was composed sometime in the middle of 1953.[72] The first dated sketches, marked 31 May 1953, show a rather advanced stage of composition and 'Aix-en-Provence, 28 juillet 1953' is written on the front page of the manuscript score.[73] However, on 31 August 1953, Xenakis made notes on sound interferences to be used in *Le Sacrifice* that also appear in the score, indicating that he may have finished this work later than is indicated on his manuscript.[74]

As the sketches, scattered across notebooks 1, 6, 8 and 10 show, Xenakis was in search of basic material that he called a 'series', based on both the Fibonacci

---

[72]   'To my master and friend Olivier Messiaen', *Le Sacrifice*, score (Paris, Salabert, 2000), p. 5.
[73]   Notebook 10, p. 1.
[74]   Notebook 1, p. 43.

Example 7.2 Xenakis, *Le Sacrifice*, series with note-lengths assigned to pitches

sequence and on intrinsic connections between pitches and note-lengths. However, this linkage as it appears in its final version was established very late in the compositional process (Example 7.2).[75]

This relationship of pitches to note-lengths is of course reminiscent of Messiaen, but beyond this clear homage (also comparable to the series of Boulez's *Structures 1a*), there is a deeper connection to Messiaen's musical poetics, based on a personal integration of Messiaen's musical interversions that had so struck Xenakis. This is not yet a matter of composing with mathematical groups as he would later do in *Metastasis*, but an evolutionary process that, so far, has not been observed by other scholars.[76]

Globally, the system of connections between pitches and note-lengths is used more freely than in *Mode de valeurs et d'intensités*; Xenakis's pitches are integrated within clusters and therefore take on the note-length of their pitch-centre, not the note-length from the initial row. The evolution of the piece is based on the idea that lengths assigned to pitches do not remain fixed but gradually change. This change occurs in different stages:

- first, an exposition of pitches, layered in Varèse-like clusters, with long note-lengths corresponding to lowest pitches (bars 1–22) and then with shorter ones in relation with highest (bars 22–37);
- then, from bar 38, the value of 34 semiquavers disappears and pitches take on shorter values as in the initial display (21 and then 13 semiquavers for E instead of 34; 8 and then 3 for B♭ instead of 13, etc.);
- from bar 63, an inversion of values may be observed as the lowest pitches become the shortest (1 semi-quaver for E and 2 for G) and the highest the longest (8 semiquavers for A and 5 for C);

---

[75] For details of genesis of 'Le Sacrifice', see Anne-Sylvie Barthel-Calvet: 'A Creative Mind in Eruption: Xenakis Composing the *Anastenaria* cycle in 1953', proceedings of the *Xenakis International Symposium*, Southbank Centre, London, 1–3 April 2011, p. 6, available at www.gold.ac.uk/ccmc/xenakis-international-symposium.

[76] Makis Solomos speaks of a 'mechanism' ('Les *Anastenaria* de Xenakis: Continuité et discontinuité historique', available at www.iannis-xenakis.org/fxe/actus/solom2.pdf, pp.14–15). In fact, Xenakis's sketches indicate no such mechanism.

- bars 74 to 76 contain an evenly arranged set of note-lengths;
- a new process of modification unfolds between bars 76 and 87 as the note-values of the four highest pitches of the set are permutated among themselves and the ones of the three lowest also;
- bars 87 to 91 again contain evenly arranged note-lengths;
- in bars 92 to 95, inversions of the original note-lengths (long for highest notes, short for lowest ones) are superimposed (but not all of them are used);
- finally, from bar 96 to the end, the low and high notes of the row are played together with the same long values.

It is also worth noting that the values of the silences belong to the Fibonacci sequence.

The process of evolution brought into play here explores the possibilities of variations offered by the permutations of note-values. Xenakis did not exactly resort to Messiaen's processes of interversion, but instead took the general idea and made it his own in order to organize the evolving textures of his work, varying their density and construction. Other connotations arise upon listening to *Le Sacrifice*: Varèse for the superposition of sound planes and also, in a way, Giacinto Scelsi with *Quatro Pezzi su una nota sola*, but this work was composed only in 1959 and, in 1953, Xenakis could have known Varèse only through recordings, as the latter only returned to Paris one year later in December 1954, for the creation of *Déserts*.

Messiaen's Place in Xenakis's Theory of Outside-time Structures

In the mid 1960s, about ten years after composing *Metastasis*, Xenakis undertook a theoretical project that he developed in two main directions. He first built a theory of musical time around the famous concept of outside-time/inside-time structures first set forth in 1963 in the fifth chapter of *Musiques formelles*.[77] To these summaries of his earlier ideas on musical time, he added the further theoretical development of pitch scales and periodical systems of other musical elements (such as note-lengths) that he called 'screens'[78] in the article 'Towards a Philosophy of Music' (1966) followed by 'Vers une Métamusique' (1967).[79] An initial, undated manuscript version of the latter is held in Xenakis's archives at

---

[77] Xenakis, *Musiques formelles*, Ch. V, pp. 183–208; *Formalized Music*, Ch. VI, pp. 155–77.

[78] Xenakis uses either the term of 'screens' ('Towards a Philosophy of Music', p. 49) or 'sieves' (*Formalized Music*, p. 278 ff).

[79] Iannis Xenakis, 'Vers une métamusique', *La Nef*, 29 (January–March 1967): pp. 117–40, summarized in *Musique architecture*, pp. 38–70, English trans. in: *Formalized Music*, Ch. VII: 'Towards a Metamusic', pp. 180–200.

the Bibliothèque Nationale de France; entitled 'Structures Harmoniques / Hors-Temps', it immediately comes across as a tribute to Messiaen:

> Le but de cet exposé est de montrer qu'un des aspects de l'œuvre de Messiaen (touche-à-tout génial)[80] s'incrit dans un des courants les plus fondamental de la pensée musicale qui prend ses sources dans les brumes de la préhistoire et qui va s'élargissant vers l'avenir à notre insu et en dépit de nous. Il s'agit des structures hors-temps.[81]

> [The goal of this paper is to show that one aspect of Messiaen's œuvre (a dabbler of genius) falls within the scope of one of the most fundamental currents of the musical thought which takes its source in the mists of prehistory and which expands towards the future without our realizing it and in spite of us: outside-time structures.]

Xenakis then goes through a highly detailed account of the evolution of music from ancient Greece to the twentieth century, considered under the double concept of outside-time/inside-time.[82] He then returns to Messiaen, writing:

> Messiaen se place à cette charnière. Que sont en vrai les modes à transpositions limitées? Une nouvelle tentative de superposer à la structure d'ordre total de la gamme tempérée une autre organisation interne plus réduite. C'est là que réside son génie talent créateur. Bâtir une nouvelle syntaxe.[83]

> [Messiaen is located at this turning point. What in truth are the modes of limited transposition but a new attempt to superimpose on the total structured order of the tempered scale another more reduced internal organization? This is where his creative genius talent lies. In building new syntax.]

Xenakis's interest in Messiaen's musical thinking is focused on the modes of limited transpositions. Because they do not determine the melodic or harmonic order of pitches, Messiaen's modes qualify as 'outside-time' structures that Xenakis formalized – as he did for the ancient Greek modes – using the abstract model of 'sieves'.[84] On page 25 of 'Structures Harmoniques/Hors-temps' – a passage that

---

[80] Here and later, the crossed out passages are Xenakis's own.

[81] File Writings 1/6, f. 1, Xenakis Archives.

[82] This part of the unpublished 'Structures harmoniques-hors-temps' may be found in 'Vers une métamusique': pp. 120–33.

[83] File Writings 1/6, f. 20.

[84] It is worth noting Xenakis's changed opinion on the usefulness of the modes of limited transposition since his days as a student in Messiaen's class (see notebook 9, pp. 22–6 mentioned above). Without going into a detailed description of sieve theory, Xenakis elaborates his idea by comparing the periodicity of musical structures (scales, initially) with

was cut from the final version of 'Vers une Métamusique' – Xenakis gave the numerical expression of the seven modes of limited transposition. For instance, mode 3 which repeats the same cell three times, has the following numerical expression in semitones:

$$0, 2, 3 \qquad\qquad 4, 6, 7 \qquad\qquad 8, 10, 11$$

As residual class 4_0 gives the values 0, 4, 8, etc.; residual class 4_2 the values 2, 6, 10, etc. and residual class 4_3 yields 3, 7, 11, etc., the mathematical formula $4_0 + 4_2 + 4_3$ expresses the whole structure of this third mode.

Giving comparable expressions of other musical modes, Xenakis stated he wanted to build a 'general symbolic expression able to unify all that was done and what will be done in time and space'.[85] At the end of 'Structures harmoniques / hors-temps', he added:

> Le dépassement actuel de la musique réside, je crois, dans ces recherches de la catégorie hors-temps atrophiée et dominée par la catégorie temporelle. Il faut rendre hommage à Olivier Messiaen d'avoir le premier (re)exploré consciemment ce domaine tombé en friche depuis plusieurs siècles. Je suis heureux de pouvoir le faire ici et de placer son travail conscient dans la lignée des grandes cultures musicales d'Europe.[86]

> [The possibility in the further development of music lies, I believe, in research in the outside-time category, nowadays forgotten and dominated by the temporal category. We have to pay homage to Olivier Messiaen to have been the first to consciously (re-)explore this terrain left fallow for several centuries. I am happy to be able to do it here and to place his lucid work in the lineage of the great musical European cultures.]

These remarks clearly show that Messiaen's musical poetics held a central position in Xenakis's important theory of music and of music history, in a sense, perhaps the only real theory developed by Xenakis, if it is considered that stochastics are more of a compositional tool. For unknown reasons, this text, conceived as a tribute to Messiaen, remained unpublished as such.[87] In the published version, entitled 'Vers une métamusique', the references to Messiaen's musical thinking were cut,

---

the residual classes of whole numbers, proposing numerical representations of repetitive forms (like modes) using the mathematical operations of union and intersection.

[85]   File Writings 1/6, f. 27.

[86]   Ibid., f. 28.

[87]   In 'Vers une philosophie de la musique' (p. 180), Xenakis wrote in a footnote: 'J'ai fait une interprétation nouvelle des modes à transposition limitée de Messiaen qui devait être publiée il y a de cela deux ans dans une collection qui n'a pas encore vu le jour.' [I have made a new interpretation of Messiaen's modes of limited transpositions that was supposed

with only sporadic allusions to Xenakis's former teacher that drastically change his argument's centre of gravity. 'Vers une métamusique' is no longer a tribute to Messiaen, where the composer is seen as a watershed in recent Western music of a process begun, according to Xenakis, in antiquity, but rather a theoretical exposition where Messiaen is hardly mentioned at all.

Xenakis returned to these ideas in a paper published in the journal of the Opéra de Paris[88] upon the première of *Saint François d'Assise*, where he again evoked Messiaen's importance, not only with the renewal of outside-time structures but also as an influence on the works of the younger generation of composers and more particularly his own compositional and theoretical choices. He presented Messiaen's contribution to the evolution of music from the standpoint of his own musical poetics:

> Intuitivement, Olivier Messiaen a réinventé d'une façon moderne la combinatoire musicale. Il appelle 'interversions' les permutations et les introduit surtout dans le domaine du temps. Neuf, original et aventureux parce qu'il monte à la lumière un concept enfoui dans la musique depuis la nuit des temps. L'usage qu'il en fait dans le *Livre d'orgue* par exemple, donne une de ses plus belles œuvres. Or les questions que soulèvent les 'interversions', puisque c'est son mot, conduisent à la combinatoire mathématique qui mène elle-même à une bifurcation remarquable. Car d'elle partent le concept de symétrie (périodicité) stricte avec comme aboutissement la théorie des groupes ainsi qu'à l'autre extrême et comme antithétique le concept d'asymétrie stricte, le hasard, la stochastique (la probabilité). Mais O. Messiaen s'est volontairement, sans doute, arrêté avant la bifurcation. Et pourtant sa musique faite ainsi est immédiate et lumineuse.[89]

> [Intuitively, Olivier Messiaen reinvented musical combinatorics in a modern manner. He calls permutations 'interversions' and uses them most often in the field of time. He is fresh, original and adventurous, because he brings to light a concept that has been buried in music since the dawn of time. The way he uses it in the *Livre d'orgue*, for instance, provides one of his most beautiful works. The questions that these 'interversions' raise (as it is his term) lead to a combinatorial mathematics which in turn lead to a noteworthy fork in the road resulting in the concepts of strict symmetry (periodicity) with group theory as a result and, on the other extreme and as an antithesis, the concept of strict asymmetry, chance, the stochastics (probability). But O. Messiaen stopped, no doubt intentionally, before reaching this point. And even so his music made this way is direct and bright.]

---

to be published two years ago in a series that has not, thus far, seen the light of day.] The text mentioned here may be 'Structures harmoniques / hors-temps'.

[88] Iannis Xenakis, 'Olivier Messiaen': p. 6.

[89] Ibid..

As surprising as it may appear, Xenakis draws a line in musical evolution involving his own compositional concepts, where Messiaen is seen as staying behind the stage he had himself reached.[90] This did not keep Xenakis from sincerely praising Messiaen's contribution to musical modernity[91] as seen from a standpoint he considered as the only valuable one. As it were, Xenakis took Messiaen for a reference as Boulez had already done with Webern, but in both cases the reading of these composers' predecessors is entirely dependent on the role those figures play in their own thinking about music.

Conclusion

In these later testimonies, Xenakis gives Messiaen a central place in his autobiographical historiography. This recognition seems like an awareness of all that he was reliant upon in his professor during his formative years, all that had played a part in the release of his own creative imagination. However, this central place accorded to Messiaen involves a particular view of Messiaen's musical poetics. Both as a pupil and later, as a recognized composer paying tribute to his master, Xenakis appears to have reacted to Messiaen's thinking with critical distance, showing attraction for only certain aspects of Messiaen's work. During his early years, in pieces such as *Zyia*, *Le Sacrifice* and even *Metastasis,* Xenakis showed particular interest in rhythmic questions involving systems of permutations and additive techniques that present undeniable links with the compositional processes that Messiaen was using in his most abstract works during the same period. Symptomatically, one of the pieces for which Xenakis took his most detailed notes in his class notebook in 1954 is the *Livre d'orgue*, a work he praised nearly 20 years later as 'one of Messiaen's most beautiful'.[92] Conversely, Xenakis showed no real interest for Messiaen's harmony, chord colours or birdsongs. Xenakis seems only to have adopted the parts of Messiaen's legacy that resonated with his own musical poetics.

---

[90]   For that matter, at the end of 'Structures Harmoniques / Hors-temps', Xenakis noted on a separate sheet, speaking about Messiaen: 'Il se rapproche par là de moi' [In this sense, he is close to me]. (File Writings 1/6, f. 18.)

[91]   Iannis Xenakis, 'Olivier Messiaen': p. 7: 'Brusquement, Debussy avec sa gamme par tons jette un regard neuf et ouvre la voie du renouvellement de ces notions et de leur abstraction. … Mais Olivier Messiaen, lui, va plus loin encore et crée consciemment de nouvelles échelles avec, comme point de départ, une idée abstraite plus générale, celle des invariants possibles lors des transpositions.' [Suddenly, with his whole-tones scales, Debussy reveals a new point of view and opens the way to the renewal of these notions and their abstractions. … But Olivier Messiaen goes further still and consciously creates new scales with a more general abstract idea as starting point: the invariability of transposition.]

[92]   Iannis Xenakis, 'Olivier Messiaen': p. 6.

Chapter 8
From France to Quebec:
Messiaen's Transatlantic Legacy

Heather White Luckow

Quebec's new music scene of the 1950s and 1960s owed much to the training of Québécois composers in France. As students, they worked under the tutelage of several legendary French teachers, of which Olivier Messiaen was arguably the most influential. Messiaen, as a pedagogue, facilitated the growth of his pupils in a direction stemming from each individual's unique talents, abilities and life experiences. As a result, the compositional styles of Quebec's Serge Garant (1929–86), Clermont Pépin (1926–2006) and André Prévost (1934–2001) are strikingly divergent, yet all three adopted and developed techniques of Messiaen, their teacher and mentor, in their own early compositions.

Garant and Pépin were close in age and studied with Messiaen concurrently: Pépin enrolled in his class from 1949 to 1952, and Garant from 1951 to 1952. Pépin was André Prévost's composition teacher at the Montreal Conservatory of Music before Prévost also went to Paris to study with Messiaen from 1960 to 1962. Garant emulated his teacher's ideas most literally, but only for a very short time. Pépin found the modes of limited transposition especially appealing, while Prévost gravitated towards the symmetrical permutations. This chapter demonstrates the gradual emergence and adaptation of these techniques in the music of the three young composers through an analysis of selected works composed before, during and immediately after they studied with Messiaen.

Several factors motivate an examination of Messiaen's influence from a compositional-technical perspective. All three students spoke of his influence in terms of compositional aesthetics and ideologies, but music analysts have not yet investigated these specific compositional techniques in their works. Thus, what has so far been known about Messiaen's influence is largely limited to what these composers have themselves chosen to mention. The following discussions of their early works not only provide tangible evidence in support of their personal accounts, but also uncover additional elements of influence that have so far been overlooked. Identifying the roots of the practices adopted from Messiaen will serve as the starting point for tracing subsequent technical developments in their music. In addition to the chords of Contracted Resonance, Hindu rhythms, modes of limited transposition, symmetrical permutations and non-retrogradable rhythms, these include innovations such as Garant's further systematization of integral serialism, Pépin's *Morsiques* (Morse code rhythmic patterns related to Messiaen's non-retrogradable rhythms), and Prévost's recursive application of symmetrical permutations.[1] As under Messiaen's influence all three composers developed unique approaches to serialist techniques, in the broadest sense, this study will shed new light on Québécois musical history and the distinctive compositional practices of the generation of composers born in the 1920s and 1930s.

Musical and cultural ties have been maintained between France and Quebec since the first French settlers proclaimed Quebec as 'New France' in the seventeenth century. The first professional musicians arriving in Quebec in the middle of the nineteenth century inspired their best pupils to complete their training in France. According to historian Gilles Potvin and musicologist Helmut Kallmann, 'thus began the continuing back-and-forth movement of young Canadian musicians who have undertaken extensive periods of study in France, chiefly in Paris, either in official institutions or with private teachers'.[2] Potvin and Kallman maintain that pedagogical travel was steady even during the Franco-Prussian War, First World War and Second World War.

The trend towards studying in France increased substantially in the twentieth century thanks to the creation of the Prix d'Europe. This annual study grant is funded by the Ministère des Affaires Culturelles du Québec and administered by the Académie de Musique du Québec. It was created by the Quebec government in 1911. Clermont Pépin won the prize in 1949, enabling him to live in Paris as a pianist from 1949 to 1955.[3] Several Québécois students went to Paris in a private capacity or on scholarships from the Quebec government or the Canada Council/ Conseil des Arts du Canada, launched in 1959 to foster and promote the study, enjoyment and production of work in the arts.[4] Serge Garant studied privately, and André Prévost studied on a scholarship. Garant's 1951–52 academic year in Paris was financed though the patronage of Madame Mimi Shea, who had recognized his talent in 1949 through a local Sherbrooke group, Jeudi Musical.[5] Prévost's 1960–61 year of study was funded through dual grants from both the government of Quebec and the Canada Council.

---

[1] Extending beyond the scope of this chapter, these later techniques are examined in Heather White Luckow, *La Marque du Maître: Messiaen's Influence on Québécois Composers Serge Garant, Clermont Pépin and André Prévost*, PhD diss. (McGill University, 2010). The dissertation is available online through McGill University's library catalogue (available at www.mcgill.ca/library). After locating the dissertation record in the catalogue, click 'digitool.Library.McGill.CA' to access the complete text.

[2] Gilles Potvin and Helmut Kallmann, 'France', in *The Encyclopedia of Music in Canada*, available at www.thecanadianencyclopedia.com.

[3] Cécile Huot, 'Prix d'Europe', in *The Encyclopedia of Music in Canada*, available at www.thecanadianencyclopedia.com.

[4] 'Canada Council/Conseil des arts du Canada', in *The Encyclopedia of Music in Canada*, available at www.thecanadianencyclopedia.com.

[5] Marie-Thérèse Lefebvre, *Serge Garant et la révolution musicale au Québec* (Montreal: L. Courteau, 1986), p. 25.

Messiaen taught more Québécois students in Paris during his tenure at the Conservatoire Nationale Supérieur de Musique than any other pedagogue, with the exception of Nadia Boulanger.[6] His reputation as an eminent composer and teacher drew the most promising young composers of the era to his analysis class at the Conservatoire. Jean Boivin attributes Messiaen's influence, in part, to the immediate access his students had to his most recent technical innovations:

> Messiaen did not hide any of the techniques used in his new compositions. The ink on the manuscripts was barely dry when a Pierre Boulez, Karel Goeyvaerts, Iannis Xenakis or Serge Garant could plunge in and gather the fuel that their excited minds demanded. This free access, referred to as his 'secret garden' by Gilles Tremblay, … contributed to the establishment of Messiaen's reputation as a master thinker amongst the younger post-war generation and made his class a distinguished place of western contemporary creation.[7]

Evidently, what Messiaen had to offer in his class extended well beyond the wealth of treasures found within his own works and those of his already well-established contemporaries. Since his classroom held talented students from a variety of cultural, academic and vocational backgrounds, he encouraged them to learn from one another, often reserving class time for the presentation of student compositions.[8] Garant was particularly struck by his classmate Boulez and later examples in this chapter illustrate Garant's employment of Boulez's most recent serial innovations at that time. In general, the music of Garant demonstrates a technical wedding of Messiaen's sense of systematization with the symmetrical schemata of Boulez. Pépin and Prévost likewise absorbed ideas from the music heard in Messiaen's class and tempered it with lessons learned from other teachers. Pépin's symphonic poems stylistically resemble the music of Stravinsky and Honegger, while Prévost's personal developments of serial reordering merge compositional techniques of Messiaen, Dutilleux and Berg.

---

[6]   A complete list of Messiaen's Québécois students was compiled according to enrolments records published by Jean Boivin in his book, *La classe de Messiaen* (Paris: Bourgois, 1995), pp. 410–32. Of the 36 former pupils of Nadia Boulanger listed in Potvin's and Kallmun's article 'France', 26 were originally from Quebec or later settled there: István Anhalt, Françoise Aubut, Pierre Beaudet, Maurice Blackburn, Richard Boulanger, Gabriel Charpentier, Gabriel Cusson, Isabelle Delorme, Andrée Desautels, Paul Doyon, Elzéar Fortier, Kenneth Gilbert, Irving Heller, Kelsey Jones, Maryvonne Kendergi, Jeanne Landry, Claude Lavoie, Roger Matton, Pierre Mercure, Pierre Mollet, Jean Papineau-Couture, Marguerite Pâquet, Michel Perrault, Rosette Renshaw, William Keith Rogers, and Yehuda Vineberg. Boivin's research of the yearly enrolment of Messiaen's students lists 14 Canadians, 12 of whom were either native or naturalized to Québec: Françoise Aubut, Jocelyne Binet, Jacques Faubert, Serge Garant, Jacques Hétu, Sylvio Lacharite, Sœur Blanche LeBlanc, Aline Legrand, Bruce Mather, Clermont Pépin, , André Prévost and Gilles Tremblay.

[7]   Boivin, *La classe de Messiaen*, p. 322.

[8]   Ibid., p. 161.

Messiaen Perspectives 2: Techniques, Influence and Reception

There is a great deal of stylistic diversity that is, to a large degree, independent of pre-compositional techniques, many of which the three composers shared. Collectively, the sound of their music spans the wide stylistic spectrum of compositional styles in Quebec at that time, where Garant's avant-garde sonorities at one end are diametrically opposed to the conservative neo-Romantic character of Pépin's music at the other. Prévost represents a balance between these two poles. His expressive tendencies aligned more with those of Pépin, yet he shared Garant's love of mathematical games and strict formal procedures.

Serge Garant

Serge Garant was born in Quebec City. His family moved through Verdun before settling in Sherbrooke when he was 11 years old. Official politically correct biographies explain that Garant was largely self-taught; although he finished grade 9 (at 14 years old), and subsequently enrolled in the local School of Arts and Trades, he found it uninteresting and chose not to continue with his studies.[9] From his own perspective, the humorous composer had a different take on his education when he quipped in an early interview that he had actually '"flunked out" of the second year of a technical school and was expelled from a Catholic seminary for questioning the authorities'.[10] His first formal composition and piano lessons with Claude Champagne and Yvonne Hubert in Montreal began only at the age of 18. Being industrious, Garant paid for both his lesson fees and the necessary commute into the city by playing the clarinet in the Sherbrooke Symphony Orchestra and saxophone in local jazz groups.[11] He discovered atonal and serial music on his own when perusing a local Sherbrooke music store and was instantly captivated. Before leaving for Paris he gave a hometown concert of Webern's Piano Variations, op. 27, and Schoenberg's Three Pieces for Piano.

While Garant's pre-Parisian music was at first jazz influenced and later inclined towards atonal techniques, the first piece he wrote in Paris during the academic year that he spent in Messiaen's class featured distinctly Messiaenic technical markers. In the first two movements of his 1951 *Concerts sur terre*, Garant acknowledged:

> Messiaen's influence was only too obvious; but I did not use any of his modes. In these two melodies there is a continual mutation of a series of chords. However,

---

[9] Lefebvre, *Serge Garant*, p. 25.

[10] Keith MacMillan and John Beckwith, *Contemporary Canadian Composers* (Toronto: Oxford University Press, 1975), p. 78.

[11] Ian Leonard Bradley, *Twentieth Century Canadian Composers*, 2 Vols (Agincourt: GLC Publishers, 1982), Vol. 2, pp. 175–6.

it is not the chords themselves that vary, but rather their colour, and this is due to the way in which the chords are distributed.[12]

To Garant's ears, the spacing and slow mutation of the chords in the first seven measures of the movement were aurally reminiscent of Messiaen's harmonic writing, as suggested by his use of the word *colour*. Considered horizontally, the upper three voices in measure 2 move in parallel motion by major third, major second and minor second, interval classes (ics) 4, 2 and 1, while the bass voice moves in contrary motion by semitone (Example 8.1). The result is a slow harmonic mutation, as the spacing of the [016] trichord in the upper voices remains fixed while only the bass changes. This gradual shift in pitch content and distribution is analogous to various hues of the passage's primary colour, since each of these harmonies is a subset-class of the chord in measure 3, the harmonic nexus and culmination of the passage. We may thus think of the mutation chords as a modal unfolding as they surreptitiously reveal the full modal colour of the nexus chord by means of their teleological motion.

There are three colouristic mutations in the movement resulting in the three nexus chords heard in measures 3, 7 and 11. As a group, these nexus chords resemble Messiaen's *accord à resonance contractée* [chords of Contracted Resonance, or CCR]. Messiaen used either his appoggiatura or genesis chord as the basis of a CCR.[13] The former was named for its voice leading, as each pitch is an appoggiatura that moves down, mostly by step, to a pitch of the genesis chord. The genesis chord is a slightly altered major ninth chord without a leading-tone whose ninth is placed at the bottom. In Example 8.2, the appoggiatura and genesis chords are placed over a contracted resonance, the combination tones of a major second dyad, to

Example 8.1   Chords of Contracted Resonance in context, melodic 'recitation tones' and linear movement primarily by ic 1 in Serge Garant's *Concerts sur terre* (1952), movement 1

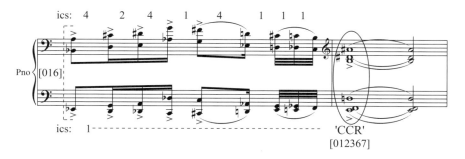

---

[12] Serge Garant, score notes for 'Concerts sur terre' in *Mélodies* (Saint-Nicolas, QC: Doberman Yppan, 1996), p. 5.

[13] Messiaen discusses his chords of Contracted Resonance in *Traité VII*, pp. 157–64.

Example 8.2   Comparison of Messiaen's CCR to similar chords in Garant's *Concerts sur terre*, movement 1

Contracted Resonance

form a CCR.[14] I have transposed Garant's three chords from *Concerts sur terre* to the bass note D for clearer comparison. All three can be considered CCRs in that they contain a contracted dyad below a more widely spaced tetrachord. The third chord most closely resembles the specific spacing of Messiaen's CCRs. In terms of interval-class content, Messiaen's appoggiatura CCR contains three semitones, while Garant's CCRs in measures 3 and 11 contain four.

In general, the work's melodic structure resembles Messiaen's music with its use of recitation pitches and its emphasis on movement by semitone and tritone, ics 1 and 6. Example 8.1 was saturated with ic 1 melodic movement and structurally emphasized one of Messiaen's two favourite melodic intervals, the descending minor sixth. Robert Sherlaw Johnson noted that this interval and the tritone were two of Messiaen's favourites, based on the composer's own writings in Chapter VIII of *Technique de mon langage musical*.[15]

The opening phrase of the second movement of Garant's *Concerts sur terre*, shown in Example 8.3, proceeds almost exclusively by ics 1 and 6. The emphasis on these two intervals and the use of B♭ and E recitation pitches are reminiscent of Messiaen's vocal writing in *Harawi*, specifically the alternation of G♯ and D in 'Syllables' at the words 'O o mon ciel tu fleuris, Piroutcha mia!' (measure 9) and

---

[14]   *Traité VII*, p. 162. These two particular chord types are explained as follows: 'Contracted resonance, such that 2 notes are compressed into a smaller interval and are moved [transposed] to the medium [range].' The chords discussed above belong to the 'second type' of CCR that Joseph Edward Harris defines in his *Musique Colorée: Synesthetic Correspondence in the Works of Olivier Messiaen*, PhD diss. (University of Iowa, 2004), pp. 69–75.

What Harris refers to as a 'first type' of CCR contains an upper pentachord, not a tetrachord. This first type of genesis chord utilizes the pentatonic collection, which Messiaen explained as a dominant ninth chord whose leading-tone is replaced by its tonic. Accordingly, this pentachord has a quintuple appoggiatura, as opposed to a quadruple one.

[15]   Robert Sherlaw Johnson, *Messiaen*, 2nd paperback edition, updated with additional text by Caroline Rae (London: Omnibus Press, 2008), p. 20.

Example 8.3   Melodic line saturated with ics 1 and 6 in the first phrase of *Concerts sur terre*, movementt 2 (1952)

the same oscillation between B♭ and E in 'L'escalier redit, gestes de soleil' at the words 'Du ciel, de l'eau, du temps, l'escalier du temps' (measures 2–4). Further support for the connection between Garant's *Concerts sur terre* and *Harawi* is provided by Jean Boivin. His compilation of Messiaen's 1951–52 class syllabus includes *Harawi*.[16] In addition, Garant's archived class notes devote more pages to *Harawi* than any other composition studied that year.[17]

While returning to Quebec by ship following his year of study with Messiaen, Garant sketched elaborate plans for a work that he left incomplete. 'Variations pour deux pianos' featured many of Messiaen's compositional techniques, including Hindu rhythms, permutation processes, non-retrogradable rhythms and rhythmic pedals. His sketches contain a page, titled *Serie* [sic] *à développements et métamorphoses* [sic] that presents 24 rows divided into two columns of 12, rather than the traditional arrangement of 12 row transpositions and their inversions that one might expect to find in a French serial composition of this era.[18] All 12 of the rows in the first column are unique, begin on D, and are partitioned with dotted lines creating segments of three, four and six pitch classes (pcs). The right-hand column lists their inversions, pairing them side by side.[19]

---

[16]   Boivin, *La classe de Messiaen*, p. 438.

[17]   Service de gestion de documents et des archives, Université de Montréal, Fonds Serge Garant (P 141), P 141 / B1, 1.

[18]   The majority of North American musicians use a single 'Babbitt' 12-tone matrix whose rows consist of the 12 prime form transpositions (P), and columns contain its inverted ones (I). A typical French 'Boulez' row calculation is divided into two separate 12 × 12 matrices. The first contains the 12 transpositions of the *originale* (O) and the second contains the inverted, or *renversement* (R) forms. Order numbers are tied to a specific pc, so that the first pc of series O–I is 1, the second is 2, the third is 3, etc. Garant often extracted the order numbers assigned to each pc in the two columns of 12 rows and recopied only these order numbers as a shorthand notation in two 12 × 12 squares. These two shorthand Latin squares are commonly referred to as a *Boulez matrix*. A representation can be found in György Ligeti, 'Pierre Boulez: Decision and Automatism in Structure Ia', *Die Reihe* 4, (1960): pp. 36–62.

[19]   See White Luckow, *La Marque du maître*, p. 93, for a reproduction of these rows.

208   *Messiaen Perspectives 2: Techniques, Influence and Reception*

The variation in segment length between rows points to Garant's use of Messiaen's *permutations symétriques* as the *métamorphoses* acting upon three key rows to generate the remaining nine rows. Messiaen codified two categories of symmetrical permutations whose purpose was to reorder or permute the 12 or 16 members of the *gamut chromatique*. Each new permutation reordering was referred to as an *interversion*, and Messiaen maximized potential *interversions* through the continuous application of the process until all possible reorderings were obtained and the procedure thereby exhausted itself. The ascending chromatic gamut of order numbers represents a single musical parameter such as pitch, duration or dynamic. He referred to the first type of permutation as éventail *ouvert* [open fan] and éventail *fermé* [closed fan], occasionally substituting the word *ciseaux* [scissors] for éventail.[20]

The second type of permutation is based on the repetitive application of an interval cycle, and it was this variety of permutations that Garant employed in his 'Variations pour deux pianos', although he did not exhaust the system as Messiaen might have done, instead choosing only the first *interversion* of each permutation. Garant divided three rows into four segments, three others into two segments; and the remaining three rows into three segments. The rows of three segments follow Messiaen's 'de 4 en 4, groupes de 3' permutation (4s – every fourth integer – in 4 segments, groups of 3). Beginning with the first pitch, Garant cycled through fourths obtaining the order numbers 5 (1+4), and 9 (5+4). At that point, he repeated the cycle from the next-to-lowest integer (2), generating the remaining segments (2, 6, 10), then (3, 7, 11) and (4, 8, 12). Rows of two segments correspond to 'de 2 en 2, groupes de 6' (2s in 2 segments, groups of 6), an extraction cycle of seconds; while those of three, to '*de 3 en 3, groups de 4*' (3s in 3 segments, groups of 4), an extraction cycle of thirds. This pattern of three interval cycles is applied three times, once to each of the primary rows.

In addition to his opening and closing fans, Messiaen drew inspiration from Çârngadeva's numbered list of 120 deçî-tâlas and shared it with his students. Example 8.4 from Garant's 'Variations' comprises an original *Candrakalâ* tâla (no. 105: ♩ ♫. ♪) and two *monnayages* [rhythmic conversions] that sub-divide the second and third variations (in the second and third measures shown) into composite groups of the same total value.[21] Two noted Messiaen scholars, Robert Sherlaw Johnson and Harry Halbreich, both remark that *Candrakalâ* was one of

---

[20]   The *éventail ouvert* and *éventail fermé* permutations will be examined more closely in the music of André Prévost.

[21]   The verb *monnayer* usually refers to the minting of money or the exchange of goods for money, or in some cases, currency exchange. In this case, I believe that Messiaen applied the term to describe a rhythmic exchange that, like a currency exchange, maintains the same total value: by exchanging the first eighth note in Example 8.4 for two sixteenths at the beginning of the example's second measure, he makes 'rhythmic change', if you will, by trading a $20 bill (the eighth) for two $10 bills (the sixteenths).

Example 8.4   Theme comprising a *Candrakalâ tâla* Hindu rhythm and two *monnayages* in Garant's incomplete 'Variations pour deux pianos'

Messiaen's most frequently used rhythms.[22] Garant applied a permutation pattern to this theme that Messiaen might have described as 'de sept en sept, groupes de quatre', or a reordering cycle of sevenths in seven segments, four rhythms in each segment, starting on 1. Messiaen would have notated the segments in a single line in this manner:

1 8 15 22 ‖ 2 9 16 23 ‖ 3 10 17 24 ‖ 4 11 18 25 ‖ 5 12 19 26 ‖ 6 13 20 27 ‖ 7 14 21 28

Garant however, chose to divide the segments by notating each in a separate row, one below the other in a rectangle as in Example 8.5. Messiaen's single row notation visually suggests performing the segments only forward and backward horizontally, whereas Garant's alternative multi-row layout allows the composer to select not only horizontal segments, but vertical and diagonal ones as well.

Nothing is known of Garant's 'Variations' aside from its existence of an unfinished manuscript and a few pre-compositional sketches found within his personal archives. However, the influence of Boulez is evident. When asked whether he found Boulez or Messiaen more influential, Garant answered simply, 'Listen, I would not really know what to attribute to whom'.[23] He remembered his 'shock' at the lecture that Messiaen gave on Boulez's Second Sonata. After that lecture, Garant explained that the Sonata 'remained on my piano throughout my time in Paris. … I looked with fascination at this monstrosity of a piece, about which

---

[22]   Johnson, *Messiaen*, p. 34. Johnson states that *Candrakalâ* and *Lakskmîça* (no. 88) were two of Messiaen's most frequently used rhythms. In a personal communication, 7 March 2009, Harry Halbreich suggested that *Candrakalâ*, *Lackskmîça* and *Râgavardhana* (no. 93) were Messiaen's three favourites.

[23]   Lefebvre, *Serge Garant*, p. 74: 'Écoutez, je ne saurais vraiment dire la part de chacun.'

Example 8.5 The compositional realization, left, of the four inversionally symmetrical readings on the right, 'Variations pour deux pianos', m. 86

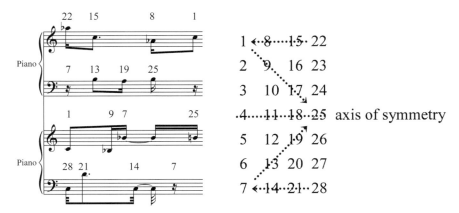

I understood almost next to nothing except the boldness of writing, complexity, invention, novelty ... everything, everything enticing me'.[24] Garant's use of his permutation squares in the following excerpt of Variations is strongly suggestive of the composer's captivation by Boulez's employment of symmetrical schemata.

In a short section from measures 86–91, Garant chose his four simultaneously performed segments according to a symmetrical design, so that right and left hands and piano 1 and 2 are each other's inverse reading. The realization of this first square is shown in Example 8.5. The right hand of piano 1 (RH 1) performs the top row backwards, from right to left, while the right hand of piano 2 (RH 2) plays the top diagonal in the opposite direction, from left to right. This pair of

---

[24] Ibid.: 'Et surtout, je me souviens du choc qu'a été pour moi la lecture de la 2ème Sonate de Boulez qui est restée sur mon piano pendant tout les temps que j'ai été à Paris. Alors, je la regardais j'étais fasciné par cette espèce de monstre auquel je ne comprenais à peu près rien mais dont l'espèce d'audace d'écriture, la complexité, l'invention, la nouveauté, tout, tout me séduisait.' Boulez and Garant remained in contact. In a letter to Garant in October 1954, Boulez discussed plans for a large Webern Festival in Paris and mentioned that he would love to receive some of Garant's most recent scores. He concluded with a challenge of sorts, with the suggestion that 'I understand your isolation, as Montreal is evidently not a [modern] music centre, at least not yet.' (Ibid, p. 49: 'Je comprends votre isolement, car Montréal n'est évidemment pas un haut lieu de la musique, du moins pas encore.') The short-term result was a Montreal concert titled 'In Memoriam Webern' that Garant assembled the following year, but in the long term, the remark was somewhat prophetic, as Serge Garant is most commonly thought of as one of the most important founding fathers of avant-garde music in Quebec.

segments reflects the pair in the left hands: the bottom row from right to left (LH 2), and the bottom diagonal from left to right (LH 1).[25]

In the next combination of four pitches/rests, the right hand of piano 1 shifts down by one position, performing the second row backwards: 23, 16, 9, 2. Mirroring this move, the left hand of piano 2 plays the penultimate row assigned the numbers 27, 10, 3, and 6, in that order. The right hand of piano 2 moves down diagonally, performing 2, 10, 18 and 26, and the left hand of piano 1 mirrors with 6, 12, 18, 24. Since there are seven rows, each line may be found in seven different positions. Garant continued his successive shifting to obtain all possible segment positions, wrapping around his square when necessary, and thus ensuring that each of the theme's 28 pitches/rests appears once in each hand. Any additional shifting beyond this point would replicate the original segment positions.

Pascal Decroupet has informally suggested that Boulez used a similar method of choosing integer strings according to symmetrical schemata.[26] An analysis by Jean-Louis Leleu explores such schemata in Boulez's *Livre pour quatuor* (1948–49).[27] The main difference between the two works is a measure of rigour. Garant's designs were used rather systematically whereas Boulez's were not. From a historical perspective, however, Boulez's influence is still very likely since his piece was composed two years before he befriended Garant in Messiaen's classroom.

Garant wrote *Caprices*, his first decidedly serial composition, in 1954, and then returned to *Concerts sur terre* in 1956 to complete its remaining three movements. After these two works, Garant moved steadily towards integral serialism. Garant's later works are based on a series of proportions or ratios that govern durations, tempi, registers and timbres.[28] Concerning his mature language, Keith MacMillan and John Beckwith write:

---

[25]　For more on Garant's ordered processing of integer strings, see White Luckow, *La Marque du Maître*, pp. 103–4.

[26]　Personal communication, 14 October 2007, 6th European Music Analysis Conference / VII. Jahreskongress der Gesellschaft für Musiktheorie, Freiburg, Germany.

[27]　Pierre Boulez, *Techniques d'écriture et enjeux esthétiques*, ed. Jean-Louis Leleu and Pascal Decroupet (Genève: Éditions Contrechamps, 2006), pp. 13–38.

[28]　This is especially true of his series *Offrande I* (1969), *II* (1970) and *III* (1971), and *Circuit I* (1972), *II* (1972), and *III* (1973) all based on the intervallic series of the theme of Bach's *Musical Offering*. Garant discusses the rigorous structures of his works in his programme notes, reprinted in Lefebvre, *Serge Garant*, pp. 185–205. For example, an earlier group consisting of *Anerca* (1962, rev. 1963) *Enneade* (1964), and *Ouranos* (1963) use 'mobile forms' in that their respective segments can be performed in any order. Otherwise, these works are strictly serial. Garant described his last two works, *Quintette* (1978) and *Plages* (1981) as similarly rigorous, and added that *Quintette* is a 'large arch, therefore completely symmetrical', and that *Plages* 'is organised from a "block" of five pitches, that, through their successive inversion and transpositions, give rise to a network of pitches covering six octaves, with the tritone F–B as its centre' (ibid.).

Garant is a confirmed subscriber to the principles of serialism. Not unlike his idol of student days, Pierre Boulez, he finds happiness in musical mathematics. Besides using twelve-tone series and the basic intervallic materials in most of his works, he frequently applies mathematical logic to such parameters of sound as duration and amplitude, or organises the relative proportions of his compositions, the degrees of sonic densities, or the choices of instrumental timbres according to pre-programmed numerical systems.[29]

The rigour associated with his 'intellectual plans' became one of his trademarks and typified his mature output.

Clermont Pépin

Clermont Pépin was born in the small town of St-Georges-de-Beauce in 1926. The trajectory of his musical education was diametrically opposed to that of Garant. Whereas Garant was self-taught and rebellious, Pépin was fortuitous as a young child in making career-building connections with local society's elite and had an impressive list of teachers before his studies with Messiaen. He studied piano, composition, conducting and chamber music at the Conservatoire de Musique du Québec à Montréal (1939–41 and 1944–46) with Arthur Letondal, Jean Dansereau, Claude Champagne, Louis Bailly and Léon Barzin; piano and composition at the Curtis Institute in Philadelphia (1941–44) with Jeanne Behrend Rosario Scalero; and piano, composition and conducting at the Senior School of the Royal Conservatory of Music (1946–49) with Lubka Kolessa, Arnold Walter and Nicholas Goldschmidt. He won the Prix d'Europe as a pianist in 1949, which in combination with other grants, allowed him to study in Paris from 1949 to 1955.

He composed two symphonic poems in Paris: *Guernica* (1952) and *Le rite du soleil noir* (1955). *Guernica* was inspired by Pablo Picasso's painting of the Basque town of Guernica after it was bombed in 1937 by the Fascists during the Spanish Civil War.[30] The second work is loosely based on Antonin Artaud's 'Tutuguri, ou Le rite du soleil noir' from his radio play *Pour en finir avec le jugement de dieu*. According to Schuster-Craig, Artaud's first drafts date back to 1936 after his experience with the Tarahumara Indians. Pépin's manner of depicting the poem's ritualistic events is not directly narrative. Since these rituals were frequently carried out under the influence of the hallucinatory drug peyote, 'both poem and music aim, rather, at suggesting a place or atmosphere, an atmosphere that is primitive, ritualistic, and violent'.[31]

---

[29] MacMillan and Beckwith, *Contemporary Canadian Composers*, p. 78.

[30] John William Schuster-Craig, *Compositional Procedures in Selected Works of Clermont Pépin (1926–)*, PhD diss., (University of Kentucky, 1987), p. 13.

[31] Schuster-Craig, *Compositional Procedures,* pp. 36–8.

Both *Guernica* and *Le rite du soleil noir* entwine the compositional techniques of Honegger and Messiaen. Stylistically, these pieces feature ostinati with shifting accents and mechanistically stuttering rhythms that are layered into multiple blocks of sound and juxtaposed like the pieces of a patchwork quilt. Because the textures are pitch-centric but harshly dissonant, the two symphonic poems evoke the primitivism of Stravinsky's *Le sacre du printemps*, which Pépin studied under Messiaen's tutelage in his two first academic years in Paris (1949–50 and 1950–51). These qualities also pertain to some of the music of Honegger, particularly *Rugby*. Honegger himself has said that while he liked football, he preferred rugby, because it is 'more spontaneous, more direct and *closer to nature* than football. ... For me the *savage, brusque, untidy and desperate* rhythm of rugby is more attractive.'[32]

Despite its savage sound, sections of *Guernica* utilize Messiaen's modes of limited transposition as the structural scaffolding underpinning the melodic themes and blocks of ostinati rhythms laid above. The second appearance of the main theme of *Guernica* borrows most heavily from Messiaen's oeuvre. The woodwind cascade in Example 8.6 contains pianistic mode 2^2 block chords that begin in a high register and descend by half and whole steps through several octaves in even eighth notes, with the exception of the lowest quarter-note voice in the reduction that moves by minor thirds. This waterfall effect is strikingly similar to measures 37–39 of Messiaen's *Turangalîla-Symphonie* with its triad-based chords in first and second inversion (Example 8.7). Given the historical context, the evidence for this specific influence is quite strong. *Guernica* was completed in 1952 and won first prize in a competition celebrating the centenary of Laval University in Quebec City that same year.[33] Presumably, Pépin composed the bulk of the work during 1951 and perhaps started sketching even earlier. According to Jean Boivin's compilation of Messiaen's course outlines, *Turangalîla* was the only piece composed by Messiaen himself that he chose to analyse with his students in the 1950–51 academic year.[34]

Aside from the fact that Pépin's eighth notes and Messiaen's sixteenths differ visually in the scores, they sound very similar in performance. Pépin's example contains a repetitive pattern of parallel descending major chords in alternating second and first inversions. Messiaen, on the other hand, changes the quality of first inversion triads from major to minor. If Pépin had split each of his quarter notes in the bottom voice into two eighth-note scale steps, he would have created alternating major and minor chord qualities as Messiaen has done. Because both examples are so brisk in speed, the chordal runs sound almost identical.

---

[32]   Geoffrey K. Spratt, *The Music of Arthur Honegger* (Cork: Cork University Press, 1987), pp. 148–9, my emphasis.

[33]   Laval University was actually founded in 1663 by Monseigneur François de Laval (the first bishop of New France) under the auspices of the King of France, Louis XIV. Originally called the Séminaire de Québec, it was renamed Université Laval in 1852, and it is the centenary of this event that was observed in 1952.

[34]   Boivin, *La classe de Messiaen*, pp. 437–8.

Example 8.6 Reduction of mode 2^2 thematic fragments and cascading woodwind scales in *Guernica*, movement 1, mm. 279–93

Example 8.7 Mode 2^2 woodwind descending scales in the 'Introduction' of Messiaen's *Turangalîla-Symphonie*, figure 6, mm. 37–9

For the analysis of passages such as the ones in Examples 8.6 and 8.7, Christoph Neidhöfer has proposed measuring intervallic relationships within modes according to the number of scale steps traversed, rather than the number of chromatic semitones, as is normally done within an atonal or serial modular-12 context.[35] For example, the mode 2^2 collection (also called the octatonic scale) is considered to be a mod 8 (modular-8) system in which each unique pc is assigned a *step class* number from 0 to 7 according to the scale's ascending pattern (C♯ = 0, D = 1, E = 2, etc., continuing to B = 7). *Step class intervals* (SCIs) name the distance between any two step classes.

According to this method, then, the single scale steps of the minor and major second of mode 2^2 in Example 8.7 are equivalent. Such equivalence enables the comparison of Messiaen's and Pépin's block chords in *Turangalîla* (Example 8.7) and the beginning of *Guernica*. In both passages, there is a downwards voice leading by successive SCIs of -1 within the context of the alternating semitones and tones of the mode 2 collection (with the exception of the lowest voice in *Guernica*, which skips every other pitch for a step class of -2). When we include the 'missing' pcs in *Guernica*'s lowest voice, each of the three voices conforms to a parallel stepwise voice leading of -1, much like *Turangalîla*.[36]

Mode 2 plays an equally significant structural role in *Le rite du soleil noir*. John Schuster-Craig has described the form as a seven-part sonata-rondo form (A–B–

---

[35] Christoph Neidhöfer, 'A Theory of Harmony and Voice Leading for the Music of Olivier Messiaen', *Music Theory Spectrum*, 27/1 (2005): 1–34.

[36] For more on Pépin's use of step classes, see White Luckow, *La Marque du Maître*, pp. 157–9.

$A'-$ C–A″–B–A‴).[37] In the re-transition leading to the final A‴ section, a single large block of sound comprises the bassoons, brass and strings. Six melodic lines march upwards by step through all three possible transpositions of mode 2.[38] Pépin superimposes two conflicting modes in the first three measures: mode 2^2 and 2^1. Harmonically however, each vertical chord conforms to a single transposition of mode 2, so that mode 2^2 is heard on strong beats 1 and 3, while 2^1 is heard on weak beats. The final four measures of the first system are especially curious, as all three modes are present melodically, yet still form single-mode harmonies (mode 2^3) on strong beats. The brackets and harmonic arrows in measures 346–8 in the middle of the second system constitute the only complete agreement between harmony and melody on mode 2^2.

Pépin returned to Montréal after completing *Le rite*. His next composition, *Variations pour quatuor à cordes*, remained faithful to Messiaen's modes while venturing into new poietic territory: serialism. While a wedding of modal and serial languages may seem unlikely, Pépin saw them as aesthetically similar for their latent emotional expression, as opposed to many ardent structuralists who embraced integral serialism in its strictest forms for its potentially expressionless aesthetic. Pépin explained:

> I am probably very sentimental at heart and very romantic. That, I think, is really one of the reasons why I went into serial music in the first place, because to me serial music is not at all intellectual. On the contrary, the more I go into it, the more I find that it opens an entire new world of emotional expression.[39]

He noted Messiaen's role in the creation of his first serial work, *Variations pour quatuor à cordes*:

> I feel obliged to say that of all of the artists with whom I've studied, Messiaen was clearly the one who enriched me the most. I'll always remember the analysis he made of Alban Berg's *Lyrische Suite*. I remember he had spent several weeks on this *Lyrische Suite* and then at one point I said to him, 'Maestro, the more you talk about this work, the more I detest it.' 'Ah!' he replied, 'now that's very interesting. Just the same, we're going to continue to study it in-depth … and you'll discuss it with me again in a year or two'. … I studied it intensely and I'm glad Messiaen encouraged me to get to know this work, since after that, I wrote my second string quartet.[40]

---

[37]   Schuster-Craig, *Compositional Procedures*, p. 29.

[38]   Ibid. Schuster-Craig mentions the coexistence of all three mode 2 transpositions from mm. 334–6 (p. 47).

[39]   A. Mason Clarke, *Thirty-four Biographies of Canadian Composers* (Montreal: Canadian Broadcasting Corporation, 1964), p. 81.

[40]   Interview with Gilles Potvin, *Anthology of Canadian Music*, Vol. 5 (Toronto: Radio Canada International, 1980). My transcription of the radio interview follows: 'Oui, je me

Although Pépin's quartet certainly employs many of Berg's techniques from the *Lyric Suite*, it still integrates Messiaen's modes into the serial fabric of Variation 7 (Example 8.8) as a sort of homage, perhaps, to his former teacher. The I_7 form of the row is labelled according to the order numbers of its pcs from 1–12. The first three measures of the example contain the first hexachord, order numbers 1–6. The second hexachord is heard from measures 19–21, order numbers 7–12, and the first reappears from measures 28–29. The hexachords are connected by mode 3 passages. Mode 3^2 interjects in measures 17 and 18, and mode 3^3 from measures 22 to 26. The D in the cello at measure 22, first beat of the second system, does not belong to mode 3^3 and is most likely a misprint, since Pépin incorporated an element of rotation that Berg used in his *Lyric Suite*. Between measures 22 and 26, the first violin part is rotated one position to the left to create the viola part, which is rotated another position to the left to yield the cello part. According to this pattern, the violin's C♯ on beat 3 of measure 22 also occurs on beat 2 of the viola, and should therefore appear on beat 1 in the cello.[41]

Example 8.8   The I_7 row with interjecting mode 3 scales in Variation VII of Pépin's *Variations*, mm. 14–29

souviendrai toujours de l'analyse qu'il avait fait, de *Suite lyrique* d'Alban Berg. Je me souviens qu'il avait passé plusieurs semaines sur cette suite lyrique, et puis un moment donné je lui ai dit "Maître, plus vous parlez de cette œuvre, plus je la déteste." Alors, il dit "bien, ça c'est très intéressant," il dit "quand-même, nous allons continuer à l'approfondir … et puis vous m'en reparlerai dans un an ou deux." … Moi, je l'ai beaucoup approfondi, et je suis content que Messiaen m'a fait connaître cette œuvre là, parce que après ça, c'est après ça que j'ai écrit mon deuxième quatuor.'

[41]   Pépin's Variations allows borrows from the structure of Berg's Lyric Suite, as well. For a complete discussion, see White Luckow, *La Marque du Maître*, pp. 160–75.

After the 1950s, Pépin experimented with other techniques, including integral serialism (*Nombres*, 1962) and music inspired by electroacoustic music (*Monade I*, 1964). His work continued to exhibit the influence of Honegger, which was duly noted by his peers.[42] In reviewing Pépin's *Monologue* (1961), Serge Garant wrote somewhat facetiously that 'the orchestration is confused, tortured and the influence of Honegger is unfortunately too obvious. I wish that Pépin would rid himself, once and for all, from the influence of this composer.'[43]

Pépin's work in the 1970s appears to have moved back towards Messiaen, and in particular, his use of birdsong in the 1960s. As Schuster-Craig recounts, 'in *Monade III* (1972), Pépin originally intended to use taped birdsongs. Technical difficulties prevented this, and passages for the ondes Martenot were substituted for the birdsong.'[44] In composing *Quasars* (1973), the composer made a definitive return to what he learned from Messiaen, featuring both non-retrogradable rhythms and their expansion through combinatory addition. The main difference between Messiaen's original non-retrogradable rhythms and Pépin's *Morsiques* is the former's employment of Hindu rhythms versus the latter's use of Morse code as source material.[45]

Schuster-Craig also notes Pépin's experiments in *Interactions* (1977) that dispensed with a traditional score in favour of graphic notation.[46] The composer's moving from one method of writing to another is described by Gilles Tremblay as 'creative evolution' that 'displays the intellectual development of one who is anxious to understand his century, searching to exploit fully the expressive possibilities of an art freed from traditional frameworks and enriched by new techniques'.[47]

---

[42]   For analytical examples detailing the direct influence of Honegger's music upon Pépin, his use of encryption and structural modelling of *Rugby* and *Symphonie pour cordes* in particular, see ibid., Chapter 4.

[43]   Lefebvre, *Serge Garant*, pp. 109–10. Originally published in the July–August 1962 edition of *Canadian Art*. Garant's full original review comment reads: 'Monologues de Clermont Pépin est l'œuvre la plus méditative et sentimentale qu'il ait écrite; mais elle produit plus bruit que d'émotion; s'efforçant d'être contemporaine dans l'expression, elle ne réussit finalement pas à dépasser le langage du 19ᵉ siècle. L'orchestration est confuse, torturée et l'influence d'Honegger est malheureusement trop évidente. Je souhaite que Pépin se dégage une fois pour toute de l'influence de ce compositeur.'

[44]   Schuster-Craig, *Compositional Procedures*, p. 9.

[45]   For a comparative analysis of Messiaen's non-retrogradable rhythms and Pépin's *Morsiques* as employed in *Quasars*, see White Luckow, *La Marque du Maître*, pp. 177–89.

[46]   Schuster-Craig, *Compositional Procedures*, pp. 102–3.

[47]   Gilles Potvin, 'Clermont Pépin', in *The Encyclopedia of Music in Canada*, available at www.thecanadianencyclopedia.com. For further research, please note that this article serves an extensive summary of Pépin's life and works.

André Prévost

André Prévost was born in 1934 in Hawkesbury, Ontario, on the Quebec–Ontario border. His family, having a long Québécois lineage, returned to the province when he was still a child and settled in St-Jérôme. He had the advantage of early musical training at the Séminaire de St-Thérèse and the Collège de St-Laurent before enrolling at the Conservatoire de Musique à Montréal in 1951.[48] There, he studied piano with Georges Savaria, bassoon with Symon Kovar, harmony, fugue and counterpoint with Isabelle Delorme and Jean Papineau-Couture and composition with Clermont Pépin.[49] Before he left the Conservatoire de Musique à Montréal in 1960 he was awarded the Sarah Fischer Award in composition (1959), the Chamber Music Award of the Fondation Les Amis de l'Art and the school's first prize in both composition and harmony (1960).[50]

André Prévost studied with Pépin from 1955 until 1960 and learned about Messiaen's techniques before he even went to France. This is evident in the second movement of his 1959 composition *Mobiles*. Prévost described this piece as his first serial composition, yet he did not use transpositions of prime, retrograde, inversion and retrograde-inversion forms of the original row. Rather, he used only the row at its original transposition (starting on G♭) both forward and backward, labelled P_6 and R_6, and the prime (P) and retrograde (R) of the first *interversion* of Messiaen's éventail *ouvert* or open-fan (o-fan) symmetrical permutation, labelled P o-fan and R o-fan. The row in measures 1–3 of the violin reads G♭–C–F–A– D♯–E–A♭–D–G–C♯–B–B♭. Starting from the central two pitches, E and A♭, he extracted dyads symmetrically from the centre towards the outsides of the row, D–D♯, G–A, etc., reversed them and placed them successively from left-to-right in the flute at measures 20–24.[51]

Prévost composed *Sonate pour violon et piano* at the beginning of his studies with Messiaen. He states in a self-analysis of the work that, 'compositional unity is assured, in part, by the form, called *repliement*, of the three movements'.[52] Through *repliement*, or folding-back, the violin and piano undergo invertible counterpoint

---

[48]   Pierre Rochon, 'André Prévost', in *The Encyclopedia of Music in Canada*, available at: www.thecanadianencyclopedia.com.

[49]   Bradley, *Twentieth Century Canadian Composers*, p. 216.

[50]   MacMillan and Beckwith, *Contemporary Canadian Composers*, p. 188.

[51]   Messiaen discussed this symmetrical permutation in several places in *Traité III*. Visual examples are found in Annex 1 of Chapter 3, beginning on p. 319. The diagrams of *ciseaux ouverts* (open scissors) and *ciseaux fermés* (closed scissors), elsewhere referred to as open- and closed-fans, appear on p. 322, examples 169 and 170. In these two examples, the permutation is applied to a 15-member chromatic gamut. The best example of application to a 12-member gamut is found on pp. 325–6, and titled 'réinterversions sur 12 valeurs, 10 fois intervertiés' (réinterversions/reapplied permutations of 12 values, permuted 10 times).

[52]   André Prévost, 'Analyse de la Sonate pour violon et piano', *Le Musicien éducateur*, 5/2 (1974): pp. 29–38. Although my analysis was originally undertaken without knowledge

at the midpoint of each movement and perform the first half in retrograde. Each movement then, reflects Messiaen's interest in bilateral symmetry and is akin to a large non-retrogradable rhythm. The Sonata's all-interval row is a *repliement*: A–G♯–Bb–G–B–F♯–C–F–C♯–E–D–E. The successive ics from the outsides to the centre are equivalent in size but inverted in direction, as indicated by the ordered pitch intervals (opis). If we place a mirror at the centre of the row (between F♯ and C), the hexachords map onto one another at R_6, meaning that either hexachord can reproduce the other by reversing it, or folding it back along that dotted line and transposing it by six semitones.

Even though Prévost conceived of the first movement as atonal – not serial – I believe that he derived the row of the second and third movements from the rotated version of the violin's opening gesture: C♯–G–Ab–D–Eb–A–Bb–E–F–B–C–F♯.[53] With C♯ at the beginning, he reordered the row by means of a *modified* o-fan permutation, pairing A–Bb, Eb–E, D–F, Ab–B, G–C, and C♯–F♯.. Instead of placing the central pairs at the beginning of the row, he alternately placed them at either end. In the third movement, the innermost pair (A–Bb) is shifted to measure 60 in prime order and Eb–E is reversed and placed in measure 64. This process is mirrored, or inverted, as the next most central pair (D–F) is placed immediately before the pair Eb–E in measures 63–64. Prévost has made Messiaen's o-fan permutation more symmetrical because every step in his reordering process is balanced on the left and right sides. It serves as a sort of procedural foreshadowing, a smaller model of the large-scale *repliement* formal structures of the following second and third movements.

In Prévost's words, 'the second movement, written in an improvisatory character, is a sort of large violin cadenza, interspersed within two piano appearances. Constructed of a 12-tone series, it prepares the third movement.'[54] The word *prepare* is highly suggestive to the analyst: what exactly in the third movement requires preparation, and how is this accomplished? Keeping in mind that Prévost was studying composition with Henri Dutilleux and Messiaen concurrently, I suggest that the answer is best understood as a creative intermingling of Dutilleux's *croissance progressive* (progressive growth) and Messiaen's symmetrical permutations. Dutilleux described *croissance progressive* as a highly surreptitious method of thematic construction, in that the listener may only perceive the building process retrospectively, once the theme appears

---

of the composer's self-analysis, I later verified my own findings with Prévost's own conception of the work and found the two to be consistent.

[53]   Prévost, 'Analyse de la Sonate pour violon et piano', p. 30. Prévost explains that the first movement is atonal and constructed somewhat freely, but that ics 1, 5 and 6 are used *somewhat systematically* (emphasis mine, here and in the translation). Other than referring to the repetitive intervallic pattern, he may also have been referring to the reorganisation of that pattern through symmetrical permutations. He writes, 'The 1st atonal movement is constructed somewhat freely. It employs the augmented fourth, the major seventh and the minor second in a way that is *quasi systematic*.'

[54]   Prévost, 'Analyse de la Sonate pour violon et piano', p. 32.

in completion.[55] Prévost's palindromic second movement comprises four trichords that continually shift position with each new row statement, gradually revealing the final trichord arrangement through a *croissance progressive*. The four trichords correspond to a left-to-right reading of the inverted form of the row shown in Example 8.9: trichord 1 = (A, G♯, B♭); 2 = (G, B, F♯); 3 = (C F, C♯) and 4 = (E, D, E♭). In this case, Prévost's 12-tone series is analogous to Dutilleux's theme, and the symmetrical permutation of the trichords, the means of *croissance progressive*. This progressive reordering process, whose directed motion stems from the prescribed unravelling of the trichords during the retrograde half of the form, *prepares* for the eventual completion of the correct order of the theme, or series, finally obtained by the beginning of the third movement.

Example 8.9 illustrates four- and eight-measure palindromes in the eight rows of the *1ʳᵉ volet* of the *partie médiane*. The palindromic relationships involved here are not immediately evident as it is not the order of the segments that is mirrored, but rather the permutation process used to determine that order. The leftmost column lists the last eight row forms, A through H (showing the order of the trichords), heard before the piece folds back upon itself and reinterprets these row reorderings as *interversions*, i.e. the way Messiaen obtained reorderings through symmetrical permutation of the trichords.

The second column describes the permutation that maps each *interversion* onto the next one in the chain. These permutations track the movement of the trichords in fixed pairs. The outermost trichords of the original row, 1 and 4 are always traced as an invariant coupling, as are the innermost trichords, 2 and 3.

I define three permutations as follows: 'Skip 1 à left–right pairs' moves the trichords in even-numbered positions into the first and second position, and the trichords in odd-numbered positions into third and fourth position (see first permutation that maps A onto B). 'Left–right pairs à Skip 1' (permutation that maps C onto D in the example) is the near-inverse of that permutation, mapping left–right adjacent pairs onto non-adjacent ones, reversing the trichords in one of them (indicated by the dotted line). 'Retrograde within pairs' simply reverses the trichords in both pairs.

There are two palindromes indicated in the third column. The permutations producing *interversions* A through D are a mirror in which the first and third operations are the retrograde of one another, as indicated by the letter *R*, and they flank a central permutation, 'retrograde within pairs'. *Interversions* E through H replicate the same permutation pattern. The fourth column casts the complete group of 8-*interversions* as a larger palindrome. The first and last permutations are each other's retrograde, *R*, as are the third and fifth. The second and sixth are equivalent, where *P* indicates 'prime'. The central 'retrograde within pairs', then, is flanked by three pairs of permutations in a mirrored arrangement: *R P R*. Notice that although the row's original trichord segment order (1, 2, 3, 4) never appears

---

[55] Caroline Potter, *Henri Dutilleux: His Life and Works* (Aldershot: Ashgate, 1997), p. 100.

Example 8.9   An illustration of the four- and eight-interversion palindromes with the eight reordered rows A–H of the *partie médiane* of Sonate pour violon et piano, movement 2

Row form	Interversion (trichord order)	Permutation type	4-interversion palindromes	8-interversion palindromes
A	1 2 4 3			
B	2 3 1 4	skip 1→left-right pairs		
C	3 2 4 1	retrograde within pairs	R	
D	4 2 1 3	left-right pairs→skip 1		
E	1 3 4 2	retrograde within pairs		R P R
F	2 3 4 1	skip 1→left-right pairs		
G	3 2 1 4	retrograde within pairs	R	
H	4 3 1 2	left-right pairs→skip 1		

within a single *interversion*, it is nonetheless replicated in a slightly-removed level of the music's structure: if we consider each trichord to be a group and each *interversion* a four-segment hypergroup, the first trichords of all the *interversions*, read from top to bottom, project the (1, 2, 3, 4) ordering at the hypergroup level, twice in succession.

Four years after the violin sonata, Prévost began a large-scale setting of Michèle Lalonde's poem *Terre des hommes* in 1964, completing it for the 1967 World Exposition in Montreal. Lalonde's poem represented the Expo theme *Man and His World* by acting as 'a sort of screen onto which the crucial preoccupations, the high hopes and the acute anxieties of contemporary man could be projected in a succession of violently antithetic metaphors'.[56] Prévost's angst over the cyclical nature of man's cruelty towards fellow man is represented by a highly internally repetitive symmetrical Latin square. In another self-analysis, *Formulation et conséquences d'une hypothèse*, he stated that the piece is based on a 'fundamental hypothesis', the Latin square.[57] He explained that 'the numbers (1 to 12 and 12 to 1) constitute the four sides of my square, since I wished to work within a

---

[56]   Frank Daley, 'Gala Program Kicks Off Expo Entertainment Binge', *The Ottawa Journal* (1 May 1967).

[57]   André Prévost, 'Formulation et conséquences d'une hypothèse', in Raoul Duguay (ed.), *Musiques du Kébèk*, (Montréal: Éditions du Jour, 1971), p. 174. This Latin square is reproduced in White Luckow, *La Marque du Maître*, p. 242.

'closed circuit' in order to avoid a huge number of possibilities and I wanted the same controlling principle acting horizontally and vertically'.[58] Prévost's words echo those of Messiaen, who employed a 'closed circuit' in his modes of limited transposition to 'reduce the number of possible transpositions'.[59]

Prévost's closed circuit of self-imposed limitations was an order-12 (12 × 12) square. The numbers 1 to 12 represent the notes of an ascending chromatic scale, where 1 is equal to C, 2 to C♯, and so forth. The permutation creating each row is an interval cycle of the same variety as in Garant's 'Variations', but Prévost has made the size of the cycled intervals equivalent to the row number. Row 1 is a semitone cycle beginning on 1, which Prévost explained as 'intervalles de secondes mineures en 1 tronçon de 12 sons' or 'minor 2nd intervals in 1 segment of 12 pitches'.[60] By the same logic, row 2 is a major 2nd cycle beginning on 2, comprising two segments of six pitches, spaced a minor second apart.

The square's internal symmetry bears remarkable resemblance to an example of interval cycle permutations found in Messiaen's *Traité*.[61] The first permutation is a cycle of thirds, followed by a cycle of seconds, a cycle of alternating fifths and sixths, and, finally, a cycle of fourths. The two central permutations involve retrogradation, and the five interversions form an inversionally symmetrical design in which interversions labelled I and V in the *Traité* are equivalent, as are II and IV. In his Latin square, Prévost obtained the 12th row through cyclic major sevenths but he might have also obtained the same pattern through inversion: minor seconds in retrograde. Therefore, row 12 is the retrograde equivalent of row 1, row 11 is the retrograde of row 2, and so on, resembling Messiaen's arrangement.

The high level of symmetry in Prévost's square creates fascinating internal self-replicative properties. Because it is entirely retrograde-invertible, any one quadrant may be used to derive the remaining three when read as four quadrants of a Cartesian plane. This can be illustrated by dividing the square into top and bottom halves and retrograding the rows in the top half. The top half may then be inverted, or folded down upon the bottom half. This relationship, known as *sigma-symmetry* in mathematics, divides the square along both diagonal axes into two inversionally symmetrical triangles.[62] Prévost was aware of these properties: he traced dotted lines throughout his Latin square, where each constitutes a non-retrogradable rhythm.

---

[58]   Prévost, 'Formulation et conséquences', p. 174.

[59]   *Traité VII*, p. 51. 'Each mode of limited transposition has a special colour, lending precisely to this impression of a closed door, or closed circuit, and also to the combinations of various sounds that when read reduces the number of transpositions.

[60]   Ibid., p. 176.

[61]   *Traité III*, pp. 324–5.

[62]   Sigma-symmetry was first defined by P.J. Owens, 'Solutions to Two Problems of Dénes and Keedwell on Row–Complete Latin Squares', *Journal of Combinatorial Theory*, 21 (1967): pp. 299–308.

Further comparison can be made between Prévost's and Messiaen's use of symmetrical permutation. Example 8.10 applies Messiaen's and Prévost's permutations to the chromatic collection and compares the results. In set B, if Messiaen referred to his own permutation as 'de 3 en 3' or '3 in 3', he might have described Prévost's innovation by the inclusion of only one additional descriptor, 'de 3 en 3 "sur" 3', or '3 in 3 "starting on" 3'. Notice here that Prévost has almost completely maintained the pitch content and order within segments, but reversed the order of those segments themselves, as indicated by the arrows. He has literally *mirrored* Messiaen's symmetrical permutations.

Example 8.10   A direct comparison between similar permutations used by Messiaen and Prévost, applied to the same original chromatic collection

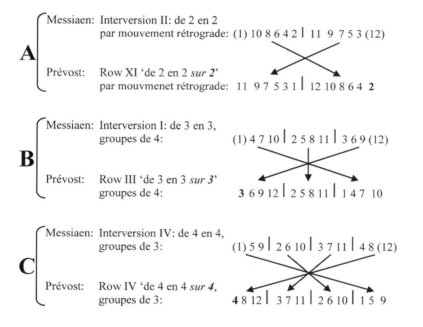

Conclusion

The notion of symmetry remained prominent in Prévost's work throughout his career. This was often generated via symmetrical generative processes or structural *repliements*. In Prévost's music, the symmetrical musical elements are replicated at every structural level of a composition, from the smallest trichords and tetrachords to the formal design of larger structures. The idea of related levels of structure in the composer's music has been hinted at by Véronique Robert in the official biographical notes released by Prévost's publisher. She explains that,

224   *Messiaen Perspectives 2: Techniques, Influence and Reception*

'Prévost's musical vocabulary reflects an essentially personal style rather than any specific school. He uses contemporary techniques but the structures of his works develop from the inherent logic of the ideas presented so as to create a sense of organic inevitability.'[63]

Garant's early music evolved at a rapid-fire pace. Only four years elapsed from the time he was a self-taught composer, then a student commuting to his first lessons in Montréal, to his year in attendance of Messiaen's classes alongside the most eminent composers of his own generation. Most of Garant's Messiaen-inspired writing occurs in the first two movements of *Concerts sur terre*, *Et je prierai ta grâce*, and 'Variations pour deux pianos', all composed during the year 1952, before he had even arrived back in Quebec.

Garant's earliest two Parisian compositions sound like, or are most esthesically similar to, the music of Messiaen. In terms of harmonic language, verticalities resembling the chords of Contracted Resonance are heard in the first movement of *Concerts sur terre*. The modes of limited transposition are not used verbatim but are intimated in this work, as is Messiaen's melodic emphasis on ics 1 and 6. In particular, the use of the recitation pitches B♭ and E in the second movement of *Concerts sur terre* has a clear correlation to the alternation of those same pcs in Messiaen's 'L'escalier redit, gestes du soleil' and to the G♯ and D in 'Syllables', both from *Harawi* (1945).

Although 'Variations pour deux pianos' resembles the music of Messiaen much less than *Concerts sur terre* from an esthesic standpoint, it more closely approximates his pre-compositional poietics through a wider use of his technical devices. These are evidenced in the sketches that show the application of a regular symmetrical permutation pattern to rows A, B and C: 'de 4 en 4, groupes de 3', 'de 2 en 2, groupes de 6', and 'de 3 en 3, groupes de 4'; and the creation of a hypothetical 'de sept en sept, groupes de quatre' permutation employed to reorder a *Candrakalâ* Hindu rhythm. The sketches additionally planned for a rhythmic pedal and non-retrogradable rhythms.

When compared to Garant or Prévost, Clermont Pépin used a much smaller number of Messiaen's techniques. However, those that he did use were employed both extensively and exactly as Messiaen himself would have done. Five of Messiaen's seven modes of limited transposition are found in Pépin's output between 1951 and 1956, namely modes 1, 2, 3, 4 and 7.[64] In *Guernica* (1952), Pepin paid homage to the falling woodwind mode 2^2 scales from Messiaen's *Turangalîla-Symphonie* that had been taught in class the previous year. The pitch content of both *Guernica* and *Le rite du soleil noir* draw heavily from modes 2 and 3. All three transpositions of mode 2 appear concurrently, both melodically and harmonically, in the retransition. Immediately preceding this, the main theme of the work is heard in mode 7^3. It is presented in two parts that are clearly delineated

---

    [63]   Véronique Robert, *André Prévost: Biography and Works* (Saint-Nicholas, QC: Dobermann-Yppan, 1999), p. 5.

    [64]   White Luckow, *La Marque du Maître*, pp. 131–72.

into the mode's two symmetrical (01234) halves. *Variations pour quatuor à cordes* (1956) is noteworthy for its use of mode 3^2 and 3^3 scales, as they are inserted within what is otherwise a completely serial composition.

Prévost's use of symmetrical permutations went beyond simple borrowing, instead becoming an inspiration from which to grow. Even early on, Prévost used the symmetrical permutations with a twist, and each incidence of modification became part of a larger string of innovation that would come to characterize his own personal language. For example, Prévost's very first use of o-fan symmetrical permutation in *Mobiles* (1959) led to his creation of a modified o-fan permutation in Sonate pour violon et piano (1960). The symmetrical permutations became the underlying basis of a completely symmetrical order-12 Latin square in *Terre des hommes* (1967). His stylistic development was one of a straight path from beginning to end.[65]

We might ask how Messiaen's influence could be so strong yet diverse. Prévost and Garant both answer this question with an apparent paradox, as they felt that Messiaen was most influential in his aim not to be influential. Instead, his challenge promoting individuality created a plurality of influence. Prévost explained that 'Messiaen never wanted to create disciples. He always encouraged us to be ourselves.'[66] Garant conveyed similar sentiments when he concluded that 'a great teacher is one who never imposes on his students but succeeds in leaving his mark on them. This mark is not necessarily stylistic, moreover, since Messiaen's teaching does not make you want to compose Messiaen's music, but rather the music that he awakens in you.'[67]

---

[65] More complete biographical information may be found at Pierre Rochon, 'André Prévost' (online).

[66] Ibid.

[67] Boivin, *La classe de Messiaen*, p. 359.

Chapter 9
Messiaen and the Spectralists

Marilyn Nonken

Spectralism is not a system. It's not a system like serial music or even tonal music. It considers sounds, not as dead objects that you can easily and arbitrarily permutate in all directions, but as being like living objects with a birth, lifetime, and death.[1]

Spectralism has effected a fundamental shift; music will never be quite the same again. Spectral music is symbiotically allied to electronic music; together they have achieved a rebirth of perception. Yet while electronic music is a well-documented technological breakthrough, spectralism in its simplest form, as color-thinking, is a spiritual breakthrough.[2]

Introduction

It is relatively easy to construct the biography of a single composer. An artist's development can be charted in relation to others and to contemporaneous historical and cultural events. Each composer leaves a distinctive footprint of scores and performances; from scores, reviews, recordings, and documented appearances, one can hypothesize the creative processes that led from one composition to the next. From life event to life event, and from work to work, we can construe the relationship between the personal and the professional, marrying psychobiography and aesthetic critique. One fortunate enough to study the contemporary repertoire may even approach the composer, or the composer's close confidantes and colleagues, to ask: How was this composition made? And why?

The evolution of a compositional movement such as spectralism, which has emerged in the last 40 years, is a more elusive essence, for an artistic movement is more like ether than flesh. The composer is born, the work is premièred; but birth of an aesthetic is harder to establish.

From a luxurious distance, one may attempt to identify spectralism's genesis, the moment at which it seemed to take on a life of its own, seemingly independent

---

[1] David Bündler, 'Gérard Grisey', interview with David Bündler, 18 January 1996, available at www.angelfire.com/music2/davidbundler/grisey.html.

[2] Jonathan Harvey, *In Quest of Spirit: Thoughts on Music* (Berkeley and Los Angeles: University of California Press, 1999), p. 39.

of any single individual or piece. One could suggest the year 1973, with the founding of the performance collective L'Itinéraire by Messiaen's students Tristan Murail, Gérard Grisey, Michaël Lévinas, and Roger Tessier. Another option would be 1979, the year that coincided with the first use of the term 'musique spectrale'.[3] Yet the act of specifying any one event must be somewhat arbitrary. Once one establishes a chain of pivotal dates and moments, something of a fictional history is created. In the quest to historicize and link these events in time, as if objects, we often lose sight of the spirit that animated the music.

In this chapter, I attempt to conjure this spirit by considering Olivier Messiaen's relationship to the spectral movement in its nascency, restricting this inquiry to the years 1967–73. At that time, spectralism had not yet been recognized as a compositional movement. Many works defining the aesthetic – Murail's *Mémoire/Erosion* (1976), *Ethers* (1978), *Treize couleurs du soleil couchant* (1979) and *Gondwana* (1980), and Grisey's epic cycle *Les Espaces acoustiques* (1974–85) – were years away. The relevance of the spectral composers would not become evident until the turn of the century, by which time they had established their own careers and their influence could be seen on major international figures such as Magnus Lindberg, Kaija Saariaho and Jonathan Harvey. But in this pivotal period, defined by Messiaen's appointment as Professor of Composition at the Paris Conservatoire in 1966 and the founding of L'Itinéraire seven years later, what became the aesthetic foundation of spectralism was laid by a handful of like-minded individuals who shared what were, at the time, novel ideas about the perception and conception of musical colour.

The Percept of Colour

In Messiaen's personal experience of music, timbre and harmony had always been closely linked. Even in his earliest works, he was extremely attuned to their mutuality and mutability, and the idiosyncratic way in which he manipulated these musical parameters uniquely defined the sound of his music. In works from the immediate post-war era, such as *Vingt Regards sur l'Enfant-Jésus* and *Turangalîla*, Messiaen used orchestration and harmony in tandem to sharply define his motivic materials and underscore his rigorously sectional forms. But in the following years, spurred towards experimentation by the activities of his students Pierre Boulez, Karlheinz Stockhausen and Iannis Xenakis, he moved away from the compositional language associated with those now-classic works. In *Réveil des oiseaux*, *Oiseaux exotiques* and the *Catalogue d'oiseaux* he began to more fully integrate birdsong into his musical vocabulary and explore more eccentric formal structures. More dramatically, he began to reconsider his use of harmony and timbre. While his former students were refining serial and stochastic

---

[3] Hugues Dufourt, 'Musique spectrale: Pour une pratique des formes de l'énergie', *Bicéphale*, 3 (1979): pp. 85–9.

techniques, all of which manipulated pitch as a musical parameter independent of timbre, Messiaen had ceased to find personal relevance in the notion of harmony as a discrete variable.

By this point, harmony and timbre had ceased to exist for Messiaen as separate perceptual elements. He had come to recognize them as contingent parts of a single, multidimensional whole: a harmonic-timbral complex from which neither component could be extracted or distilled. His preoccupation with these kinds of complexes is evidenced by the compositions from the early 1960s. Dating from the period directly preceding Murail's study with him, *Chronochromie*, *Sept Haïkaï* and *Couleurs de la Cité céleste* demonstrate his radical new focus. 'I don't think I've ever gone so far with the sound-colour relationship', Messiaen told Claude Samuel with regard to *Couleurs*.[4] So that his intent could not be misinterpreted, Messiaen wrote in the work's preface: 'The form of the work depends entirely on colours. The melodic and rhythmic themes, the complexes of sounds and timbres evolve in the manner of colours.' As Paul Crossley has noted:

> Plainsong Alleluias, Greek and Hindu rhythms, permutations of note-values, birdsong of different countries: all these accumulated materials are placed at the service of colour and the combinations of sounds that represent it.[5]

That a musical work could be based on progressions of harmonic-timbral complexes (based on colours, and not primarily defined by pitch relationships) was an idea notably detached from the aesthetic debates then percolating at centres for new music. At the Internationale Ferienkurse für Neue Musik at Darmstadt, the Cologne Courses for New Music and, as Murail recalls, in Parisian circles, debates regarding compositional technique were dominated by two approaches. One was the systematic approach of the serialists, a group dominated by Boulez that also included other former students of Messiaen, such as Stockhausen, Gilbert Amy and Jean Barraqué. Even prior to the conception of the Institut de Recherche et Coordination Acoustique/Musique (IRCAM) in 1970, these figures were powerful advocates for a post-Schoenbergian serial aesthetic. The other approach, which presented itself as the antithesis to serialism and other formalized compositional techniques, was the aleatoric approach associated with John Cage. In Paris, its foremost advocate was André Boucourechliev, who had spent six months in America (1963–64) becoming familiar with the philosophies of Cage and Earle Brown. Although the ideological bases underlying postwar serialism and aleatoricism were in many ways oppositional, the compositional methodologies of the serialists and chance composers were based on common assumptions of music as systematically organized information constructed of independent musical parameters. The serialists focused on the permutations of

---

[4]   *Music and Color*, p. 139.

[5]   Paul Crossley, liner notes to *Messiaen: Des Canyons aux étoiles... / Oiseaux exotiques / Couleurs de la Cité céleste* (CBS Records, M2K 44762, 1988).

pitched, rhythmic, dynamic, registral and timbral elements. While leaving much to chance, the aleatoric composers similarly isolated these elements, specifying in their scores, for example, absolute durations but not pitches, or specific pitches but neither their registers nor dynamics. In this way, both approaches assumed the inherent discreteness, or singularity, of each element.

In unique contrast, Messiaen embraced musical colour as a hybrid of timbre and harmony and as a component of multidimensional complexity. His musical colour was an unmeasurable, unnotatable variable, and one not easily reconciled with compositional methodologies, the 'permutational orthodoxies of the avant-garde', that demanded parametric discreteness.[6]

'Demand' is an apt word to use. Integrally serial and aleatoric methods can be described as techniques that explore different degrees to which the composer controls the nature of the work and performance. At one extreme, Boulez sought something approaching absolute control. His stated goal was to reduce music to its elementary particles, then re-assemble them. By unraveling and then reweaving the musical fabric fibre by fibre, he sought to create music free of stylistic reference and historical association.

> I wanted to eradicate from my vocabulary absolutely every trace of the conventional, whether it concerned figures and phrases, or development and form; I then wanted gradually, element after element, to win back the various stages of the compositional process.[7]

If Boulez sought absolute control, Cage sought its renunciation, 'giving up control so that sounds can be sounds'.[8] His *Cheap Imitation* for two pianos (1969), for example, is based upon his 1947 adaptation of Satie's *Socrate*. Manipulating the earlier work's variables independently, Cage maintained the original phrase structure but transposed some of the notes and also varied the dynamic scheme. Unlike Boulez, Cage sought no specific result, but he similarly based his procedures (operations directed by the *I-Ching*) on abstract musical elements, treated independently.

Messiaen could not conceive his musical fundamentals in this manner. He wanted to assert control over certain elements (such as rhythm and the development of temporal values), but also realized that there were other musical elements, such as colour, that he wanted to treat more intuitively. He thus saw himself as treading the nebulous ground between the oppositions of freedom and rigour. Responding to the poor reception of *Chronochromie*, he wrote:

---

[6] Jonathan Croft, 'The Spectral Legacy', *Journal of the Royal Musical Association*, 135/1 (2009): p. 195.

[7] Pierre Boulez, 'Necessité d'une orientation esthétique (II)', *Canadian University Music Review / Revue de Musique des Universités Canadiennes*, 7 (1986): p. 61.

[8] John Cage, *Silence: Lectures and Writings by John Cage* (Middletown, CT: Wesleyan University Press, 1973), p. 72.

Messiaen and the Spectralists 231

My permutations of durations are rigorous, my birdsongs are entirely free. Rigor is implacable, but so too is freedom. Mingling them together shocks audiences of all persuasions. ... *Freedom!* Doubtless we're afraid of this word. In the end it is freedom which triumphs in my music.[9]

Messiaen's freely idiosyncratic approach to composition reflected his own experience. As a listener incapable of perceptually segregating harmony from timbre, and as a mature artist reconciled with his own perceptual abilities, he now allowed his own experience of musical colour more fully to inform his evolving compositional technique. And as the scholarly discourse regarding compositional systems and the role of the composer intensified, he focused ever more tightly on musical perception and the experience of the listener.

By the 1960s, Messiaen's synaesthetic experience and approach to composition became a primary topic of his lectures and interviews.[10] A particularly relevant statement followed the Paris première of *Chronochromie* at the Théâtre des Champs-Élysées. The audience's extraordinarily negative response to the work provoked the critic René Dumesnil to liken its reception to that of Stravinsky's *Le sacre du printemps*, which took place nearly 50 years earlier in the same hall. Responding to criticisms of both form and content (all now 'at the service of colour'), Messiaen justified his compositional methods by appealing to the concept of a psychological universal:

> Neoclassicists expect clear tonal cadences, while old-fashioned dodecaphonists miss the greyness of the 'series'. And when I speak quite straightforwardly of resonant harmonies being 'purple flecked with orange and red and surrounded with violet', they look at me smilingly as if this were a dangerous illusion. However, these connections between sound and colour are not a purely subjective phenomenon: I myself feel them intensely – and I know, having had the experience, that others also feel them.[11]

Messiaen's appeal to a shared psychological reality granted his aesthetic argument unique authority. Conveniently, his highly personal stance also enabled him to avoid becoming entangled in skirmishes over compositional systems. As Christopher Dingle said:

> By referring to chords in terms of colours, Messiaen put all harmonies, from common triads to twelve-note complexes, on an equal footing that made their common musical labels redundant. He was thus able to side-step the entire dogmatic debate of the time about what was and was not appropriate material

---

[9] PHNS, p. 245.

[10] Christopher Dingle, *The Life of Messiaen* (Cambridge: Cambridge University Press, 2007), p. 164.

[11] PHNS, p. 244, from an unpublished interview conducted in 1964.

for a composer; he was composing neither tonally, nor atonally, nor modally, but using different areas of colour.[12]

Messiaen's work in the late 1960s was thus doubly innovative. He had developed a personal approach to composition emphasizing musical colour, which dominated every aspect of his musical vision, from the most immediate perception of individual works to his conception of the art form itself. Ever the professional, Messiaen discussed musical colour largely with regard to his own compositions, his creative process and the reception of his work. Yet his compositional innovations held weighty implications for other composers. His provocative statements on musical colour, when considered in relation to his compositions from the period, would prompt others to critically evaluate existing compositional approaches and suggest unexplored avenues for scholarly research and artistic exploration. Messiaen's work heralded what would be recognized as 'the new thinking, spectralism in music: the art of composing with harmonic and inharmonic series, fused conglomerates of sound'.[13]

The Concept of Colour

In 1967, Messiaen was renowned throughout the world as a composer, performer and pedagogue. He had already produced several works recognized as postwar masterpieces; upon his appointment to Professor of Composition (having taught harmony and aesthetics at the Conservatoire since 1941, and only unofficially offering courses in composition), he had been at work for months on his most massive choral work, *La Transfiguration de Notre-Seigneur Jesus-Christ*. On the other hand, Murail (b. 1947) was just beginning his career as a composer. Unsure of his future in music, he was drawn to what Messiaen offered: a musical aesthetic based on the projection in space and time of sound-complexes defined by harmonic-timbral colour. The two composers had arrived simultaneously, and independently, at a similar aesthetic within which timbre and harmony were inseparably linked, within which form could be dictated by the transformation of harmonic-timbral material. Both intuitively felt that vibrantly coloured sound-complexes could provide a basis for musical structure, and that these complexes and their transformations, as perceived, could assume the integral role previously reserved for tones and tonal relationships.

Prior to 1967, Murail had devoted his university studies not to music but to Arab languages and economics, enrolling at the École Nationale des Langues Orientales Vivantes and the Institut d'Études Politiques, both in Paris. He had studied piano and organ but had not felt compelled to pursue composition with any teacher at the university level. However, he had developed a fascination with

---

[12] Dingle, *The Life of Messiaen*, pp. 163–4.

[13] Harvey, *In Quest of Spirit*, p. 39.

Messiaen's music. He had familiarized himself with much of the piano music and, at the keyboard, made his way through works such as the *Messe de la Pentecôte* and *Oiseaux exotiques*.[14] He had attended no live performances of Messiaen's music but was entranced by the recordings he had heard, notably of the *Trois Petites Liturgies de la Présence Divine*, and while he did not have a thorough grasp of Messiaen's theoretical writings and compositional techniques, Murail sensed that the composer's conception of music mirrored his own. By the time he heard of Messiaen's appointment, he had come to realize that Messiaen was his 'only option' as a teacher.[15] Thereupon, at 20 years old, Murail applied for admission to the Conservatoire National Supérieur de Musique. He submitted with his application materials the piano solo *Comme un oeil suspendu et poli par le songe....*

Comme un oeil suspendu et poli par le songe... (Like an eye suspended and polished by the dream...) predates Grisey's first mature work (*Dérive*, 1972) by five years. It is the first opus in Murail's catalogue, but it should not be dismissed as mere juvenilia. While not representative of Murail's mature aesthetic stance, *Comme un oeil suspendu et poli par le songe...* documents the young composer's responses to the music of Messiaen and the French post-serialists and tantalizingly reveals a protospectral concern with harmony, timbre and time.

Historically, *Comme un oeil suspendu et poli par le songe...* marks the first point of intersection between Murail and Messiaen, and it evidences a rare affinity between the two: a commonality of artistic concerns remarkable considering their difference in age (nearly 40 years) and accumulated experience. Unpublished, the work remained largely unknown for decades and was only released by the composer for publication and performance in 2003.

Lasting approximately six minutes, *Comme un oeil suspendu et poli par le songe...* is in many ways imitative of Messiaen's style. Figures abound that are reminiscent of his non-retrogradable and pseudo-symmetrical constructions. The score features palindromic constructions and rhythmic motives presented in successive variation, altered through the use of additive values. Passages of slow-moving, dense chords evoke the brassy, chorale-style writing of *Turangalîla*, and virtuoso flourishes immediately bring to mind the composer of the *Vingt Regards*. Indeed, Murail fluidly and sensitively appropriated Messiaen's gestural language, in a manner openly derivative yet highly intuitive. Murail achieved a similar feel of metric freedom and stasis in this première opus, with which he aligned himself with Messiaen and not with the composers of the post-serial and aleatoric factions then in vogue.

The work's central section features Murail's most sophisticated adaptation of Messiaen's techniques. This section is constructed from four series of chords, each progressively longer, which are juxtaposed against a cycling filigree pattern. This chordal progression is notated on the second of three staves.

---

[14] Marilyn Nonken, 'An Interview with Tristan Murail', 15 May 2008 (unpublished).

[15] Ibid.

Example 9.1 Murail, *Comme un oeil suspendu et poli par le songe...*, page 2, systems 3–4

As the section begins, three chords are introduced, marked *mf* and *bien timbré*; of these, the second is articulated twice (Example 9.1). They are closely related harmonically: each has four notes, and each includes the harmonic intervals of tritone, major third and half-step. The chords are similar, but each is unique, distinguished by its individual intervallic content. The second has more of a quartal sound when compared to the others, due the heightened presence of the perfect fourth/fifth; and the third sounds more dissonant, due to its emphasis of the minor second/major seventh. The first chord, contextually, is distinguished by its tertian sound, owing to the presence of both minor and major thirds and their complements. Essentially, this chord progression is a progression of sonorous colours. Each sonority presents a subtly different hue. As shown in Example 9.2, with the chords marked in boxes labelled A, B and C, these harmonies can be categorized as belonging to three unique set classes, with similarly unique intervallic content.

The passage shown in Example 9.1 begins a section comprising more than a third of this short work, in which a progression of harmonic-timbral complexes unfolds, embedded in a thicket of birdlike motives and momentary flourishes notated on the uppermost and lower staves. The course of the section as a whole is driven not by the development of rhythmic ideas, nor the variation nor exploration

Example 9.2   Murail, *Comme un oeil suspendu et poli par le songe…*, chords, set-class and interval-class content, page 2, system 3 to page 4, system 2

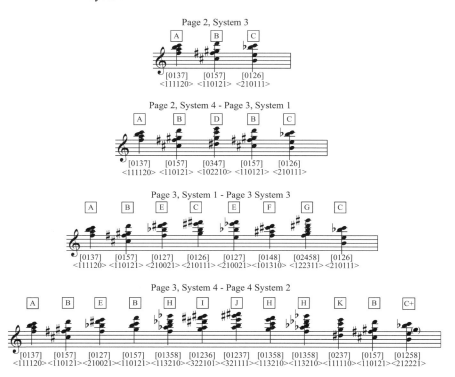

of motivic materials, nor any kind of directed or 'functional' harmonic progression. These three chords recur four times, as the identical incipits of four progressively longer chordal progressions, within which nearly every chord is unique. Of all the chords presented, only two are transpositions, containing the same intervallic content but simply reproduced at a different pitch level. Virtually each expansion of the harmony incorporates not a transposition of a sonority previously heard, but a new chord with an audibly distinctive harmonic content. Each change of chord heralds a change in colour. Murail's method, then, admittedly intuitive, was to effect chromatic shifts through voice-leading processes, maintaining the outer intervals of the chords while manipulating the inner voices. A brilliant chromaticism is achieved, in which each successive harmony varies subtly from its predecessor, in terms of actual pitches (as in transposition) and absolute intervallic content.

This central section's four phrases are outlined in Example 9.2. This reveals in the nomenclature of set theory the subtle harmonic and intervallic variations underlying what is heard as a kaleidoscopic play of colours. The initial chords (A, B and C) appear as such, with variations produced by voice-leading identified by successive letter names (D–K), unique set-class descriptors (which appear in square brackets under the chords in Example 9.2), and individual interval vectors (which appear under the set-class descriptors for each chord). One sees the palindromic processes as well as those of harmonic and registral expansion. While the aggregate is largely saturated, the result is not the greyness Messiaen deplored but the brilliance of a rainbow. The passage articulates what Debussy described as a music *de couleurs et de temps rythmés*.

Murail has recalled how Messiaen, through his words and his music, revealed to him and his peers the potential of colour as a structuring force in music. Messiaen's example suggested an alternative to other compositional approaches:

> I had musical ideas, sound images that I wanted to express, and I could not do that with the serial or twelve-tone technique … . Messiaen's classes … [were] kind of a shock for most of us, because we saw that there were possibilities other than serialism. You didn't have to think about music in terms of accompanied melody or counterpoint … [but rather] the importance given to timbre, as a way of structuring the form.[16]

As *Comme un oeil suspendu et poli par le songe...* reveals, Murail was not a thoroughly schooled composer at this point. Preparing for the Conservatoire's formidable entrance exams, he studied briefly with Julien Falk, an academic better known for his *Technique de composition musicale: Théorique et pratique* (1958) than for his musical compositions. More of a tutor in theory and analysis, Falk did not intervene in the actual writing of the work, in which Murail was empowered by intuition and compelled by an innate musical sense. This was recognized by Messiaen, who read through the work at the piano and complemented the young composer on his talent.[17] Due to its embryonic status, Murail's first work is thus impressive for its unusual focus on timbre and harmony, and resonance and register, all of which facilitate the perception of musical colours and their transformation. These factors distinguish *Comme un oeil suspendu et poli par le songe…* as not just a historical curiosity, but as a serious protospectral study. Murail's première opus is particularly valuable in that it captures something of that raw essence – a spirit drawn to and inspired by Messiaen – which would mature into the spectral attitude.

The Perceiving Body, The Conceiving Spirit

Messiaen's treatment of colour as a harmonic-timbral complex was a formative influence on the French spectralists. Yet almost as influential on the developing aesthetic was Messiaen's recognition of the role played by the listener's perception

---

[16] Tristan Murail, 'Seminar at Ostrava Music Days', available at www.newmusicostrava.cz/en (2003).

[17] Nonken, 'An Interview with Tristan Murail'.

of colour. Foreshadowing by nearly 20 years the sentiments of music theorists lamenting the mismatch between avant-garde 'compositional grammars' and psychological 'listening grammars', or the gap between certain compositional systems (such as integral serialism) and what can be considered innate cognitive constraints,[18] Messiaen and his students situated their compositional endeavours within the context of a sounding, profoundly physical reality. In this way, the spectral attitude was neither anti-serial nor anti-aleatoric nor anti-avant garde. Murail maintained:

> At a certain point, the 'spectral movement' was seen as a reaction against the 'avant-garde'. And clearly, it was a reaction against certain composers who believed that they were the avant-garde. But, in reality, it was a reaction against their refusal to make even the slightest concessions to the phenomena of auditory perception. Abstract combinations on paper are not musical research. As a result, we fought against this type of musical behavior.[19]

Grisey would further note how spectralism distinguished itself by taking into account, in the very processes of composition, the psychological reality of the listener: 'Especially at the beginning, [a goal] was to try to find a better equation between concept and perception – between the concept of the score and the perception the audience might have of it.'[20] He would describe this equation as the 'perfectly parallel relation between the perceiving body and the conceiving spirit'.[21] In seeking this ideal relation, the spectralists expanded upon Messiaen's approach, motivated to acknowledge in music the complexities of human perception and their relation to the sound itself. From its inception, then, spectralism was a strongly ecological attitude, considering the mutual relation between the listening perceiver and the affordances of the musical environment.

The spectral appeal to ecology has been viewed sceptically, as a rhetorical flourish through which Grisey, Murail and Dufourt sought to convey their attitude's moral and ethical superiority over serialism.[22] Theorist Eric Drott suggests that the spectral composers, by strategically employing the language of social change, allied their goals with those of left-wing political causes (such as the environmentalism, anti-consumerism, anti-imperialism and the 'politics of difference' surrounding

---

[18] See Fred Lerdahl, 'Cognitive Constraints on Compositional Systems,' *Contemporary Music Review*, 6/2 (1992): pp. 97–121, and Lerdahl and Ray Jackendoff, *A Generative Grammar of Tonal Music* (Cambridge, MA: MIT Press, 1987).

[19] Tristan Murail, 'After-Thoughts', *Contemporary Music Review*, 19/3 (2002): p. 6.

[20] Grisey and Bündler, 'Gérard Grisey'.

[21] Gérard Grisey, 'Did You Say Spectral?', trans. Joshua Fineberg, *Contemporary Music Review*, 19/3 (2000): p. 2.

[22] Eric Drott, 'Spectralism, Politics, and the Post-Industrial Imagination', in Björn Heile (ed.), *The Modernist Legacy: Essays on New Music* (Farnham: Ashgate, 2009), pp. 46–56.

238   *Messiaen Perspectives 2: Techniques, Influence and Reception*

feminist, gay and anti-racist movements), courting anti-establishment favour and assuming a political stance designed to situate their compositional endeavours in relation to the socio-political culture at large. Certainly, there are parallels among the seismic shifts that occurred simultaneously in both political and aesthetic arenas, and the composers associated with spectralism were no doubt profoundly influenced by the chaotic events associated with May 1968 and its aftermath. Yet it is inaccurate to characterize their references to 'ecology' and 'environment' as essentially metaphorical. In summoning these terms, they were more akin to scientists than political theorists; the spectral interest in ecology reflected a new awareness of the mutual relationship between the listener and the environment and was motivated primarily by aesthetic and artistic concerns. In their music (as in Messiaen's), the spectralists sought not to construct an 'imagined' ecology,[23] but to explore a very real one. Thus, their perspective today is more fruitfully considered in relation to advances made in ecological psychology and their musicological applications.[24]

Messiaen developed his compositional techniques over years of experimentation, mainly by appealing to his intuition. He created distinctive timbral colours by conceiving a spectrum for each note he orchestrated: 'a chord, not a classified chord but a complex of sounds which is designed to give the note its timbre'.[25] (In 1976, he would comment on setting the song of the Blackcap: 'I had to invent chords on each note in order to translate the special timbre.')[26] Yet Murail did not want to rely, as he had in *Comme un oeil suspendu et poli par le songe...*, solely on intuition:

> We did not want to be completely intuitive like the aleatoric composers or like Giacinto Scelsi, or even György Ligeti . We were interested in those experiences but we wanted to build something more .[27]

Working methodically, the composers of the Groupe de l'Itinéraire became involved with advanced research in acoustics and psychoacoustics, fertile fields renewed by the emerging technologies of digital recording and data processing. Seeking to decompose sounds to their most elementary particles, they used the computer to analyse the acoustic spectrum of recorded sounds in such unprecedented detail that it seemed to reveal the fingerprints of these sounds. Using a fast Fourier transform, descriptive data was generated about selected sounds, which were then depicted using a spectrogram. The resultant graphic representations of timbre

---

[23]   Ibid., p. 46.

[24]   See, for example, Eric F. Clarke, *Ways of Listening: An Ecological Approach to the Perception of Musical Meaning* (New York: Oxford University Press, 2005).

[25]   *Music and Color*, p. 102.

[26]   PHNS, p. 311.

[27]   Ronald Bruce Smith and Tristan Murail, 'An Interview with Tristan Murail', *Computer Music Journal*, 24/1 (2000): p. 12.

unveiled something akin to an anatomy of colour, exposing its components and their evolution throughout the birth, lifetime and death of the sonic event. Developing techniques detailed extensively elsewhere,[28] spectralist composers exploited this technology to build upon newly conceived fundamentals of music. The techniques they advanced, such as additive synthesis, led them to invent new worlds of harmonic-timbral colour. And although much has been written about them, their techniques and the role of computer-assisted analysis remained the means to an end. The spectral characteristics of real-world sounds, those of the natural environment, continued to serve as the point of departure:

> Where analyses of 'real' sounds are used as a starting point for compositional processes, the ambiguity between mimesis or the original timbre and the metaphorical use of the spectrum as harmonic material is precisely and explicitly the point: our perception drifts between timbre and harmony.[29]

Ultimately, what renders any music 'spectral' would be its basis, in some way, in the exploration of the spectrum or a group of related spectra.

In January 1973, L'Itinéraire was formed as a musical collective offering an alternative to Boulez's Domaine Musical. Their rhetoric emphasized the unity of technique and technology, as well as the equality of composers and their interpreters, and they dedicated themselves to exploring how technology could transform composition, performance and musical perception. On their programmes were works for both acoustic instruments and live electronics, and for the latter they often used equipment that they built themselves specifically for the occasion.[30] Featuring works of Messiaen and their own members, their programmes also included the French premières of compositions by composers little known in Paris but similarly fascinated with colour, such as Scelsi, George Crumb and Salvatore Sciarrino.

The initial group of Murail, Grisey, Dufourt, Tessier and Lévinas would be joined by Jean-Claude Risset, a student of Jolivet who had pursued psychoacoustic research at Bell Labs as a colleague of Max V. Mathews. For years, Risset had studied the acoustics of brass instruments, which demonstrated empirically for the first time how dramatically instrumental harmonics (partials) change, depending on pitch, duration and dynamic. His scientific focus was shared by the composers

---

[28]   See, for example, Viviana Moscovich, 'French Spectral Music: An Introduction', *Tempo*, 200 (1997): pp. 21–7; Eric Daubresse and Gérard Assayag, 'Technology and Creation: The Creative Evolution', *Contemporary Music Review*, 19/2 (2000): pp. 61–80; Joshua Fineberg, *Spectral Music: History and Techniques* (Amsterdam: Overseas Publishers Association/ Harwood Academic Publishers, 2000), constituting *Contemporary Music Review*, 19/3; and Smith and Murail, 'Interview with Tristan Murail': pp. 11–19.

[29]   Jonathan Croft, 'The Spectral Legacy': p. 194.

[30]   Smith and Murail, 'An Interview with Tristan Murail': p. 11.

in the collective, who concurred with his conviction that 'the control of timbre can bring about the creation of new musical architectures'.[31]

While many spectral innovations can be attributed to the technologies and techniques associated with computer-assisted composition, the core components of Messiaen's compositional philosophy, which underscored works such as *Couleurs de la Cité céleste* and are mirrored in the earliest works of Murail, would become central to the new compositional attitude. All musical factors would be viewed in the service of the harmonic-timbral complex and its development over time. Pitch, dynamic, duration and articulation would not be considered as independent parameters, but as elements integrally related in the creation of colour; on the larger scale, processes of harmonic-timbral transformation would assume dramatic proportions, literally serving as the basis of a musical form. Crucially, the machinations of harmonic-timbral colour were designed to be accessible to the listener. Musical processes and transformations were composed out with a heightened awareness of the listener's experience and with the recognition of concrete auditory phenomena.

The spectral composers shared with Messiaen the goal of creating music that would have the listener engage directly with what sound itself could become (*le devenir des sons*), not with the metaphorical interpretation of thematic and motivic material, nor with the mechanics of codified musical forms, nor with the abstractions established by a rigid compositional system. By continuing the 'search for expression through the material itself, without hidden or conventional reference',[32] and by attempting to create music free from the trappings of historical reference and tradition, the goal of Messiaen's aesthetic descendents was not so different from that of Boulez. However, spectralist composers sought to create this music not by constructing a fully determined music *ex nihilo* via a comprehensive compositional system (to 'win back' what had been lost), but by exploring more fully the potential inherent in sound itself, in all its unnotatable and previously inaccessible sonic complexity. It would privilege, above all, the concept and percept of musical colour.

---

[31] Jean-Claude Risset, 'Exploration du timbre par analyse et synthèse', in Jean-Baptiste Barrière (ed.), *Le timbre: Métaphore pour la composition* (Paris: IRCAM/ Christian Bourgois), pp. 125–6.

[32] Daniel Pressnitzer and Stephen McAdams, 'Acoustics, Psychoacoustics, and Spectral Music,' *Contemporary Music Review*, 19/2 (2002): p. 58.

Intermède 2

Chapter 10

The Tombeaux of Messiaen: At the Intersection of Influence and Reception

Robert Fallon

Part 1: Commentary and Descriptive Overview

Reputations of artists rise, fall and sometimes rise again, their mutability matched by their opacity. What exactly is an artistic reputation and how can its rise, fall and specific content be described? There are no easy answers for such complex questions. Reputation can be traced, however, by the way people esteem or otherwise respond to an artist: it is a byway of reception history. When such reception is expressed in art, it becomes an influence. An artist (or artwork) may leave a mark on another artist, who in turn reflects and further shapes the reputation of the earlier artist. Artistic influence is reflected in the conscious or unconscious adoption of a portion of another artist's signature identity. Larger than traditional notions of musical style, this signature identity may embrace an artist's associations with media (live, recorded, internet, video), spheres of purpose (ritual, secular, occasional, dance, concert, commerce) and creative principles (order/ disorder, objectivity/subjectivity, beauty/repellence).

In the case of Olivier Messiaen, there are numerous widely acknowledged spheres of influence, such as his seminal roles in shaping hyperserialism, advocating natural resonance, expanding the vocabulary of rhythm, and substantially expanding the repertory for the piano, organ, ondes Martenot, and mallet percussion. His delight in symmetries and mechanical processes has proved infectious, as has his use of poetic imagery involving colours, rainbows, and visions. Messiaen's influence is felt in the way that these words themselves appear to belong to him; it is obvious, for example, that he is a source for works like Euricio Carrapatoso's *Modes of Unlimited Expression I* and *II*. His presence also inevitably hovers behind all birdsong in contemporary music. He may even be credited as a driving force behind larger artistic or cultural currents such as the return of representation in the classical tradition, the taking of nature as model and subject, and the unabashed incorporation of religious thought into musical modernism. Messiaen's influence on composers is easily asserted, but how is it documented?

The measurement of artistic influence poses problems along every labyrinthine turn. Arriving at the centre of the labyrinth promises insight into neither art nor influence, it seems, but rather confrontation with bull-headed critics hungering after proof, accuracy and better methodology. In a two-page article on musical

244   *Messiaen Perspectives 2: Techniques, Influence and Reception*

influence, for example, critics David Beard and Kenneth Gloag take to task one of the few monographs on the subject. 'Why assume that using the past is the same as being influenced by the past?' they ask. 'How he has transferred [Harold] Bloom's theories into a musical context requires greater theoretical reflection.'[1] And so it's back to the entrance to try again to explain how art responds to art. Back inside, one greets another critic, Lawrence Kramer, who begins an essay on the subject by saying 'Talk about musical influence has traditionally been cheap'. continues by calling theories of influence a 'cult of aesthetic heroism', and ends by dismissing the subject: 'influence isn't important'.[2]

When regarded as a form of reception, however, influence is important indeed, for it provides the stuff of narrative history and thus the context in which art is understood. In the opening pages of his *Oxford History of Western Music,* Richard Taruskin asserts that 'the historian's trick is to shift the question from "What does it mean" to "What has it meant?"'[3] My focus here fixes specifically on what Messiaen has meant to later composers. As memory is a form of history, so their commemorations to Messiaen trace a musical history of his legacy, in contrast to a reception history located beyond the scores.[4] Taruskin also writes of the need to address both the poietic (production-centred) and esthesic (reception-centred) perspectives on music:

> If it is true that production and reception history are of equal and interdependent importance to an understanding of cultural products, then it must follow that types of analysis usually conceived in mutually exclusive 'internal' and 'external' categories can and must function symbiotically.[5]

The texts discussed here, tombeaux written for Messiaen, reside at the intersection of production and reception and thus offer a unique path for negotiating a labyrinth as daunting as Messiaen's reputation and influence.

The most common way of studying issues of influence can be effective but is usually tightly circumscribed. Such studies typically focus on the influence of a single composition or composer on another. I take a different approach here. Partly inspired by movements in the humanities that embrace empirical data, such as the digital humanities movement and the quantitative literary history of Franco

---

[1]   David Beard and Kenneth Gloag, *Musicology: The Key Concepts* (New York: Routledge, 2005), p. 93.

[2]   Lawrence Kramer, 'Influence', in *Interpreting Music* (Berkeley and Los Angeles: University of California Press, 2011), pp. 113, 122, 127.

[3]   Richard Taruskin, *Oxford History of Western Music*, Vol. 1 (Oxford and New York: Oxford University Press, 2005), p. xxv.

[4]   For a study that focuses on a handful of tombeaux in the context of musical politics, see Peter J. Schmelz, 'What Was "Shostakovich", and What Came Next?', *The Journal of Musicology*, 24/3 (Summer 2007): pp. 297–338.

[5]   Taruskin, *Oxford History of Western Music,* Vol. 1, p. xxvii.

Moretti, I have collected a large pool of works whose authors acknowledge the influence of Messiaen by variously naming their pieces *homages, tombeaux,* or *memorials,* or by dedicating them to Messiaen, or in some other way unequivocally linking them to Messiaen. Although many of these pieces were not composed in response to Messiaen's death, I call them all *tombeaux* because no single word addresses all forms of artistic tribute. I explore these tombeaux as the juncture where artistic production is simultaneously artistic reception.[6]

The tombeaux of Messiaen serve here as texts that reveal the contour and content of Messiaen's artistic legacy as received and recreated by composers. Given the large number of pieces discussed here, however, no individual text or context is explored in depth. Rather, as an exercise in reception history, depth is sacrificed to accommodate breadth, which affords the ability to make generalizations. The tombeaux are listed in the second part of this chapter: Table 10.1 names 23 tributes to Messiaen by non-classical artists and Table 10.2 lists 134 homages in the classical tradition.[7] While these lists are, of course, not comprehensive, their large size and scope (spanning 60 years and some 25 countries on four continents), can at least be seen as representative of Messiaen's musical memorials. The collection of pieces in Table 10.2 could facilitate a number of future studies. Does Messiaen mean something different to French composers than to Japanese composers? What features of Messiaen do these groups tend to honour? What sort of American composer honours him and what sort does not? How has his reputation changed over time? The lists may also prove useful to musicians searching for repertory and particularly in programming concerts celebrating Messiaen. In this chapter, however, my objectives are only to demonstrate that the tombeau occupies a fruitful intersection between musical reception and production, to present the lists of works that undeniably show Messiaen's influence, to unpack the variety of ways that such works honour him and, most importantly, to aggregate these works' particular forms of Messiaen reception into a broad portrait of his influence.

The tombeaux reveal that composers find Messiaen's most characteristic quality in the realm of harmony: resonant bell sounds, unusual colours, and complex chords are ubiquitous in these works. His second most commonly imitated trait is his trademark slow tempo and meditative but intense mood; the rich harmonies are often long held and sometimes open onto a profound silence. The third most influential quality concerns his instrumentation: the harmonies result from a taste for winds, brasses and piano – but most of all the percussion of gongs and mallet instruments. Piano solos and, to a much lesser extent, organ pieces also constitute the tombeaux. Fourth, two melodic figures stick with many composers: birdsong generally, of course, and Messiaen's 'Boris' motif or the

---

[6] Messiaen himself participated in this tradition in his *Tombeau de Paul Dukas*, for piano.

[7] The dates in both tables may represent different events. Where possible, the date of completion of a composition is given. For some entries, the year represents the date of publication or the only date I have found for the composition.

246   *Messiaen Perspectives 2: Techniques, Influence and Reception*

somewhat longer 'Chant d'extase' theme (or something reminiscent of it), both of which cadence with descending tritones. After these traits, one also hears the occasional dance-like rhythm, evocation of plainchant, repetition of chords, and simultaneous extremes of range. The compositions most commonly alluded to are, perhaps surprisingly, from Messiaen's pre-1950 period, especially the *Vingt Regards*. Finally, the imagery that composers write to remember him includes the exotic (especially the Asiatic), cathedrals, mountains landscapes, rainbows, stars and heaven. Of equal significance is what the tombeaux exclude. As Messiaen deliberately avoided discussion of faith in *Technique* and the *Traité*, saying 'We treat technique and not sentiment' (*Technique*, Preface), so he effectively staged his own musical reception. This study of his tombeaux reveals that Messiaen is received by composers largely as a paragon of compositional craft rather than a model for spirituality, as a titan of technique rather than a guru of musical nature and supernature. In this way, his is a modernist legacy, appealing to later composers principally on an aesthetic basis rather than one consciously mediated by contexts and concepts.

The Troubles with Tombeaux

The great variety of tombeaux challenges any assumptions that they equally honour the honouree and problematizes any approach to writing reception history that relies on them. Whether these compositions are representative of the composers is beside the point. Rather, the accumulation of approaches to Messiaen evinced in these works reveals a portrait of Messiaen as painted by his artistic heirs, a portrait perhaps as much of his influence as of their reception of his music. The large number of tombeaux reflects the strength of his influence as being among the greatest of any twentieth-century composer, though I leave such comparisons to other studies. Subtler forms of influence – the normal fare of analytical studies – also fall outside this chapter. For example, Messiaen's bird style is parodied in Ohana's *Office des oracles*, his rhythmic principles may inform parts of Boulez's Second Piano Sonata, while his third mode of limited transposition appears to launch the second movement of Ligeti's Piano Concerto.[8] With the large body of works addressed here, however, such specific analysis is impractical. Addressed as a whole, influence must address categories larger than rhythms and modes.

Many of the tombeaux presented here imitate Messiaen's style and many were written to express sorrow over Messiaen's death, thus skewing the mood and means of expressing it toward a sobriety that may not capture the full range of emotion that Messiaen's example inspires in younger composers. The most common title among these pieces is *homage* (or *hommage*); the next most common includes

---

[8] See Caroline Rae, 'Messiaen and Ohana: Parallel Preoccupation or Anxiety of Influence?' in this volume, Antoine Goléa, *Rencontres avec Pierre Boulez* (Paris: René Julliard, 1958), pp. 82–3, and Richard Steinitz, *György Ligeti: Music of the Imagination* (Boston: Northeastern University Press, 2003), p. 326.

some form of the word *memory* (in Latin, French or English), followed in turn by a dedication, and then by the word *tombeau*. I balk at giving weight to the significance of the word *tombeau*, because I agree with Michael Fling's assessment in his book *Musical Memorials for Musicians: A Guide to Selected Compositions* that 'these works are known by a plethora of descriptive terms'.[9] To most composers today, there appears to be no significant generic tradition distinguishing words such as *Trauermusik, musique funèbre, dirge, commemoration, elegie, homage, tombeau* and '*à la mémoire de…*', though each of these, originating with the *déploration,* has its own history. Each of these terms implies the work honours the composer, often with a meditative mood.

Beyond issues of nomenclature are those of scope, because Messiaen's influence extends to all the arts. In literature, Messiaen's mother and brother wrote poems about him, as have Oni Buchanan, Daniel Abdal-Hayy Moore, Alex Skovron, Mark Wilson and others. Zdzisław Nardelli's novel *Otchlan ptaków* tells the story of the *Quartet for the end of Time*, inscribing history into fiction written by an eye-witness of the première. Other writings do similar work. For his 50th birthday in 1958, for example, the German journal *Melos* published tributes from 17 of Messiaen's students under the name 'Hommage à Messiaen'. These half-page essays acknowledge Messiaen's good-natured personality and discriminating but non-judgmental teaching style, and suggest the dominant perspective on him valued his ability to expose his students to the sounds from all of time and space. Declaring his distaste for Messiaen's focus on the world's musical 'objects', Stockhausen complains that 'Messiaen ist ein glühender Schmelztiegel' [Messiaen is a blazing melting pot].[10] In the visual arts, set and scene designers have worked not only on his opera but also on ballets of his music; dancers and choreographers such as Trajal Harrell, Patricia Malavard and Roland Petit have set his music in motion. Painters, sculptors and photographers have crafted their work in response to his, as in the work of Cartier Bresson, Arturo Martin Burgos, Michael Canning, Charles Cater, Dirk Castelein, Kim Cypert, Mike J. Davis, Barry Fantoni, Paul Helm, Stephen Hutchings, Marilyn Kalish, Anton Mendizabal, Toshiko Nishimoto,

---

[9]   Michael Fling, *Musical Memorials for Musicians: A Guide to Selected Compositions* (Lanham, MD and London: Scarecrow Press and the Music Library Association, 2001), p. xi. Other honourifics include dedications (whether 'dedicated to Messiaen' or simply 'to Messiaen') and works designated as 'in the manner of', 'on a theme of', or 'with the modes of' Messiaen. As Fling writes, 'Today, however, a composer is as likely to use a generic title such as "Sonata" for such a work, and to identify it as a memorial piece only in a dedicatory phrase or prefatory note' (*Musical Memorials*, p. xii). Such forms of recognition that are not part of the work's title make them difficult to find, as are the less frequently acknowledged quotations. For an amusing essay on *tombeaux*, see Richard Toop, 'Dedicated to…', liner note in *From Vienna*, Arditti String Quartet, Arditti Quartet Edition 21 (1994), Montaigne Auvidis CD MO 782027.

[10]   Karlheinz Stockhausen, contribution to 'Hommage à Messiaen', *Melos: Zeitschrift für Neue Musik*, 12 (December 1958): p. 392.

248   *Messiaen Perspectives 2: Techniques, Influence and Reception*

Catherine Parker, Tom Philips, Daniel P. Ramírez, Tony Renner, Mark Rowan-Hull and Eric Prenshaw, whose photographs honour the cover of this book.

Another sphere of artistic influence includes commemorative events, such as the recital, festival and conference, and commemorative media, such as the recording, book and documentary. These also appear in different guises. *Hommage à Messiaen* is both the title of a CD of Messiaen's piano music recorded by Pierre-Laurent Aimard and one of organ music performed by Colin Andrews. *A Tribute to Olivier Messiaen* is a recording with works by Messiaen, Dukas, Zuidam and Dalbavie stemming from a commissioning and recording project curated by George Benjamin. Recordings may, however, also honour the composer by their title alone when the works fail to refer to him directly, as in the CD *Autuor de Messiaen,* with music by Murail, Reverdy and Tremblay. Tributes may also have ulterior motives, since they can associate a lesser-known artist with a greater-known one like an opening act for the marquee name. An unusual example comes from New England Conservatory's Department of Contemporary Improvisation, which produced a concert of improvisations on Messiaen entitled *Across Time: A Third Stream Tribute to Olivier Messiaen.* This concert undoubtedly served both to legitimate Third Stream and to legitimate Messiaen in non-classical spheres of music. Of course, another form of commemorative media includes scholarship (such as this chapter), concert reviews, magazine features, circulating anecdotes and textbook stylizations of a composer. This is the stuff of reception history.

Tombeaux capture a composer's reputation at a particular time. David Drew's commissions to honour Stravinsky in a 1971 issue of *Tempo,* for example, show how a younger generation of composers valued him as an Apollonian composer of canons, rather than the Dionysian composer of his early ballets. These tribute canons include Luciano Berio's *Autre fois (berceuse canonique pour Igor Stravinsky*), Edison Denisov's *Canon en Mémoire d'Igor Stravinsky*, Alfred Schnittke's *Canon for Two Violins, Viola and Violoncello – In memoriam of Igor Stravinsky* and Elliott Carter's *Canon for 3 – In memoriam Igor Stravinsky.*

Further examples continue to complicate the lowly homage. Jonathan Harvey's *Bird Concerto with Pianosong* presents its vestige of Messiaen not in its title or any dedication or programme note from the composer, but from three less direct sources: the composer's prior work *Tombeau de Messiaen*, his participation in a body of bird-based pieces heavily associated with Messiaen, and his publisher's comments that link the work to Messiaen. Similarly, Qigang Chen's *Instant d'un opéra de Pékin*, for piano, was composed for the Olivier Messiaen piano competition, and Ramon Humet's *Escenas de Pájaros (Scenes of Birds)* won the International Olivier Messiaen Composition Prize. In what way do such works honour Messiaen and associate the identity and musical orientation of a younger composer with him? Can Ian Krause's *Piano Murmurs* be regarded as a tombeau, since its first incarnation honoured him, but its revision withdrew the honour? Finally, there are undoubtedly many compositions that are indebted to Messiaen but that refrain from naming him explicitly. One such example is Marta Ptaszynska's *Awakening Birds*, the title of which alludes to Messiaen's

Réveil des oiseaux. Though the score abstains from mentioning him, she says the connection to Messiaen is obvious.[11] For those who do not speak French or know that she studied with Messiaen, however, the work's status as a tombeau could be lost. A similar example can be found in Reza Vali's *Toward that Endless Plain: Concerto for Persian Ney and Orchestra*, which includes birdsong, movement titles referring to 'the Abyss' and a spiritual journey told in music. Vali regards these traits as connected to Messiaen, though the score does not mention him. How many composers have not composed tombeaux to Messiaen, but could, like Vali, say "I became a composer because of Messiaen'?[12]

Musical covers and quotations are common gestures of recognition. But how do covers, which typically convey a sense of tribute, differ from arrangements, which suffer from a sense of being derivative? Is this form of tribute outside the classical tradition a form of disrespect within it? The band Ruins has quoted Messiaen in their song 'Messiaen' and has covered his 'Amen des étoiles, de la planète à l'anneau'. David Sherr and the Bel Air Jazz Ensemble have similarly reworked *Le Merle noir*. Both of these groups along with the Lilliput Orkestra, Spooky Actions and Naked City have paraphrased the *Quartet for the end of Time*'s 'Danse de la fureur pour les sept trompettes'. Whether the attraction is the evocation of apocalypse or the unison melody in parallel but asymmetrical phrases, these covers are clearly meant to honour Messiaen. Yet when classical musicians perform the *Vocalise-étude* on trumpet, trombone and saxophone or when the cello movement from the *Quartet for the end of Time* is heard on the organ, classical purists may perceive these tributes as desecrations. Is Yvonne Loriod's remix of Messiaen sketches in *Feuillets inédits* ontologically different from these paraphrases? On the other hand, quotations of Messiaen always seem to honour him, whether it's the *Vingt Regards* heard in the electronica of Advokaten Le Messiaen or in the piano quartet of Donald Sloan's *Tributaries*.

Are homages that adopt Messiaen's harmonies and timbres a sign of Messiaen's influence or a sign of the later composer's weakness of invention? The 14 movements of Helmut Sosha's *Le Tombeau de Messiaen*, for piano, sound very much like Messiaen. Are such works suitable for concert performance or are they mere exercises in style imitation? Clearly, there is no blanket answer. Very often, however, such works are comparative triflings, occasional works completed not for a composer's portfolio but to fill a commission or occupy space on a tribute concert.

What is to be made of a conspicuous lack of acknowledgement? Claude Vivier and François-Bernard Mâche never dedicated a work to Messiaen, though both were his students and were significantly shaped in his musical image. Dutilleux's colours and Gubaidulina's spirituality would seem to have taken inspiration from Messiaen, but their works offer no explicit acknowledgement of his influence. Carter shared a fascination with rhythm, but never dedicated any of his many homages to

---

[11] Personal communication, 25 October 2012.
[12] Personal communication, 18 October 2012.

250   *Messiaen Perspectives 2: Techniques, Influence and Reception*

Messiaen. And despite Lutosławski's avowed appreciation of Messiaen, he left no music for him. Does such silence speak to an anxiety of influence?

The End of Time Ensemble

A special type of homage resides in the many works written for clarinet, violin, cello and piano, a nearly proprietary instrumentation that usually points to the *Quartet for the end of Time*. Messiaen did not originate this ensemble; at least two works for this configuration predate Messiaen's work: Paul Hindemith's Quartet (1938) and Walter Rabl's Quartet, op. 1 (1896). In a sense, any such work is part of Messiaen's legacy as much as the Pierrot ensemble points to Schoenberg's *Pierrot Lunaire*. As the Pierrot ensemble has formed the core of many contemporary music groups, such as the Fires of London, the New York New Music Ensmble, Da Capo Chamber Players, and eighth blackbird, the *Quatuor pour la fin du Temps* has engendered groups such as Tashi (later called the Tashi Quartet), the Antares Ensemble, the Mercury Quartet, the Ebb and Flow Quartet, Ensemble QAT, the Lyra Ensemble, the Contrasts Quartet (formerly the Eberli Ensemble) and the Akoka Quartet (not to be confused with David Krakauer and Matt Haimovitz's Akoka). Although the four instruments comprise a subset of the Pierrot ensemble, the breadth of the literature for this group merits its own name: the End of Time ensemble.

Related to these groups, but with only clarinet and cello as its core instruments, is Akoka, an ensemble formed by clarinettist David Krakauer and cellist Matt Haimovitz 'to create a new project centred around Olivier Messiaen's *Quartet for the end of Time*'. Their project has taken the form of a concert in which Messiaen's quartet is framed by two improvisations with the purpose of representing the experience of Henri Akoka, the Jewish clarinettist who played the première of the work in a Nazi prisoner-of-war camp. The programme notes for Akoka's concert highlight its political resonance: 'As the forces of fundamentalism, intolerance and violence intensify in today's world, this project is all the more timely.'[13] Akoka's overtly political framing of Messiaen puts it in the company of various studies and recordings that portray the *Quartet for the end of Time* as a site of remembrance of the Holocaust or resistance to violent political repression.[14] This political slant to Messiaen reception is, however, notably lacking among the tombeaux.

Figure 10.1 charts the creation of about 150 works for End of Time ensemble. Among the most famous composers who have written for it are Thomas Adès, Samuel Adler, Milton Babbitt, Peter Maxwell Davies, Aaron Jay Kernis, Fred

---

[13]   See www.bernsarts.com/akoka/akoka.html.

[14]   See, for example, Steven Honigsberg's inclusion of 'Louange à l'éternité de Jésus' on his 1997 CD *Darkness and Light*, Vol. 2 (part of the Holocaust Museum Series) and the performance of 'Vocalise, pour l'Ange qui annonce la fin du Temps' on the commemorative DVD *Holocaust: A Music Memorial Film from Auschwitz* (2005). See also Leslie Sprout, 'Messiaen, Jolivet, and the Soldier-Composers of Wartime France', *The Musical Quarterly*, 87/2 (Summer 2004): pp. 259–304.

Lerdahl, Per Norgård, Krzystof Penderecki, Bernard Rands and Chinary Ung. Many of these works clearly nod to Messiaen and perhaps were composed with the prospect of being programmed on the same concert as the *Quatuor*. They include bird themes (Alexandra Gardner's *Crows*, Andrew Schultz's *L'Oiseau fantastique*), time themes (Detlev Glanert's *Yakub iki: Zeit des Wartens*, Ian Wilson's *Timelessly this*, Sydney Vale's *Quartet for the Beginning of Time*) and spiritual themes (Dimitri Terzakis's *Seelenbilder*, Jean-Michel Ferran's *Sept visions de l'apocalypse*, Judith Bailey's *Visions of Hildegard*, Zygmunt Krauze's *Quatuor pour la Naissance*). Other works have been written for the End of Time ensemble as soloists with orchestra, such as Takemitsu's *Quatrain* and Charles Wuorinen's *Tashi* (both from 1975).

The name *Quartet for the end of Time* has itself been subject to endless permutations. There have been Trios and Quintets for the End of Time. There is a *Quartet for the Beginning of Time* (Mark Alburger), a *Quartet for the End of Space* (Pauline Oliveros and friends), a *Quartet for the Love of Time* (William Kraft) and a *Quartet for the New Beginnings* (Katrina Curcin). George Crumb's *Vox Balaenae* is, like the *Quartet*, in eight movements, with two movement titles riffing off of Messiaen's work: the first is called 'Vocalise (...for the beginning of time)' and the last is named 'Sea-Nocturne (...for the end of time)'. In a different sort of twist, Trajal Harrell has also set the *Quartet for the end of Time* to dance.

The Tashi Quartet undoubtedly has helped to popularize the End of Time ensemble. Formed by pianist Peter Serkin, clarinetist Richard Stolzman, violinist Ida Kavafian and cellist Fred Sherry, Tashi was founded in 1973 explicitly to perform the *Quartet for the end of Time*. But it also commissioned works for this instrumentation. Universal Edition has claimed the End of Time ensemble to be a novelty, promoting Johannes Maria Staud's *Lagrein* (2008), for example, to be for 'an ensemble for which hardly anyone has written since Olivier Messiaen's *Quatuor pour la fin du Temps*'.[15] Shortly after the 1976 release of Tashi's recording of the *Quatuor*, however, increasing numbers of composers took up this ensemble, as shown in Figure 10.1.

End of Time ensemble works and performing groups represent a different type of homage from the works discussed below. Though on a much smaller scale, Messiaen must be credited with establishing this group in a manner analogous to Haydn's string quartet, Mozart's piano concerto, or Schubert's Lied. Here style is beside the point; the tribute may be direct or indirect and exists in the work's instrumentation alone.

Figure 10.1 shows three spikes in the history of this instrumentation. The first is after 1992 (the year Messiaen died); the second is around 2001 (possibly for the tenth anniversary of his death or for Y2K fears of apocalypse – see Jean-Michel Ferran's 2002 *Sept visions de l'apocalypse*); and the third around 2008 (for the Messiaen centennial). The correspondence of these dates with events associated

---

[15] Universal Edition Spring 2008 Newsletter (www.universaledition.com/tl_files / News_Dateien/Newsletter_pdf/2008_02_en.pdf).

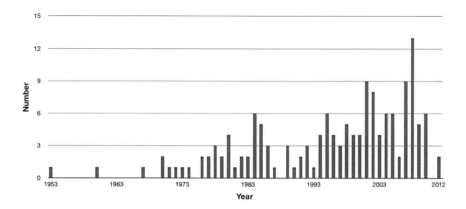

Figure 10.1   The number of works composed each year for the same instrumentation as the *Quartet for the end of Time*, from 1953 to 2012

with Messiaen suggests that these works were composed with him in mind, even when the work and its programme note do not mention him.

In tracking Messiaen's reputation by way of the tombeaux, interesting comparisons arise between the curve of the End of Time ensemble pieces, shown as they appear over the last 60 years in Figure 10.1, and the curve of the 134 tombeaux (drawn from Table 10.2) over roughly the same period, as shown in Figure 10.2. The first spike in Figure 10.1, in 1984, was caused not by anything related directly to Messiaen, but by the recording Tashi made of the *Quatuor pour la fin du Temps* and the group's sudden popularity, which enabled it to commission works for itself. The trough appearing around the time of Messiaen's death in 1992 shows that few End of Time ensembles were active at this time, giving composers little reason to write for this instrumentation. Curiously, it appears that existing Pierrot ensembles did not generally associate themselves with Messiaen's *Quartet* and thus did not add to the End of Time ensemble repertory. Shortly after his death, however, increasing numbers of such pieces were composed, peaking briefly with six works in 1995, a trend corresponding to the increasing number of scholarly studies of Messiaen's work. This growth of interest is a sure sign of a growing reputation and, however well known Messiaen was before his death, the trend confirms the truth behind the macabre quip that artists have to die to become famous. The continued growth in numbers of pieces from the mid-1990s suggests that various End of Time ensembles were forming and commissioning new works. Unlike at Messiaen's death, a spike appears at the centenary of his birth in 2008, showing that the association between Messiaen and this ensemble had cemented and that a sufficient number of ensembles existed to generate a growth spurt in commissioned works. The continued creation of new pieces for End of Time ensemble demonstrates that the reputation of a composer may affect the existence of particular performing ensembles, which in turn strongly mediate the works written in a new genre.

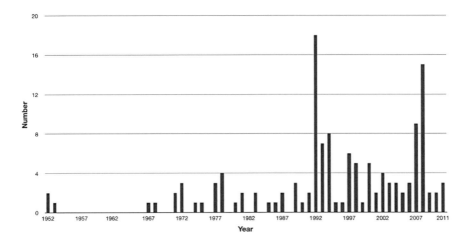

Figure 10.2   The number of tombeaux composed each year from 1952 to 2011

By contrast, Figure 10.2's spikes around 1992 and 2008 highlight the lack of mediation by ensembles and the more direct connection between a composer's writing a tombeau and key dates in the trajectory of the honouree's fame (death and centenary birth). The greater volatility in the curves of Figure 10.2 over the general growth shown in Figure 10.1 shows the dependence of tombeaux on key anniversaries and that, at least in Messiaen's case, death and centenary provide roughly equivalent occasions for celebrating his life and crafting a reputation for him through art.

Prominent Works

Of all of Messiaen's tombeaux, several stand out as being particularly prominent, successful and representative. Describing them in ascending order from solo instruments to orchestral forces, I find grounds for asserting that, as enumerated above, Messiaen's musical legacy resides principally in bell-oriented harmonies, percussion instruments, birdsong and contemplative tempi. The trappings of Messiaen's poetic paratexts survive in the titles of this repertory as well, but his Christian faith and inspiration from the natural world are largely absent.

Non-classical
Before surveying some of the more notable compositions written for Messiaen, it is well worth recognizing that his influence has extended to musicians working in non-classical idioms, such as jazz, rock and electronica (see Table 10.1). Björk's 'Cover Me', for example, quotes Messiaen's 'Les Bergers' and evokes his 'charm of impossibilities' in the line 'I'm going to prove the impossible really exists'. Radiohead's Jonny Greenwood, who plays the ondes Martenot on the soundtrack

to the film *There Will Be Blood*, has written: 'I came to think of Messiaen and my favourite bands like The Pixies, New Order, The Fall as all being in the same category somehow … and I still do.'[16] This influence can be heard on the song 'Pyramid Song' from Radiohead's album *Amnesiac*. Its parallel chords, distended and foreshortened phrases, floating feeling, homophonic texture, and lyrics on death and heaven apparently honour a *louange* movement from the *Quartet for the end of Time*. Finally, Matt Haimovitz and David Krakauer have improvised both with one another and with Josh Dolgin (aka Socalled), combining their classical training with klezmer and noise-oriented improvisation.

John Zorn has honoured Messiaen both as a classical composer and as a jazz musician. With his band Naked City, including core players Bill Frissell, Fred Frith, Wayne Horvitz and Joey Baron, Zorn's 'Notre Dame de l'Oubli (for Olivier Messiaen)' seems to turn the iambic rhythm of the last movement of the *Quartet for the end of Time* into a heartbeat. They covered 'Louange à l'eternité de Jésus' on their album *Grand Guignol*, setting the cello line with an ethereal electronic sound and the piano part with a gong-like sonority. Zorn's classical tributes to Messiaen include *Duras: Duchamp*, which alludes to various moments in the *Quartet for the end of Time,* and *Aporias: Requia for piano and orchestra*. *Aporias* takes Stravinsky's *Requiem Canticles* as a source for the whole, but relates individual movements to other artists. The fanfaric seventh movement, 'Religioso (Olivier Messiaen)', does not share much with Messiaen's sound world, though traces of gongs and birdsong polyphony betray the tribute. In a sketch for the work, Zorn associated Messiaen with 'oriental rhythm in long strophes', 'dense wind chords', and a 'tam-tam'.[17]

As in the realm of classical composition, many non-classical musicians borrow broadly from Messiaen without necessarily quoting his work or composing a homage. The 'Orchestral Intro' from the 2010 album *Plastic Beach* by Gorillaz appears to paraphrase Messiaen's *Les Offrandes oubliées*, a connection perhaps facilitated after 2007, when bandleader Damon Albarn toured with ondes Martenot player Thomas Bloch. A still more general influence appears in the music of Israeli drummer Asaf Sirkis and his trio Inner Noise, who mix modern jazz with slow, densely chromatic harmonies on a church organ. Perhaps most profoundly and pervasively, electric bass player Anthony Jackson has acknowledged Messiaen as a key influence ever since 1967, when he heard Messiaen's own recording of *La Nativité du Seigneur*, an experience that, he says, changed his life.[18]

---

[16]   Jonny Greenwood, 'New Jonny Greenwood: "Future Markets" Plus Greenwood Q&A', interview with Stereogum (7 December 2007), http://stereogum.com/7412/new_jonny_greenwood_future_markets/news/.

[17]   See Figure 4.5 in John Brackett, *John Zorn: Tradition and Transgression* (Bloomington & Indianapolis: Indiana University Press, 2008), p. 153.

[18]   For more on Anthony Jackson and Messiaen, see Sander van Maas, 'Unfolding the Pocket, Neutralizing the Lyrical: Contrabass Guitarist Anthony Jackson and the Aesthetics of Modernism', *Dutch Journal of Music Theory*, 13/3 (2008): pp. 207–19.

Organ

Most *hommages* for organ were written by organist-composers like Messiaen. At well over 30 minutes, the longest organ work on the list is Bengt Hambraeus's *Missa pro organa: In memoriam Olivier Messiaen.* The work, however, does not pay homage to Messiaen's style. Although he studied with Messiaen, Hambraeus elected a musical language far more dense and dissonant in this work than most of Messiaen. Naji Hakim, who succeeded Messiaen as titular organist at Paris's Trinité church, composed a three-movement *Le Tombeau de Olivier Messiaen*, which is closely allied to Messiaen's style in its layered textures, modal harmonies and devotional titles. It opens with a reminiscence of 'Dieu parmi nous' and includes quotations from several other works. Overall, its aggressiveness, textures and harmonies are most like 'Force et agilité des corps glorieux' and 'Joie et clarté des corps glorieux'. Lionel Rogg's *Hommage à Messiaen* is a slow, seamless meditation with soft colours in the model of 'Desseins éternels' from *La Nativité.* The organist-composer Eduard Terényi has written several works related to Messiaen by their common interest in mysticism, colour, birds and chant; his music is most akin to *L'Ascension.*[19]

Piano

With Yvonne Loriod serving in bookend roles as muse and interpreter, Messiaen's contribution to the piano repertory of the twentieth century rivals, if not surpasses, that of Debussy, Ravel, Rachmaninoff and Bartók. Many composers (usually pianists themselves) have channelled their tombeaux into this instrument, with its history of short character pieces. Of these works, Jonathan Harvey's *Tombeau de Messiaen,* for piano and digital audio tape, stands apart for its length, power, and strong foothold it has found in the repertory. It is dedicated to its first interpreter, Philip Mead, and 'to Jake (aged 10 hours)', a reference to birth in the face of death that recalls Messiaen's repeated theme of resurrection. Also evoking Messiaen is the DAT part, which 'consists of piano sounds tuned to twelve natural harmonic series', perhaps pointing to Messiaen's focus on natural resonance as the basis for his harmonies. Bell-like sounds begin the work. Over a sequence of chords with modal allusions, Harvey writes 'Delicate and coloured', thus connecting his harmonies to Messiaen's synaesthesia. The piece includes a bird-like passage and the score mentions bells in relation to a tritone. Rapidfire arpeggiation of unfolding chords are left to vibrate, creating a dark, beautiful and substantial work.

Two other works that have entered the repertory are Tristan Murail's *Cloches d'adieu, et un sourire* and Toru Takemitsu's *Rain Tree Sketch II: In memoriam Olivier Messiaen.* Murail's title not only alludes to a Messiaen prelude and an early song (or late orchestral work) by his teacher, but also sounds much like the carillon heard in 'Cloches d'angoisse et larmes d'adieu' or *Visions de l'Amen.*

---

[19] For more on Terényi, see Anamaria Mădălina Hotoran, 'Musical and Spiritual Affinities: Olivier Messiaen and Eduard Terényi', available at www.wseas.us/e-library/conferences/2010/Iasi/AMTA/AMTA-34.pdf.

256 Messiaen Perspectives 2: Techniques, Influence and Reception

Takemitsu's *Rain Tree Sketch II* is not only his last piano work, but has been called his best. Allusions to Messiaen include whole-tone scales, moments of silence, use of dotted notes to elongate a phrase, fleeting reminiscences of the *Vingt Regards*, the performance indications 'Celestially Light' and 'Joyful', sounds of a carillon and Messiaen-like harmonies, textures and phrasings.

The *Vingt Regards* is again the touchstone in Gérard Pesson's 'Trop d'étoiles', which recalls the melody of 'Regard de la Vierge' or perhaps 'Chant d'extase'. György Kurtág's '…humble regard sur Olivier Messiaen…' is sparse, slow and meditative in a low register, but very short, like 'Regard du silence' or (again) 'Chant d'extase'. Though dedicated not to Messiaen but to Yvonne Loriod, George Benjamin's *Sortilège* repeats a descending tritone cadence reminiscent of 'Chant d'extase'. Despite a brief passage of avian fantasy, its sound world is otherwise distant from Messiaen.

Gerald Levinson's brief *Pièce pour l'anniversaire de Olivier Messiaen* masterfully recreates Messiaen's rich, smooth, custardy harmonies beneath the slow-motion melody of the Birthday Song, a nod to the 'Boris' theme and a touch of birdsong. Composed long before Messiaen's death, it shows that the complex chords and slow tempo found in many of the tombeaux are not motivated exclusively by the wish to express grief, but in fact comprise his signature style. Messiaen's last student, Qigang Chen, composed his *Instant d'un opera de Pékin* for the Messiaen Piano Competition. His music draws mainly from Chinese opera, but includes this procedure: 'Parallel melodic lines without changing mode contrasted by "Messiaen-style" modulations'.[20]

A final example of a piano tombeau, Augusta Read Thomas's 'Cathedral Waterfall' comes, like several other pieces listed in Table 10.2, from a collection of short pieces dedicated to different composers or artists. It is paired and contrasted with a piece written for Pierre Boulez. 'Cathedral Waterfall' does not exhibit the soft, resonant harmonies of Messiaen's music that characterize many other homages. Rather, Thomas's chords are harsher and more brilliant, reminiscent of Messiaen's late style, as from the Pièce for piano quintet. Yet like several other works, 'Cathedral Waterfalls' allows these severe chords to ring with long-held durations, rather like a greatly slowed down 'Noël' or parts of 'Regard de l'Onction terrible' from the *Vingt Regards*. The work taps into Messiaen's style with its title and the imagery in the author's note, which mentions bells, colour, cathedrals and nature. It projects a meditative mood with its long-held, granitic chords and uses the tritone structurally, focusing on F in the first half and B in the second half.

Chamber Ensemble

Among homages for chamber ensembles, the obvious point of reference is the *Quartet for the end of Time*. Messiaen wrote other chamber works, of course, including the *Thème et variations*, *Visions de l'Amen*, *Merle noir*, the Pièce and

---

[20] From the liner note of the CD *Autuour de Messiaen*, Ensemble Parallèle, New Music Ensemble, cond. Nicole Paiement (MSR Classics MS 1151).

The *Tombeaux of Messiaen* 257

arguably several others, but his most famous work is undoubtedly the *Quartet*. Here I briefly describe duet, trio, quartet and quintet tombeaux in turn.

Joan Tower has acknowledged that Messiaen provided her with a model for how to compose in a modern but not serial idiom. '*Très Lent* was written as an *hommage* to Olivier Messiaen', she wrote, 'particularly to his *Quartet for the end of Time,* which had a special influence on my work.' She continues by explaining what she took from Messiaen for this piece:

> When I was the pianist for the Da Capo Chamber Players, we frequently performed Messiaen's quartet over a seven-year period. During this time, I grew to love the many risks Messiaen took – particularly the use of very slow 'time', both in tempo and in the flow of ideas and events. *Très Lent* is my attempt to make 'slow' music work.[21]

The tempo is indeed very slow, set at $\eighthnote$ = 40. The instrumentation, for cello and piano, recalls the fifth movement of the *Quartet for the end of Time.* In measure 11, the piano begins the characteristic ♫. rhythm from the final movement of the *Quartet.* Like the *Quartet,* the cello plays long, sustained notes in an intense, sorrowful, improvisatory style over somewhat dissonant chords in the piano.

At over 30 minutes, Peteris Vasks's *Episodi et Canto perpetuo: Hommage à O. Messiaen,* for violin, violoncello and piano, rivals Bengt Hambraeus's *Missa pro organa* in length. Like the *Quartet,* it is in eight movements. In his programme note, Vasks says the work 'describes a difficult journey through the realms of distress, disappointment and the suffering of love, which, in particular, forms the central point of the *canto*'.[22] The work suffers from being highly derivative of Messiaen (and, at times, of George Crumb). Like parts of the *Quartet*, Vasks's work begins with long, quiet, meditative and static octaves in the strings. The third movement's asymmetrical dance in unison recalls Messiaen's 'Danse de la fureur' and the fourth movement's fugue recalls the sixth movement of the *Vingt Regards.* The fifth movement carries a cello melody like the *Quartet* and the sixth recollects bits and pieces of the earlier movements, like the *Quartet*'s penultimate movement. It ends with the violin and cello in octaves in a high tessitura, *pianissimo,* very much like the end of the *Quartet.* It's an effective work made worse by its insistent adherence to Messiaen's model.

From the grand bouquet of pieces composed for End of Time ensemble, I choose only Toru Takemitsu's *Quatrain II* to discuss here, a work he wrote following *Quatrain* for Tashi as soloists with orchestra. The perennial description of Takemitsu as a cross between Debussy and Messiaen is apt here and he

---

[21] See Joan Tower's program note in the score to *Très Lent (Homage to Messiaen)* (G. Schirmer, 1994).

[22] Peteris Vasks, quoted in Peter T. Köster, 'Works with Violincello', liner note to Peteris Vasks, *Works with Violoncello,* David Geringas (cello) (2008), Hänssler Classic CD 93.229.

quotes 'Chant d'extase' or the gestures from examples 95 to 99 in *Technique of My Musical Language*. In a passage where the clarinet jumps ever downward, Takemitsu evokes moments from 'Abîme des oiseaux'.

In the programme note to her work *Trois visions de l'arc-en-ciel*, for End of Time ensemble and percussion (her own instrument), Marta Ptaszynska writes:

> My piece is an homage to Olivier Messiaen, who was my teacher and mentor. Therefore, I tried to implement in my music several features characteristic to Messiaen's harmonic and melodic language. However, there is no exact quotation of his music in my work. Rather, I tried to capture the Messiaen-like flavour of beautiful and celestial sonorities.

Ensemble Works

Requiring more effort to compose than short piano pieces, orchestral works generally rely less heavily on Messiaen's style, presenting a more individual sound to better showcase the composer. While David Patterson's sublimely peaceful recreation of Messiaen's music in *In Memoriam Messiaen* is an exception to this rule, works such as George Benjamin's *Invention* and *Ringed by the Flat Horizon* do not strongly point to Messiaen, except perhaps in their complex harmonies. Michèle Reverdy's *Anacoluthes: Hommage à Olivier Messiaen* offers a similar example. It borrows the idea of multiple piano cadenzas from her teacher while insisting on her own intuitive stamp on form. Her programme note explains what she took from his music: 'To give homage to Olivier Messiaen, I decided to work along the lines that his teaching and the deep study of his works have left in me: the taste for rhythmic study, melodic freedom, controlled harmonic writing, a passion for timbre'. Similarly, Gérard Grisey's *Modulations* nods to Messiaen in its embrace of complex but resonant chords and use of metallic percussion and brass. A passage of delicate wind chimes, followed by rich, brilliantly scored harmonies near the end may further honour Messiaen, but the absence of rhythmic and melodic gestures positions this music as a strong statement of independence.

Reza Vali's 'Lament, *in Memoriam Olivier Messiaen*' from *Folk Songs (Set No. 10)*, opens with a low, resonant tone like a tam-tam, followed by low chimes and other percussion, as might be heard in *La Transfiguration*. In what Vali calls a 'funeral dirge', a soprano sings Vali's achingly simple lyrics in Persian:[23]

Páránde boodi yo nághme soroodee	You were a bird
Jáhân áz nághme ye chod pornemoodee.	and filled the world
	with your beautiful songs.

---

[23] Like the poem, the transliteration and English translation are Vali's; the score provides a note on pronunciation. The Persian version is in three rhyming couplets while the English is in two tercets and a quatrain, as shown.

Ázeeze joo nom be mânânde páránde pâr goshoodee	Like a bird
Be ân don yâ ye deegár pâr goshoodee.	you opened your wings
	and took flight
	toward other worlds.

Válee pesvâke toválee pes va ke tomeerâs mâ nád	But your voice will remain
Dár â vâze párende tâ be âchár bâzomânâd.	forever echoing
	in the song of each bird.

Like Messiaen's own gravestone, the lyrics compare Messiaen to a bird. The song closes with a recessional of the opening, with bells giving way to gongs in a symmetrical structure characteristic of Messiaen. The rhythm that Messiaen derived from the retrograde of râgavardhana, as announced in example 5 of the *Technique* and made famous as the opening of the piano part in the *Quartet for the end of Time*, repeats in several instruments and in local as well as structural ways. Often measured to prime numbers of a small durational unit, it expands and contracts in the manner of Messiaen's *personnages rythmiques*.

Gerald Levinson wrote *Chant des rochers*, for 11 wind instruments, harp, piano and percussion, for Messiaen's 70th birthday. In his liner note to the recording, he explains the work's many modes of recognizing his teacher:

> The piece is an homage to Messiaen by way of the mountain landscapes which were so dear to him. Its basic 'sound images' evoke the majestic and craggy peaks and glaciers of the Dauphiné where Messiaen (and Berlioz) found inspiration. Some of these are derived from the sounds of Tibetan ritual music, a mountain music par excellence. The central section is a kind of musical puzzle in which a coded message to Messiaen is inscribed into the music, using a musical alphabet of his invention. It is accompanied by two layers of wind chords marking out permutations of a series of durations whose values constantly add up to 70. Finally, each word is separated from the next by a silence (filled in by soft gong strokes) whose duration is given by the numerological value of the letters of the word, so that in effect (at least fancifully), the message is articulated twice: once in sounds and again in the silences. This work, written while Messiaen was at the height of his powers, is one of two homages I have paid him my music; the other is the Adagio-finale of my Second Symphony, dedicated to him in memoriam in 1994.[24]

The work is flavoured with the same reedy, complex chords that define Messiaen's *Sept Haïkaï*.

Six orchestral works clearly summon Messiaen's spirit. Eduardo Soutullo's triptych, *All the Echoes Listen*, *But in Vain*, and *They Hear No Answering Strain*, dedicates each movement to Messiaen, Takemitsu and Grisey. Melodies in *All the*

---

[24] Gerald Levinson, liner note to *Music of Gerald Levinson*, Orchestra 2001 and James Freeman (cond.) (2005), Albany Records, CD Troy742.

260   *Messiaen Perspectives 2: Techniques, Influence and Reception*

Echoes Listen have the 'Chant d'extase' contour and *They Hear No Answering Strain* sounds a five-note descending octatonic scale in strings, much like *Le Tombeau resplendissant*. Marc-André Dalbavie's *La Source d'un regard* opens with a repeated, bell-like tolling of four complex, ringing sonorities; the musical progress is slow and gentle. Melodic turns characteristic of Messiaen sound shortly before a fast section, and the piece intones 'Puer natus est', a chant that Messiaen occasionally paraphrased. Leo Samama writes in his liner note for the CD that, 'Apart from a few references to chords such as Messiaen used in *Vingt Regards sur l'Enfant-Jésus*, Dalbavie's new work focuses entirely on an extended melodic line.' He calls this line a lamentation and 'a kind of prehistoric song'. Its colourful, restless orchestration and spectralist harmonies and texture adopt Messiaen's sonorous, complex harmonies. Robert Zuidam's *Adam-Interludes* bathes in rich, Messiaen-like harmonies in the first movement and cleverly resets his 'Thème de Dieu' from the *Vingt Regards* in the final movement. Zuidam writes of how he hears Messiaen's spirituality:

> It is the peculiar mixture of worldliness and a predilection for mysticism and exoticism which have always fascinated me about Messiaen's music. Titles that allude to concepts like 'heaven', 'vision' or 'angel' normally set off alarm bells for me because the programme often ends up overshadowing the music. But one searches in vain for a kind of New Age 'wooliness' in Messiaen's music. It is always vigorous and focused, ecstatically jubilant, like the birds, to sing the beauty of God's creation. Spirituality always benefits his music; it is the driving force that opens up heaven's gates of inspiration to him.[25]

Two final works set more independent courses. Bruno Mantovani's *Le Sette Chiese* (2002) is a series of nine movements for ensemble, each titled for a part of the Seven Churches complex in Bologna. The central movement, which also begins the second of three parts, is 'Basilique des saints Vital et Agricola' and is written 'in memory of Olivier Messiaen'. Mantovani's programme note reads: 'Appropriate to this sober, oblong area [the basilica], I composed a piece of church music for brass, which flows into a percussion trio with undefined extent.' The instrumentation and homorhythmic textures evoke *Et exspecto ressurectionem mortuorem*, composed for performance in another sacred building, the Sainte-Chapelle. Much of the percussion trio sounds pleasantly like the polyphonic tappings of a chorus of busy woodpeckers. Like Takemitsu's *Quatrain,* Jonathan Harvey's half-hour *Bird Concerto with Pianosong*, for solo piano, chamber orchestra and live electronics, stands on the border of what I regard as a tombeau. The piece is hardly conceivable without Messiaen – it seems to outdo him at bird

---

[25]   Robert Zuidam, quoted in Leo Samama, 'Dukas, Messiaen, Dalbavie and Zuidam: An Explosion of Colour', trans. Josh Dillon, liner note to *Horizon 2: A Tribute to Olivier Messiaen*, Royal Concertgebouw Orchestra, George Benjamin (cond.) (2008), RCO Live 09003.

representation, with recordings of 40 species of California birds – yet it bears no clear marks of his style. In his programme note, Harvey writes: 'If the songs and objects of the score can bring some inkling of how it might feel to be a human in the mind of a bird, or vice-versa, then I would be happy.' To me, it brings to mind Harvey's feelings about Messiaen. The music consists almost entirely of birdsong samples or birdsong on the solo piano. Touches of Asian melody remind his audience of Messiaen's airs of Eastern exotica.

Conclusion

Although the references to Messiaen described above, ranging from modes to mountains, may at first seem to touch on every aspect of Messiaen, his cosmology offers much more: caverns, lightning, flowers, atoms and planets resonate with fugues, mechanical processes, folksongs, mythology, death, resurrection, afterlife, biblical stories, love songs, musical alphabets, rhythmic retrogradation and modes of duration and dynamics. By and large, these qualities and others – notably a strong religious inclination – are lacking among Messiaen's tombeaux and, I suggest, in his legacy generally.

Instead, Messiaen's influence is most pronounced in younger composers' use of complex but resonant harmonies (Dalbavie, Grisey, Harvey, Levinson, Murail, Patterson), exquisitely slow tempi (Kurtág, Pesson, Rogg, Sloan, Thomas, Tower), melodic ideas often including birdsong (Hummel, Johnson, Soutullo, Takemitsu, Schultz, Zorn) and distinctive use of instruments, especially metallic percussion (Dao, Kremski, Louvier, Palej, Ptaszynska, Vali). Another form of his legacy stems less from his works than from their success, namely the nearly inescapable association of Messiaen with the End of Time ensemble. Their repeated focus on specific style traits paints Messiaen as a respected technician rather than the man of faith he projected himself to be in his music and public persona. Composers remember Messiaen's compositions, not their messages; audiences, by contrast, often respond to his faith, love of nature and values of joy and wonder.

As artistic repositories of memory, these tombeaux open themselves to the influence of the past. They are cultural products doing the work of cultural reception. Though created in order to receive, they nevertheless create in turn. Tombeaux filter the past, creating the reputation of the earlier artist and filtering the range of associations with which later artists, critics and historians bring to that œuvre. Simultaneously proliferating and limiting his influence, the tombeaux recompose Messiaen, writing history in their own notes.

Part 2: Lists of Music Composed in Recognition of Messiaen

Table 10.1   Music composed in recognition of Messiaen in jazz, rock and electronica traditions

Date	Group	Title	Notes
1981	Larry Ochs/Rova Saxophone Quartet	Paint Another Take of the Shootpop	Dedicated to Olivier Messiaen and Otis Redding.
1995	Björk	Cover Me	Quotes Messiaen's 'Les Bergers' from *La Nativité du Seigneur*. Note: this song exists in long, short, remixed and instrumental versions on different albums.
1999	Jason Kao Hwang and Dominic Duval	Messiaen – Speaking of Birds, improvisation for violin and viola	
	Loops	Melodic Minor Messiaen Samba	
	Keith Yaun Quartet	Amen: Improvisations on Messiaen	
2001	Misha Alperin	Emptiness	Dedicated to Olivier Messiaen.
	Christian Muthspiel and Wolfgang Muthspiel	Messiaen Remixed	
2002	Ruins	Messiaen	
2003	Lilliput Orkestra	Castrum (pour Olivier Messiaen)	
2004	Divide by Pi	Hommage à Messiaen	
	John Hagen	Messiaen	
2006	Berger Knutsson Spering	Messiaen	
2007	Akoka	Akoka	Inspired by Henri Akoka, clarinetist of the premiere of the *Quartet for the end of Time*, the core members of Akoka are David Krakauer and Matt Haimovitz.
	Socalled	Meanwhile (A Messiaen Remix)	Performed in collaboration with Akoka.
2008	Gene Ess	Messiaen Shuffle	Dedicated to Olivier Messiaen, in modes 4 and 5 simultaneously, from album *Modes of Limited Transcendence*.
	David Sherr and the Bel Air Jazz Ensemble	'Au Revoir Merle Noir' and 'Quartet for the End of Time/Otherworld Music'	
2010	Katya Sourikova	Homage to Messiaen	

Date	Group	Title	Notes
	Mats and Morgan Band	Advokaten Le Messiaen	
	Team Hegdal	When Sun Ra Met Messiaen	
2011	David Fiuczynski	Flam! Pan-Asian MicroJam for JDilla and Olivier Messiaen	
	Raul Gubert	eye space outside	Dedicated to Olivier Messiaen, with an accompanying painting by Gubert.
2012	Stephen Godsall	Black Messiaen	
	Anders Koppel	Messiaen & the Asparagus Chase	

Table 10.2   Music composed in recognition of Messiaen in classical traditions

Date	Composer	Title	Notes
1952	Pierre Boulez	*Structures* Ia, for two pianos	Series derived from Messiaen's *Mode de valeurs et d'intensités*.
	Karlheinz Stockhausen	*Klavierstück 2*, for piano	Acknowledged influence of Messiaen's use of neumes on this piece, a step toward his concept of 'groups'.
1953	Iannis Xenakis	*Anastenaria*, part 2: *Le Sacrifice* [*I Thysia*], for orchestra	'À mon maître et ami Olivier Messiaen'. *Anastenaria* also includes *Procession aux eaux Claire* and *Metastasis*.
1967	Tristan Murail	*Comme un oeil suspendu et poli par le songe...*, for piano	'*Comme un oeil...* carries the influence of Messiaen – the piece was written for the entrance exam of the Conservatoire National de Musique de Paris, therefore before my studying with Messiaen. An allusion to the composer is found several years later and more consciously in *Cloches d'adieu...*, written as a homage to the composer shortly after his death. The 'bells' heard in the piece belong to the universe of 'spectral' music and to that of Messiaen' (from Murail's website).
1968	Gerd Zacher	*Die Kunst einer Fuge,* 'Timbres-durées', for piano	Dedicated to Messiaen.

Date	Composer	Title	Notes
1971	George Crumb	*Vox Balaenae*, for amplified flute, amplified cello, amplified piano and rattles	Movement titles such as '...for the beginning of time' and '...for the end of time' recall Messiaen's *Quartet for the end of Time*, as does the imitation of animal vocalization.
	Poul Rovsing Olsen	*Many Happy Returns*, op. 70, 'Messiaen', for solo piano	
1972	Guy Lacour	*28 Studies on Modes with Limited Transposition by Olivier Messiaen*, for saxophone	
	Alain Louvier	*Çandrakâla*, for six percussionists	'Dédié à Olivier Messiaen – utilise ce très beau rythme, significant "la beauté de la Lune" et symbolisant la triade Terre/Soleil/Lune, que Messiaen emploie beaucoup depuis son *Quatuor pour la fin du Temps*' (from Louvier's website).
	Alain Louvier	*Shima*, for six percussionists	'Dédié à Olivier Messiaen – utilise ce très beau rythme, significant "la beauté de la Lune" et symbolisant la triade Terre/Soleil/Lune, que Messiaen emploie beaucoup depuis son *Quatuor pour la fin du Temps*' (from Louvier's website).
1974	Gerald Levinson	*Pièce pour l'anniversaire d'Olivier Messiaen*, for piano	
1975	Toru Takemitsu	*Quatrain*, for clarinet, violin, cello and piano soloists with orchestra	Intended as a homage, using the End of Time ensemble as a solo quartet.
1977	Gérard Grisey	*Les espaces acoustiques: Modulations*, for orchestra	'Pour Olivier Messiaen, à l'occasion de son soixante-dixième anniversaire'.
	Toru Takemitsu	*Quatrain II*, for clarinet, violin, cello and piano	Instrumentation and several motives allude to Messiaen.
	Adolfo Ventas	*Estudios para saxofón: 28 caprichos basados en los modos de transposición limita de Messiaen*, for saxophone	
1978	George Benjamin	*Sortilèges*, for piano	Dedicated to Yvonne Loriod, it is stylistically similar to Messiaen.
	John Speight	*Hommage à Olivier Messiaen*, for piano	
	Eduard Terényi	*Chaconne: Hommage à Messiaen*, for organ	

Date	Composer	Title	Notes
	Gilles Tremblay	*Compostelle I*, for 18 instruments	Written for Messiaen's 70th birthday.
1980	George Benjamin	*Ringed by the Flat Horizon*, for orchestra	Dedicated to Olivier Messiaen.
1981	Herbert Bielawa	*Blackbirds: Prelude and Fugue on a Theme by Olivier Messiaen*, for organ	
	McNeil Robinson	*Hommage à Messiaen*, for organ	
1983	Young-Jo Lee	*Variations for Piano on the Theme Baugoge*	Incorporates themes from Messiaen and other composers.
	Gerald Levinson	*Chant des rochers*, for 11 wind instruments, harp, piano and percussion	For Messiaen's 70th birthday, commissioned by French Ministry of Culture.
1985	Peteris Vasks	*Episodi e canto perpetuo*, for violin, cello and piano	'Hommage à O. Messiaen'.
1986	William Bolcom	*Twelve New Etudes*, 'Hymne à l'amour', for piano	Quotes Messiaen.
	Hubert Prati	*Échelles modales: D'après les modes à transpositions limitées d'Olivier Messiaen*, for saxophones	
1987	François Bru, rev. Robert Hériché	*Gammes sur des modes extra-Européens*, for flute	'Des gammes orientales au jazz en passant par Olivier Messiaen'. A book of études for flute.
	William Kraft	*Quartet for the Love of Time*, for clarinet, violin, cello and piano	Title and instrumentation allude to the *Quartet for the end of Time*.
1989	William Bolcom	*Symphony No. 5*, mvt. 3, 'Hymne à l'amour'	Quotes Messiaen.
1989	Andrew Ford	*8 Australian Birds Discover the Music of the 20th Century*, Mvt. 8: 'A Common Mynah Mocks Messiaen', for piano	
	Dianne Goolkasian	*Rondo*, for organ	'Homage to Olivier Messiaen'.
	Henri Pousseur	*Méthodicare*, for keyboards (piano, but also, at least partially, harpsichord, chromatic harp, synthesizer, etc.), tome 3, vol. 2, fascicle 3, mvt. 2: 'Petite liturgie (une pensée pour Olivier Messiaen)'	
1990	Alexander Goehr	*Sing, Ariel*, for mezzo-soprano, 2 sopranos and 5 players	Written in homage to Messiaen, his teacher.

Date	Composer	Title	Notes
1991	Angels Alabert	*Cinc variacions*, for piano	'Cinc variacions per a piano sobre el 3er i 4t mode i ritmes d'O. Messiaen'.
	Matilde Capuis	*Breve dialogo*, for clarinet, violin, cello and piano	'Al quartetto O. Messiaen'.
1992	Peter James Amsel	*Hommage à Messiaen*, for guitar	
	Christian Asplund	*To Messiaen*, for solo organ	
	Simon H. Fell	*Requiem pour Olivier Messiaen*	
	Michael Finnissy	*A solis ortus cardine: In memory of Olivier Messiaen*, for piano	
	Malcolm Forsyth	*Tre Vie*, mvt. 2: 'Ommaggio a Messiaen', concerto for alto saxophone and orchestra	
	Bengt Hambraeus	*Missa pro organo: In memoriam Olivier Messiaen*	
	Peter Michael Hamel	*Vom Klang Des Lebens (Of the Sound of Life)*, mvt. 8: 'In memoriam Olivier Messiaen', for alto flute and piano	Part of a series of such works dedicated to famous composers.
	Bertold Hummel	*Trio*, op. 95c, for flute, oboe, piano	In memoriam Olivier Messiaen.
	Georg Kröll	*Hommage à Messiaen*, for piano	
	Theo Loevendie	*Lerchen-Trio*, for clarinet, cello, piano	In memoriam Olivier Messiaen.
	Laurent Mettraux	*Hommage à Olivier Messiaen*, pour orgue	
	Francis Miroglio	*Et les bleu-violets sont dans le si…: À la mémoire d'Olivier Messiaen*, for piano	
	Jean-Pierre Mougin	*Éternité*, for piano	'Pour Olivier Messiaen'. Revised 2001.
	Tristan Murail	*Cloches d'adieu, et un sourire…: In memoriam Olivier Messiaen*, for piano	
	Toru Takemitsu	*Rain Tree Sketch II: In memoriam Olivier Messiaen*, for piano	
	Reza Vali	*Folk Songs, Set No. 10*, 'Lament', for chamber orchestra	In memoriam Olivier Messiaen.

Date	Composer	Title	Notes
	David Vayo	*Prayer*, for organ	In memoriam Olivier Messiaen.
1993	Robert Bauer	*One-part Invention with Colour: Hommage à Olivier Messiaen*, for piano	
	Mariangeles Sánchez Benimeli	*Tres Caprichos*, mvt. 2: 'Homenaje a Olivier Messiaen', for guitar	
	Qigang Chen	*Un pétale de lumière: Tribute to Olivier Messiaen*, for flute and orchestra	
	Naji Hakim	*Le tombeau d'Olivier Messiaen*, for organ	Composer succeeded Messiaen as organist at the Trinité church in Paris.
	Don Sloan	*Tributaries*, mvt. 3: 'Homage to Messiaen', for violin, viola, cello and piano	
	Eduard Terényi	*In solemnitate corporis Christi: In memoriam Olivier Messiaen*, for organ	
	Eduard Terényi	*Messiaenesques*, for organ	
1994	Amando Blanquer	*Symphony No. 3*, 'Transparencies for Messiaen'	
	Anders Brodsgaard	*Hymns I* and *II*, for piano	In memoriam Messiaen.
	Jonathan Harvey	*Le Tombeau de Messiaen*, for piano and digital audio tape	
	Gerald Levinson	*Symphony No. 2*, 'Adagio-Finale'	In memoriam Messiaen.
	Gert Oost	*The Voice of Silence*, for chorus	'Homage to Olivier Messiaen'.
	Lionel Rogg	*Hommage à Messiaen*, for organ	
	Joan Tower	*Très lent*, for cello and piano	'*Très lent* is written as an homage to Olivier Messiaen, particularly to his *Quartet for the end of time,* which had a special influence on my work' (from the score).
	Heinz Wehrle	*Un instant pour Olivier Messiaen: Omaggio a Paul Hindemith*, for organ	
1995	George Benjamin	*Three Inventions for Chamber Orchestra*, mvt. 1, originally entitled 'Tribute'	Dedicated 'In memory of Olivier Messiaen'.
1996	Robert Sherlaw Johnson	*Pour le tombeau de Messiaen*, for piano	

Date	Composer	Title	Notes
1997	Eurico Carrapatoso	*Cinco Elegias*, op. 11, mvt. 4: 'A Messiaen', for wind quintet	
	Nicole Chambard	*7 Petits Regards sur la Sainte Vierge: En hommage à Olivier Messiaen*, for piano	
	György Kurtág	*Játékok*, Vol. 2: *... humble regard sur Olivier Messiaen...*, for piano	
	Manfred Trojahn	*Danse: Pour violon et piano; Pastiche en hommage à Olivier Messiaen*	Revised 2000. Also in a version for clarinet and piano.
	John Zorn	*Duras: Duchamp*	'Inspired by the romantic writings of Marguerite Duras and the mystical music of Olivier Messiaen' (from the Tzadik website of John Zorn).
	Wolfgang Zoubek	*Piano Trio No. 2*	Hommage à Messiaen.
1998	Theo Brandmüller	*Nirwana-Fax II*, for flute (piccolo), clarinet, cello, percussion, piano (celesta)	In memoriam Olivier Messiaen.
	Alexander Goehr	*'...kein Gedanke, nur ruhiger Schlaf' (In memoriam Olivier Messiaen)*, op. 61a, for chamber ensemble	From *Schlussgesang*, op. 61, rearranged by the composer.
	Andre Juarez	*Studio Panorama: Obras electroacústicas*, 1994–1997	Messiaen revisited (collective composition for ensemble, tape and live electronics).
	Detlev Müller-Siemens	*light blue, almost white*, for 11 players	In memoriam Olivier Messiaen. Part of a series of such pieces.
	John Zorn	*Aporias: Requia for Piano and Orchestra*, mvt. 7: 'Religioso (Olivier Messiaen)'	
1999	Aenon Loo	*Last Days: Hommage à Messiaen*	
2000	David Cope	*Début du temps after Messiaen*, for piccolo, clarinet and strings	Messiaen listed as an author on the work.
	Avner Dorman	*Piano Sonata No. 2*	Second movement inspired by the works of Messiaen.
	Peter Klatzow	*Le Tombeau de Messiaen*, for two pianos and electronic sounds	

The Tombeaux of Messiaen

Date	Composer	Title	Notes
	Ian Krause	*Piano Murmurs*, for violin, clarinet, cello and piano	Premièred as 'Hommage à Messiaen', but was revised and renamed.
	András Soós	*Elfelejtet melódiak/ Forgotten Melodies* No. 3, 'A megfordíthatatlan dallam', for three unspecified instruments	Hommage à Messiaen.
2001	Masami Akita [aka Merzbow]	*Nakasendow*, for musique concrète/electronics	'Track 1 based on "Mode de valeurs et d'intensités" pour piano by Olivier Messiaen' (from record sleeve).
	Jonathan Harvey	*Bird Concerto with Pianosong*, for piano and electronics	London Sinfonietta, who recorded it, called it 'Harvey's homage to Messiaen'; Harvey's own programme note does not mention Messiaen.
2002	David Briggs	*Improvisations 3*, Variation 6, Adagio, for organ	Hommage à Olivier Messiaen.
	Alexandre Danilevski	*Tombeau de Messiaen*, for organ	
	Bruno Mantovani	*Le Sette Chiese*, mvt. 5: 'Basilique des saints Vital et Agricola (à la mémoire d'Olivier Messiaen)', for 25 players	This movement begins part 2 and is the fifth of nine pieces based on the Seven Churches complex in Bologna (i.e. at the very centre of this architecturally oriented work).
	Pedro da Silva	*Rapsodie sur un Thème d'Olivier Messiaen*, for guitar	
2003	Mike Garson	*Homage to Messiaen*, for piano	
	Thomas Daniel Schlee	*String Trio*, op. 75, mvt.: 'Invocation'	'An homage to Schlee's highly regarded former teacher Olivier Messiaen in commemoration of the 100th anniversary of his birth. This movement, composed somewhat earlier than the others, was the departing point for the work' (from Bärenreiter's website).
	Augusta Read Thomas	*Six Piano Études*, mvt. 3: 'Cathedral Waterfall – Homage to Olivier Messiaen', for piano	
2004	Henco De Berg	*Cinq Méditations*, for organ	'Hommage pour Olivier Messiaen' (improvisation).

Date	Composer	Title	Notes
	Michel Gonneville	...*L'oiseau du cri à la quête des ailes...*, for clarinet	'Les allusions à Messiaen (L'abîme des oiseaux) et aux trois courtes pièces pour clarinette de Stravinsky se sont imposées d'elles-mêmes, preuve que cette oie a de la culture et de l'humour' (from composer's programme note).
	Liviu Marinescu	*Homage Collage*, mvt 3: Messiaen, for clarinet and piano (1st version) or flute and piano (2nd version)	
2005	Eduardo Soutullo	*All the Echoes Listen*, for orchestra	Dedicated to Messiaen, Takemitsu and Grisey. Part of a triptych with *But in Vain* (2006), and *They Hear No Answering Strain* (2008).
	Sydney Vale	*Quartet for the Beginning of Time*, for clarinet, violin, cello and piano	Title and instrumentation allude to Messiaen's *Quartet for the end of Time*.
2006	David Patterson	*In memoriam Messiaen*, for wind ensemble and percussion	
	Helmut Sosha	*Le Tombeau de Messiaen*, for piano	
	Eduardo Soutullo	*But in Vain*, for orchestra	Dedicated to Messiaen, Takemitsu and Grisey. Part of a triptych with *All the Echoes Listen* (2006) and *They Hear No Answering Strain* (2008).
2007	Theo Brandmüller	*Norge*, for organ	Dedicated to Messiaen for his 100th birthday.
	Marc-André Dalbavie	*La source d'un regard*, for orchestra	'Conceived as a tombeau for Messiaen' (composer's website at billaudot.com), the work was composed for the Royal Concertgebouw Orchestra's 100th anniversary tribute to Messiaen.
	Nguyen-Thien Dao	*Duo vivo*: *Hommage à Olivier Messiaen*, for two percussionsists	
	Toshio Hosokawa	*Stunden-Blumen: Hommage à Olivier Messiaen*, for clarinet, violin, cello and piano	'Contrary to the end of time, I would like to create a piece that implies the "beginning of time" or its "origins"' (from the programme note on the IRCAM website).
	Wilhem Latchoumia	*Tombeau de Messiaen*, for piano and tape	
	Armando Luna	*Carnaval*, mvt. 3: 'Messiaen', for harp duo	

Date	Composer	Title	Notes
	Marco Lo Muscio	*Meditazione Estatiche*, no. 1, 'Homage to Messiaen', for organ	
	Andrew Violette	*Rave*, mvt. 1: 'Intro, Messiaen and the Sitar', for violin, electric violin and keyboards	
	Robert Zuidam	*Adam-Interludes*, for orchestra	Composed for the Royal Concertgebouw Orchestra's 100th anniversary tribute to Messiaen. 'As Messiaen often had done, Zuidam has chosen biblical themes, although he has chosen to concentrate on the historical elements (the "herebefore") instead of the hereafter Messiaen so often illuminated. Musically speaking there are two references to Messiaen: the tinkling triangle in the beginning of the *Adam interludes*, which refers to the end of Messiaen's *Éclairs sur l'Au-delà...*, while in the third part of Zuidam's composition, chords of the *Thème de Dieu* are mirrored' – from Astrid de Jager, trans. Terri Hron, 'Première: Robert Zuidam – Adam interludes' (www. muziekcentrumnederland .nl/ en/contemporary/news/article/ artikel/67//volgende/4/).
2008	Daniel Akiva	*3 Préludes after Messiaen*, for guitar	
	Simon Bertrand	*Le jardin des délices: Triptyque pour Olivier Messiaen*, for clarinet, violin, cello and piano	
	Theo Brandmüller	*Nachtflug mit Messiaenfenster*, for violin, viola, cello and piano	
	Nicolas Gilbert	*Le temps des impossibles (Hommage à Olivier Messiaen)*, for piano	
	Alain Kremski	*Souvenir: Lullaby for a Tibetan Child*, for piano and singing bowls	Dedicated to Olivier Messiaen. After hearing Kremski's recordings with Tibetan gongs and cymbal, Messiaen wrote: 'Je les ai écoutées avec une attention soutenue et je peux vous assurer qu'il s'agit là d'un monde absolument nouveau'.

Date	Composer	Title	Notes
	Olivier (Oli) Lawrence Morris	*Toccata on a French Theme*, for organ	'To Olivier Messiaen'.
	Robert Palej	*Souffle de lumière: Un hommage à Messiaen*, for wind ensemble	
	Milica Paranosic	*I am a Bird*, multimedia performance piece for dancers, vocalists, instrumentalists, electronics, visual projection	Dedicated to Olivier Messiaen.
	Bob Priest	*Smile*, for violin, viola and cello	Composed for a festival of Messiaen's music and named after Messiaen's early song 'Un sourire'.
	Marta Ptaszynska	*Trois visions de l'arc-en-ciel*, for clarinet, violin, viola, cello, piano and percussion	'My piece is an homage to Olivier Messiaen, who was my teacher and mentor. Therefore, I tried to implement in my music several features characteristic to Messiaen's harmonic and melodic language. However, there is no exact quotation of his music in my work. Rather, I tried to capture the Messiaen-like flavor of beautiful and celestial sonorities' – from the composer's programme note.
	Michèle Reverdy	*Anacoluthes: Hommage à Olivier Messiaen*, for 7 players	
	Michaël Sebaoun	*In Memoriam Messiaen*, for piano	
	Eduardo Soutullo	*They Hear No Answering Strain*, for orchestra	Dedicated to Messiaen, Takemitsu and Grisey. Part of a triptych with *All the Echoes Listen* (2005) and *But in Vain* (2006).
	Fabian Watkinson	*Le Tombeau d'Olivier Messiaen*, for string trio	
	Hagihara Yoshiaki	*Music for Timetable – for Stations on the Yamanote Line*, 'Tamachi Station – for Olivier Messiaen', for electronics	
2009	Thuridor Jonsdottir	*Flute Concerto (in Memoriam Messiaen)*	
	Frank Pesci	*O Sacrum Convivium (Hommage à Messiaen)*, for mixed voices	
2010	Giuseppe Perna	*To Olivier Messiaen*, no. 1 and no. 2, for piano	

Date	Composer	Title	Notes
	Eric Schaefer	*Für Olivier Messiaen*, for violin solo	
2011	Susan Alcorn	*Olivier Messiaen's Morning Conjugal Death Waltz*, for electronics with voice	
	Marco Lo Muscio	*Mystic Pieces,* no. 2, 'Mystical Alleluia in Memory of Messiaen', for organ	
	Gérard Pesson	*Musica Ficta*, 'Trop d'étoiles (à la manière d'Olivier Messiaen)', for piano	

PART III
Reception

Perspectives on Reception

Christopher Dingle and Robert Fallon

In repeated efforts to communicate his message and control his image, Messiaen taught his audience how to think about his music. In 1944 he organized his *Technique* into chapters addressing Rhythm, Melody, and Harmony. In 1962, he said his music was about Rhythm, Birds, Colour and Freedom. In 1970, this became Rhythm, Birds, Colour and Tristan, while in 1986, he settled on Rhythm, Birds, Colour and Faith. These self-fashioned categories have significantly shaped Messiaen reception, guiding the structures of many subsequent books and documentaries in the decades since his death. These companion volumes of *Messiaen Perspectives* represent the first overview of the composer structured in a manner unrelated to these four categories, choosing instead the somewhat neutral perspectives of Sources, Influences, Techniques, Influence and Reception as a broadly chronological, and thus historical, framework in which to examine the man, music and milieux.

A composer's reception consists in whatever posterity attends to and thus ultimately influences his music more than anything he himself can control. For example, in much of the nineteenth century J. S. Bach was generally regarded as a technician of counterpoint; only after publication of the Bach Gesamtausgabe began in 1851, with volume after volume of his cantatas, did his image change into that of a devout Lutheran and consummate church musician. The vagaries of Messiaen reception have shown similar changes. For years, Messiaen was anthologized or discussed mainly for two highly unrepresentative works. When hyperserialism dominated compositional circles in the third quarter of the twentieth century, Messiaen was valued for his short, enigmatic *Mode de valeurs et d'intensités* – or rather for its pre-compositional primer that influenced the development of hyperserialism. The other work most valued by theorists and musicologists was the first movement to the *Quatuor pour la fin du Temps*, which fascinated analysts for its highly organized but completely independent individual lines. Today such techniques seem less important than the work's emotional content and broader message. More of the work is now anthologized than the first movement alone and it is valued less for its formal procedures than for its remarkable genesis and gripping experience in performance. To take another example of Messiaen's changing fortunes, his *Couleurs de la Cité céleste* enjoyed a vogue among conductors in the 1960s, while now *Oiseaux exotiques* is more likely to be programmed. The birds that made Messiaen a laughing stock in the 1950s are beloved as a source of wonder in this age of environmental awareness.

278   Messiaen Perspectives 2: Techniques, Influence and Reception

As important as reception studies are, there remains an alarming paucity of them in Messiaen studies.[1] The four chapters collected here, in fact, represent the first concerted effort to map what his music has meant and how it has taken hold in different places. Yet there is much more to do: Why was Messiaen's burial not met with greater fanfare in France? What accounts for a far stronger record of inquiry thus far among Anglophone countries than in Messiaen's home country? What exactly has been the position of the Vatican in regard to Messiaen's music and how has it been received by faith communities worldwide? The forthcoming second edition of the *Grove Dictionary of American Music* has commissioned an article on Messiaen's engagement in American musical life, not least due to the World premières in America of well-known works such as *Turangalîla-Symphonie*, *Méditations sur le mystère de la Sainte Trinité*, *Des Canyons aux étoiles...*, *Livre du Saint Sacrement* and *Éclairs sur l'Au-Delà...*. A brief dictionary entry cannot, however, do justice to a topic as large as his reception in America.

Of the four chapters on reception, the first two provide documentary evidence from Italy and Spain on how Messiaen was reviewed, perceived and positioned in relation to musical and cultural politics, while the second two investigate responses to two tangible but very different products of his legacy – Utah's Mount Messiaen and the *Traité* itself. Raffaele Pozzi's in-depth exposition of Messiaen's soujourns and reviews in Italy shows that he was first represented as a conservative, religious musician and, later, as a radical composer championing freedom. He was also characterized as the link between Webern and post-war serialists. Pozzi furthermore speaks to how Godfredo Petrassi, Luigi Dallapiccola, adherents to the aesthetics of Benedetto Croce, fascism and the Catholic Church all viewed Messiaen. Germán Gan-Quesada's history of Messiaen's reception in Spain shares much with Pozzi's chapter. As in Italy, Messiaen puzzled the musical world in Spain for being at once Catholic and modern, a rare or impossible mixture in the mindset of the day. Gan-Quesada provides a political backdrop around Franco and a survey of responses to Messiaen by prominent Spanish composers such as Amando Blanquer that help to track his activities and assessments in Spain, where he was called a 'great master' as early as 1951.

Messiaen reception in the United States warrants its own book to account for the earliest performances of his music in 1936; his being championed by Leopold Stokowski, Serge Koussevitzky, Pierre Monteux and Kent Nagano; his stays in Tanglewood, Aspen and Berkeley; his trip to Utah to compose *Des Canyons*; his American students; and his engagements with various orchestras and premières across the country. On the whole, America has welcomed Messiaen and proved

---

[1]   Existing studies that explore or include aspects of Messiaen reception include: Wolf-Günter Leidel, 'Messiaen-Rezeption in Ostdeutschland vor und nach der Wende: Ein Gespräch', in Michaela Christine Hastetter (ed.), *Musik des Unsichtbaren: Der Komponist Olivier Messiaen (1908–1992) am Schnittpunkt von Theologie und Musik* (St Ottilien, Germany: EOS, 2008); PHNS; Leslie Sprout, 'Messiaen, Jolivet, and the Soldier-Composers of Wartime France', *The Musical Quarterly*, 87/2 (Summer 2004): pp. 259–304.

fertile ground for his music and ideas. Robert Fallon writes the history of one such gesture of welcome, the dedication of Mount Messiaen in Utah, and accounts for how this mountain may relate to Messiaen's legacy and love of nature. Conversely, Jean Boivin has written on Messiaen's love of culture – his *Traité*, whose reception he tracks through four key reviewers, for whom it displays an impressive range of Messiaen's reading (including Aquinas, Ronsard, Bergson and Einstein) but also a fragmentary organization and unpolished analytical apparatus. Boivin suggests that one reason Messiaen has long received scant attention in France concerns the difficulty many there find in critiquing a famous compatriot. He dares scholars, however, to rise to the challenge of analysing Messiaen's music without undue reliance on the terms that Messiaen set for his own reception.

Chapter 11
The Reception of Olivier Messiaen in Italy: A Historical Interpretation[1]

Raffaele Pozzi

It was in the years following the Second World War that Olivier Messiaen first began to receive close attention in Italy. This was no coincidence. The outbreak of war, the fall of fascism and the end of the war caused a very marked cultural change. neoclassicism, whose anti-romantic spirit had originally paved the way to a form of modernity vigorously upheld in Italy by Alfredo Casella, had already fallen into crisis by the end of the 1930s. The neoclassical *rappel à l'ordre* was increasingly perceived as an aesthetic orientation that had by now outlived its time, politically disengaged when not actually compromised with a regime that had steered Italy towards racial laws and the war.[2]

Crucial works from those years such as *Canti di prigionia* (1938–41) by Dallapiccola or the *Coro di morti* (1940–41) by Petrassi[3] give clear evidence of such concerns, although in stylistically different ways. Even Casella was forced to acknowledge the existence of this historic and linguistic crisis in his entourage, noting in the *Serenata* for piano (1940) by Camillo Togni, his pupil, a strong 'veering

---

[1]   This chapter is a new version of the paper entitled 'The Reception of Olivier Messiaen in Italy: A Historical Interpretation' presented at the Messiaen 2008 International Centenary Conference (Birmingham Conservatoire, 20–24 June 2008). The contents of the paper – already published in January 2008 in the form of an extended abstract on the site of the British conference www.conservatoire.bcu.ac.uk/messiaen – were the subject of discussion during the Convegno internazionale di Studi Italia/Francia, 'Musica e cultura nella seconda metà del XX secolo', held in Palermo on 23 and 24 June 2008.

[2]   On the relationship between neoclassicism and the ideological-political sphere in the twentieth century, see Raffaele Pozzi, 'L'ideologia neoclassica', in *Enciclopedia della musica*, Vol. I, *Il Novecento*, ed. J.-J. Nattiez (Turin: Einaudi, 2001): pp. 444–70. For the first historical criticisms levelled at neoclassicism in Italy, see Luigi Rognoni, 'Il Concerto di Petrassi', *Rivista musicale italiana,* 40/3–4: p. 357, and Luigi Dallapiccola, 'Prime composizioni corali' (1961), in Dallapiccola, *Appunti, incontri, meditazioni* (Milan: Edizioni Suvini Zerboni, 1970), p. 134.

[3]   On the *Coro di morti* of Petrassi interpreted in this light, see Raffaele Pozzi, 'Leopardi e l'ansia di rinnovamento: Il Coro di morti (1940-41) di Goffredo Petrassi', in E. Tonani (ed.) *Storia della lingua italiana e Storia della musica: Atti del IV Convegno dell'Associazione per la Storia della Lingua Italiana* (Sanremo, 29–30 April 2004) (Florence: Franco Cesati Editore, 2005), pp. 131–41.

towards Vienna', as he drew closer to the language of Schoenberg.[4] Owing to these upheavals and their interweaving with the prevailing historical climate, atonality and dodecaphony began to be identified ideologically with anti-fascism and later with the Marxist positions that were to influence music deeply in Italy after 1945.[5]

In France, too, the 1936 appeal for a new 'sincerity, generosity and artistic conscientiousness' contained in the manifesto of the group La Jeune France, of which Messiaen was a founding member, sharply distanced itself from neoclassical formalism. Three years later, on 17 March 1939, in an article published in the *Page musicale*, Messiaen would be even more explicit:

> Lazy are those composers who produce too much without giving themselves enough time to reflect, to mature their hasty conceptions. Lazy, those artisans who produce pseudo-Fauré, pseudo-Ravel. Lazy those maniacs of fake-Couperin, the manufacturers of *Rigaudon* and *Pavane*. Lazy those hateful contrapuntists with their return to Bach, who remorselessly offer us dry and lacklustre lines, poisoned by an appearance of atonalism.[6]

The importance given to the spiritual conception that was gaining currency in the Jeune France group – which had emerged from the preceding experience with La Spirale, founded in 1935 under the leadership of Georges Migot, where Messiaen, Jolivet and Daniel-Lesur had already met – was grasped in Italy by Guido Maggiorino Gatti. In an article written in 1938, entitled 'Situazione della musica', Gatti pointed out some new trends.[7] Amongst these, he noted the return to an aesthetics of content, of some 'spiritual attitudes which had been considered outdated, consigned once and for all to the scrap heap of the 19th century'.[8]

With evident reference to the decline of neoclassicism, seen as being the style of modernity, Gatti continues by emphasizing the existence at a compositional

---

[4]   For Casella's reaction to Togni's *Serenata* for piano, see *Carteggi e scritti di Camillo Togni sul Novecento Italiano*, Fondazione Giorgio Cini di Venezia, Archivio Camillo Togni, Studi di Musica Veneta, I (Florence: Olschki, 2001), p. 8.

[5]   On the importance of the ideological component underlying adoption of dodecaphony in Italy, see Pozzi, 'L'ideologia neoclassica', p. 464; and Pozzi 'Musica nuova per una nuova società. Colloquio con Giacomo Manzoni di Raffaele Pozzi', in Raffaele Pozzi (ed.) and Giacomo Manzoni, *Musica e progetto civile: Scritti e interviste, 1956–2007* (Milan: Ricordi-LIM (Le Sfere), 2009), p. 447 ff.

[6]   Messiaen's article is cited in Raffaele Pozzi, *Il suono dell'estasi: Olivier Messiaen dal* Banquet céleste *alla* Turangalîla-Symphonie (Lucca: LIM, 2002), p. 79.

[7]   On the relationship between the La Spirale and Jeune France groups, see Serge Gut, *Le Groupe Jeune France* (Paris: Honoré Champion, 1977), p. 16; more recently, see the study by Nigel Simeone, 'La Spirale and La Jeune France: Group Identities', *The Musical Times*, 143/1880 (Autumn 2002): pp. 10–36.

[8]   Guido Maggiorino Gatti, 'Situazione della musica' (1938), in Luigi Pestalozza (ed.), *La Rassegna musicale: Antologia* (Milan: Feltrinelli, 1966), p. 376.

level of 'a greater sense of responsibility. Creation is not desired merely for immediate and easy enjoyment; playfulness is no longer possible when so many elements of meditation and attainment have come into question'.[9] In this way, claims Gatti, a renewed interest in the religious dimension of music forcefully emerges. Here, the experience of Olivier Messiaen finds its setting: he is defined as an 'extremely pure artist whose austerity and restraint do not help to widen the circle of his admirers. (Messiaen belongs, together with Daniel-Lesur, Jolivet and Baudrier, to the "Jeune France" group, which aims to restore spiritual and, in a certain sense, traditional values)'.[10] Using the case of Messiaen as a point of departure, Gatti asks himself, 'Yet among those Italians who only yesterday wrote Symphonies and Partite and Divertimenti of a chilly agnosticism, how many today seek in the holy scriptures the inspiring spark of fantasy, the heartening word?'[11]

In Italy, the prevailing taste in music during the 1930s can be clearly understood from the programming of the Festival Internazionale di Musica in Venice. During this period, the influential Venetian meeting had several times turned to French musicians, whose music revealed a deep-seated neoclassical orientation. In 1932, there were performances in Venice of music by Marcel Delannoy, Jacques Ibert, Francis Poulenc, Albert Roussel and Henri Tomasi; in 1934, by Darius Milhaud; in 1936 by Pierre Octave Ferroud and Albert Roussel; and in 1937, by Jean Françaix and Darius Milhaud.[12]

In the early 1930s, Messiaen had barely begun his creative path and, according to an article written by Armand Machabey in 1933 and published in the *Rassegna musicale*, he was considered to be a young composer making 'his first attempts' (along with musicians who would not go very far, such as Georges Hugon and Jean Cartan, who died at an early age).[13]

Messiaen acquired greater standing in the following decade. In 1946, in the dramatically changed framework of historical crisis and aesthetic rethinking, Messiaen took part for the first time in the ninth Festival di Musica Contemporanea in Venice, a festival that assumed noteworthy symbolic value in the 'artistic and spiritual rebirth of Italy' after the years of fascism and war, as Giovanni Ponti, Extraordinary Commissioner for the Biennale, writes in his presentation of the exhibition.

The writer Massimo Bontempelli echoes these words in the same presentation, establishing a connection between socio-historical evolution and shifts in scientific thinking and the language of the arts and music, all united by a straining towards freedom, a genuine key word in both the political and artistic debate of the post-war

---

[9] Ibid.

[10] Ibid.

[11] Ibid.

[12] See the official programmes of the second (3–15 September 1932 – X), third (8–16 September 1934 – XII), fourth (6–13 September 1936 – XIV) and fifth (6–12 September 1937 – XV) Festival Internazionale di Musica di Venezia.

[13] Armand Machabey, 'Il sinfonismo francese contemporaneo' (1933), in Luigi Pestalozza (ed.), *La Rassegna musicale*, p. 207.

284   *Messiaen Perspectives 2: Techniques, Influence and Reception*

period: 'The ongoing social upheavals', writes Bontempelli, 'strive for increasing growth and conquest of individual freedom. ... In music, too, revolutions that begin with chromaticism, whose victory dates back to the Renaissance, right up to Schoenberg and Dallapiccola, are a quest for ever greater freedom'.[14] This, for the writer, is also what lies behind the latest linguistic development, 'The destiny of dodecaphony which, for now (in other words, as long as the musical tradition of the equal temperament endures), is the utmost freedom attainable.'[15]

At the IX Festival, the centrality of the debate on the renewal of musical language and on dodecaphony is patently evident in a review by Goffredo Petrassi:

> As was to be expected, the IX Festival di Musica Contemporanea in Venice was marked by an unusually lively debate, both among the general public with regard to the music performed and among the musicians themselves .... Dodecaphony was the main protagonist and, as in all disputes, there were the mystic-martyrs of the twelve-tone music, the violent opponents and those who smilingly stood by watching the hotheads of the two factions.[16]

While not wishing to take an openly partisan stand, and acknowledging the positions of both the 'tonalists' and the 'twelve-toners', Petrassi broadly examines the causes of the heated discussions that erupted during the Venice meeting. In the virulent diatribes of the festival, he sees a 'dramatic reflection, expressed in technical terms, of the profound crisis which affects the very nature of man', and ends with a consideration that attempts to highlight the link between the aesthetic realm and the historical-existential dimension, which excludes the limited or instrumental use of the differing views expressed: 'All technical upheavals or so-called crises of art are based on the transformation of the individual and society, so it would be absurd to consider them as phenomena confined to a particular field for the exclusive use of those involved'.[17]

The appearance of Messiaen in the Festival of Venice's programme in 1946, indicative of his evolution and the changed political and cultural climate, spread a new image of the composer. The promising young symphonist of the early 1930s, the austere traditionalist and spiritual musician of the Jeune France group presented by Gatti, became a ground-breaking representative of post-war musical renewal. Thus began that reception phenomenon, in many ways misleading, that would associate Messiaen with the birth of the serial avant-garde: a 'myth-misunderstanding', a genealogy spawned in those same avant-garde circles during

---

    [14]   Giovanni Ponti and Massimo Bontempelli, 'Presentazione', in *Programma ufficiale del IX Festival internazionale di Musica contemporanea, 15–22 Sept. 1946* (Venice: Grafiche Fantoni, 1946), pp. 5, 7.

    [15]   Ibid.

    [16]   Goffredo Petrassi, 'Il nono Festival Musicale di Venezia', in Raffaele Pozzi (ed.) and Goffredo Petrassi, *Scritti e interviste* (Milan: Edizioni Suvini Zerboni, 2008), p. 89.

    [17]   Ibid.

the 1950s. One must remember, however, that in wartime Paris a generically avant-garde spirit and desire for innovation inspired a group of Messiaen's young pupils, who nicknamed themselves Les Flèches. They included Pierre Boulez, Maurice Le Roux, Yvonne Loriod, Serge Nigg and Jean-Louis Martinet, and attended the courses in analysis run by the composer in the house of Guy-Bernard Delapierre that were later to become legendary, and also, in some cases, the official course in harmony at the Paris Conservatoire.[18] After the war, Messiaen came to Italy where, in the new historical and cultural climate, he was hailed as an innovator. Since there was, however, no real understanding of his symbolist eclecticism, the composer's complex poetics were placed in the ambiguous and misleading ideological domain of the avant-garde. That same coterie of Jeune France is described in the programme of the Venice Festival as a 'group of young avant-garde musicians' with Messiaen as its guiding figure.[19]

In the festival's cautiously anonymous profile on the composer, he would appear to be interested in Gregorian chant, Hindu rhythms, quarter-tones and birdsong. Readers are reminded of his use of 'a particular language, which is not linked to any school', summed up in a treatise, *'Tecnica del mio linguaggio musicale'*, which is cited with numerous inaccuracies and translation errors.[20] For example, one can read:

> The processes of this language are melodic (binary, ternary anacruses and endings) and harmonic (limited transposition modes) and rhythmic (added values), augmented rhythms that cannot be shortened. His bizarre terminology has given rise to some criticism, perhaps wrongly since Messiaen only understood its technicalities later, having experimented with them for years with no preconceptions.[21]

Lastly, the composer is defined as being a Catholic: his works bear 'the sign of the Christian faith' and 'implicitly sing the Mysteries of Christ'; his creativity tends towards 'Unity' and 'the quest for an Ideal', positions that meaningfully evoke 'what is lacking in the variable and tormented natures of our age'.[22]

The work programmed at Venice, *Poèmes pour Mi* for voice and piano – mistakenly announced as a work from 1945 instead of 1936 – was the result of the 'fundamentally harmonistic atonalism' of the composer, based on 'compact chromatic density' and 'forms that are wide-ranging, fleshy and often for the organ'.[23] The observer finds 'dodecaphonic passages' there, which 'assume rather

---

[18] Pozzi, *Il suono dell'estasi*, p. 114.
[19] *Programma ufficiale del IX Festival*, p. 35.
[20] Ibid.
[21] Ibid.
[22] Ibid.
[23] Ibid.

286 *Messiaen Perspectives 2: Techniques, Influence and Reception*

colouristic movements and whose intention seems to be, above all, the criterion of creating a climate of sound'.[24]

The mistakes in this presentation, far more than the correct information, provide noteworthy indications of the backdrop against which Messiaen's problematic reception in Italy began. The desire for change, and the identification of Messiaen with the avant-garde's new ideological framework, bound up with the term atonal-dodecaphonic, meant that even the work *Poèmes pour Mi* was absorbed into this current, thus confirming how little was known or theoretically understood about dodecaphony in Italy at this time.[25] Messiaen thus came to seem ambivalent: on the one hand, he was considered a musician of the avant-garde, of radical modernism, interested in the quarter-tone, belonging to the 'technical' atonal-dodecaphonic party; on the other, a Catholic composer, organist at the Trinité in Paris, thus tied to a politically conservative praxis and image, in many ways similar to that of a pre-bourgeois musician.

In 1946, the composer also began to give telling information about himself, thus enhancing the profile of a musician linked to the contemporary milieu. The periodical *Musica*, in fact, distributed a questionnaire among Italian and foreign composers, entitled 'Panorama musicale 1939–1946', in which they were asked which of their works had been composed during the war years, and if war events had had 'a particular influence' on them. Presented to Italian readers as 'one of the most controversial contemporary composers' and 'today considered in France to be the most significant composer of the post-war period', Messiaen responded by recounting his experience in the Görlitz concentration camp and the by now legendary circumstances that had inspired his *Quatuor pour la fin du Temps*. He also mentioned his *Visions de l'Amen*, the *Trois Petites Liturgies de la Présence Divine*, with the diatribe that had accompanied its performance, and two as yet unpublished works, *Harawi* and a 'Symphony for a full-size orchestra' which was to become the *Turangalîla-Symphonie*. Having said that, he then revealed the following:

> The most important period for me was the liberation of Paris. At that time, I was alone in Paris, and when I went to work, I had to walk through the streets for long stretches in the midst of the fighting and, of course, I participated in the general fever, the emerging joy. I have never composed so much, nor so quickly. In five months, from May to October 1944, I wrote my piano solo *Vingt Regards sur*

---

[24] Ibid.

[25] On dodecaphony in Italy, refer to the 1999 Seminar on 'Problemi e aspetti della musica del Novecento', coordinated by Raffaele Pozzi at the DAMS – University of Bologna, whose findings were presented at the Quinto Colloquio del 'Saggiatore musicale' (Bologna, 23–25 November 2001) in a study session entitled 'Sulle strade della dodecafonia: Gino Contilli, Riccardo Malipiero, Mario Peragallo, Camillo Togni', with papers by Luca Conti, Andrea Di Giacomo, Virginia Guastella, Maria Melchionne and Anna Scalfaro. For a synthesis, see Luca Conti, 'La Scuola di Vienna e la dodecafonia nella pubblicistica italiana (1911–1945)', *Nuova Rivista Musicale Italiana*, 37/2 (2003): pp. 155–96.

l'Enfant-Jésus. This work is undoubtedly the most exacting and distinctive that I have ever created. It is exceptionally long: twenty parts, two and a half hours![26]

After the remarkable success of *Vingt Regards*, which the composer associated with the 'emerging joy' for the liberation of Paris, increasing attention was paid to Messiaen soon after the war in Italy, where there was felt to be a close link between the needs for change at both a political-cultural and linguistic-musical level.

From this point of view, it came as no surprise that the French musician should arouse the interest and admiration of Luigi Dallapiccola, a major protagonist in the so-called revival of post-war Italian music, whose work *Canti di prigionia* was performed in London in July 1946, together with Anton Webern's *Cantata* and Messiaen's *Quatuor pour la fin du Temps*, at the XX Festival of the International Society for Contemporary Music (SIMC), the first to take place since the outbreak of war. In one of his presentations for the Venice Festival, Dallapiccola cites a review by Thérèse Lavanden, published on 9 August 1946 in the *Tribune de Genève*, where she writes:

> A stream of burning spirituality illuminates, by contrast, the three works that, in our opinion, are the most significant to be heard in the festival, because emanating from diverse temperaments, they convey to the listener the same message: that of an invincible belief in the revival of eternal values on which man has based his sovereignty.
>
> [Un courant de brûlante spiritualité illumine au contraire les trois œuvres qui sont à notre sens, les plus significatives entendues au festival; parce que émanées de tempéraments très divers, elles transmettent à l'auditeur un message identique: celui d'une croyance invincible dans la renaissance des valeurs éternelles sur lesquelles l'homme a fondé sa souveraineté.][27]

When Messiaen returned to France on 27 April 1947 after a tour of Italy with Yvonne Loriod, he wrote to Dallapiccola expressing interest in his music:

> Dear Friend, I have often thought, with deep gratitude to you, believe me, of all those concerts in Florence, Rome and Turin that you so kindly provided. I have often thought also of the package of your works that your editor in Milan sent me too late in Turin. I wish that I could speak of you here and go some way to repaying a little the kindnesses you have done for me: for this, I need your works. Those I possess, which I bought in Rome, are not enough. Isn't it possible to catch up with the package, couldn't your Milanese publisher send it to me, this selection of your works made by so carefully by you? Either by my

---

[26]   Olivier Messiaen, 'Panorama musicale, 1939–1946', in *Musica*, 2/1 (1947): p. 29.

[27]   Luigi Dallapiccola, 'Presentazione dei *Canti di Prigionia*', in *Programma ufficiale del IX Festival*, p. 30.

publisher, Durand & Cie. ... or via Alberto Mantelli ... (who has offered to get it to me by one of his friends who comes frequently to Paris) – or by any other means. I am sorry to torment you so. See to this, please, and I hope that my wish will finally come true. Again all my thanks, dear friend, and my grateful admiration. Olivier Messiaen

[Cher Ami, j'ai souvent repensé, avec une profonde reconnaissance pour vous, croyez-le, à tous ces concerts de Florence, Rome et Turin que vous m'avez si gentiment fournis. J'ai souvent repensé aussi à ce lot de vos œuvres que votre éditeur de Milan m'a adressé trop tard à Turin. Je voudrais tant pouvoir parler de vous ici et vous rendre un peu les bontés que vous avez eu à mon égard: pour cela, il me faut vos œuvres. Ce que j'en possède, et que j'ai acheté à Rome, ne suffit pas. N'est-il pas possibile de rattraper cela et votre éditeur Milanais ne peut-il vraiment pas m'envoyer ce lot, ce choix de vos œuvres fait par vous avec tant de soin? Soit par l'intermédiaire de mon éditeur Durand et Cie. ... soit par l'intermédiaire de Alberto Mantelli ... (qui s'est offert à me le faire parvenir par un de ses amis venant fréquemment à Paris) – soit par tout autre moyen. Je m'excuse de vous tourmenter ainsi. Voyez cela, je vous prie, et j'espère bien que mon souhait finira par se réaliser. Encore tous mes remerciements, cher Ami, et ma reconnaissante admiration. Olivier Messiaen.][28]

In March 1947, Messiaen and Yvonne Loriod's Italian tournée had touched on the cities of Florence, Rome and Turin where some of his *Préludes*, *Vingt Regards* and *Visions de l'Amen* were performed. Nonetheless, after the performance of the *Quatuor* in London – at the above mentioned XX Festival of the SIMC – Dallapiccola initially expressed some reservations about Messiaen. In a review written on 10 August 1946, he writes:

Olivier Messiaen seeks out the magical, and turns to the extremely distinctive, refined and voluptuous atmospheres of certain music from the Orient. But here an embarrassing question arises. Among Eastern peoples, some music has a magic, religious function and there is no doubt that the music knows exactly what effect its sounds produce on those who take part in the religious rites. But transported, even if transformed, into our European world, these sounds lack one of the two given figures (the listener), who certainly does not react in the same way as the Oriental listener.[29]

---

[28]   Letter to Dallapiccola, dated 27 April 1947, in Fiamma Nicolodi (ed.), *Luigi Dallapiccola: Saggi, testimonianze, carteggio, biografia e bibliografia* (Milan: Edizioni Suvini Zerboni, 1975), pp. 73–4.

[29]   Luigi Dallapiccola, 'Musica contemporanea a Londra', *La Lettura* (Milan, 10 August 1946): p. 6.

In another review from that same London festival, Dallapiccola expresses further perplexities about the music he has heard that are extremely significant from our point of view: 'This literary side leads Messiaen to care and fret far more about the atmosphere than the construction and, every now and again, you run into passages which feel much too arbitrary and improvised.'[30] These reservations about the composer's literary or even technical verbalizations were shared by other authoritative observers. In July 1946, Guido Maggiorino Gatti had criticized 'an excessively theorizing rigourism and an occasionally vexatious mystagogy, expressed in countless preambles and directions'.[31] Whereas Goffredo Petrassi, in his review of the 1946 Venice Festival, observes that *Poèmes pour Mi* are by no means sufficient to form a true opinion about Messiaen: 'We must await the performance of some major orchestral work before we can realize the effective force of his music, beyond the literature and incense fumes with which the author loves to surround his works.'[32]

Orientalism and magic for Dallapiccola, theorizing rigourism and didactic excess for Gatti, literature and incense fumes for Petrassi: these first, ambiguous displays of reception with regard to Messiaen – coupled with the varying reservations shown towards a complex composer who was difficult to place, who verbalized extensively and who theorized on music – became part of the lively critical and aesthetic debate of post-war Italy. Even so, these reactions disclose a striking political and ideological aspect. The music criticism influenced by Benedetto Croce's idealistic aesthetics took the view that atonality represented the destruction of the centrality of lyrical intuition when creating music, in favour of technical formalism. The altercation between the Crocean critic, Alfredo Parente, and Luigi Dallapiccola in the *Rassegna musicale* of 1939 was significant from this point of view and was settled through a debate *pro* or *contra* linguistically innovative contemporary music. It should be noted that this clash intensified in the post-war period, often assuming marked ideological and political connotations in the period from the 1950s to the 1970s.[33]

At the Festival of Venice in 1946, a conflict exploded between the proponents of renewal – who viewed dodecaphony as a language of liberation, and who were led with increasing authority by Luigi Dallapiccola – and the defenders of tradition in a conservative sense. From his initial reservations about Messiaen, Dallapiccola now began to welcome his music, motivating his reasons in clear terms. In 1947 he writes:

---

[30] Luigi Dallapiccola, 'Musiche al Festival della S.I.M.C.', *Sipario* (Varese, August–September 1946): p. 78.

[31] Guido Maggiorino Gatti, 'Il Festival della S.I.M.C.', *Il Mondo*, Florence, no. 31 (6 July 1946): p. 8.

[32] Petrassi, 'Il nono Festival', p. 92.

[33] For the diatribe between Dallapiccola and Alfredo Parente, see *La Rassegna musicale*, pp. 377–84.

After the London audition of *Quatuor pour la fin du Temps*, we expressed some reservations (not on his personality or genial talent) about a literary aspect which we thought weighed worryingly on his music (an element which is perhaps more sensitive for us Italians than for others: the d'Annunzio phenomenon is still too close to be forgotten!). ... Messiaen is a musician who is fully aware of his tasks: his technical research, perhaps more determinedly oriented towards the modal and rhythmic fields than the harmonic, is so vast that he appears to be the first to be convinced that many years will pass before these rhythms can be heard and expressed by performers with the spontaneity used by him in intuitively creating them.[34]

As confirmation of what has been said, it is interesting how Dallapiccola couples the risk of a literary kind of heteronomy in Messiaen's music with what he calls 'the d'Annunzio phenomenon'. With his nationalistically decadent myths, d'Annunzio had in effect profoundly influenced Italian cultural history in the first half of the twentieth century and, in the new post-war atmosphere, Dallapiccola clearly meant to distance himself from that model, which in his eyes was so seriously compromised with the recent past.

On the other hand, it should be noted how Dallapiccola's interest in Messiaen's technical research methods, particularly the rhythmic studies, seems to have influenced, or at any rate stimulated, his compositional writing, as Dietrich Kämper has hypothesized.[35] This is true for his *Quaderno musicale di Annalibera* for piano (1952), *Goethe Lieder* for mezzo-soprano and three clarinets (1953), and *Cinque Canti* for baritone and eight instruments (1956). In these works, from the rhythmic point of view, beyond principles of syntactic and formal symmetry that recall both Webern and Messiaen, Dallapiccola uses irregular imitations or canons that aim to go beyond the regular meter and *tactus*: compositional procedures, therefore, that converge with the concept of *musique amersurée* to which Messiaen had dedicated specific theoretical reflections in *Technique de mon langage musical*.[36] On this topic, Dallapiccola clearly explains how his writing in the *Cinque canti* addresses 'frequent elimination of the "tempo forte" of the beat, which leads to a wider-ranging and freer style'.[37]

With Dallapiccola, the reception of Messiaen in Italy thus took a determined step in the direction of linguistic innovation, at a time when such innovation would assume intense ideological connotations as a reaction to the 20-year period of fascism, and in opposition to the reigning aesthetic idealism of Benedetto Croce's

---

[34] Luigi Dallapiccola, 'Olivier Messiaen', *Il Mondo europeo*, no. 40 (Rome-Florence, 1 April 1947): p. 14.

[35] Dietrich Kämper, *Luigi Dallapiccola: La vita e l'opera* (Florence: Sansoni, 1985), pp. 174–5.

[36] *Technique*, Chapters 1 and 6.

[37] Dallapiccola, 'A proposito dei *Cinque canti*', in Fiamma Nicolodi (ed.), *Parole e musica* (Milan: Il Saggiatore, 1980), p. 494.

epigones. Among the opposing aesthetic factions, the figure of Messiaen was accepted and understood only in part, due to the essence of his nature, which could not easily find its place in this arena. On the one hand, the spiritual and religious needs, the constant references to the extra-musical realm in Messiaen's vision, were overshadowed or more radically blocked by the formalist and anti-Crocean tendencies of the dodecaphonic-serial avant-garde in the post-war period; on the other hand, the Crocean or post-Crocean circles felt puzzled and dubious about the composer's technical and self-analytic verbalizations.

In this sense, the position of Massimo Mila is significant. An authoritative musical critic and anti-fascist intellectual who had originally espoused Crocean views, even though elaborated in an original way, Mila was an attentive observer of twentieth-century and contemporary music. In 1951, when reviewing *Cinq Rechants, Mode de valeurs et d'intensités, Île de feu 2* and *Neumes rythmiques*, he perceives an aspect in *Cinq Rechants* that is:

> by far the happiest and most persuasive ... that we have happened to hear by Messiaen. ... That refinement of timbres and rhythms which in instrumental compositions is so often dressed up with irksome esoteric pretension, is clarified and justified in the choral writing with an authentically primitive simplicity. The rigorous use of exotic scales – Javanese, Balinese, or whatever the devil they may be – fortunately protects the melody from those slumps 'à la Massenet' which infest his *Visions de l'Amen* and [*Vingt*] *Regards sur l'Enfant-Jésus*.[38]

Mode de valeurs et d'intensités and *Neumes rythmiques*, on the other hand, are severely criticized by Mila:

> Of the piano pieces, two are essays in creative impotence theorized with that learned bizarreness which Messiaen's talent so often delights in; *Île de feu 2*, however, which is 'dedicated to Papua', when it is properly performed (not exactly the easiest thing in the world), should produce something like the pianistic equivalent of a volcanic eruption in the middle of a tropical island.[39]

It is interesting to note what happened after this reprimand in 1951 with regard to the presumed influence of Massenet in *Visions* and *Vingt Regards*, and the even more critical comment, for differing reasons, on the 'learned bizarreness' of *Neumes rythmiques* and *Mode de valeurs*, the latter of which was destined to establish the 'myth-misunderstanding' of Messiaen as the father of the serial

---

[38] Massimo Mila, '*Cinq Rechants, Mode de valeurs et d'intensités, Île de feu 2, Neumes rythmiques*', *La Rassegna musicale*, 21/4 (October 1951): p. 335. Mila's association of Messiaen with Massenet may have been prompted by the composer's own reference to him in Chapter 13 of *Technique*.

[39] Ibid.

avant-garde.[40] In his later review of the *Turangalîla-Symphonie* in Turin, published in 1955 in the *Espresso*, Mila distances himself in a different way, influenced by the swelling tide of ideology fed by Darmstadt's serial avant-garde. His article, meaningfully entitled 'Webern + Messiaen: La musica di domani', opens with the observation that many people now look to Messiaen as the spearhead of the contemporary music scene, capable of defusing 'the sterile squabble' between conservatives and supporters of dodecaphony. He notes, in fact, how the Sainte-Trinité organist has by now become the standard-bearer of those 'young extremists' (Boulez, Goeyvaerts, Maderna, Nono and Stockhausen) who want to surpass even dodecaphony by 'exploring electronic sounds'.[41]

Mila then describes some crucial points in the aesthetics and poetics of Messiaen, as guided by the work *Esthétique de la musique contemporaine* by Antoine Goléa[42] who, as everybody knew, had worked from 1952 to 1953 as Messiaen's assistant and translator in Darmstadt. He expresses his total surprise at the distance between the 'extremely simple' language and, on occasion, 'openly confessed banality' of *Turangalîla* and the 'exotic and esoteric' claims of the composer's declaredly aesthetic vision. For Mila, the symphony is a kind of cheerful 'Carnival on Broadway', which presents themes in the Gershwin mould and uses brass instruments reminiscent of the symphonic jazz performed by Paul Whiteman.[43]

Lastly, Mila asks himself: 'Can this fine Trinité organist be so guileless as not to perceive the hybrid nature of the materials he puts together in his compositions?'[44] Against the aesthetic categories of eclecticism, the naïve, the plural and an intentionally heteronymous and impure music like Messiaen's, Mila sets the opposite categories of aesthetic autonomy and absolute music, blatantly unsuitable for understanding compositions such as *Visions* and *Vingt Regards* or, more to the point, *Turangalîla*. In fact, despite his revised Crocean vision (such as his aesthetic of the 'unconscious expression' in music), Massimo Mila seems to criticize *Turangalîla* with arguments close to the aesthetic purism of the avant-garde.[45] This tendency, influenced by the growing ideological weight of the avant-garde and shared by much of Italian progressive criticism, prevented the fledgling emergence of Messiaen in post-war Italy from putting down solid roots.

Nonetheless, the 'father of the avant-garde' myth invented by representatives of the avant-garde itself clearly created proselytes. It concentrated on the much-

---

[40]   For this misundertood image of Messiaen as the 'father' of serialism, see Pozzi, *Il suono dell'estasi*, p. 13.

[41]   Massimo Mila, 'Webern + Messiaen: La musica di domani', *L'Espresso*, 4 December 1955, reprinted in *Cronache musicali, 1955–1959* (Turin: Einaudi, 1959), p. 414.

[42]   Antoine Goléa, *Esthétique de la musique contemporaine* (Paris: Presses universitaires de France, 1954).

[43]   Mila, 'Webern + Messiaen', p. 414.

[44]   Ibid.

[45]   For the concept of 'unconscious expression', see Mila, *L'esperienza musicale e l'estetica* (Turin: Einaudi, 1956), pp. 124–7.

discussed *Mode de valeurs,* whose modal organization was mistaken for a serial one – Hence the image of Messiaen as a figure of transition between Webern and the younger serial avant-garde generation. The Webern-Messiaen line, a genealogy propagated in Darmstadt, was not only presented by Mila but also endorsed by a representative of the Italian avant-garde like the composer Aldo Clementi. In an article published in 1957, not by chance entitled 'Dopo la dodecafonia, verso un nuovo stile', Clementi writes:

> Going beyond Webern, yet with no affinity whatsoever, Messiaen organizes even the other 'parameters' in series: durations, modes of attack, dynamics. But in parallel, his mystical and exotic nature leads him to research modalities and rhythms stemming from the Orient and other regions, or even to speculate about birdsong: the result is a new form of descriptivism reminiscent of impressionism. Nonetheless, the function of this musician is extraordinarily important: the path towards a radical pulverizing and organization of different values has now been paved. He is, though not in the essential musical gesture, the true unifying link between Webern and the new generation.[46]

The ongoing reception of Messiaen in avant-garde circles, effectively synthesized by Mila's formula 'Webern + Messiaen: La musica di domani', is also confirmed in the 1969 book by Mario Bortolotto, *Fase seconda. Studi sulla Nuova Musica*, which records numerous critical passages from the debate of those years. Guided by Clementi's above-mentioned statements, the latter's *Composizione n. 1* for piano is viewed as a work that rethinks Webern's 'great Viennese lesson', in particular the last movement of the Variations op. 27, by means of Messiaen's *Mode de valeurs* and the Première Sonate by Boulez. Webern–Messiaen–Boulez: the genealogical lineage is traced and Clementi's *Composizione n. 1* is placed within it, even though this work's compositional process owes very little to those models, recalling them only very superficially.[47]

After 1946, Messiaen returned only once to the Festival Internazionale di Musica Contemporanea in Venice, for a memorable performance in 1957 of *Trois Petites Liturgies de la Présence Divine* conducted by Marcel Couraud, a concert of spiritual music where Dallapiccola's *Canti di prigionia* was also performed. In his reception in the 1950s, the figure of Messiaen was gradually eclipsed by a generation of serial and post-serial avant-garde composers. His historical position and image did not attain the autonomous and original value they deserved: at the cost of misunderstandings and the dismissal of fundamental aspects of his

---

[46]   Aldo Clementi, 'Dopo la dodecafonia, verso un nuovo stile', *L'esperienza moderna*, 1/3-4 (1957): p. 45.

[47]   Mario Bortolotto, *Fase seconda: Studi sulla Nuova Musica* (Torino: Einaudi, 1969), p. 178. The compositional process in *Composizione n. 1* by Aldo Clementi, unlike *Mode de valeurs*, is based on acceleration and deceleration of durations, visually predetermined on millimetred paper.

294   *Messiaen Perspectives 2: Techniques, Influence and Reception*

aesthetics, to all intents and purposes he became a talented forerunner of the avant-garde, of Boulez and Stockhausen. His work as a teacher took on – in Italy and elsewhere – mythical and ritual contours; his own pupils contributed to that hagiographic narrative.

Enwrapped as he was in this modernist teleology and in a certain sense confined to it, Messiaen's return in the 1960s to the central stage of the Festival Internazionale di Musica in Venice did not lead to a wider diffusion and understanding of his music. In Venice, the following works were performed: in 1961, *Le Merle noir* by Severino Gazzelloni and Frederic Rzewski; *Chronochromie* in 1962; *Sept Haïkaï* in 1964; *Cinq Rechants* in 1968. Apart from *Le Merle noir*, all these performances appeared as Italian premières.[48]

Giacomo Manzoni's review of the Italian premiere of *Chronochromie* in Venice in 1962 gives a further indication of the atmosphere in that period among the ranks of the militant avant-garde. First of all, it should be said that the composer, in his work as a critic, frequently referred to Messiaen as being close to Boulez, even though today the profound distance separating the aesthetic concepts and creative processes of the two musicians is patently clear. Right from the article on the first performance of *Le marteau sans maître* in 1956 at the XXIX Festival of the SIMC in Baden-Baden, Manzoni sees the 'extreme rhythmic variety' of *Le Marteau* as surpassing 'Messiaen at his boldest'. On the other hand, Manzoni observes, the 'cult of the beautiful sound' in Boulez follows in the wake of Debussy and Messiaen, to the latter of whom Boulez is bound by a certain 'calligraphic need' that leads to 'Orientalisms' that he would be the first to introduce in a systematic way into New Music.[49]

Manzoni's critical comment on *Chronochromie* thus sets further distance between himself and a composer who is yet again depicted as being but a moment of transition towards the new music of Boulez, but whose best work is not in line with the aesthetics and ideology of a radical avant-garde, often politically active on the Left. In this sense, Messiaen seems to hark back to the stream of historic and 'primitivistic' modernism from the first half of the century. Hence, *Chronochromie* is judged negatively by Manzoni:

> as being the latest orchestral composition by the fifty-three-year-old French musician, who has served such an important function in the evolution of today's music, even if we clearly do not share his positions (once again, yesterday

---

[48]   See the official programmes of the 20th (11 September–2 October 1957), 24th (9–27 April 1961), 25th (10–24 April 1962), 27th (6–16 September 1964), and 31st (7–14 September 1968) Festival Internazionale di Musica Contemporanea in Venice.

[49]   For references to the Boulez–Messiaen relationship, see articles by G. Manzoni, 'Il XXIX Festival della SIMC di Baden-Baden' [1956], 'Maderna resta un primattore' [1964], 'A che punto è la "Nuova Musica"' [1965], now in Pozzi (ed.) and Giacomo Manzoni, *Musica e progetto civile: Scritti e interviste (1956–2007)*, pp. 23, 149–50, 163.

evening, while listening to *Chronochromie*, we recognized how much the music of Pierre Boulez owes to the maestro from Avignon).[50]

Messiaen's best works are thus considered to be *Trois Petites Liturgies* or *Turangalîla* where 'he gave us quite different proof of the genuineness of his expressive world, in which the naturalist tendency blends with the ambitious aim of introducing the musical concepts of Eastern peoples (static forms, obsessive repetitions, taut sounds, subtly varied rhythms) into European music'.[51]

In addition to feeling Messiaen's music derived from a linguistic purism of a formalist nature, the avant-garde also expressed misgivings about Messiaen that stemmed from that same avant-garde's closeness to Marxist positions and the Partito Comunista Italiano (PCI), whose electoral support was growing in the 1960s and reached its height in 1976 (34.4 per cent, one Italian in three, voted for the PCI). The Communist Party at that time had a profound effect on the organization of music and many representatives of advanced experimental music (Berio, Gentilucci, Maderna, Manzoni, Nono and so on) were sympathizers or members of the PCI.

Hence the musical avant-garde grew up in Italy, between the 1960s and 1970s, expressing political values that were essentially secular and, on occasion, anti-religious. The presentation of Messiaen included in Armando Gentilucci's *Guida all'ascolto della musica contemporanea* – which was widely read at that time and had an important role in spreading twentieth-century music in Italy – is meaningful from this standpoint. Gentilucci writes:

> The other aspect of his music, in other words the aspect that goes beyond the exoticism of timbre and polyrhythm, lies in its universalistic religiosity, achieved musically by means of an 'atmospheric' mysticism (and this is the worst aspect, which explains in fact how a musician who has always been in the forefront of French avant-garde groups could for so many years have filled the post of church organist). As previously mentioned, Messiaen's pupil, Boulez, will benefit from those interesting experiments carried out in the field of rhythm and timbre, transferring them into the bosom of a rigorous post-Webernism.[52]

In expressing his opinion, Luigi Nono also referred to this orientation, this ideological atmosphere, clearly rebuffing Messiaen's mysticism and assimilating it with what for him was the equally unbearable mysticism of Stockhausen. To

---

[50]   Manzoni, 'Una "prima" di Messiaen con uccelli e torrenti', *L'Unità* (Milan, 18 April 1962).

[51]   Ibid.

[52]   Armando Gentilucci, *Guida all'ascolto della musica contemporanea* (Milan: Feltrinelli, 1969), p. 276.

296   Messiaen Perspectives 2: Techniques, Influence and Reception

all intents and purposes, due to the musical modalities used, he sees a kind of colonial-style plunder and usurpation in the French composer's exoticism.[53]

If the religiousness of the Sainte-Trinité organist caused bafflement and suspicion among the progressive avant-garde circles of the Italian Left, the modern language with which Messiaen expressed that religiousness was clearly destined to arouse similar feelings in the opposing front of the Catholic Church. With the *Motu proprio* by Pope Pius X in 1903 – a text on liturgical matters that would inspire the position of the Church with regard to sacred music throughout the twentieth century – and those documents relating to music in the *Sacrosanctum Concilium* of the Second Vatican Council in 1963, the position of the Roman Catholic Church followed the course of the Gregorian and neo-Palestrinian myths proclaimed by the Cecilian movement. The paths of modern music and religious music had divided dramatically. The level of ecclesiastical conservatism is exemplified by the Cecilian Don Raffaele Casimiri, who in 1933 had railed against music that was 'novecentista' and 'modernist' (a word that evokes other more serious forms of wretchedness), 'music that is often algebraic and erotic' which circulates within 'a certain caste of so-called young musicians'.[54]

Among these young musicians, Goffredo Petrassi was an active composer who, from an opposing point of view, complained in 1946 about how 'an average kind of sacred music, a sort of kitty available to one and all' had come about, in which 'Franckian after-effects and harmonic impressionism' merge, and in which 'the shadow of Puccini weds Parsifalian mysticism of a poor nature' and Gregorian chant is 'reviewed through Liberty-style aestheticism and a certain academic stance that tries to justify such contamination with austere and professional posturing'.[55] It should be noted that Petrassi's criticism comes from a composer with a modern orientation, a practising Catholic, one of the most noteworthy twentieth-century authors in Italy, who lived in Rome until the age of 99 without the Vatican ever showing any interest in his music.

The Church's neglect of Petrassi helps us to understand how the anti-modernist policy of the pre-conciliar Church and, following the Second Vatican Council's extreme open-mindedness in principle, its non-artistic liturgical and musical practice based on simplistic models of commercial light music, were not positions that could support and promote Messiaen's music.[56] As the different reception in other countries shows, organ music was an important means of awareness and dissemination of his music. In Italy, however, the control of ecclesiastic authority

---

[53]   Luigi Nono, *Scritti e Colloqui*, ed. A. I. De Benedictis and V. Rizzardi, Vol. 2 (Lucca: Ricordi-LIM, 2001), pp. 87, 97, 113.

[54]   Raffaele Casimiri, 'Arte novecentista', *Note d'Archivio per la storia musicale*, 10/1 (1933): p. 58.

[55]   Petrassi, 'Sulla musica religiosa', in *Scritti e interviste*, pp. 84–5.

[56]   On the post-conciliar positions of the Catholic Church, see Raffaele Pozzi, 'Liturgia d'arte o liturgia pop? La questione della musica contemporanea nel culto cattolico dopo il Concilio Vaticano II', *Musica e Storia*, 13/3 (2005): pp. 489–514.

over musical liturgy was, by reason of its closeness to the political centre of Catholicism, more marked than elsewhere. Consequently, the potential insertion of improvisations and pieces of advanced, modern writing, such as those offered by Messiaen during the liturgy in the Church of the Sainte-Trinité in Paris, had no following. To all of this should be added other reasons for his neglect, such as the extremely self-absorbed Italian tradition of organ playing, and even the structural features of Italian organs, which, as an expression of this tradition, are frequently not suitable for the performance of Messiaen's organ works.

It is perhaps no coincidence that in a 1971 interview with Messiaen in Italy by Leonardo Pinzauti, he was questioned on the emerging scenario of the 'Messa beat' ('Beat Mass') in Catholic liturgical music. His level-headed answer shows the obedience of the believer but, at the same time, extreme severity: 'What, for example,' asks Pinzauti, 'do you think about certain Masses that are celebrated with so-called pop music, electric guitars, drums, etcetera?' Messiaen replies: 'This is certainly not the kind of music that I would write. But Christ has come for everyone, even bad musicians.'[57]

With the crisis of the avant-garde and the new postmodern cultural wave, which appeared in Italy in the late 1970s, Messiaen's intrinsically multiform aesthetics found a musical environment that was potentially more receptive. Berio was among the first to express this different atmosphere. In his *Intervista sulla musica* in 1981, he spurns 'the combinatory extremism' of Boulez, 'inherited', as he puts it, from Messiaen and Cage. Furthermore, with regard to compositions such as the still stubbornly coupled '*Mode de valeurs* and the first volume of *Structures*', he claims that they are 'the most well-known and least listenable results' of those years.[58]

During the 1980s, numerous works by the French composer were presented in Florence, Milan, Rome, Turin (at the Festival di Settembre Musica) and Venice. Some articles appeared and a seminar on Messiaen's works for piano, curated by this author, was proposed in November 1987 at one of the historic centres of the musical avant-garde in Rome, the Associazione 'Nuova Consonanza'. Subsequently, in 1988, the XXIV Festival Pontino di Musica, offered a memorable performance of *Quatuor pour la fin du Temps*. In 1989, the XXVI Festival of Nuova Consonanza, in collaboration with the Orchestra di Santa Cecilia, programmed a performance of the *Turangalîla-Symphonie* in Rome, in the course of a cycle dedicated to *Mito del primitivo nella musica moderna*, curated by Diego Carpitella.[59]

---

[57]   Leonardo Pinzauti, 'A colloquio con Olivier Messiaen', *Nuova Rivista musicale italiana*, 5/6 (November–December 1971): p. 1031.

[58]   Luciano Berio, *Intervista sulla musica*, ed. Rossana Dalmonte (Bari: Laterza, 1981), p. 65.

[59]   For articles in the 1970s, see C. Marinelli, 'Lettura di Messiaen', in *Aspetti della musica d'oggi*, ed. Giorgio Pestelli, Quaderni della Rassegna musicale no. 5 (Turin: Einaudi, 1972), pp. 97–146; and Raffaele Pozzi, 'Messiaen: Il suo tempo verrà', *Musica e Dossier*, no. 34 (November 1989): pp. 72–5. See also the programme of the 26th Festival di Nuova Consonanza: Diego Carpitella (ed.), *Il mito del primitivo nella musica moderna*

A 1983 review by Fedele d'Amico of the Paris première of Messiaen's opera *Saint François d'Assise* reveals continuity with a critical orientation, strongly rooted in Italy, that is guided by strict adherence to an aesthetic concept of musical autonomy. D'Amico notes the reverence that Messiaen enjoys on the international scene and proclaims, not without irony, all his scepticism with regard to the 'imperious invitation to accept dogmatically, even prior to his musical works, analyses of their language and description of their meanings which he himself dictates and that our ear is unable to verify'.[60] Despite the composer's 'unfaltering fanaticism' and 'visionary convictions', d'Amico, overcoming all preclusion, reveals his appreciation for *Saint François d'Assise*. A critical need to understand the specificity of an essentially static dramatic concept seems to thrust its way forward, like it or not, irrespective of categorization in 'schools' or aesthetic or political-ideological factions. D'Amico writes:

> The fact is that a Wagner, a Bruckner, a Mahler, by forcing us to follow the thread of a discourse, can be much more tiring than this *San Francesco*, where there is no discourse, and our imagination merely has to pass from one image to another, all of them invented for this purpose.[61]

And he ends, 'Messiaen may not be what one would call a pure-bred composer of operas. But among the works of the last twenty-nine years, try to find even one that is worth this: I couldn't.'[62]

The problems with regard to Messiaen's reception, the meagre knowledge of his music and its relatively limited diffusion in Italy stemmed from a convergence of different historic and cultural factors that clashed with the composer's complex and multiform aesthetics. The emergence of Messiaen in the post-war period, during those years of heated ideological debate and political and cultural conflict, led to a form of censorship that emerged from the critical circles that espoused the idealism of Benedetto Croce and opposed technical and theoretical approaches to the arts and music. Messiaen was moreover incorporated into the genealogy of serial music and, for this reason alone, as a driving force and 'father' to the serialism of Boulez and Stockhausen, accepted into the circles of the radical avant-garde who were often influenced by secular-Marxist and anti-religious ideological tendencies. Too religious for a left-wing avant-garde, too modern for a Catholic church that was anti-modernist or had gradually slid, after the Second Vatican Council, into a liturgy that absorbed the musical forms and modes of commercial

---

(Rome: Semar, 1989), with contributions by G. Cane, D. Carpitella, M. Dall'Ongaro, G. Giuriati, R. Pozzi.

[60] Fedele d'Amico, 'Un uccello di nome Marimba', *L'Espresso*, 18 December 1983, reprinted in Luigi Bellingardi (ed.), *Tutte le cronache musicali*, '*L'Espresso*', Vol. 3 (1977–89) (Roma: Bulzoni), pp. 2047, 2049.

[61] Ibid.

[62] Ibid.

pop music, Messiaen has received modest institutional attention in Italy, even though the emotion aroused by his works still inspires audiences at his concerts. Increasingly, these works are regarded in Italy as among the most noteworthy, 'classic' if you will, fruits of twentieth-century music.

Chapter 12

Three Decades of Messiaen's Music in Spain: A Brief Survey, 1945–1978

Germán Gan-Quesada

Introduction

Retracing the reception of Messiaen's music in Spain is a very difficult task. Achieving a coherent panorama is hindered by the scarcity of its programming, the paucity of Spanish-language references to the European avant-garde, and the ideological and aesthetic premises in force among music critics and musicologists. Nevertheless, exploring the reception of Messiaen in Spain reveals much about late twentieth-century Spanish musical tastes and broadens the sources available to Messiaen scholars.[1]

I focus mainly on critical sources from Madrid and Barcelona that have heretofore been largely neglected and limit myself to a definite period, marked between the composer's first visit to Spain in 1949 and two more stays, in 1974 and 1976,[2] just around the end of Francoism and the subsequent beginning of a difficult period of political and socio-cultural normalization.[3] These are, indeed, three main milestones in the process of reception of Messiaen and his œuvre in the country. In the middle of this period, the biennium 1964–65 – when the first Biennial for Contemporary Music and the International Society for Contemporary Music (ISCM) Festival were held in Madrid – marks a significant, but not absolute, turning point of acceptance.

Integrating this survey into a more general approach to the peculiarities of Spanish music around the middle of the twentieth century would greatly exceed the scope of this text.[4] However, I propose a possible further development of this research, providing a very brief digression about the possible influence of Messiaen on some Spanish composers during the 1950s and 1960s, a small sign

---

[1] For further discussion of the state of Messiaen reception, see 'Perspectives on Reception' at the beginning of Part III of this volume.

[2] These three visits have been briefly noted in PHNS, pp. 182–5, 301 and 322.

[3] For a brief approach to more recent times, see Germán Gan Quesada, 'Pájaros en el cielo hispano: Apuntes sobre la recepción inicial de la música de Olivier Messiaen en España', *Scherzo*, 236 (December 2008): pp. 130–34.

[4] Leon Botstein, 'Music in History: The Perils of Method in Reception History', *The Musical Quarterly*, 89/1 (Spring 2006): pp. 1–16.

302   *Messiaen Perspectives 2: Techniques, Influence and Reception*

of a wider historical context in which the composer from Avignon takes only a partial, but highly representative, place.

First Steps along a Difficult Path: 1949–1964

After the outbreak of the Spanish Civil War, Madrid and Barcelona, and to a much lesser extent smaller towns such as Valencia, Bilbao or Seville, kept something of the musical vitality they had enjoyed prior to the war. They showed in their concerts an undeniable taste for the great nineteenth-century repertoire and for Spanish 'new' works well-rooted in romantic, nationalistic or moderate neoclassical models, such as Joaquín Rodrigo or Ernesto Halffter's compositions. For the progressively minded, performances of music by composers such as Bartók, Stravinsky, Hindemith or the members of Les Six were like sparse and fleeting oases in this desert landscape, usually appearing in minority public institutions or in strictly private ones. They were often sceptically greeted or directly rejected because of their harshness, lack of expressiveness, intellectual or 'abstract' condition or even simply the racial origin or political tendencies of their composers.

The updating of musical models and listening attitudes from 1953 was a large step forward, normalizing, with great difficulty, this sporadic presence of new music through the initiative of conductors such as Ataúlfo Argenta and institutions such as the Ateneo of Madrid and the Group 'Manuel de Falla' (the latter was sponsored by the Institut Français in Barcelona). However, introducing Stravinsky's or Bartók's works as the 'true advanced music' simultaneously closed the doors to real avant-garde composers until the 1960s or, in Messiaen's case, to composers not easily classed in such a rough dichotomy.

The first evidence of Messiaen's music in Spanish musical media, so far as I know, was published in November 1945 in the Madrilenian periodical *Ritmo*, the principal Spanish music journal of its time. It is an article signed by Paul Loyonnet, a regular contributor to *Ritmo* on French music who, after defining the immediate postwar situation in Paris as one of stylistic hesitation and overcoming of the materialist avant-garde, puts forward Jolivet, Françaix and, above all, Messiaen as exponents of this 'new spirit'. He also comments on Messiaen's fervent Catholicism and alludes to referents nearer to Spanish readers in characterizing his music, no doubt in order to win their affection:

> [Messiaen] tries to find again, through Indian modes, the sense of a subtle vocalization, which, winding and with fleeting outlines, makes the audience lose every notion of time and of common ways of thinking. I guess such a doctrine will not surprise my Spanish readers: Flamenco is the survival of a millenial art that intends identical magic purposes; and the Spain of the great mystics Saint John of the Cross and Saint Theresa is very present in Messiaen's artistic mysticism.

[Trata de volver a encontrar, a través de los modos indios, el sentido de la vocalización sutil, que, sinuosa, de fugaces contornos, hace perder a los oyentes toda noción del tiempo y de la ordinaria manera de pensar. Creo que semejante doctrina no podrá extrañar ni chocar a mis lectores españoles: el flamenco es la supervivencia de un arte milenario que se propone idénticos fines mágicos; y la España de los grandes místicos San Juan de la Cruz y Santa Teresa está muy presente en el misticismo artístico de Messiaen].[5]

But which works by Messiaen could actually be known by the supposed readers of these words, if we take into account the actual programming of his works and, moreover, the non-existence of a market for foreign scores in Spain and the weakness of the national broadcasting system? Probably none. Although performances of some of Messiaen's works in Spain around 1950 can be confirmed,[6] only the first trip by Olivier Messiaen and Yvonne Loriod to Spain in February 1949,[7] at the request of the Institut Français in Barcelona[8] and Madrid, evoked a certain response in the country.

They arrived in Barcelona on 19 February. Five days later Yvonne Loriod performed three pieces from the *Vingt Regards* and, together with the composer, the whole *Visions de l'Amen*. The critical response was rather positive, if not extensive, both for the performances and the ambitious scope of the works. However, in terms of the music itself, the anonymous critic of *La Vanguardia Española* observed that 'although these works revealed his author's efforts to remove himself from tradition and achieve novelty at all costs … they make only a sensation of vague expressiveness'.[9]

The performance the next day (25 February) of *Trois Tâla* [*sic*] by the Barcelona Municipal Orchestra, conducted by Eduard Toldrà with Yvonne Loriod and Ginette

---

[5]   Paul Loyonnet, 'Las tendencias actuales de la música en París', trans. from the French original by Antonio Iglesias, *Ritmo*, 191 (November 1945): pp. 4–5.

[6]   For instance, 'Paysage', was performed by Ginette Guillamat and Carmen Díez Martín in the Ateneo of Madrid in November 1948, as were a piano piece by Alexander Borovsky (Madrid, 21 March 1949), and *La Mort du Nombre* (18 July 1951) and *Trois Mélodies* (1953/54 season) around 1950 in the exclusive concerts held at the Casa Bartomeu in Barcelona.

[7]   PHNS, pp. 184–5. Taking advantage of his stay in Madrid, on 1 March Messiaen met the poet Gerardo Diego and the composers Eduard Toldrà and Joaquín Rodrigo. See www.fundaciongerardodiego.com.

[8]   The Institut Français in Barcelona, directed by Pierre Deffontaines, was at that time very interested in musical activities. It sponsored the visits to Barcelona of Arthur Honegger and Francis Poulenc in March 1949 and André Jolivet in May 1950. It also scheduled Messiaen's music in some of its evening concerts, such as the *Thème et variations*, performed by Henry Merckel and Marie-Louise Pugnet-Guillard on 30 November 1950.

[9]   'Aunque revelaron el esfuerzo del autor para alejarse de lo tradicional y conseguir a toda costa la novedad … no sin dejar la sensación de lo vagamente expresivo'. [Unsigned], 'Música – Instituto Francés. Audición de obras de Olivier Messiaen', *La Vanguardia Española* (25 February 1949): p. 2.

Martenot as soloists, a year after its Parisian première, aroused even less sympathy. Loriod's recollection to Peter Hill and Nigel Simeone was of an 'immense success: the public threw their hats, programmes and flowers onto the stage!'[10] Despite this, the exceptional presence of Messiaen in Barcelona and programme notes that underlined Messiaen's art as being 'as interesting as [it is] personal',[11] one of the most influential critics of the town, U. F. Zanni, painted a different picture. Writing two days later in *La Vanguardia Española*, he stated that the audience, which was much more at its ease with the rest of the program (D. Scarlatti, Haydn and Turina), had satisfied nothing more than its curiosity about the strange ondes Martenot and acknowledged the challenging task of the performers.[12]

The composer Xavier Montsalvatge (1912–2002), by contrast, preferred to reserve his judgement, waiting for the possibility of listening to a more comprehensive sample of Messiaen's music. Nonetheless, he noted the 'duel of applause and stampings, protests and *bravos*, livened up with some high and piercing hisses'[13] that went throughout the performance. And what about the music?

> As regards Messiaen's 'Tres ritmos', it's a music spiced with all the resources of the Strawinskyan cuisine, with its rhythmical and tonal superpositions: in brief, brain divorced from heart …. The composer adds it's only an essay on rhythmical language. And that's all indeed, an attempt that doesn't acomplish its goal. Too much rhythmical energy, too many dissonances and nothing beyond.

> Only those who did not want to be accused of being not very advanced applauded and the rest, those who, as Messiaen himself would think, have not yet developed their auditive sensibility, protested, and did it really noisily.

> [En cuanto a los 'Tres ritmos', de Olivier Messiaen, es obra salpimentada con los ingredientes que tanto abundan en la cocina strawinskiana. Todo en ella tiende a las superposiciones rítmicas y tonales. El cerebro divorciado del corazón … el autor añade que se trata de un ensayo de lenguaje rímico. Y en eso queda todo, en un ensayo que no llega a la feliz realización. Mucha fuerza rítmica, muchas disonancias, y de allí no se pasa.

---

[10] PHNS, p. 185.

[11] Oriol Martorell, *Quasi un segle de simfonisme a Barcelona*, I (Barcelona: Beta Editorial, 1995), p. 161. A copy of the programme of this concert is held at the Biblioteca i Arxiu de l'Orfeó Català (Barcelona) and digitalized at http://bibliotecadigital.palaumusica. org/cdm4/document.php?CISOROOT=/programes&CISOPTR=29492&REC=1.

[12] U. F. Zanni, 'Música – Palacio de la Música. La Orquesta Municipal: Segundo concierto de invierno', *La Vanguardia Española* (27 February 1949): p. 13.

[13] 'duelo de aplausos y pateos, protestas y bravos, amenizados con algún silbido agudo y penetrante. Xavier Montsalvatge, 'Una música nueva: Olivier Messiaen', *Destino*, 604 (5 March 1949): p. 19.

> Aplaudieron los que se consideraron obligados a ello para que no se les tache de poco avanzados, y protestaron, ruidosamente por cierto, aquellos que, como diría Messiaen, no tienen suficientemente desarrollada la sensibilidad auditiva.][14]

Regardless of how much that opinion could be judged as negative, it is not, perhaps, the worst that Messiaen's *Trois Tâla* might have generated in Spain. After regarding Stravinsky's Concerto in D as a 'genial act of insanity' ['genial acto de demencia'], Arturo Menéndez Aleyxandre, correspondent of *Ritmo* in Barcelona, preferred 'not to write a word' about Messiaen's music.[15] Perhaps we should not regret his silence if we take into account his opinion, only four months earlier, about a composition so 'dangerous' as Albert Roussel's Trois Pièces for piano, which he deemed to be like a 'house under construction about to collapse … whose fragility remains standing miraculously. All this belongs to that "Neoclassicism" that is not even *music for music's sake*, but *noise for noise's* sake'.[16] Certainly, if Menéndez Aleyxandre had thrown his hat onto the stage of the Palau de la Música Catalana on listening to Messiaen's *Trois Tâla*, it would not have been with good intentions.

By contrast, Madrilenian critics were more enthusiastic in greeting the Messiaen-Loriod concert on 28 February at the Institut Français in Madrid where they met, amongst other personalities, the well-known Hispanist Maurice Legendre (see Illustration 12.1).[17] While they recorded the audience reaction as being 'curious and warm',[18] it should not be inferred that there was a higher degree of understanding of Messiaen's music. The comments, both by Antonio Fernández-Cid in *Arriba* and Regino Sáinz de la Maza in *ABC*, restrict themselves to following a precise ideological premise: the positive value of Messiaen's music was not the music itself, which was judged as esoteric and as a 'hyper-complex language, even hostile to the average listener'.[19] Rather the worth of Messiaen's

---

[14] Zanni, 'Música – Palacio de la Música': p. 13.

[15] Arturo Menéndez Aleyxandre, 'Crónicas de conciertos: Barcelona', *Ritmo*, 220 (May 1949): p. 14.

[16] 'que por su descoyuntada estructura compararíamos a una casa en construcción que acaba de hundirse … cuya fragilidad se mantiene en pie por milagro. Todo ello pertenece a ese "neoclasicismo" que ya no es *la música por la música*, sino *el ruido por el ruido*'. Arturo Menéndez Aleyxandre, 'Crónicas de conciertos. Barcelona', *Ritmo*, 217 (January 1949): p. 6.

[17] Directed by Paul Guinard, the Institut Français in Madrid also organized three sessions on 'French modern music' during the first half of 1950. The last one (4 May 1950) was entrusted to André Jolivet, who performed and conducted works by Messiaen, among others, after a seminar entitled 'Le groupe Jeune France et son influence sur la musique contemporaine'. See Serge Fohr (ed.), *L'Institut Français de Madrid: 100 ans de culture et d'enseignement /El Institut Français de Madrid: 100 años de cultura y de enseñanza* (Madrid: Institut Français de Madrid, 2010).

[18] Antonio Fernández-Cid, 'Olivier Messiaen, autor e intérprete, en Madrid', *Arriba* (1 March 1949): p. 3.

[19] 'lenguaje complicadísimo, hostil incluso para el auditor medio'. Ibid.

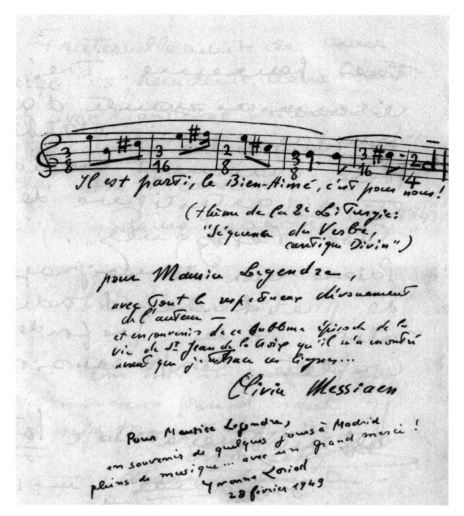

Illustration 12.1   Dedication by Olivier Messiaen and Yvonne Loriod to Maurice Legendre, director of the 'Casa de Velázquez' in Madrid (28 March 1949)[20]

music was found in its 'emotive force', its non-calculating, friendly character and, most of all, its religious background:

> In a time in which musical inspiration delights itself in trivial subjects, in more or less refined stylizations of coarseness or is placed in the sheer intellectual joke

---

[20]   I am grateful to Dr Yvan Nommick, former Artistic Director of the 'Casa de Velázquez', for bringing this document to my attention. Casa de Velázquez, Madrid.

that bans sensibility and exalts energy and mere movement to the category of dogma, the attitude of this mystic, of this music visionary who aspires to make from music a vehicle of communication with Divinity, is astonishing.

[En una época en que la inspiración musical se complace en los temas triviales, en estilizaciones más o menos refinadas de lo vulgar o se sitúa en el puro juego intelectual, que proscribe la sensibilidad y se eleva a la categoría de dogma la energía y el puro movimiento, resulta sorprendente la actitud de este místico, de este visionario de la música que aspira a hacer de ella vehículo de comunicación con lo divino.][21]

By spring 1951, *Ritmo* had already published the first interview with Messiaen in a Spanish journal, provided by Henri Collet, a long established figure in Spanish musical circles. He presented, in a brief space, some of the technical and aesthetic keys of the composer's music for Spanish readers. In Collet's opinion, Messiaen was without a doubt a 'maestrazo' ['great master'].[22] However, this status was not clear to an anonymous commentator (possibly Enrique Franco) writing in *Cuadernos hispanoamericanos* on the 1953 performance of *L'Ascension* in Rome. The author of the article distrusted Messiaen's 'so misty, literary, ambiguous and, in brief, a-musical' comments and, especially, his sensualist and overflowing religious conception. This was in constrast to Palestrina, Monteverdi, Bach, Franck or Manuel de Falla, and also to neo-Thomist winds that blew in Spanish theological thought. He was even harder on Messiaen's musical substance, which was esentially 'impure' and, therefore, blameworthy:

From a strictly musical point of view, it seems a music of exasperated and exasperating Debussyism, upon which all possible and impossible musical influences are built up: Gregorian chant, Stravinsky, Schönberg, Hinduist music, quarter-tone music …. Everything assimilated and unsteady, the product of a music of irritating and disturbing sonic sensuality, sometimes declamatory, sometimes of a weak romanticism, not to be hidden by its sparkling sonic clothing. No doubt it is interesting music, to be read at the desk or played at the piano, but it says nothing to us and leaves only a vague memory of physical discomfort.

[Desde un punto de vista estrictamente musical, parece música de un debussysmo exasperado y exasperante, sobre el cual se sostienen inestablemente todas las influencias posibles e imposibles: el gregoriano, Strawinsky, Schönberg, la música india, los cuartos de tono …. Todo asimilado y perfectamente inestable, producto de una música de una sensualidad exarcebada y desconcertante, a veces declamatoria, a veces de un romanticismo de baja ley, que la rutilante

---

[21] Regino Sáinz de la Maza, 'Un gran músico francés en Madrid', *ABC* (2 March 1949): p. 19.

[22] Henri Collet, 'Olivier Messiaen', *Ritmo*, 235 (April–May 1951): p. 4.

308 *Messiaen Perspectives 2: Techniques, Influence and Reception*

vestidura sonora no basta a ocultar. Música interesante, sin duda, para leer en la mesa de trabajo o al piano, pero que prácticamente no nos dice nada, de la que no queda sino un vago recuerdo de malestar físico.][23]

In 1953, the priest Federico Sopeña (1917–91), one of the biggest names in Spanish music and musicology at this time, pointed out that Messiaen's stay in Madrid four years earlier 'was not very fruitful'.[24] And yet that was not the whole truth: some Spanish performers incorporated Messiaen's music into their concert programmes after 1950. Notable examples were the organist Ramón González de Amezúa, the pianist Conchita Rodríguez and, even more relevant, the Aragonese pianist Pilar Bayona (1898–1979). Bayona was a former champion of Impressionist repertoire and of Spanish composers such as Jesús Guridi, Óscar Esplá or Fernando Remacha. Moderately modernist in her programmes in the 1950s, she performed music by Bartók, Britten and the Groupe des Six. Between April 1950 and May 1959 there are records of performances on at least eight occasions – two for national broadcasting – of pieces from *Vingt Regards* ('Le baiser de l'Enfant-Jésus' and, more often, 'Regard des prophètes, des bergers et des Mages') and the prelude 'Un reflet dans le vent'. After 1964, she added 'La colombe' and 'Île de feu 1' to her repertory.[25]

Not surprisingly, Sopeña's book *La música europea contemporánea* (1953) makes no effort to analyse Messiaen's music. He mentions the organ and religious works – which he labelled five years later as 'questionable' and 'too literary' compared to the 'spiritual content' of late-period Bartók and, of course, the ethic and music of Manuel de Falla[26] – to attack, in somewhat ridiculous terms, existentialist trends and mass culture, which were contrary to the National Catholic and authoritarian premises of the Francoist regime:

> I want to set up against those thousands of Sartrian youngsters, hysterical and crying, equally hysterical and crying at an Armstrong 'jazz'-concert as at a performance of Berg's 'Wozzeck', there are a few hundred – they will be thousands soon – that need a solemn, meditative air, a hard-working silence to follow Messiaen's metaphoric and mystic language.

---

[23] [Unsigned], '¿Es un gran músico Messiaen?', *Cuadernos Hispanoamericanos*, 48 (December 1953): pp. 373–4.

[24] Federico Sopeña, *La música europea contemporánea: Panorama y diccionario de compositores* (Madrid: Unión Musical Española, [1953]), p. 90.

[25] Pilar Bayona owned several scores of Messiaen's works: *Préludes*, *Île de feu 1* and *Vingt Regards*, now kept in the Archivo Pilar Bayona (pilarbayona.es/castellano.htm) in Madrid.

[26] Federico Sopeña, *La música en la vida espiritual* (Madrid: Taurus, 1958), pp. 23 and 26.

[Me interesa que frente a esos millares de jovenzuelos sartrianos, histéricos, gritadores, igualmente histéricos y gritadores en un concierto de 'jazz' con Armstrong que ante el 'Wozzeck' de Berg, haya unos cientos, víspera de millar, que necesitan un aire grave, meditativo, un silencio trabajador para seguir el lenguaje metafórico y místico de Messiaen.][27]

Aside from these poetic ramblings, obviously founded upon ideological prejudices and on a very limited acquaintance with Messiaen's music, very few interesting contributions can be found in Spanish musical literature from these years. An exception is the positive reception of the Parisian première of *Réveil des oiseaux* by René Dumesnil, published in *Ritmo* in summer 1954, which lauds the work's 'treasures of patient observation and timbral inventiveness'.[28]

This situation was to improve slowly from the second half of the 1950s, thanks almost entirely to the official initiatives of the two heads of the Institut Français in Spain. Seminars and concerts on French contemporary music and, as a result, performances of Messiaen's works, were held by Jean-Étienne Marie and Béatrice Berg (March 1954), the pianist Violette Abel (April 1955), the vocal duo Ruf-Nifemecker/Douay-Dupuy (May 1955) and the Danish-born composer Gunnar Berg and his wife, Béatrice Berg-Duffourt (January–February 1957). The latter played the *Quatre Études de rythme* without provoking any remarkable response.[29]

Finally, in autumn 1959, ten years after *Trois Tâla*, Messiaen's orchestral music again reached Spanish audiences, performed, as before, by the Barcelona Municipal Orchestra conducted by Eduard Toldrà. On this occasion, Toldrà warned the season-ticket public about the 'iconoclast' nature of his music.[30] The work was *L'Ascension*, given on 23 October and 29 November. At last, the music critics – the same two mentioned in relation to *Trois Tâla* – seemed to bow to the evidence, as did the audience. U. F. Zanni described the piece as 'a noble work, sensitive, well-illustrative of its religious subjects, as varied as possible, and tempting in its spirit and writing'.[31] Menéndez Aleyxandre, who had previously stated 'I'd-rather-not-

---

[27] Sopeña, *Panorama*, p. 91.

[28] 'tesoro de paciente observación y de ingeniosidad en el empleo de los timbres'. René Dumesnil, 'Una nueva obra de Olivier Messiaen. "Le réveil des oiseaux"', *Ritmo*, 263 (August–September 1954): pp. 10–11.

[29] Likewise, the Spanish première of *Cantéyodjayâ* (Madrid, July 1956) also seems to have gone almost unnoticed. It was played by Pedro Espinosa – the second Spanish musician to attend Darmstadt Internationale Ferienkurse für Neue Musik in 1958 – at a seminar on Contemporary Piano Music held by Margot Pinter and organized by the Spanish Section of the ISCM.

[30] Sempronio, 'La semana en libertad', *Destino*, 1158 (17 October 1959): p. 33.

[31] 'obra noble, sensible, ilustrativa de los temas religiosos inspiradores, variada, dentro de lo posible, y seductora por su espíritu y por la escritura'. U. F. Zanni, 'Música – Palau de la Música: El violinista Newman y la Orquesta Municipal', *La Vanguardia Española* (25 October 1959): p. 31.

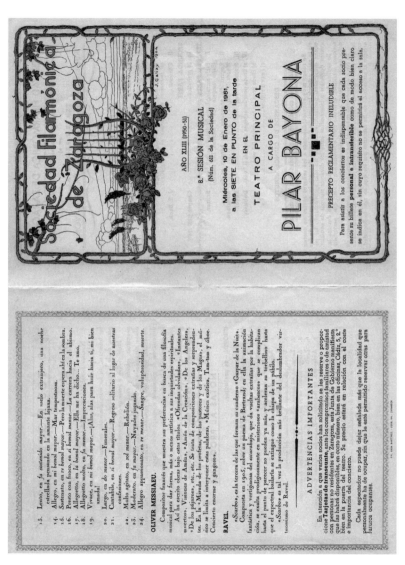

Illustration 12.2a Concert programme of the Pianist Pilar Bayona (Zaragoza, 10 January 1951), featuring 'Regard des prophètes, des bergers et des Mages' by Olivier Messiaeu (sic) [front and back cover]

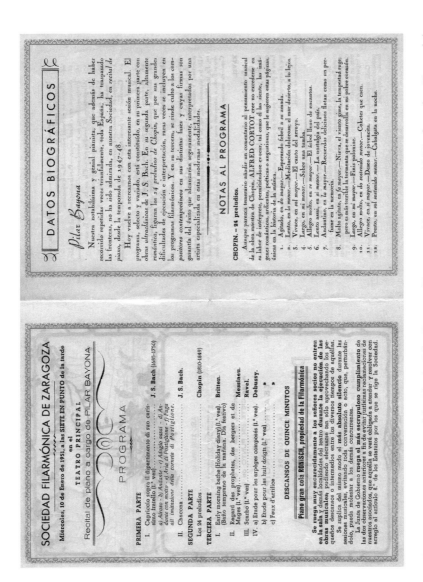

Illustration 12.2b Concert programme of the Pianist Pilar Bayona (Zaragoza, 10 January 1951), featuring 'Regard des prophètes, des bergers et des Mages' by Olivier Messiaeu (sic) [inside pages]

312   *Messiaen Perspectives 2: Techniques, Influence and Reception*

say-a-word', labelled it as 'daring, but emotive and convincing ... with a rather unadorned language, but deep and well provided with beauty and colour'.[32]

In fact, *L'Ascension* was at that time the most frequently broadcast music by Messiaen in Spain. From 1954 onwards, Radio Nacional de España often scheduled it during Holy Week and public recording sessions were held this same year in Seville and Barcelona. A recording of *Turangalîla-Symphonie*, with commentary by François Paliard of the Institut Français, was broadcast from Barcelona on 3 December 1956, and recordings of works such as the *Trois Petites Liturgies* (18 November 1959), *Chronochromie* (17 January 1961) and *La Nativité du Seigneur* (16 February 1962) were presented at Jeunesses Musicales, years before their first live performances in Spain. Messiaen's repertoire in the country, nevertheless, was largely restricted to older works. For instance, in spring 1960, only such early compositions as *Visions de l'Amen* and the *Thème et variations* were performed in Madrid. The critics were still not without prejudice in judging the first of these. For instance, Enrique Franco branded it as 'excessive, full of Lisztian reminiscences, very often banal – and always rhetorical'.[33]

The critical uneasiness provoked by the music of the composer from Avignon, whose stylistic evolution could not be followed by the Spanish public and critics from such a small portion of his catalogue, was also conditioned by two main premises. First, Messiaen was 'too modern', yet also too deeply rooted in tradition actually to be an avant-garde composer. Second, his spirituality seemed unlikely to fit the new Catholic framework postulated by the Second Vatican Council.

Nonetheless, Montsalvatge went on deepening his appraisal of Messiaen's music as he began to hear new works by the composer: Montsalvatge himself was renovating his musical language. The 'originality and freedom of concept'[34] that he found in Messiaen's compositions were for him a mirror in which to reflect on his music, even in cases – like the Spanish première of the *Livre d'orgue* by Montserrat Torrent (Barcelona, 7 March 1962) – where the dimensions and complexity of the work prohibited a clear assessment.[35]

---

[32]   'audaz, pero emotiva y convincente ... lenguaje algo descarnado, pero profundo y con buena dosis de belleza y color'. Arturo Menéndez Aleyxandre, 'Barcelona. La Orquesta Municipal', *Ritmo*, 306 (October–November 1959): p. 10.

[33]   'excesiva de proporciones, llena de reminiscencias lisztianas, banal en muchas ocasiones, retórica en todas'. Enrique Franco, 'Estreno de "Progressus", de Luis de Pablo, por Conchita Rodríguez y Pedro Espinosa – Concierto extraordinario de la Filarmónica', *Arriba* (1 April 1960): p. 17.

[34]   'originalidad y libertad de concepto'. Xavier Montsalvatge, 'Los últimos conciertos del Festival Internacional – La Orquesta Municipal, dirigida por Rafael Ferrer, en el Palacio de la Música, y la Agrupación Coral de Pamplona, en el Tinell', *La Vanguardia Española* (31 October 1965): p. 56.

[35]   Xavier Montsalvatge, 'Los Conciertos: En la iglesia de la Concepción: obras modernas al órgano, interpretadas por Montserrat Torrent', *La Vanguardia Española* (9 March 1962): p. 28.

Indeed, new works by Messiaen began to be performed in Spanish auditoria in the beginning of the 1960s. For instance, the *Trois Petites Liturgies* were performed in Madrid on 2 April 1963 by the Chorus of Radio Nacional de España, with Pedro Espinosa and Françoise Deslogères as soloists, and conducted by Alberto Blancafort. On this occasion, the influential Federico Sopeña – who had claimed in 1961 that Messiaen should be in charge of the composition classes of the newly formed 'Música en Compostela' courses[36] – referred openly to the aforementioned 'impure' religiosity of Messiaen, anchored to an obsolete historical circumstance.[37] Sopeña even reinforced these opinions faced with Messiaen's most recent compositions, such as *Chronochromie*, played by Maurice Le Roux and the Spanish National Orchestra in the opening concert of the first – and last – Biennial for Contemporary Music (Madrid, 28 November 1964).[38]

All these fluctuating judgements, therefore, say a lot about the discontinuity and fragmentary nature of the reception of Messiaen's music in Spain at this time. They might also be seen, however, in the light of the paucity of information available to the Spanish media for their critical task. What useful resources, from a starting point of Messiaen's piano music of the 1940s and the *Trois Tâla*, could Montsalvatge draw upon in order to evaluate the 'harmonic acidity' ['acidez armónica'][39] of *Oiseaux exotiques*, on the occasion of its Spanish first performance?[40] Needless to say, with such a scarce framework of reference, only this kind of critical reaction could be expected:

> It's a music – actually, a series of organized sounds – entirely descriptive, but the useless description of some kind of infernal aviary, wherein it's sure that these winged animals live an apotheosis of ornithological madness.

> [Se trata de una música – en realidad una serie de sonidos organizados – totalmente descriptiva, pero una descripción inútil de una especie de pajarera

---

[36] Federico Sopeña, 'Música en Compostela: Resumen y perspectiva', *ABC* (30 August 1961): p. 36.

[37] Federico Sopeña, 'Música – Conciertos sacros: estreno de Oliver (sic) Messiaen', *ABC* (4 April 1963): p. 81.

[38] Federico Sopeña, 'La Orquesta Nacional, en la Bienal', *ABC* (1 December 1964): p. 85. Although a possible seminar by Messiaen and a concert by Yvonne Loriod were widely advertised by the press, they never took place. Instead, *Le Merle noir* was played by Severino Gazzelloni and Frederic Rzewski on 3 December.

[39] Xavier Montsalvatge, 'El XII Festival Internacional de Música y Danza de Granada – Resumen de los conciertos iniciales: Preponderancia de la música y los músicos españoles, con un elevado índice de aplausos a su favor', *La Vanguardia Española* (28 June 1963): p. 32.

[40] Given on 24 June 1963 by the Spanish National Orchestra conducted by Rafael Frühbeck de Burgos and with Pedro Espinosa featuring as soloist, at the International Festival of Music and Dance, Granada.

314   *Messiaen Perspectives 2: Techniques, Influence and Reception*

infernal, donde seguramente los alados animales viven una apoteosis de locura ornitológica.][41]

The lack of reliable bibliographical sources translated into Spanish also contributed to the confusion for quite some time. Only the publication, in 1965, of the Spanish version of Claude Samuel's *Panorama de l'art musicale contemporaine* (1962) allowed a reasonably updated approach to Messiaen.[42] Other introductory books available in Spain simply offered very general and out of date remarks on his music[43] and the Spanish translation of the *Technique de mon langage musicale* would have to wait until 1993.[44] No doubt, the planned translation of Antoine Goléa's *Rencontres avec Olivier Messiaen* (1960) could have remedied this musicological shortage, but it was never to be carried out.[45]

Messiaen and some Spanish Composers in the 1960s

The younger generation of Spanish musicians expressed enthusiasm for Messiaen's music. The so-called 'Generation of 51', comprising composers such as Cristóbal Halffter, Luis de Pablo, Ramón Barce or Carmelo Bernaola, stood out in the Spanish compositional panorama because of their eagerness for avant-garde music, their constant presence in small, but very active, publications and concert promotion organizations, and their persistent attendance at new music activities.[46] Through these, they achieved a partial acquaintance with Messiaen's music in the broader European post-war avant-garde.

---

[41]   So wrote the music critic Juan José Ruiz Molinero in the Granada journal *Ideal* (25 June 1963); quoted by José Luis Kastiyo and Rafael del Pino, *El Festival Internacional de Música y Danza de Granada (1952–2001)*, Vol. 1 (Granada: INAEM, 2001), p. 219.

[42]   Claude Samuel, *Panorama de la música contemporánea* (Madrid: Guadarrama, 1965), pp. 252–60.

[43]   Manfred Gräter, 'Olivier Messiaen', in *Guía de la música contemporánea* (Madrid: Taurus, 1966; German original, 1955), pp. 179–85; Hans Heinz Stuckenschmidt, *La música del siglo XX* (Madrid: Guadarrama, 1970; German original, 1969), pp. 167–8.

[44]   Olivier Messiaen, *Técnica de mi lenguaje musical*, trans. Daniel Bravo López, (Paris: Alphonse Leduc, 1993).

[45]   This translation was intended as the sixth number of a 'Libros de Música' collection, edited by the music critic Fernando Ruiz Coca between 1964 and 1966 for the publishing house Rialp.

[46]   Germán Gan Quesada, '*A la altura de las circunstancias*… Continuidad y pautas de renovación en la música española', in Alberto González Lapuente (ed.), *Historia de la música en España e Hispanoamérica*, Vol. 7, *La música en España en el siglo XX* (Madrid: Fondo de Cultura Económica, 2012), pp. 169–231.

Cristóbal Halffter (b. 1930) had tried to study with Messiaen in 1956.[47] He was unsuccessful, but he would receive classes from Jolivet and Tansman years later. Although Alberto Blancafort (1928–2004) preferred to study with Nadia Boulanger, both Luis de Pablo (b. 1930) and Carmelo Alonso Bernaola (1929–2003) attended Messiaen's course at Darmstadt in 1961 and each used *Technique de mon langage musical*, in self-study and during studies with Petrassi in Rome respectively.[48] In fact, Jean Boivin mentions only three Spanish pupils in his study about Messiaen's class at the Conservatoire: José Romero de Tajada[49] (Harmony) 1945–46, the pianist Manuel Carra (Introduction to Music Philosophy) 1958–59 and Amando Blanquer (1929–2005). Blanquer attended what was now the Music Analysis class for two years: 1961–62, when he was awarded a second prize, and 1962–63.[50] Already acquainted with Messiaen's theoretical work from his formative times in Valencia, Blanquer stayed in Paris between 1958 and 1962 and studied with Daniel-Lesur and Pierre Wissner before moving to study with Petrassi in Rome for two more years. He often recalled the composer's teachings, his 'great lesson, the lesson of freedom in musical creation'[51] and paid hommage to his former teacher in his third symphony, subtitled 'Transparences for Messiaen' and premièred in May 1994. Yet only Blanquer's piano works from the early 1960s, such as *Tres piezas breves* (1960) and *Variaciones para piano* (1963), show evident influences of Messiaen's modality and rhythm,[52] whereas the *Quatre preludis per a piano* (1975) look back to Messiaen's own early piano preludes.

As an occasional student, and through his friendship with Alain Messiaen, Joan Guinjoan (b. 1931) was able unofficially to attend some classes between 1962 and 1964.[53] The Catalonian composer would not forget this teaching: years later, he

---

[47] Hubert Daschner, *Spanische Musik auf der Höhe ihrer Zeit. Cristóbal Halffter* (Saarbrücken: PFAU Verlag, 2000), p. 61.

[48] José Luis García del Busto, *Carmelo Bernaola: La obra de un maestro* (Madrid: Fundación Autor – Diputación Foral de Bizkaia, 2004), pp. 62 and 64.

[49] More likely 'Tejada'.

[50] Jean Boivin, *La Classe de Messiaen* (Paris: Bourgois, 1995), pp. 412, 420 and 423. The cover of this book reproduces a photograph, shot by Robert Doisneau, that portrays Messiaen's class in 1961. Both this image and the one included in Anik Lesure and Claude Samuel, *Olivier Messiaen: Le livre du centennaire* (Lyon: Symétrie, 2008), p. 218, cut out its top left corner, in which Amando Blanquer appears almost hidden, as shown in M.ª Luisa Blanes Nadal, *Amando Blanquer: Vida y obra; Una aproximación a su repertorio pianístico* (Alicante: Instituto Alicantino de Cultura Juan Gil-Albert, 2006), p. 50.

[51] 'su gran lección, la de la libertad en la creación musical'. Amando Blanquer, 'Del diario íntimo', in *Primer encuentro de composición musical: Valencia 1988; Textos y ponencias* (Valencia: Generalitat Valenciana – Conselleria de Cultura, Educació i Ciència – Àrea de Música del IVAECM, 1989), pp. 37–42, p. 39.

[52] Blanes, *Amando Blanquer*, pp. 46–50.

[53] Xavier García and Agustín Charles Soler, *Joan Guinjoan* (Barcelona: Generalitat de Catalunya–Departament de Cultura, 1999), p. 32; José Luis García del Busto (ed.), *Joan Guinjoan: Testimonio de un músico* (Madrid: Fundación Autor, 2001), p. 46.

Example 12.1   Luis de Pablo, Sonata para piano, op. 3 (1958), bars 1–4[54]

made use of Messiaen's works as musical examples in a conference series about contemporary music in the Conservatorio Superior de Barcelona (May 1967), composed some works for ondes Martenot (*Dynamiques-Rythmes*, 1968; *Phobos*, 1978) and, as conductor of the contemporary music ensemble Diabolus in Musica, frequently performed Messiaen's music after 1974.

Luis de Pablo provides an instance of Messiaen and his music being held in especially high esteem.[55] He knew French modern music relatively well from the early 1950s through his contacts with Maurice Ohana and Jean-Étienne Marie. From 1957, Messiaen's piano and vocal music had made a deep impression,[56] as he recalled in 1991: 'I simply couldn't understand how a piano could sound in such a way.'[57] Some of Luis de Pablo's works of these years certainly have a 'messiaenesque' flavour. Even more than the 'strange cohabitation between Messiaen and Gregorian chant' of his *Missa Pax Humilium* (1956),[58] a good sample of this imprint can be seen in his one-movement Piano Sonata op. 3, composed in 1958 and premi+èred in 1960 by Pedro Espinosa (Example 12.1).

---

[54]   Unión Musical Española, UME 19508, 1960.

[55]   Piet de Volder, *Encuentros con Luis de Pablo: Ensayos y entrevistas* (Madrid: Fundación Autor, 1998), pp. 140–42.

[56]   José Luis García del Busto, *Luis de Pablo* (Madrid: Espasa-Calpe, 1979), p. 35.

[57]   'No podía comprender cómo era posible que un piano sonara de esa manera.' Volder, *Encuentros*, p. 140.

[58]   'extraño contubernio entre Messiaen y el gregoriano'. García del Busto, *Luis de Pablo*, p. 31.

Illustration 12.3 Luis de Pablo, 'Clave y ejemplo', *La Estafeta literaria*, 188 (1 March 1960): 20

318   *Messiaen Perspectives 2: Techniques, Influence and Reception*

It is clear from an examination of its first section ('Invención rítmica libre' – 'Free rhythmical invention'), that the invention is not entirely 'free'. Bar by bar, its patterns are based upon non-retrogradable rhythms, while its intervallic field is constructed upon a dodecaphonic series. This will later reveal itself to be polarized around its final pitch, A♭.[59]

In November 1958, Luis de Pablo had no doubts in admitting something so evident, almost anywhere but in Spain, as the route of dodecaphony as a 'legitimate evolution' of music and its being a 'live and updated path' for composition.[60] He included Messiaen as the only representative of the older generation in a cycle of conference-concerts held in the Ateneo of Madrid throughout 1960 and 1961 in which a series of younger composers (Berio, Boulez, Nono, Pousseur, Stockhausen and so on) was featured. His approach to the *Trois Petites Liturgies*[61] did not insist upon the virtues of their rhythmic and melodic-harmonic features but, rather meaningfully, considered them as an earlier step on the way towards a generalized serialism. From a more emotive viewpoint, Messiaen was an example of intellectual teaching and eager innovation from a mediating composer intertwining German and French traditions.[62]

Towards a Definitive Consolidation: 1965–78

From 1965 onwards, the number of Messiaen's works introduced to Spanish audiences did not tail off. Works such as *Quatuor pour la fin du Temps*,[63] *Les Offrandes oubliées*,[64] *Hymne*,[65] *Cinq Rechants*[66] and *Couleurs de la Cité céleste*[67]

---

[59] Mario Bortolotto, 'Agudeza y arte de teclado. Sobre las obras para piano de Luis de Pablo', in José Luis García del Busto (ed.), *Escritos sobre Luis de Pablo* (Madrid: Taurus, 1987), pp. 46–50.

[60] Luis de Pablo, 'El dodecafonismo: una técnica y una visión musical', *Acento cultural*, 2 (December 1958): pp. 49–53.

[61] He owned and studied a score of the *Trois Petites Liturgies* from the late 1940s; Ana Useros and César Rendueles, *Luis de Pablo: A contratiempo* (Madrid: Círculo de Bellas Artes, 2009), p. 15. The composer has also offered a recent commentary of the *Trois Petites Liturgies* in order to illustrate Messiaen's music; see Luis de Pablo, *Una historia de la música contemporánea* (Madrid: Fundación BBVA, 2009), pp. 30–33.

[62] Luis de Pablo, 'Clave y ejemplo', *La Estafeta literaria*, 188 (1 March 1960): p. 20.

[63] Barcelona, 18 January 1965; Madrid, 9 December 1965, The Gabrieli Consort. I have not been able to confirm a possible earlier performance of the *Quatuor* (Barcelona, 28 March 1960), scheduled at the 'First Series of Chamber Music Concerts' of Jeunesses Musicales and Club 49.

[64] Madrid-Barcelona, 7–8 May 1970, Orchestre de Paris, Serge Baudo.

[65] Madrid, 20–21 March 1971, Orquesta de Radiotelevisión Española, Igor Markevitch.

[66] Barcelona, 10 March 1972; Madrid, 14 March 1972, Solistes des Choeurs de l'ORTF, Marcel Couraud. A previously scheduled performance (Madrid, 11 January 1971) was cancelled.

[67] Madrid, 24 May 1974, Soloists of the Orquesta de Radiotelevisión Española, M.ª Elena Barrientos (piano), Odón Alonso.

were premièred in Spain, part of a slow but determined process that allowed more diverse understanding of his music. This greater understanding came both from a general aesthetic perspective – as displayed by the poet, composer and philosopher Juan Eduardo Cirlot (1916–73) in several articles published in Barcelona journals[68] – and from positions rooted in theological allegory. For example, the master of the chapel of Seville Cathedral, organist Norberto Almandoz (1893–1970), possessed an odd spiritual proximity to Messiaen. He had studied with Eugène Cools in Paris and, in the last five years his life, devoted several writings to Messiaen[69] and examined specific compositions such as *Réveil des oiseaux*[70] and the orchestral version of *L'Ascension*.[71]

The growing trickle of Spanish premières of these and other compositions points to a new appreciation of Messiaen, who encountered his first public recognition in the country. Although several potential commissions never reached fruition,[72] his appointment as Honorary Academic of the Real Academia de Bellas Artes de San Fernando in April 1973 and the awarding of the Luigi Dallapiccola Composition Prize in Barcelona in 1978 reflected a growing interest in the composer in Spain.

No doubt Messiaen's two visits to Spain around 1975 decisively reinforced this hard-won recognition. During the first trip, in autumn 1974,[73] he attended the Spanish première of the *Turangalîla-Symphonie* in Madrid on 19–20 October, performed by the Orquesta de Radiotelevisión Española conducted by Odón Alonso with Yvonne and Jeanne Loriod as soloists. On this occasion, the programme notes represented his visit as extremely important,[74] as did the

---

[68] Juan-Eduardo Cirlot, 'Los azules de Francia', *La Vanguardia Española* (11 June 1965): p. 7. He discusses the synaesthetic nature of *Cinq Rechants*. Enric Granell, *Juan Eduardo Cirlot: L'habitació imaginària* (Madrid/Barcelona: Ediciones Siruela-Centre d'Arts Santa Mònica, 2011).

[69] Norberto Almandoz, 'La personalidad de Olivier Messiaen', *ABC* (Seville) (19 June 1964): p. 61.

[70] Norberto Almandoz, '"El despertar de los pájaros", de Olivier Messiaen, curioso concurso', *ABC* (Seville) (6 May 1969): p. 76.

[71] Norberto Almandoz, '"La Ascensión", de Olivier Messiaen', *ABC* (Seville) (16 May 1969): p. 44.

[72] PHNS, p. 322 only mentions the commission of a *Salve regina* for a three-voice children's choir on the occasion of the composer's visit to Montserrat Abbey in October 1976. Two more commissions were intended, nevertheless, in these years, both thought to be premièred ad the Semana de Música Religiosa in Cuenca: a solo cello work for Reine Flachot in 1966 (Federico Sopeña, 'Concierto de Reine Flachot en el Ateneo', *ABC* (7 November 1965): p. 104) and a new organ work in 1971, encouraged by Sopeña, by then National Delegate for Music ('Interesantes planes de colaboración musical hispano-francesa', *La Vanguardia Española* (11 June 1971): p. 51).

[73] PHNS, p. 301.

[74] Programme notes reproduced in Enrique Franco, *Escritos musicales* (Madrid: Fundación Albéniz, 2006), pp. 247–52.

320 Messiaen Perspectives 2: Techniques, Influence and Reception

Spanish media in interviews[75] and articles that related several tributes paid to the composer at the French Embassy and at the Institut Français in Madrid.[76] In the pages of *Destino*, a journal of moderately progressive attitude, Xavier Montsalvatge showed his approval of *Turangalîla*'s 'bright and joyful expression of compositional freedom'.[77] By contrast, Sopeña's successor as music critic for *ABC*, Antonio Fernández-Cid (1916–95) – who had already objected to a certain 'poetic of excess' in the work[78] – supported his predecessor's preferences for Messiaen's 'pentagrams of a deeper, mystic and poetic sign'.[79]

Messiaen's later appearance had a much reduced impact. On this occasion, it was Barcelona,[80] where the Spanish première of *Et exspecto resurrectionem mortuorum*[81] had opened the International Festival of Music on 4 October 1976. A little later, the Messiaen–Loriod duo performed a selection of the *Vingt Regards* and *Visions de l'Amen* in a half-empty Palau de la Música Catalana, as they had done 27 years before. Now, however, they were greeted by 'very warm applause and bravos for the artists'.[82]

After years of fluctuating appreciation, Montsalvatge managed at last to summarize a resolute opinion, widely disseminated in the Spanish musical panorama, about the 'modern classicism' of Olivier Messiaen:

> Olivier Messiaen's stay at the Festival represents an undeniable event. He is, as is well known, one the principal composers in the world, whose works still attract

---

[75]   Concha Gil de la Vega, 'El maestro Messiaen: "No es la primera vez que vengo a España, antes ya estuve en Barcelona"', *La Vanguardia Española* (20 October 1974): p. 67; Amelia Die, 'Olivier Messiaen, músico místico', *ABC* (16 November 1974): p. 147; Manuel Chapa Brunet and José Luis Pérez de Arteaga, 'Conversación con Olivier Messiaen', *Reseña de literatura, artes y espectáculos*, 81 (January 1975): pp. 43–6, published earlier in *Ritmo*, 446 (November 1974): pp. 4–7.

[76]   Antonio Fernández-Cid, 'Olivier Messiaen, huésped de Madrid', *ABC* (18 October 1974): p. 90.

[77]   'luminosa y jubilosa manifestación de libertad compositiva'. Xavier Montsalvatge, 'La "Sinfonía Turangalila" de Olivier Messiaen', *Destino*, 1934 (26 October 1974): pp. 57–8.

[78]   Antonio Fernández-Cid. 'De Beethoven a Messiaen, pasando por Brahms, Chopin y Prokofieff, en Lucerna', *ABC* (7 September 1967): p. 70. At the time of a performance of *Turangalîla* at the Lucerne Festival, Fernández-Cid corroborated his first impression about the work from hearing it at the European première at Aix-en-Provence in 1950.

[79]   'pentagramas de signo más profundo, místico y poético'. Antonio Fernández-Cid, 'Odón Alonso dirigió a Yvonne y Jeanne Loriod y la orquesta de la RTV. E. el estreno madrileño de "Turangalila-Sinfonía", de Messiaen', *ABC* (22 October 1974): pp. 95–6.

[80]   PHNS, p. 322.

[81]   Orquestra Ciutat de Barcelona, Jean-Pierre Dupuy (piano), Gilbert Amy.

[82]   'ovaciones fogosísimas y bravos dedicados a los artistas'. Xavier Montsalvatge, 'El Festival Internacional de Música: Olivier Messiaen, compositor e intérprete', *La Vanguardia Española* (28 October 1976): p. 63.

controversy, even if they have already entered the catalogue of French music of the middle of the century. They are pieces of the highest significance and of a stylistic stability that the composer has been able to maintain throughout, without giving up a thoughtful evolution, independent from the main trends of contemporary music.

[La presencia del compositor Olivier Messiaen en el Festival representará un acontecimiento innegable. Se trata, es bien sabido, de uno de los primeros compositores mundiales, cuya obra continúa suscitando polémicas aun estando ya insertas en el catálogo de la música francesa de la mitad de nuestro siglo como piezas de la más alta significación y de una estabilidad estilística que el artista ha sabido mantener sin renunciar a una meditada evolución, independiente de las principales corrientes de la música contemporánea.][83]

Epilogue

After 1976, Messiaen visited Spain twice more, first in 1986 for a concert performance of his *Saint François d'Assise* (Madrid, 30 September) and then three years later, when his *Petites Esquisses d'oiseaux* were played by Yvonne Loriod (Madrid, 14 May 1989). Loriod was, in fact, the most celebrated guest when the Spanish capital's Autumn Festival paid tribute to the composer in 1994. The festival closed with the Spanish première of *Éclairs sur l'Au-Delà...* on 15 October (Spanish National Orchestra, Antoni Wit). Loriod also performed the piano part of *Des Canyons aux étoiles...*, again in Madrid, on 9 June 1999.

With these performances, 50 years of Messiaen in Spain in some respects came to a close. Much work on the composer remains to be done in Spanish musicology, and not only about reception issues.[84] Compositions such as *La Transfiguration*

---

[83]   Montsalvatge, Xavier, 'En el marco del Festival: Olivier Messiaen', *La Vanguardia Española* (24 October 1964): p. 54.

[84]   Not surprisingly, no Spanish contribution is recorded in Vincent P. Benitez, *Olivier Messiaen: A Research and Information Guide* (New York and London: Routledge, 2008). At least some relevant aesthetical and analytical essays should be added, nevertheless: José María Sánchez-Verdú, 'Estudios sobre la presencia del canto gregoriano en la composición musical actual a través del análisis de obras de O. Messiaen, G. Ligeti y C. Halffter', *Música*, 4–6 (1997–99): pp. 25–65. Yvan Nommick, 'Tradición, modernidad y sincretismo en el *Quatuor pour la fin du Temps* de Olivier Messiaen', *Quodlibet*, 25 (February 2003): pp. 14–44. Jordi-Agustí Piqué i Collado, 'Olivier Messiaen (1908–1992): La música-color o la contemplació del Misteri com a revelació del sentit', in *Teologia i Música: propostes per a un diàleg* (Barcelona: Publicacions de l'Abadia de Montserrat, 2006), pp. 236–61. This includes discussion of the 'Offrande et Alleluia final' from the *Livre du Saint Sacrement*. Trinidad Lull Naya, 'La extraordinaria contribución al mundo de la música de Olivier Messiaen', *Música y educación*, 75 (October 2008): pp. 14–22; 'Olivier Messiaen y el sonido-color', *Archivo de Arte Valenciano*, 90 (2009): pp. 213–22; 'Las

have yet to be performed in Spanish auditoria, while *Concert à quatre* was only heard in 2012.[85] Despite the lack of a suitable commemoration of the 20th aniversary of Messiaen's death, the huge success achieved by the five performances of *Saint François d'Assise* in July 2011 in Madrid surely confirm that the 'Spanish debt' to the figure and creative output of the composer of Avignon is beginning to be paid off.

---

formas gregorianizantes en el primer ciclo vocal de Olivier Messiaen: *Poèmes pour Mi*', *Quodlibet*, 49 (January–April 2011): pp. 49–73; 'Liszt, el gran ausente en el pensamiento musical de Olivier Messiaen', *Archivo de Arte Valenciano*, 92 (2011): pp. 279–93. Miguel Gironés, '*Préludes pour piano*, de Olivier Messiaen: Un acercamiento desde el análisis de conjuntos', *Quodlibet*, 46 (January–April 2010): pp. 3–14.

[85] Alicante, 21 September 2012, Orquesta Nacional de España, Juan Carlos Garvayo (piano), Robert Silla (oboe), José Satorres (flute), Ángel Luis Quintana (violoncello), Rubén Gimeno.

Chapter 13
Placing Mount Messiaen[1]

Robert Fallon

Although Olivier Messiaen's fondness for birds is far better known than his affinity for mountains, his music is nonetheless filled with a geological theme. Both birds and mountains connote high elevation and lead toward the heavens, but birds sing rapidly in a high tessitura, while rocks and mountains complement them with a ponderous tempo, a low tessitura, and an absence of melody. Messiaen's mountains represent, among other things, a form of time. He described 'superimposed times' in natural terms, referring to 'the immensely long time of the stars, the very long time of mountains, the average time of man, the short time of insects, and the very short time of atoms'.[2] The *Vingt Regards sur l'Enfant-Jésus* refers to stalactites and the *Messe de la Pentecôte* to caverns. A melody in *Livre d'orgue* traces the contours of the French Alps, the same landscape that opens the entire *Catalogue d'oiseaux*. The colours of *Couleurs de la Cité céleste* are those of gemstones listed in the Book of Revelation. The solemn, dense harmonies in *Et exspecto resurrectionem mortuorum* were his 'chords of granite'. *La Transfiguration de Notre-Seigneur Jésus-Christ* reflects on the biblical miracle on Mount Tabor, scenes from *Saint François* take place on Mount Verna, and *Livre du Saint Sacrement* contains birdsong notated on Israel's Mount of Temptation. Shortly before composing *Des Canyons aux étoiles...*, Messiaen planned a 'concerto des montagnes' that was to name its three movements after mountains in France, Iran and Switzerland.[3] Messiaen's commitment to the world beneath our feet even led him to invent an instrument, the geophone, to reproduce the song of the earth.

Summering in the foothills of the French Alps, where he found an environment conducive for composing, he allied himself intimately with the majesty of mountains:

> I love all of nature, and I love all landscapes, but I have a predilection for mountains because I spent my childhood in Grenoble and saw, from an early age, the mountains of the Dauphiné.[4]

---

[1]   I am grateful to Lenore Kitts, who helped me to research Mount Messiaen in Utah and interview Julie Whitaker in New York City.

[2]   See Olivier Messiaen, *Conférence de Bruxelles* (Paris: Alphonse Leduc, 1958), pp. 11–12, or *Traité I*, pp. 13–28.

[3]   PHNS, pp. 284–5.

[4]   *Music and Color*, p. 34.

In the reception of his music, Messiaen's love of these mountains has engendered an alpine love of Messiaen. Every summer since 1998, the Messiaen au Pays de la Meije music festival has honored him high in the French Alps, where Messiaen used to hike and write in his notebooks. The Meije glacier is shown on the cover to the score of *Livre d'orgue*.

The mountain most closely bound to Messiaen, however, is Mount Messiaen in the American Southwest, located among the geological wonders that he celebrated in *Des Canyons aux étoiles...*. The unusual naming of Mount Messiaen is intimately linked to the composition of *Des Canyons aux étoiles...*, one of his most admired works for large ensemble. Commissioned by Alice Tully for the American Bicentennial, Messiaen chose as a subject the most beautiful natural feature he could find in America. Though Hawaii came in a close second, Messiaen ultimately chose to celebrate three geologic wonders in southern Utah: Cedar Breaks, Bryce Canyon and Zion Park. These names are featured in the concluding movements of the three parts of the twelve-movement composition. Located near Cedar Breaks National Monument, Mount Messiaen was dedicated in response to his having recognized this landscape in *Des Canyons*.

Mountains do not normally honour composers; it is usually composers who honour mountains. Whether Beethoven's Mount of Olives, Mussorgsky's Bald Mountain in Kiev, Strauss's Bavarian Alps, Çetin Isiközlü's Mount Ararat, or Alan Hovhaness's Mount St Helens, such works often summon the musically sublime. Edmund Burke associated the sublime with a sense of terror. But sublime terror, I feel, is nearly absent from Messiaen's emotional range; his is the benign aesthetic of wonder, even in the face of granite monoliths.[5] Other composers have also celebrated Utah's mountains. Mount Timpanogos, outside of Provo, is the subject both of William F. Hanson's opera *The Legend of Timpanogos* (1937) and a 1992 ballet with a New Age electronic score by Michael Babbitt and choreography by Jacqueline Colledge.[6] Insofar as I am aware, only one other mountain has been named for a composer, and the naming took place after the dedication of Mount Messiaen: a peak on the southwest shore of Lake Agnes, about 50 miles northwest of Boulder, Colorado is called Mount Mahler.[7]

Helped by the lustre of Mount Messiaen, *Des Canyons* precipitated a new branch of Messiaen iconography, inspiring the publication of photographs of Messiaen in the Alps and at Cedar Breaks, a stream of CD, score and book cover art featuring mountains and conveying a sense of earthly grandeur and wide open

---

[5]   For a study of Messiaen's sometimes terrifyingly mechanical music, see Christopher Dingle, 'Sacred Machines: Fear, Mystery and Transfiguration in Messiaen's Mechanical Procedures', this volume.

[6]   For a fascinating cultural history of Mount Timpanogos, see Jared Farmer, *On Zion's Mount: Mormons, Indians, and the American Landscape* (Cambridge, MA: Harvard University Press, 2008).

[7]   See Robert C. Michael, 'Naming Mt. Mahler', *Pomona College Magazine*, 40/3 (Spring 2004): p. 55, available at pomona.edu/magazine/pcmsp04/AVfirstperson.shtml.

spaces. The 2001 edition of the *Grove Dictionary of Music* finds Messiaen's eponymous mountain a suitably impressive image to conclude the biographical section of his entry: 'Among the many honours bestowed on him during his last quarter century was the naming of a Utah mountain Mount Messiaen'. A widely viewed documentary, Olivier Mille's *Olivier Messiaen: La Liturgie de cristal* (2007), finds mountains so important to his identity that it opens with four minutes of spacious, spectacular mountain footage before cutting to and from scenes of Messiaen himself and eventually of Mount Messiaen.[8] From the first minutes of this film, one is led to associate Messiaen above all with the defamiliarizing strangeness of bare, craggy peaks.

As important as mountains were to Messiaen personally and as closely as he has come to be identified with them, Mount Messiaen and the canyons he painted in music suffer from a kind of identity crisis. Alain Périer's early monograph, *Messiaen,* for example, includes a cover picture of the Grand Canyon, even though the Grand Canyon plays no role whatsoever in Messiaen's music.[9] Or again, the cover image on the programme book of the première depicts a landscape like Monument Valley, a cowboy badlands with buttes rather than the life-filled canyons and hoodoos that inspired Messiaen during his stay in Utah.[10] Périer calls Mount Messiaen 'Messiaenax' and mistakenly says it's near the town of 'Pasowon', rather than Parowan. The webpage of French violinist Christophe Boulier also calls it 'Messiaenax' and claims it is near Salt Lake City.[11] In fact, Salt Lake City is 244 miles (410 km) from Mount Messiaen, a distance similar to Paris–Basel or London–Blackpool; Las Vegas is considerably closer. Such carelessness riddles the reception of Messiaen's mountains and runs counter to his own efforts to recreate the place in his music, for as much as his theological perspective is expressed in metaphor, the metaphor often begins with real-world places, actual birdsong and specific rock formations.

Mount Messiaen, or rather the *idea* and *existence* of a mountain named in the composer's honour, often exerts a special force on those who first learn about it. Acknowledging that his mountain is more an outcropping of impressive rocks than an entire mountain, however, Messiaen said that 'It is not necessary to exaggerate the importance of Mount Messiaen'.[12] Yet nor is it necessary to ignore its significance or to discourage inquiry into how the mountain affects attitudes to Messiaen. I have found that the existence of the named mountain impresses

---

[8]   Olivier Mille (dir.), *Olivier Messiaen: La Liturgie de Cristal*, 2002, DVD (2007), Ideale Audience International DVD9DS44. For a photograph of Mount Messiaen, see Catherine Massip (ed.), *Portrait(s) d'Olivier Messiaen* (Paris: Bibliothèque Nationale de Musique, 1996), p. 36, or Alain Périer, *Messiaen* (Paris: Éditions du Seuil, 1979), p. 168.

[9]   Alain Périer, *Messiaen*.

[10]   For a reproduction of this cover, see PHNS, p. 301.

[11]   See www.christophe-boulier.com/pages/compositeurs.html.

[12]   Brigitte Massin, *Olivier Messiaen: Une poètique du merveilleux* (Aix-en-Provence: Editions Alinea, 1989), p. 84.

and intrigues people, raises Messiaen's stature for them and evokes a moment of incredulity from the very novelty and seeming magnitude of the honour. Aware that the unusual power of Mount Messiaen opens such a cognitive empty space, I fill that space here by asserting how Mount Messiaen has become a place that, like Messiaen's music, transforms banal materiality into significant fantasy through an ecological accrual of memories and lived experience.

To this end, I have visited the mountain, interviewed Julie Whitaker, who led the dedication in Messiaen's name, and researched its dedication, problematic description, and the geology and human geography of the area. I have found useful some of the ideas of humanistic geographer Yi-Fu Tuan, whose *Space and Place: The Perspective of Experience* argues that the process of understanding a place comes from a sensitively felt, first-hand experience with it, in all its factors, ranging from the observer's age and mood to the place's relationship to time.[13] I write this sometimes first-hand account to fill out the story of Mount Messiaen, to explain and problematize its significance to fellow music tourists, and to facilitate the tourism itself.

Let me begin with directions for the journey.

From the intersection of Center Street and South Canyon Road (Rt. 143) in Parowan, Utah, drive south on Rt. 143. The trailhead to the pinnacles of Mount Messiaen is 8.8 miles down the road on the left. The turn onto this dirt road is not marked and not easily seen. Rt. 143 is a winding road, one lane in each direction. Shortly before the trailhead, the road curves sharply to the left – at which point the northern peaks first become visible, looming above the road – and then immediately curves right. Due to the cover of the trees, the peaks are not readily seen from this stretch of the road. After turning left onto the dirt logging road, follow it as it jogs left, then right. The cliffs are immediately to the left of the trail and the dedicatory plaque is located to the right of the trail amidst some trees. The plaque is embedded onto the southern face of a small boulder about 40 yards northeast of where the dirt road quietly begins off of Rt. 143. It is orientated so that if you are reading the plaque, you are facing the white sandstone pinnacles, which extend from about 37° 45'15" N to 37° 44'30" N along the meridian at 112° 50'10" W.[14] From the trailhead, the entrance to Cedar Breaks is a further 7.1 miles south from Parowan. At 11.2 miles is Sunset View, the dramatic lookout at Cedar Breaks where Messiaen experienced the 'Gift of Awe' evoked in the fourth movement of *Des Canyons*.

---

[13]   Yi-Fu Tuan, *Space and Place: The Perspective of Experience* (Minneapolis: University of Minnesota Press, 1977).

[14]   Photographs of Mount Messiaen are available at www.robertfallon.org.

Naming Mount Messiaen[15]

Naming Mount Messiaen was not a simple act of speaking it into existence. From idea to dedication took four years of ambitious effort, and the première of *Des Canyons* in Utah, proposed in the mid-1970s, did not take place until almost 30 years after the dedication, in 2007. The organizational dynamo behind the dedication was Julie Whitaker, who spent summers in Parowan as a child, grew up in Salt Lake City and learned to appreciate Utah from living in Paris for two years. 'Why did I do it?' she asked in my interview. 'Because I said I would!' Whitaker was a dancer and taught English at a prestigious private school in Manhattan. Her creativity and enterprising spirit appears to run in her family. Her ancestor was John Taylor, a Utah politician and third president of the Church of Latter Day Saints (LDS). A musician whose hymns are still printed in the LDS Hymnbook, he also published a missionary newspaper in France from 1851 to 1852 with the title *L'Étoile du Déséret*, a highly evocative but false cognate with *Des Canyons aux étoiles…* and its first movement 'Le Désert'. Whitaker's brother, Lyman, is a sculptor of kinetic art. In his studio near Zion Park, he models his large copper and steel sculptures, which move in the wind, on forms inspired by nature. He cast the dedicatory plaque and set it into the small boulder at a short distance from the foot of Mount Messiaen. Whitaker's husband is Michael Burke, also a sculptor, as well as a writer and former Columbia University professor with dozens of publications and exhibitions. His father was Kenneth Burke, the literary critic, philosopher and poet who wrote music criticism for *The Dial* and *The Nation* in the 1920s and 1930s.[16]

The story of the creation of Mount Messiaen has been told once before, in an article by Harriet Watts published in *Decade* (and republished in *Tempo*) in 1979.[17] Watts's article is, frankly, misleading. She claims that Mount Messiaen is located at White Cliffs, aka Lion's Peak. A Lion Peak exists at 38° 38' and 112° 20'40" while a Lion Rock appears on maps at 38° 12' and 112° 07', but neither is the location of Mount Messiaen. According to Whitaker, Watts meant to write 'Cougar's Peak', though that is a local name. As for the White Cliffs, Whitaker confessed to me: 'I just called them that.' Locating Mount Messiaen based on

---

[15]   The information in this section comes from my interview with Julie Whitaker, held at her home in New York City on 14 September 2007, and from the numerous letters and notes she generously shared with me that document her project, which she called Utah Salutes Messiaen.

[16]   For an account of this criticism, see Jeffery Carroll, 'The Song above Catastrophe: Kenneth Burke on Music', *KB Journal: The Journal of the Kenneth Burke Society*, 7/2 (Spring 2001), available at kbjournal.org/carroll.

[17]   Harriet Watts, 'Interview with Olivier Messiaen on the Influence of Landscape on his Latest Symphony, *From the Canyons to the Stars*', *Decade: The Magazine of Contemporary Arts and Culture* (March/April 1979): p. 8. This interview was also printed as 'Canyons, Colours and Birds: An Interview with Olivier Messiaen', *Tempo*, 179 (March 1979): pp. 2–8.

the names in Watts's article is thus a fool's errand. Such confusion about this landscape, as also portrayed on a book cover of the Grand Canyon and programme book cover of Monument Valley, extends even to definitions of what a mountain may be. Geologists have reached no consensus on the definition, as gleaned from the vague entry in the *Oxford English Dictionary*: 'A large natural elevation of the earth's surface, *esp.* one high and steep in form (larger and higher than a hill) and with a summit of relatively small area.' No minimum height, elevation, slope or shape is specified, reflecting the surprising state of perpetual rootlessness I find at the heart of Mount Messiaen. Despite its flaws, Watts's article includes an interview with Messiaen, who offers a response to the mountain less humble than that quoted above:

> Ah, it's just incredible and very touching. When I told my impresario [Herbert Breslin] about it, he was amazed. When I told my publisher M. Leduc in Paris about it, he was astounded, too. He couldn't imagine that there would be a mountain anywhere with my name; at first he laughed, but then he almost cried. And we plan to go back there soon. It's a great excuse to see Utah again, and, in any case, it seems to me that I now have the obligation to present myself before those three cliffs. They're there waiting for me.

Unfortunately, Messiaen never saw his mountain in person.

On 1 May 1972, Messiaen had travelled to Utah for ten days' research into *Des Canyons aux étoiles…*, which premièred on 20 November 1974. While Messiaen was visiting Utah and composing *Des Canyons*, Whitaker was living at 39 Rue de la Harpe in Paris's Fifth Arrondissement, where she became acquainted with Messiaen's music. Back in New York during the holiday season of 1975–76, she learned that *Des Canyons* had been inspired by the landscapes of southern Utah. In her chronology of the event, she writes, 'I thought it would be great fun to name a mountain for him somewhere in that beautiful landscape'[18] and in a letter dated 20 May 1976, she described to a friend how the naming came about:

> Messiaen attended the music conferences at Tanglewood last summer. In one of his speeches he described the country of Southern Utah as the most beautiful, sensuous and bizarre, that he had ever visited. As a result, he wrote a symphony inspired by that country. I was delighted and honoured to learn of this. I too find the country strange and exciting. So – I decided that something should be named for him. When I was in Southern Utah, Parowan to be exact, I contacted the Mayor and asked him if he didn't agree. He did. In fact, he offered his own mountain for the occasion. It is indeed a beautiful mountain, located about 15 miles from a national park called Cedar Breaks, which Messiaen specifically mentioned in an interview as one of the areas which had so moved him.

---

[18] Julie Whitaker-Burke, 'Utah Salutes Messiaen Chronology', unpublished.

Placing Mount Messiaen 329

> When I returned to New York, I spoke with some friends, pianists who had spent the last year in Paris, and asked them if they knew how I might get in touch with Messiaen. They gave me the name and address of Denise Tual, a woman who had made a film, sponsored by the French Ministry of Cultural Affairs, of Messiaen's life and work.

At the advice of piano-duo team Arthur Gold and Robert Fizdale, Whitaker contacted the producer of the documentary *Olivier Messiaen et les oiseaux*, Denise Tual, who forwarded her proposal to Messiaen in February 1976. On 7 March 1976, Messiaen responded with a gracious letter acceding to the festival. He reports he is very happy and honoured, and even suggests that, in lieu of a mountain, a pathway for birdwatchers would suffice, or a mountain or just a rock at one of the three parks, or even just a street in her hometown of Parowan, north of Cedar Breaks.

Whitaker's initial plan was to dedicate the mountain, screen Tual's film and throw a festival of Messiaen's music in September 1976, the bicentennial year for which *Des Canyons* was commissioned. Whitaker's mother spoke with Utah Governor Scott Matheson and learned that national landmarks cannot be named after living persons without an act of Congress. She thus sought advice from Kendall Gurr (1926–2012), mayor of Parowan from 1970 to 1978. Gurr owned the mountain at the time and offered it for the occasion, since he was able to give it any name he wished.

In May 1976, Tual arranged to have her film subtitled in English with the help of the French Minister of Cultural Affairs, and French President Giscard d'Estaing was told of the planned festival in preparation for his visit to the United States that month. Whitaker also sought the help of photographer Jean Cartier, who was working at French Cultural Services in New York. In June, discussions focused on televising the mountain's dedication, with Tual suggesting that both Messiaen and Pierre Boulez should be present and that Whitaker would participate in the televised event. Both Whitaker and Tual agreed, however, that the September target date was too early to make all necessary arrangements.

In the late summer, Whitaker's ideas for the festival grew. She met with Charles Bestor of the University of Utah School of Music, who suggested that a week-long festival take place at Snowbird, a mountain resort outside of Salt Lake City, that would be integrated into the school's summer coursework. She contacted personnel at the University of Utah who could show Tual's film and reached out to the Museum of Fine Arts about exhibiting paintings inspired by southern Utah, such as those by Jimmy Jones. She envisaged a festival with Messiaen lecturing on his music at the University of Utah, culminating in a performance of *Des Canyons*. The festivities would include performances by Yvonne Loriod, the sceening of Tual's film, and dance and painting inspired by southern Utah.

In November 1976, Whitaker formally invited Messiaen to the festival called 'Utah Salutes Messiaen', with the hope that the Utah Symphony would participate. The Messiaens' expenses were to be underwritten by French Cultural Services in

New York. He accepted the invitation in a letter of 4 December 1976, requested that *Des Canyons aux étoiles…* be on the program with his wife Yvonne Loriod as the piano soloist and committed to being present from 7 to 13 August 1977.

On 14 February 1977, however, Messiaen requested the August date be moved to November, presumably because August interfered with his summer *vacances,* during which he composed at his home in the south-east of France. The proposed date for the festival, however, would have conflicted with the regular concert season of the Utah Symphony, and thus presented more problems. For the conductor of *Des Canyons* he suggested Seiji Ozawa, Zubin Mehta, Pierre Boulez, Pierre Dervaux, Miltiades Caridis, Odon Alonso and Louis Lane, and provided their addresses. He detailed the instrumentation and also suggested *Hymne, Réveil des oiseaux*, *Oiseaux exotiques*, and *Et exspecto resurrectionem mortuorum* for a second orchestral concert. Another delay soon followed. Writing to Whitaker on 1 May 1977, he explained how he injured himself in a fall: 'Il y a un mois, j'ai pris mon pied dans un arceau de fer destiné à empêcher les parkings. et j'ai fait une chute grave.'[19] Indeed, in March 1977, Messiaen tripped outside the Guy Moquet Métro station, broke his glasses, bloodied his face and cut his ankle. He required immediate stitches on his eyebrows, nose, and lips and underwent surgery on his ankle the following month.[20] Nonetheless, having received photos of Mount Messiaen from Whitaker, he wrote of his enthusiasm: 'C'est vraiment magnifique et je me réjouis de voir un jour l'original.'[21] Due to his injuries, however, he also requested the dedication and festival be rescheduled for a year later, November 1978 instead of 1977.

The next month, Whitaker wrote to Messiaen that the Utah Symphony had agreed to cooperate fully with the project, when in fact she had secured only the collaboration of composer Charles Bestor, then chair of the University of Utah's Department of Music, which in turn collaborated at times with the Symphony. Feeling a need to raise money for the festival, she travelled to Washington, DC to meet with Utah Senators Jake Garn and Orin Hatch to request funding. Congressman Dan Marriott wrote a letter of support for her as well, but assumed the funding would come from the French government. Whitaker sought to involve the senators as a way of gaining legitimacy for the festival. The politicians supported her project in person, but did not arrange for any financial assistance. She sent letters to potential donors and wrote to Seiji Ozawa and Zubin Mehta, asking them to conduct the Utah Symphony outside its regular season, and founded a non-profit organization called Utah Salutes Messiaen to solicit funds for the festival. Her partner Michael Burke (they married in 1979) created a letterhead with a drawing that resembles the most widely circulated photograph of the mountain.

---

[19] 'A month ago, I caught my foot in an iron hoop meant to prevent parking, and I took a serious fall.'

[20] PHNS, p. 316.

[21] 'It's truly magnificent and I look forward to seeing the original one day.'

After writing to him at the end of February, Whitaker met with Maurice Abravanel, conductor of the Utah Symphony, in his home in March, where, she says, 'he attacked me for my impudence: "Young lady, do you not know that you cannot mix art and politics? How dare you!"' Abravanel was put off by the idea of a young woman organizing the festival without his consent and with the involvement of senators and other political dignitaries. His opposition to the festival sank the ambitious project.

In April 1977, Whitaker wrote to Messiaen to announce that the festival was cancelled for lack of funding and lack of Abravanel's cooperation (and thus the participation of the Utah Symphony), though the naming of the mountain would still take place in August. She invited the Messiaens to stay in her parents' home. On 19 June, Whitaker visited Messiaen at his home in Paris, where she was served wine from one of his student's vineyards and marvelled at the photographs of birds adorning the walls. When she described her difficulties in obtaining Abravanel's cooperation, he exclaimed, 'Abravanel est fou!'

In July 1978, his schedule booked tight with 70th birthday celebrations in Japan, Poland, France, and the United States, Messiaen sent a telegram to Whitaker saying that he could not participate in the 5 August christening of the mountain. The naming ceremony then took place without him. Most of those present were members of the Parowan Cultural Committee, the group of friends of Julie Whitaker's parents who gave themselves the authority to name the mountain, with the blessing of the mayor and owner of the mountain, Kendall Gurr, and the governor of Utah, Scott M. Matheson. The committee's name appears on the dedicatory plaque. 'We, my sister and I and my brothers – we all laughed', Whitaker recalled. 'We called ourselves the Parowan Cultural Committee .... There was no Cultural Committee. It was our family! It was a joke.' The committee may have been formed in jest, but the desire to name the mountain was quite serious, as the ordeal over the festival makes clear.

The dedication celebration was televised by station KTVX news. At 6:00 pm, they unveiled the bronze plaque, cast by Julie's brother Lyman, and held a ribbon-cutting ceremony.[22] At 7:30 the exhibition of Jean Cartier's photos of Utah opened at the local high school. At 8:00, the ceremony continued with a prayer, a reading of Utah Governor Scott Matheson's declaration of 'Olivier Messiaen and the Beauty of Southern Utah Day', a speech by Whitaker about Messiaen, and a performance of Messiaen's *Chants de terre et de ciel* by Naomi and Lowell Farr, musicians on the faculty of the University of Utah. The combined choirs of three local church wards sang 'Battle Hymn of the Republic' and 'This is America'. A reception at the Whitaker home followed at 9:00 pm. Whitaker wrote to Messiaen about the event in September and informed him of the governor's declaration.

For his part, Messiaen noted the events of that day in his diary:

---

[22] The plaque is now under the jurisdiction of the Utah Department of Transportation (UDOT), which calls it the Olivier Messiaen Marker.

332 Messiaen Perspectives 2: Techniques, Influence and Reception

5 August. In the morning the naming of Mount Messiaen – unveiling of the plaque on the rock. In the evening, a performance of my *Quatuor pour la fin du Temps* by students of the Aspen Conservatory, a showing of the film by Denise Tual, *Messiaen et les oiseaux,* an exhibition of photos by J. S. Carter [sic] on southern Utah.[23]

Nearly 30 years after the collapse of the festival, the approach of Messiaen's centenary finally mobilized the Utah Symphony to honor Messiaen. Jason Hardink, Principal Symphony Keyboard of the Utah Symphony, and Jeff Counts, then Artistic Administrator, proposed a Messiaen Festival in collaboration with other Salt Lake ensembles. Hardink had long championed Messiaen's piano music in recital. On 27 April 2007, conductor Keith Lockhart and the Utah Symphony at last gave the Utah première of *Des Canyons aux étoiles*.... The Symphony invited Julie Whitaker as a special guest and publicly recognized her at the concert for her central role in naming Mount Messiaen.

Before and After Mount Messiaen

Despite the dedication and the 2007 festival, 'Mount Messiaen' remains an unofficial name; it cannot be found on any map of this vast, sparsely populated desert landscape. To make sense of such open space, geographer Yi-Fu Tuan says one must pause and 'get to know it better and endow it with value'.[24] On my pilgrimage to discover, experience and make sense of Mount Messiaen, the values I carried with me into southern Utah were musical and historical, and the values I gathered there were geological. The on-site mixture of memory and experience, of music and mountain, constitute the meaning I found in Mount Messiaen. The geology and human history of the area directed my thoughts and, reciprocally, my knowledge of Messiaen determined the meaning of the landscape. The empty space did not passively absorb my projections of Messiaen and become the place that now so shapes Messiaen reception. Rather, the literal, physical geology also moulded my figural understanding of Messiaen. I had expected to find Mount Messiaen easily, but it was difficult to find. I had expected it to be overtly grandiose, but the spires are modest in relation to the national parks honoured in *Des Canyons.* Turned outward toward nature, I found that nature directed my thoughts into myself, into a difficult and humble experience of my own musically and geographically informed interiority. Messiaen's values of quietude were mine and were often shared by the land; in turn, the humility of my experience there and of the hidden mountain renewed my appreciation for Messiaen's modesty – the long pauses between movements, the meditative tempi, the simple monodies, the exaltation of birdsong rather than his own music. At stake here are the definitions

---

[23]   PHNS, p. 320. Messiaen was mistaken about the performance of the *Quatuor.*

[24]   Tuan, *Space and Place,* p. 6.

of space and place. Experiencing Mount Messiaen created a contiguity of space and place where imagination and the physical environment formed a hermeneutic circle, each enlightening the other in the production of an intriguing but enigmatic memorial in Messiaen reception.

Let me now continue on the journey.

Geology is inescapable in this country. Roadside gift shops feature semi-precious stones and the National Park Visitors Centres are packed with books on local geological history. By flooding, uplifting and erosion, the surrounding peaks rose and took on their peculiar shapes. As Messiaen well understood, geology unfolds history: it is the biography of the planet. Geology's most fundamental assumption is the principle of *uniformitarianism*, the belief that the world today behaves with the same processes that were at work millions of years ago building and destroying mountains, seas, plains and shores. Like much of Messiaen's music, geology is not teleological. Its concern with deep time may explain Messiaen's fascination with it, but its prevalence in the region's culture explains my own geologically-informed interpretation of Mount Messiaen, of which I now offer a second history, one that long predates the dedication ceremony. In his celebrated book of American geology, *Annals of the Former World*, John McPhee has explained geological time in this striking formulation:

> Geologists will sometimes use the calendar year as a unit to represent the time scale, and in such terms the Precambrian runs from New Year's Day until well after Halloween. Dinosaurs appear in the middle of December and are gone the day after Christmas. The last ice sheet melts on December 31st at one minute before midnight, and the Roman Empire lasts five seconds.[25]

I follow a similar geological chronology as I meld Messiaen's desert mountain into my own experience of the landscape.

Zooming in from a satellite's perspective, Mount Messiaen occupies the south-west corner of the Colorado (meaning 'red-coloured') Plateau. Occupying a circle at the Four Corners, where southern Utah, northern Arizona, south-west Colorado, and north-west New Mexico intersect at right angles, the Colorado Plateau fragmented into smaller plateaus due to faulting. Bryce is on the Paunsaugunt Plateau, while Zion is on the older, 28- by 50-mile Markagunt Plateau. The sand dunes that became Zion's Great White Throne and Three Patriarchs formed as long ago as 240 million years, when the land was roughly where Honduras sits today. The dunes formed the bed of the ancient Lake Flagstaff, the silt coming from erosion from the Ancestral Rockies. The lake's shellfish secreted the calcium carbonate that, when crushed, glued the sand into stone. Some 50 to 16 million years ago, uplift drained the seas. The Pacific and North American Plates slammed into one another, raising the elevation to about 10,000 feet in

---

[25] John McPhee, *Annals of the Former World* (New York: Farrar, Straus, Giroux, 1998), p. 89.

some places, including Cedar Breaks and Mount Messiaen. The faulting created the south-western escarpment of the Colorado Plateau, which geologists call the Grand Staircase. Rising from old age to youth as it moves from south to north and from a lower to a higher elevation, the lowest step is the Grand Canyon, while its highest step is Bryce Canyon and, indeed, Mount Messiaen. In the middle is Zion Canyon and the White Cliffs. Other steps in the Grand Staircase are called the Chocolate, Vermillion, Gray and Pink Cliffs. Following the uplift, erosion from wind, rain and the Green, Colorado and Virgin Rivers unglued the stone, carrying away the silt, cracking the rock and oxidizing the iron. Erosion sculpted astonishing shapes and revealed the colours from the earth. Water once created the rocks and, reversing itself like Messiaen's non-retrogradable rhythms, now disintegrates them, temporarily creating the parkland formations visited today.

In wild landscapes lacking in spatial coordinates, orientation comes from relating park landmarks to one another. The main entrances to the three parks create an 'r' shape on the map, with Cedar Breaks in the north-west, Zion about 25 miles due south and Bryce about 35 miles due east. The three geological wonders celebrated in *Des Canyons* require a progressively higher perspective and occupy a progressively lower elevation. Ending the first part, 'Cedar Breaks and the Gift of Awe' is inspired by the most precipitous drop of the three parks, some 2,500 feet, starting at about 10,450 feet above sea level. At the end of the second part, 'Bryce Canyon and the Red-Orange Rocks' celebrates the hoodoos of Bryce, whose elevation is over a thousand feet below that of Cedar Breaks. Towers, spires, knobs, hammers and holy steeples rise from the red desert. Concluding the entire work is 'Zion Park and the Celestial City', named for the Mormon dream of a homeland free of religious persecution, a place 100 million years older than Bryce Canyon. The progression of movements traces a spiritual journey from the canyons to the stars and beyond toward heaven, after the medieval reconception of Ptolomy's geocentric cosmology. This upward and outward motion is paralleled by the experience of visiting the parks. One looks down from the rim of Cedar Breaks. At Bryce, one may look down or, after walking the trails, look up at the hoodoos. In the floor of Zion Park, eyes rise to see the tops of the tremendous monoliths.

Bryce and Cedar Breaks are part of the Claron Formation, a rock layer created during the late Paleocene and Eocene Epochs about 50–60 million years ago and notable for its pink colour – the Pink Cliffs of the Grand Staircase. McPhee has explained the source of the brilliant reds in the rocks of Utah. On account of constantly shifting sea levels some 300 to 200 million years ago, huge quantities of plant and animal life were buried. He writes:

> Their carbon would be buried with them – isolated in rock – and so the amount of oxygen in the atmosphere would build up. All over the world, so much carbon was buried in Pennsylvanian time that the oxygen pressure in the atmosphere quite possibly doubled. … Where could [the oxygen] go? After carbon, the one other thing it could oxidize in great quantity was iron – abundant, pale-green

Placing Mount Messiaen

ferrous iron, which exists everywhere, in fully five per cent of crustal rock; and when ferrous iron takes on oxygen, it turns a ferric red.[26]

Colour therefore correlates to the time the rock was created, a linkage between colour and time that Messiaen had previously explored in his orchestral works *Chronochromie* and *Couleurs de la Cité céleste*.

The first people presumed to see these colours, nomadic Paleo-Indians, arrived 15,000 years ago and stayed for 5,000 years. About 2,000 years ago, the Fremont peoples and ancestral Puebloans carved abstract petroglyphs and pictographs into the rock; they left the area some 800 years ago, replaced by the Utes, Paiutes and Navajo. The first Europeans to explore the area were on the 1776 Dominguez-Escalante Expedition, which passed through nearby Cedar City. In the early nineteenth century, trappers and mountain men lived here, followed soon by Mormons in 1849, shortly after they settled in Salt Lake City. Mormons founded Parowan in 1851, which served as home to 862 people in 1871 and 1,640 when Messiaen visited the area in the early 1970s. In the 1850s, Ebenezer Bryce settled near the eponymous hoodoos and lamented that the area was 'a helluva place to lose a cow'. Indeed, the spires are gothic and labyrinthine; they invite tourists like Messiaen on a spiritual journey. The US Army explored the area in 1859, followed by Major John Wesley Powell's expedition from 1869 to 1872. By 1919 Zion was declared a National Park; Bryce followed in 1928 and Cedar Breaks became a National Monument in 1933. Wallace Stegner's essay 'High Plateaus' begins by distinguishing this region from other icons of the American West, such as the Great Basin, the Rockies and the mesas, and devotes four paragraphs to the French, German and Japanese tourists who populate the parks today. Prefiguring Messiaen's experience, Stegner said that 'what most recommends the plateaus and their intervening valleys and deserts is space, emptiness, silence, awe'.[27]

Mount Messiaen is found about eight miles north of Cedar Breaks, forming with the other parks the top of a kind of asymmetrical, Nordic cross. The only geological description of Mount Messiaen appears in Herbert Gregory's *Geology of Eastern Iron County, Utah* (1950):

> The Kaiparowits formation in the drainage basin of Parowan Creek is represented by detached masses brought into view by faulting, and its characteristic erosion forms are cliffs, steep canyon walls, and sharply outlined mesas, ridges, and picturesque pinnacles. In general view the formation in this area appears as thick

---

[26]   Ibid., 30.

[27]   Wallace Stegner and Page Stegner, 'High Plateaus' in *American Places* (New York: Penguin Classics, 2006), p. 137. Incidentally, Stegner also wrote a biography of one of the most important chroniclers of the American West, Pulitzer-winner Bernard DeVoto, father of music theorist Mark DeVoto.

irregular beds of sandstone and huge lenses of conglomerate, white or yellow-gray in colour.[28]

A thick talus apron rises to the base of Mount Messiaen's 300-foot cliffs (elevation c. 9,025 feet), serving as a buffer between the vertical stone and horizontal canyon road. The mountain is topped with an earthen red hat, though its prominent spires are white sandstone and conglomerate. Rising above Rt. 143 in what is sometimes called 'Colour Country', surrounded by Engelmann spruce and subalpine fir, quaking aspen and various mountain grasses and flowers, Mount Messiaen appears on the route of what Reader's Digest has called one of the most beautiful drives in America.[29]

On my pilgrimage in late July 2007, I felt Stegner's silence, but also heard the wind, the rustling birch trees, the twittering and screaming swallows. I saw a raven and White-throated Swifts at Cedar Breaks, as I did at Mount Messiaen. I heard the call of the Pinyon Jay and, I think, the clear, quick chirrup of a Snowy Tree Cricket. At Zion's Weeping Rock, I heard a crystalline Canyon Wren. At Bryce I saw chipmunks, mule deer, Blue Grouse, swallows and a flicker. I heard the songs of two iridescent green hummingbirds on Navajo Loop Trail, many swallows, a Scrub Jay.

At the base of Mount Messiaen's pinnacles is sand. Seen from the west, I count nine pinnacles. Though the smaller square-shaped ones are indistinct, the view may be represented with these typographic shapes: ⌂∏∏∏∏∏∏ÅΔ – a miniature range far more expansive than the three peaks seen in the earliest photographs. The right-most peak looks like a beehive with a tip of red earth topped by Christmas trees; to the left of it is the peak some call the Rock Frog. Between the pathway and the near-vertical cliffs is a small arch known locally as the Jug Handle. The sandstone here has been mined for silica. Below the pinnacles are black-and-white cliffs, city-like in appearance, in intricate formations, several with small spires. Mount Messiaen is the most prominent geological feature of Parowan Canyon and serves in retrospect as an excellent, intimate prelude or postlude to a visit to Cedar Breaks. Trips to Bryce Canyon and Zion Park require of travellers at least one further day each.

Like the ellipses in the title of *Des Canyons aux étoiles…*, my search for Mount Messiaen yielded not a single place but a sense of endlessness, a problematic mountain. Expecting three pinnacles, I found nine, plus a red mountaintop. I then discerned the mountain's indistinct boundaries, an increasing mass of rock and earth that could not be confined to a preconception of what a mountain is (as shown above, it is unclear what a mountain is).

---

[28]   Herbert E. Gregory, *Geology of Eastern Iron County, Utah*, published as the *Utah Geological and Mineralogical Survey Bulletin*, 37 (February 1950): p. 51.

[29]   Robert J. Dolezal, *The Most Scenic Drives in America: 120 Spectacular Road Trips* (Pleasantville, NY: Reader's Digest, 1997), p. 134.

The unreality of the landscape invites figurative thinking. The Paiutes had referred to the hoodoos, for example, as Legend People. I, too, began to link geology, history and spirituality into a web of theological metaphor, of spiritual place, as *Des Canyons* invites this spiritual journey, its deserts, rocks and stars used both as reality and symbol. Mount Messiaen's stone is highly friable, embodying the crumbling of mountains and time that occupies the heart of Messiaen's message, a message to look from the impermanent earth to the longer-lasting stars and beyond to the eternity of heaven. The sandstone pinnacles are capped with durable limestone that prevents the rock below it from dissolving and that suggests a separation of the wheat from the chaff based on what endures. As one of the pinnacles is said to have recently been home to a hermit, one of the birds in *Des Canyons* is a Hermit Thrush and one of the layers of rock in the Grand Canyon is called Hermit Shale. Another is called Bright Angel Shale. This is a region where the outside reflects what is inside. The oldest layers of rock at the bottom of the Grand Canyon are the Pre-Cambrian schists called Brahma and Vishnu, named for Hindu gods that Messiaen referred to in his music. His music is frequently labelled with colours, as in the movement titled 'Bryce Canyon and the Red-Orange Rocks'. In person, with shifting light and ubiquitous, personality-laden rock coming in all tints and shades, the uncanny colours come to life. In addition to visual colour, an obvious attraction for Messiaen must have been the verbal colour from the Old Testament nomenclature that the Mormon settlers gave to Zion Canyon and its stupefying stone sites: Temple of the Patriarchs, Angel's Landing, Cathedral Mountain, Great White Throne, Altar of Sacrifice and The Organ. Before the Mormons, in 1776, the Fransiscan Fathers Sylvestre Velez de Escalante and Atanasio Dominguez had named the river that created Zion Canyon after the mother of their New Testament God: the Virgin River. At Bryce one finds Fairyland Point, Silent City, Cathedral – all of them with names that resonate in Messiaen's all-consuming, fantastic Christian cosmology of nature and culture.

Working over my memories of visiting Mount Messiaen, I construct the sights and sounds, the open air, the colours, the maps and roads of the landscape, into something that evokes Messiaen's music. Cultural critic Andreas Huyssen has said: 'Remembrance as a vital human activity shapes our links to the past, and the ways we remember define us in the present. As individuals and societies, we need the past to construct and to anchor our identities and to nurture a vision of the future'.[30] My memories and re-memories shape and reshape the experience of the pilgrimage to Mount Messiaen. The vacant landscape wants filling; it calls upon identities and metaphors to impart significance to it. It is undifferentiated *space* that pulls in meaning and progressively turns with memories and experience into a *place*. This process, too, like the uplift and the eroding rain, forms Mount Messiaen. The motivation for the memories we construct, however, depends on

---

[30] Andreas Huyssen, 'Monument and Memory in a Postmodern Age', in James E. Young (ed.), *The Art of Memory: Holocaust Memorials in History* (New York: Prestel: 1994), p. 9.

Messiaen Perspectives 2: Techniques, Influence and Reception

who makes them. Julie Whitaker wished to express her exuberant gratitude that a famous Frenchman had recognized the quiet corner of her childhood. The Utah governor identified Messiaen for his purposes of promoting the scenic beauty of the region, undoubtedly with an eye towards advancing the area's strong tourism industry. Both of them probably felt that the European sophistication afforded by a celebrated composer bestowed on southern Utah a cultural legitimacy that the otherwise meagre cultural offerings of a desert town sparsely settled by religious outcasts could not offer. The area's culture clearly centres on its evocative nature.

Given the local, familial history behind Julie Whitaker's naming of Mount Messiaen, it is surprising that the mountain has come to add so profoundly to Messiaen's lustre. Its inherent grandeur and apparent permanence, its novelty and monumentality differentiate it from other possible memorials, such as a plaque or statue. In this irony, Mount Messiaen is an 'anti-monument' that, as James E. Young has observed in his book *The Art of Memory*, challenges the notion of monuments themselves. An anti-monument resists the normal work of monuments, which is to evoke the memory of the person or event commemorated. Instead of declaring the memory, it places the burden of creating the memory onto the visitor.[31] In this way, the memory of Messiaen, the meaning of his music and his career, is always unfinished and always changing with each new individual's virtual or real encounter with Mount Messiaen, the monument that reflects back to us our thoughts on Messiaen reception. The pinnacles and talus do not collect, interpret or preserve Messiaen for us. Rather, they provide a slate (or white sandstone) onto which we project our understanding of Messiaen. But the slate is not blank. The colours, shapes, sounds and names all point the musical tourist suggestively toward agents in Messiaen's cosmology.

The mountain begs for substance and significance. In this way, it is the opposite of the *lieu de mémoire* discussed by Pierre Nora, which absorbs the responsibility of remembering, removing the burden from the individual and society. Its significance emerges most palpably from the interplay of space and time, where two billion years of geology are visible in the two vertical miles of stone along the Grand Staircase, giving a sense that all of time is immediately accessible. The meaning emerges from the transhistorical traces of placenames given by Paiutes, Spanish and Mormon explorers, all of whom named the wondrous geology after supernatural or biblical people and places.

Reflecting on Mount Messiaen and my experience there, my memories seek to identify with Messiaen as the mountain itself is identified with him. I think on recreating his process of making metaphors from mountains, the process that led him to compose his music and that led Julie Whitaker to name the mountain, the process that now makes people marvel at the earth honouring an artist. None of it would have been possible without the gravity-defying rock formations of Bryce, Zion and Cedar Breaks. As Jared Farmer has written in his 2008 book *On Zion's*

---

[31]   James E. Young, 'The Art of Memory: Holocaust Memorials in History', in Young (ed.), *The Art of Memory*, p. 37.

Mount: Mormons, Indians, and the American Landscape, certain places join two landscapes: 'a perceptual landscape overlaps the physical one. These layers of reality are not glued together in smooth and permanent contiguity; instead, they are fastened together at points. Landmarks are these fastening-points. We use them for orientation. They are the icons of our mental maps'.[32] Similarly, the reception of Mount Messiaen takes shape both in its orogenesis and in the reception of this very chapter as it was written and is now read.

Such is the process of Mount Messiaen's continual uplift and erosion – but what does the mountain mean? The problematic identity of Mount Messiaen arises not only from its protracted naming process, tumultuous geological genesis or its history of misrepresentation. The very relationship of Mount Messiaen to an ever-mutable sense of time works against its identity. On one level, a visitor is unlikely to sit long hours there or visit day after day – perhaps a local could do so, but not a music tourist. On another level, the pervasive sense of geological time subverts the sense of the place. 'Permanence is an important element in the idea of place', writes Tuan.[33] 'If we see the world as process', he says, 'constantly changing, we should not be able to develop any sense of place.'[34] The synoptic sense of time emerging from a geological perspective indeed destabilizes Mount Messiaen's sense of place. Its very site is also problematic. It cannot be seen as a whole from the road, but only as the northerly pinnacles or, near the entrance, the southerly pinnacles. Nor can the red top easily be seen from the canyon floor. Like a house with no front yard, it feels too close to the road – too present on one side and too hidden on the other, intimate but mysterious. Mount Messiaen blends into an ever-expanding range of pinnacle upon pinnacle, the red mountaintop dropping off to an army of white sandstone sentinels. It is in the open desert, but hiding in narrow Parowan Canyon. Is it three peaks, or nine, or the whole ridge? Mount Messiaen seems intent on slipping away from emplacement and on disorienting the pilgrim. At its foot, it invites a kind of inverse vertigo from craning the neck to look directly upward, upward in that quintessentially Christian direction, the upward abyss of Gothic cathedrals, light and birds that define Messiaen's music.

Mount Messiaen is a return gift, honouring the composer as he honoured Utah. It is rock commensurate with the composition. But it is also a memory, a memorial of Messiaen. Moreover, it is a memory of a memory, for Messiaen's music evokes the sounds and emotions of his visit, as captured in *Des Canyons*. There seems little more ephemeral in this world, however, than a memory of a memory. In the end, as in the mind, music and mountain sound as one, saying that soon, after thousands of years, the significant pinnacles will wash, like a memory, away....

---

[32] Farmer, *On Zion's Mount*, p. 6.

[33] Tuan, *Space and Place*, p. 140.

[34] Ibid., p. 179.

Chapter 14

Genesis and Reception of Olivier Messiaen's *Traité de rythme, de couleur, et d'ornithologie*, 1949–1992: Toward a New Reading of the Composer's Writings[1]

Jean Boivin

An Exceptional Treatise

Early in the autumn of 1994, the first *tome* of Olivier Messiaen's vast *Traité de rythme, de couleur, et d'ornithologie* was published posthumously by Alphonse Leduc in Paris.[2] The following six *tomes* appeared at regular intervals up to 2002. The publication was a highly anticipated event. As early as 1949 Messiaen began compiling notes concerning various aspects of rhythm, an element of musical discourse that fascinated him as much as a composer as in his capacity as professor at the Paris Conservatoire, where he taught from 1941 to 1978. Over the years, the project grew to incorporate large sections devoted to birdsongs, modes and harmonic colours, as well as analyses of excerpts from the repertoire and of some of his own compositions. The entire treatise comes to over 3,200 pages divided into seven *tomes*, the fifth of which is published in two separately bound parts.

Messiaen unfortunately passed away on 27 April 1992, before completing the treatise, whose conception encompasses a period of 43 years, as the complete title specifies. The composer's extraordinary creative energy, particularly remarkable in the last 15 years of his life, when many important works came to life, apparently

---

[1] This chapter is a revised translation of a French contribution to a collection of essays on various composers' writings entitled *Écrits de compositeurs, 1850–2000: Questions, méthodes et perspectives de recherche*, Michel Duchesneau, Valérie Dufour and Marie-Hélène Benoit-Otis (eds) (Paris: Vrin, 2013). I sincerely thank Heidi Bishop for allowing the editors to include it in this volume. I am also deeply grateful to Jon-Tomas Godin and Catrina Flint for giving me a hand with the translation.

[2] Olivier Messiaen, *Traité de rythme, de couleur, et d'ornithologie, 1949–1992*, in 7 volumes (or tomes) and 8 parts, preface by Pierre Boulez, Foreword by Alain Louvier (Paris: Alphonse Leduc, 1994, 1995, 1996, 1997, 2000, 2001, 2002). See also Melody Baggech, *An English Translation of Olivier Messiaen's* Traité de rythme, de couleur, et d'ornithologie, *volume 1*, DMA thesis (University of Oklahoma, 1998).

did not give him time to perfect his manuscript. One can also presume that he was not entirely satisfied with it. Yet the very precise instructions he left his wife in 1991 show without a doubt that he wanted this lifetime's work published.

It therefore fell to Yvonne Loriod to sort out the various sections of what can be called the most substantial treatise born of a composer's pen in any period. She was of course the person best qualified to complete this colossal compilation and editing task: a favoured interpreter of Messiaen's music from a young age, she had been one of his very first students.[3] Furthermore, she had assisted Messiaen at the Conservatoire on various occasions by playing the works he was analysing in his class, either solo or four hands with him. In her daunting task of manuscript preparation, Loriod was helped by the composer Alain Louvier, also a former student (in the mid-1960s). Louvier wrote the Foreword, as well as the introductory text to each volume. He explains that Yvonne Loriod 'wished neither to compile nor to summarize, preferring to risk certain partial repetitions'.[4] We shall return to certain consequences of this editorial choice.

The *Traité de rythme, de couleur, et d'ornithologie* appears as the sum of the theoretical and aesthetic thought of a man who claimed to be at once a composer, ornithologist and rhythmist. Specialists of his *oeuvre* will find in its pages the keys necessary to understanding his development as a composer, especially in the two decades that followed the Second World War. Furthermore, the *Traité* testifies, more than any other document, to the content of Messiaen's legendary Conservatoire music analysis classes. Yet this original and monumental treatise has not elicited as much reaction from music scholars or informed commentators as might have been expected, even though it offers an excellent chance to observe the close ties that unite the writings of a composer and his musical creations. This network of correspondences is even more apparent since the composer in question doubled, as we know, as an influential pedagogue, whose impact on many generations of musicians was, and remains, considerable.

The limitations of the present publication preclude the presentation of a detailed overview of the contents of the *Traité*. I propose instead to explore its reception, with particular reference to a few significant texts that both underscored its publication and allow us to evaluate its contents. But first, a glance at Messiaen's literary œuvre as a whole is in order.

Messiaen as Writer

Messiaen was prolific on many levels. Born in 1908 and educated at the Paris Conservatoire, he rapidly crafted a coherent intellectual system and an original

---

[3] For more details on Messiaen's pedagogical activities, see Jean Boivin, *La classe de Messiaen* (Paris: Bourgois, 1995).

[4] Alain Louvier, Foreword to *Traité I*, p. viii. (This text is repeated in each subsequent volume.) Louvier also wrote a short postface at the end of *Traité VII*, pp. 328–9.

Genesis and Reception of Traité de rythme, de couleur, et d'ornithologie   343

compositional technique for himself, which he laid out in the important treatise *Technique de mon langage musical* (1944), written remarkably early in his career, during the war, as an answer to questions from his first students.[5] Many young composers around the world have been inspired by these pages dedicated to modes of limited transposition, non-retrogradable rhythms and Contracted Resonance chords, whose workings and expressive potential Messiaen presents. In this first composition treatise, Messiaen centres the discussion on his own music, but enhances the text with a handful of examples chosen among his favourite composers, already revealing a propensity towards approaching the repertoire in a creative manner.

Complementing these pedagogically minded pages are the numerous verses authored by Messiaen, from the first *Mélodies* (1930) to the opera *Saint François d'Assise* (1983). Moreover, he wrote a number of prefaces to his scores as well as programme notes, often elaborate, destined to accompany a concert performance, a recording or the published score.[6] Often careful to specify the source of his inspiration, Messiaen also granted a number of interviews that led to publications, whose texts he meticulously revised (such is the case with the series of conversations with Claude Samuel, reworked and re-issued on several occasions).[7] The lectures given in Brussels (1958), Paris (*Conférence de Notre-Dame*, 1977) and Kyoto (1985), which bear witness to 30 years of evolution as a composer, have also been diligently published by Alphonse Leduc, respectively in 1960, 1978 and 1988.[8] We find traces of them, sometimes overt, in the *Traité*.[9] To all of this we can further add

---

[5]   Messiaen had previously participated in a multi-author theoretical work called *Vingt leçons de solfège moderne dans les sept clés* (Paris: Lemoine, 1933), which also included texts by Claude Arrieu, Georges Hugon and Georges Dandelot. A few years later, Messiaen wrote *Vingt leçons d'harmonie: Dans le style de quelques auteurs important de l'histoire harmonique de la musique depuis Monteverdi jusqu'à Ravel* (Paris: Leduc, 1939).

[6]   Regarding the programme notes, see Yves Balmer, 'Entre analyse et propagande: Olivier Messiaen et son usage des notes de programme' in Michel Duchesneau, Valérie Dufour and Marie-Hélène Benoit-Otis (eds), *Écrits de compositeurs (1850–2000): Questions, méthodes et perspectives de recherche* (Paris: Vrin, 2013), pp. 27–47.

[7]   See the bibliography for full details. Brigitte Massin's book, *Olivier Messiaen: Une poétique du merveilleux* (Aix en Provence: Alinéa, 1989) is also mostly based on interviews with the composer.

[8]   *Conférence de Bruxelles* (Paris: Leduc, 1958); *Conférence de Notre-Dame* (Paris: Leduc, 1978); *Conférence de Kyoto* (Paris: Leduc, 1988). The first of these publications included an English translation, while the Paris lecture was translated by Leduc only in 2001 (having earlier appeared in Almut Rößler's *Contributions to the Spiritual World of Olivier Messiaen*, trans. Babara Dagg and Nancy Poland (Duisberg: Gilles & Francke, 1986), and the Kyoto Lecture in 2011.

[9]   For example, Messiaen quotes his *Conférence de Bruxelles* at the beginning of *Traité II* (p. 7), while excepts from the 1977 Notre-Dame lecture were chosen by Yvonne Loriod to serve as an introduction to the chapter on plainchant, an opening for which Messiaen had only drafted an outline (*Traité IV*, pp. 66–9). An excerpt from the same lecture and another

344 *Messiaen Perspectives 2: Techniques, Influence and Reception*

a few critiques written early in his career,[10] various homages and prefaces as well as a short book dedicated to Mozart's piano concertos that appeared in 1987.[11] The *Traité* finally afforded the beginnings of an understanding of Messiaen's approach at the Paris Conservatoire.

Together, this documentation constitutes an excellent example of the 'construction of a new association between the musical work and its Idea but also between the work and its creator, between the work and the listener', to quote the well-worded call for papers to a conference on composers' writings held in Montreal in 2008 that was one of the impulses behind the present chapter.[12] The monumental *Traité de rythme, de couleur, et d'ornithologie* stands as a crowning achievement of an already substantial textual corpus, which allows us to sound out Messiaen's interior landscapes and wide fields of interest, to understand better the aesthetic and theoretical concepts that underpin his works, to apprehend his opinion of other composers and to learn what he retained of their works. It is, therefore, rather intriguing to read Boulez's statement in the preface to the treatise, that Messiaen 'did not leave many reflections on his methods. He published *Technique de mon langage musical* but, apart from his teaching, he never revealed his points of view, commented on his thinking or his works. It is surprising that such a pedagogue left nothing on himself, on his evolution.'[13] Apparently, Boulez considers all of these texts and interviews granted over the course of decades insignificant or insufficiently informative – for a veteran composer and thinker such as himself.

---

from the 1985 *Conférence de Kyoto* are quoted in the 'Prologue sur la couleur' of the final *tome* of the treatise (*Traité VII*, p. 8).

[10] Regarding Messiaen's early contributions to music criticism, a lesser known aspect of his activities, see the brilliant editing, translation and discussion by Stephen Broad, *Olivier Messiaen: Journalism 1935–1939* (Farnham: Ashgate, 2012).

[11] Olivier Messiaen, *Les 22 concertos pour piano de Mozart*, Foreword by Jean-Victor Hocquard (Paris: Librairie Séguier, Archimbault/Birr, 1987). For a list of Messiaen's writings, consult the comprehensive bibliography in PHNS, pp. 402–5. I thank these two scholars, authors of the most extensive Messiaen biography to date, for their help. See also, Vincent Benitez, *Olivier Messiaen: A Research and Information Guide* (New York: Routledge, 2008).

[12] 'Édification d'un nouveau rapport entre l'œuvre musicale et son Idée, mais aussi entre l'œuvre et son créateur, entre l'œuvre et l'auditeur.' Michel Duchesneau, Jonathan Goldman et al., call for papers to the multidisciplinary conference 'Écrits de compositeurs 1850–2000', held in March 2008 at the Observatoire International de la Création et des Cultures Musicales (now the Observatoire Interdisciplinaire de Création et de Recherche en Musique), Université de Montréal, available at www.aieq.qc.ca/bulletins/2007/mai/colloque.oicm.pdf.

[13] 'Il n'a pas laissé beaucoup de réflexions sur sa démarche. Il a publié *Technique de mon langage musical* mais, son enseignement mis à part, il n'a pas exposé ses points de vue, commenté sa pensée ou ses œuvres. On peut s'étonner qu'un tel pédagogue n'ait rien laissé sur lui-même, sur son évolution.' Pierre Boulez, preface to the *Traité I*, p. vi; this two-page text is reprinted in each subsequent volume.

Genesis and Reception of Traité de rythme, de couleur, et d'ornithologie   345

Whatever the case, and before examining more explicit commentaries, we must go back to the beginning.

The Genesis of the *Traité*

The history of this posthumous publication is interesting in itself. On the one hand, according to Louvier, Yvonne Loriod 'rigorously' respected the detailed outline, in seven *tomes*, and the precise instructions that her husband gave her in 1991: 'Assembling chapters written at very different times, she remained faithful to the presentation of the manuscript (paragraphs, sub-chapters, underlined terms, etc.).'[14] On the other hand, she took certain initiatives, such as reproducing certain short texts published elsewhere,[15] inserting Messiaen's notes on incomplete chapters or even alternate versions of chapters he had decided to re-write.[16]

Loriod and Louvier provided some rationale for their additions and editorial choices.[17] Dating precisely the various sections of the *Traité* remains, however, quite problematic. My study of Messiaen's pedagogical career leads me to believe that much of the content of the *Traité* was communicated orally by Messiaen to his students at the Paris Conservatoire, or occasionally abroad, for instance during lectures in Darmstadt in the early 1950s.[18] Two former Messiaen students, Pierre Boulez and Alain Louvier, also suggested such a close link between the treatise and his teaching in their respective introductory texts, while Harry Halbreich, enrolled in the class in the 1950s, has found in it 'many times nearly the exact formulation' as in his course notes.[19] Biographers Peter Hill and Nigel Simeone, who had access to Messiaen's diaries, have for their part discovered annotations that support this theory as well.[20]

---

[14]   Louvier, Foreword, *Traité I*, p. viii. Regarding the fifth volume, whose main topic is birdsong, Yvonne Loriod had to make a difficult choice between numerous transcriptions of the call of a given species. She was assisted in this task by the ornithologist Jacques Penot, to whom Messiaen also turned in 1956 when he was preparing to compose the first parts of *Catalogue d'oiseaux* (1956–58). See PHNS, p. 218.

[15]   This happens, for example, in a brief homage to Debussy at the beginning of the sixth *tome*, entirely devoted to this key composer (*Traité VI*, p. xiii), or in the introduction to Chapter 3 of the seventh *tome*, which focuses on the relationship between sound and colour (*Traité VII*, p. 97–9).

[16]   Thus, annexed to *Traité III* (1996) one can find the first version of the chapter on rhythmic permutations that opens the same volume (Annex 1, pp. 319–43), as well as sparse notes taken by Messiaen on different subjects, such as the I-Ching, Leitmotivs and communicable language, intended for an unwritten chapter on language (Annex 2, pp. 347–61).

[17]   Especially in *Traité VII*, p. 55.

[18]   See Boivin, *La classe de Messiaen*, Chapters 4 and 5.

[19]   Harry Halbreich, *L'œuvre d'Olivier Messiaen* (Paris: Fayard, 2008), p. 547.

[20]   For example, see PHNS, p. 207.

346   *Messiaen Perspectives 2: Techniques, Influence and Reception*

From the late 1940s onward, when he held a class in musical analysis and aesthetics, Messiaen regularly taught courses on Greek meter and Hindu rhythms, themes that permeate a large part of the first volume of the treatise. This emphasis on rhythm, which contributed to the pedagogue's reputation, becomes even more pronounced in the mid-1950s, and many sections of the first volumes were likely written in this decade.[21] The German musicologist Stefan Keym claims that the lion's share of the work was conceived in the 1940s and 1950s, arguing that Messiaen only rarely cites passages of his own works composed after 1960.[22] The principal exceptions concern compositions such as *Couleurs de la Cité céleste*, *La Transfiguration de Notre-Seigneur Jésus-Christ* and the *Méditations sur le mystère de la Sainte Trinité*. However, on certain occasions, Yvonne Loriod apparently took it upon herself to refer to later works such as the opera *Saint François d'Assise*, *Un Vitrail et des oiseaux* and the final completed work, *Éclairs sur l'Au-Delà...*, interesting additions to the treatise, in fact, based on short presentation texts written by Messiaen.[23]

A large part of the *Traité* would therefore have been written many decades prior to its publication, in fact mostly during the 1950s.[24] Biographers Simeone and Hill again confirm this hypothesis when they inform us that Messiaen wrote in his diary in 1957 that he had, among other projects, to 'finish the *Traité du rythme* [sic]'.[25] Nevertheless, 17 years later, in November 1974, Messiaen notes in his diary that he had worked on the chapter concerning birdsongs, and had once again consulted Alain Daniélou's book on Indian music.[26] Then, in early 1992, only a few months before his death, and despite considerable suffering, he once again added material to the volume on birdcalls.[27] As for Yvonne Loriod, she indicates

---

[21]   The *Conférence de Bruxelles*, which happens to focus on rhythm, was given in 1958. The especially careful writing in the first *tome*, on Time (with a capital 'T') and duration, reflects their importance for Messiaen.

[22]   Stefan Keym, 'Olivier Messiaen: *Traité de rythme, de couleur, et d'ornithologie (1949–1992)*, en 7 tomes, Paris, Alphonse Leduc, 1994-2002', *Musiktheorie*, 19/3 (2004): pp. 269–74. Composition dates of Messiaen's works allow an approximate dating of some passages of the treatise. Thus, according to Yvonne Loriod, Messiaen wrote the sections concerned with symmetrical permutations as preparation for composing *Chronochromie*, and would therefore have penned them before 1959 (*Traité III*, pp. 317–43).

[23]   In these three specific cases, the musical excerpts involve sections written *hors tempo* [out of tempo], added to Volume III, published in 1996 (*Traité III*, pp. 397–403).

[24]   A note supplied by Yvonne Loriod in the final volume (*Traité VII*, p. 55) suggests a writing process in three stages, the first going back to c. 1955. A chapter on the calls of the birds of France, not included in the original outline, would have appeared between 1956 and 1960. Messiaen then never stopped accumulating material (to the point where the fifth volume, totalling to 1310 pages, needed to be split into two parts).

[25]   PHNS, p. 224. This formulation of the title was probably unconsciously corrected in the French edition, which gives 'Finir *Traité de rythme*'; PHNS (Fr. edn), p. 290.

[26]   Ibid., p. 303.

[27]   Ibid., p. 380.

Genesis and Reception of Traité de rythme, de couleur, et d'ornithologie   347

that the passage concerning modes of limited transposition, which only appears in the final volume, was written after 1975, during what she terms the 'third period' of analysis of these modes by the composer, the first period going back to the writing of the *Technique*, and the second to the composition of *Oiseaux exotiques* in 1956.[28] From all of this we can deduce that Messiaen wrote a large part of the treatise while he was teaching analysis at the Conservatoire, then continuously perfected the text, added material and rewrote certain parts until the end of his life. It seems that he worked on it more zealously just after having retired from the Conservatoire in June 1978.[29]

A Surprisingly Small Group of Substantial Reviews

Considering all of the factors that make this posthumous treatise an exceptional work, including its central theme (i.e. rhythm), the scarcity of in-depth and detailed reviews published in music journals is surprising. The comments I found most worthy of attention are those that go beyond a simple description of the contents, sincere praise for Messiaen and his editor or an invitation to read, as heartfelt as it may be. More interesting in my view is the *critical*, or at least reasonably objective and informed, account (or *compte rendu*) of this posthumous treatise. I will therefore ignore those texts that limit themselves to announcing the publication of one of the volumes and summarize its contents, as in some of Jean-Noël von der Weid's notices in the Swiss journal *Dissonanz/Dissonance*[30] or Jean Roy's review in *Le monde de la musique*.[31]

It should also be noted that since the publication of the first volumes of the treatise, various Messiaen scholars have referred to it, particularly in valuable collections of specialized essays published since 2007. These musicological

---

[28]   Note at the bottom of page 107 in *Traité VII*. On p. 99, in another footnote, Loriod refers to the year 1978 as the beginning of this 'period'.

[29]   One of the last sections penned by Messiaen, in winter 1992, only months before his death, is the analysis of Act I, scene 3 of Debussy's *Pelléas et Mélisande* (footnote by Loriod, *Traité VI*, p. xi).

[30]   Jean-Noël von der Weid, reviews of the first four volumes of the *Traité de rythme* in three issues of *Dissonanz/Dissonance*, 43 (February 1995): pp. 43–4 (*tome* I); 48 (May 1996): p. 48, (*tome* II); and 54 (November 1997): p. 40 (*tomes* III and IV). To these we can add a brief but enthusiastic review by Adélaïde de Place in *Piano*, 17 (2003–04): p. 185, one by Philippe A. Autexier in *Dix-huitième siècle*, 30 (1998): p. 691, which only covers *tome* IV (in which Mozart's music is discussed), a review of *tome* I by Francis Cousté in *L'éducation musicale*, 422 (November 1995): p. 22, and one by François Sabatier in *L'Orgue*, 234: pp. 42–3. I would like to thank Jean Leduc, from Alphonse Leduc publishers, for having shared some of these texts – all fairly brief but often very well written – of which I had been unaware.

[31]   Jean Roy, 'Traité: Messiaen et les autres', *Le Monde de la musique*, 77 (June 2003): p. 14.

348   *Messiaen Perspectives 2: Techniques, Influence and Reception*

studies are mostly focused on particular aspects of the composer's work or thought rather than on the *Traité de rythme* itself, mostly used as a source of information. This being said, a few authors evaluate, however briefly, the importance of its contents, and thus deserve mention here. For instance, Andrew Shenton refers frequently to the first volume in order to explain the concept of musical time in Messiaen's music,[32] while Gareth Healey examines the various theoretical works to which Messiaen occasionally refers in the treatise.[33] For his part, Philippe Albèra provides an interesting synthesis of Messiaen's rhythmic theory in a richly illustrated book published for the centenary of the composer's birth.[34]

Let us now turn to the reviews that I would like to discuss in more detail. The most comprehensive, also among the most compelling contributions, comes from the British musicologist and Messiaen specialist Christopher Dingle. In four articles written between 1995 and 2004 for *Tempo*, he reviewed all seven *tomes* of the *Traité*.[35] Another British writer, Roger Nichols, author of one of the first English-language books on Messiaen,[36] commented on the first two *tomes* for *The Musical Times* in 1996.[37] I will also consider two German-language reviews that cover the seven *tomes* in one single stroke. The first, by Theo Hirsbrunner, who also authored a biography of the composer,[38] was published in 2003.[39] A year later, *Musiktheorie* published a substantial critical essay by Stefan Keym.[40]

---

[32]   Andrew Shenton, 'Observations on Time in Olivier Messiaen's *Traité*', in Christopher Dingle and Nigel Simeone (eds), *Olivier Messiaen, Music, Art and Literature* (Aldershot: Ashgate, 2007).

[33]   Gareth Healey, 'Messiaen – Bibliophile', in Christopher Dingle and Nigel Simeone (eds), *Olivier Messiaen, Music, Art and Literature* (Aldershot: Ashgate, 2007).

[34]   Philippe Albèra, 'Le rythme repensé', in Anick Lesure and Claude Samuel (eds), *Olivier Messiaen: Le livre du centenaire* (Lyon: Symétrie, 2008).

[35]   Being very long, the titles of these reviews, several of which also cover other publications, are abbreviated in the following references (full details are in the bibliography). Christopher Dingle, review of *tome* I, *Tempo*, 192 (April 1995): p. 29; review of *tomes* II and III, *Tempo*, 202 (October 1997): pp. 25–6; review of *tome* IV, *Tempo*, 205 (July 1998): pp. 26–7; review of *tome* V, Vols 1 and 2, and *tomes* VI and VII, *Tempo*, 227 (January 2004): pp. 41–5.

[36]   Roger Nichols, *Messiaen*, 2nd edition (London: Oxford University Press, 1986; first published 1975).

[37]   Roger Nichols, 'And a little child shall lead them', *The Musical Times*, 137 (July 1996): pp. 17–19.

[38]   Theo Hirsbrunner, *Olivier Messiaen, Leben und Werk*, 2nd edition (Laaber: Laaber Verlag, 1999; first published 1988).

[39]   Theo Hirsbrunner, 'Olivier Messiaen: *Traité de rythme, de couleur, et d'ornithologie (1949–1992)*, in 7 Bänden (Alphonse Leduc, Paris, 1994–2002), "Privatuniversum mit weitem Horizont"', *Dissonanz/Dissonance*, 81 (June 2003): pp. 40–41. The subtitle could be translated as 'A private world with a wide horizon'.

[40]   Keym, Stefan, 'Olivier Messiaen'. Keym also wrote the entry on Messiaen in Ludwig Fischer (ed.), *Die Musik in Geschichte und Gegenwart*, 2nd edition (Kassel:

Genesis and Reception of Traité de rythme, de couleur, et d'ornithologie   349

In France, curiously, apart from the few *invitations à la lecture* that have already been mentioned, Messiaen's treatise has not generated to my knowledge any in-depth commentary, except for the text published by Alain Louvier in *Musurgia, analyse et pratique musicales* in 1995, just after the publication of the first volume; although this journal devoted to music analysis would have been a perfect venue for a detailed appreciation, Louvier simply submits the Foreword that can be read at the beginning of each of the *tomes*, with minor modifications.[41] I will not here discuss for obvious reasons my own review of the first four volumes of the *Traité de rythme*, published in Canada in 1998,[42] although it may well be one of the few texts in French that qualifies as a critical review. Since some of the observations I made in 1998 can be found among the comments of authors I discuss in the following pages, I will refer to it only indirectly. As for Harry Halbreich, he took advantage of the revision of his 1980 monograph (whose reissue coincided with the centenary) to add four pages on the *Traité*. Apart from a few penetrating observations to which I shall return, the Belgian musicologist essentially describes the contents of each volume, albeit with all the enthusiasm he is known to possess for the work, taken as a whole, of his former teacher.[43] The only other French commentary that I shall quote at some length, written by Jacques Viret, was published in Switzerland in 1995 and covers the first volume. A slightly expanded version circulated among French organists.[44]

Well-deserved Praise

After having read through a part, or the whole, of the work, the majority of authors that I have named comment – as I did – on the breadth of Messiaen's culture, and see him as a humanist, an intuitive artist possessed with an uncommon intellectual

---

Bärenreiter, 2001), Vol. 12: pp. 63–81, as well as a book on Messiaen's unique opera, published in 2002: *Untersuchungen zur musiktheatralen Struktur und Semantik von Olivier Messiaens Saint François d'Assise* (Hildesheim: Georg Olms Verlag, 2002).

[41]   Alain Louvier, 'Olivier Messiaen, le *Traité de rythme, de couleur, et d'ornithologie*, Paris, Alphonse Leduc, 1994', *Musurgia, analyse et pratique musicales*, 2/1 (1995): pp. 162–4. Louvier supplements his general Foreword with an introductory text tailored to each volume.

[42]   Jean Boivin, 'Le *Traité de rythme, de couleur, et d'ornithologie* d'Olivier Messiaen, tomes I, II, III et IV', *Circuit: Musiques contemporaines*, 9/1 (1998): pp. 17–25.

[43]   Halbreich, *L'œuvre d'Olivier Messiaen*, pp. 546–50. The first version, simply entitled *Olivier Messiaen*, was published in Paris by Fayard-Sacem.

[44]   J. V. [Jacques Viret], 'Un grand traité posthume de Messiaen (Olivier Messiaen, *Traité de rythme, de couleur, et d'ornithologie (1949–1992)*, tome I, Paris, Éditions Alphonse Leduc, 1994)', *Revue musicale de Suisse romande*, 1995/4 (December 1995): p. 65. The Swiss-born, naturalized French musicologist and organist has himself made me aware of the slightly extended version that appeared in *L'Orgue francophone*, the bulletin of the Fédération francophone des amis de l'orgue: 'Olivier Messiaen, *Traité de rythme, de couleur, et d'ornithologie (1949–1992)*, tome I' (June 1995): pp. 88–9. I thank him for this information.

350 *Messiaen Perspectives 2: Techniques, Influence and Reception*

curiosity, who refers in turn to Pierre Ronsard, Brahma, Paul Éluard, Confucius, Paul Claudel, Henri Bergson, Rainer Maria Rilke, Thomas Aquinas and Albert Einstein, to name only a few.[45] This is certainly the opinion Alain Louvier expresses in his Foreword, and one finds the term 'universalism' in more than one review. Messiaen's prose is also an object of admiration. Thus Jean-Noël von der Weid remarks on 'the beauty of the style, combining diligence and poetry' in the first volume.[46] Many commentators are also struck by the astonishing – and revealing – links that the analyst draws between works of widely divergent styles, sometimes composed centuries apart, certainly a typical trait of his teaching.

The originality of the *Traité de rythme* lies in part in its unusual length. Theo Hirsbrunner, who recognizes the importance Messiaen had as a pedagogue and therefore looks quite favourably on this posthumous publication, praises the considerable effort involved in editing the notes left by Messiaen in order to create a cohesive whole.[47] He admits the risk was considerable, but believes that only a complete restoration of *all* aspects of Messiaen's pedagogical material could properly convey his thinking. Publishing only isolated excerpts, and potentially seeing them turn into dogmas, would have been contrary to the spirit of his patient and tolerant teaching.[48] What interests Hirsbrunner is the substance of the courses at the Conservatoire, and the treatise therefore complements, in his view, our knowledge of Messiaen's teaching. In this sense, the German musicologist underscores the value of the lengthy analyses, and particularly the 'full page' musical examples.[49] Even though a generous discussion of rhythmic procedures such as non-retrogradable rhythms and development by augmentation or diminution had already been laid out in *Technique*, Hirsbrunner calls attention to the fact that the examples come not only from Messiaen's works alone, but also bear the signature of Beethoven, Debussy, Ravel, Jolivet, Boulez or Stockhausen.[50] In fact, the seven volumes contain an impressive number of musical examples, including complete orchestral pages, complemented by several lists and tables, devoted, for example, to plainchant neumes, Hindu deçi-tâlas, rhythmic permutations, Carnatic scales (*échelles karnatiques*) or colour chords (*accords-couleurs*). Christopher Dingle justly remarks that this unusual quantity of musical illustrations distinguishes itself clearly from the prevalent, and unfortunate, tendency in the world of music publication today, and is to the credit of the publishers, Alphonse Leduc. This

---

[45] See also Jean Boivin, 'Messiaen's Teaching at the Paris Conservatoire: A Humanist Legacy', in Siglind Bruhn (ed.), *Messiaen's Language of Mystical Love* (New York: Garland, 1998).

[46] Von der Weid, 'Le traité tant attendu', *Dissonanz/Dissonance*, 43 (February 1995): p. 43.

[47] 'Ein geschlossenes Ganzes'. Hirsbrunner, 'Olivier Messiaen: *Traité de rythme*': p. 40.

[48] Ibid.

[49] Ibid.

[50] Ibid. This last remark refers to *tome* II of the *Traité*.

Genesis and Reception of Traité de rythme, de couleur, et d'ornithologie   351

generosity also accounts for the treatise's great length and enriches its contents.[51] It is, in fact, a major asset.

Other qualities are stressed by the authors discussed in this brief survey, such as the clarity of discourse, the value of the digressions, the attention to detail or the abundant technical information Messiaen offers on his own music. However, we should move on to traits that are not so widely admired, such as the treatise's overall structure or the methodological ground on which it was erected. These, for the very reason they incite critical comments, may teach us more of the work under study and the expectations it created.

Faults in the Armour

Commentators generally agree that the incomplete state of the *Traité de rythme* generates some difficulties for the reader, whether specialist or simple enthusiast. One may be briefly tempted to dwell on the misprints, the few awkward formulations, or on the typesetting or punctuation idiosyncrasies. The numerous repetitions revealed by a careful reading of the entire treatise will undoubtedly appear more significant.[52] In his Foreword, Alain Louvier warns us of the inevitable consequences arising from the staggering quantity of material that Messiaen gathered over the years. Then again, some of the cross-references and repetitions are explained by the subdivision of the treatise into precise themes and sub-themes (Greek meter, Hindu deçi-tâlas, non-retrogradable rhythms, rhythmic characters, rhythmic pedals and canons, symmetrical permutations, plainchant, birdsong, Debussy, modes, sound-colour, etc.), themes that are often permeable to one another.[53] This being said, one may also safely claim that reiteration is an integral part of this composer's creative process.

As pertains to the theoretical sources Messiaen claims, Stefan Keym rightly notes that the composer remained true to the treatises to which he referred as a young composer, such as the writings of Dom Mocquereau, those of his teacher Maurice Emmanuel or Albert Lavignac and Lionel de la Laurencie's *Encyclopédie*

---

[51]   Christopher Dingle, '*Traité de rythme, de couleur, et d'ornithologie (1949–1992) – Tome V, volumes 1 & 2, Tome VI & Tome VII* by Olivier Messiaen', *Tempo*, 227 (January 2004): p. 42.

[52]   For example, see Shenton, 'Observations on Time in Olivier Messiaen's *Traité*', p. 176. Dingle prefers to qualify those repetitions as 'inevitable longueurs' [sic] ('*Traité de rythme, Tomes V, VI & VII*': p. 45).

[53]   Throughout the treatise, Messiaen invokes for example modes of limited transposition when he analyses his own works, yet the concept is only described in detail in *tome* VII. In the same vein, many Debussy examples are provided in the first two *tomes* when a whole *tome*, the sixth, is reserved for this composer; the same passages can therefore be cited and commented on in different volumes.

de la musique, published between 1913 and 1931.[54] Jacques Viret does not hesitate, for his part, to pronounce these sources outdated.[55] As for Roger Nichols, he expresses a profound discomfort when reading the numerous quotations on time that Messiaen gathers, observing that 'there seem to be certain facts he chose not to know and indeed certain authors he chose not to credit'.[56] How could there be no reference, asks Nichols, to Stravinsky's *Poétique musicale*, where 'psychological' and 'ontological' time is also discussed? Messiaen was evidently not a trained historian, admits the British musicologist. Still, some sweeping affirmations remain surprising, such as when Messiaen states that he was the only composer, for 30 years, to have used non-retrogradable rhythms. How does he know, Nichols wonders?[57]

An Analyst Quite Out of the Ordinary

But it is when 'Messiaen the analyst' is the topic of discussion that potential readers should perhaps be better informed of the actual content of the treatise. One may wonder why so few reviewers feel the need to send a clear warning. In his first review, Christopher Dingle identifies 'many delights to come'[58] in the table of contents for the whole treatise (printed in the first volume) and expresses his eagerness to read what promises to be 'many in-depth analyses of a remarkably disparate group of composers'.[59] Yet the publication of subsequent volumes does not lead him openly to re-evaluate the treatment reserved for works of major importance in Messiaen's development, such as Stravinsky's *Le sacre du printemps* or Debussy's *Prélude à l'après-midi d'un faune*.[60] These pages could in fact disappoint readers with high expectations. For although the corresponding sections were written with a care not necessarily found elsewhere, and while the point of view and metaphors may certainly be found original as well as fascinating,

---

[54]   Keym, 'Olivier Messiaen: *Traité de rythme*': p. 271. Messiaen was likely familiar with the entire work, but had paid closer attention to the article on India written by Joanny Grosset, published in the first volume, 'Antiquité – Moyen Âge'; Joanny Grosset, 'Inde', in Albert Lavignac and Lionel de la Laurencie (eds), *Encyclopédie de la musique et Dictionnaire du Conservatoire*, Part 1, *Histoire de la musique, Antiquité-Moyen âge*, Vol. 1 (Paris: Delagrave, 1921): pp. 257–341.

[55]   Viret, 'Un grand traité posthume de Messiaen': p. 65.

[56]   Nichols, 'And a little child shall lead them': p. 17.

[57]   Ibid., p. 18.

[58]   Ibid.

[59]   Dingle, '*Traité de rythme, de couleur, et d'ornithologie (1949–1992) – Tome I* by Olivier Messaien ...', *Tempo*, 192 (April 1995): p. 29.

[60]   Respectively in *Traité II*, pp. 95–147, and *Traité VI*, pp. 28–40; *La Mer*, another key work for Messiaen, is also discussed in *Traité VI*, in two separate places (pp. 22–7 and pp. 181–97).

Genesis and Reception of Traité de rythme, de couleur, et d'ornithologie   353

it still would be a stretch to speak here of 'in-depth' analyses of these landmark scores. Even considering the fact that the *Traité* does not really stand as a music analysis treatise, unexplained gaps still emerge between 'chosen passages'. As could be expected, the rhythmic parameter is given particular attention. Yet, as Stefan Keym aptly observes, the musical texts are in fact studied according to varying criteria, haphazardly selected, without any effort at systematization.[61]

This is particularly true of Messiaen's analysis of the *Rite of Spring*, regularly proposed at the Conservatoire and long since famous *in absentia*, so to speak, thanks to his students' accounts. While Hirsbrunner surprisingly fails to even mention this long-awaited analysis, Nichols judges this chapter to be not only crucial to an understanding of Messiaen's views on rhythm, but also fascinating in itself; he furthermore calls for a comparison with Boulez's analysis.[62] As for Dingle, after having noted that Messiaen's view on the works he analyses is 'personal in the extreme', he points out that, in the case of the *Sacre*, the reader is immediately supplied with an alternative version of the analysis of the 'Sacrificial Dance', Messiaen's response to criticisms formulated by some doubtful students.[63]

The pianist Peter Hill for his part concludes that the *Traité*, and in particular the section devoted to the analysis of *The Rite of Spring,* displays 'how Messiaen's passion for theory allowed him to summarize multiple influences without losing his authenticity'.[64] Yet, in this composer's view, effect sometimes wins over abstract consideration. After having provided a few examples of 'astonishing digressions' that contrast with analytical passages where the discourse is 'purely theoretical',[65] Hill underlines that at the very end of the 'Sacrificial Dance', Messiaen considers that a new ostinato, in the bass, partially destroys the logic of the 'rhythmic characters' whose functioning he has just described. And the composer of the *Turangalîla-Symphonie* estimates that 'so close to the end, such a fault is nearly a quality, since it imbues the final measures ... with an absolutely necessary

---

[61]   Keym, 'Olivier Messiaen: *Traité de rythme*': pp. 271 and 273. Nichols writes for his part: 'I am bound to say that at times [Messiaen] has a tendency to see what he wants to see' ('And a little child shall lead them': p. 18).

[62]   Pierre Boulez, 'Stravinsky demeure', text notably published in Paule Thévenin (ed.), *Relevés d'apprenti* (Paris: Seuil, 1966), pp. 75–145. Since Boulez's text was apparently provoked by what he considered Messiaen's unsatisfactory view of sections of the score, this comparison has been sketched by Keym ('Olivier Messiaen: *Traité de rythme*': p. 271) and by Gareth Healey, 'Messiaen and the Concept of "Personnages"', *Tempo*, 58/230 (October 2004): pp. 10–19.

[63]   Dingle, '*Traité de rythme, de couleur, et d'ornithologie (1949–1992), Tome II & Tome III* by Olivier Messaien ...', *Tempo*, 202 (October 1997): p. 26. Nichols also notices the presence of these two versions ('And a little child shall lead them': p. 18), as I myself did in *Circuit* ('Le *Traité de rythme*': p. 22). For some reactions on this specific Messiaen's analysis, see Boivin, *La classe de Messiaen*, pp. 282–95.

[64]   'Épilogue: La pensée musicale', in PHNS, fr. edn, p. 494 (this new chapter was written by Hill alone, specifically for the French edition of the book).

[65]   Ibid., pp. 494 and 495.

conclusive strength'.[66] In Peter Hill's opinion, the statement is remarkable: 'This type of comment is quite rare in the *Traité*; most of the time, Messiaen wavers between passionate speculation and abstract theory, preferring to keep secret this place *where intention intersects with means.*'[67]

On a more general level, and despite a favourable prejudice towards Messiaen and his music, Christopher Dingle remains objective and also expresses some reserve. For example, terms such as 'masculine' and 'feminine' used to describe Mozart's melodic phrases are judged outmoded.[68] Dingle also suggests that the model of Mozartian accentuation presented will not be unanimously accepted, no more than Messiaen's interpretation of plainchant in terms of flux and reflux.[69] *Tome VI*, devoted to another much admired composer, Claude Debussy, is surprisingly brief, regrets Dingle. Yet it is Messiaen's 'ease with this material, the breadth and depth of [his] knowledge and insight that makes [this volume] a delight to read'.[70] Dingle also remarks that quite a few pages – mostly dealing with Debussy's piano music or the *Chansons de Bilitis* – consist of Yvonne Loriod's transcriptions of annotations found in Messiaen's scores.[71] This confers on several passages a certain dryness that does not escape Stefan Keym, who judges that the final three volumes are particularly fragmentary, comprising a series of notes and comments rather than discursive passages.[72]

Even the majority of British or German commentators, though part of a culture that saw the birth and rise of the discipline, use the term *analysis* to designate those sections of the treatise centred on specific musical compositions. In this they merely respond to the term *analyse* used by Messiaen and repeated by both Yvonne Loriod and Alain Louvier, who, as we know, collaborated closely in the editing process.[73] A more appropriate term to designate these passages would be

---

[66] Cited in PHNS, fr. edn, p. 496. Emphasis added.

[67] Ibid., p. 496. Emphasis added.

[68] Dingle, '*Traité de rythme, de couleur, et d'ornithologie (1949–1992) – Tome IV* by Olivier Messaien ...', *Tempo*, 205 (July 1998): p. 27. Nichols remarks in his 1996 review of the first two *tomes* that Messiaen's views on accentuation in Mozart, announced in the upcoming tome IV, will enable readers to 'judge for [them]selves whether a young pupil called Stockhausen had reason to be impatient' ('And a little child shall lead them': pp. 18–19). See Boivin, *La classe de Messiaen*, p. 109, and Claude Samuel, *Permanences d'Olivier Messiaen* (Arles: Actes Sud, 1999), p. 311.

[69] Dingle, '*Traité de rythme, Tome IV*': p. 27.

[70] Dingle, '*Traité de rythme, Tomes V, VI & VII*': p. 43.

[71] Yvonne Loriod stresses that these analyses were 'entirely written in his scores' (*Traité VI*, p. xii, footnote).

[72] Keym, 'Olivier Messiaen: *Traité de rythme* ...': p. 269.

[73] See the introduction to *Traité VI*, p. ix. Louvier makes a remark on this subject that reveals much about his own perception of the discipline: 'If we analyse the first Prélude ('Danseuses de Delphes') with structural analysis tools, intervallic or harmonic, interest is scarce' (ibid.). Louvier prefers to picture Messiaen sitting at the piano, revealing laws of

Genesis and Reception of Traité de rythme, de couleur, et d'ornithologie   355

'commentary', employed in one instance by Roger Nichols. Or one could prefer to distinguish, as Stefan Keym does, between what is based in turn on metaphor, on rigorous technical elucidation or on subjective description. Whatever the case, we may agree with Theo Hirsbrunner when he sums up that 'often we cannot consider these analyses as scientific, but stimulating they most certainly have been'.[74]

On the whole, Nichols finds Messiaen more interesting 'and even provocative' when he discusses music by other composers, in part because what he reveals about his own music could already be found in other books – though in less detail than in the *Traité* – but also because 'there was in Messiaen an abiding, childish curiosity about the world and all that is therein'.[75] And if Nichols judges that Messiaen sometimes goes to great lengths to make music by earlier composers fit 'into pre-ordained patterns', he also proves that 'he has the true teacher's gift ... of making you look anew at things you thought you knew and encouraging you to approach new things in a positive spirit'.[76] Hence the term 'elucidator' so aptly adopted by Dingle.[77]

Christopher Dingle reveals himself to be more demanding when he examines those chapters that Messiaen devotes to his own works, particularly in the part of the fifth *tome* regarding birdsong and 'œuvres aux oiseaux' such as the *Sept Haïkaï* or the *Catalogue d'oiseaux*, a piano cycle frequently used as an example. Dingle writes that here:

> Messiaen's comments provide ample information on what material is actually in the music, and where it has come from. In this, he is punctilious and extremely illuminating. However, ... Messiaen says precious little about how this material is used within the compositional process. There is nothing about why a certain grouping of birds might be chosen for a particular chorus, nothing about why an individual bird may be presented at one pitch rather than another, and nothing about the function of this material within the broader compositional structure.[78]

One will remember Peter Hill's remark regarding the secret and protected place where 'intention intersects with means'. In fact, Dingle explains that according

---

acoustics and harmonic resonance, and 'discovering what is essential: Debussy composes first and foremost with sound' (ibid.).

[74]   'Man mag diese Analysen Messiaens oft nicht wissenschaftlich nennen, anregend sind sie auf jeden Fall'. Hirsbrunner, 'Olivier Messiaen, *Traité de rythme*': p. 41; my translation. Hirsbrunner is at this point discussing the Debussy volume.

[75]   Nichols, 'And a little child shall lead them': p. 18. I dare say that in 1998 I expressed the opposite view since I judged that, at least in the first *tomes*, Messiaen's analyses could be found more satisfactory and detailed when he dealt with his own works (Boivin, 'Le *Traité de rythme*': pp. 22–3).

[76]   Ibid.

[77]   Dingle, '*Traité de rythme, Tome IV*': p. 26.

[78]   Dingle,'*Traité de rythme, Tomes V, VI & VII*', *Tempo*, 227 (January, 2004), p. 43.

to Messiaen's British students, the composer 'simply did not comprehend such questions, for he could not conceive of the music being any other way'.[79] Dingle touches here on a sensitive and particularly important point. And he goes further when he adds that this observation is equally valid for 'so much of [Messiaen's] analysis of his own music'.[80] In this respect, *tome V* is in Dingle's eyes 'a touch frustrating', 'as with the other *Tomes*' he concedes, so to speak, under his breath, in the last of four texts he offers on the *Traité de rythme*.[81] This caveat put aside, Dingle's overall evaluation remains highly positive. Like the long 'Prêche aux oiseaux' in *Saint François d'Assise*, which the listener traverses with patience '*en route* to the splendours of the third act', the two large parts of *tome V* (devoted to birdsong) stand as obstacles in the path of the reader before reaching the rich sixth and seventh *tomes*.[82]

Harry Halbreich, clearly more conciliatory, pronounces himself entirely satisfied with this gigantic fifth volume, which he judges, surprisingly, to be 'a particularly attractive read'.[83] Its second part, on non-European birds, already valuable for a detailed analysis of the *Sept Haïkaï*, ends with 'a precious anthology (thirty pages, we want even more!) of the composer's most beautiful ornithological memories; here is the domain of the freshest, purest poetry, a true Franciscan oasis'.[84]

A Particularly Harsh Review

My research to this point has allowed me to uncover only one text drawing negative conclusions. And this is no understatement, as we shall now see. In only two paragraphs published in December 1995 in the *Revue musicale de Suisse romande* and dealing only with the first *tome*, Jacques Viret admits to his 'perplexity in front of this large treatise that Messiaen himself had talked about for forty years', and does not hesitate to offer this advice: 'the musicologist wishing to educate himself on Hindu or Ancient Greek rhythm should go look elsewhere'.[85] This first *tome*, the writer continues, 'confirms, in all, a fact that we already knew or sensed. Doubtlessly, no one will deny that Messiaen was one of the great composers of the twentieth century. But neither the thinker nor the theorist is any match for the

---

[79]   Ibid.

[80]   Ibid.

[81]   Ibid.

[82]   Ibid.

[83]   Halbreich, *L'oeuvre d'Olivier Messiaen*, p. 549.

[84]   Ibid.

[85]   'Avouons notre perplexité devant ce gros traité dont Messiaen lui-même parlait depuis quarante ans', and 'Le musicologue désireux de s'informer sur la rythmique hindoue ou sur celle de la Grèce antique ira se documenter ailleurs.' Viret, 'Un grand traité posthume de Messiaen': p. 65.

artist.'[86] The greater part of the treatise is viewed by the French-Swiss musicologist, specializing in Gregorian chant and Renaissance organ music,[87] as mere 'notes or course preparations', stating that 'the pious zeal with which [Yvonne Loriod] assembled and preserved any and all written texts … is, in [his] opinion, in no way justified with respect to the interest of the contents'.[88] And 'three-quarters at least [of the first *tome*] are quotations haphazardly taken, rarely commented and sometimes originating from such obsolete authors as the Abbé Moreux, Alexis Carrel or Dom Mocquereau'.[89] In the end, Messiaen is declared 'unable to wield the writer's pen in a logical and discursive manner. With regards to theory he certainly said everything important he had to say in his brief treatise, *Technique de mon langage musical*, which appeared in 1944.'[90]

This last opinion is not shared by such Messiaen specialists as Stefan Keym, Theo Hirsbrunner or Christopher Dingle. The first observes in his own review that the symmetrical permutation process developed by Messiaen at the end of the 1940s and over the following decade forms the heart of *tome III* of the posthumous treatise, which notably contains an analysis of the *Quatre Études de rythme* and of *Chronochromie*. *Technique* was written many years prior to this important development and obviously contains no mention of it. The same thing goes for the 'special chords', complex aggregates of 7 to 12 tones that played a key role in Messiaen's music beginning in the 1950s, and only described in *tome VII* of the *Traité*.[91] Along the same lines, Hirsbrunner notes that in *tome III*, Messiaen offers rhythmic analyses of works that influenced the serial music of the 1950s, such as the *Études de rythme* and *Livre d'orgue*, but that he also lingers on later

---

[86] 'Tout cela confirme en somme un fait que l'on savait déjà ou pressentait. Personne sans doute ne niera que Messiaen ait été l'un des grands compositeurs du XXe siècle. Mais en lui ni le penseur ni le théoricien ne sont à la hauteur de l'artiste.' Ibid.

[87] Once a student of Jacques Chailley, Jacques Viret is an emeritus teacher of musicology at the Université de Strasbourg.

[88] 'Le pieux zèle avec lequel elle a tout conservé des textes rédigés (souvent, semble-t-il, des notes ou dossiers de cours) n'est à notre avis guère justifié par l'intérêt intrinsèque du contenu.' Viret, 'Un grand traité posthume de Messiaen': p. 65.

[89] 'Les trois quarts au moins [du premier tome] sont un remplissage de citations tous azimuts, rarement commentées et provenant parfois d'auteurs aussi surannés que l'Abbé Moreux, Alexis Carrel ou Dom Mocquereau.' Ibid. Francis Cousté, is another reviewer who found authors such as Alexis Carrel, Armand Cuvillier, Gisèle Brelet or the Abbé Moreux 'dated' ('Olivier Messiaen, *Traité de rythme, de couleur, et d'ornithologie: 1949–1992*: Tome I', review, *L'éducation musicale*, 422 [November 1995]: p. 22).

[90] 'L'imaginatif et le poète qu'il était se révélait inapte à manier la plume de l'écrivain d'une manière logique et discursive. S'agissant de théorie il a certainement tout dit ce qu'il avait d'essentiel à dire dans son bref traité, *Technique de mon langage musical* paru en 1944.' Ibid. On the opposite side of the spectrum, the same *tome* brings Halbreich to praise the 'exceptional quality of Messiaen's style, that of a great writer' (*L'oeuvre de Messiaen*, p. 547).

[91] Keym, 'Olivier Messiaen: *Traité de rythme*': p. 273.

358 *Messiaen Perspectives 2: Techniques, Influence and Reception*

'discoveries', such as the communicable language used in the *Méditations sur le Mystère de la Sainte Trinité* for organ. These developments may not have had as spectacular an impact [*Wirkung*] as the earlier ones, writes Hirsbrunner, but they are nonetheless worth presenting in detail.[92]

A Question of Transparency

Space permits neither discussion of the *Traité*'s peculiar overall structure (other than to remark that the table of contents only provides a cursory glance at its subject matter and that a few hidden treasures lie in its pages), nor detailed engagement with the *tome* devoted to colours, a subject in itself that garners the attention of Keym and Dingle. More interesting in my point of view is the philological question pertinently raised by Stefan Keym when he observes that Yvonne Loriod's name does not appear on the cover page, despite her role as principal editor. Neither is that role clarified in any proper introduction. Her direct and avowed interventions are limited to a few remarks and footnotes, particularly in the last three *tomes*, truly the most fragmentary of the entire set.[93] Messiaen clearly emerges as the sole author of the whole, Keym notes.[94] It is tempting to observe that Loriod's participation generates some awkward moments, since the speaking 'I' of the sentences sometimes disappears behind an absent 'he'.[95] A similar lack of transparency in the editorial work has also been noted by Christopher Dingle and Robert Fallon, this time regarding the publication of some of Messiaen's scores – either posthumous or early works – which are also due to Yvonne Loriod.[96] Those who knew her well would probably argue that in her view, every word and note ever written by Messiaen was precious and had to be brought to light, which had clearly become her mission after his death. Morover, she alone could hardly be held accountable for a lack of knowledge of the academic norms of editorial propriety.

---

[92] Hirsbrunner, 'Olivier Messiaen: *Traité de rythme*': pp. 40–41.

[93] Keym, 'Olivier Messiaen: *Traité de rythme*': p. 269.

[94] Ibid.

[95] For example, in the 'plan general résumé du tome V', the last two sections have the following titles: 'Mes plus beaux souvenirs ornithologiques' ('My most beautiful ornithological memories') and 'Les chants d'oiseaux dans l'œuvre d'Olivier Messiaen' ('Bird songs in Olivier Messiaen's oeuvre'); *Traité V:1*, p. 3.

[96] Robert Fallon expresses this dilemma well when discussing the late *Concert à quatre*, left unfinished by the composer but completed by Yvonne Loriod (the second movement being an adaptation for oboe and strings of a *mélodie* composed 60 years earlier). No indication is given of the state in which Messiaen left the scores that were published posthumously and it is impossible to be certain that he would have approved of the way they were completed or revised (Robert Fallon, 'Various Messiaen Editions', *Notes*, 60/3 (March, 2004): pp. 795–801).

Messiaen and the Critics, or Putting an End to the 'Messiaen Case'

As I pointed it out earlier, the most significant contributions relevant to the reception of the *Traité* – and of Messiaen's writings as a whole – have been made by scholars in the UK, Germany, and to a lesser extent, in the United States.[97] It would seem that Messiaen's compatriots are more reticent to issue a reasonably objective appraisal of his writings. Jacques Viret's withering review would then be the exception that proves the rule. Could Messiaen have become some sort of icon in his own country, one whom it would be improper to criticize publicly? After all, this composer displayed throughout his life – and right to the very end – an astonishing level of creative vitality, which commands admiration and respect ... whatever one really thinks of his prose or his music.[98] Furthermore, the composer's historic importance is today nearly unanimously recognized, as shown by the many activities organized around the world to celebrate the centenary of his birth in 2008. All this may be at the root of hesitation, on the part of French music critics, to express any serious reservation on any aspect of his work. This prudent stance is particularly noticeable in what we may call the 'Messiaen scholars', still a rare entity in France.

One may nonetheless wonder, today as in the spring of 1945, following the premiere of *Vingt Regards sur l'Enfant-Jésus* and *Trois Petites Liturgies*, at the high point of the small media storm labelled 'Le cas Messiaen',[99] whether the composer's prolific textual complements to his scores are truly necessary for the appreciation of his music. One may ask oneself whether these texts and assertions – detailed programme notes, theoretical explications, score annotations, presentations and interviews – whether all this abundant material was not meant in the end, at least in part, to control, to 'fix' the discourse on his music. This effort at setting the limits of commentary – probably subconscious – appears as one of the cornerstones of a remarkably consistent process. An incessant dialogue between texts and music is thus established from the beginning, one that the gigantic and late *Traité de rythme, de couleur, et d'ornithologie* nurtures and strengthens – and

---

[97]   I exclude my own review of the first four volumes, published in Canada.

[98]   It could actually be argued that Messiaen's music has suffered from overexposure in France, and particularly in Paris, especially since the 10th anniversary of his death in December 2002.

[99]   A performance of *Visions de l'Amen* in Paris on 25 March 1945, preceded by an introduction to the work by the composer, and the premiere of *Vingt Regards sur l'Enfant-Jésus* the following day, each of the 20 piano pieces again introduced by Messiaen, provoked a rather touchy response from the *Figaro* critic Clarendon – alias Bernard Gavoty. Gavoty's review became the starting point of a flurry of texts in many newspapers and journals written by detractors of Messiaen's music (and also, perhaps especially, of his prose), but also by enthusiastic supporters. A performance of *Les Corps glorieux* on 15 April 1945, and the premiere of *Trois Petites Liturgies* ten days later, the latter's lyrics and introductory remarks all by Messiaen, only revived the polemic. See Chapter 5 of PHNS, pp. 142ff.

360   *Messiaen Perspectives 2: Techniques, Influence and Reception*

sometimes obscures. Of course, the unease the composer felt when faced with another's interpretation of his work is not a unique phenomenon, but it extended to the nearly obsessive care he put into reviewing the texts of the interviews he granted[100] and the endless revision of this immense treatise, destined by this very fact to remain incomplete.

Conclusion: Re-reading Messiaen

The sheer number of documents Messiaen left us creates a veritable maze for the inquisitive reader, in which, we now know, the factual mixes with the imaginary, the true is juxtaposed with the approximate (or even the false or unverifiable). Recent research, while shedding light on certain errors and voluntary omissions on the composer's part, particularly concerning his biography,[101] shows that it is difficult – but not impossible – to engage the music without necessarily taking into account what Messiaen revealed about his intentions and his vocabulary, what he believed to be the *content* of his compositions, of their sound as well as their network of associations.[102] Though some scholars now manage this separation, the literature pertaining to his body of work remains strongly shaded by the composer's own discourse, by these fundamental texts coined in such abundance in this last treatise.

Now that Messiaen and his *œuvre* truly are a part of history, an opportunity may come to undertake new studies on the strong ties that have formed throughout the years between his writings and his musical works. Even if the actions taken by the composer during his lifetime may have rendered the task more complicated, we must avoid confusing the two terms of the equation. Will we dare to go further and propose a true critique of his theoretical work, including his fundamental posthumous *Traité*, without provoking a defensive response from exegetes and disciples, admirers and former students alike?

Each commentator has his own vision of Messiaen and his output, both musical and theoretical. And each reaction to the *Traité* reflects these preconceptions. Thus,

---

[100]   See Nichols, 'And a little child shall lead them': p. 19; see also Claude Samuel, *Permanences d'Olivier Messiaen* (Arles: Actes Sud, 1999), p. 11.

[101]   See PHNS, for example Chapters 4 ('Messiaen's war: 1940–1944') and 9 ('Public Controversy, Private Happiness: 1959–1963'), as well as the interesting articles by Yves Balmer, ' "Je suis né croyant...": Aux sources du catholicisme d'Olivier Messiaen', in Sylvain Caron and Michel Duchesneau, with the collaboration of Marie-Hélène Benoit-Otis (eds), *Musique, art et religion dans l'entre-deux-guerres* (Lyon: Symétrie, 2009); see also, Balmer, 'Entre analyse et propagande', pp. 27–47.

[102]   This would be an interesting angle from which to re-examine edited collections by Bruhn (*Messiaen's Language of Mystical Love* (New York: Garland Publishing Inc.,1998)), Dingle and Simeone (*Olivier Messiaen: Music, Art and Literature* (Aldershot: Ashgate, 2007)), Robert Sholl (*Messiaen Studies* (Cambridge: Cambridge University Press, 2007)) or Lesure and Samuel (*Olivier Messiaen: Le livre du centenaire*, 2008).

Genesis and Reception of Traité de rythme, de couleur, et d'ornithologie   361

while the critic from the *Revue musicale de Suisse romande*, after reading no more than the first *tome*, condemns what he describes as 'unreadable compilations and self-analyses',[103] Theo Hirsbrunner sees in the whole treatise not only a colossal work of theory, but also a lived history of nearly the entire twentieth century',[104] lived from a French point of view of course, the musicologist hastens to add, but nonetheless attributable to a broad-minded musician. Dingle and Keym also conclude their respective reviews with considerations on the *Traité*'s value as a legacy.[105] As for Adélaïde de Place, she considers it 'essential for any composer, any musicologist, any performer, and quite simply for any musician'.[106]

Reading the *Traité de rythme, de couleur, et d'ornithologie* teaches us a great deal about Messiaen the man and about his music, about his full cultural baggage as much as his unexpected documentary lapses. And the reviews expose both the richness and the fragmentation of his discourse, sometimes erudite – filled with musical, literary, philosophical and scientific references – and sometimes undeniably naïve. The truth is, we ask a great deal from composers who are also theorists or writers, especially in the twentieth and twenty-first centuries. We expect them to be at once rigorous and frank, to use solid reasoning but also to complement their *exposés* with carefully doled-out unpublished revelations. In itself, the project that Messiaen undertook as early as 1949 is in every regard remarkable. One may legitimately wish that he had had a more rigorous attitude (i.e. more 'musicological'), a more refined prose, a more concise thought. But viewed from another angle, this would be unfair. Messiaen was first and foremost a creator. Even his unquestionable exploits as a pedagogue were in large part due to his status as a particularly cultured and lucid *composer*.

And whatever we may say about the posthumous *Traité*'s structure and composition, who other than Yvonne Loriod could have completed such a project? Without her and those who assisted her (including the personnel at Alphonse Leduc), this final bequest from a respected composer and complex artist would have stayed unpublished. As more than one reviewer has pointed out, the *Traité* compels recognition as a precious document, if only because it preserves tangible traces of a profoundly influential teaching practice. Therein lies a vast and rich field of inquiry, one that must remain neither unexplored nor simply shallowly observed. Given the size and the complexity of this posthumous work, we are barely beginning to come to terms with its contents and its impact.

---

[103]   Viret, 'Un grand traité posthume de Messiaen': p. 65.

[104]   'Fast ein ganzes Jahrhundert miterlebte Musikgeschichte, aus Französischer Sicht freilich, aber doch von weitem Horizont.' Hirsbrunner, 'Olivier Messiaen: *Traité de rythme*': p. 41. Emphasis added.

[105]   Jean Roy develops this line of thought even further ('Traité: Messiaen et les autres': p. 14).

[106]   Adélaïde de Place, 'Olivier Messiaen: Le *Traité de rythme, de couleur, et d'ornithologie*', *Piano*, 17 (2003): p. 185.

Appendix:
A Critical Catalogue of Messiaen's Musical Works

Christopher Dingle and Robert Fallon

> The posthumous publishing of such music not only does nothing for Messiaen's reputation, but contradicts the composer's well-founded and carefully considered judgment on what was superfluous and what was genuine to his whole creative enterprise.[1]

Does it matter what composers think of their own music? Scholarship since the Second World War has tended to respond to the authority of the composer by pulling in two not entirely compatible directions. On the one hand, musicologists create critical editions, striving to discern as precisely as possible what composers intended to write in their scores and, increasingly, how they expected or wanted them to be performed. Leaving aside the partial nature of even the best urtext score, there is a presumption by many, for understandable reasons, that composers are not just the primary, but the sole authorities for their own music. On the other hand, every newly discovered musical jotting by a major composer is eagerly devoured, studied and performed regardless of whether the composer remotely intended it as anything more than a doodle. As is clear in extreme cases such as Mahler's Tenth Symphony, the composer's wishes are sacrosanct in all things except whether a particular piece of music is to be disseminated and performed. This contradiction is not only entirely understandable, but is also one that the editors share: we seek to discern a composer's thoughts while simultaneously being fascinated by discoveries, no matter how trifling.

The three arrangements of Messiaen's worklist given below provide new perspectives on his musical output that seek to respect Messiaen's conception of his œuvre, while also enumerating the odds and ends of his catalogue. The second and third arrangements are relatively straightforward. The second presents Messiaen's works known to have been performed, listed in chronological order of their première, rather than the more usual completion date. This highlights how, for instance, *Cantéyodjayâ* waited several years for its first performance, in marked contrast to the *Quatre Études de rythme*, which were performed and recorded while

---

[1] See Julian Anderson's chapter, 'Messiaen and the Problem of Communication', in *Messiaen Perspectives 1*.

the ink was barely dry on the page. The third list groups Messiaen's acknowledged works by genre and size of performance forces, which may facilitate performers seeking to explore his music.

We started, though, with the first list, which attempts to clarify Messiaen's core œuvre and, in a series of annotations, to layout the evidence for discerning his own view of his output. While Messiaen was still alive, the content of his body of musical works was reasonably clear, with a very strong sense of œuvre defined by the man himself, both in worklists and also in the extent to which he did, or did not, discuss a given piece. For those coming to his music afresh today, his catalogue of works has become increasingly blurred due to the proliferation of posthumous publications and newly discovered manuscripts. Between Messiaen's death in 1992 and Yvonne Loriod's death in 2010, his worklist became increasingly difficult to negotiate. Loriod had facilitated the publication not only of scores that Messiaen had been working on in his last months of life, but also of music that Messiaen himself had not chosen to publish.[2] Knowledge of the posthumous discoveries has been invaluable, and often reveals the behind-the-scenes work of his activities, from student exercises to occasional pieces and revisions of existing works. Nonetheless, whether given alphabetically or chronologically, an unfettered complete listing obscures the sense of a coherent body of works that Messiaen himself had cultivated. The first list below is an attempt to recapture that sense of an œuvre in which some pieces of music were acknowledged by Messiaen as *works* while others fulfilled different functions. So far as can be discerned, Messiaen's view of a *work* could be understood as a statement of compositional thought, or, alternatively, as a piece clearly intended for performance and posterity. Another way of viewing this would be to say that, had he been so inclined, these are the pieces to which Messiaen would have assigned opus numbers.

The editors do not intend this list of acknowledged works to discourage performance of any of Messiaen's music – quite the opposite. We simply hope this list will clarify which works Messiaen fully endorsed, which ones he forgot or had reservations about, and which pieces lay beyond his control. It might be thought that this can be conveyed merely by following one of the composer's own listings. However, these are problematic in two respects. First, there are a couple of pieces, such as *Chant des déportés*, for which a strong case can be made that Messiaen would have included them in his œuvre even though they do not appear in any of his lists. Second, the best known listing is the one in *Technique*, where he also provided star ratings like a Michelin guide. Despite its obvious limitation that its latest entry was composed in 1943, this worklist also includes numerous pieces that have remained unpublished and, in some cases, may never have been performed. Given that Messiaen was only in his mid-30s when he

---

[2]   Some of the issues of authorship involved with these new publications is addressed in a review of eight posthumously published Messiaen scores; see Robert Fallon, 'Various Messiaen Editions', *Notes* 60/3 (March 2004): pp. 795–801.

Appendix 365

wrote *Technique*, it appears that some of the pieces may have been included to bulk out an otherwise modest worklist for someone making such bold and public revelations. Though many of these unpublished pieces disappeared from Messiaen's own later lists, the point is that the evidence for constructing a list of his acknowledged works is sometimes contradictory.

In considering for the first list which of Messiaen's pieces he would have considered *works*, we have needed to discern as best we can various issues of authorial intention. The editors seek to represent what we think Messiaen would have thought about his works, a useful (if imperfect) task in light of some 15 compositions published posthumously in his name as well as a growing body of transcriptions and newly discovered manuscripts. These range from, on the one hand, a fully completed work for large forces such as *Chant des déportés* to single pages of a birdsong transcription. Peter Hill has noted that much of what is contained in the *cahiers* is not just transcription, but is immediately filtered through Messiaen's immense musicality and could be played as a perfectly musical study. Nonetheless, if Messiaen's worklist is to include every *fauvette* he notated, then, aside from seeing the wood for the trees, there will be a problem seeing the works for the birds.

Needless to say, there are various pieces where the authorial intention is equivocal or uncertain. These are discussed in the annotations constituting the fourth part of this appendix. The annotations set out the evidence and the rationale for the decisions made in the first listing. Some works provoked lively discussion, and our eventual decision should not be viewed as a definitive judgement. Rather, this catalogue highlights that there are debates and discussions to be had about several of Messiaen's pieces.

For the sake of clarity, the lists do not enumerate a work's individual movements. Yet one persistent question about Messiaen's works – and their status as *works* in his view – concerns whether individual movements can be performed apart from the piece from which they are drawn. Performers often wonder whether it is 'legitimate' to perform, for example, only the cello movement from the *Quatuor pour la fin du Temps* or the solo horn movement from *Des Canyons aux étoiles…*. As is common practice, 'may' vocalists sing selections from the song cycles, and organists play choice movements from the organ cycles? 'Can' the opera *Saint François d'Assise* be excerpted or be given in concert performances? Such questions obviously have been and will be answered variously by individual performers. Since the early nineteenth century, however, the touchstone for answering such questions has involved the composer's presumed intention, which can be gleaned from Messiaen and Yvonne Loriod's own practice. There is little doubt that Messiaen valued the integrity of a musical work and sometimes expressly instructed performers not to excerpt his music. Yet in his efforts to promote his music, or for purely artistic reasons, Messiaen and Loriod often performed partial works. In particular, Loriod frequently performed selections from the *Préludes*, *Vingt Regards* and *Catalogue d'oiseaux*. Similarly, there were numerous occasions when Messiaen or Loriod accompanied individual songs from the cycles or even performed a transposition by the composer of the entirety of *Harawi* for a male singer.[3] Sometimes, though, Messiaen's sanctioning of individual movements being performed reflected the fact that a piece was in need of support. *Turangalîla-Symphonie* provides a clear instance of this. Before the official première, three movements were given several performances under the title '*Trois Tâla*'. When the score was published in 1953, it included suggestions of various combinations of movements that could be performed rather than the whole piece. These were removed in the 1990 revised score, and Messiaen was later unequivocal that the work should be performed as a whole: 'The *Trois Tâla* never existed. Through the publisher Durand I forbade the improper use of this title. Besides, I have never been of the view that my *Turangalîla* should be split into separate pieces.'[4] Similarly, Messiaen attended various concert performances of three or four scenes from *Saint François d'Assise* in the latter half of the 1980s, but this was a time when he despaired of the work receiving a second full production. He stated that the work should be performed in its entirety, but, early in its life, this was clearly more an ideal or aspiration rather than an unbreakable condition.

This critical worklist addresses only Messiaen's work as a composer. Music in pedagogical works (such as examples in *Technique* and the *Traité*, *Solfège* (1933), *Vingt leçons de solfège moderne* (1934), *Vingt leçons d'harmonie* (1939) or *Chant donné* for *64 leçons d'harmonie offertes en homage à Jean Gallon* (1953)) have been omitted unless there is a tradition of performance by authoritative interpreters with a direct link to the composer. Messiaen's extensive work as an improviser is problematic for a list such as this. Music for projects such as *Matins du monde* (1948 and 1953) or *Le Mystère de Dieu* (1967) was improvised and partially planned.[5] However, with no manuscript notes or recording available for these or his numerous Sunday improvisations, no entry is provided in this catalogue.[6] Where Messiaen sanctioned a commercial release of his improvisations or where a manuscript has come to light (for example *Tristan et Yseult*), this has been included. A list of works planned but not composed by Messiaen appears in Hill and Simeone's *Messiaen*; a discography of Messiaen as performer is available as an appendix to Christopher Dingle's essay 'Messiaen as Pianist: A Romantic in a Modernist World'; and a bibliography of Messiaen's

---

[3]   PHNS, pp. 206–7.

[4]   Letter to Karl Schweitzer, 23 March 1980, cited in PHNS, p. 174.

[5]   For more on *Matins du monde*, see Robert Fallon, 'Birds, Beasts and Bombs in Messiaen's Cold War Mass', *The Journal of Musicology*, 26/2 (2009): pp. 186–7. For more on *Le Mystère de Dieu* and its relationship with *Méditations sur le mystère de la Sainte Trinité*, see Anne Keeley's chapter 'In the Beginning Was the Word? An Exploration of the Origins of *Méditations sur le mystère de la Sainte Trinité*' in *Messiaen Perspectives 1*.

[6]   Some unauthorized recordings of Messiaen's improvisations have circulated, notably a 2 CD set briefly available on the La Praye label. Frustratingly, this gave no indication of the dates and, hence, the liturgical setting and inspiration for each.

writings is provided within Vincent Benitez's *Olivier Messiaen: A Research and Information Guide.*[7] Inevitably, all catalogues of works are provisional in content and partial in viewpoint. As new discoveries emerge in the future, we hope that the following listings and annotations will prove useful to scholars as they seek to determine where pieces are situated within Messiaen's output.

---

[7] PHNS, p. 430; Christopher Dingle, 'Messiaen as Pianist: A Romantic in a Modernist World', in Scott McCarrey and Lesley Wright (eds), *Perspectives on the Performance of French Piano Music* (Farnham: Ashgate, forthcoming); Vincent Benitez, *Olivier Messiaen: A Research and Information Guide* (New York and London: Routledge, 2008). Benitez's book also includes a list of works, but provides different information and in a different order from that given here.

Lists and Annotations of Messiaen's Works

1. **Complete List of Messiaen's Works (listed by authorial status, then date of composition)**
2. **Messiaen's Works, Listed by Year of Première (listed alphabetically within each year)**
3. **Messiaen's Acknowledged Works, Listed by Instrumentation**
4. **Annotations (listed alphabetically)**

Key

pr. = premièred
c. = composed (this indicates the date(s) when Messiaen was specifically composing the work in question)
pb. = published
unpb. = unpublished
r. = revised publication
* = a piece for which an annotation has been provided. These are located alphabetically in Section 4. Entries without asterisks have relatively straightforward histories where the authorial status is clear one way or the other (e.g. clearly an acknowledged work on the one hand or a student exercise on the other).

Notes

1. Where no date is given, none exists or is known with certainty. For some early works, such as *Le Banquet céleste*, the date of première is presumed to be the earliest known performance.
2. Determining a work's precise title can frequently be difficult. In particular, the graphic presentation on the covers of scores and other sources is often ambiguous about the status of supplementary title information, which often (though not always) suggests a work's genre, for example '*Méditation symphonique*'. In recognition that these are not subtitles in the sense of modern scholarly usage, we have placed this titular information in parentheses and in italics. Similarly, we have not treated instrumentation as part of the title. For instance, the title of the Pièce written in 1991 does not include the words 'pour piano et quatuor à cordes'. Alternate names are given in square brackets. We have not included information on the sources of the texts in Messiaen's vocal works or any other collaborators.

1. Complete List of Messiaen's Works
(listed by authorial status, then by date of composition)

i. Messiaen's Acknowledged Works
ii. Other Pieces
    a. Score Known to Exist
    b. Pieces Incorporated into Works in Section (i)
    c. Location of Score is Unknown
    d. Select Arrangements
    e. Alternate Names of Select Works and Pieces

i. Messiaen's Acknowledged Works

La Dame de Shalott, piano*
c. 1917; pr.; unpb.; recorded by Yvonne Loriod, 1975

Le Banquet céleste, organ*
c. 1928; pr. 1935; pb. 1934; r. 1960

Préludes, piano
c. 1928–29; pr. 1930 (6 mvts), 1937 (complete); pb. 1930; r. 1945

Diptyque (*Essai sur la vie terrestre et l'éternité bienheureuse*), organ
c. 1929; pr. 1930; pb. 1930

Trois Mélodies, soprano and piano
c. 1930; pr. 1931; pb. 1930

Les Offrandes oubliées (*Méditation symphonique*), orchestra
c. 1930; pr. 1931; pb. 1931

Les Offrandes oubliées (*Méditation symphonique*), piano reduction by Messiaen*
c. 1930; pr.; pb. 1931

La Mort du Nombre, soprano, tenor, violin and piano
c. 1930; pr. 1931; pb. 1931

Le Tombeau resplendissant, orchestra*
c. 1931; pr. 1933; pb. 1997

Apparition de l'Église éternelle, organ
c. 1932; pr. 1932?; pb. 1934; r. 1985

Hymne au Saint-Sacrement [Hymne], orchestra*
c. 1932 [lost 1942 and re-composed from memory 1946]; pr. 1933; pb. 1974

Thème et variations, violin and piano
c. 1932; pr. 1932; pb. 1934

Fantaisie burlesque, piano*
c. 1932; pr. 1933; pb. 1932

L'Ascension (*Quatre méditations symphoniques*), orchestra*
c. 1932–33; pr. 1935; pb. 1948

L'Ascension (*Quatre méditations symphoniques*), organ*
c. 1933–34; pr. 1935; pb. 1934

Vocalise-étude, high voice and piano*
c. 1935; pr. 1935; pb. 1935

Pièce (*pour le Tombeau de Paul Dukas*), piano*
c. 1935; pr. 1936; pb. 1936 in *La Revue musicale*; r. 1996

La Nativité du Seigneur (*Neuf méditations*), organ
c. 1935; pr. 1936; pb. 1936

Poèmes pour Mi, dramatic soprano [*grand soprano dramatique*] and piano
c. 1936; pr. 1937; pb. 1937

Poèmes pour Mi, dramatic soprano [*grand soprano dramatique*] and orchestra
   (orchestration of so prano and piano version)
c. 1937; pr. 1937 (part), 1949 (whole); pb. 1939

O sacrum convivium! (*Motet au Saint-Sacrement*), four-voice mixed chorus or
   four soloists with organ ad libitum or soprano and organ
c. 1937; pr. 1938; pb. 1937

Chants de terre et de ciel, soprano and piano
c. 1938; pr. 1939; pb. 1939

Les Corps glorieux (*Sept Visions brèves de la Vie des Ressuscités*), organ
c. 1939; pr. 1943; pb. 1942

Quatuor pour la fin du Temps, violin, clarinet, cello, piano
c. 1940–41; pr. 1941; pb. 1942

Rondeau, piano*
c. 1943; pr. 1943; pb. 1943

Visions de l'Amen, two pianos
c. 1942–43; pr. 1943; pb. 1950

Trois Petites Liturgies de la Présence Divine, solo piano, solo ondes Martenot,
celesta, vibraphone, percussion, women's chorus, strings
c. 1943–44; pr. 1945; pb. 1952; r. 1952 [sic], 1990

Vingt Regards sur l'Enfant-Jésus, piano
c. 1944; pr. 1945; pb. 1947

Harawi (*Chant d'amour et de mort*), voice and piano
c. 1945; pr. 1946; pb. 1949

Chant des déportés, chorus and orchestra*
c. 1945; pr. 1945; pb. 1998

Turangalîla-Symphonie, solo piano and solo ondes Martenot and large orchestra
c. 1946–48; pr. 1949; pb. 1953; r. 1990 (pb. 1994)

Cinq Rechants, 12 mixed voices
c. 1948; pr. 1950; pb. 1949

Cantéyodjayâ, piano
c. 1949; pr. 1954; pb. 1953

Quatre Études de rythme, piano*
c. 1949–50; pr. 1950; pb. 1950

Messe de la Pentecôte, organ
c. 1950–51; pr. 1951; pb. 1951

Livre d'orgue, organ
c. 1951–52; pr. 1953; pb. 1953

Le Merle noir, flute and piano
c. 1952; pr. 1952; pb. 1952

372 *Messiaen Perspectives 2: Techniques, Influence and Reception*

Réveil des oiseaux, solo piano and orchestra
c. 1953; pr. 1953; pb. 1955; r. 1988 (pb. 1999)

Oiseaux exotiques, solo piano and small orchestra
c. 1955–56; pr. 1956; pb. 1960; r. 1985 (pb. 1995)

Catalogue d'oiseaux (*Chants d'oiseaux des provinces de France. Chaque soliste est présenté dans son habitat, entouré de son paysage, et des chants des autres oiseaux qui affectionnent la même région.*), piano
c. 1956–58; pr. 1957 (partial), 1959 (complete); pb. 1964

Chronochromie, large orchestra
c. 1959–60; pr. 1960; pb. 1963

Verset (*pour la fête de la Dédicace*), organ
c. 1960; pr. 1961; pb. 1961

Sept Haïkaï (*Esquisses japonaises*), solo piano and small orchestra
c. 1962; pr. 1963; pb. 1966

Couleurs de la Cité céleste, solo piano, three clarinets, three xylophones, brass orchestra and metallic percussion
c. 1963; pr. 1964; pb. 1967

Et exspecto resurrectionem mortuorum, orchestra of woodwinds, brass, and metallic percussion
c. 1964; pr. 1965; pb. 1967

La Transfiguration de Notre-Seigneur Jésus-Christ, mixed chorus, seven instrumental soloists and very large orchestra
c. 1965–69; pr. 1969; pb. 1972

Méditations sur le mystère de la Sainte Trinité, organ
c. 1969; pr. 1972; pb. 1973

La Fauvette des jardins, piano
c. 1970; pr. 1972; pb. 1972

Des Canyons aux étoiles..., solo piano, horn, xylorimba, glockenspiel and orchestra
c. 1971–74; pr. 1974; pb. 1978

Saint François d'Assise (*Scènes Franciscaines*), opera
c. 1975–83; pr. 1983; pb. 1983 (libretto), 1988–1992 (full score), 2007–12 (vocal score)

Livre du Saint Sacrement, organ
c. 1984; pr. 1986; pb. 1989

Petites Esquisses d'oiseaux, piano
c. 1985; pr. 1987; pb. 1988

Un Vitrail et des oiseaux, solo piano and small orchestra*
c. 1987; pr. 1988; pb. 1992

La Ville d'En-Haut, solo piano and small orchestra*
c. 1987; pr. 1989; pb. 1994

Un Sourire, orchestra*
c. 1989; pr. 1991; pb. 1994

Pièce, piano and string quartet*
c. 1991; pr. 1991; pb. 1992

Éclairs sur l'Au-Delà…, large orchestra*
c. 1987–91; pr. 1992; pb. 1998

Concert à quatre, solo flute, solo oboe, solo cello, solo piano, orchestra*
c. 1990–92 [Note: completed by Yvonne Loriod]; pr. 1994; pb. 2003

ii. Other Pieces

a) Score Known to Exist

Fugue [1926, sur un sujet d'Henri Rabaud]*
c. 1926; pr.; pb. 1926

Prélude, organ*
c. 1927–28?; pr. 1999; pb. 2002

Offrande au Saint-Sacrement, organ*
c. 1928–29?; pr. 1999; pb. 2001

Fugue pour le Concours de Rome
c. 1930; pr.; unpb.

La Sainte-Bohème, mixed chorus and orchestra*
c. 1930; pr.; unpb.

Fugue pour le Concours de Rome
c. 1931; pr.; unpb.

La Jeunesse des vieux, mixed chorus and orchestra*
c. 1931; pr.; unpb.

Fantaisie, violin and piano*
c. 1933; pr. 1935; pb. 2007

Morceau de lecture à vue (*pour les examens de piano de l'École normale de Musique: Déchiffrage I*), piano*
c. 1934; pr. 1934; pb. 1934 in *Le Monde musical*; 2005 facsimile in PHNS

Fête des belles eaux, six ondes Martenot*
c. 1937; pr. 1937; pb. 2003

Deux Monodies en quarts de ton, ondes Martenot*
c. 1938; pr.; unpb.

Portique pour une fille de France [Chœurs pour une Jeanne d'Arc], large chorus and small mixed chorus, a cappella*
c. 1941; pr. 1941; unpb.

Timbres-durées, musique concrète*
c. 1952; pr. 1952; pb. in fragments; recording released 2004

La Fauvette Passerinette, piano*
performing realization by Peter Hill
c. 1961; pr. 2013; unpb.

Monodie, organ*
c. 1963; pr. 1998; pb. 1998

Prélude, piano*
c. 1964; pr. 2000; pb. 2002

Improvisations [for *L'Âme en bourgeon*], organ*
c. improvised 1977; pr. 1977; unpb., recorded improvisations released on Erato STU 71104 (LP)

[Three] Improvisations, organ
c. improvised 1985; pr. 1985; unpb., recorded improvisations released as Olivier
  Messiaen: Quartet for the end of Time / Improvisations on Image Entertainment
  ID5085GCDVD (DVD)

Chant dans le style Mozart, clarinet and piano*
c. 1986; pr. 1986; unpb.

Un oiseau des arbres de Vie*
c. 1988?; unpb.

b. Pieces Incorporated into Works in Section (i)

Pièce, oboe and piano*
c. 1945; pr. 1945; pb. 1949 as the fifth movement, 'L'amour de Piroutcha', of
  Harawi

Tristan et Yseult (*musique de scène*), organ*
  c. 1945; pr. 1945; unpb. (improvised); used as 'Thème d'Amour' in *Harawi*

Trois Tâla, piano solo and orchestra*
c. 1946–48; pr. 1948; pb. 1953 within *Turangalîla-Symphonie*

Mode de valeurs et d'intensités, piano
c. 1949; pr. 1950; pb. 1950; see annotation for *Quatre Études de rythme**

Neumes rythmiques, piano
c. 1949; pr. 1950; pb. 1950; see annotation for *Quatre Études de rythme**

Île de feu 1
c. 1950; pr. 1950; pb. 1950; see annotation for *Quatre Études de rythme**

Île de feu 2
c. 1950; pr. 1950; pb. 1950; see annotation for *Quatre Études de rythme**

Pièce (à la mémoire de Jean-Pierre Guézec), horn*
c. 1971; pr. 1971; pb. 1978 as sixth movement of *Des Canyons aux étoiles…*

Sigle, flute*
c. 1982; pr. 1982; pb. 1998 within seventh movement of *Éclairs sur l'Au-Delà…*,
  also 2007 (facsimile in Fr. edn of PHNS)

c. Location of Score is Unknown

Deux Ballades de Villon, voice and piano
c. 1921; pr.; unpb.

La Tristesse d'un grand ciel blanc, piano
c. 1925; pr.; unpb.

Andantino, string quartet
c. 1926/27; pr.; unpb.

Pièce pour orgue sur un thème de Laparra, organ
c. 1927; pr.; unpb.

Esquisse modale, organ
c. 1927; pr.; unpb.

Adagio, organ, violin and cello
c. 1927; pr.; unpb.

Variations écossaises [?Pièce pour orgue sur un thème écossais], organ
c. 1928; pr.; unpb.

Fugue en ré mineur, orchestra
c. 1928; pr.; unpb.

Jésus (*Poème symphonique*)
c. 1928; pr.; unpb.

Le Banquet eucharistique, orchestra*
c. 1928; pr. 1930; unpb.

L'Hôte aimable des âmes, organ
c. 1928; pr.; unpb.

Prélude en trio sur un thème de Haydn, organ
c. 1929; pr.; unpb.

Simple Chant d'une âme, orchestra
c. 1929–30; pr.; unpb.

L'Ensorceleuse, cantata for soprano, tenor, bass-baritone and piano (or orchestra)*
c. 1931; pr. 1931; unpb.

Messe, eight sopranos and four violins
c. 1933; pr.; unpb.

Musique de scène pour un Œdipe [Dieu est innocent], ondes Martenot*
c. 1942; pr. 1942; unpb. (improvisation?); Lucien Fabre's play *Dieu est innocent*
published in 1945

d. Select Arrangements

Apparition de l'Église éternelle, arr. David Miller for Wind Ensemble

Chants de terre et de ciel, arr. Cliff Colnot for voice, flute, clarinet, violin, viola,
cello, piano and 2 percussionists

Feuillets inédits, arrangement by Yvonne Loriod for ondes Martenot and piano of
unpublished pieces*

La Nativité du Seigneur, mvts 6 & 7, arr. Owen Murray for classical accordion

e. Alternate Names of Select Works and Pieces

Chœurs pour un Jeanne d'Arc – title given by Messiaen in *Technique* to the
choruses written for *Portique pour une fille de France*

Dieu est innocent – title of play for which Messiaen wrote *Musique de scène pour
un Œdipe*

La Mer – see *L'Ensorceleuse*

Œdipe – see *Musique de scène pour un Œdipe*

Oraison – title for extract from *Fête des belles eaux*

Prismes (*Six Poèmes*) – original title for *Chants de terre et de ciel*

2. Messiaen's Works, Listed by Year of Première
(listed alphabetically within each year)

1930s

Le Banquet eucharistique, orchestra
pr. 1930; c. 1928; unpb.

Diptyque (*Essai sur la vie terrestre et l'éternité bienheureuse*), organ
pr. 1930; c. 1929; pb. 1930

Préludes, piano
pr. 1930 (6 mvts), 1937 (complete); c. 1928–9; pb. 1930; r. 1945

L'Ensorceleuse, soprano, tenor, bass-baritone and piano (or orchestra)*
pr. 1931; c. 1931; unpb.

La Mort du Nombre, soprano, tenor, violin and piano
pr. 1931; c. 1930; pb. 1931

Les Offrandes oubliées (*Méditation symphonique*), orchestra*
pr. 1931; c. 1930; pb. 1931

Trois Mélodies, soprano and piano
pr. 1931; c. 1930; pb. 1930

Apparition de l'Église éternelle, organ
pr. 1932?; c. 1932; pb. 1934; r. 1985

Thème et variations, violin and piano
pr. 1932; c. 1932; pb. 1934

Fantaisie burlesque, piano*
pr. 1933; c. 1932; pb. 1932

Hymne au Saint-Sacrement [Hymne], orchestra*
pr. 1933; c. 1932 [lost 1942 and re-composed from memory 1946]; pb. 1974

Le Tombeau resplendissant, orchestra*
pr. 1933; c. 1931; pb. 1997

Morceau de lecture à vue (*pour les examens de piano de l'École normale de Musique: Déchiffrage I*), piano*
pr. 1934; c. 1934; pb. 1934 in *Le Monde musical*; 2005 facsimile in PHNS

L'Ascension (*Quatre méditations symphoniques*), orchestra*
pr. 1935; c. 1932–33; pb. 1948

L'Ascension (*Quatre méditations symphoniques*), organ*
pr. 1935; c. 1933–34; pb. 1934

Le Banquet céleste, organ*
pr. 1935; c. 1928; pb. 1934; r. 1960

Fantaisie, violin and piano*
pr. 1935; c. 1933; pb. 2007

Vocalise-étude, high voice and piano*
pr. 1935; c. 1935; pb. 1935

La Nativité du Seigneur (*Neuf méditations*), organ
pr. 1936; c. 1935; pb. 1936

Pièce (*pour le Tombeau de Paul Dukas*), piano*
pr. 1936; c. 1935; pb. 1936 in *La Revue musicale*; 1996

Fête des belles eaux, six ondes Martenot*
pr. 1937; c. 1937; pb. 2003

Poèmes pour Mi, dramatic soprano [*grand soprano dramatique*] and piano
pr. 1937; c. 1936; pb. 1937

Poèmes pour Mi, dramatic soprano [*grand soprano dramatique*] and orchestra (orchestration of soprano and piano version)
pr. 1937 (part), 1949 (whole); c. 1937; pb. 1939

O sacrum convivium! (*Motet au Saint-Sacrement*), four-voice mixed chorus or four soloists with organ ad libitum or soprano and organ
pr. 1938; c. 1937; pb. 1937

Chants de terre et de ciel, soprano and piano
pr. 1939; c. 1938; pb. 1939

1940s

Portique pour une fille de France [Chœurs pour une Jeanne d'Arc], large chorus and small mixed chorus, a cappella*
pr. 1941; c. 1941; unpb.

Quatuor pour la fin du Temps, violin, clarinet, cello, piano
pr. 1941; c. 1940; pb. 1942

Musique de scène pour un Œdipe [Dieu est innocent], ondes Martenot*
pr. 1942; c. 1942; unpb. (improvisation?); Lucien Fabre's play *Dieu est innocent* published in 1945

Les Corps glorieux (*Sept Visions brèves de la Vie des Ressuscités*), organ
pr. 1943; c. 1939; pb. 1942

Rondeau, piano*
pr. 1943; c. 1943; pb. 1943

Visions de l'Amen, two pianos
pr. 1943; c. 1943; pb. 1950

Chant des déportés, chorus and orchestra*
pr. 1945; c. 1945; pb. 1998

Pièce, oboe and piano*
pr. 1945?; c. 1945; pb. 1949 as the fifth movement, 'L'amour de Piroutcha', of *Harawi*

Tristan et Yseult (*musique de scène*), organ*
pr. 1945; c. 1945; unpb. (improvised) – became 'Thème d'Amour' in *Harawi*

Trois Petites Liturgies de la Présence Divine, solo piano, solo ondes Martenot, celesta, vibraphone, percussion, women's chorus, strings
pr. 1945; c. 1943–44; pb. 1952; r. 1952 [sic], 1990

Vingt Regards sur l'Enfant-Jésus, piano
pr. 1945; c. 1944; pb. 1947

Harawi (*Chant d'amour et de mort*), voice and piano
pr. 1946; c. 1945; pb. 1949

Turangalîla-Symphonie, solo piano and solo ondes Martenot and large orchestra
pr. 1949; c. 1946–48; pb. 1953; r. 1990 (pb. 1994)

1950s

Cinq Rechants, 12 mixed voices
pr. 1950; c. 1948; pb. 1949

Quatre Études de rythme, piano*
pr. 1950; c. 1949–50; pb. 1950

Messe de la Pentecôte, organ
pr. 1951; c. 1950–51; pb. 1951

Le Merle noir, flute and piano*
pr. 1952; c. 1952; pb. 1952

Timbres-durées, musique concrète
pr. 1952; c. 1952; pb. in fragments; recording released 2004

Livre d'orgue, organ
pr. 1953; c. 1951–52; pb. 1953

Réveil des oiseaux, solo piano and orchestra*
pr. 1953; c. 1953; pb. 1955; r. 1988 (pb. 1999)

Cantéyodjayâ, piano
pr. 1954; c. 1949; pb. 1953

Oiseaux exotiques, solo piano and small orchestra*
pr. 1956; c. 1955–56; pb. 1960; r. 1985 (pb. 1995)

Catalogue d'oiseaux (*Chants d'oiseaux des provinces de France. Chaque soliste est présenté dans son habitat, entouré de son paysage, et des chants des autres oiseaux qui affectionnent la même région.*), piano
pr. 1957 (partial), 1959 (complete); c. 1956–58; pb. 1964

1960s

Chronochromie, large orchestra
pr. 1960; c. 1959–60; pb. 1963

Verset (*pour la fête de la Dédicace*), organ
pr. 1961; c. 1960; pb. 1961

Sept Haïkaï (*Esquisses japonaises*), solo piano and small orchestra
pr. 1963; c. 1962; pb. 1966

Couleurs de la Cité céleste, solo piano, three clarinets, three xylophones, brass
orchestra and metallic percussion
pr. 1964; c. 1963; pb. 1967

Et exspecto resurrectionem mortuorum, orchestra of woodwinds, brass, and
metallic percussion
pr. 1965; c. 1964; pb. 1967

La Transfiguration de Notre-Seigneur Jésus-Christ, mixed chorus, seven
instrumental soloists and very large orchestra
pr. 1969; c. 1965–69; pb. 1972

1970s

La Fauvette des jardins, piano
pr. 1972; c. 1970; pb. 1972

Méditations sur le mystère de la Sainte Trinité, organ
pr. 1972; c. 1969; pb. 1973

Des Canyons aux étoiles..., solo piano, horn, xylorimba, glockenspiel and
orchestra
pr. 1974; c. 1971–74; pb. 1978

1980s

Sigle, flute*
pr. 1982; c. 1982; pb. 1998 within seventh movement of *Éclairs sur l'Au-Delà...*,
also 2007 (facsimile in Fr. edn of PHNS)

Saint François d'Assise (*Scènes Franciscaines*), opéra
pr. 1983; c. 1975–83; pb. 1983 (libretto), 1988–1992 (full score), 2007–12 (vocal
score)

Chant dans le style Mozart, clarinet and piano*
pr. 1986; c. 1986; unpb.

Livre du Saint Sacrement, organ
pr. 1986; c. 1984; pb. 1989

Petites Esquisses d'oiseaux, piano
pr. 1987; c. 1985; pb. 1988

Un Vitrail et des oiseaux, solo piano and small orchestra*
pr. 1988; c. 1987; pb. 1992

La Ville d'En-Haut, solo piano and small orchestra*
pr. 1989; c. 1987; pb. 1994

1990s

Pièce, piano and string quartet*
pr. 1991; c. 1991; pb. 1992

Un Sourire, orchestra
pr. 1991; c. 1989; pb. 1994

Éclairs sur l'Au-Delà..., large orchestra*
pr. 1992; c. 1987–91; pb. 1998

Concert à quatre, solo flute, solo oboe, solo cello, solo piano, orchestra*
pr. 1994; c. 1990–92; pb. 2003

Monodie, organ*
pr. 1998; c. 1963; pb. 1998

Offrande au Saint-Sacrement, organ*
pr. 1999; c. 1928–29?; pb. 2001

Prélude, organ*
pr. 1999; c. 1927–28?; pb. 2002

Prélude, piano*
pr. 2000; c. 1964; pb. 2002

La Fauvette Passerinette, piano*
performing realization by Peter Hill
pr. 2013; c. 1961; unpb.

3. Messiaen's Acknowledged Works, Listed by Instrumentation

i. Vocal Works: opera; chorus and orchestra; solo voice(s) and instruments (by size of ensemble); a cappella; song (by date of composition).
ii. Instrumental Works: orchestra with soloist(s) (by size of ensemble); orchestra (by size of ensemble); chamber (by size of ensemble); organ (by duration); piano (by duration); other.

i. Vocal Works

Opera

Saint François d'Assise (*Scènes Franciscaines*), opéra

Chorus and Orchestra

La Transfiguration de Notre-Seigneur Jésus-Christ, mixed chorus, seven instrumental soloists and very large orchestra
pr. 1969; c. 1965–69; pb. 1972

Chant des déportés, chorus and orchestra*
pr. 1945; c. 1945; pb. 1998

Trois Petites Liturgies de la Présence Divine, solo piano, solo ondes Martenot, celesta, vibraphone, percussion, women's chorus, strings
pr. 1945; c. 1943–44; pb. 1952; r. 1952 [sic], 1990

Solo Voice(s) and Instruments

Poèmes pour Mi, dramatic soprano [*grand soprano dramatique*] and orchestra (orchestration of voice and piano version)
pr. 1937 (part), 1949 (whole); c. 1937; pb. 1939

La Mort du Nombre, soprano, tenor, violin and piano
pr. 1931; c. 1930; pb. 1931

Messiaen Perspectives 2: Techniques, Influence and Reception

O sacrum convivium! (*Motet au Saint-Sacrement*), four-voice mixed chorus or four soloists with organ ad libitum or soprano and organ [also listed under a cappella]
pr. 1938; c. 1937; pb. 1937

A Cappella

O sacrum convivium! (*Motet au Saint-Sacrement*), four-voice mixed chorus or four soloists with organ ad libitum or soprano and organ [also listed under solo voice(s) and instruments]
pr. 1938; c. 1937; pb. 1937

Cinq Rechants, 12 mixed voices
pr. 1950; c. 1948; pb. 1949

Song

Trois Mélodies, soprano and piano
pr. 1931; c. 1930; pb. 1930

Vocalise-étude, high voice and piano*
pr. 1935; c. 1935; pb. 1935

Poèmes pour Mi, voice and piano
pr. 1937; c. 1936; pb. 1937

Chants de terre et de ciel, soprano and piano
pr. 1939; c. 1938; pb. 1939

Harawi (*Chant d'amour et de mort*), voice and piano
pr. 1946; c. 1945; pb. 1949

ii. Instrumental

Orchestra with Soloist(s) (by size of ensemble)

Concert à quatre, solo flute, solo oboe, solo cello, solo piano, orchestra*
pr. 1994; c. 1990–92; pb. 2003
[7.5.7.5; 4.5.3.1; flute solo, oboe solo, piano solo, cello solo; celesta, glockenspiel, xylophone, xylorimba, marimba, 7 percussion; 16.16.14.12.10]

Turangalîla-Symphonie, solo piano and solo ondes Martenot and large orchestra
c. 1946–48; pr. 1949; pb. 1953; r. 1990 (pb. 1994)
[3.3.3.3; 4.5.3.1; piano solo, ondes Martenot solo, glockenspiel, celesta, vibraphone, 5 percussion; 16.16.14.12.10]

Réveil des oiseaux, solo piano and orchestra*
c. 1953; pr. 1953; pb. 1955; r. 1988 (pb. 1999)
[4.3.4.3; 2.2.0.0; piano solo, celesta, xylophone, glockenspiel, 2 percussion; 8.8.8.8.6]

Des Canyons aux étoiles…, solo piano, horn, xylorimba, glockenspiel and orchestra
pr. 1974; c. 1971–74; pb. 1978
[4.3.4.3; 3.3.3.0; piano solo, glockenspiel, xylorimba, 5 percussion; 6.0.3.3.1]

La Ville d'En-Haut, solo piano and small orchestra*
pr. 1989; c. 1987; pb. 1994
[5.4.5.3; 6.4.3.1; piano solo, glockenspiel, xylophone, xylorimba, marimba, 4 percussion]

Sept Haïkaï (*Esquisses japonaises*), solo piano and small orchestra
pr. 1963; c. 1962; pb. 1966
[2.3.4.2; 0.1.1.0; piano solo, xylophone, marimba, 4 percussion; 8.0.0.0.0]

Un Vitrail et des oiseaux, solo piano and small orchestra*
pr. 1988; c. 1987; pb. 1992
[4.4.5.3; 0.1.0.0; piano solo, xylophone, xylorimba, marimba, 5 percussion]

Couleurs de la Cité céleste, solo piano, three clarinets, three xylophones, brass orchestra and metallic percussion
pr. 1964; c. 1963; pb. 1967
[0.0.3.0; 2.4.4.0; piano solo, xylophone, xylorimba, marimba, 3 percussion]

Oiseaux exotiques, solo piano and small orchestra*
c. 1955–56; pr. 1956; pb. 1960; r. 1985 (pb. 1995)
[2.1.3.1; 2.1.0.0; piano solo, glockenspiel, xylophone, 5 percussion]

Orchestra (by size of ensemble)

Éclairs sur l'Au-Delà…, large orchestra*
pr. 1992; c. 1987–91; pb. 1998
[10.4.10.4; 6.5.3.3; crotales, glockenspiel, xylophone, xylorimba, marimba, 10 percussion; 16.16.14.12.10]

Chronochromie, large orchestra
pr. 1960; c. 1959–60; pb. 1963
[4.3.4.3; 4.4.3.1; glockenspiel, xylophone, marimba, 3 percussion; 16.16.14.12.10]

L'Ascension (*Quatre méditations symphoniques*), orchestra*
pr. 1935; c. 1932–33; pb. 1948
[3.3.3.3; 4.3.3.1; timpani, percussion; 16.16.14.12.10]

Les Offrandes oubliées (*Méditations symphoniques*)*
pr. 1931; c. 1930; pb. 1931
[3.3.3.3; 4.3.3.1; timpani, percussion; strings]

Le Tombeau resplendissant, orchestra*
pr. 1933; c. 1931; pb. 1997
[3.3.3.3; 4.3.3.1; timpani, percussion, strings]

Hymne au Saint-Sacrement [Hymne], orchestra*
pr. 1933; c. 1932 [lost 1942 and re-composed from memory 1946]; pb. 1974
[3.3.3.3; 4.3.3.0; timpani, percussion; strings]

Un Sourire, orchestra*
pr. 1991; c. 1989; pb. 1994
[4.4.3.3; 4.1.0.0; xylophone, xylorimba, 2 percussion; 16.16.14.12.0]

Et exspecto resurrectionem mortuorum, orchestra of woodwinds, brass and
 metallic percussion
pr. 1965; c. 1964; pb. 1967
[5.4.5.4; 6.4.4.2; 6 percussion]

Chamber (by size of ensemble)

Pièce, piano and string quartet*
pr. 1991; c. 1991; pb. 1992

La Mort du Nombre, soprano, tenor, violin and piano
pr. 1931; c. 1930; pb. 1931

Quatuor pour la fin du Temps, violin, clarinet, cello, piano
pr. 1941; c. 1940; pb. 1942

Visions de l'Amen, two pianos
pr. 1943; c. 1943; pb. 1950

Thème et variations, violin and piano
pr. 1932; c. 1932; pb. 1934

Fantaisie, violin and piano*
pr. 1935; c. 1933; pb. 2007

Le Merle noir, flute and piano*
pr. 1952; c. 1952; pb. 1952

Organ (by duration)

Livre du Saint Sacrement, organ
pr. 1986; c. 1984; pb. 1989

Méditations sur le mystère de la Sainte Trinité, organ
pr. 1972; c. 1969; pb. 1973

La Nativité du Seigneur (*Neuf méditations*), organ
pr. 1936; c. 1935; pb. 1936

Les Corps glorieux (*Sept Visions brèves de la Vie des Ressuscités*), organ
pr. 1943; c. 1939; pb. 1942

Livre d'orgue, organ
pr. 1953; c. 1951–52; pb. 1953

Messe de la Pentecôte, organ
pr. 1951; c. 1950–51; pb. 1951

L'Ascension (*Quatre méditations symphoniques*), organ*
pr. 1935; c. 1933–34; pb. 1934

Diptyque (*Essai sur la vie terrestre et l'éternité bienheureuse*), organ
pr. 1930; c. 1929; pb. 1930

Apparition de l'Église éternelle, organ
pr. 1932?; c. 1932; pb. 1934; r. 1985

Verset (*pour la fête de la Dédicace*), organ
pr. 1961; c. 1960; pb. 1961

Le Banquet céleste, organ*
pr. 1935; c. 1928; pb. 1934; r. 1960

Piano (by duration)

Catalogue d'oiseaux (*Chants d'oiseaux des provinces de France. Chaque soliste est présenté dans son habitat, entouré de son paysage, et des chants des autres oiseaux qui affectionnent la même région.*), piano
pr. 1957 (partial), 1959 (complete); c. 1956–58; pb. 1964

Vingt Regards sur l'Enfant-Jésus, piano
pr. 1945; c. 1944; pb. 1947

Préludes, piano
pr. 1930 (6 mvts), 1937 (complete); c. 1928–29; pb. 1930; r. 1945

La Fauvette des jardins, piano
pr. 1972; c. 1970; pb. 1972

Quatre Études de rythme, piano*
pr. 1950; c. 1949–50; pb. 1950

Petites Esquisses d'oiseaux, piano
pr. 1987; c. 1985; pb. 1988

Cantéyodjayâ, piano
pr. 1954; c. 1949; pb. 1953

Les Offrandes oubliées (*Méditation symphonique*), piano reduction by Messiaen
pr.; c. 1930; pb. 1931

Fantaisie burlesque, piano*
pr. 1933; c. 1932; pb. 1932

Pièce (*pour le Tombeau de Paul Dukas*), piano*
pr. 1936; b. 1935; c. 1935; pb. 1936 in *La Revue musicale*; r. 1996

Rondeau, piano*
pr. 1943; c. 1943; pb. 1943

4. Annotations

(listed alphabetically)

* Asterisks on titles above refer to this list

L'Ascension *(Quatre méditations symphoniques)*

Thanks to the worklist in *Technique*, where Messiaen wrote the dates the wrong way round, it was thought for some time that the orchestral version of *L'Ascension* was an arrangement of the organ version. In fact, not only did the orchestral version come first, but the organ transcription appears to have been viewed by Messiaen as just that, a transcription, similar to the piano reduction of *Les Offrandes oubliées* and following a standard practice of composers, until recordings became the usual way of disseminating their works, of making arrangements of orchestral music. This is complicated by the fact that the third movement of the organ version is an original piece, 'Transports de joie'. However, Messiaen tended gently to encourage performance of other organ cycles in preference to *L'Ascension*. For instance, in a letter about a recital planned to coincide with the first performance of *La Transfiguration*, he stated that '*L'Ascension* dates from 1933 and I think it would be better to give a more characteristic work. You could ask Marie-Claire Alain to play *La Nativité du Seigneur* or ask Raffi Ourgandjian to play either *Les Corps glorieux* or the *Livre d'orgue*.'[1]

Le Banquet céleste, *organ;* **Le Banquet eucharistique**, *orchestra*

Although not the first piece by Messiaen to appear in print, *Le Banquet céleste* is the earliest music by Messiaen for which he sought publication. The *Préludes* prompted Dukas to recommend to René Dommange, managing director of the publishing house Durand & Cie, that Messiaen be contracted to them; they were published in June 1930. The first *work* actually to appear in print was the *Diptyque* in May 1930. The very first *music* by Messiaen to appear in print, though not at his prompting, was his fugue for the 1926 concours, which was published by Heugel (see Fugue [1926] below). As an organ work, *Le Banquet céleste* contributed to the misperception that Messiaen began his career as an organist-composer. However, it was actually adapted from a section of the orchestral work *Le Banquet eucharistique*. He told Brigitte Massin, 'When I was in Paul Dukas's class, I composed a work initially conceived for orchestra, and afterwards

---

[1] Nigel Simeone, 'Towards "un success absolument formidable": The Birth of Messiaen's *La Transfiguration*', *Musical Times*, 145 (Summer 2004): p. 21.

a second version for organ, at least of a passage taken from this work. [It had] a single beautiful moment, and this I kept and made into a little piece for organ, *Le Banquet céleste*.'[2] Even if the score of *Le Banquet eucharistique* comes to light, there would be little case for including it in the list of acknowledged works, for Messiaen's assessment was damning: 'It was a very long work, neither very well scored, nor very well constructed. ... I wrote in sonata form, but it was an entirely unsuccessful sonata form, with a development, but terribly scholarly, ... it was truly a great naivety.'[3] Similarly, he told Almut Rößler that he 'found it bombastic, in other words, not good. I kept only the 2nd theme of it and rewrote it for organ. The 1st theme and the development – a proper one à la Beethoven – I discarded.'[4] It seems likely that, as well as salvaging the best part of the orchestral piece, Messiaen adapted this music for organ also to sharpen his compositional knowledge of an instrument that was still relatively new to him. Messiaen revised *Le Banquet céleste* in 1960, changing the time signature from $\frac{3}{4}$ to $\frac{3}{2}$, doubling the length of all notated durations and adding a metronome marking ($\flat$ = 52) as organists were playing it too quickly.

Chant des déportés, chorus and orchestra

Chant des déportés was commissioned by Henri Rabaud, the Director of Music at Radio France, for a concert celebrating the release of prisoners from the concentration camps. For many years, few people knew that this fascinating piece existed. After the single performance on 2 November 1945 conducted by Manuel Rosenthal with the 21-year-old Pierre Boulez at the piano, the score for *Chant des déportés* was deposited in the library at Radio France and forgotten. According to Yvonne Loriod, Messiaen mentioned his sorrow at the apparent loss of the work to an interviewer in 1991, who promised to look for it, and, to the composer's delight, subsequently found the piece in the Radio France library, exactly where it had been tucked away after the performance 46 years earlier.[5] Although it did not appear in worklists, *Chant des déportés* evidently remained in Messiaen's thoughts. The fact that it was thought lost, rather than set aside, that this was a source of regret for Messiaen, and that it was a comment from him that prompted its rediscovery provides enough evidence to believe that he would have overseen publication and added this to his official catalogue had he lived longer.

---

[2]   Brigitte Massin, *Olivier Messiaen: Une poétique du merveilleux* (Aix-en Provence: Alinéa, 1989), pp. 44 and 46.

[3]   Ibid., p. 45.

[4]   Almut Rößler, *Contributions to the Spiritual World of Olivier Messiaen*, trans. Barbara Dagg and Nancy Poland (Duisberg: Gilles and Francke, 1986), p. 140.

[5]   Sleeve note to Jade CD *Messiaen Inédits*, 7432167411-2.

Annotations

Chant dans le style Mozart*, clarinet and piano*

Written in 1986 for the Conservatoire harmony examination, Yvonne Loriod recorded this piece in 1999, saying that she 'could not resist the charm' of the piece.[6] That may be so, but Messiaen himself made no reference to this pedagogical exercise. Given that he did not regard pastiche as true composition – hence his antipathy to neoclassicism – no case can be made for regarding this as an acknowledged Messiaen work, even if it is charming music.

Chœurs pour une Jeanne d'Arc *– see Portique pour une fille de France*

Concert à quatre*, solo flute, solo oboe, solo cello, solo piano and orchestra*

The *Concert à quatre* was left unfinished at Messiaen's death and was completed by Yvonne Loriod with advice from George Benjamin and Heinz Holliger. Loriod provides a reasonably detailed description of the completion process in a preface to the score, though the publisher, Alphonse Leduc, should have supported her in making full editorial notes. In reality, the published work is essentially a performing edition, akin to Deryck Cooke's work on Mahler's Tenth Symphony. There is nobody who would have been better placed to make the completion than Loriod, and much of it involved merely fleshing out the orchestration, though there are some striking touches in the final movement.[7] The work would undoubtedly have been different had Messiaen lived to complete it, not least in there being at least one more movement, but also because he is likely to have treated his material with greater freedom, especially the birdsong. However, unlike some of the pieces discovered since his death, there is abolutely no question at all that Messiaen intended the *Concert à quatre* to be a part of his œuvre.

La Dame de Shalott*, piano*

This is another work for which cases can be made both for inclusion and exclusion from the list of acknowledged works. In Messiaen's own lists, notably in *Technique*, it is the earliest piece mentioned, dated 1917, with a gap of four years before the next piece, *Deux Ballades de Villon*. In his 1967 conversations with Claude Samuel, Messiaen said of *La Dame de Shalott*, 'It's obviously a very childish piece, but neither quite silly nor completely devoid of sense. I still regard it with a certain tenderness.'[8] In 1986 he also said that 'the undefined style and naive form

---

[6] Ibid.

[7] For more on this, see Chapter 24 of Christopher Dingle, *Messiaen's Final Works* (Farnham: Ashgate, 2013).

[8] Claude Samuel, *Conversations with Olivier Messiaen*, trans. Felix Aprahamian (London: Stainer & Bell, 1976), p. 1.

make me laugh'.[9] It was recorded by Yvonne Loriod as part of her complete survey of the piano works for Erato. However, Loriod's recording was not included in the 1988 Erato box set of Messiaen's works and he made no attempt to have a score published. Asked by Samuel in 1967 whether it was published, Messiaen exclaimed 'Oh no! It's just the stammering of a child',[10] while in the 1986 edition of the interview, he amended his answer: 'No. It's just a little souvenir.'[11] However, in the notes for Loriod's recording, Messiaen states: 'Despite its extraordinary naivety, this work is nonetheless my op. 1.'[12] Regardless of his reluctance to publish the work, Messiaen's continued willingness to discuss *La Dame de Shalott* suggests a different status from his other pieces of juvenilia and, in the context of this listing, the mention of it being his 'op. 1', even if taken with a grain of salt, is crucial for its inclusion as an 'acknowledged work'.

Deux Monodies en quarts de ton, ondes Martenot

These pieces stemmed from Messiaen's brief involvement with Wyschnegradsky. For a long time thought to be lost, a photocopied score has come to light in the Médiathèque Hector Berlioz at the Paris Conservatoire as part of the Fonds Jeanne Loriod. They are discussed by Christopher Brent Murray in his PhD thesis.[13] After his initial enthusiasm for quarter-tones, Messiaen's apparent absence of interest in these pieces means that, while they are intriguing, it is hard to make a case for placing them in the list of acknowledged works.

Éclairs sur l'Au-Delà…, large orchestra

Although not published until just after Messiaen's death, there is no doubt that this is a fully acknowledged work.

L'Ensorceleuse, soprano, tenor, bass-baritone and piano (or orchestra)

It seems reasonably certain that the score for Messiaen's Prix de Rome cantata exists somewhere, but it is yet to come to light. When it does, aside from its intrinsic value, it will be fascinating to see whether any of the material was re-used in later works. Nonetheless, given his own assessment, in a letter to Langlais dated 3 August 1931 – 'My cantata was good as music, but poor as theatre; the

---

[9] *Music and Color*, p. 19.

[10] Samuel, *Conversations with Olivier Messiaen*, p. 1.

[11] *Music and Color*, p. 19.

[12] Olivier Messiaen, notes to Erato LP set OME1.

[13] Christopher Brent Murray, *Le développement du langage musical d'Olivier Messiaen: Traditions, emprunts, expériences*, PhD thesis (Université-Lumière Lyon 2, 2010).

Annotations 395

judgement was fair'[14] – and the fact that he made no attempt to have the piece performed or published after its reading for the jury, it cannot be regarded as an acknowledged part of his œuvre.

Quatre Études de rythme, *piano*

The four rhythmic studies were composed in the order *Modes de valeurs et d'intensités*, *Neumes rythmique*, *Île de feu 1* and *Île de feu 2*. Messiaen had wanted them to be published as a set, but they were issued as separate works, with no indication that they collectively formed a larger work. However, they were already given the collective title *Quatre Études de rythme* by the time that Messiaen came to record them in 1950. The order on that recording does not follow the order the composer later specified as definitive (presumably because of how they spread across the four sides of 78 rpm discs). Messiaen later stated that 'the four Études were published separately, but should always be played' in the following order: *Île de feu 1*, *Modes de valeurs et d'intensités*, *Neumes rythmique* and *Île de feu 2*.[15] They were finally published as a set in 2008. It should be noted that, despite Messiaen viewing the four pieces as a set, their long history as individual publications poses orthographical challenges (in terms of italicization, etc.) as the individual studies can legitimately be regarded both as movement titles and titles of works in their own right.

Fantaisie, *violin and piano*

Written in 1933, this piece was clearly intended as a follow-up to the *Thème et variations*, and was first performed in 1935. It is unclear why it was neither published, nor appears to have been performed again in the composer's lifetime. By the time of the first performance, one of the principal themes had been reused in 'Alléuias sereins d'une âme qui désire le ciel', the second movement of *L'Ascension*. It was published in 2007 and quickly engendered a spate of performances and recordings. Despite the music's considerable drama and beauty, Messiaen's apparently complete disinterest in the piece after its initial performance explains its absence from the list of acknowledged works.

Fantaisie burlesque, *piano*

A case could be made for saying that this quirky piece should not appear in the list of acknowledged works. Messiaen was relatively scathing about the *Fantaisie burlesque*, stating that, 'In 1932, my old classmates from Paul Dukas's composition

---

[14] Marie-Louise Jaquet-Langlais, *Ombre et lumière: Jean Langlais, 1907–1991* (Paris: Combre, 1995), p. 64.

[15] Liner notes to Yvonne Loriod's 1968 recording of *Quatre Études de rythme*, Erato STU 70433. For full discographical details, see the appendix to *Messiaen Perspectives 1*.

396 *Messiaen Perspectives 2: Techniques, Influence and Reception*

class found me too serious, too contemplative: they thought I didn't know how to laugh. I wanted to prove them wrong... and failed to do so.'[16] It received no stars in the worklist in *Technique*. The final repeated tonic chords are omitted from Yvonne Loriod's recording for her complete survey of the piano works released by Erato in 1975, a set for which Messiaen undoubtedly had artistic input. Moreover, it was omitted from Erato's big box set of Messiaen's music gathered together to celebrate the composer's 80th birthday, another project for which he had artistic input. Nonetheless, as a work published by Messiaen and performed by Loriod it deserves recognition as an acknowledged work.

La Fauvette Passerinette, piano (*performing realization by Peter Hill*)

Peter Hill discovered this work in advanced sketch form among the huge amount of photocopied material that he brought back from Paris after working in the Messiaen archive in the early 2000s. Messiaen had mapped-out the materials for a piece, presumably intended for the never-composed second *Catalogue d'oiseaux*, in which a Fauvette Passerinette was the clear protagonist. While many pages of the *cahiers*, for example, could be played as pieces of music for performance (and some performers have already done so), this is a much more planned and sophisticated work, with Messiaen writing 'page à copier' (page to copy) on some parts, suggesting they were finished. Hill is explicit that this is a performing realization, acknowledging that Messiaen doubtless would have refined his plans in putting the work together. It is nonetheless a valuable addition to the catalogue, even if it cannot be regarded as an acknowledged work in this context.

Fête des belles eaux, six ondes Martenot

This is one of those pieces for which a case can be made both for inclusion and exclusion from the list of acknowledged works. This occasional work from the 1937 Exposition Internationale in Paris remained unpublished at Messiaen's death despite its circulation among and performances by Jeanne Loriod and her students. Messiaen's programme note for a concert at Notre-Dame des Blancs-Manteaux (Paris, 24 April 1974) makes clear that he did not think especially highly of the work:

> Severe and precise timings had been imposed on my work (as well as the title) and the commission was rushed: I therefore had to write *Fête des belles eaux* in just a few days, forever adjusting the form so that it would fit the required timings precisely. The only point of interest in this extremely rushed composition was that it was for a sextet of ondes Martenot. ... Musically, in this rushed and careless work, there is just one valuable page – that I love (and that I've always

---

[16] Olivier Messiaen, 'Fantaisie burlesque', programme note reproduced in the booklet to Accord CD 461 645-2.

loved): because for me it represents a departure from the dimension of time, a humble attempt at true Eternity. But that is just a personal opinion – and even if it is a worthy opinion, one page is not enough to justify the whole of a score.[17]

This strongly recalls Messiaen's comments to Brigitte Massin about *Le Banquet eucharistique* having 'a single beautiful moment'. In *Fête des belles eaux* the 'one valuable page' is the music that would later become the cello 'Louange' in *Quatuor pour la fin du Temps*. Like *Le Banquet céleste*, the cello 'Louange' appears to be a case of salvaging the best bit of an otherwise weak work. While it is not surprising that a piece for six ondes Martenot did not attract a publisher in 1937, Messiaen's name surely carried enough weight in later life to publish it had he wished to do so. In 1974 he noted in his diary that he should 'correct *Fête des belles eaux* and offer it to Durand', but Hill and Simeone state that this appears not to have happened.[18] In a sense, this sums up the work's status. No doubt encouraged by his sister-in-law, ondiste Jeanne Loriod, Messiaen appears to have thought periodically about trying to get *Fête des belles eaux* published, but was either frustrated or it was not enough of a priority. It was eventually published by Leduc in 2003. In his chapter in *Messiaen Perspectives 1*, Julian Anderson is unequivocal: 'the posthumous publishing of such music not only does nothing for Messiaen's reputation, but contradicts the composer's well-founded and carefully considered judgment on what was superfluous and what was genuine to his whole creative enterprise'. Nonetheless, *Fête des belles eaux* did feature in Messiaen's worklists, and he actually awarded it a star in the entry in *Technique*, though this may have been in recognition of the 'one valuable page' mentioned above. On balance, though, the music's equivocal status and Messiaen's poor view of it tips it away from being regarded as an acknowledged work.

Feuillets inédits, ondes Martenot and piano

After Messiaen's death Yvonne Loriod arranged these four pieces for ondes Martenot and piano. Loriod is open about the way the pieces were put together, for they combine short re-discovered pieces by the composer with birdsong from his *cahiers*, with the instrumentation reflecting that they were for her and her sister, Jeanne, to play. Given her constant desire to defer to her husband and direct credit to him in all manner of things, she presumably did not want to have any acknowledgment when the harmonies, melodies and rhythms are entirely Messiaen's. However, Durand should have insisted that the work be described as

---

[17]   Cited in Jacques Tchamkerten, 'From Fête des Belles Eaux to Saint François d'Assise: The Evolution of the Writing for Ondes Martenot in the Music of Olivier Messiaen', in Christopher Dingle and Nigel Simeone (eds), *Olivier Messiaen: Music, Art and Literature* (Aldershot: Ashgate 2007), p. 66.

[18]   PHNS, p. 303.

398   *Messiaen Perspectives 2: Techniques, Influence and Reception*

'Messiaen, arranged by Yvonne Loriod-Messiaen' or 'Messiaen, in a performing realization by Yvonne Loriod-Messiaen'.

Fugue *[1926, sur un sujet d'Henri Rabaud]*

Clearly a student exercise, and remaining unmentioned in the list in *Technique*, this fugue is far from an acknowledged work. However, it has the distinction of marking the first time that Messiaen's music appeared in print, though not at his own prompting. Featured alongside other four-part fugues by his classmates Pierre Revel and Jean Rivier, it was published by Editions Heugel in a collection of the entries by Paris Conservatoire students who had won a premier prix in the 1926 *concours de fugue*.

Hymne au Saint-Sacrement *[Hymne], orchestra*

The story of the *Hymne au Saint-Sacrement* is complex. Full details are given in Dingle's article on Messiaen's early orchestral works.[19] It was first performed in 1932, and received subsequent performances in the 1930s, but the score and material were lost in 1942. Messiaen subsequently reconstructed the piece from memory, giving it the more succinct title *Hymne*. The changed title reflected, at least in part, slight dissembling on Messiaen's part that led Leopold Stokowski to think this was a brand new work. When it was recorded by Erato in 1971, it was given the full title of *Hymne au Saint-Sacrement*, confirming that these works are one and the same. Regardless of whether the work as it now stands is more expressive of Messiaen's musical thought in 1932 or 1946, there is no question that it is an acknowledged compositional statement. Unusually, it was published not by a French publisher but the relatively obscure US firm Broude Bros. This may have been due to concern on Messiaen's part that Durand would attempt to reassert rights to the work they had lost. It is worth noting that Messiaen included a hyphen in 'Saint-Sacrement' for this work and in the subtitle for *O sacrum convivium!*, yet omitted it for the title of *Livre du Saint Sacrement*.

Improvisations *[for L'Âme en bourgeon], organ*

A rare example of Messiaen not only improvising in a non-sacred context (though his mother's poetry was arguably sacred to him), but also allowing a recording of his improvisations to be commercially released. In that respect, these improvisations were published, but Messiaen never referred to these (or any other) improvisations in the same terms as any of his fully realized musical works, and these were never listed in any worklist compiled by him. As such, they do not qualify as an acknowledged work.

---

[19]   Christopher Dingle, 'Forgotten Offerings: Messiaen's First Orchestral Works', *Tempo*, 241 (July 2007): pp. 2–21.

Annotations

La Jeunesse des vieux, *mixed chorus and orchestra**

Written as part of his 1931 attempt to win the Prix de Rome, this choral setting of a text by Catulle Mendès is fascinating, but so far as is known, Messiaen made no attempt either to have it performed or published and, as such, it falls short of qualifying as an acknowledged work, even if it is to be hoped it will be performed in the future. For further details, see the chapter 'Messiaen and the Prix de Rome' by Christopher Brent Murray and Laura Hamer in *Messiaen Perspectives 1*.

Monodie, *organ*

This short piece was written in 1963 for a teaching manual, *Nouvelle méthode de clavier* by Noémie Pierront and Jean Bonfils (Messiaen's assistant at the Trinité) published by Schola Cantorum. Messiaen made no reference to its existence and it does not appear in any of his official listings of works. Leduc obtained permission to publish *Monodie* separately in 1996, but it did not appear until 1998, in an edition providing no explanation regarding its provenance.[20]

Morceau de lecture à vue *(pour les examens de piano de l'École normale de Musique: Déchiffrage I), piano*

While this listing generally omits pedagogical works, this sight-reading piece warrants inclusion, though not as an acknowledged work, as several authorities have thought it warranted attention: Yvonne Loriod regarded it highly enough to include it in the *Feuillets inédits* for piano and ondes Martenot; Peter Hill has performed it publicly on numerous occasions; Matthew Schellhorn, who studied Messiaen's piano works with both Loriod and Hill, recorded it in 2008.[21]

Musique de scène pour un Œdipe [Dieu est innocent], *ondes Martenot*

Any sign of Messiaen's involvement in 1942 in Lucien Fabre's play *Dieu est innocent* may not have come to light until recently had he not mentioned this piece in his listing in *Technique*. However, it is entirely possible that, like the music for *Tristan et Yseult* a few years later, the music for *Dieu est innocent* was at least partially improvised and, thus far, no record of the musical content exists.

---

[20]   Contrary to the statement by Yvonne Loriod in a note for Naji Hakim's 1999 recording for the CD *Messiaen Inédits* (Jade 7432167411-2) that 'the work has never been played in concert or recorded until now', the first known public performance and broadcast, at Christopher Dingle's instigation, was by Gillian Weir during a complete cycle of Messiaen's organ works at Westminster Cathedral in spring 1998.

[21]   Signum Classics, SIGCD126.

400   *Messiaen Perspectives 2: Techniques, Influence and Reception*

Offrande au Saint-Sacrement, organ

The *Offrande au Saint-Sacrement* was discovered by Yvonne Loriod after Messiaen's death and published in 2001. The date of composition is uncertain, with Naji Hakim suggesting that it dates from between 1930 and 1935.[22] In the preface to the score, Olivier Latry suggests it was written in 1928, as there are some stylistic resemblances with *Le Banquet céleste* and the registration appears to be influenced by Tournemire. Christopher Brent Murray has uncovered mentions of two organ works that Messiaen submitted for Conservatoire examinations, and suggests that either could match the posthumously published Prélude (see below). The first is a 'Prélude pour orgue', submitted on 25 January 1928. The title of the second is uncertain, there simply being mention of 'deux pièces pour piano et une pièce pour orgue' for the submission of 25 January 1929.[23] It seems possible, though, that the 'pièce' submitted from 1929 could be the *Offrandes au Saint-Sacrement*, and the 1928 'Prélude' is the piece discussed below, as no further references to other unknown organ works have come to light thus far. Messiaen wrote 'Bien' on the manuscript, indicating that it was a finished work. However, it was not mentioned in the worklist in *Technique*, which includes various unpublished works from his student years and early career. Messiaen may have forgotten about its existence, which is reason in itself for excluding it from the list of acknowledged works.

Les Offrandes oubliées (*Méditation symphonique*), piano reduction by Messiaen

While it is a fully acknowledged work, a case could be made for regarding Messiaen's piano arrangement of *Les Offrandes oubliées* not as a work in its own right, for it was almost certainly not written with the intention of being given independent concert performance. Rather, this is one of the last vestiges of the common practice from the era before recordings became prevalent. At a time when the only way to hear music was as it was physically being performed, piano transcriptions were the means by which the majority of people got to know much of the orchestral repertoire. If the composer did not provide a transcription, the publisher would pay someone else to do it as this was a vital promotional tool. In catalogues of piano transcriptions of French orchestral works, Messiaen's reduction of *Les Offrandes oubliées* appears to take its place alongside, among numerous others, Debussy's versions of *Prélude à l'après-midi d'un faune* and *La mer* or Dukas's transcription of *The Sorceror's Apprentice*. If Messiaen had been inclined to give works opus numbers, then the piano reduction of *Les Offrandes oubliées* would have the same number as the orchestral version, with a supplementary letter.

---

[22]   Sleeve note to Jade CD *Messiaen Inédits*, 7432167411-2.

[23]   Christopher Brent Murray, *Le développement du langage musical d'Olivier Messiaen*, pp. 173–4 and 176–7.

Un oiseau des arbres de Vie, *orchestra*

This piece was intended as the third movement of *Éclairs sur l'Au-Delà...* in what was originally a 12-movement scheme. It was completed in short score, with indications of orchestration and labelled 'Bien'. However, at some point Messiaen discarded it. This is the only known instance of a completed movement being dropped from a work.[24] It is possible that he may have used it at a later date had he lived, though it is equally likely that he felt that it simply could not match the exuberant 'L'Oiseaux-Lyre et la Ville-Fiancée', the third movement in *Éclairs*. As such, while entirely characteristic, there is not enough evidence to regard this movement as an acknowledged work.

Pièce, *oboe and piano*

Pièce was written in 1945 as a test piece for the oboe *concours* at the Paris Conservatoire. While the score is yet to be located, according to Loriod it was re-worked note-for-note as 'L'amour de Piroutcha', the fifth movement of *Harawi*. The range of that song fits the oboe perfectly, complete with emphatic low B♭s. Nonetheless, while a fine addition to the oboe repertoire, it cannot be regarded as an acknowledged work in this version.

Pièce (à la mémoire de Jean-Pierre Guézec), *horn*

Written in 1971, shortly after the death of the Canadian composer and former Messiaen student Jean-Pierre Guézec, this piece was renamed 'Appel interstellaire' and incorporated as the sixth movement of *Des Canyons*. Though it was performed at Guézec's memorial concert, Messiaen's repurposing of the music before publication and not sanctioning later performances of it clearly suggest he did not regard it as a piece independent of the larger work.

Pièce (pour le Tombeau de Paul Dukas), *piano*

This memorial was originally only available in the special musical supplement of *Revue Musicale* dedicated to Dukas, where it was just called *Pièce*, with Messiaen giving the title as above in the worklist in *Technique*. Durand published it in 1996, 'fingered and revised by Yvonne Loriod-Messiaen'. In the process Loriod made some changes, notably adding many more dynamic markings, a *legatissimo* instruction, a metronome mark, fingerings and pedalling. In addition, the ties across the barlines for the final B major chord are removed. These are sensible modifications, and may well have been discussed with Messiaen when Loriod recorded it for her 1975 complete survey of his piano works on Erato. However,

---

[24]   For full discussion of the genesis of *Éclairs*, including this movement, see Chapter 11 of Christopher Dingle, *Messiaen's Final Works*.

402   *Messiaen Perspectives 2: Techniques, Influence and Reception*

since Loriod was not experienced in modern editorial conventions, Durand should have ensured that editorial notes accompanied this edition.

Pièce, piano and string quartet

This piece was written for a concert celebrating the 90th birthday of Universal Edition's Alfred Schlee, at which Berio, Birtwistle, Boulez, Ligeti, Pärt, Pousseur, Schnittke and others also offered their musical tributes. While there is no evidence suggesting a link between this work and another, it is possible that, had he lived longer, Messiaen may have incorporated it into a larger structure, as happened with some earlier occasional pieces, notably the *Pièce* for oboe incorporated into *Harawi* and the *Pièce pour cor (à la mémoire de Jean-Pierre Guézec)*, which became the 'Appel interstellaire' from *Des Canyons*.

Portique pour une fille de France, large chorus and small mixed chorus a cappella

Listed in *Technique* as *Chœurs pour un Jeanne d'Arc*, the circumstances of the two choruses Messiaen wrote for the spectacle *Portique pour une fille de France* are discussed in the chapter 'Olivier Messiaen and *Portique pour une fille de France*' by Lucie Kayas and Christopher Brent Murray in *Messiaen Perspectives 1*. As a far from idiomatic (if fascinating) pair of pieces written for a larger occasional work that Messiaen did not even hear performed, there is no firm evidence for viewing this as an acknowledged work, despite the cryptic listing in *Technique*.

Prélude, organ

Discovered by Yvonne Loriod after Messiaen's death, the *Prélude* was published in 2002. The date of composition is uncertain. Olivier Latry suggests late 1929 in the preface to the score, noting its stylistic similarity to the *Diptyque* and the inclusion of notes outside the range of most Parisian organs, but available on an instrument at the Conservatoire. In the notes to Latry's recording, Paul Griffiths suggests that it was written at the time of *La Nativité*.[25] However, Christopher Brent Murray has uncovered mentions of two organ works that Messiaen submitted for Conservatoire examinations, suggesting that either could match this prelude. The first is a 'Prélude pour orgue', submitted on 25 January 1928. The title of the second is uncertain, there simply being mention of 'deux pièces pour piano et une pièce pour orgue' for the submission of 25 January 1929.[26] It seems possible, though, that the 1928 Prélude is this work, while the 'pièce' submitted a year later could be the *Offrandes au Saint-Sacrement*, as no further references to other

---

[25]   Paul Griffiths, sleeve note to Deutsche Gramophon CD set 471 480-2.

[26]   Christopher Brent Murray, *Le développement du langage musical d'Olivier Messiaen*, pp. 173–4 and 176–7.

unknown organ works have come to light thus far. While clearly a complete work, Messiaen did not mention the *Prélude* in the worklist in *Technique*, which includes various unpublished works from his student years and early career. Messiaen may have forgotten about its existence, which is reason for it to be excluded from the list of acknowledged works.

Prélude, *piano (1964)*

While it was to be expected that various pieces from the 1920s and 1930s would turn up after Messiaen's death, a completed work for solo piano from 1964 was entirely unexpected. Although it contains birdsong, it is not in the manner of a *Catalogue d'oiseaux* piece. The reason for its neglect by Messiaen can only be speculated. A standalone piece seems most unlikely, given his predilection for monumental works in this period. It therefore seems possible that this was the start of a larger project. If so, it may be that commissions prevented Messiaen from making further progress. The complete absence of any reference to it by Messiaen (even, it seems, in private) means that a case for regarding this as an acknowledged work is hard to make.

Rondeau, *piano*

The Rondeau was written (concurrently with *Visions de l'Amen*) for the Conservatoire piano *concours* in February 1943. Unusually for Messiaen, it has an abstract, generic title. Despite being easy to overlook alongside the big Loriod-inspired cycles – *Visions de l'Amen* and the *Vingt Regards* – Messiaen clearly desired the Rondeau to be part of his catalogue, for he did not publish all such pedagogical works.

La Sainte-Bohème

Written as part of his 1930 attempt to win the Prix de Rome, this choral setting of an extract from a text by Théodore de Banville is fascinating, but, so far as is known, Messiaen made no attempt either to have it performed or published. As such, it falls short of qualifying as an acknowledged work, even if it is to be hoped it will be performed in the future. For further details, see the chapter 'Messiaen and the Prix de Rome' by Christopher Brent Murray and Laura Hamer in *Messiaen Perspectives 1*.

Sigle, *flute*

This single page for flute was written in December 1982 at the request of Rolf Liebermann, who commissioned *Saint François d'Assise*. It has not been formally

404   *Messiaen Perspectives 2: Techniques, Influence and Reception*

published,[27] and was not mentioned by Messiaen, so it cannot be regarded as an acknowledged work in this format. However, he incorporated this example of his bird style into the seventh movement of *Éclairs*, slightly adjusting the final run to fit the movement's harmony.[28]

Un Sourire, orchestra

Although not published until just after Messiaen's death, there is no doubt that it was a fully acknowledged work and Messiaen himself declared it to SACEM.[29]

Timbres-durées, musique concrète

Messiaen's sole attempt at *musique concrète* is fascinating and earned him short-lived renown as a pioneer of the medium. However, it also has the unique distinction of being the only piece he withdrew from his catalogue. As such, it cannot be included in the list of acknowledged works. For further discussion, see Christopher Brent Murray's chapter 'Olivier Messiaen's *Timbres-durées*' in *Messiaen Perspectives 1*.

Le Tombeau de Jean-Pierre Guézec – see Pièce (à la mémoire de Jean-Pierre Guézec)

Le Tombeau resplendissant, orchestra

Le Tombeau resplendissant is an especially unusual case in Messiaen's output and, of all the works that appear in standard lists, it is the one for which the strongest case can be made for excluding it from the list of acknowledged works. Although it was assigned to a publisher upon completion, and thus was technically published, it was all but withdrawn after its first performance in 1933 and does not appear to have received another performance until February 1984. No commercial recording was made until 1994 and no score was published until 1997. In marked contrast to *Les Offrandes oubliées*, the *Hymne au Saint-Sacrement* and *L'Ascension*, which he actively promoted, there is currently no evidence that Messiaen made any attempt at all to have this work performed. Moreover, its omission from, for instance, Marius Constant's 1971 recording of early orchestral works for Erato – a project for which Messiaen wrote the notes and was almost certainly consulted from its inception – provides circumstantial evidence that this was a work that had fallen from favour. It appeared on various worklists as 'material on hire', though this may simply be because Durand had it on its books. Unlike *Les Offrandes oubliées* and the *Hymne au Saint-Sacrement*, *Le Tombeau resplendissant* received

---

[27]   The manuscript is reproduced in PHNS, Fr. edn, p. 426.

[28]   See Chapter 18 of Dingle, *Messiaen's Final Works*, for details.

[29]   Ibid, p. 113.

Annotations 405

no stars in the worklist in *Technique*. Messiaen never spoke of it, which may be significant (as with his silence on other aspects of his career in the 1930s) or was an oversight that turns *Le Tombeau resplendissant* into a Cinderella work within his catalogue. Assuming the work did fall out of favour with Messiaen following the first performance, this could have been for two mutually compatible reasons. First, there may have been a purely artistic decision, Messiaen feeling that, as with *Le Banquet eucharistique*, *Le Tombeau resplendissant* fell short of expectations. In the broadest terms, it can be viewed as repeating the approach of *Les Offrandes oubliées*, but opening with an additional turbulent section. Second, Messiaen may have become uncomfortable with the subject matter of the work, which, based on his mother's death, is extremely personal and anguished.

Tristan et Yseult (*musique de scène*), *organ*

In February 1945 Messiaen recorded the incidental music for Lucien Fabre's play *Tristan et Yseult*. Played on the organ, the music was partly improvised, but one written fragment survived in Messiaen's papers, titled *Tristan et Yseult – Thème d'Amour*. This would be re-used later the same year as the cyclic love theme in *Harawi*. There is no reason to regard this music as an acknowledged work.

Trois Tâla, *solo piano and orchestra*

This is the title given by Messiaen to the three movements from *Turangalîla* that were performed in advance of the première of the symphony as a whole. PHNS states that these correspond to movements 3, 4 and 5 of the completed symphony.[30] However, there is a possible contradiction in this account. On p. 169, PHNS cites Messiaen's diary from 9 January 1947 noting that 'Raynaud is copying the *Trois Tâla*' as 'evidence that movements 3, 4 and 5 of *Turangalîla* were not only composed but also orchestrated by this date'. However, Messiaen's two working plans for the symphony from the back of his 1947 diary do not include the eventual fifth movement, 'Joie du sang des étoiles', which was the last to be composed. Rather, the 'Final' is to be played twice in Messiaen's ten-movement plan.[31] It is also possible that, in 1947, Messiaen was referring to the three movements now called 'Turangalîla'. It is unclear whether 'Joie du sang des étoiles' was complete by the time the *Trois Tâla* were first performed in February 1948. Later in life Messiaen was unequivocal: 'The *Trois Tâla* never existed. Through the publisher Durand I forbade the improper use of this title'.[32]

---

[30] PHNS, pp. 169 and 171.
[31] See ibid., pp. 171–2.
[32] Letter to Karl Schweitzer, cited in PHNS, p. 174.

La Ville d'En-Haut, solo piano and small orchestra

Although not published until just after Messiaen's death, there is no doubt that it was a fully acknowledged work and Messiaen himself declared it to SACEM.[33]

Un Vitrail et des oiseaux, solo piano and small orchestra

Although not published until just after Messiaen's death, there is no doubt that it was a fully acknowledged work and Messiaen himself declared it to SACEM.[34]

Vocalise-étude, high voice and piano

It might be thought that as an apparently pedagogical, utilitarian work, completely abstract with no text and published as no. 151 in a series of such studies compiled by A. L. Hettich, the *Vocalise-étude* would not belong in the list of acknowledged works. In these ways it is similar in nature to the *Monodie* for organ. However, despite its modest and uncharacteristic nature, Messiaen clearly retained a fondness for this piece throughout his life. For instance, he awarded it a star in the worklist in *Technique* and gave permission for Jeanne Loriod to perform it on ondes Martenot. Crucially, it was this work that Heinz Holliger played to Messiaen in 1984 to demonstrate circular breathing. That encounter sowed the seed for the *Concert à quatre*, and Messiaen's orchestration of the *Vocalise-étude*, which was fully complete at his death, became the second movement.

---

[33] PHNS, p. 361.
[34] Ibid., p. 358.

Select Bibliography

Albèra, Philippe, 'Le rythme repensé', in Anick Lesure and Claude Samuel (eds), *Olivier Messiaen: Le livre du centenaire* (Lyon: Symétrie, 2008).

Almandoz, Norberto, 'La personalidad de Olivier Messiaen', *ABC* (Seville) (19 June 1964): 61.

—, '"El despertar de los pájaros", de Olivier Messiaen, curioso concurso', *ABC* (Seville) (6 May 1969): 76.

—, '"La Ascensión", de Olivier Messiaen', *ABC* (Seville) (16 May 1969): 44.

Anderson, Julian, 'In Harmony: Julian Anderson Introduces the Music and Ideas of Tristan Murail', *The Musical Times*, 134/1804 (June 1993): 321–3.

—, 'A Provisional History of Spectral Music', *Contemporary Music Review*, 19/2 (2000): 7–22.

Autexier, Philippe A., 'Olivier Messiaen, *Traité de rythme, de couleur, et d'ornithologie: 1949-1992*: Tome IV' (review), *Dix-huitième siècle*, 30 (1998): 691.

Baggech, Melody, *An English Translation of Olivier Messiaen's* Traité de rythme, de couleur, et d'ornithologie*, Volume 1*, DMA thesis (University of Oklahoma, 1998).

Balmer, Yves, '"Je suis né croyant…": Aux sources du catholicisme d'Olivier Messiaen', in Sylvain Caron and Michel Duchesneau, with the collaboration of Marie-Hélène Benoit-Otis (eds), *Musique, art et religion dans l'entre-deux-guerres* (Lyon: Symétrie, 2009).

Baltensperger, André, *Iannis Xenakis und die stochastische Musik* (Berne: Paul Haupt, 1996).

Barthel-Calvet, Anne-Sylvie, *Le rythme dans l'œuvre et la pensée de Iannis Xenakis*, PhD thesis, 4 Vols (École des Hautes Etudes en Sciences Sociales, Paris, 2000).

—, '*MÉTASTASSIS-Analyse* : Un texte inédit de Iannis Xenakis sur *Metastasis*', *Revue de Musicologie*, 89/1 (2003): 129–87.

—, 'De l'ubiquité poïétique dans l'œuvre de Iannis Xenakis: Espace, Temps, Musique, Architecture', *Intersections*, 29/2 (2009): 9–51.

—, 'A Creative Mind in Eruption: Xenakis Composing the *Anastenaria* Cycle in 1953', proceedings of the *Xenakis International Symposium*, Southbank Centre, London, 1–3 April 2011, available at www.gold.ac.uk/ccmc/xenakis-international-symposium.

—, 'Xenakis et le sérialisme: L'apport d'une analyse génétique de Metastasis', *Intersections: Revue Canadienne de Musique*, 31/2 (2011): 3–22.

—, 'Le regard de Xenakis sur Debussy', in Myriam Chimènes and Alexandra Laederich (eds), *Regards sur Debussy* (Paris: Fayard, 2013).

Bauer, Amy, 'The Impossible Charm of Messiaen's *Chronochromie*', in Robert Sholl (ed.), *Messiaen Studies* (Cambridge: Cambridge University Press, 2007).

Beard, David and Gloag, Kenneth, *Musicology: The Key Concepts* (New York: Routledge, 2005).

Bellingardi, Luigi (ed.), *Tutte le cronache musicali, 'L'Espresso'*, Vol. 3 (1977–89) (Roma: Bulzoni).

Benitez, Vincent P., 'Simultaneous Contrast and Additive Designs in Olivier Messiaen's Opera *Saint François d'Assise*', *Music Theory Online*, 8/2 (August 2002).

—, 'Aspects of Harmony in Messiaen's Later Music: An Examination of the Chords of Transposed Inversions on the Same Bass Note', *Journal of Musicological Research*, 23/2 (April–June 2004): 187–226.

—, 'Messiaen as Improviser', *Dutch Journal of Music Theory*, 13/2 (2008): 129–44.

—, *Olivier Messiaen: A Research and Information Guide* (New York and London: Routledge, 2008).

Benjamin, George, 'The Master of Harmony', in Peter Hill (ed.), *The Messiaen Companion* (London: Faber and Faber, 1995).

Berio, Luciano, *Intervista sulla musica*, ed. Rossana Dalmonte (Bari: Laterza, 1981).

Bernard, Jonathan, 'Messiaen's Synesthesia: The Correspondence between Colour and Sound Structure in His Music', *Music Perception*, 4/1 (Fall 1986): 46.

Blanes Nadal, M.ª Luisa, *Amando Blanquer: Vida y obra. Una aproximación a su repertorio pianístico* (Alicante: Instituto Alicantino de Cultura Juan Gil-Albert, 2006).

Blanquer, Amando, 'Del diario íntimo', in *Primer encuentro de composición musical: Valencia 1988; Textos y ponencias* (Valencia: Generalitat Valenciana – Conselleria de Cultura, Educació i Ciència – Àrea de Música del IVAECM, 1989).

Bloom, Harold, *The Anatomy of Influence: Literature as a Way of Life* (New Haven: Yale University Press, 2011).

Boivin, Jean, *La classe de Messiaen* (Paris: Bourgois, 1995).

—, 'Messiaen's Teaching at the Paris Conservatoire: A Humanist's Legacy', in Siglind Bruhn (ed.), *Messiaen's Language of Mystical Love* (New York: Garland, 1998).

—, 'Le *Traité de rythme, de couleur, et d'ornithologie* d'Olivier Messiaen, tomes I, II, III et IV', *Circuit: Musiques contemporaines*, 9/1 (1998): 17–25.

—, 'Musical analysis according to Messaien: a critical view of a most original approach', in Christopher Dingle and Nigel Simeone (eds), *Olivier Messiaen: Music, Art and Literature* (Aldershot: Ashgate, 2007).

—, 'Convictions religieuses et modernité musicale au Québec avant la révolution tranquille: L'example de Nadia Boulanger et d'Olivier Messiaen, pédagogues et transmetteurs du renouveau musical', in Sylvain Caron and Michel Duchesneau (eds), *Musique, art et Religion dans l'Entre-deux-guerres* (Lyon: Symétrie, 2009).

Bortolotto, Mario, *Fase seconda: Studi sulla Nuova Musica* (Torino: Einaudi, 1969).

—, 'Agudeza y arte de teclado: Sobre las obras para piano de Luis de Pablo', in José Luis García del Busto (ed.), *Escritos sobre Luis de Pablo* (Madrid: Taurus, 1987).

Botstein, Leon, 'Music in History: The Perils of Method in Reception History', *The Musical Quarterly*, 89/1 (Spring 2006): 1–16.

Boulez, Pierre, 'Contrepoint', in François Michel, François Lesure and Vladimir Fedoron (eds), *Encyclopédie de la Musique* (Paris: Fasquelle, 1958).

—, 'Stravinsky demeure', in Paule Thévenin (ed.), *Relevés d'apprenti* (Paris: Seuil, 1966).

—, 'Necessité d'une orientation esthétique (II)', *Canadian University Music Review/Revue de Musique des Universités Canadiennes*, 7 (1986): 46–79.

—, 'Preface', in Olivier Messiaen, *Traité de rythme, de couleur, et d'ornithologie, Tome I* (Paris: Alphonse Leduc, 1994), p. vi; this two-page text is reprinted in each subsequent volume.

—, *Techniques d'écriture et enjeux esthétiques*, ed. Jean-Louis Leleu and Pascal Decroupet (Genève: Éditions Contrechamps, 2006).

Brackett, John, *John Zorn: Tradition and Transgression* (Bloomington & Indianapolis: Indiana University Press, 2008).

Bradley, Ian Leonard, *Twentieth Century Canadian Composers*, 2 Vols (Agincourt: GLC Publishers, 1982).

Broad, Stephen, 'Messiaen and Cocteau', in Christopher Dingle and Nigel Simeone (eds), *Olivier Messiaen: Music, Art and Literature* (Aldershot: Ashgate, 2007).

—, *Olivier Messiaen: Journalism. 1935–1939* (Farnham: Ashgate, 2012).

Bruhn, Siglind (ed.), *Messiaen's Language of Mystical Love* (New York: Garland Publishing Inc., 1998).

—, *Messiaen's Contemplations of Covenant and Incarnation: Musical Symbols of Faith in the Two Great Piano Cycles of the 1940s* (Hillsday, NY: Pendragon, 2007).

—, *Messiaen's Explorations of Love and Death: Musico-Poetic Signification in the 'Tristan Trilogy' and Three Related Song Cycles* (Hillsdale, NY: Pendragon, 2008).

—, *Messiaen's Interpretations of Holiness and Trinity: Echoes of Medieval Theology in the Oratorio, Organ Meditations and Opera* (Hillsdale, NY: Pendragon, 2008).

Bündler, David, 'Gérard Grisey', interview with David Bündler, 18 January 1996, available at www.angelfire.com/music2/davidbundler/grisey.html.

Cage, John, *Silence: Lectures and Writings by John Cage* (Middletown, CT: Wesleyan University Press, 1973).

[Unsigned], 'Canada Council / Conseil des arts du Canada', *The Encyclopedia of Music in Canada*, available at www.thecanadianencyclopedia.com.

Carpentier, Alejo, *La música en Cuba* (Mexico [City]: Fondo de Cultura Económica, 1946).

—, 'Revelación de un compositor', *El Nacional* (Caracas, 29 April 1956), reproduced in 'Ese músico que llevo dentro', *Obras completas de Alejo Carpentier*, Vol. 10 (Mexico City: Siglo veintiuno, 1987): 214–17.

Carpitella, Diego (ed.), *Il mito del primitivo nella musica moderna* (programme of the 26th Festival di Nuova Consonanza) (Rome: Semar, 1989).

Carroll, Jeffery, 'The Song above Catastrophe: Kenneth Burke on Music', *KB Journal: The Journal of the Kenneth Burke Society*, 7/2 (Spring 2001), available at kbjournal.org/carroll.

Casimiri, Raffaele, 'Arte novecentista', *Note d'Archivio per la storia musicale*, 10/1 (1933): 58.

Chapa Brunet, Manuel and Pérez de Arteaga, José Luis, 'Conversación con Olivier Messiaen', *Reseña de literatura, artes y espectáculos*, 81 (January 1975): 43–6.

Cheong, Wai-Ling, 'Messiaen's Triadic Colouration: Modes as Introversion', *Music Analysis*, 21/1 (2002): 53–84.

—, 'Rediscovering Messiaen's Invented Chords', *Acta Musicologica*, 75/1 (2003): 85–105.

—, 'Neumes and Greek Rhythms: The Breakthrough in Messiaen's Birdsong', *Acta Musicologica*, 80/1 (2008): 1–32.

Cirlot, Juan-Eduardo, 'Los azules de Francia', *La Vanguardia Española* (11 June 1965): 7.

Clarke, A. Mason, *Thirty-four Biographies of Canadian Composers* (Montreal: Canadian Broadcasting Corporation, 1964).

Clarke, Eric F., *Ways of Listening: An Ecological Approach to the Perception of Musical Meaning* (New York: Oxford University Press, 2005).

Clementi, Aldo, 'Dopo la dodecafonia, verso un nuovo stile', *L'esperienza moderna*, 1/3–4 (1957): 45.

Collet, Henri, 'Olivier Messiaen', *Ritmo*, 235 (April–May 1951): 4.

Conti, Luca, 'La Scuola di Vienna e la dodecafonia nella pubblicistica italiana, 1911–1945', *Nuova Rivista Musicale Italiana*, 37/2 (2003): 155–96.

Cousté, Francis, 'Olivier Messiaen, *Traité de rythme, de couleur, et d'ornithologie: 1949–1992*: Tome I', *L'éducation musicale*, 422 (November 1995): 22.

Crispin, Judith (ed.), *Olivier Messiaen: The Centenary Papers* (Newcastle upon Tyne: Cambridge Scholars Publishing, 2010).

Croft, Jonathan, 'The Spectral Legacy', *Journal of the Royal Musical Association*, 135/1 (2009): 191–7.

Crossley, Paul, liner notes to *Messiaen: Des Canyons aux étoiles… / Oiseaux exotiques / Couleurs de la Cité céleste* (CBS Records Inc., M2K 44762, 1988).

Daley, Frank, 'Gala Program Kicks Off Expo Entertainment Binge', *The Ottawa Journal* (1 May 1967).

Dallapiccola, Luigi, 'Musica contemporanea a Londra', *La Lettura* (Milan, 10 August 1946): 6.

—, 'Musiche al Festival della S.I.M.C.', *Sipario* (Varese, August–September 1946): 78.

—, 'Olivier Messiaen', *Il Mondo europeo*, no. 40 (Rome–Florence, 1 April 1947): 14.

—, *Appunti, incontri, meditazioni* (Milan: Edizioni Suvini Zerboni, 1970).

—, 'A proposito dei Cinque Canti', in Fiamma Nicolodi (ed.), *Parole e musica* (Milan: Il Saggiatore, 1980).

Daschner, Hubert, *Spanische Musik auf der Höhe ihrer Zeit: Cristóbal Halffter* (Saarbrücken: PFAU Verlag, 2000).

Daubresse, Eric and Assayag, Gérard, 'Technology and Creation: The Creative Evolution', *Contemporary Music Review*, 19/2 (2000): 61–80.

Delaere, Mark, 'Olivier Messiaen's Analysis Seminar and the Development of Post-War Serial Music', *Music Analysis*, 21/1 (2002): 35–51.

Devillers, P. and Ouellet, H., *Noms français des oiseaux du monde avec les equivalent latins et anglais: Commission internationale des noms français des oiseaux* (Sainte-Foy, Québec and Chabaud, Bayonne, France: Multimondes, 1993).

Die, Amelia, 'Olivier Messiaen, músico místico', *ABC* (16 November 1974): 147.

Dingle, Christopher, *Olivier Messiaen:* La Transfiguration de Notre-Seigneur Jésus-Christ: *A Provisional Study*, MPhil thesis (University of Sheffield, 1994).

—, *Traité de rythme, de couleur, et d'ornithologie (1949–1992) – Tome I* by Olivier Messiaen; *Music and color – Conversations with Claude Samuel*; Messiaen: *L'Apparition de l'Église éternelle, La Nativité du Seigneur*. Olivier Messiaen (organ); Messiaen: Complete organ works. Gillian Weir (organ)', *Tempo*, 192 (April 1995): 20–32.

—, *Traité de rythme, de couleur, et d'ornithologie (1949–1992), Tome II & Tome III* by Olivier Messiaen; *La classe de Messiaen* by Jean Boivin, *Tempo*, 202 (October 1997): 25–6.

—, *Traité de rythme, de couleur, et d'ornithologie (1949–1992) – Tome IV* by Olivier Messiaen; *Le tombeau de Paul Dukas for piano solo, doigtés et révision de Yvonne Loriod-Messiaen*, *Tempo*, 205 (July 1998): 26–7.

—, '"La statue reste sur son piédestal": Messiaen's *La Transfiguration* and Vatican II', *Tempo*, 212 (April 2000): 8–11.

—, *Traité de rythme, de couleur, et d'ornithologie (1949–1992) – Tome V, volumes 1 & 2, Tome VI & Tome VII* by Olivier Messiaen, *Tempo*, 227 (January 2004): 41–5.

—, 'Forgotten Offerings: Messiaen's First Orchestral Works', *Tempo*, 241 (July 2007): 2–21.

—, 'Frescoes and Legends: The Sources and Background of *Saint François d'Assise*', in Christopher Dingle and Nigel Simeone (eds), *Olivier Messiaen: Music, Art and Literature* (Aldershot: Ashgate, 2007).

—, *The Life of Messiaen* (Cambridge: Cambridge University Press, 2007).

—, *Messiaen's Final Works* (Farnham: Ashgate, 2013).

—, 'Messiaen as Pianist: A Romantic in a Modernist World', in Scott McCarrey and Lesley Wright (eds), *Perspectives on the Performance of French Piano Music* (Farnham: Ashgate, forthcoming).

Dingle, Christopher and Simeone, Nigel (eds), *Olivier Messiaen: Music, Art and Literature* (Aldershot: Ashgate, 2007).

Dolezal, Robert J., *The Most Scenic Drives in America: 120 Spectacular Road Trips* (Pleasantville, NY: Reader's Digest, 1997).

Drott, Eric, 'Spectralism, Politics, and the Post-Industrial Imagination', in Björn Heile (ed.), *The Modernist Legacy: Essays on New Music* (Farnham: Ashgate, 2009).

Dubois, Théodore, *Traité de contrepoint et de Fugue* (Paris: Heugel & Cie., 1901)

Duchesneau, Michel, Dufour, Valérie and Benoit-Otis, Marie-Hélène (eds), *Écrits de compositeurs, 1850–2000: Questions, méthodes et perspectives de recherche* (Paris: Vrin, 2013).

Dufourt, Hugues, 'Musique spectrale: pour une pratique des formes de l'énergie', *Bicéphale*, 3 (1979): 85–9.

Dumesnil, René, 'Una nueva obra de Olivier Messiaen: "Le réveil des oiseaux"', *Ritmo*, 263 (August–September 1954): 10–11.

Dupré, Marcel, *Cours complet d'improvisation à l'orgue*, Vol. 2, *Traité d'improvisation à l'orgue*, English trans. John Fenstermaker (Paris: Alphonse Leduc, 1974).

Dutilleux, Henri, 'Regards croisés', in Jean Roy and Frédéric Duval (eds), 'Maurice Ohana le musicien du soleil', *Le monde de la musique*, no. 2 [special edition] (1994): 18.

Dutilleux, Henri and Cadieu, Martine, *Constellations: Entretiens* (Paris: Michel de Maule, 2007).

Emmanuel, Maurice, *Histoire de la langue musicale* (Paris: H. Laurens, 1951).

Fallon, Robert, 'Various Messiaen Editions', *Notes*, 60/3 (March 2004): 795–801.

—, *Messiaen's Mimesis: The Language and Culture of the Bird Styles*, PhD diss. (University of California, Berkeley, 2005).

—, 'Birds, Beasts and Bombs in Messiaen's Cold War Mass', *The Journal of Musicology*, 26/2 (2009): 175–204.

Fanning, David, 'Messiaen: Vingt Regards sur l'Enfant-Jésus; Peter Hill', *Gramophone* (September 1992): 137.

Farmer, Jared, *On Zion's Mount: Mormons, Indians, and the American Landscape* (Cambridge, MA: Harvard University Press, 2008).

Ferro, Sergio, Kebbal, Chérif, Potié, Philippe and Simonnet, Cyrille, *Le Corbusier: Le Couvent de la Tourette* (Marseille: Parenthèses, 1988).

Ferguson, Sean, 'De-composing Tristan Murail: The Collected Writings, 1980–2000 (Review of 'Models and Artifice: The Collected Writings of Tristan Murail', *Contemporary Music Review*, 24 (2/3) April/June 2005)', *Circuit: musiques contemporaines*, 17/1 (2007): 115–20.

Fernández-Cid, Antonio, 'Olivier Messiaen, autor e intérprete, en Madrid', *Arriba* (1 March 1949): 3.

—, 'De Beethoven a Messiaen, pasando por Brahms, Chopin y Prokofieff, en Lucerna', *ABC* (7 September 1967): 70.

—, 'Olivier Messiaen, huésped de Madrid', *ABC* (18 October 1974): 90.

—, 'Odón Alonso dirigió a Yvonne y Jeanne Loriod y la orquesta de la RTV. E. el estreno madrileño de "Turangalila-Sinfonía", de Messiaen', *ABC* (22 October 1974): 95–6.

Fineberg, Joshua, *Spectral Music: History and Techniques* (Amsterdam: Overseas Publishers Association / Harwood Academic Publishers, 2000), constituting *Contemporary Music Review*, 19/3.

—, *Classical Music, Why Bother? Hearing the World of Contemporary Culture through a Composer's Ears* (New York: Routledge, 2006).

Fineberg, Joshua and Michel, Pierre (eds), 'Models and Artifice: The Collected Writings of Tristan Murail', *Contemporary Music Review*, 24/2–3 (April/June 2005).

Fling, Michael, *Musical Memorials for Musicians: A Guide to Selected Compositions* (Lanham, MD and London: Scarecrow Press and the Music Library Association, 2001).

Fohr, Serge (ed.), *L'Institut Français de Madrid: 100 ans de culture et d'enseignement / El Institut Français de Madrid: 100 años de cultura y de enseñanza* (Madrid: Institut Français de Madrid, 2010).

Forte, Allen, 'Olivier Messiaen as Serialist', *Music Analysis*, 21/1 (2002): 3–34.

Franco, Enrique, 'Estreno de "Progressus", de Luis de Pablo, por Conchita Rodríguez y Pedro Espinosa: Concierto extraordinario de la Filarmónica', *Arriba* (1 April 1960): 17.

—, *Escritos musicales* (Madrid: Fundación Albéniz, 2006).

Gan Quesada, Germán, 'Pájaros en el cielo hispano: Apuntes sobre la recepción inicial de la música de Olivier Messiaen en España', *Scherzo*, 236 (December 2008): 130–34.

—, '*A la altura de las circunstancias…* Continuidad y pautas de renovación en la música española', in Alberto González Lapuente (ed.), *Historia de la música en España e Hispanoamérica*, Vol. 7, *La música en España en el siglo XX* (Madrid: Fondo de Cultura Económica, 2012).

García, Xavier and Charles Soler, Agustín, *Joan Guinjoan* (Barcelona: Generalitat de Catalunya–Departament de Cultura, 1999).

García del Busto, José Luis, *Luis de Pablo* (Madrid: Espasa-Calpe, 1979).

— (ed.), *Joan Guinjoan: Testimonio de un músico* (Madrid: Fundación Autor, 2001).

—, *Carmelo Bernaola: La obra de un maestro* (Madrid: Fundación Autor – Diputación Foral de Bizkaia, 2004).

Gatti, Guido Maggiorino, 'Il Festival della S.I.M.C.', *Il Mondo*, Florence, no. 31 (6 July 1946): 8.

Gedalge, André, *Traité de la fugue, 1re partie: De la fugue d'école* (Paris: Enoch & Cie, 1901).

Gentilucci, Armando, *Guida all'ascolto della musica contemporanea* (Milan: Feltrinelli, 1969).

Gil de la Vega, Concha, 'El maestro Messiaen: "No es la primera vez que vengo a España, antes ya estuve en Barcelona"', *La Vanguardia Española* (20 October 1974): 67.

Gill, Frank and Wright, Minturn, *Birds of the World: Recommended English Names* (Princeton: Princeton University Press, 2006).

Gillock, Jon, *Performing Messiaen's Organ Music: 66 Masterclasses* (Bloomington: Indiana University Press, 2009).

Gironés, Miguel, '*Préludes pour piano*, de Olivier Messiaen: Un acercamiento desde el análisis de conjuntos', *Quodlibet*, 46 (January–April 2010): 3–14.

Glayman, Claude, *Henri Dutilleux: Music – Mystery and Memory; Conversations with Claude Glayman*, trans. Roger Nichols (Ashgate: Aldershot, 2003).

Goléa, Antoine, *Esthétique de la musique contemporaine* (Paris: Presses universitaires de France, 1954).

——, *Rencontres avec Pierre Boulez* (Paris: René Julliard, 1958).

Granell, Enric, *Juan Eduardo Cirlot: L'habitació imaginària* (Madrid/Barcelona: Ediciones Siruela-Centre d'Arts Santa Mònica, 2011).

Gräter, Manfred, 'Olivier Messiaen', in *Guía de la música contemporánea* (Madrid: Taurus, 1966; German original, 1955).

Greenwood, Jonny, 'New Jonny Greenwood: "Future Markets" plus Greenwood Q&A', interview with Stereogum (7 December 2007), available at stereogum. com/7412/new_jonny_greenwood_future_markets/news/.

Gregory, Herbert E., *Geology of Eastern Iron County, Utah*, published as the *Utah Geological and Mineralogical Survey Bulletin*, 37 (February 1950).

Griffiths, Paul, '*Saint François d'Assise*', in Peter Hill (ed.), *The Messiaen Companion* (London: Faber and Faber, 1995).

——, 'Messiaen, Olivier', in Stanley Sadie and John Tyrrell (eds), *The New Grove Dictionary of Music and Musicians*, 2nd edition (London: Macmillan, 2001), Vol. 15, 491–504.

Grisey, Gérard, '*Tempus ex Machina*: A Composer's Reflection on Musical Time', *Contemporary Music Review*, 2/1 (1987): 239–275.

——, 'Did You Say Spectral?', trans. Joshua Fineberg, *Contemporary Music Review*, 19/3 (2000): 1–3.

Grisey, Gérard and Bündler, David, 'Gérard Grisey', available at www.angelfire. com/music2/davidbundler/grisey.html (March 1996).

Grosset, Joanny, 'Inde', in Albert Lavignac (ed.), *Encyclopédie de la musique et dictionnaire du Conservatoire*, Part 1: *Histoire de la musique, Antiquité-Moyen âge* (Paris: Delagrave, 1921): 257–341.

Grunenwald, Alain, '*T'Harân-Ngô*: Conversation avec Maurice Ohana', *Arfuyen*, no. 2 (1975): 58.

Gut, Serge, *Le Groupe Jeune France* (Paris: Honoré Champion, 1977).

Halbreich, Harry, *Olivier Messiaen* (Paris: Fayard, 1980).

——, *L'œuvre d'Olivier Messiaen* (Paris: Fayard, 2008).

Harcourt, Marguérite d' and Harcourt, Raoul Béclart d', *La musique des Incas et ses survivances* (Paris: Paul Guethner, 1925).

Harris, Joseph Edward, *Musique Colorée: Synesthetic Correspondence in the Works of Olivier Messiaen*, PhD diss. (University of Iowa, 2004).

Select Bibliography 415

Harvey, Jonathan, *In Quest of Spirit: Thoughts on Music* (Berkeley and Los Angeles: University of California Press, 1999).

Healey, Gareth, 'Messiaen and the Concept of "Personnages"', *Tempo*, 58/230 (October 2004): 10–19.

—, 'Messiaen: Bibliophile', in Christopher Dingle and Nigel Simeone (eds), *Olivier Messiaen: Music, Art and Literature* (Aldershot: Ashgate, 2007).

—, *Messiaen's Musical Techniques: The Composer's View and Beyond* (Farnham: Ashgate, 2013).

Hill, Camille Crunelle, 'Saint Thomas Aquinas and the Theme of Truth in Messiaen's *Saint François d'Assise*', in Siglind Bruhn (ed.), *Messiaen's Language of Mystical Love* (New York: Garland, 1998).

Hill, Peter (ed.), *The Messiaen Companion* (London: Faber and Faber, 1995).

—, 'Piano Music II', in Peter Hill (ed.), *The Messiaen Companion* (London: Faber and Faber, 1995).

Hill, Peter and Simeone, Nigel, *Messiaen* (New Haven and London: Yale University Press, 2005). [PHNS]

—, *Olivier Messiaen: Oiseaux Exotiques* (Aldershot: Ashgate, 2007).

—, *Messiaen*, French trans. Lucie Kayas (Paris: Fayard, 2008). [PHNS, fr. edn]

Hirsbrunner, Theo, *Olivier Messiaen, Leben und Werk*, 2nd edition (Laaber: Laaber Verlag, 1999; first published 1988).

—, 'Olivier Messiaen: *Traité de rythme, de couleur, et d'ornithologie, 1949–1992*, in 7 Bänden (Alphonse Leduc, Paris, 1994–2002), "Privatuniversum mit weitem Horizont"', *Dissonanz/Dissonance* 81 (June 2003): 40–41.

Hotoran, Anamaria Mădălina, 'Musical and Spiritual Affinities: Olivier Messiaen and Eduard Terényi', available at www.wseas.us/e-library/conferences/2010/Iasi/AMTA/AMTA-34.pdf.

Huot, Cécile, 'Prix d'Europe', in *The Encyclopedia of Music in Canada*, available at www.thecanadianencyclopedia.com.

Huyssen, Andreas, 'Monument and Memory in a Postmodern Age', in James E. Young (ed.), *The Art of Memory: Holocaust Memorials in History* (New York: Prestel: 1994).

Jaquet-Langlais, Marie-Louise, *Jean Langlais: Ombre et lumière* (Paris: Combre, 1995).

Johnson, Robert Sherlaw, *Messiaen*, 2nd paperback edition, updated and additional text by Caroline Rae (London: Omnibus Press, 2008; first published 1975). [Note: Pagination is identical to the first (1989) paperback edition up to p. 195.]

Kämper, Dietrich, *Luigi Dallapiccola. La vita e l'opera* (Florence: Sansoni, 1985).

Kastiyo, José Luis and Pino, Rafael del, *El Festival Internacional de Música y Danza de Granada, 1952–2001*, Vol. 1 (Granada: INAEM, 2001).

Keym, Stefan, 'Olivier Messiaen', in Ludwig Fischer (ed.), *Die Musik in Geschichte und Gegenwart*, 2nd edition (Kassel: Bärenreiter, 2001), Vol. 12: 63–81.

—, *Untersuchungen zur musiktheatralen Struktur und Semantik von Olivier Messiaens Saint François d'Assise* (Hildesheim: Georg Olms Verlag, 2002).

—, 'Olivier Messiaen: *Traité de rythme, de couleur, et d'ornithologie, 1949–1992*, en 7 tomes, Paris, Alphonse Leduc, 1994–2002)', *Musiktheorie*, 19/3 (2004): 269–74.

—, '"The Art of the Most Intensive Contrast": Olivier Messiaen's Mosaic Form up to its Apotheosis in *Saint François d'Assise*', in Robert Sholl (ed.), *Messiaen Studies* (Cambridge: Cambridge University Press, 2007).

Kopp, David, 'Pentatonic Organization in Two Piano Pieces of Debussy', *Journal of Music Theory*, 41/2 (Fall 1997): 261–87.

Köster, Peter T., 'Works with Violincello', liner note to Peteris Vasks, *Works with Violoncello*, David Geringas (cello) (2008) Hänssler Classic CD 93.229.

Kramer, Lawrence, *Interpreting Music* (Berkeley and Los Angeles: University of California Press, 2011).

Lacassagne, R. A., 'Ohana et Messiaen, un regard neuf sur le piano', *La musique* (15 April 1975).

Latry, Olivier and Mallié, Loïc, *L'œuvre d'orgue d'Olivier Messiaen: Œuvres d'avant-guerre* (Stuttgart: Carus, 2008).

Le Corbusier, *Choix de lettres*, ed. Jean Jenger (Basel: Birkhäuser, 2002).

Lefebvre, Marie-Thérèse, *Serge Garant et la révolution musicale au Québec* (Montreal: L. Courteau, 1986).

Leidel, Wolf-Günter, 'Messiaen-Rezeption in Ostdeutschland vor und nach der Wende: Ein Gespräch', in Michaela Christine Hastetter (ed.), *Musik des Unsichtbaren: Der Komponist Olivier Messiaen (1908–1992) am Schnittpunkt von Theologie und Musik* (St Ottilien, Germany: EOS, 2008).

Lerdahl, Fred, 'Cognitive Constraints on Compositional Systems', *Contemporary Music Review*, 6/2 (1992): 97–121.

Lerdahl, Fred and Jackendoff, Ray, *A Generative Grammar of Tonal Music* (Cambridge, MA: MIT Press, 1987).

Lesure, Anik and Claude Samuel, *Olivier Messiaen: Le livre du centennaire* (Lyon: Symétrie, 2008).

Levinson, Gerald, liner note to *Music of Gerald Levinson*, Orchestra 2001 and James Freeman (cond.) (2005) Albany Records, CD Troy742.

Ligeti, György, 'Pierre Boulez: Decision and Automatism in Structure Ia', *Die Reihe* 4 (1960): 36–62.

Louvier, Alain, foreword to Messiaen, Olivier, *Traité de rythme, de couleur, et d'ornithologie – Tome I* (Paris: Alphonse Leduc, 1994), p. viii (text is reprinted in each subsequent volume).

—, 'Olivier Messiaen, le *Traité de rythme, de couleur, et d'ornithologie*, Paris, Alphonse Leduc, 1994', *Musurgia, analyse et pratique musicales*, 2/1 (1995): 162–4.

Loyonnet, Paul, 'Las tendencias actuales de la música en París', trans. from the French original by Antonio Iglesias, *Ritmo*, 191 (November 1945): 4–5.

Lull Naya, Trinidad, 'La extraordinaria contribución al mundo de la música de Olivier Messiaen', *Música y educación*, 75 (October 2008): 14–22.

—, 'Olivier Messiaen y el sonido-color', *Archivo de Arte Valenciano*, 90 (2009): 213–22.

—, 'Las formas gregorianizantes en el primer ciclo vocal de Olivier Messiaen: *Poèmes pour Mi*', *Quodlibet*, 49 (January–April 2011): 49–73.

Maas, Sander van, 'Unfolding the Pocket, Neutralizing the Lyrical: Contrabass Guitarist Anthony Jackson and the Aesthetics of Modernism', *Dutch Journal of Music Theory*, 13/3 (2008): 207–19.

—, *The Reinvention of Religious Music: Olivier Messiaen's Breakthrough Toward the Beyond* (New York: Fordham University Press, 2009).

Mâche, François-Bernard, 'L'Hellénisme de Xenakis', in *Un demi-siècle de musique... et toujours contemporaine* (Paris: L'Harmattan, 2000).

— (ed.), *Portrait(s) de Iannis Xenakis* (Paris: Bibliothèque Nationale de France, 2001).

—, 'Xenakis et la musique indienne', *Filigrane*, 10 (2009): 21–6.

MacMillan, Keith and Beckwith, John, *Contemporary Canadian Composers* (Toronto: Oxford University Press, 1975).

Manzoni, Giacomo, 'Una "prima" di Messiaen con uccelli e torrenti', *L'Unità* (Milan, 18 April 1962).

Marinelli, C., 'Lettura di Messiaen', in *Aspetti della musica d'oggi*, ed. Giorgio Pestelli (Quaderni della Rassegna musicale no. 5) (Turin: Einaudi, 1972).

Martorell, Oriol, *Quasi un segle de simfonisme a Barcelona*, Vol. I (Barcelona: Beta Editorial, 1995).

Massin, Brigitte, 'Écrire aujourd'hui pour le piano', *Panorama de la musique* (March–April 1980): 12–13.

—, *Olivier Messiaen: Une poétique du merveilleux* (Aix-en-Provence: Alinea, 1989).

Massip, Catherine (ed.), *Portrait(s) d'Olivier Messiaen* (Paris: Bibliothèque nationale de France, 1996).

Matossian, Nouritza, *Iannis Xenakis* (London: Kahn & Averill, 1986).

McPhee, John, *Annals of the Former World* (New York: Farrar, Straus, Giroux, 1998).

Menéndez Aleyxandre, Arturo, 'Crónicas de conciertos: Barcelona', *Ritmo*, 217 (January 1949): 6.

—, 'Crónicas de conciertos: Barcelona', *Ritmo*, 220 (May 1949): 14.

—, 'Barcelona: La Orquesta Municipal', *Ritmo*, 306 (October–November 1959): 10.

Messiaen, Olivier, *Vingt leçons d'harmonie (dans le style de quelques auteurs important de l'histoire harmonique de la musique depuis Monteverdi jusqu'à Ravel)* (Paris: Leduc, 1939).

—, 'Contre la paresse', *La Page musicale* (17 March 1939): 1.

—, 'Le rythme chez Igor Strawinsky', *La Revue musicale*, 191 (June 1939): 91–2.

—, *Technique de mon langage musical*, 2 Vols (Paris: Alphonse Leduc, 1944; single volume edition published 1999).

—, 'Panorama musicale 1939–1946', in *Musica*, II/1 (1947): 29.

—, *Technique of my musical language*, 2 vols, trans. John Satterfield (Paris: Alphonse Leduc, 1956; single volume edition published 2001).

—, *Conférence à Bruxelles* (Paris: Alphonse Leduc, 1958).

418   *Messiaen Perspectives 2: Techniques, Influence and Reception*

—, *Conférence de Notre-Dame* (Paris: Alphonse Leduc, 1978).
—, *Les 22 Concertos Pour Piano de Mozart*, foreword by Jean-Victor Hocquard (Paris: Librairie Seguier, Archimbault/Birr, 1987).
—, *Conférence de Kyoto* (Paris: Alphonse Leduc, 1988).
—, *Técnica de mi lenguaje musical*, trans. Daniel Bravo López (Paris: Alphonse Leduc, 1993).
—, *Traité de rythme, de couleur, et d'ornithologie – Tome I* (Paris: Alphonse Leduc, 1994) [*Traité I*].
—, *Traité de rythme, de couleur, et d'ornithologie – Tome II* (Paris: Alphonse Leduc, 1995) [*Traité II*].
—, *Traité de rythme, de couleur, et d'ornithologie – Tome III* (Paris: Alphonse Leduc, 1996) [*Traité III*].
—, *Traité de rythme, de couleur, et d'ornithologie – Tome IV* (Paris: Alphonse Leduc, 1997) [*Traité IV*].
—, *Traité de rythme, de couleur, et d'ornithologie – Tome V, 1er Volume – Chants d'Oiseaux d'Europe* (Paris: Alphonse Leduc, 1999) [*Traité V:1*].
—, *Traité de rythme, de couleur, et d'ornithologie – Tome V, 2ème Volume – Chants d'Oiseaux Extra-Européens* (Paris: Alphonse Leduc, 2000) [*Traité V:2*].
—, 'Discours de réception à l'Institut de France-Mercredi 2 mai 1984', in François-Bernard Mâche (ed.), *Portrait(s) de Iannis Xenakis* (Paris: Bibliothèque Nationale de France, 2001).
—, *Traité de rythme, de couleur, et d'ornithologie – Tome VI* (Paris: Alphonse Leduc, 2001) [*Traité VI*].
—, *Traité de rythme, de couleur, et d'ornithologie – Tome VII* (Paris: Alphonse Leduc, 2002) [*Traité VII*].
Messiaen, Olivier (et al.), *Vingt leçons de solfège moderne dans les sept clés* (Paris: Lemoine, 1933).
Michael, Robert C., 'Naming Mt. Mahler', *Pomona College Magazine*, 40/3 (Spring 2004): 55, available at pomona.edu/magazine/pcmsp04/AVfirstperson.shtml.
Mila, Massimo, '*Cinq Rechants, Mode de valeurs et d'intensités, Île de feu 2, Neumes rythmiques*', *La Rassegna musicale*, 21/4 (October 1951): 335.
—, *L'esperienza musicale e l'estetica* (Turin: Einaudi, 1956).
—, *Cronache musicali 1955–1959* (Turin: Einaudi, 1959).
Montsalvatge, Xavier, 'Una música nueva. Olivier Messiaen', *Destino*, 604 (5 March 1949): 19.
—, 'Los Conciertos. En la iglesia de la Concepción: obras modernas al órgano, interpretadas por Montserrat Torrent', *La Vanguardia Española* (9 March 1962): 28.
—, 'El XII Festival Internacional de Música y Danza de Granada – Resumen de los conciertos iniciales: Preponderancia de la música y los músicos españoles, con un elevado índice de aplausos a su favor', *La Vanguardia Española* (28 June 1963): 32.
—, 'En el marco del Festival – Olivier Messiaen', *La Vanguardia Española* (24 October 1964): 54.

—, 'Los últimos conciertos del Festival Internacional – La Orquesta Municipal, dirigida por Rafael Ferrer, en el Palacio de la Música, y la Agrupación Coral de Pamplona, en el Tinell', *La Vanguardia Española* (31 October 1965): 56.

—, 'La "Sinfonía Turangalila" de Olivier Messiaen', *Destino*, 1934 (26 October 1974): 57–8.

—, 'El Festival Internacional de Música – Olivier Messiaen, compositor e intérprete', *La Vanguardia Española* (28 October 1976): 63.

Moscovich, Viviana, 'French Spectral Music: An Introduction', *Tempo*, 200 (1997): 21–7.

Murail, Tristan, 'After-Thoughts', *Contemporary Music Review*, 19/3 (2002): 5–10.

—, 'Seminar at Ostrava Music Days', available at www.newmusicostrava.cz/en (2003).

Murray, Christopher Brent, *Le développement du langage musical d'Olivier Messiaen: Traditions, emprunts, expériences*, PhD thesis (Université-Lumière Lyon 2, 2010).

Music and Color – see Samuel, Claude, *Olivier Messiaen: Music and Color*.

Neidhöfer, Christoph, 'A Theory of Harmony and Voice Leading for the Music of Olivier Messiaen', *Music Theory Spectrum*, 27/1 (Spring 2005): 1–34.

Nichols, Roger, *Messiaen*, 2nd edition (Oxford: Oxford University Press, 1986; first published 1975).

—, 'Messiaen: *Eclairs sur l'au-delà*', *Musical Times*, 135/1812 (February 1994): 116–17.

—, 'And a little child shall lead them', *The Musical Times* 137 (July 1996): 17–19.

Nicolodi, Fiamma (ed.), *Luigi Dallapiccola. Saggi, testimonianze, carteggio, biografia e bibliografia* (Milan: Edizioni Suvini Zerboni, 1975).

Nommick, Yvan, 'Tradición, modernidad y sincretismo en el *Quatuor pour la fin du Temps* de Olivier Messiaen', *Quodlibet*, 25 (February 2003): 14–44.

Nono, Luigi, *Scritti e Colloqui*, ed. A. I. De Benedictis and V. Rizzardi, Vol. 2 (Lucca: Ricordi-LIM, 2001).

Owens, P. J., 'Solutions to Two Problems of Dénes and Keedwell on Row-complete Latin Squares', *Journal of Combinatorial Theory*, 21 (1967): 299–308.

Pablo, Luis de, 'El dodecafonismo: una técnica y una visión musical', *Acento cultural*, 2 (December 1958): 49–53.

—, 'Clave y ejemplo', *La Estafeta literaria*, 188 (1 March 1960): 20.

—, *Una historia de la música contemporánea* (Madrid: Fundación BBVA, 2009).

Périer, Alain, *Messiaen* (Paris: Éditions du Seuil, 1979).

Pestalozza, Luigi (ed.), *La Rassegna musicale: Antologia* (Milan: Feltrinelli, 1966).

Petersen, Nils Holger, 'Saint François and Franciscan Sprituality', in Siglind Bruhn (ed.), *Messiaen's Language of Mystical Love* (New York: Garland, 1998).

Petrassi, Goffredo, 'Il nono Festival Musicale di Venezia', in R. Pozzi (ed.), *Scritti e interviste* (Milan: Edizioni Suvini Zerboni, 2008).

PHNS – see Hill, Peter and Simeone, Nigel.

420   *Messiaen Perspectives 2: Techniques, Influence and Reception*

Pinzauti, Leonardo, 'A colloquio con Olivier Messiaen', *Nuova Rivista musicale italiana*, 5/6 (November–December 1971): 1031.

Piqué i Collado, Jordi-Agustí, 'Olivier Messiaen (1908–1992): La música-color o la contemplació del Misteri com a revelació del sentit', in *Teologia i Música: propostes per a un diàleg* (Barcelona: Publicacions de l'Abadia de Montserrat, 2006).

Place, Adélaïde de, 'Olivier Messiaen: Le *Traité de rythme, de couleur, et d'ornithologie*', *Piano* 17 (2003): 185.

Ponti, Giovanni and Bontempelli, Massimo, 'Presentazione', in *Programma ufficiale del IX Festival internazionale di Musica contemporanea, 15–22 Sept. 1946* (Venice: Grafiche Fantoni, 1946).

Pople, Anthony, 'Messiaen's Musical Language: An Introduction', in Peter Hill (ed.), *The Messiaen Companion* (London: Faber and Faber, 1995).

—, *Messiaen: Quatuor pour la fin du Temps* (Cambridge: Cambridge University Press, 1998).

Potter, Caroline, *Henri Dutilleux: His Life and Works* (Aldershot: Ashgate, 1997).

Potvin, Gilles, 'Clermont Pépin', in *The Encyclopedia of Music in Canada*, available at www.thecanadianencyclopedia.com.

Potvin, Gilles and Kallmann, Helmut, 'France', in *The Encyclopedia of Music in Canada*, available at www.thecanadianencyclopedia.com.

Pozzi, Raffaele, 'Messiaen: Il suo tempo verrà', *Musica e Dossier*, no. 34 (November 1989): 72–5.

—, 'L'ideologia neoclassica', in *Enciclopedia della musica*, Vol. I, *Il Novecento*, ed. J.-J. Nattiez (Turin: Einaudi, 2001): 444–70.

—, *Il suono dell'estasi: Olivier Messiaen dal* Banquet céleste *alla* Turangalîla-Symphonie (Lucca: LIM, 2002).

—, 'Leopardi e l'ansia di rinnovamento: Il Coro di morti (1940–41) di Goffredo Petrassi', in E. Tonani (ed.), *Storia della lingua italiana e Storia della musica: Atti del IV Convegno dell'Associazione per la Storia della Lingua Italiana* (Sanremo, 29–30 April 2004) (Florence: Franco Cesati Editore, 2005).

—, 'Liturgia d'arte o liturgia pop? La questione della musica contemporanea nel culto cattolico dopo il Concilio Vaticano II', *Musica e Storia*, 13/3 (2005): 489–514.

— (ed.), and Goffredo Petrassi, *Scritti e interviste* (Milan: Edizioni Suvini Zerboni, 2008).

— (ed.), and Giacomo Manzoni, *Musica e progetto civile: Scritti e interviste, 1956–2007* (Milan: Ricordi-LIM (Le Sfere), 2009).

Pressnitzer, Daniel and McAdams, Stephen, 'Acoustics, Psychoacoustics, and Spectral Music', *Contemporary Music Review*, 19/2 (2002): 33–60.

Prévost, André, 'Formulation et conséquences d'une hypothèse', in Raoul Duguay (ed.), *Musiques du Kébèk* (Montréal: Éditions du Jour, 1971).

—, 'Analyse de la Sonate pour violon et piano', *Le Musicien éducateur*, 5/2 (1974): 29–38.

Prost, Christine, 'Catalogue raisonné', *La Revue musicale*, no. 351–2 (1982): 52–3.

Rae, Caroline, 'Debussy et Ohana: Allusions et références', *Cahiers Debussy*, no. 17–18 (1993–94): 103–20.

—, 'The Piano Music of Maurice Ohana', *Revista Musica*, 6/1–2 (Saõ Paulo, May–November1995): 44–74.

—, *The Music of Maurice Ohana* (Aldershot: Ashgate, 2000).

—, 'Henri Dutilleux and Maurice Ohana: Victims of an Exclusion Zone', *Tempo*, 212 (April 2000): 22–30.

—, 'The Works of Messiaen's Final Years', in Robert Sherlaw Johnson, *Messiaen*, 2nd paperback edition, updated and additional text by Caroline Rae (London: Omnibus Press, 2008).

Reber, Henri, *Traité d'Harmonie* (Paris: Colombier, 8th edition, n. d.; first edition 1862).

Reigle, Robert and Whitehead, Paul (eds), *In Spectral World Musics: Proceedings of the Istanbul Spectral Music Conference* (Istanbul: Pan Yayıncılık, 2008).

Risset, Jean-Claude, 'Exploration du timbre par analyse et synthèse', in Jean-Baptiste Barrière (ed.), *Le timbre: métaphore pour la composition* (Paris: IRCAM/ Christian Bourgois).

Robert, Véronique, *André Prévost: Biography and Works* (Saint-Nicholas: Dobermann-Yppan, 1999).

Roberts, Paul, 'La musique de piano de Maurice Ohana', *La Revue musicale*, nos 391–3 (1986): 27–50.

Rochon, Pierre, 'André Prévost', in *Encyclopedia of Music in Canada*, available at www.thecanadianencyclopedia.com.

Rognoni, Luigi, 'Il Concerto di Petrassi', *Rivista musicale italiana*, 40/3–4: 357.

Rößler, Almut, *Contributions to the Spiritual World of Olivier Messiaen*, trans. Barbara Dagg and Nancy Poland (Duisburg: Gilles und Francke, 1986).

Roy, Jean, 'Traité: Messiaen et les autres', *Le Monde de la musique*, 77 (June 2003): 14.

Sabatier, François, 'Olivier Messiaen, *Traité de rythme, de couleur, et d'ornithologie, 1949–1992*', review, *L'Orgue*, 234: 42–3.

Sáinz de la Maza, Regino, 'Un gran músico francés en Madrid', *ABC* (2 March 1949): 19.

Samama, Leo, 'Dukas, Messiaen, Dalbavie and Zuidam: An Explosion of Colour', trans. Josh Dillon, liner note to *Horizon 2: A Tribute to Olivier Messiaen*, Royal Concertgebouw Orchestra, George Benjamin (cond.) (2008), RCO Live 09003.

Samuel, Claude, *Panorama de la música contemporánea* (Madrid: Guadarrama, 1965).

—, *Entretiens avec Olivier Messiaen* (Paris: Pierre Belfond, 1967).

—, *Conversations with Olivier Messiaen*, trans. Felix Aprahamian (London: Stainer and Bell, 1976).

—, *Musique et couleur: Nouveaux entretiens avec Claude Samuel* (Paris: Pierre Belfond, 1986).

—, *Olivier Messiaen: Music and Color; Conversations with Claude Samuel*, trans. E. Thomas Glasow (Portland, OR: Amadeus, 1994).

—, *Permanences d'Olivier Messiaen* (Arles: Actes Sud, 1999).

Sánchez-Verdú, José María, 'Estudios sobre la presencia del canto gregoriano en la composición musical actual a través del análisis de obras de O. Messiaen, G. Ligeti y C. Halffter', *Música*, 4–6 (1997–99): 25–65.

Santa, Matthew, 'Defining Modular Transformations', *Music Theory Spectrum*, 21/2 (1999): 200–29.

Sauvage, Cécile, *Oeuvres complètes* (Paris: La Table Ronde, 2002).

Schmelz, Peter J., 'What Was "Shostakovich", and What Came Next?', *The Journal of Musicology*, 24/3 (Summer 2007): 297–338.

Schubert, Peter, 'A Lesson from Lassus: Form in the Duos of 1577', *Music Theory Spectrum*, 17/1 (1995): 1–26.

Schuster-Craig, John William, *Compositional Procedures in Selected Works of Clermont Pépin (1926–)*, PhD diss. (University of Kentucky, 1987).

Sempronio, 'La semana en libertad', *Destino*, 1158 (17 October 1959): 33.

Shenton, Andrew, 'Composer as Performer, Recording as Text: Notes Towards a "Manner of Realization" for Messiaen's Music', in Robert Sholl (ed.) *Messiaen Studies* (Cambridge: Cambridge University Press, 2007).

—, 'Observations on Time in Olivier Messiaen's *Traité*', in Christopher Dingle and Nigel Simeone (eds), *Olivier Messiaen, Music, Art and Literature* (Aldershot: Ashgate, 2007).

—, *Olivier Messiaen's System of Signs: Notes towards Understanding his Music* (Aldershot: Ashgate, 2008).

— (ed.), *Messiaen the Theologian* (Farnham: Ashgate, 2010).

Sherlaw Johnson, Robert – see Johnson.

Sholl, Robert (ed.), *Messiaen Studies* (Cambridge: Cambridge University Press, 2007).

—, 'Making the Invisible Visible: The Culture, Theology and Practice of Olivier Messiaen's Improvisations', paper given at the annual meeting of the American Musicological Society, Washington, D.C., October 2005.

Simeone, Nigel, 'La Spirale and La Jeune France: Group Identities', *The Musical Times*, 143/1880 (Autumn 2002): 10–36.

—, 'Towards "un success absolument formidable": The birth of Messiaen's *La Transfiguration*', *Musical Times*, 145 (Summer 2004): 21.

Simundza, Mirjana, 'Messiaen's Rhythmical Organisation and Classical Indian Theory of Rhythm I–II', *International Review of the Aesthetics and Sociology of Music*, 18/1–2 (June 1987): 117–44 and 19/1 (June 1988): 53–73.

Smith, Richard Langham, 'Ohana on Ohana: An English Interview', *Contemporary Music Review,* 8/1 (1993): 123–9.

Smith, Ronald Bruce and Murail, Tristan, 'An Interview with Tristan Murail', *Computer Music Journal*, 24/1 (2000): 11–19.

Solomos. Makis. 'Les *Anastenaria* de Xenakis: Continuité et discontinuité historique', available at www.iannis-xenakis.org/fxe/actus/solom2.pdf.

Solomos, Makis and Hoffmann, Peter, 'Xenakis et Messiaen', in Christine Wassemann Beirão, Thomas Daniel Schlee, Elmar Budde (eds), *La Cité céleste: Olivier Messiaen zum Gedächtnis* (Berlin: Weidler, 2006).

Sopeña, Federico, *La música europea contemporánea: Panorama y diccionario de compositores* (Madrid: Unión Musical Española, [1953]).

—, *La música en la vida espiritual* (Madrid: Taurus, 1958).

—, 'Música en Compostela: Resumen y perspectiva', *ABC* (30 August 1961): 36.

—, 'Música – Conciertos sacros: estreno de Oliver [sic] Messiaen', *ABC* (4 April 1963): 81.

—, 'La Orquesta Nacional, en la Bienal', *ABC* (1 December 1964): 85.

—, 'Concierto de Reine Flachot en el Ateneo', *ABC* (7 November 1965): 104.

—, 'Interesantes planes de colaboración musical hispano-francesa', *La Vanguardia Española* (11 June 1971): 51.

Spratt, Geoffrey K., *The Music of Arthur Honegger* (Cork: Cork University Press, 1987).

Sprout, Leslie, 'Messiaen, Jolivet, and the Soldier-Composers of Wartime France', *The Musical Quarterly*, 87/2 (Summer 2004): 259–304.

Stegner, Wallace and Stegner, Page, 'High Plateaus', in *American Places* (New York: Penguin Classics, 2006).

Steinitz, Richard, *György Ligeti: Music of the Imagination* (Boston: Northeastern University Press, 2003).

Stockhausen, Karlheinz, contribution to 'Hommage à Messiaen', *Melos: Zeitschrift für Neue Musik*, 12 (December 1958): 392.

Stuckenschmidt, Hans Heinz, *La música del siglo XX* (Madrid: Guadarrama, 1970; German original, 1969).

Taneiev, Sergei Ivanovitch, *Convertible Counterpoint in the Strict Style*, trans. G. Ackley Brower (Boston: Bruce Humphries Publishers, 1962).

Taruskin, Richard, *Oxford History of Western Music*, Vol. 1 (Oxford and New York: Oxford University Press, 2005).

Tchamkerten, Jacques, 'From *Fête des Belles Eaux* to *Saint François d'Assise*: The Evolution of the Writing for Ondes Martenot in the Music of Olivier Messiaen', in Christopher Dingle and Nigel Simeone (eds), *Olivier Messiaen: Music, Art and Literature* (Aldershot: Ashgate 2007).

Togni, Camillo, *Carteggi e scritti di Camillo Togni sul Novecento Italiano*, Fondazione Giorgio Cini di Venezia, Archivio Camillo Togni, Studi di Musica Veneta, Vol. I (Florence: Olschki, 2001).

Toop, Richard, 'Dedicated to…', liner note in *From Vienna*, Arditti String Quartet, Arditti Quartet Edition 21 (1994), Montaigne Auvidis CD MO 782027.

Tournemire, Charles, *Précis d'éxécution, de registration et d'improvisation à l'orgue* (Paris: Eschig, 1936).

Tuan, Yi-Fu, *Space and Place: The Perspective of Experience* (Minneapolis: University of Minnesota Press, 1977).

[Unsigned], 'Música: Instituto Francés. Audición de obras de Olivier Messiaen', *La Vanguardia Española* (25 February 1949): 2.

[Unsigned], '¿Es un gran músico Messiaen?', *Cuadernos Hispanoamericanos*, 48 (December 1953): 373–4.

Useros, Ana and Rendueles, César, *Luis de Pablo: A contratiempo* (Madrid: Círculo de Bellas Artes, 2009).

J. V. [Viret, Jacques], 'Un grand traité posthume de Messiaen (Olivier Messiaen, *Traité de rythme, de couleur, et d'ornithologie, 1949–1992*, tome I, Paris, Éditions Alphonse Leduc, 1994)', *Revue musicale de Suisse romande*, 1995/4 (December 1995): 65.

—, 'Olivier Messiaen, *Traité de rythme, de couleur, et d'ornithologie (1949– 1992)*, tome I', *L'Orgue francophone* (June 1995): 88–9.

Volder, Piet de, *Encuentros con Luis de Pablo: Ensayos y entrevistas* (Madrid: Fundación Autor, 1998).

Watts, Harriet, 'Interview with Olivier Messiaen on the Influence of Landscape on his Latest Symphony', *From the Canyons to the Stars*, Decade: The Magazine of Contemporary Arts and Culture (March/April 1979): 8.

Weid, Jean-Noël von der, 'Le traité tant attendu' (review of *Traité* I), *Dissonanz/ Dissonance*, 43 (February 1995): 43–4.

—, 'Olivier Messiaen, *Traité de rythme, de couleur, et d'ornithologie: 1949–1992*, Tome II', review, *Dissonanz/Dissonance*, 48 (May 1996): 48.

—, 'Olivier Messiaen, *Traité de rythme, de couleur, et d'ornithologie: 1949–1992*, Tomes III & IV', review, *Dissonanz/Dissonance*, 54 (November 1997): 40.

White Luckow, Heather, *La Marque du maître: Messiaen's Influence on Québécois Composers Serge Garant, Clermont Pépin and André Prévost*, PhD diss. (McGill University, 2010).

Whittall, Arnold, *Exploring Twentieth-century Music: Tradition and Innovation* (Cambridge: CUP, 2003).

Xenakis, Françoise, 'Ce que je sais de lui', in François-Bernard Mâche (ed.), *Portrait(s) de Iannis Xenakis* (Paris: Bibliothèque Nationale de France, 2001).

Xenakis, Iannis, 'La Crise de la musique sérielle', *Gravesaner Blätter*, 1, 1955: 2–4.

—, *Musique Formelles: Nouveaux principes formels de composition musicale* (Paris: Richard-Masse, 1963). First published in *La Revue Musicale*, 253–4 (1963).

—, 'Zu einer Philosophie der Musik' '/Towards a Philosophy of Music', *Gravesaner Blätter*, 29 (1966): 23–38/39–52.

—, 'Vers une métamusique', *La Nef*, 29 (January–March 1967): 117–40, resumed in *Musique Architecture*, English trans. 'Towards a Metamusic' in Iannis Xenakis, *Formalized Music: Thought and Mathematics in Composition* (New York: Pendragon, 1991).

—, 'Vers une philosophie de la musique', *Revue d'esthétique*, 21/2–3–4 (1968): 173–210.

—, 'W strone filozofii Muzyki', *Res Facta*, 2 (1968).

—, *Musique. Architecture* (Tournai: Casterman, 1971).

—, 'Olivier Messiaen', *Opéra de Paris*, 12 (November 1983): 6–7.

—, *Arts/Sciences: Alloys; The Thesis Defense of Iannis Xenakis*, trans. Sharon Kanach (New York: Pendragon Press, 1985).

—, *Formalized Music: Thought and Mathematics in Composition* (New York: Pendragon, 1991).

—, *Keleütha: Écrits* (Paris: L'Arche, 1994).

—, *Musique de l'architecture*, Sharon Kanach (ed.) (Marseille: Parenthèses, 2006).

Young, James E. (ed.), *The Art of Memory: Holocaust Memorials in History* (New York: Prestel: 1994).

Zanni, U. F., 'Música: Palacio de la Música; La Orquesta Municipal: Segundo concierto de invierno', *La Vanguardia Española* (27 February 1949): 13.

—, 'Música: Palau de la Música; El violinista Newman y la Orquesta Municipal', *La Vanguardia Española* (25 October 1959): 31.

Discography

Autuour de Messiaen, [various composers], Ensemble Parallèle, New Music Ensemble, cond. Nicole Paiement, 2005, MSR Classics MS 1151.

Grisey, Gérard, *Le Noir de l'Etoile*, Les Percussions de Strasbourg, rec. 2003, Paris, Cité de la Musique, Accord SACD 476 1052.

Horizon 2: A Tribute to Olivier Messiaen, [various composers], Royal Concertgebouw Orchestra, George Benjamin (cond.), rec. 2008, RCO Live 09003.

Levinson, Gerald, *Music of Gerald Levinson*, Orchestra 2001 and James Freeman (cond.), 2005, Albany Records, CD Troy742.

Messiaen, Olivier, *Cantéyodjayâ*, Yvonne Loriod (pno), [?live] rec. 1958, Paris Adès CD 13.233-2 (originally released as Véga C30A139).

—, *La Fauvette des jardins*, Yvonne Loriod (pno), rec. 8 February 1973, Paris, Église Notre-Dame du Liban, Erato STU 70796; Warner 2564 62162-2 (18 CDs).

—, *Des Canyons aux étoiles… / Oiseaux exotiques / Couleurs de la Cité celeste*, Paul Crossley (piano), London Sinfonietta, Esa-Pekka Salonon (cond.), rec. 1988, CBS Records M2K 44762.

—, *Messiaen Inédits*, Yvonne Loriod (piano), etc., 1999, Jade CD 7432167411-2.

Murail, Tristan, *Comme un oeil suspendu et poli par le songe…*, Marilyn Nonken (piano), rec. 2003, Metier MSV CD 92097.

Mille, Olivier (dir.), *Olivier Messiaen: La Liturgie de Cristal*, 2002, DVD (2007), Idéale Audience International DVD9DS44.

Vasks, Peteris, *Works with Violoncello*, David Geringas (cello), 2008, Hänssler Classic CD 93.229.

Notes on Contributors

Anne-Sylvie Barthel-Calvet is a former student of the École Normale Supérieure (Paris), of the University of Paris–Sorbonne and the University of Strasbourg. She graduated from the École des Hautes Etudes en Sciences Sociales (Paris) with a PhD dedicated to *Le rythme dans l'œuvre et la pensée de Iannis Xenakis*. She is Maître de Conférences and Director of the *Licence de Musique* (BMus) at the Music Department of the Université de Lorraine (France), in Musicology of Contemporary Music. A specialist in the life and music of Iannis Xenakis, she devotes her research to the analytical, historical and aesthetic aspects of the works of this composer.

Barthel-Calvet has written numerous articles and is currently preparing two books – including a biography for the French publisher Fayard – on Xenakis. She works, too, on the elaboration of new analytical tools relevant to twentieth-century music, and studies musical life and cultural politics in the twentieth century, with many contributions on subjects such as twentieth-century opera, the Musica Festival in Strasbourg, the Donaueschingen Festival at the time of Heinrich Strobel and an edition of the memoirs of RTF's director Henry Barraud.

Since December 2012, Barthel-Calvet has been involved in a research programme supported by the National Research Agency (ANR) in France on musical gesture in contemporary music. Her recent publications include 'De l'ubiquité poïétique dans l'œuvre de Iannis Xenakis : Espace, Temps, Musique, Architecture' in *Intersections : Canadian Journal of Music* (29/2); 'Xenakis et le sérialisme: L'apport d'une analyse génétique de *Metastasis*', *Intersections : Canadian Journal of Music* (31/2); 'Un stratège de l'avant-garde: le rôle de Heinrich Strobel dans le redémarrage des *Donaueschinger Musiktage* après 1945', in Jean-Paul Aubert, Patrick Marcolini, Serge Milan and Jean-François Trubert (eds), *Avant-gardes: Frontières, mouvements; Délimitations, historiographie*, Vol. 1 (Sampzon, Delatour, 2012).

Jean Boivin is Full Professor of Music History at the Université de Sherbrooke (Quebec, Canada). He received his PhD in musicology from the Université de Montreal in 1992. He also completed graduate studies at the University of Paris–Sorbonne. His book *La classe de Messiaen* (Christian Bourgois, 1995) was published to acclaim by French music critics and awarded the French Académie des Beaux-Arts's Prix Bernier. Boivin has given lectures on Olivier Messiaen's career, teaching and influence at a variety of international conferences in Italy, Belgium, Britain, Canada and the United States. He has contributed chapters to *Messiaen's Language of Mystical Love* (Garland, 1998), *Musique: Une encyclopédie pour le XXIᵉ siècle*, Vol. 1 (Einaudi, 2001; Actes Sud / Cité de la musique, 2003),

Olivier Messiaen: Music, Art and Literature (Ashgate, 2007), Musique, arts et religion dans l'entre-deux-guerres (Symétrie, 2009) and Écrits de compositeurs: Questions, méthodes et perspectives de recherche (Vrin, forthcoming).

The author of a number of articles on various aspects of twentieth-century music, including the impact on Canadian composers of twentieth-century European music and pedagogues (such as Messiaen, Nadia Boulanger and Pierre Boulez), Boivin is the recipient of two Opus prizes (given by the Québec Music Council). He is an active member of the research group Observatoire Interdisciplaire de Création et de Recherche en Musique (OICRM, Montreal). He is currently writing a book on modern and avant-garde music in Québec.

Roderick Chadwick is a lecturer at the Royal Academy of Music in London and combines his teaching and research activity with a wide-ranging career as a pianist. He has performed at venues including Manchester's Free Trade Hall, Wigmore Hall in London, Seoul Arts Centre, Tokyo Opera City Concert Hall and Auditorium du Louvre, as well as at festivals such as Aldeburgh and Huddersfield. Olivier Messiaen's music features prominently in his repertoire, and in 2007–08 he was Artistic Advisor to the Royal Academy for their involvement in the London Southbank Centre's Messiaen centenary celebrations. He has broadcast extensively on BBC Radio 3 and recorded on the Guild, Métier, Naxos and Victor (Japan) labels. Recordings of works by Finnissy, Godowsky and Stockhausen are due for release in 2013.

He recently published an article on Gloria Coates's piano music in the Komponisten in Bayern series and contributed the paper 'Les Mains de Pierre: Boulez, Ernst and Messiaen' to the Southbank's Boulez Symposium *Exploring the Labyrinth*. His ongoing collaboration with composer Alex Hills on a project exploring piano resonance has just culminated in the première of 'After and Before' with the ensemble Plus Minus at London's King's Place.

Christopher Dingle is Reader in Music and Co-ordinator of Research Degrees at Birmingham Conservatoire, UK. A specialist in the life and music of Olivier Messiaen, he is author of the acclaimed biography *The Life of Messiaen* (Cambridge University Press, 2007) and *Messiaen's Final Works* (Ashgate, 2013). He co-edited *Olivier Messiaen: Music, Art and Literature* (Ashgate, 2007) and is contributing two chapters to McCarrey and Wright (eds), *Perspectives on the Performance of French Piano Music* (Ashgate, forthcoming). He was the organizer of the Messiaen 2008 International Centenary Conference hosted by Birmingham Conservatoire, having previously conceived and organized the Messiaen 2002 International Conference in Sheffield.

Dingle is also a specialist in the history and practice of music criticism. He is the editor of the *Cambridge History of Music Criticism* (Cambridge University Press, forthcoming), and co-author with Chris Morley of *The Cambridge Introduction to Music Criticism* (Cambridge University Press, forthcoming). He is also working on a research project exploring evolutions in British newspaper criticism since the

Second World War. He is a member of the review panel for *BBC Music Magazine*, has broadcast on BBC Radio 3 and has written for *Tempo, Music & Letters, The Guardian, The Independent, The Herald* and *Organists' Review*. He was a member of the jury for the *BBC Music Magazine Awards* in 2008 and 2011.

Robert Fallon is Assistant Professor and Coordinator of Musicology at Carnegie Mellon University School of Music in Pittsburgh, Pennsylvania. His research interests include nature and theology in Messiaen's music and thought, ecocriticism, the pressures of globalization and place on musical composition and reception, and contemporary music in France, the United States and Turkey. He has previously edited *Ars Lyrica: Journal of the Lyrica Society for Word-Music Relations*. His book chapters on Messiaen appear in *Messiaen the Theologian* (Ashgate, 2010), *Musique, arts et religion dans l'entre-deux-guerres* (Symétrie, 2009), *Messiaen Studies* (Cambridge University Press, 2007), *Olivier Messiaen: Music, Art, and Literature* (Ashgate, 2007) and *Jacques Maritain and the Many Ways of Knowing* (Catholic University of America Press, 1999). He has also contributed articles to the *Grove Dictionary of American Music* and published in the *Journal of the American Musicological Society,* the *Journal of Musicology, Modern Fiction Studies, Tempo* and *Notes*. He has provided programme notes or pre-concert talks for the Pittsburgh Symphony, San Francisco Opera, New York City Opera, Carnegie Hall and the Kennedy Center and is a frequent contributor to The Allegheny Front radio programme on music and the environment.

He is co-founder of the AMS Ecocritical Musicology Study Group and is the 2004 recipient of the Paul A. Pisk Prize given by the American Musicological Society. He holds a PhD from the University of California at Berkeley.

Germán Gan-Quesada completed his PhD in History of Art-Musicology at the University of Granada in 2003 with the thesis *Cristóbal Halffter's Work: Musical Composition and Aesthetic Backgrounds* and is, at present, Lecturer and Academic Coordinator of the Departament d'Art i Musicologia at the Universitat Autònoma de Barcelona. He has received grants from, among others institutions, the Archive Manuel de Falla and Paul Sacher Stiftung, and his research topics include twentieth-century Spanish Music and Contemporary Music Aesthetics.

He has published essays on Spanish contemporary music (Joan Guinjoan, José María Sánchez-Verdú, Mauricio Sotelo, Ramon Lazkano, Elena Mendoza), Spanish music criticism around 1930 and about the process of reception in Spain of European repertories in the early and mid-twentieth century; furthermore, he is editor of the Spanish board of the series Komponisten der Gegenwart.

Among his forthcoming publications are chapters on post-war avant-garde music in Spain for the new *Historia de la música española e iberoamericana* (Fondo de Cultura Económica), music historiography during the Francoist regime (Brepols), and twentieth-century Spanish string quartets (*Contemporary Music Review*). He has recently contributed papers to the Second and Third International Robert Gerhard Conferences (Barcelona and Alcalá de Henares), and to the International Conferences Music and Propaganda in the Short Twentieth Century (Pistoia) and Rethinking Stravinsky: Sounds and Gestures of Modernism (Salerno), and has been member of the Scientific Comittee of the 8th Spanish Society for Musicology International Conference.

David Kopp is Associate Professor in the Department of Composition and Theory, and Director of Graduate Studies at the Boston University Music School. He holds an undergraduate degree from Harvard College, a master's degree in piano performance (with Charles Rosen) from Stony Brook University, and a PhD in musicology and music theory from Brandeis University, with additional studies at the École Normale de Musique, Paris, and with Nadia Boulanger and her circle. He has also taught at Harvard University, Yale University, MIT and the University of Washington. Kopp is the author of *Chromatic Transformations in Nineteenth-century Music* (Cambridge University Press, 2002) and has articles in the *Journal of Music Theory* and *In Theory Only*, among others. Recent publications include two essays, 'Intermediate States of Key in Schumann', in *Rethinking Schumann* (Oxford University Press, 2011) and 'Chromaticism and the Question of Tonality', in *The Oxford Handbook of Neo-Riemannian Theories* (OUP, 2011, recipient of a Society for Music Theory publication award). He is currently chair of the Performance and Analysis Interest Group of the Society for Music Theory. As pianist he has performed extensively as soloist and chamber musician and has recorded for the New World, CRI and ARTBSN labels.

Christoph Neidhöfer is Associate Professor and Chair of the Department of Music Research at McGill University in Montreal, Canada. He holds undergraduate and master's diplomas in music theory, composition and piano performance from the Musikhochschule in Basel and a PhD in music theory from Harvard University. His research focuses on twentieth- and twenty-first-century theory and analysis, sketch studies, aesthetics of serialism, and tonal counterpoint. He has published articles on the music of Milton Babbitt, Luciano Berio, John Cage, Bruno Maderna, Olivier Messiaen, Arnold Schoenberg and Igor Stravinsky, among others, and is co-author (with Peter Schubert) of the textbook *Baroque Counterpoint* (Prentice Hall, 2006).

Marilyn Nonken is Associate Professor of Music and Music Education at New York University's Steinhardt School of Culture, Education and Human Development, where she is also Director of Piano Studies. A student of David Burge at the Eastman School, she received a PhD degree in musicology from Columbia University. Her writings on twentieth- and twenty-first-century music, music perception, and contemporary performance practices have been published in *Tempo, Perspectives of New Music, Contemporary Music Review, Agni, Current Musicology, Ecological Psychology, Music and Medicine, The Journal of Hand Therapy,* and the *Journal of the Institute for Studies in American Music,* and she is currently preparing a monograph on spectral piano music for

Cambridge University Press. Upon her 1993 New York recital debut, she was heralded as 'a determined protector of important music' (*New York Times*), and she has performed at venues including Carnegie Hall, Lincoln Center, and IRCAM. Festival appearances include Résonances and the Festival d'Automne (both Paris), When Morty Met John, Making Music, Interpretations, and Works & Process at the Guggenheim (all New York), American Sublime (Philadelphia), The Festival of New American Music (Sacramento), Musica Nova Helsinki, Aspects des Musiques d'Aujourd-hui (Caën), Messiaen 2008 (Birmingham, UK), New Music Days (Ostrava), Musikhøst (Odense) and the William Kapell International Piano Festival and Competition. She has recorded for New World, Bridge, Mode, Kairos, Lovely Music, Albany, Metier, Divine Art, BMOP Sound, Innova, CRI, Tzadik and New Focus. Recent releases include *Tristan Murail: The Complete Piano Music*, Messiaen's *Visions de l'Amen* (with Sarah Rothenberg), and *Voix Voilées: Spectral Piano Music*.

Raffaele Pozzi studied piano at the Conservatorio di Santa Cecilia and musicology at the Università di Roma 'La Sapienza' and King's College London. He published the Italian edition of the writings of Edgard Varèse (*Il suono organizzato*, Unicopli-Ricordi, 1985), has written about Elliott Carter (in David Schiff, *Elliott Carter*, ESI, 1990), Goffredo Petrassi (*Scritti e interviste*, Edizioni Suvini Zerboni, 2008), Giacomo Manzoni (*Musica e progetto civile: Scritti e interviste, 1956–2007*, Edizioni Ricordi-LIM, 2009) and has contributed to the proceedings of important international meetings, including *La musica come linguaggio universale: Genesi e storia di un'idea* (Olschki, 1990) and *Tendenze e metodi nella ricerca musicologica* (Olschki, 1995).

Pozzi has submitted entries on twentieth-century Italian authors for the *New Grove Dictionary of Opera* (Macmillan, 1992) and for the *New Grove Dictionary of Music and Musicians* (Macmillan, 2001) for which he wrote, in cooperation with J. C. G. Waterhouse, 'Italy – twentieth-century Music'. He contributed the article 'L'ideologia neoclassica' to the volume on the twentieth century of the *Enciclopedia della Musica*, edited by Jean-Jacques Nattiez (Einaudi, 2001).

He has given particular attention in his scientific work on the twentieth century to the figure and the works of the composer Olivier Messiaen, about whom he has written the first Italian book, entitled *Il suono dell'estasi: Olivier Messiaen dal Banquet céleste alla* Turangalîla-symphonie (Libreria Musicale Italiana, 2002). Having previously taught the history of modern and contemporary music at the University of Bologna, he is currently Professor of Musicology and Methodology of Musical Education at the University of Roma Tre.

Caroline Rae is Senior Lecturer in Music at Cardiff University and has been Visiting Lecturer at the universities of Paris–Sorbonne, Paris 8, Rouen and Cologne as well as Visiting Scholar at St John's College Oxford. The author of *The Music of Maurice Ohana* (Ashgate, 2000), editor of the revised and expanded edition of Robert Sherlaw Johnson's *Messiaen* (Omnibus, 2008) and co-editor of 'Dutilleux at 95' for *Contemporary Music Review* (2010), she has published numerous articles on twentieth-century music in France, as well as on the writings and musical activities of Alejo Carpentier. She is currently preparing a new study of André Jolivet and an interdisciplinary monograph *Magic Realism, Music and Literature*, both forthcoming with Ashgate. Also a pianist, she has performed internationally as well as in the UK and gives lecture-recitals relating to her research interests. A pupil of Dame Fanny Waterman, she later studied with Yvonne Loriod-Messiaen under a French Government Scholarship in Paris as well as at the Hochschule für Musik und Theater in Hanover. She maintained a two-piano duo with the late Robert Sherlaw Johnson for many years, their programmes focusing on French repertoire, notably Messiaen's *Visions de l'Amen*. She broadcasts for BBC Radio 3, discussing twentieth-century French music, and with the BBC National Orchestra of Wales was co-organizer of the 2008 BBC Discovering Dutilleux Festival, which took place in the presence of the composer, as well as the André Jolivet Composer Portrait and Paul Sacher Perspectives season 2011–12. She is also programming consultant for the Philharmonia Orchestra of London. Caroline is the sister of composer and writer Charles Bodman Rae.

Heather White Luckow is a freelance writer and composer. She holds an undergraduate degree in Music Theory/Composition from Memorial University of Newfoundland and a PhD in Music Theory from McGill University, Montreal, where she worked under the direction of Christoph Neidhöfer. Aside from her dissertation *La marque du maître: Messiaen's Influence on Serge Garant, Clermont Pépin and André Prévost*, her research interests include the music of Joni Mitchell, history of music theory, music theory pedagogy, and the perception of time in music. She is currently examining the confluence of drug use, mental illness and popular music with her husband, a specialist in addiction medicine. Heather has presented her research at national meetings of the Society of Music Theory and the International Association for the Study of Popular Music, as well as the Messiaen 2008 International Centenary Conference and the 6th European Music Analysis Conference / VII. Jahreskongress der Gesellschaft für Musiktheorie.

Index

Abravanel, Maurice 331
Aimard, Pierre-Laurent 39, 248
Akoka Ensemble 250
Alain, Marie-Claire 391
Albèra, Philippe 348
aleatory 151, 166, 168, 171, 229–30, 233,
    237–8
Alonso Bernaola, Carmelo 314–15
d'Amico, Fedele 298
Amy, Gilbert 229
Anderson, Julian 397
d'Annunzio, Gabriele 290
Argenta, Ataúlfo 302

Bach, J. S. 77–9, 277, 282, 307
Barraqué, Jean 229
Bartók, Bela 95, 171, 308
Bayona, Pilar 308, 310–11
Beard, David 244
Beethoven, Ludwig van 184, 187, 392
Benitez, Vincent 2, 61, 367
Benjamin, George 77, 109, 168, 248, 256,
    258, 393
    Invention 258
    Ringed by the Flat Horizon 258
    Sortilège 256
Berg, Alban 216
    Lyric Suite 216
Bermat, Alain 156
Björk 2, 253
Blanquer, Amando 278, 315
Bloch, Thomas 254
Bloom, Harold, 149, 151, 244
Boivin, Jean 176, 182, 192, 203, 207, 213,
    279, 315, 349
Bontempelli, Massimo 283–4
Boucourechliev, André 229
Boulanger, Nadia 157, 182, 203

Boulez, Pierre 35, 104, 155, 176, 195, 203,
    209–11, 228–30, 239–40, 246, 256,
    292, 294, 297–8, 329, 344–5, 392
    Le marteau sans maître 294
    Second Piano Sonata 246
Broad, Stephen 3
Brown, Earle 229
Bruhn, Siglind 2
Burke, Edmund 324
Burke, Kenneth 327
Burke, Michael 327, 330

Cage, John 229–30, 297
Capdevielle, Pierre 179
Carpentier, Alejo 170
Carter, Elliott 249
Casella, Alfredo 156, 281
Casimiri, Raffaele 296
Castro, Sergio de 157
Chen, Qigang 248, 256
Cheong, Wai-Ling 69
Clementi, Aldo 293
Cocteau, Jean 14, 78
Colassi, Irène 179
Conservatoire *see* Paris Conservatoire
Constant, Marius 159, 404
Counts, Jeff 332
Couraud, Marcel 177–9, 293
Crispin, Judith 3
Croce, Benedetto 278, 289–92, 298
Crossley, Paul 229
Crumb, George 150, 239, 251, 257

Dalbavie, Marc-André 248, 260–61
Dallapiccola, Luigi 278, 281, 284, 287–90,
    293, 319
Daniel-Lesur 157, 160, 164, 282–3, 315
Darmstadt, Ferienkurse für Neue Musik
    229, 292–3, 315, 345

Index

Debussy, Claude 33, 95, 151, 153–4, 161–3, 166, 172–4, 184, 187–8, 236, 255, 257, 294, 307, 352, 354, 400
  Chansons de Bilitis 354
  En blanc et noir 162
  Études 162
  Pelléas et Mélisande 185–6
  Prélude à l'après-midi d'un faune 185, 188, 352, 400
  Préludes 162, 184, 187
de Place, Adélaïde 361
Dieudonné, Annette 182
Dingle, Christopher 52, 79, 98, 231, 348, 350, 352–8, 361, 366, 398
Domaine Musical, Concerts du 154–5, 159, 239
Donaueschingen Musiktage 26
Drott, Eric 237
Dufourt, Hugues 35, 237, 239
Dukas, Paul 83, 248, 391, 395, 400–401
Dumesnil, René 231, 309
Dupré, Marcel 83–4, 86–7
Dutilleux, Henri 154, 157, 162, 168–9, 203, 219–20, 249

Emmanuel, Maurice 351

Falla, Manuel de 157, 302, 307–8
Fallon, Robert 258
Fanning, David 20, 22
Farmer, Jared 338
Fernández-Cid, Antonio 305, 320
Fineberg, Joshua 35–6
Fleming, René 1
Fling, Michael 247
Forest Divonne, Pierre de la 156–7
Françaix, Jean 283, 302
Francis of Assisi, St 14, 25
Franco, Francisco 278, 301, 308

Garant, Serge 149, 151, 201–12, 217, 222, 224–5
  Concerts sur terre 204–7, 211, 224
Gatti, Guido Maggiorino 282, 283, 284, 289
Gentilucci, Armando 295
Gillock, Jon 2
Gloag, Kenneth 244
Goehr, Alexander 10, 33, 48

Goeyvaerts, Karel 203, 292
Goldbeck, Fred 181
Goléa, Antoine 292, 314
Gorillaz 254
Greenwood, Jonny 253
Gregory, Herbert 335
Grisey, Gérard 34–37, 40, 42–4, 48, 150, 228, 233, 237, 239, 258–9, 261
  Espaces acoustiques, Les 42, 228
  Prologue 42
  Partiels 35, 37, 42
  Modulations 258
  '*Tempus ex Machina*: A Composer's Reflection on Musical Time' 34, 36–7, 42, 48
Guézec, Jean-Pierre 401
Guinjoan, Joan 315
Gurr, Kendall 329, 331

Haimovitz, Matt 250, 254
Hakim, Naji 255, 400
Halbreich, Harry 42, 48, 208, 345, 349, 356
Halffter, Ernesto 302, 314–15
Hambraeus, Bengt 255, 257
Hardink, Jason 332
Harvey, Jonathan 150, 228, 248, 257, 261
  Bird Concerto with Pianosong 248, 260–61
  Tombeau de Messiaen 250, 255
Healey, Gareth 3, 348
Hill, Peter 2, 20, 26, 38, 42, 52, 76, 304, 345–6, 353–4, 356, 365–6, 396, 397, 399
Hindemith, Paul 37, 250, 302
Hirsbrunner, Theo 348, 350, 353, 355, 357–8, 361
Holliger, Heinz 109, 168, 393, 406
Honegger, Arthur 203, 213, 217
  Rugby 213
Humet, Ramon 248
Huyssen, Andreas 337

IOU (International Ornithologists' Union) 113–16
IRCAM 229
Italy 278, 281–99
  cultural politics 281–4, 289–92, 295–8
Itinéraire, Groupe de l' 228, 238–9

Index

Jackson, Anthony 254
Jeune France, La 13–14, 30, 78, 156–8, 160, 282–5
Johnson, Robert Sherlaw 2, 3, 26, 114, 206, 208
Jolivet, André 151, 160, 170, 174, 239, 282–3, 302, 315, 350
Josquin Desprès 164
Joy, Geneviève 154

Kallmann, Helmut 202
Kavafian, Ida 251
Keym, Stefan 346, 348, 351, 353–4, 357–8, 361
Krakauer, David 250, 254
Kramer, Lawrence 244
Kurtág, György 256, 261

Latry, Olivier 400, 402
Lavanden, Thérèse 287
Le Corbusier (Charles-Édouard Jeanneret) 177–8, 182, 186–7, 190, 192
Le Jeune, Claude 164
Lévinas, Michaël 228, 239
Levinson, Gerald 256, 259, 261
Ligeti, György 36, 176, 238, 246
Liszt, Franz 9, 173, 312
Lockhart, Keith 332
Loriod, Jeanne 319, 394, 396–7, 406
Loriod, Yvonne 9, 47, 51–2, 109, 114–15, 154, 168, 249, 255–6, 285, 287–8, 303–6, 319–21, 329–30, 342, 345–6, 354, 357–8, 361, 364–5, 392–4, 396–403
Louvier, Alain 261, 342, 345, 349–51, 354
Loyonnet, Paul 302
Lutosławski, Witold 151, 250

Maas, Sander van 2
Machabey, Armand 283
Machaut, Guillaume de 164, 187
Mâche, François-Bernard 15, 191, 249
McPhee, John 333–4
Mahler, Gustav 298, 324, 363, 393
Mantovani, Bruno 260
Manzoni, Giacomo 294, 295
Marxism 282, 295, 298
Massenet, Jules 291

Matossian, Nouritza 182
Menéndez Aleyxandre, Arturo 305, 309
Messiaen, Olivier
  agrandissement asymétrique 15–16, 18–20, 81, 108, 110
  biography
    Italy, Messiaen in 287, 288, 293
    Prix de Rome entry 394, 399, 403
    relationship with Yvonne Loriod 51–2, 255, 330, 342, 345, 361, 397–8, 401, 403
    Spain, Messiaen in 303, 305, 320–21
    teaching 36, 150, 161, 176, 187–8, 194, 201, 203, 225, 247, 294, 315, 318, 345, 350, 355, 361, 399
    U.S.A., Messiaen in 278, 328
  birdsong *see also* Messiaen, Olivier, *cahiers de notations de chants d'oiseaux* 16–17, 23–9, 44, 51–2, 54–6, 64, 168, 185, 231, 243, 253, 323, 346, 403
    list of birds 113–46
  cahiers de notations de chants d'oiseaux xvii, 365, 396–7
  chromatic saturation 41–4
  colour 3, 14, 23, 25–31, 38, 44, 56, 58, 151, 205, 228–36, 245, 277, 323, 335, *see also* harmony; modes of limited transposition
  communicable language, see *langage communicable*
  counterpoint 44, 48, 77–110, 164, 168
    fugue 79–80, 82–3, 109, 257, 391, 398
    rotational array 78, 96–103
  form 34, 44, 52–7, 66, 75–6, 84, 105, 392, 396
    palindromes 61, 219, 236, 290
  harmony 17, 28, 41–4, 57–9, 62, 64, 66, 70–71, 73–4, 86, 95
    Contracted Resonance chords 56, 62, 66, 68, 201, 205, 224, 343
    modes of limited transposition 58, 84, 197
    Total Chromatic chords 41–2, 56, 61–3, 68, 70

Transposed Inversion chords
(*renversements transposés*) 9,
38, 55–6, 61–2, 70, 72
Turning chords 105, 108
historiography 1–4, 11, 77–8, 149–51,
227–8, 243–6, 251–3, 261, 277–9,
324–5, 332–3, 338–9, 360–61,
363–7
improvisation 83–4, 366, 374–5, 398
interversion *see* permutation
langage communicable 358
mechanical procedures 13–31, 243
melody 41, 43, 89, 94–5, 105, 109,
164, 215, 256, 277, 323
nature 13–15, 20, 29, 48, 162, 246,
261, 323–4, *see also* birdsong
orchestration 11, 150, 228, 393, 401, 406
permutation 16–17, 27–8, 30, 84–5, 99,
151, 199, 208, 223, 231
plainchant 10, 17, 23, 55, 67, 71, 184,
350, 354
rhythm 3, 10, 16, 19, 27, 55, 277
additive rhythm 10
Hindu (Indian) rhythms 28, 229,
259, 346
personnages rythmiques 15–17, 19,
43, 150, 185
serialism 22–5, 185, 277, 284, 293
theology 20–21, 23, 30, 115, 325
timbre 23, 26, 34–5, 38–39, 54, 56,
178, 228–9
WORKS
L'Ascension 79, 255, 307, 309, 312,
319, 391, 395
Banquet céleste, Le 391–2, 397, 400
Banquet eucharistique, Le 391–2, 397,
405
Cantéyodjayâ 23, 363
Catalogue d'oiseaux 15–16, 18, 20,
23–4, 33, 46, 54, 59, 60–61, 171,
228, 323, 355, 365, 396
Chant dans le style Mozart 393
Chant des déportés 364, 392
Chants de terre et de ciel 80–81, 93, 331
Chœurs pour une Jeanne d'Arc see
Portique pour une fille de France
Chronochromie 1, 16, 25, 27–8, 38, 170,
229–31, 294–5, 312–13, 335, 357

Cinq Rechants 169, 177, 291, 294, 318
Concert à quatre 105–6, 109, 114, 168,
173, 322, 393, 406
Corps glorieux, Les 255
Couleurs de la Cité céleste 38, 229,
240, 277, 318, 323, 335, 346
Dame de Shalott, La 393–4
Des Canyons aux étoiles... 2, 11, 24,
159, 161, 278, 321, 323–4, 326–30,
332, 334, 336–7, 339, 365, 401
Deux Monodies en quarts de ton 394
Diptyque 391, 402
Éclairs sur l'Au-Delà... 4, 11, 17, 25,
114, 160–61, 168, 278, 321, 346,
394, 401, 404
L'Ensorceleuse 394
Et exspecto resurrectionem mortuorum
1, 260, 320, 323, 330
Fantaisie 395
Fantaisie burlesque 395
Fauvette des jardins, La 11, 33–49, 115
Fauvette Passerinette, La 396
Fête des belles eaux 396–7
Feuillets inédits 249, 397, 399
Fugue (*1926, sur un sujet d'Henri
Rabaud*) 391, 298
Harawi 114, 169, 206–7, 224, 286,
366, 401–2, 405
Hymne au Saint-Sacrement [*Hymne*]
160, 318, 330, 398, 404
Jeunesse des vieux, La 399
Improvisations (for *L'Âme en
bourgeon*) 398
Livre d'orgue 15–16, 24–6, 183, 185,
187, 191, 193, 199–200, 312,
323–4, 357
Livre du Saint Sacrement 23, 278, 323,
398
*Méditations sur le mystère de la Sainte
Trinité* 278, 346, 358
Merle noir, Le 72, 249, 256, 294
Messe de la Pentecôte 84–5, 87, 185,
187, 233, 323
Monodie 399, 406
Morceau de lecture à vue 399
Musique de scène pour un Œdipe 399
Nativité du Seigneur, La 88, 91, 254, 312
O sacrum convivium! 171

Offrande au Saint-Sacrement 400
Offrandes oubliées, Les 15, 160, 254, 318, 391, 400, 404–5
Oiseau des arbres de Vie, Un 401
Oiseaux exotiques 1, 48, 113, 228, 233, 277, 313, 347
Petites Esquisses d'oiseaux 51–76, 173, 321
Pièce (à la mémoire de Jean-Pierre Guézec) 401–2
Pièce (pour le Tombeau de Paul Dukas) 401
Pièce (oboe and piano) 401–2
Pièce (piano and string quartet) 402
Poèmes pour Mi 1, 95–6, 285–6, 289
Portique pour une fille de France [Chœurs pour une Jeanne d'Arc] 402
Prélude (organ) 400, 402–3
Prélude (piano, 1964) 403
Préludes 83, 161, 288, 365, 391
Quatre Études de rythme 16, 27, 192, 309, 357, 363, 395
   Île de feu 1 114, 308, 395
   Île de feu 2 16, 27, 291, 395
   Mode de valeurs et d'intensités 16, 22–3, 192, 195, 277, 291, 293, 297
   Neumes rythmiques 291
Quatuor pour la fin du Temps 1, 4, 15–16, 20, 25, 29, 113–14, 116, 250–52, 277, 286–8, 290, 297, 318, 332, 365, 397
Réveil des oiseaux 20, 26, 113, 115, 228, 249, 309, 319, 330
Rondeau 403
Sainte-Bohème, La 403
Saint François d'Assise 15, 17, 23, 28, 33, 153, 168, 175–6, 199, 198, 321–3, 343, 346, 356, 365–6
Sept Haïkaï 162–3, 229, 259, 294, 355–6
Sigle 403
Sourire, Un 404
Timbres-durées 404
Tombeau resplendissant, Le 260, 404–5
Transfiguration de Notre-Seigneur Jésus-Christ, La 4, 11, 15, 17, 21, 23–5, 27–8, 96–8, 232, 258, 321, 323, 346

Tristan et Yseult (musique de scène) 366, 399, 405
Trois Petites Liturgies de la Présence Divine 77, 233, 286, 293, 295, 312–3, 318, 359
Trois Tâla 303, 305, 309, 313, 366, 405
Turangalîla-Symphonie 1, 4, 15–16, 25, 169, 174, 185, 187, 193, 213–4, 224, 228, 233, 278, 286, 292, 295, 297, 312, 319–20, 353, 366, 405
Ville d'En-Haut, La 114, 406
Vingt Regards sur l'Enfant-Jésus 16, 20, 79–80, 82, 88–9, 92, 171, 187, 228, 233, 246, 249, 256–7, 260, 286–8, 291–2, 303, 308, 320, 323, 359, 365
Visions de l'Amen 160, 255–6, 286, 288, 291, 303, 312, 320
Vitrail et des oiseaux, Un 22, 168, 346, 406
Vocalise-étude 249, 406
Writings and pedagogical works
   Solfège 366
   Technique de mon langage musical 9–10, 58, 84, 88, 206, 246, 258–59, 277, 290, 314–15, 343–4, 350, 357, 364–5
   Traité de rythme, de couleur, et d'ornithologie 2, 9–10, 25, 41, 51–2, 54–5, 57–8, 64, 114, 184, 222, 146, 341–61
   Vingt leçons d'harmonie 10, 366
   Vingt Leçons de Solfège Moderne 366
Mila, Massimo 291–3
Mille, Olivier 325
Mocquereau, Dom 351, 357
modernism 188, 199, 200, 243, 246, 257, 278, 281–2, 286, 294, 296–8, 308, 312, 316, 320
Montsalvatge, Xavier 304, 312–13, 320
Moretti, Franco 245
Mount Messiaen 323–39
Mozart, W.A. 150, 185, 251, 344, 354
   Don Giovanni 184
   Nozze di Figaro, Le 105
Murail, Tristan 34–6, 43, 149–51, 228–9, 232–40, 248, 255, 261

440   *Messiaen Perspectives 2: Techniques, Influence and Reception*

Cloches d'adieu, et un sourire 255
Comme un oeil suspend et poli par le songe... 234–6, 238
Gondwana 35, 228
Territoires de l'oubli 43
Murray, Christopher Brent 394, 399–400, 402–4

Nancarrow, Conlon 36
Nardelli, Zdizisław 247
Neidhöfer, Christoph 214
neoclassicism 14, 78–9, 109–10, 231, 281–3, 302, 305, 393
Nichols, Roger 1, 2, 348, 352–3, 355
Nono, Luigi 292, 295, 318
Nora, Pierre 338
Norgård, Per 251

Ohana, Maurice 153–74
    24 Préludes 161, 171–3
    Avoaha 170
    Célestine, La 153, 170
    Cinq sequences 165
    Cris 169
    Lys de madrigaux 171
    Messe 155–6, 164, 166–7
    Offices des oracles 166, 168, 246
    Sibylle 169
    Signes 159, 163, 168
    Silenciaire 161
    Syllabaire pour Phèdre 159, 163, 169–70
    T'Harân-Ngô 160
Ourgandjian, Raffi 391

Pablo, Luis de 14–18
Paris Conservatoire (C.N.S.M.D.P.) 83, 157, 161, 176–7, 182, 203, 232–3, 236, 285, 315, 341–2, 344–5, 347, 350, 353, 393–4, 398, 400–403
Patterson, David 258, 261
Pépin, Clermont 201–4, 212–18, 224
    Guernica 212–14, 224
    Rite du soleil noir, Le 212–14, 224
    Variations pour quatuor à cordes 215, 225
Périer, Alain 325
Pesson, Gérard 256, 261
Petichet 13, 33

Petrassi, Goffredo 278, 281, 284, 289, 296, 315
Picasso, Pablo 10, 212
Pinzauti, Leonardo 297
Pius X (pope) 296
Potvin, Gilles 202
Prévost, André 151, 201–4, 218–25
    Mobiles 218, 225
    repliement, use of 218–19, 223
    Sonate pour violon et piano 218, 221, 225
    Terre des homes 221, 225
Ptaszynska, Marta 248, 258, 261

Rabaud, Henri 392
Radiohead 2, 253–54
Rameau, Jean-Philippe 158
Ravel, Maurice 77, 172–3, 255, 282, 350
Reverdy, Michèle 248, 258
Risset, Jean-Claude 239
Rodrigo, Joaquín 302
Rogg, Lionel 255, 261
Roland-Manuel 77
Rosenthal, Manuel 392
Roussel, Albert 158, 283, 305
    Trois pieces 305

Saariaho, Kaija 150, 228
Saguer, Louis 186
Sainte-Trinité, Église de la 255, 286, 292, 297, 299
Samuel, Claude 5, 13, 23, 30, 78, 229, 314, 343, 393–4
Scelsi, Giacinto 37, 196, 238–9
    Quatro Pezzi su una nota sola 196
Schaeffer, Pierre 179–80
Scherchen, Hermann 179, 181
Schoenberg, Arnold 157, 204, 250, 282, 284
Schola Cantorum 156, 158, 164, 166, 399
Serkin, Peter 251
Shea, Mimi 202
Shenton, Andrew 54, 348
Sherry, Fred 251
Sholl, Robert 2, 84
Sirkis, Asaf 254
Six, Les 302, 308
Skrowaczewski, Stanisław 157
Slonimsky, Nicolas 185

Sopeña, Federico 308, 313, 320
Sosha, Helmut 249
Soutullo, Eduardo 259, 261
Spain 164, 170, 301–22
  cultural politics 301–2, 307–9, 312,
    314, 318, *see also* Messiaen,
    biography, Spain – Messiaen in
spectralism 33–49, 150–51, 227–40, 260
Stegner, Wallace 335–6
Stockhausen, Karlheinz 10, 36, 228–9,
    247, 292, 294–5, 350
Stokowski, Leopold 278, 398
Stolzman, Richard 251
Stravinsky, Igor 10, 79, 95, 160, 185, 187,
    203, 248, 302, 307, 352
  Concerto in D 305
  Noces, Les 79
  Requiem canticles 254
  Sacre du printemps, Le (*Rite of Spring*)
    160, 185, 187, 193, 213, 231, 352–3
  Symphony of Psalms 79
Strobel, Heinrich 181

Takemitsu, Toru 150, 251, 257–9, 261
  Quatrain 251
  Quatrain II 257
  *Rain Tree Sketch II: In memoriam
    Olivier Messiaen* 255–6
Taneiev, Sergei 94
Taruskin, Richard 244
Tashi 250–52, 257
Taylor, John 327
Terényi, Eduard 255
Tessier, Roger 228, 239
Thomas Aquinas, St 21, 25

Thomas, Augusta Read 257
Toldrà, Eduard 303, 309
Tournemire, Charles 83–4, 400
Tower, Joan 257, 261
Tremblay, Gilles 150, 203, 217, 248

Vali, Reza 249, 258–9, 261
Varèse, Edgar 161, 170, 196
Vasks, Peteris 257
Viret, Jacques 349, 352, 356, 359
Von der Weid, Jean-Noël 347, 350

Watts, Harriet 327–8
Webern, Anton von 157, 189–90, 200, 210,
    278, 287, 290, 292–3, 295
  Piano Variations, op. 27: 184, 204, 293
Whitaker, Julie 326–32, 338
Whitaker, Lyman 327, 331
Wyschnegradsky, Ivan 185, 394

Xenakis, Iannis 30–31, 149, 175–201
  Fibonacci sequence, use of 190–94
  Metastasis 176, 179, 181, 189, 193,
    195–6, 200
  notebooks 175, 178, 183–7, 189–93,
    195, 200
  Le Sacrifice 179–80, 187–8, 194–6, 200
  Zyia 177, 179–80, 190, 192–4, 200

Yi-Fu Tuan 326, 332, 339

Zanni, U. F. 304, 309
Zodiaque, Le 156–60
Zorn, John 254, 261
Zuidam, Robert 248, 260

Contents of *Messiaen Perspectives 1: Sources and Influences*

Introduction
Christopher Dingle and Robert Fallon

PART I SOURCES

Perspectives on Sources
Christopher Dingle and Robert Fallon

1   Olivier Messiaen and the Prix de Rome as Rite of Passage
    Laura Hamer and Christopher Brent Murray

2   Olivier Messiaen and *Portique pour une fille de France*
    Lucie Kayas and Christopher Brent Murray

3   Formal Genesis in the Sketches for *Visions de l'Amen*
    Yves Balmer

4   From Music for the Radio to a Piano Cycle: Sources for the *Vingt Regards sur l'Enfant-Jésus*
    Lucie Kayas

5   My Collaboration with Olivier Messiaen and Yvonne Loriod on *Harawi*
    Sigune von Osten

6   Olivier Messiaen's *Timbres-durées*
    Christopher Brent Murray

7   From *Réveil des oiseaux* to *Catalogue d'oiseaux*: Messiaen's *Cahiers de notations des chants d'oiseaux*, 1952–59
    Peter Hill

8   In the Beginning Was The Word? An Exploration of the Origins of *Méditations sur le mystère de la Sainte Trinité*
    Anne Mary Keeley

Intermède

9   Yvonne Loriod as Source and Influence
       Christopher Dingle

PART II INFLUENCES

Perspectives on Influences
Christopher Dingle and Robert Fallon

10   Messiaen and Mozart: A Love without Influence?
       Christopher Dingle

11   Messiaen and the Romantic Gesture: Contemplations on his Piano Music
       and Pianism
       Caroline Rae

12   Messiaen and the Problem of Communication
       Julian Anderson

13   Messiaen and *Art Sacré*
       Stephen Broad

14   Messiaen, the *Cinq Rechants* and 'Spiritual Violence'
       Philip Weller

15   Messiaen in Retrospect
       Hugh Macdonald

Appendix: Yvonne Loriod Discography
Christopher Dingle